The Interpretation of Early Music

by the same author

A Performer's Guide to Baroque Music
Wagner's 'Ring' and its Symbols
String Playing in Baroque Music

THE INTERPRETATION
OF EARLY MUSIC

by

ROBERT DONINGTON

NEW VERSION

FABER AND FABER
3 Queen Square
London

First published in 1963
by Faber and Faber Limited
3 Queen Square London WC1
Second edition 1965
Revised version 1974
Reprinted with corrections 1975 and 1977
Printed in Great Britain
by Unwin Brothers Limited
The Gresham Press, Old Woking, Surrey

ISBN 0 571 04789 0

In grateful memory
of
ARNOLD DOLMETSCH

Contents

CONTENTS

8

CONTENTS

PART TWO: EMBELLISHMENT

VII. THE PLACE OF EMBELLISHMENT

CONTENTS

CONTENTS

CONTENTS

CONTENTS

CONTENTS

CONTENTS

15

CONTENTS

CONTENTS

CONTENTS

CONTENTS

PART FIVE: DYNAMICS

BOOK FOUR: INSTRUMENTS

CONTENTS

CONTENTS

CONTENTS

CONTENTS

Roger North, *Memoires of Musick . . . 1728*; Hereford Cathedral Library, MS. R.11.xlii, first sentence:

'In matters of Antiquity there are two extreams, 1. a totall neglect, and 2. perpetuall guessing; between which proper evidences are the temper; that is, if there be any, to make the best of them; if none, to desist.'

NEW THINKING ON EARLY INTERPRETATION

I. Our Changing Attitude

1. A LITERARY REINCARNATION

This book, in the virtual reincarnation to which it has now been subjected, takes the place of a third edition of the volume long since known to my students, with tolerant affection, as 'the fat book': officially, *The Interpretation of Early Music* (London, 1963 and New York, 1964).

The Interpretation of Early Music: New Version is thus the lineal descendant of the old *Interpretation*, and inherits from it everything which seems to me to have withstood the test of time. The old book is still here, but after having been submitted to the most scrupulous re-examination and renewal. Around it is built a structure of new information and new ideas so extensive that it far exceeds what could have been passed off merely as a revised edition. It seemed most accurate to publish the present volume as the new book it substantially is, while retaining in its title a sufficient indication that the old book has been incorporated in the new book like prawns in aspic, which is not at all the same dish as merely prawns alone.

It is nearly a dozen years now, as I write these words in the Spring of 1973, since first I finished the manuscript of *The Interpretation of Early Music*. And even as I write these words, Faber and Faber have in preparation yet another volume of mine, not entirely slim, but much slimmer than the original 'fat book', and slimmer still than this. Its title is *A Performer's Guide to Baroque Music* [published late 1973]; and since it is obvious from this title that it covers something of the same subject from another point of view, I shall take the opportunity of explaining in what way it differs from the present volume, and in what way the two books are designed to be complementary to one another. But first a word about this present book.

2. THE CHANGING ENVIRONMENT OF EARLY INTERPRETATION

About as many years were needed previously for completing my work on *The Interpretation of Early Music* as have now elapsed since first I handed it over to Faber and Faber for publication: nearly a dozen years. That is almost a quarter of a century, all told, since first I set to; and the environment in which we come to our performances of early music has been changing steadily all this time.

During the twelve years of preparation, it still seemed very necessary, and I think it was, to make out a case, and to buttress it with argument and evidence, for interpreting early music on its own merits as mature art: as an art not requiring to be patronisingly adapted to our modern habits of performance; but on the contrary, requiring of us a very considerable effort of adaptation in order to avoid the gross inadvertent modernisation which our prevailing habits must otherwise entail. This case has hardly to be made nowadays to the kind of musician hopefully most likely to be using such a book, and certainly most prominent in the performance of baroque and earlier music today. But there are many other excellent musicians not yet by any means persuaded of it; and I have therefore retained it here, as Chapter I of Book One, where the older stratum begins.

A certain spaciousness undoubtedly set in as I wrestled over those twelve years with my recalcitrant material. The mere bulk of the contemporary quotations spread itself over a full half of my original book; but this bulk makes it possible to absorb their suggestive atmosphere rather than merely snatching at their information, and perhaps thereby misunderstanding it. I have kept virtually the whole of these contemporary quotations, *i.e.* the historical material, intact, and I have also added others to round out the picture. The next step on from there, of course, is reading the contemporary treatises in full, available as they now are, but as they were not then, in numerous facsimiles, reprints, and translations with valuable commentaries often added. Yet even read comfortably at home in facsimile editions, the contemporary authorities can be quite hard going, and I hope that the organised introduction to them offered here may make them the more readily approachable.

In my discussion of the evidence, I did not further extend the length by telling the reader over again in my own words what he has just been told (and can turn back to) in some contemporary quotation. This policy has been maintained for the older stratum of the present book; for its newer stratum, I have somewhat relaxed my methods, and wherever fresh evidence is introduced, it is quite likely to be summed up, and not merely referred to, in the ensuing discussion. Moreover, a much greater proportion of the new material of the book is discursive rather than merely descriptive.

But none of the original spaciousness, and none of the new discursiveness, results from any voluntary extravagance in words. On the contrary, I felt, long as the book is, that I have had to confine myself to the barest elements of early interpretation, so wide is the topic even when restricted, as I have basically restricted it, to the baroque period. There are many glances before and after, many instructive comparisons with adjacent periods, for which I have kept the door open by using the word 'early' in my title; but the hundred and fifty years or so of baroque music are the main objective. If I have taken up a considerable diversity of stances, it was in order the better to gain a perspective view.

The changing environment of our approach to early music is not only a matter of attitude, but of knowledge. A comparison between the Select Bibliography as it has now been re-cast and as it stood originally would tell a story of expansion in all dimensions, and would be some measure of our debt to very numerous and often very good workers, many of whom had not yet entered the field a dozen years ago. But it is still, and indeed more rigorously than ever before, a Select Bibliography. We have now the monumental services of the two new RISM volumes for printed writings on music down to and including 1800 to help us in locating and checking material of whose existence we are aware; and to help us in finding out what is relevant, we have the benefit of an inclusive survey, the *Bibliography of Performance Practices* (ed. Mary Vinquist and others, for which see my Select Bibliography, under Vinquist), which even so has had to make some exclusions. Knowledge has exploded, here as elsewhere, and one of the purposes of this present new version of my *Interpretation* is to go over the enormous field for what is most relevant and most valuable.

I have followed the latest scholarship both carefully and respectfully. There are certain matters on which I think one or other of my colleagues may have misread some extremely complicated and ambiguous evidence, bringing back an element of disagreement for which the remedy now is to press on with the argument until we can again reach as much agreement as the nature of the case allows. There are very many more matters on which we have between us successfully modified or extended our knowledge, even though the foundations of it have not been seriously in doubt ever since the pioneering work of Arnold Dolmetsch a long generation ago.

Whatever has been newly questioned or newly contributed by my colleagues or myself, in articles, books or other offerings, has been brought up for consideration somewhere here in this new version of my old book. I have been glad to find my old book standing up so solidly on the whole, after all these years; but I am all the more concerned to give it the benefit now, in this topical reincarnation, not only of new information but of new thinking. I have attempted to accomplish this in the following ways.

3. THE CONSTRUCTION AND FUNCTION OF THIS PRESENT BOOK

There is a certain completedness about an existing book, with which it can be an artistic blunder to interfere. I was therefore very willing to agree with my publisher's wish to avoid re-setting the existing matter, while sparing no effort at revising it for its new existence as the kernel of the present book. A very large number of small to moderate changes have been made, on most of its pages, by taking out words, lines or paragraphs, and substituting others. I was thus able to bring it all well up to date without disturbing an order and arrangement which have proved very workable, having grown almost autonomously though not unlaboriously at the time, as the contents slowly accumulated and still more slowly suggested to me what ought to be juxtaposed with what.

Of these very numerous small to moderate changes, some are of important substance, others are of significant emphasis, while still others are merely different ways of expressing matters which we should put a little otherwise now because of wider changes in our general attitude. But together these changes in the existing matter amount to a very thorough overhaul indeed in the light of recent knowledge.

For the convenience and economy of not having to re-arrange, re-set, and re-cross-reference the older stratum, I am asking the reader to accept (as in the second edition of the old book) a certain overflow into Postscripts at chapter endings, and a further and much more considerable overflow into Appendixes at the end of this present book. All these, however, are cross-referenced in the main body of the text, and indexed in the ordinary fashion.

It is in the Appendixes to the present book (themselves cross-referenced to the main text) that I have entered most substantially upon those many and important issues of early interpretation which have been making the controversial news in the conferences and publications of recent years. I have watched some of these controversies from the judicial comfort of an observer's chair; but in others (ornaments is one example, and rhythm is another) I have had an active share, making friends rather than enemies in the course of it, I am glad to say, but with keen thrusts given and taken, and points conceded and contested on every side. I now stand back a little to assimilate the situation and sum up what I think has come out of it all at this stage of the argument.

Not only in these topical Appendixes, but in the reborn body of the text, the consequences of our strenuous discussions will be apparent. There is no conclusion given there which I have not examined freshly, and altered unhesitatingly wherever I found good cause to do so. If I have left unaltered a statement which has meanwhile been challenged, this means that I have weighed the challenge, but not agreed with it. I have left nothing unaltered through mere default. In most cases where questions have arisen, I have set out my answers, if not in the text, then in one of the cross-referenced Appendixes. *The Interpretation of Early Music: New Version* does therefore give one man's considered opinion in the light of what has newly happened in this still eventful and adventurous area of musicology.

Other matters, not at the moment controversial, but nevertheless opening out in new and sometimes unexpected directions, will also be found explored in certain of the new Appendixes. One of these new explorations of mine of which I did not quite expect the extent of the resulting findings has been the problem of accidentals, not in the remote middle ages, not even in the renaissance, but in the baroque; and I have given it some partial reconsideration here. Another is certain lingering influences, of more practical importance than I had previously appreciated, from the remnants of mensural notation in baroque music: the effect of time-signatures on French recitative, for example, led me to a particularly unforeseen conclusion; the continued use of 'black notation' and 'white notation', and the effect of those, was not quite what I had expected either.

My discussion of these and other matters, and indeed my re-worked book as a whole, can make no possible claims in the direction of exhaustiveness; but the view has widened a little, and although still uneven, it is so far as it goes a comprehensive view. I have touched, however inadequately, on anything which has occurred to me as likely to be looked up by interested parties. Suggestions from readers concerning errors and omissions are always welcome.

4. HOW CONTROVERSIAL IS EARLY INTERPRETATION?

If so many issues of early interpretation have been in hot and recent dispute, the reader is entitled to ask how far he can depend upon the contents of the present book as a sufficiently sound and uncontroversial representation of the facts. My reply would be that he can indeed depend upon the facts in so far as common human fallibility permits. Most of the facts are given in the shape of actual quotations, in English translations (where needed) which I have gone out of my way to make as painstakingly literal as I can, with the original language added in parenthesis where I have felt the slightest doubt. The quotations (musical and verbal) from our point of view *are* the main facts, together with some subsidiary evidence from pictures, financial accounts and surviving instruments, *etc.*, which may bear on our problems from other angles. I have not wittingly distorted or omitted a fact known to me as relevant.

As to where we go from the facts, it is possible to speculate solidly, and it is possible to speculate fancifully; and we can have no guarantee of our own or anybody else's reliability in the matter. Much of the evidence is so badly expressed that we cannot even be sure what are some of the facts upon which we are seeking to base our explanations. Under these circumstances, we need feel neither surprise nor shame at falling into controversy. And I have certainly no wish to underestimate the value of the controversy still continuing, itself a sign of healthy growth, when I suggest that it is nevertheless possible now to bring within the two covers of this book a large and settled body of accepted knowledge.

Moreover, of those particulars which are not yet settled, there is a considerable proportion which were not settled at the time, and should not be settled now. Much that is now in flux always was in flux and should remain in flux. The options open to an early performer within the boundaries of a style were often very wide; and it is not our business to narrow the outer boundaries of style, but to clarify them. The more we can discover what variations of detail were practised then within a given context, the more flexibly we can now match our options to theirs; yet the more we can give to our interpretations that sharpness of focus which comes from great precision and appropriateness of style.

The reader will find that my recommendations, though properly cautious from the scholarly point of view, are usually quite definite. There is usually a way of doing things which is better authenticated and better musicianship within the given context. It may be flexible, but it is not vague. It can be taught with precision and it can be taught with confidence, and the great majority of my colleagues are so teaching it.

Wherever there is a minority opinion of sufficient scholarly substance, I have drawn attention to it. There are certainly some incompatible conclusions as yet unreconciled. There are also conclusions which might both be right in different contexts, or in the same context if they fall within the flexibility proper to the style. And again there are conclusions which we may just not be able to draw with certainty, from lack of sufficiently unambiguous evidence surviving. But then, these are quite likely to settle themselves practically enough provided we can keep them within the known general boundaries of the style.

We shall never get everything altogether right. That does not matter; for in music, as elsewhere, good enough is good enough. I am confident that nowadays we can, if we so desire, make our interpretations of early music good enough. This book is designed to point that way, in plenty of detail.

5. THE INTRODUCTORY CHAPTERS: ANOTHER KIND OF CONTROVERSY?

The six chapters which make up the present Introduction: New Thinking on Early Interpretation, are entirely new material. They might well be regarded as having another kind of controversial bearing: not on account of the facts here to be retailed, nor even my reading of the facts; but on account of my careful reconsideration of the general principles with which we may wish to approach the interpretation of early music, as illustrated by some recent performances which have indeed aroused a considerable amount of topical controversy.

It is here, in this Introduction, that I have done most to bring my own general thinking on early interpretation up into the current mood of 1973. I do not find myself substantially disagreeing with my former self; but I have some thoughts to add which I hope may be of interest, since, topical as they are, they point on towards what I think may be the unfolding future of our ideas and methods for the interpretation of early music.

6. THE SELECT BIBLIOGRAPHY

My Select Bibliography, like everything else, has been given the most intensive reconsideration. A few of the old entries have been left out, either because they are less necessary now than they were, or because they have been superseded, or merely to reduce wherever possible a list of relevant reading-matter which is inevitably growing longer all the time, and which tends to defeat its own purpose if it is made any longer than it has to be. A much larger number of new entries has been added as being both valuable and relevant; but this double criterion has been applied still more rigorously than before. Even the most valuable items have been excluded when their relevance to my subject is slight, or indirect, or lies chiefly in the relaying of existing knowledge.

My late wife, Gloria Rose, who did so much to make my previous Bibliography thorough and accurate, spent an even longer amount of skilled working-time in tracking down new bibliographical information, and in checking over again what was here before, by unremitting reference to original sources. Surprisingly often the results have been unexpected (but rather less surprisingly, perhaps, when I add that her new researches took her just on four months of hard labour and harder patience). The essential principle of describing only what has been seen, and describing it just as it has been seen, was pushed to all practicable lengths.

We were able, before this revision was completed, to compare our entries with those which are in the new RISM volumes. Valuable tool as RISM is, it does not and it cannot set to rest all bibliographical uncertainties, nor is it without mistakes; but it has enabled us to solve some long-standing problems for which the information required was not hitherto available. The debt of gratitude which we all owe to it is very great.

A particularly time-consuming attempt has been made, in working over the present Select Bibliography, to record (to 1973) the commercially motivated multiplication (a recent phenomenon) of photographic facsimile reprints; and none of these has been listed as existing merely because announced for sale in a publisher's catalogue or advertisement, until we could personally assure ourselves that the young hopeful had actually seen the light of day, and if so, what state of the original it represented, from what degree of editing if any it benefited, *etc.*

Readers are again invited to send me any queries on bibliographical as on other matters, care of my publishers.

7. THE COMPLEMENTARY FUNCTION OF THE SMALLER BOOK

I now turn to the different but complementary function of my smaller book, *A Performer's Guide to Baroque Music*. Though sharing some elements in common, this is not a summary of the present, larger book, but takes many fresh angles on much fresh material.

The intention of the *Performer's Guide* is to offer to busy practitioners and hard-pressed teachers and students a severely utilitarian course of instruction in the basic know-how of baroque performance. This instruction is very far from being on an elementary level; on the contrary, it goes quite searchingly into the most advanced procedures of rhythmic alteration, ornamental elaboration and the other newly fashionable conventions of baroque performance. But it does this and much else as briefly and as simply as the complicated nature of the material allows.

This larger *Interpretation* aims to give a perspective view of the great panorama of baroque performance, with some glances forward and backward for greater depth of field. That smaller *Guide* is not concerned with perspective or with depth of field. It is concerned with getting conveniently and efficiently into the editor's study as he prepares his score, into the conductor's music-room as he learns it, into the class-room where its applied principles may be taught systematically and into the rehearsal-room where it may be turned to actual music.

Gone, then, is the spaciousness of this larger book; gone are the humanist asides, the ample contemporary quotations, the instructive comparisons with periods before and after. In their place stand concise surveys and working rules-of-thumb, with only sufficient quotation from the contemporary treatises to elucidate the original methods and support my current recommendations, themselves condensed as much from my own practical experience as from my reading in the contemporary documents. Some of the quotations used there are reduced extracts from those in this present book; others come from different sources, particularly in connection with matters which, for practical reasons, needed not briefer but more extended treatment in that smaller book, or which have become more extensively known to me from my own and other continuing researches. These researches are also reflected in the present book; but not necessarily in the same detailed applications, owing to the difference of function between the larger and the smaller books.

There is, in that smaller book, a much more deliberate attempt to give direct and explicit advice to the editors of baroque music, and also to that intelligent and increasing class of performers intent on following the best baroque precedent by being so far as possible their own editors.

There is a much expanded discussion of singing, and particularly of the crucial art of *bel canto* voice-production as it is now being energetically recovered from its serious decline during the first half of the twentieth century. The historical gramophone recordings made early in this century by the last altogether undiminished exponents of the *bel canto* technique are brought to bear upon a study of their methods which seemed more in place there than here, though I have, of course, considered here the ruling principles involved for their technical and general relevance to early interpretation.

There is also a still more expanded discussion of the technique of handling baroque accidentals editorially: a wider problem for baroque (and not merely for medieval and renaissance) music than we had altogether appreciated, and remaining so throughout that period although greatly decreasing towards the end of it. This was a problem already recognised and confronted in the first and second editions of the original *Interpretation*, but not yet sufficiently seen through to its logical conclusions. The present book includes as an Appendix some considerable amplification of the subject, but the more detailed findings of my recent researches into baroque accidentals will be found, where I think they most conveniently belong, as practical examples in the *Performer's Guide*.

There is, in the *Performer's Guide*, a particularly sustained and concentrated new attempt to give lucid instructions for applying in practice those quite complicated conventions for modifying the notated rhythms in performance, which also receive much intensive consideration here. Recent controversies about ornaments are not discussed there as they are here; but they are, where necessary, incorporated in the information given.

There is, on the other hand, much less there than here on the necessary and important art of realising an appropriate, imaginative and well-contrived accompaniment, whether prepared or improvised or a little of each, on a continuo bass. That is a subject which receives particularly full and systematic consideration in this present, larger book, and I hope that readers within whose responsibilities it falls will give it their careful attention, since I have dealt here with many practical aspects of the matter which did not lie within the scope of F. T. Arnold's magnificent *Art of Accompaniment from a Thorough-Bass* (London, 1931).

In my smaller book, I have said enough to suggest the chief virtues and vices in this most enticing branch of baroque performance. But my wife, Gloria Rose, had for some time been collecting a quantity of rather unexpected new evidence, much of it in the form of ordinary figured-bass accompaniments, partly or wholly realised in ordinary notation by baroque musicians, and surviving in ordinary working manuscripts of the baroque period. She had also assembled some very interesting pictorial evidence. It was our hope to collaborate in a forthcoming book on continuo accompaniment, largely based on her new material; and there, for the moment, this matter rests. I should only add here that the new material reassuringly confirms and amplifies my old recommendation to give the accompaniment a texture in good and well-sustained and even lightly imitative part-writing, wherever possible and suitable, as very commonly it is. An Appendix to the present volume shows certain examples of such written-out baroque accompaniments.

A fuller discussion by me of the special problems of *String Playing in Baroque Music*, with recorded illustrations by Yehudi Menuhin, George Malcolm and myself is now (1977) available under that title from Faber.

The *Performer's Guide* gives throughout more prominence than the *Interpretation* to actual instruments; it uses more excerpts from actual music and fewer quotations from musical examples in baroque treatises; it is altogether less directed towards general principles, and more toward particular applications. Both that smaller and this larger book are suitable as textbooks for teaching, both in class and individually; but the courses to which they are most suitable, and the levels of study at which they are most readily applicable, are different. It is a difference not only of length but of approach; and teachers will no doubt judge for themselves which approach (or approaches) can best be adapted to their own purposes.

Scholars will not, I hope, overlook the smaller book, since there is new matter for them there which is not included in the present book, as well as the other way round. In both books, it is ultimately the performer whose interests I have tried to serve, and ultimately by the same method of using scholarly means to musicianly ends.

The performer; and thereby the listener.

II. Prospects for Authenticity

1. TWO UNDERLYING ASSUMPTIONS RECONSIDERED

What best pleases the performer will generally best please the listener, since musical enjoyment is apt to be shared enjoyment. What best pleases a great many especially of our younger performers today is anything that has the air and glamour of authenticity; and a very welcome development this is. But it makes it all the more desirable to think out as clearly as possible just what we mean by authenticity.

There were two large assumptions concerning authenticity which gave to *The Interpretation of Early Music*, twelve years ago, its point of view and its underlying character.

The first assumption was that early music really is best served by matching our modern interpretations as closely as possible to what we believe (on historical grounds transmitted by surviving contemporary evidence) to have been the original interpretations.

The second assumption was that (over and above the irreducible minimum of inadvertent modernisation which must attend our best efforts, simply because we can never quite find out what went on so many generations ago) there will ordinarily have to be a large element of deliberate compromise, since practical and especially economic conditions will seldom permit it to be otherwise; the which compromise had therefore better be made as knowledgeably and intelligently as possible.

How, then, do these two assumptions stand up today?

2. THE ASSUMPTION CONCERNING HISTORICAL AUTHENTICITY

The first assumption, that we can best serve early music by matching our modern interpretation as closely as possible to what we know of the original interpretation, may be called the doctrine of historical authenticity.

This is in better standing today than ever before, and much better than a dozen years ago. The doctrine of historical authenticity is now unquestionably respectable, though not universal. The great conservatories of music, for example, where the finest of our young musicians receive their professional training, have not yet given to this doctrine the weight of their unreserved support, though they would probably subscribe to it as a general principle, and in many cases are implementing it in some areas, for example in teaching harpsichord as well as piano.

Precedents now exist (as at Brooklyn College in the City University of New York) for regular full courses in Performance Practice under a director with the diplomatic function of maintaining good relations with his colleagues teaching individual instruments: a relationship raising problems of cooperation as well as of demarcation, but none that cannot be solved. The tendency to recognise early interpretation as a special area with its own material for tuition is an evident one by now, and the pace is increasing.

It has long been taught or assumed that early methods of performance and early standards of technique were necessarily inferior to modern methods and standards. It is now increasingly being taught or assumed that, on the contrary, early methods and standards may be superior for their own music. We should not underestimate the significance of this change of attitude, which is radical and requires a considerable time to become generally established.

A merely tacit assumption, however, that early methods, instruments and techniques are superior for early music ignores the possibility that there might be exceptions to that basic truth. This new and fashionable habit of mind is indeed much sounder than its previous opposite, and gives better results; but it still flies somewhat in the face of probability. In course of musical history, there must, we should suppose, have been some flaws upon which we have made genuine improvements. And in fact there were many, often of a very substantial order. In most instances (for example, with early brass and wood-wind) it may under many circumstances be worth accepting and overcoming the authentic deficiencies for the sake of the authentic appropriateness so closely associated with them; but not necessarily in all instances.

A homely illustration is plastic substitutes for harpsichord quill which sound no less well but are more easily available and more reliable; even the most historically-minded makers seem to be using them successfully. Again, while researches into original alloys for stringing harpsichords have certainly been instructive, early seventeenth-century bowed instruments had bottom strings of uncovered gut, whose reluctance to get into vibration is disadvantageous, and is perhaps the reason why early violin parts such as Monteverdi's so seldom go down on to the G string. That is no superiority, and a return to it might be an advance historically but a retrogression musically. This does not necessarily rule it out; but it is just the sort of small point which may set us asking whether we do not want to draw the line somewhere, and if so, where.

An uncritical assumption that whatever is old is best is no more reasonable than an uncritical assumption that whatever music has fallen into oblivion merits revival, as if oblivion itself were a mark of value and a sufficient claim upon our modern attention. But the basic assumption that early music is worth reviving, and on its own terms, gains ground all the time. I stand by that, and more musicians than ever before are evidently in agreement.

3. THE ASSUMPTION CONCERNING NECESSARY COMPROMISE

The second assumption, that compromise is largely unavoidable, is less generally agreed to than it was, and I am glad to say it.

There are now very numerous groups obdurately opposed to compromise, and for that very reason successful up to a much greater extent in avoiding it. Sometimes they pay more of a price than I would be prepared to pay in lowered standards of technique or musicianship or vital energy. Sometimes, on the contrary, they triumph over the attendant difficulties, and do us all a very great service indeed.

The first of such groups to pioneer successfully and on a significant scale was that led by my own great teacher, Arnold Dolmetsch, with whom I studied forty and more years ago after he had eventually settled down in Haslemere, England. There was a substantial amount of unavoidable compromise at that time, if only because those were such pioneering days, and some things were simply not yet recovered or discovered; but remarkably little compromise that was avoidable (we did not, however, use gut bottom strings on our bowed instruments for early seventeenth-century music). It is only quite recently that groups of so little willingness to compromise have become numerous and in a manner normal. They make it their business (and normal is a very proper word for this) to seek out the original instruments, the original conventions, the original techniques and idioms, just so far as it is physically and mentally possible to recover them.

But whereas, at the time of my own apprenticeship under Arnold Dolmetsch, harpsichordists were birds of some rarity, viol players and recorder players only occurred here or there in scattered clusters, lutenists were singletons of most uncommon provenance, violinists using early bows and fittings, mainly gut strings and a baroque conception of tone and articulation, were virtually a local species at Haslemere, while early brass and most early wood-wind (reeds above all) were hardly yet to be heard again in the land: whereas forty years ago, in short, the resources were either not available at all, or confined to a small minority movement necessarily somewhat assertive in the face of superior odds, now the attack is mounted everywhere with forces extraordinarily numerous and well equipped, and in many instances highly competent in addition.

Within the last dozen years, the most notable achievements have been in the field of wind instruments. These are now being manufactured in satisfactory reproductions, and mastered with a satisfactory standard of technique, on a scale which has opened up new possibilities. Of course, only the most proficient players can get them reliably in tune; but this was always so, as certain rather over-worked quotations from the eighteenth century have long assured us. It is quite magnificent, and quite a novelty, to hear cornettos ringing out now so brilliantly and accurately, crumhorns buzzing along so precisely, long trumpets and sackbuts like silver and bronze streaks of sound, serpents as smooth as turtle-doves, and shawms effortlessly raising the dead, but not at the same time necessarily the pitch. From all this, medieval, renaissance and early baroque music has taken great advantage.

Much solid progress has also been made with the wind instruments of the later baroque orchestra, and some progress with that most recalcitrant problem, the string foundation. Arnold Dolmetsch long ago refitted and even made violins to baroque design, and outcurved bows to go with them (just as advanced makers like Richard Hart are doing again today). He got us playing, too, with a fine sense of baroque string style, which we almost took for granted, but which unfortunately did not pass (as so much of his remarkable pioneering did pass) into common practice. It has taken almost these full forty years before this crucial problem of transparent string sonority and incisive string articulation has been picked up again quite in the same radical spirit of adventure.

Meanwhile, one mistaken tradition has grown up of teaching as authentically baroque a certain dryness and abruptness (almost ruthlessness) of string style (cellos and basses particularly), in the reaction (necessary in itself) against too much richness and smoothness; for there is, indeed, a certain romantic legacy remaining in string style which we still need for our Wagner and our Strauss, our Mahler and our Elgar, but which is incongruous for our baroque revival.

If we compare Menuhin's style with Kreisler's, a generation back, we may notice particularly the reduction in *portamento*, that swift but deliberately audible joining of some notes by *glissando* which was so normal a resource in romantic violin playing. They all did it: the Lener Quartet, for example, whom it would be hard to equal today for great quartet playing, though no modern quartet would perhaps wish to be quite so romantic in their Beethoven. Perhaps they should be, since Beethoven also was a romantic composer. At their worst, the romantic fiddlers were sentimental; at their best, they were out of this world for aural nectar and ambrosia. For all that, I would not wish them on to our baroque revival.

In good orchestras, string sections now play accurately in tune. So rare was this forty years ago that orchestras in which it happened, such as the Berlin Philharmonic or the Vienna Philharmonic, were acclaimed for the bloom and the warmth of their string tone as if this were some high miracle of Germanic artistry. It was simply that we were so habituated to the tinny sound which is the acoustic beating of many strings playing almost but not quite in unison that we did not even recognise the disease until mercifully it became cured, with improved proficiency in the back desks. Warmth of string sound is something we can now take for granted in good orchestras everywhere; and that has been as good for our Bach playing as it has for our Wagner.

Nevertheless, there can also be a kind of thickness of string sound which is good for Wagner but not good for Bach. It is due partly to wide vibrato; partly to long and swift bow-strokes as opposed to slower, shorter and more into the string; partly to holding too many notes too ruthlessly to the end with no graceful tapering down of the sound; partly to other and almost unanalysable (because habitual) such assumptions in the player's mind about the sonority and articulation proper to his instrument. Proper they are, but for Wagner or for Schoenberg rather than for Bach or for Monteverdi. It was in reaction against these habitual assumptions that the hard style of string playing grew up of which I have spoken. But that, on the other hand, is too hard to be altogether musicianly, and it too is not quite what the contemporary evidence suggests or the music implies.

Allied to this hard school, but lacking its considerable virtues of robustness and energy, is the school which mistakes under-playing for authentic playing. As a reaction against over-playing, this too has its place in the history of the baroque revival; but it is really quite as un-baroque in its failure to achieve a singing line, a *cantabile* of sustained shapeliness and warmth (yet with a razor-edge articulation in the proper places). An overall lack of continuity between unslurred notes, and non-slurring carried to the remarkable extreme of bowing every note of a trill separately: these are misunderstandings of the contemporary evidence, rather than neglect of it. But they are much in need of reconsideration. *Cantabile* and robustness are both very important elements in baroque music.

No fiddler carried on quite that blend of subtle poetry, fiery colouring, lucid transparency and keen cutting edge which was at once so singular to Arnold Dolmetsch's personality and so convincingly baroque. But the leader of the Alarius ensemble reaches something of the same fiery glow and clarity, though not, of course, the same personal singularity; and, from the side of theory, David Boyden's classic *History of Violin Playing* (London, 1965) has provided a stronger foundation than we ever had before, on which there largely rests, for example, the wonderful baroque fiddling of Sonya Monosoff.

On the side of practice, there has probably been less accomplished

41

by way of radical achievement with the strings than has been accomplished with the woodwind and still more with the keyboards. Baroque-fitted violins, it is true, grow more common; but that understanding of baroque violin-playing which would be a truly radical reform is confined still to very few modern performers. The most extensive advances towards a baroque style of string playing for baroque music have not so far resulted from radical reforms at all, but from that general inclination towards a sharper, leaner fashion in fiddling which I have mentioned above.

It is fairly common now, especially with the younger players, to hear a most agreeably relaxed and ringing sonority and crisp articulation which does reasonably well for baroque music. It can often be further improved in rehearsal by a few timely hints about bow strokes, speeds and pressures; but it is fundamentally suitable. It will let the music breathe, neither suffocating it with too much richness nor clamping it down with too much hardness. In a word, it will sound sufficiently natural to the baroque style, though it is not actually a baroque sound, for which more drastic changes are needed, as with Sonya Monosoff.

The hard style is fairly common too; but far commoner than either is an average solidity which has the sustained weight for a nineteenth-century symphony or string quartet, but which in baroque music is a little like an otherwise good cake which has not quite risen properly. That is a factor which cannot usually be much improved in a limited space of rehearsal, being too ingrained into the player's technique; but given time, this technical consideration can be worked through, in technical terms, provided that there is not some corresponding temperamental disinclination on the mental plane. Temperamental differences are perfectly legitimate, and no disparagement is implied, but it is of course very important to choose colleagues for a baroque performance who are temperamentally inclined to a style of fiddling relaxed enough, yet with enough inner electric tension, for the purpose on hand. There are more of them around now among whom to choose.

The possibilities for mounting an almost uncompromisingly baroque performance are, in short, much greater today than they were twelve years ago (to say nothing of forty years ago): not only within the limited requirements of chamber music, but on the ambitious scale of large works with full baroque orchestra (and that is a wonderful sonority when it is successfully achieved, early wind instruments, baroque-style fiddling and all). And not only under rare and special circumstances, but under much more ordinary artistic and commercial circumstances, since the practical and economic odds are no longer nearly so unfavourable as they used to be. Original methods of performance are the fashion now, and this in itself has greatly increased the possibilities.

42

Thus my second basic assumption of twelve years ago, that considerable compromise is necessary and should be planned with knowledge and intelligence, now holds less force, though it still holds some force. For many excellent musicians of the reforming party, the advanced principles of twelve years ago have become the established norms of the present day; and I am hopeful that this book, in its new version, may serve today as a more or less standard presentation of the case for the reforming party.

III. Authenticity and Personality

The case for the reforming party rests largely on the case for historical authenticity, but not entirely, and I think that the question calls for some reconsideration here.

What are the motives for historical authenticity? One of them is a rightful curiosity. If the establishment has assumed that modern skills and instruments are improvements on early skills and instruments, then the younger generation, questioning the establishment as its habit is, has to find out for itself, and is doing so with great and welcome enthusiasm. The reforming party is immeasurably the stronger for this fresh support.

Another motive, although on an unconscious level, for historical authenticity consists of an elusive and not very welcome contamination by an odd sort of misplaced morality. When 'it goes better like this' becomes 'it ought to go like this', historical purity has somehow got to seem like moral purity. It is as if we should feel guilty for enjoying ourselves against the small, still voice of authenticity. Or perhaps just for enjoying ourselves; for there can be a fear of joy and a flight from emotion, in which early music may seem a safe refuge although it is not. If letting go robustly touches on guilty misgivings, then underplaying may feel safer and be rationalised as historical authenticity. But authenticity is not really more virtuous than anachronism. It is just in the main much more musicianly; and robust enjoyment is a part of it.

Then has morality no part in music? It has, I think, a part. There is an integrity in being true, each of us, to our own personal visions of the music; and there is an honesty in not wilfully misrepresenting it. But as to the integrity, this is hardly a case, if indeed there are any such, for setting up to know best for other people. And as to the honesty, musicians seldom see themselves as wilfully misrepresenting the music; they are more likely to misrepresent it unwittingly.

It is certainly helpful and honourable to provide a sufficient minimum of information in our programme notes and prefaces; but this is rather from scholarly convention and practical convenience than from moral obligation. We give better value if we do, but it is not worse morality if we do not. Giving explicitly or implicitly false information is, perhaps, another matter, and in a bad case might almost amount to fraudulent misrepresentation. Even when done in ignorance, this might be blameworthy, since an editor really ought not to enter the field without a reasonable knowledge of his difficult job, which is full of traps for the inexperienced worker. But this still does not make bad scholarship or bad musicianship the same as bad morality.

Moral judgement is a very insidious substitute for artistic judgement. It may run counter to my own integrity if I perform publicly on violins those contrapuntally low-lying fantasies for viols whose transparent eloquence will, as I know from unfortunate experience, be obscured and misrepresented by this apparently harmless change of scoring. I would pass adverse artistic judgement on it if I heard it done. But moral judgement? Where lies the injury to another person which would make a moral issue of it? Or of playing Bach on the piano, as so many pianists do with unquestionable integrity and artistry? Or of giving the young clarinettists who are so much commoner than violinists, in American high schools and colleges, baroque trio sonatas to enlarge their musical horizons? Or of transcribing baroque music for the wind bands whose repertoire so needs improvement and many of whose directors are so eager to improve it? Our artistic advice as to where and how to do such things is perfectly proper, but it is likely to be acceptable in proportion as it is unmoralistically conveyed.

A living composer may feel injured and frustrated if his explicit intentions are wilfully disregarded, even though it is not unknown for such disregard to do better for his music than he has done himself, and for him to admit this afterwards. A baroque composer may not ever have had such explicit intentions, which run somewhat counter to the baroque attitude; being dead, he cannot suffer in his feelings; his music, lying both legally and morally within the public domain, is ours to use as best we like and can. It was a fashion some years ago to perform Shakespeare in modern dress, which shocked some people while interesting others. Those who like early music in modern dress do no more injury, though they may give no more pleasure, to those of us who like it better so to speak (I do not mean literally) in period costume. Yet, of course, I know for myself how hard it is not to feel morally outraged.

Moral outrage tempts one to moralism, and moralism to disapproving and repressive attitudes. But Milton, great Puritan as (on one side) he was, had a wise answer for this perennial dilemma of conscientious minds. 'And though all the winds of doctrine were let loose to play upon the earth, so Truth be in the field, we do injuriously by licensing and prohibiting to misdoubt her strength,' he wrote against censorship in his *Areopagitica* of 1644. 'Let her and Falsehood grapple; who ever knew Truth put to the worse, in a free and open encounter.' It is a magnificent faith, which we must believe to be ultimately valid however often it is temporarily belied. But then Milton added, with sudden insight, that which does most to make his faith believable: 'Yet it is not impossible that she may have more shapes than one.' It is not impossible that good interpretation of early music may have more shapes than one.

That thought should take much of the sting out of the controversy in which we musicologists, like all scholars of all times and places, are so often involved. But if moral indignation in such matters of art is misplaced indignation, it is certainly a tribute to the importance of art in our daily lives, so much more than mere entertainment value and passing diversion. If we did not mind so much about how these things are done, we should not be much good at doing them; and perhaps the heat of controversy is not too high a price to pay for the intensity which our strong feelings enable us to put into our work. Anyhow, controversy is unavoidable.

I am of an age now when it is a little easier to tolerate controversy in a spirit of acceptance; and of course it can lead to valuable conclusions if it is accepted. Ironically enough, I must be one of the few musicians of my generation who actually was brought up from early youth in the uncompromising assumption, now so fashionable, that you cannot get too authentic for the good of the music; and I must confess, looking back on it, that moral goodness was distinctly part of the insinuation. But artistic goodness was nevertheless being practised as well as preached, as I sat literally at Arnold Dolmetsch's feet, down on the floor among the music-stands, and treated rather like an unofficially adopted cat by his talented and friendly family.

The Dolmetsch tradition may have become inevitably diluted now by its enormous growth, to which many more musicians are indirectly indebted at this time than have ever directly heard of it. But at that time, under the formidable old genius himself, it was highly concentrated; and there I drew in what I could of a vision of the true inwardness of baroque music unsurpassed, very possibly unequalled, in modern times. My training was not exactly systematic; but presently I was playing in Arnold Dolmetsch's concerts, later in his pupil Marco Pallis' concerts, and later still in my own, filling in the gaps meanwhile at the British Museum, the Bodleian, the Fitzwilliam Museum, the Bibliothèque Nationale or wherever else the needed knowledge lay. Against all this I could not nor should I wish to turn.

But Arnold Dolmetsch was not a fanatic: merely a man ahead of his day (and already sixty-five when I as a shy schoolboy first encountered him). He had ears too sharp for a comfortable fanatic. Thus when my ears tell me that it is time to compromise a little, I will do so, remembering how Thomas Morley (*A Plaine and Easie Introduction to Practicall Musicke*, London, 1597, marginal rubric on p. 88) insisted, in the very middle of his great learning, on calling 'the eare the most just judge of al musicke'.

When the early wood-wind (even if available) cannot on some occasion be got in tune, it may be a wise (or necessary) compromise to use modern counterparts. When the early wood-wind are available and are in tune, but are ineffective against the dry acoustics of an excessively unresonant (and in this respect un-baroque) hall, it may still be wiser (as I learnt from David Lasocki, a player of both early and modern flutes and a most articulate spokesman for the younger generation) to use modern counterparts. When the harpsichord is too feeble or the harpsichordist has too untutored a touch to give adequate support, electrical amplification may be a virtual necessity. When it is a choice between indifferent fiddlers devoted to authenticity and excellent fiddlers only able to give limited rehearsal time, there may be more gain than loss in using the excellent fiddlers if they are willing to be adaptable within that practical limitation.

It would seem that authenticity can be taken within a certain margin of opinion; and this needs, perhaps, some further elucidation. The decisions just mentioned are largely questions of expediency; but an issue of principle is more deeply at stake, to which I shall next turn.

2. A TOPICAL ISSUE OF PRINCIPLE

The issue of principle to which I refer, although of the broadest relevance to early interpretation, has come up topically in connection with early Italian opera, revivals of which in different manners by different musicologists (and some who are not musicologists) have been attracting such fine audiences, and arousing such fine controversy, in recent years. Universities have been the chief scenes of such revivals, from J. A. Westrup's brilliant pioneering of Monteverdi at Oxford forty years ago, to Alan Curtis' sophisticated, sensitive and musicianly performances at Berkeley and elsewhere recently. But recently, too, Monteverdi and Cavalli have been taking fashionable audiences by storm in fashionable opera-houses; and from a later stage of baroque opera, Alessandro Scarlatti and Handel have also been having their notable successes.

With Handel, and again with Alessandro Scarlatti, there are the usual baroque problems of instrumental sonority and articulation, and there are the special operatic problems of *bel canto* casting, and in particular the casting of the castrato parts (whether transposed or at their proper pitch); but we are not forced unavoidably into facing a broader issue of principle. It is far otherwise with Monteverdi or Cavalli.

Monteverdi's *Orfeo* (perf. Mantua, 1607) was regarded as having provided so memorable an occasion that the score was published twice

(Venice, 1609 and 1615); and it contains a reasonably indicative although by no means complete record of the music and its instrumentation. The great majority of seventeenth-century operas, however, after the earliest years of novelty, were not printed at all (except quite often, in France, as mere vocal reductions); they survive as rough working manuscripts in which only the voice parts and the bass line are reasonably certain to be notated more or less in full, the rest of the music being either notated in varying degrees sketchily, or in places not notated at all. Whether to fill out this sketchy manuscript with modern composing to complete the music is therefore not a matter of choice, but of necessity. The opera cannot be revived at all in any acceptable degree of completeness unless it is done, and the only realistic questions are how boldly or timidly, how well or badly it is going to be done. We cannot avoid the issue of principle which this fact brings up in a particularly acute and disputable form.

The issue is: how far should the personality of the modern performer blend with the personality of the early composer?

3. A BLEND OF PERSONALITIES

History and artistry so often go hand in hand that we may easily overlook the possibility of their sometimes conflicting. Neither historical nor any other kind of knowledge can recreate the music for us. We have to live it for ourselves. That not only involves our artistry; it involves our personality.

No music other than electronic can be performed without a blend of personalities between performer and composer: or if they are one and the same person, between these aspects of his personality. Baroque music, with its great reliance on the performer's initiative (and with all its composers long since dead) requires this blend of personalities in high degree; baroque opera, in especially high degree.

We are not morally obliged to follow history. But we are artistically obliged to draw upon our own resources of musical personality. We cannot so much as realise a continuo accompaniment without revealing a personality self-effacing or ostentatious or somewhere felicitously in between, and a musicianship inventive or pedestrian or good decent average. We cannot either add or refrain from adding free ornamentation or specific ornaments without showing our personal inclination in the matter, to say nothing of our knowledge. We cannot take over, as baroque notation allows and requires us to take over, virtually the whole responsibility for the expression, without giving thereby the plainest indication of our taste and quality; of our awareness of baroque styles or our unawareness; of our empathy with history or our lack of empathy; and of whatever leanings towards the classic or the romantic temperament we may personally harbour. *Le style, c'est l'homme* is no doubt only one side of a very complicated picture; but it is a side we cannot afford to overlook.

One complication for the interpretation of early music is that the style is never only one man, but at the very least two, and these two separated by several eventful generations of musical and human history. An early painting is an early painting if it survives at all; an early composition is just some more or less intelligible marks on paper until it becomes music again through a modern interpreter. In quite another sense of the word, intervening events have left their mark, on his personality and ours, and on our current musical awareness. It is naïve to think that we can shed the intervening centuries like a garment, and interpret Monteverdi and Cavalli as though these centuries had never been.

And yet seeking out the mood and idioms of Monteverdi or Cavalli is the one approach which takes us some way back into that distant world. We can get some way back by pursuing the historical approach; and nowhere at all by neglecting the historical approach.

We can get back if we have enough historical empathy, supported by enough practical information. But that empathy, that feeling of our way into idioms and moods historically quite distant from our own, is itself powered by our own present musicianly desires. It seems that we very much desire this nostalgic delight in experiencing, almost although not quite as though we could return in time, the artistic emotions of past musicians and past audiences. It seems that we seek this marriage of antiquity with modernity; but it also seems that no forced marriage will serve. We must do no violence either to the given music, or to our own musicianship.

This means in practice a performance historically oriented, but not at all costs historical.

4. EARLY MUSIC IN THE HERE AND NOW

To reproduce every historical feature which can be reproduced is desirable when our purposes are equivalent to those of a fine historical museum: unfamiliar experience; educational instruction; rightful curiosity; something for the record; something to broaden the mind. But these are not quite the purposes of a great opera-house or concert-hall. Their purposes are incidentally educational, and certainly include broadening the mind by unfamiliar experience. But perhaps the difference is that the emphasis is on the experience rather than on the unfamiliarity.

The music has to come down to us reasonably intact. But it does have to come to us, and as an experience of the here and now. The beauty of it is that when past music, or any music, really comes to us in the here and now, it catches us up into a world where, in a certain manner, time is not. There is a magic in that world whereby, in some important although not of course literal sense, the borders of space and time dissolve, so that we become in our feelings at once of the twentieth century and of other centuries.

We do not shed our individuality, which is indeed of the twentieth century. But we are made more aware than usual of emotional states which do not attach solely to our individuality, because our ancestors have repeatedly passed through them before, and our descendants will again. These are emotions common to our human condition. Nothing could possibly feel more private and personal: it is as though the music were our very own, so closely identified do we become with it and so intimately are we absorbed into any deep hearing of it. But not exclusively our own, since anyone else in the audience who is as absorbed as we is communing with the music no less privately and no less personally. Thus what we commune with is public property for those capable of sufficient musical response, and they have never been very few. Great music has always been with us, and audiences for it.

Emotions so fundamental that they have always been with us are archetypal in the Platonic sense, which is also the (Hellenistic and renaissance) Neoplatonic sense, and the modern Jungian sense. They evoke in us a feeling of recognition, as though we have known them all our lives, which indeed we have in Plato's meaning of forms laid up in heaven, or in an analytical psychologist's meaning of behaviour-patterns laid down in the unconscious.

It is not, therefore, unfamiliarity alone which we find in Monteverdi or Cavalli, although there is an important element of that. It is also, and more fundamentally, familiarity. There is a relief in shedding, not our individuality, but something of its time-bound and place-bound limitations. There is a delight in responding to emotions older and bigger than our short life-spans, and more enduring, beginning as they did at the childhood of our race and stretching as we may hope into the illimitable future. Here are dreams, but dreams a great deal more solid and tough than our mere perishable mortality; and here are we, sharing them effortlessly with Monteverdi's or Cavalli's original audiences. Such dreams are of the inner stuff of life; indeed, such dreams are the very pattern of what life feels like from the inside. No wonder we do not depend upon the smaller details of historical authenticity for sharing them. They are themselves a shared element in our human heritage. From this point of view, we are merely members of Monteverdi's or Cavalli's wider audience.

Nevertheless we are of a different century. We have to work hard for that blend of personalities across the centuries on which such successful communion with the past depends. Early opera only differs from other music of a like antiquity in making us work even harder than usual before we can perform it in any acceptable degree of completeness.

Thus it is that early opera forces us to face openly what is always an issue in early music, but an issue which we often take more or less for granted. It is quite possible to realise a trio sonata, but hardly possible to realise an opera, without appreciating how inevitably one's own personality takes its proper share. But it is important to appreciate that it is a proper share, since trying to be self-effacing, while no less personal a decision than any other, may lead in practice to a more monotonous interpretation. We have so many contemporary accounts of early Italian operas having strongly moved great audiences, even to the point of tears, that monotony is the one outcome of which we can be certain that it was not the baroque ideal (which is not of course to say that it never happened).

Not whether our modern personalities should share in the interpretation of early music, but how best they can share: this is the question brought into the foreground by our topical experiences with early seventeenth-century opera.

IV. Authenticity in Early Opera

1. EARLY OPERA AN EXTREME THOUGH NOT A SPECIAL CASE

Our method here, as usual, may be to ask what is the contemporary evidence on which we can exercise our modern judgement.

There is not much contemporary evidence. Few accounts of payments to opera instrumentalists have been found, for example (Denis Arnold did his best with two fragmentary ones, '*L'Incoronazione di Poppea* and Its Orchestral Requirements', *Musical Times*, CIV, 1963, p. 177). General descriptions and particular references are slightly more numerous, but usually less specific (they are well sampled and discussed by Gloria Rose, 'Agazzari and the Improvising Orchestra', *Journal of the American Musicological Society*, XVIII, 3, 1965, pp. 382–393, summarised in Appendix IV of the present book). There is enough evidence altogether to suggest a considerable quantity and variety of instruments; not enough to pin down what quantity and what variety, in what contexts.

There are therefore legitimate differences of modern opinion (themselves revealing of personality as well as of scholarly competence) in this respect. But no opinion can diminish the large theatres and popular audiences, above all in seventeenth-century Venice, which were not compatible with very small instrumental forces. We may have, indeed, a fair representation, or at the most one not too misleadingly above the average, in the 'forty instruments' including 'recorders, trumpets, drums, viols, and violins' mentioned in *Le nouveau mercure galant . . . au mois de avril de l'année 1679* (Paris, 1679, pp. 66–67, 71) for the performance in that year of Pallavicini's *Nerone* in Venice at the theatre of S. Giovanni Cristostomo; for all these instruments and a few others do get mentioned somewhere or other in the manuscript scores of the Contarini Collection (Biblioteca Marciana, Venice), which contains operas produced in Venice from 1639 to 1692; while manuscripts of Venetian operas in the Nationalbibliothek at Vienna confirm horns, cornettos, trombones and theorbos. Cesti's *Pomo d'oro* (Vienna, 1667, but in Venetian style) was a festival opera, and somewhat special: its very varied orchestra included regals and chamber-organ. Moderate to fairly large forces: that seems to have been the historical situation, to which our modern responses have been very various.

One of the least successful of recent Monteverdi editors has been Bruno Maderna: not because he has been too modern, but because he has been too Victorian, cramping the rhythmic freedom of the recitative with symmetrical accompaniments and obbligatos, negating the tonal architecture, the dramatic key-changes and the skilful tessitura by wilful transpositions and alterations of order, and altogether failing to match his personal musicianship with the given music, as I described in a detailed review (*Notes*, XXV, 1, Sept. 1968, pp. 112–114) and a more general article ('The Robustness of Early Opera', *Opera*, Jan. 1970, pp. 16–22). His performing versions tend to fall quite flat, in spite (or because) of their ambitious decking.

And one of the most successful of recent Monteverdi and Cavalli editors, at Glyndebourne and other famous opera-houses, has been Raymond Leppard. The praise and the criticism he encounters alike show how real the issues are; and while some of the criticism is merely of inadequate information in his published editions, there has also been criticism of his workmanship, particularly of his transpositions and translocations of order.

That realisations of early opera should be liable to criticism is little wonder, when we recall that opera-composers during much of the seventeenth century did not write down, but left to be worked out more or less by concerted improvisation in rehearsal, or to be provided by some other musician: the entire realisation of the continuo, and not just at the harpsichord, but on a group of many instruments of which some at times might certainly be melodic; the melodic orchestral parts for many or all of the sinfonias and ritornellos, often notated only as a bass and a treble line, or only as a bass line, or not at all, sometimes indicated merely by the word 'sinfonia' or 'ritornello' without any music notated, sometimes required where in no way indicated (and all this likewise with the dances); much, at least, of the choice of instruments, and the scoring for them; much free ornamentation expected to be mainly improvised (and differently on different occasions) by singers; and whatever else a practical performance has to have decided, but the sketchy notation of the manuscripts in no way decides. To have to realise early music on such a scale as this does not make a special case of it; but it is certainly an extreme case.

For improvisation to have covered in the original performances some of the features just mentioned, it would have, at the very least, to have been preconcerted very thoroughly indeed; and while it can be shown (as by Gloria Rose in the article just mentioned) that such concerted improvisation did actually occur, we do not yet know to what lengths it was carried, or between what dates. Some of the orchestral material lacking from the manuscript scores, for example, might well have been written down separately at the time, but subsequently lost. Either the composer himself or other composers might have provided

53

it, perhaps at a late stage in the proceedings; for we know that such a delaying or sharing out of the responsibility was a common occurrence in early opera (in France, it was quite usual to have the extensive dance music handed to another composer, as when Lully composed the dances for Cavalli's *Ercole Amante*, performed at Paris in 1662).

Yet what may once have existed is of no help to us now if it has not survived; and the practical situation remains the same on either hypothesis, or on a combination of both. The modern interpreter must take responsibility for deciding what is required, and for providing it. He cannot provide it in any musicianly way unless he pours his own personality into the work, and has plenty to pour. The result is almost bound to displease some critics, while pleasing others; but it is my belief that for creative musicianship and fundamental appropriateness alike, Raymond Leppard comes extremely well out of the controversy.

2. COMBINING MUSICIANSHIP AND MUSICOLOGY

Some of the recent disparagement of Raymond Leppard has had such a satirical edge to it that I have wondered if it was not a little tinged with envy: the envy of the book-bound scholar for the fancy-free (and in this case very successful) artist. It is a picture not quite fair to either party; but an uneasy relationship between, on the one hand, scholars and scholar-performers, and on the other hand, unscholarly or at least unscholastic regular performers, is as old as these professions themselves. Indeed, this book is very largely conceived as a contribution towards building new bridges between them.

Professional musicians, with their consummate manual skills and their profoundly intuitive certainties, may find it extremely hard to understand, and sometimes extremely hard to endure, their counterparts the professional scholars, with their no less practised critical equipment, their factual knowledge and their long-tested habits of intellectual caution. Conversely, a musicologist whose historical interest is keener than his intuition may undervalue the uncanny sureness which a good musician often brings to bear even in comparatively unfamiliar music, so that the musicologist ends by irritating the musician rather than guiding him diplomatically along. These difficulties on either side are perfectly genuine, due partly to background and training, still more to temperament. They cannot be eliminated, but they can be ameliorated by a certain deliberate cultivation of mutual recognition and respect.

The basis for this mutual respect lies in the fact that a musicologist working with fine professional performers can and should be learning from them all the time, as well as teaching them. His strength lies in the things that he knows, which they would never hit upon simply by the light of their own musicianship (depending as these things largely do on factual information); their strength lies in their ability to take up this information and mould it into a living musical line of extraordinary sureness, subtlety, warmth and expressiveness.

A musicologist who does not allow his own conceptions of the music to be affected in his turn by what happens in this living act of performance may be wasting an excellent opportunity. His own musicianship will take him a long way, but theirs is probably better (to say nothing of their technique), since their very trade hangs upon it; and accepting this quite as a matter of course should help the partnership, making it easier for them to see the point of him and his fund of good and often unexpected practical suggestions. His facts and their imaginations should get along very well together.

In so far as all this is combined in one and the same person, so much the better, and indeed this has to be so in some degree. An unmusical musicologist is not acceptable in this line of work.

Yet a great performer may be untutored in much that a good musicologist has to offer. Mutual respect is of the essence here, since it is not quite easy for an accomplished performer to take advice which may strike him on first acquaintance as bookish and impertinent. Only by trying it out in rehearsal may he perhaps find it, to his surprise, 'opening doors and windows on Purcell's music', as I remember being told by the Zorian Quartet on one such occasion, at the start of which I had certainly been regarded with suspicion. It is absolutely natural; but we are getting much more accustomed now to this kind of team-work. It needs a spirit of give and take on two sides, of course, not only on one. But the partnership of practising musicians with practical musicologists has become a familiar occurrence of our time, and its usefulness may grow to be increasingly appreciated.

There is room for it. There seems something a little wasteful, for example, in spending the morning at Hanover on good discussions of the appoggiatura in Handel's operas, and the evening in hearing an almost appoggiatura-less performance. Some new feat of diplomacy seems needed to cross this pointless void. And I do not only mean diplomacy from the musicological side. A little more alertness from the musician's camp, a little more awareness of the modern trend in the interpretation of early music, might also be in keeping with the times.

The lack of that awareness is what leads to just such a misuse of fine creative energies as Bruno Maderna falls into in his role as a revivalist of early opera. Not alone Bruno Maderna, of course; it has been a common failing at least since Vincent d'Indy, Respighi and others began taking a modern interest in early opera; and there are many more recent (hence less readily pardonable) examples.

Thus there is the misused opportunity of the recording under Angelo

Ephrikian of Peri's *Euridice* (Florence, 1600), a much-to-be-desired opera if ever there was one. The start is merely quiet and unadventurous. Then string accompaniments begin to invade the recitative, with independent part-writing of so monumental an incongruity that Peri goes almost out of the picture, and wraiths of Puccini, of late Beethoven and (when trombones take up) of Don Juanesque Mozart float by in disconcerting splendour; for it is genuine personal expression, of no little beauty of invention, but so incompatible with the given music that nothing artistic can come of it. The cause (confirmed by the excessively slow tempos) is evidently a failure to understand what manner of free and unfettered thing Italian recitative of the early period is. What you do not know, you have to make up; and this is an excellent example of the shifts to which a fine musician may be driven whenever he has wandered in ignorance or wilfulness outside the implications of the given music.

A most apposite and agreeable contrast is presented by the Archive recording, under Charles Mackerras, of Cavalieri's *Rappresentatione di anima, et di corpo* (Rome, 1600). This, too, is on my definition an opera (a sacred opera), though the recitative is neither so extensive nor so masterly, and there is a great deal of chorus. But the interpretation intended was certainly operatic; and I can hardly imagine it being better done than on this recording. All manner of early baroque instruments are thrown in with true early baroque abandon; but the mercurial freedom of the recitative is in no way hampered, and the voices float gloriously on the orchestral colouring. There is a very great understanding of early Italian recitative. There is also a robustness which is absolutely baroque, congruous and desirable.

I shall return shortly to the instrumentation used for this recording, so different from the other, in its realisation, that the two operas sound aeons apart, rather than products, as they were, of that one notable year 1600. It is not only musicological knowledge which accounts for this difference; but it does account for a great part of it, aided as it is by uncommonly fine musical inspiration and excellent conducting by Charles Mackerras in the Cavalieri recording. Such can be the benefits of combined musicianship and musicology.

3. THE MUSICOLOGICAL CONTRIBUTION

The musicological contribution has to do with supplying the historical knowledge of what goes congruously with what. The musicianly contribution has to do with knowing in one's bones what goes with what. Nothing can turn out right without the second; but very little is likely to turn out right without the first.

AUTHENTICITY IN EARLY OPERA

When Bruno Maderna, lacking the musicological qualifications which might otherwise have alerted him, poured his undoubtedly creative personality into Monteverdi, the result was destructive musically, because Bruno Maderna was too far out of touch with what the given music of Monteverdi itself implies and needs. Historical authenticity was destroyed, and much more than historical authenticity. For was this, in any case, really Bruno Maderna's personality? One would not think so, from his own music; and perhaps he was merely pouring in what he thought he ought to be pouring in. Not only is there an artistic incongruity; there is something very like an artistic insincerity. It does not work. It worries me, not I hope as a moralist, but certainly as a musicologist and equally as a musician. Not of this kind are the liberties I am inclined to advocate.

When Benjamin Britten poured his personality into Purcell, the result was creative musically; and it works like a charm. When I was younger, it used to worry me musicologically, and I suppose moralistically. Purcell with Britten's piano accompaniments does not always come out quite Purcell any more; for Britten was a genius, and made everything he touched his own. There is decidedly an affinity with transcription here. Authenticity is respected only on a deeper level, where musicology does not count for very much, but artistry and integrity do. The artistry is amazing, the integrity is unmistakable, and I am able nowadays to let myself enjoy it (though not as first preference) in spite of my remaining reservations as a musicologist. What we get here is an altered experience of the music: an experience powerfully modified by Britten's personality. But in no way is the music destroyed. On the contrary, there is indeed a deep-lying artistic congruity between the two composers.

When Raymond Leppard pours his personality into Monteverdi or Cavalli, on the other hand, the result is to serve these seventeenth-century composers really much better in themselves, because he does know better what their given music in itself implies and needs. He has enough of the musicologist in him to leave the music mostly as it was. There is certainly an element of transcription, as there is bound to be with any sufficient reconstruction of such early opera; but it has I think been much exaggerated by some of my severer colleagues. The result is unmistakable Monteverdi or Cavalli (whereas, for example, Stravinsky's *Pulcinella* on alleged Pergolesi is unmistakable Stravinsky). At the same time, these are indeed unmistakable Raymond Leppard reconstructions. There is no missing the characteristic finger-prints, the strong and inventive musical personality. But then, how valuable to have a strong and inventive musical personality; and how rare.

There is a remarkable artistic conviction and consistency in Raymond

Leppard's reconstructions. Is there also an artistic congruity with the given music? Close enough, I think, or they would not be so vastly enjoyable. They do not deceive the ear quite as good reproductions of antique furniture may deceive the eye; but there the difference is that we have not got the genuine antique performances on which to model our reconstructed performances. I would myself prefer rather more solid orchestration at times, rather less pizzicato from the string section and sforzato plucking from the continuo section, some substantial added woodwind parts and more trumpet and timpani parts, occasionally a firmer, less gimmicky harpsichord part, sometimes more melodic or even lightly contrapuntal inner parts in the orchestra: while others, as their criticisms have made plain on musicological grounds which I think are quite mistaken, would prefer less of everything.

Sometimes it is not Raymond Leppard's composed string parts, but the rather un-baroque opaqueness of their performance, which sounds a little incongruous: the old and difficult problem, to which I have referred above, of getting a baroque sonority and articulation from a modern string section.

Against that, there is the quite excellently Italianate pronunciation and enunciation which Raymond Leppard (perhaps assisted by a good vocal coach working under him) is getting from his singers: a rare virtue indeed under most modern circumstances and one especially important in this early Italian style of opera. There is a kind of theatricality, a kind of dramatisation with the voice and the words and the pure sounds of the Italian language, which the singers under Raymond Leppard at Glyndebourne are getting better than almost any (and far better than most) of the singers in the other performances discussed in this present chapter.

Raymond Leppard is not exactly a case of neutral musicology; but then, is there really such a thing as neutral musicology when it comes to actual performance? There are certainly performers whose personality shows chiefly in their not being willing to show any personality; but this, though negative, is not neutral either. Could neutral musicology bring Monteverdi or Cavalli back from far-away seventeenth-century Venice, just as they were with nothing left out and nothing else added besides? Not so, for there is much which is left out from the manuscripts themselves and which must be added with inspiration, if we are not to have a most unhistorically dull performance on our hands. The inspiration can only be our own; we have none other.

The point about these Raymond Leppard performances is not the occasionally arguable detail, but the glorious impetus and essential authenticity of the evening's work as a whole. To have got Monteverdi and Cavalli across with such valid excitement to these large, fashionable and very enthusiastic audiences is no mean achievement in practical musicology.

4. FLEXIBILITY A PART OF AUTHENTICITY

A very different approach to the interpretation of early Italian opera is taken by an editor and performer whose previous achievements were already admirable, but in the realm of chamber music and more particularly Dutch and French keyboard music. This is Alan Curtis. True to his own artistic personality, Alan Curtis uses for his very individual recording of Monteverdi's *Poppea*, for example, forces so small as to make a chamber opera out of this great and popular masterpiece, whose original performance at Venice, 1642, was under far from chamber-music conditions in the particularly large public theatre of SS. Giovanni e Paolo. He uses a single lute, or a single harpsichord, for very much of the continuo accompaniment; for much more, he adds only a string bass (and that not at all in recitative).

His accompaniments themselves are not merely congruous with the given music; they are of a lyrical inventiveness beyond the ordinary. And if this were, say, a chamber cantata of the mid-seventeenth century, such instrumentation could be authenticated historically (early in the century from title-pages, later in the century from a few passing references and pictures).

Or we can think of this recorded performance, intimately relayed into our own living rooms on high-fidelity equipment ('almost as if we were producing a radio drama', Alan Curtis describes it on the record sleeve), in the spirit of that wonderful Lament of Ariadne, when it was transferred from Monteverdi's opera into the function of a chamber cantata, having been published by Monteverdi for this purpose together with his two celebrated Love Letters in Representative Style (*Lamento d'Arianna . . . due Lettere Amorose in genere Rappresentativo*, Venice, 1623); that same lament of which Bonini wrote around 1650 (*Discorsi*, Florence, Biblioteca Riccardiana, MS. 2218 f. 87 v.) that 'there was not a house which, possessing harpsichords or theorbos, did not have [a copy of] the lament of that [opera, *i.e.* Monteverdi's otherwise lost *Arianna*]'. That was, in short, using an excerpt from an opera as chamber music.

But as an opera, Monteverdi's *Arianna* was performed in 1608 at Mantua in a theatre specially erected to hold an audience of 'at least 5000 spectators' (Nino Pirrotta, in *Claudio Monteverdi e il suo tempo*, n.p., 1969, p. 47), so that Federico Follino's estimate of 6000 in his *Compendio*, Mantua, 1608 (given in A. Solerti, *Albori*, Milan, 1904–5, II, p. 145) would not have been much more exaggerated. One does suspect some exaggeration in both accounts. Nor were most baroque audiences that large. But neither were they ordinarily of chamber size. They were less often of hundreds than of thousands.

Thus it was not for nothing that Doni around 1635 (*Trattato della musica scenica*, ed. A. F. Gori, Florence, 1763, pp. 69–70), like so many other baroque writers, distinguished between the three different styles to be used *ne' Teatri* (in theatres), *nelle Chiese* (in Churches) and *nelle camere* (in chambers). Accompaniment by a solo lute or a solo harpsichord is not authenticated historically for a large public opera-house such as the theatre of SS. Giovanni e Paolo in which *Poppea* was first performed, nor would it have been satisfactory acoustically. On the contrary, Doni himself (p. 110) expressed some fear that in such circumstances what he calls 'the multitude of instruments' might 'excessively cover the voices' for those at the back of the hall: and we shall want to avoid that misfortune. But opera is opera: it is not chamber music; and an orchestral accompaniment of sufficient sonority (though hopefully of due discretion) has always been historically and artistically a part of it. There must somewhere be a happy mean.

The chamber-music reticence and refinement which come naturally to Alan Curtis do not make a neutral musicologist of him. On the contrary, his obvious commitment to his own intensely personal vision of Monteverdi or Cavalli is what brings excellence to his performances. They are not, in the respects just mentioned, very historical; but they are very musicianly.

And what would be most historical in these respects? Charles Mackerras, aided by some of the most advanced instrumental group-work devoted to historical performance on the present Viennese scene, where players of early instruments seem particularly to flourish, has come, I think, in the Archive recording mentioned above of Cavalieri's *Rappresentatione di anima, e di corpo*, as near as anyone to the kinds of sound I would actually expect to hear in a very early Italian opera, if I could be carried back to the original performance.

A sinfonia ringing out on strings (the violins have baroque 'short-neck' fittings), recorders, pommers (shawms), crumhorns, dolcian (early bassoon), zink (cornetto), trombones (sackbuts), (chamber) organ, harpsichord, lutes, drums and cymbals is a joyful and authentic sound indeed. So are choruses similarly accompanied. A four-part vocal ensemble with four viols (all sizes), violone, double-bass, lira da braccio and wooden (chamber) organ is an exquisite colouring; while the use of different solo voices variously accompanied by chamber organ, harp and cello, or by lira da braccio, lute and viola da gamba, or by lira da braccio, theorbo and violone, or by other combinations of the kind, gives diversity and resonance enough, without seeming to run into any danger of covering the voices. It is really a wonderful performance: very authentic; and its full-bodied impetus is one aspect of its authenticity.

In all this, one of the chief principles to emerge is the wide range of possibilities left open to the performer. The key word here, as so often, is flexibility. Nothing was more characteristic of the baroque habits of musicianship than their extreme adaptability. But this is not to suppose that anything goes. The choice lies with the performer. But so does the responsibility for making a suitable choice: musicianly; inventive; practical for the acoustic circumstances; and above all, congruous with the given music. Flexibility is not so easy to live with as rigidity, but it is much more interesting; and it is a very large part of the challenge of early interpretation.

5. KEEPING WITHIN THE IMPLICATIONS OF THE MUSIC

It may be as well to sum up the suggestions of the present argument here before passing to its concluding portion.

A musicologist can hope to achieve a very considerable measure of objectivity, and it is very desirable that he should do so. But he cannot be impersonal. Music itself is not impersonal. Music touches people: in one of its aspects, music is a communication between people. In this aspect, attempting an authentic interpretation of early music is like attempting to open up communication with our ancestors.

Nevertheless we make this attempt not in their interests but in ours, and for the sake not of the historical record but of our own present experience.

We can distinguish between historical authenticity and essential authenticity, in the following manner.

Historical authenticity is attainable up to the limits of our knowledge: it is relatively desirable, as a means to our own better experience; it is sometimes expendable, when genuinely outweighed by artistic considerations. Essential authenticity is attainable up to the limits of our musicianship: it is absolutely desirable, as comprising the experience which is the end desired; and it is not expendable at all, being the sum of the necessary artistic considerations.

Music is like any other artefact in being partly shaped by historical conditioning, partly cast in the mould of our enduring human nature. It is fascinating in its differences, which we cultivate by attempting historical authenticity. But it is accessible through its similarities, which we recognise by responding to its essential implications. That is what I have here described as essential authenticity; and though it is not divorced from historical conditioning, it goes much deeper.

As music wells up from the deep unconscious, through layers of the subconscious nearer to conscious craftsmanship and conscious purpose, it takes on the historical imprint of its own time and place. But the deep unconscious perceives no distinctions of time or place, and our contact with it brings us as close as we can get in this mortal world to an experience of eternity.

Like everything else which springs from that eternal fountain beloved of the Muses, music trails a glory not only of its own time and place. It is not ultimately our acquired historical sense which responds to music. It is our innate sense of archetypal meaning. The music may have come about as a historical occurrence, but it comes down to us as an autonomous artefact; and we have that within us which wants to respond to it in the present tense.

Our response to early music is not rigidly determined. Just as we can convey the same meanings in other words, so we can bring out genuine implications of the same music in other interpretations. And this is valuable; for human nature has many shadings, and while we are archetypally alike, we are not individually alike.

But there are also outer limits to our valid interpretations. There are boundaries of style. Beyond them we miss the genuine experience of the music, and substitute only a plausible counterfeit. For in that outer darkness, anything goes. There are no limits to what a performer may find himself making up to replace the genuine idioms which he does not know or will not use. Thus there may be brilliance, but it will be artificial; there may be expression, but it will be contrived; and the audience may be pleased, but rather in default of the genuine article than from comprehending satisfaction.

The genuine article is any interpretation which lies within the implications of the music. To pick up the implications of the music needs good musicianship; to be in a position to pick up the implications of the music needs good knowledge of the style. Hence it is a sound working principle: keep it flexible; but keep it within the boundaries of the style.

Getting to know the boundaries of style depends on historical evidence such as the contemporary quotations in this present book deploy. But is historical authenticity the only authenticity? Or can we also pick up something in the implications of the music for which the contemporary evidence prepares us, but which is not in the contemporary evidence, having more to do with the timelessness of early music than with its history?

I am sure that we can, and that good performers have done it all along without having to think about it. However, it is still better to know what we are doing; and I shall close these introductory chapters with a recent experience of mine which made me take a hard look at this very question.

V. Past and Present

1. A PROBLEM OF PROJECTION

In the early spring of 1971, I was commissioned by Sandor Salgo to prepare a new realisation of John Blow's *Venus and Adonis* (perf. London, *c.* 1684) for the Carmel Bach Festival of that summer. Time was short: I had other commitments, and could not get to it at once; when I did, I worked continuously and in state of unusual emotion, but without any opportunity for reconsideration or revision, except that when it came to actual rehearsal, I used the blue pencil on a number of small miscalculations. But my Muse was friendly, and decided to see me through. The performances under Sandor Salgo and the production by John Olon-Scrymgeour were alike admirable; audience and press proved favourable; and I was a happy man.

Venus and Adonis is called a masque in the manuscripts, but can properly be viewed as a miniature opera, because there is genuine dramatic development, and because the music is integral and not merely incidental to this development, so that the drama unfolds as much in the music as in the words. It is, of course, a very fine piece of work, and it has been known to us for some time in an excellent modern edition by Anthony Lewis (*Éditions de l'Oiseau-Lyre*, Monaco, 1949): reliable, informative and musicianly in every way.

The original circumstances of performance were domestic in more senses than one. Here was 'a masque for the entertainment of the King', as the chief manuscript has it. We are further given the interesting information that Venus was sung by Moll Davies, who had been for some time a professionally experienced actress and was then his mistress; and that Cupid was sung by their gifted but scarcely experienced little daughter, Lady Mary Tudor, who may only have been nine years of age and cannot have been more than eleven years of age at the time.

The manuscripts show the solo voice-parts with continuo bass; some three-part and four-part choruses; and for instruments, four-part writing suggestive of strings (but not necessarily excluding other instruments). There is also a little obbligato work for flute (i.e. recorder) accompanying Venus, and very hard it is to concert successfully when Venus is on stage and the orchestra is on the floor or in a theatre pit.

But that was precisely the problem: the original performance, though we know nothing about it directly, is most unlikely to have had pretty Moll Davies and little Lady Mary Tudor on a public stage or with a substantial theatre orchestra. We may wish, and at Carmel we did wish, to bring the opera out of its probable origins as an essentially private and small-scale entertainment, into modern use as a fully public presentation in a moderately large auditorium, and for a moderately large audience not in touch either with its original court setting or with its musical idiom. We had, in short, a problem of projection.

2. BRINGING OUT THE TRAGIC IMPLICATIONS

But why should we concern ourselves with thus making over an early work of music, tailored to suit a small and private occasion, in order to fit it for a larger and more public occasion?

The answer, I suppose, is that *Venus and Adonis*, though we can imagine it to have been very successful entertainment at that intimate royal party in 1684 or so, is not altogether tailored for a small occasion. There is more than mere courtly sentiment in the conflict of wills which sends Adonis off with such seeming casualness to his lethal hunt: Venus as nagging woman is very amusing, but behind her looms the formidable goddess, the mythological Great Mother in her destructive aspect, and behind that gallant huntsman lies the sacrificial god of ancient ritual and legend, prey to the devouring boar as Osiris to his black brother Set and many another embodiment of those age-old, archetypal roles.

We can none of us in our deeper responses take Venus quarrelling with her recalcitrant Adonis in quite the spirit of light-hearted banter in which they are outwardly presented. Blow has already shown us his awareness of the deeper undercurrent in the heartfelt simplicity of their opening scene together. We have had plenty of frivolous irony in Cupid's jibes at the amorous, inconstant courtiers, as the Prologue caricatures the obsequious flattery of the contemporary French opera prologue. We get enchanting wit and warmth and delicacy for the Little Cupids, while Venus waits delightedly on stage for her lover to come back from the hunt. But when he comes back, wounded to the death, a greatness comes over the music just as it comes over Purcell's *Dido and Aeneas* at Aeneas' departure and Dido's lament; and in range at least, if not in feeling (where they are equal), it is Blow who makes the most of his poignant opportunity.

It is the implications of this great music which invite us to take Blow's *Venus and Adonis* out of its aristocratic and social role as a mere 'masque for the entertainment of the King', and to make it over into the moving little drama in music which it can be for a modern audience. This is not to be done by changing its nature, but by bringing out that side of its nature which carries these more serious implications. The wit and the delicacy are another side, and are just as important to the mixture. But the challenge is to body out the strength implied by the tragic side, without eclipsing the sparkle apparent in the entertaining side.

To call this brief and exquisite masterpiece a tragi-comedy would be to put the matter the wrong way round. It is a comical pastoral which ends (as pastorals do not ordinarily end) in tragedy. Neither the librettist nor the composer has softened down the tragedy, and it is a question of what we can best do to bring it out in all its majesty and stature by our interpretation.

3. THE ROBUST ASPECT OF BAROQUE OPERA

What would a seventeenth-century opera director have done, confronted with this quite practical problem in theatrical projection? We know more or less what he would have done, since baroque revivals of operas were frequent, and scarcely ever without substantial alterations either to suit altered circumstances, or to take advantage of available singers, or merely for the pleasure of having something new. A seventeenth-century opera director would have done unhesitatingly as he saw fit in the interests of his own performance. That was the baroque attitude, and it may with perfect historical propriety be our attitude now. The chief difference is that we shall have more difficulty now in keeping within the boundaries of the style. But it can be done.

There was a seventeenth-century revival of *Venus and Adonis*, about which we know nothing except that the manuscripts which are our only evidence for it do show considerable changes, judged by Anthony Lewis to be for the worse. His study of the sources is scrupulous, his presentation of them is consistently accurate, his realisation of the harpsichord continuo is skilled and imaginative, and it was no part of his purpose to suggest possibilities for further amplification in performances for larger modern audiences.

I have, in fact, conducted performances at the University of Iowa in a version not greatly modified from this, with further orchestration for the overtures and dances, but with the continuo improvised skilfully at the harpsichord by Gloria Rose, and supported otherwise only by a cello. I shall have more to say below about the authenticity and advisability of this; but in a somewhat reticent and chamber-music way, these performances gave considerable enjoyment to all concerned. For an audience of chamber-music dimensions and chamber-music connoisseurship, performance with almost chamber-music forces may suit some conditions and some purposes very well, though I do not now think that the implications of this music can be brought out to their fullest extent by such a chamber-music realisation.

For the Carmel Bach Festival, at all events, we had other conditions and other purposes in view. We needed more sonority, just as we needed more variety, for our larger and less habituated audiences. We needed the essential authenticity to keep within the implications of the music; and at the same time we needed the imaginative orchestration to make good public theatre of the little piece. That has always been one of Raymond Leppard's strongest arguments, and I quite agree with him. If an opera is to be projected, it has to be good theatre. If it is to be good theatre, it has to be musically as well as visually highlighted. It was so in the baroque period and remains so now.

In the baroque period, there were indeed certain operatic performances virtually under chamber-music conditions, in one of the smaller salons of a princely palace: the first performance of Peri's *Euridice* on 6 October 1600, at the Palazzo Pitti in Florence, was of this kind, the audience being a very select few. And then again there were performances under extremely ambitious conditions, in palatial halls or actual theatres of the amplest size, to say nothing of the stage-machinery: the performance of Caccini's *Rapimento di Cefalo* three days later, 9 October 1600, at the Palazzo Vecchio, also in Florence, was reported to have entertained, at vast expense, an audience of nearly 4000 persons with a cast, chorus and orchestra of 'more than a hundred musicians' (Francesco Settimani, *Diario*, entry for 9 Oct. 1600, VI, f. 221, Florence, Archivio di Stato: Caccini himself put it at a mere seventy-five, *Nuove Musiche*, Florence, 1602, p. 19, so that the number of musicians seems to have grown a little in the telling; but it was not small). That is where the element of robustness in early opera comes in; and it was certainly the robust public performances, and not the refined private performances, which were most typical of seventeenth-century opera.

Thus when one asks, why not perform an early Italian opera just as it appears in surviving prints or manuscripts, the answer is that this is not the least what happened in the seventeenth century on big occasions, and not entirely what happened even on small occasions. If, therefore, taking such a manuscript at its face value, we perform it as it is, we shall not perform it as it was; we shall perform it as a more or less arbitrary sketch of what it was.

And when one asks concerning Blow's *Venus and Adonis*, why not perform it as it is, the answer is that this cannot quite happen either, but that we can indeed perform it as or nearly as it is in Anthony Lewis' edition, which is a faithful reflection of the chief manuscript (British Museum Add. 22100), with its continuo bass well realised and sufficient suggestions included for tempo and expression. This version may give us (though there can be no complete historical certainty about it) a very fair approximation to what happened at the original performances, supposing that they were indeed mounted under the modest circumstances at which their domestic context hints. The result will be rather more, on the one hand, than the mere sketch to be literally extracted from an early Italian opera manuscript; but considerably less, on the other hand, than a full baroque performance of Restoration theatre music under public circumstances.

It seems to me that such a relatively (it cannot be wholly) literal performance of Blow's *Venus and Adonis* may be one good way of experiencing the music, which I should entirely endorse for those who prefer it so; but that it is not the only way which can be regarded either historically or artistically as authentic. Much ampler and robuster performances could have happened at the time, and may properly and successfully happen now.

4. THE CONTINUO ACCOMPANIMENT

By far the most critical problem of such an operatic realisation is what to do with the continuo accompaniment.

What we do with the overtures and dances can make a big difference to their sonority and to their variety; but so long as it is kept relatively historical, and absolutely congruous with the implications of the given music, it is not going to change their basic character.

But what we do with the continuo accompaniment of the recitative and the arias can change their basic character. We have to be extraordinarily careful not to spoil and denature this early recitative by incongruous counter-attractions in the shape of accompanying melodies; for though it is much more arioso than later Italian recitative, and will tolerate and invite considerably more melodic interest in its accompaniment, it will not tolerate it everywhere, or too independently anywhere. The arias are not quite so vulnerable to misjudged counter-melody; but there is very little actual aria in Blow's operatic texture. Arioso is the real substance of this style of opera.

It is unhistorical, and as I now think inartistic, to think that we can solve the problem of continuo accompaniment in the seventeenth century, as we can and should normally solve it in the eighteenth century, by handing it over to a harpsichord (or other instrument of harmony) with the support of a cello (or other bass instrument of melody), reinforced or not reinforced by a double-bass. This sonority, which is so excellent and so indispensable for dry recitative, and so satisfactory for the developed type of (mainly da capo) aria which goes with it, and of which the bass-line generally gives such strong sound already by being melodically very active: this conventional continuo of harpsichord and cello does not seem to have been at all prominent during the greater part of the seventeenth century, and perhaps first became habitual in the sonatas and other chamber music, mainly during the later decades. We have certainly no cause to take it for granted in Blow's little opera of *c.* 1684; and this was the first large question which I felt had to be brought up for consideration before I decided on the general texture of my new realisation.

My argument with myself concerning the continuo accompaniment unfolded somewhat as follows.

5. DIFFERENT VARIETIES OF CONTINUO ACCOMPANIMENT

We have, first, an interesting and relevant comparison here in the contemporary French *ballets de cour*, and on the grander scale, in the operas of Lully. It is becoming more and more evident that the continuo group in a French theatre orchestra of the Lully period, so far from being confined to harpsichord and bass, included a considerable assortment of instruments, melodic as well as harmonic.

This French continuo group goes under the name of *petit choeur*, in contrast to the orchestra as a whole, which goes under the name of *grand choeur*. We also find the word *symphonie*, in one of its many meanings, used of this inner group, by contrast with *grand symphonie* sometimes used for the orchestra as a whole. An example is the complaint by Alexandre Toussaint de Limojon, Sieur de Saint Disdier (*La ville et la république de Venise*, Paris, 1680, p. 419) that 'the *Symphonie*' then heard by him in his experiences of Venetian opera was 'a small affair, inspiring more melancholy than gaiety: it is composed of Lutes, Theorbos and Harpsichords, which accompany the voices with admirable precision'. The translation 'orchestra' (Donald Grout, *Short History of Opera*, 1947, ed. of 1965, pp. 99) is therefore misleading here, since it is not the orchestra as a whole (based as that would have been primarily on bowed strings) to which de Limojon is referring.

In this period of Lully, there was more resemblance between current French opera and previous Italian opera than between current French and current or at least emerging Italian opera; and this is nowhere more important than in recitative, both as to its character, and as to its accompaniment.

Early baroque Italian recitative, and all baroque French recitative, has a certain fluid melodiousness, of arioso character, which requires a corresponding shapeliness and mobility for its accompaniment. Where it is most free and speech-like, it needs, certainly, most care not to tie its freedom down by rhythmically measured counter-melodies; but it never is so free and speech-like as later Italian recitative, and it will therefore admit more varied sonority and more well-judged melodiousness of accompaniment, especially in its most arioso passages.

This difference of character is also connected with its difference of

68

instrumentation. That is why it was in the later, not in the earlier style of Italian recitative (nor generally in French), that there arose the standard continuo accompaniment of harpsichord and cello (with or without reinforcement by a double-bass). This is indeed a very clear sound, not unsonorous if well produced; but less sonorous than the earlier (and persisting French) mixed continuo groups. With only two (or three) players needed, the accompaniment can follow with extreme closeness the very swift, free and speech-like rhythm essential to a proper delivery of dry recitative; for which reason, too, such recitative should never be conducted (just the changes of harmony indicated to help the continuo players keep their place). Anything rhythmically melodious in the accompaniment is hampering; but ample and imaginative arpeggiation on the harpsichord is needed for sufficiently sustained support. Dry it was called, and dry in this sense it is: *recitativo secco* in contrast with the *recitativo accompagnato* supported, and kept to stricter rhythm, by its written-out orchestral accompaniment.

The standard continuo accompaniment by harpsichord and melodic bass is therefore integral to the dry category of later Italian baroque recitative, as well as common in later Italian baroque aria. On grounds both of historical and of musicianly authenticity, it is imperative to retain it there, and extremely desirable to retain in addition its traditional, zestful performance by a skilled harpsichordist more or less improvising his own accompaniment above the (hopefully) figured bass, which in recitative he must know how to fill out with the most sonorous yet tactful of arpeggiation, but not with counter-melody such as would impede the singer's freedom of rhetorical declamation.

And if some modern listeners find this a little tedious at times, so did some baroque listeners. The best we can do, now as then, is to make the performance really lively, because really declamatory, and get our modern audiences really used to it, as indeed is happening already on a growing scale. And incidentally, our accompaniment of dry recitative needs as much improvement today (especially by much fuller and bolder and more prolonged though not unremitting arpeggiation) in Mozart as it does in Handel.

But none of this standardisation of the continuo accompaniment (*i.e.* as harpsichord and melodic bass) had yet set in at the date of Blow's *Venus and Adonis*, within the life-time of Lully. Indeed, it never did set in with baroque French opera, so different from late baroque Italian opera. Blow's recitative in *Venus and Adonis* bears no resemblance to the later baroque Italian *secco* recitative, with its dry declamation and correspondingly dry accompaniment. Blow's recitative is Italianate as Luigi Rossi's recitative is Italianate, in the middle of the seventeenth century (that is to say, never very far from arioso); or French as Lully's recitative is French in the last third of the century (and the second of these is not so very much removed musically from the first, wholly French though it is in its adaptation to that very different language). Blow's recitative, again, is fully adapted to the English language; but its musical relationship to recent Italian and contemporary French recitative is unmistakable, and its implications for accompaniment are similar.

Thus we have a historical context suggesting ampler possibilities of accompaniment for *Venus and Adonis* than only harpsichord and bass. History here does not only permit us to be more flexible in our instrumentation; history invites us to be more flexible. Baroque interpretation was always adaptable to the practical circumstances of the case. To be baroque we are required to be adaptable.

One of the circumstances requiring adaptability is the considerable likelihood, under modern conditions, of encountering a harpsichord too weak to give adequate sonority even in a moderate hall, and a harpsichordist innocent of the technique for getting a strong and sustained sonority even out of a harpsichord (old or new) good enough and well enough maintained to be capable of producing it (and Carmel had a weak harpsichord though a fine harpsichordist). Electrical amplification should then be used; but even so, it will not make a thin, metallic harpsichord tone sound full and warm, though it will make it louder, which can be a very great advantage indeed so far as it goes.

There would be relevant French precedent for requesting as continuo instruments several lutes (at least two, perhaps with two or three cellos or gambas, a pair of violins and a pair of flutes) in addition to harpsichord; for French influence was general enough at the Restoration court in England, where, moreover, large groups of lutenists (up to forty) had appeared in masques. But Carmel had no spare money for any Herculean effort at assembling massed lutenists; and while some guitarists might quite possibly have been got together, we have considerable evidence from title pages had elsewhere that (at least in seventeenth-century Italian solo song) the guitar was preferred rather for light and unsophisticated than for serious accompaniment.

6. WHAT TO GIVE TO THE CONTINUO INSTRUMENTS

Suppose, then, that the problem were to be approached from the other end, simply by asking what could best be done with the normal, small but excellent modern orchestra actually available at Carmel? Here is a medium capable of all the necessary sonority and variety: not indeed technically or acoustically the same as a historical baroque orchestra of the same size, because of the modifications undergone by so many instruments in the meantime; but perfectly able to serve a comparable function. It cannot give quite the same experience of the music, but it can give another experience very close, possibly as good in its own kind, and certainly within the musicianly boundaries of the style. And just as it is best, when the decision to play harpsichord solos on the piano has been opted for, to conceive them pianistically; so it is best, when the decision to prepare an orchestral accompaniment has been opted for, to conceive it orchestrally. Nothing is gained by refusing to make idiomatic use of any medium selected, for that merely gets the worst of both worlds and the best of neither.

I had some although not very much relevant experience to fall back upon. When preparing an abridged version of Lully's *Amadis* for performance under rather similar circumstances (except in being amateur) at the University of Iowa in 1965, I gave some portions of its protracted French recitative to a continuo of harpsichord and cello, with disappointing results in a not very large auditorium although my written part was quite a full one, and nicely played on a very fair instrument. Other portions I supported to better effect with string or wind parts or both (besides those portions of the score where Lully or his assistants had already notated instrumental parts). I also gave the woodwind and even the trumpets and timpani plenty to do in some orchestral and dance passages. Since many of my wind parts were independent additions, I went beyond what we can yet regard as historically certain, but not beyond what we can regard as historically possible, on the basis of evidence some of which is very hard to explain on any other hypothesis. I again refer the reader to Gloria Rose ('Agazzari and the Improvising Orchestra', *Journal of the American Musicological Society*, XVIII, 3, 1965, pp. 382–393), and also to Jürgen Eppelsheim, *Das Orchester in den Werken Jean-Baptiste Lullys* (Tutzing, 1961, esp. pp. 150 ff., 173–174, 215, and Anhang 25–26).

The uncertainty is not as to whether a mixed group of continuo instruments functioned in early Italian opera, and also in French opera even after the change in this respect began in Italian opera (probably quite late in the seventeenth century and on into the eighteenth); we know that this was so. Nor is there any uncertainty about this mixed continuo group having commonly included instruments of melody (*e.g.* violins, flutes) as well as instruments of harmony (*e.g.* harpsichords, theorbos): this, too, we know.

References so far discovered are indeed very scanty; but so is all evidence on early operatic performance, and the search is still proceeding. But we might have a typical Italian grouping of this small but mixed size prescribed for an *Accademia* (something like a small serenata) by Francesco Bonini Romano (*Carillo tradito del vagante academico gelato* . . . Bologna, 1635, libretto only, p. 3) under the rubric: *Sinfonia*

71

di viole, violini, tiorbi e clavicembali, sinfonia of viols, violins, theorbos, and harpsichords. And we certainly have a typical French grouping in the one quoted by Eppelsheim (*op. cit.*, p. 215) for the opera at the Palais-Royal at Paris so late as 1712, in a *petit choeur* of two violins, two flutes, two cellos (*basses de violon*), one gamba (*basse de viole*), two theorbos and one harpsichord, allied to a *grand choeur* of nineteen strings and eight wind (flutes, oboes, bassoon). The description in Diderot and D'Alembert's *Encyclopédie* (III, Paris, 1753, p. 362, s.v. CHOEUR) is still nearly the same; and this was quite certainly the approximate situation throughout the history of French baroque opera.

The uncertainty is as to what these mixed continuo groups played, and in what passages, for operas of different dates and places. What did they have on their music stands in front of them? Doni complained around 1635 (*Trattati*, ed. A. F. Gori, Florence, 1763, II, pp. 110–113) of 'the trouble and time it takes to make so many copies of the tablature of the bass' as one of the disadvantages of 'all this multitude of instruments' who have to improvise above it as a result of the composer 'sparing the trouble of instrumental pieces written expressly', instead of which 'the tablature of a simple Basso continuo suffices'. At this time, tablature (*intavolatura*) generally meant some sort of compressed score, but here 'a simple Basso continuo' may literally be meant, since this would indeed suffice. Thereon the players of harmony instruments could obviously have improvised their harmonic (but not unmelodious) accompaniments, as usual. But the players of melody instruments?

They, too, would have been trained in 'counterpoint' (i.e. composition), and could therefore have improvised their melodic parts on a continuo bass. And so it seems they did, boldly for instrumental passages, discreetly for accompanying voices, at least in Italy during the first half of the seventeenth century, since Agazzari in 1607 (copied by the German, Praetorius, in 1619), Doni around 1635 and Pietro della Valle in 1640 all describe it, and there are places in contemporary opera scores requiring it (Gloria Rose, *loc. cit.*). Remarkable, but I think proven. Later in the seventeenth century, and in French opera: historically possible, artistically attractive, but not proven. The whole problem there stands open for the time being, at once frustrating and challenging.

I am never one to resist an interesting challenge; but the irony is that my attack of historical conscience in restricting much of my continuo accompaniment in Lully's *Amadis* to a rather ineffectual harpsichord and cello seems to have been merely a case of misinformed conscience, since I did not know enough then either about the Italian improvising orchestra or about the French *petit choeur* of ten instruments or so for continuo accompaniment. It all goes to show that reticence is not in itself a sure road to authenticity, with which it is quite often but mistakenly confused. An enquiring and venturesome turn of mind is sometimes as necessary for penetrating into history as that indispensable caution which is its proper complement and restraining mentor. Intuition is fallible, reason is limited, and it can really be very difficult to balance them just right in any given case; but I am sure that we do need both reason and intuition for our modern interpretation of early music.

What my reason and my intuition between them made of *Venus and Adonis* will be told in the next (the final) Chapter of this Introduction.

VI. Present and Future

It was at this point that I asked myself the deliberate question: can we hear something in the implications of the music which is not so much historical as essential, having to do less with its origins in past history than with its timeless essence?

Our experience of music is not altogether a time-bound or a place-bound experience. The more we get it in the here and now, the more it takes us out of our immediate selves and into those regions of archetypal but intimate awareness which we share with others of our kind. In a successful encounter with early music, we must be feeling really very much as our ancestors were feeling when they were getting it in what was, there and then, the here and now. Their personalities were different in that they lived different life-stories under different environmental conditioning; but also the same in that their human birth-right was the same. It is the sameness even more than the otherness which reaches us across the centuries in those indescribable but nevertheless specific responses caused in us by their music.

We respond: not all quite similarly, thank God; but there is something there which is constant enough to be recognised with broad agreement. We call it the music, but we do not mean only the notes and the pauses, the voices and the instruments. We mean the acoustic experience, but still more do we mean the emotional experience which the music implies. No one who has not got an ear for the implications of the music will ever make a musician; and if we do not always hear quite ear to ear, this is not so much because we have different musicianships as because we have different characters. We like things a little differently from one another. But then again, we are also a little apt to exaggerate these differences.

What astonishes me is not how much we fall out over our individual interpretations, but how confidently we assume that there must be a right interpretation implicit in the music, with all the others wrong. Our confidence in the music itself telling us what to do with it is absolutely justified: in the long run, there would be no other way of finding out. It is only that we do have to allow a certain margin for temperament, this way or that. The music does not so much tell us its own interpretation as tell us the outer boundaries within which our interpretations may be congruous with its implications. This leaves room for a considerable flexibility. But we can live with that.

2. BODYING OUT THE MUSIC

In taking up Blow's *Venus and Adonis* with the experience of Lully's *Amadis* behind me, and this clearer formulation of my attitude in front of me, I was able to do a more consistent job of work. I would set out my formulation something like this: I wanted to keep substantially within the historical possibilities, and absolutely within the implications of the music.

It seemed to me, as I set to work, not only that I could hear but that I was hearing my way into the implications of the music, with a certain familiar sense of conviction which I have had before, when realising continuo accompaniments; only more so. Such a conviction, I am aware, may easily be an illusion and is bound to be a personal conviction; but it is really all we have to go on in the end, after using our musicological knowledge to the best of our ability.

Alan Curtis, in editing *Poppea*, had a vision of chamber-music intensity, and followed it, although it led him somewhat away from the historical probabilities of that original, big public performance in the theatre of SS. Giovanni e Paolo; yet he is a musicologist who rightly attaches much weight to historical authenticity, and follows it in other respects more closely than Raymond Leppard or (in this instance) myself. Winton Dean, again, is a musicologist of the minutest accuracy and the keenest vision; yet he justifiably advocates staged performances of Handel's oratorios (originally unstaged through external circumstances), *i.e.* performances which in this respect are quite as unhistorical from the literal standpoint as they can be triumphant from the artistic standpoint. The external circumstance, likewise, of Lully's monopoly over opera restricted Marc-Antoine Charpentier to progressively fewer musicians for his theatre music, a historical disability which we should probably wish to rectify in modern performance.

J. S. Bach, for other reasons, frequently used more restricted forces than he would himself have chosen or than we have any need, merely from too literal a sense of historical correctitude, to impose on him today. It is perhaps a misjudgement in this respect which caused, for example, Nikolaus Harnoncourt with his Concentus Musicus to record Bach's B minor Mass in a performance of great sweetness and beautifully baroque wind colourings, but no truly baroque cutting-edge to the very few (baroque-fitted) violins, and no truly baroque grandeur or weight anywhere, such as is needed to meet the implications of this music not just for sweetness but for big and even terrifying power.

This misjudgement was corrected in the Concentus Musicus recording of J. S. Bach's *St. Matthew Passion*. Here the orchestra used is of more normal baroque proportion. There are twelve violins, presumably six firsts and six seconds. The gain in artistic congruity from this fact alone is quite crucial. The choral forces are also stronger and better, including the boy sopranos from King's College, Cambridge; there is weight enough to sound powerful, yet not ponderous, and the counterpoint comes through true and clear. The gloriously baroque wind colourings are a delight in themselves, and almost impeccably in tune. This is good baroque-style interpretation because it has sufficient baroque robustness as well as sensitive baroque sonority.

In short, while history is indeed important to our trade as musicologists, history is not all-important. Artistry is also important, and probably should always have the last word.

If Alan Curtis moved from a robuster original performance towards a smaller-scaled modern performance, I went the other way round: from a smaller-scaled original performance (most of whose original accompaniment seems not unlikely to have been on lutes and harpsichord) towards a robuster modern performance, in which, however, I used a considerable amount of reticent string-quartet accompaniment among other textures, and mostly with piano or mezzo-forte dynamics at that, being anxious not to overweight Blow's ecstatically free vocal line in the course of making it over for more public use.

For instrumental passages, I was somewhat weightier with my orchestration. I scored for double woodwind (but without clarinets); two trumpets and timpani; two horns (on account of the hunting scenes); strings and harpsichord. My intention throughout was a warm and varied sonority, congruous with the given music, but suiting it to an audience of moderate or even of considerable size.

The colouring of my orchestration was to some extent worked out in consultation with the producer for these Carmel performances, John Olon-Scrymgeour, who had many excellent ideas for bringing out by skilful stagecraft the contrasting moods and underlying symbolism of the action, the poetry, the myth and the music. He asked of me, and I gave him (on very ordinary baroque precedent), certain orchestral colourings for certain dramatic moods; and conversely, certain of my orchestral colourings were brought out by him, at my request, in dramatic images and movements on the stage. We were closely in touch, too, with our brilliant young choreographer and lead dancer, Rhonda Kay Martin. Above all did I follow Sandor Salgo's advice as conductor, and Priscilla Salgo's as director of the Festival Chorale.

To practise my own precept, let me now state succinctly just what I did, and to what. With regard to what we have to work upon, Anthony Lewis in his edition chiefly used, and made reliably available, the best source (Brit. Mus. MS Add. 22100). I too chiefly used this source, and also the other manuscript sources which he collated, and to which he gives references (they are in the British Museum, at Westminster Abbey, and at Christ Church, Oxford). I worked from photographic copies of the manuscripts. I made no cuts, no changes of order, and only one brief transposition for a passage (the Huntsman's Song) of difficult tessitura.

I notated a new harpsichord realisation, the Carmel harpsichordist not wishing to improvise his own, and a written-out part being needed anyhow for the singers to learn from, as also for rehearsals. I added (but very reticently, as I think this music requires) vocal cadenzas and other ornamentation. I introduced extensive woodwind, trumpet and timpani parts (some doubling Blow's written parts, some newly composed as independent counter-melodies, or occasionally as main melodies where Blow wrote none) for overtures, ritornellos, dances and choruses: indeed I noticed that one manuscript (that in Westminster Abbey, p. 5 and elsewhere) employs in several places the rubric 'Cho: Instruments and voices', thus confirming that Blow's choruses were not meant, any more than Lully's, to be sung unaccompanied, though no accompaniment is actually shown in any of the *Venus and Adonis* manuscripts.

I have accompanied with various instruments of melody (often string quartet with or without double-bass, sometimes strings and woodwind) many of the arias, and most portions of the recitative which fall (as on the whole Blow's recitative does fall) into a more or less tuneful arioso and therefore measured movement not in danger of being hampered by the presence of some independent movement in the accompanying parts. I have been very careful on this point, and felt quite satisfied in the theatre that most of this instrumentation added appropriately both to the sonority and to the emotional power of the music, without getting in the way. Where it did get in the way, I cut it out, either at rehearsal, or by subsequent revision.

Finally, I have composed instrumental ritornellos for the orchestra in the following situations: where requested (though not notated) by the rubric 'Ritornello' (Christ Church MS 1114, after 'Haste, haste away'); where notated only as a bass part, no upper parts being supplied (West. Abbey MS, Brit. Mus. MS Add. 31453, same places); and where neither requested nor notated, but suggested by normal seventeenth-century precedent (and especially as prelude, interludes and postlude for the final chorus, in order to give this beautiful closing scene enough length to carry its own great weight of grievous emotion).

In a word, I bodied out the given music. I gave it a more varied orchestration than anything literally suggested by the manuscripts; and in so doing I composed some harmony and much melody in free addition to what is there already. The additions to the harmony chiefly derive from a very extensive use of suspensions, appoggiaturas and accented passing notes, along the lines recommended for suitable passages of continuo in my Chapters on accompaniment below; the additions to the melody chiefly derive from the need for good and enjoyable part-writing in using melodic instruments within continuo ensembles. I carried the same principles a stage further for the existing instrumental passages, where my wind parts become important to the texture; and a stage further still in the ritornellos which I have composed in a few places where none exist, but a rubric in one of the manuscripts or an implication in the given music suggests a need for them.

And how, then, does all this differ from what I have criticised Bruno Maderna above for doing incongruously to Monteverdi, and Angelo Ephrikian for doing incongruously to Peri? Precisely, I hope, in not being incongruous. I hope that what I have done is congruous with the given music.

This is, of course, quite an optimistic claim. But I took certain precautions, to which I have long been accustomed, and which are broadly as follows.

3. TWO WORKING RULES FOR CONGRUOUS REALISATION

There are, I think, two main working rules which may help in making a realisation congruous with the given music, so that we bring it out more richly in its own true colours, rather than less effectively in an incongruous disguise. These rules are simple to state, but extremely important to observe; and the first of them is really just a matter of being sufficiently firm-minded, although the second is not quite so easy.

The first working rule is to keep the original intact in all possible respects, other than in very small particulars or for very strong reasons. As very small particulars, I instance a few improvements made by me in Blow's part-writing, which is quite careless at some times and quite clumsy at others; for Dr. Burney's celebrated criticism of Blow's crudities, though partly anachronistic and irrelevant, was not wholly so, as I found a little painfully while realising Blow's sometimes very awkward and exasperating basses. As strong reasons, I instance the cuts and shifts I made to produce an abridged version (mentioned above) of Lully's *Amadis*, because for that occasion it was abridge or nothing, and a complete performance was not in question. With Blow's *Venus and Adonis*, I cut nothing out, I shifted nothing around, and I transposed only one insignificant passage of a dozen or so bars to solve a singer's problem.

The second and more difficult working rule is to bring in nothing as amplifying matter which is not related in the most direct and intimate way with the existing matter of the given music. This does not mean that counter-melodies have always to grow thematically out of the given melodies, though in many cases they can do this to good advantage. It does mean that they must convey an unmistakable impression of belonging to the given music. Often a counter-figuration works better than a counter-melody; but the same principle of belonging congruously applies. And if it is a good and congruous figuration, or melody, it is of the utmost importance to stay with it so far as possible, and not to confuse the impression by adding further material unnecessarily. All this applies to realising a continuo bass in the ordinary way, where just the same precautions have habitually to be taken; but all the more does it apply in these much rarer and more ambitious realisations with which early opera may confront us.

To judge what amplifying material is really congruous requires considerable experience as well as sufficient musicological know-how; and to invent it requires a friendly Muse, which she may not be every day of the week. But because she was friendly this time, I felt I was able to amplify Blow's given music (without changing him around) by merely letting flow what seemed to add itself naturally and almost autonomously in the extraordinary pleasure of that summer's work.

I worked as an artist works, half awarely, half intuitively. I worked without forgetting what I know as a musicologist; but I do not think that any of us could make living contact with early music, whether in small matters or in large, if it were not for that dimension in music itself which is not historical but archetypal. Nothing can be more precious than personal individuality: nothing shows more plainly the influence of the time and place in which we formed our personalities; and yet we are not only individuals. We are men and women; we are heirs to mankind. And one part of our inheritance is our ability to recognise the meanings conveyed both consciously and unconsciously by works of art.

There can be a recognition of what an early piece of music means. Whatever we may do to instruct and clarify our recognition by means of scholarly information, it is still recognition, in Plato's sense of recognising what after a fashion we already knew but did not know that we knew. From the recognition comes the response; and from the response we can begin to work out an interpretation or a reconstruction or a combination of both. On the small scale or the large, it is through the perceptiveness of our response, supported by the amplitude of our historical information, that we may hope to approach somewhere in the direction of an essential authenticity.

My large-scale bodying out of *Venus and Adonis* may therefore illustrate what I should regard as about the farthest extreme likely to be successful in our modern presentation of baroque music, and that only under somewhat exceptional circumstances: but these were somewhat

79

exceptional circumstances. The other extreme is the least degree of modern realisation which will give us an acceptably complete performance. The degree of such necessary and minimum realisation itself varies from piece to piece, and from little to much: but it can never be negligible. Our modern personalities must unavoidably enter in; and what Michael Tippett once described to me as 'the temper of our times'.

There does not have to be only one right way of doing things. If Raymond Leppard and Alan Curtis can both give moving performances of Monteverdi or Cavalli, and they can, there is evidently a considerable margin for personal preference. 'A musician cannot move others,' wrote C. P. E. Bach in that much-quoted *Essay* of his (Berlin, 1753, III, 13), 'without himself being moved'; and, of course, I and my audiences at Carmel were also moved. I was glad to be called 'inspired and scholarly' by the critic of the *Monterey Peninsula Herald*; and glad when Robert Commanday wrote in the *San Francisco Chronicle*, having previously 'heard a harpsichord-accompanied performance of the unadorned score and found it interesting only in an esoteric way', that 'the Blow-Donington *Venus and Adonis* is a viable theatre piece which has beautiful things to say to the modern audience'. For if that is so, there has been genuine communication between past and present; and the method has worked.

I would describe this method as, in some significant degree, a re-experiencing of the music *sub specie aeternitatis*, in the light of its enduring essence. But in varying degrees, what else can our modern interpretations be but some such vision filtered through the fine lens of our modern imaginations? There can be no historical authenticity in the absolute. There can only be a continuous spectrum from the least regardful of our inadvertent modernisations to the most scrupulous of our combined knowledge and insight.

But there is a great difference between inadvertent interpretations and deliberate interpretations; and it is knowledge and insight which make the difference. No one can literally get outside himself, or outside his time. But we can get messages from the past: partly by intuitive recognition; partly through our knowledge of the contemporary evidence. My faith in the high value of that knowledge remains exactly what this present book shows it to be. Prepared by such knowledge, we can listen to what early music itself has to tell us about its own implications.

And that is, ultimately, what I mean by keeping within the boundaries of style.

4. THE SHAPE OF THINGS TO COME

As I introduce this new version of my old *Interpretation*, this attempt to review what now seems most important for the felicitous interpretation of early music, I am aware of two complementary aspects, each important in its different way. One is the great body of factual information now at our disposal, surveyed with such method and accuracy as I could achieve in the many pages which follow. The other is that growing understanding of the spirit, without which all our knowledge would be unprofitable learning indeed.

Neither our knowledge of the facts nor our understanding of the spirit has reached finality, or ever will. Perhaps it is part of the fascination of our search that it never can be completed. But there are, of course, areas of greater or lesser certainty.

I am not sure how much more we can hope to extract directly from the contemporary treatises. They have been worked over very thoroughly by now; and indeed, there is much repetitiveness in all the variety of their instructions, since they were concerned with practices in which there were considerable elements of uniformity as well as of variability. But musical manuscripts in their vast and largely unexplored proliferation must still hide many clues, particularly for accidentals, for instrumentation, and for contemporary realisations of accompaniment and ornamentation (in quantities only recently suspected). Accounts of payments to musicians, descriptions in letters or ambassadorial reports and similar documentary evidence, and even pictures so far unnoticed, will undoubtedly bear at least a small crop of further suggestive material. On the borders, too, of scholarship and craftsmanship, the reeds and mouthpieces and bores of wind instruments, the strings and scaling and thicknesses of harpsichords, the technique and methods of *bel canto* voice production: these and other areas are yielding fresh secrets all the time. For mere knowledge alone there is no end in sight.

For understanding our knowledge, no end is possible. Never will there be a newer version of this book in which it will be possible to say: now we have it. Yet in certain more limited respects it may already be possible to say, with all due regard for human fallibility, that we do seem to have it. In the well stressed and well nuanced execution of the standard form of cadential trill, for example, either you have it or you do not have it, but once you do have it there is no uncertainty. Your own good musicianship gets the point of it, and that is that. There is nothing more to understand. Matters are very nearly as obvious with appoggiaturas in recitative, and I was delighted when Stanley Sadie wrote (*Musical Times*, Jan., 1972, p. 61, in a mainly favourable review of Colin Davis' new *Figaro* at Covent Garden) that 'the omission of many of the obligatory appoggiaturas in recitative is sheer bad grammar'.

These details are indeed exceptional in our being able to say of them, virtually, that they can only be either right or wrong. Over the entire area of early interpretation, all that we can usually claim is that we are somewhere within the outer boundaries of the style, where great though not unlimited variability prevailed at the time, and should therefore be allowed to prevail again now. But how can we be certain of boundaries so elusive? How can our history be sufficiently authenticated? How can our sense of style, depending as it does on so much more than our piecemeal historical knowledge, be sufficiently authentic?

I would never make any claim to certainty in this broader sense. But it is just in this broader sense that I think our understanding is increasing with the years, and will go on increasing. As I look around, I feel that the present generation of musicians is far more with it (and I do not only mean the young generation: it is in the air altogether). No doubt plenty of new mistakes are being made; but it was Bernard Shaw who once wrote that the man who never made a mistake never made anything. And that goes as much for Alan Curtis, with his unhistorically reticent instrumentation in Monteverdian opera, as it does for Raymond Leppard, with his somewhat arbitrary transpositions and translocations and what my admired friend Winton Dean calls, amusingly but as I think over-critically in this case (*Musical Times*, Jan., 1972, p. 59), 'the Straussian bolster'.

All this, and indeed most of this long Introduction, is topical talk, which as more years pass by and this book hopefully becomes due one day for a yet newer version, will recede from topicality and become history in its turn. But now it needs to be talked about, because it is on the outcome of these present debates that the shape of things to come in our interpretation of early music depends. I put in my own topical plea now, with Alan Curtis for more sonority, with Raymond Leppard for more judiciousness, with Nikolaus Harnoncourt and his Concentus Musicus for more tension: or rather, since no man can change his basic temperament and we can each only follow the best of our personal visions when interpreting both style and evidence, I put in my plea for an open mind as we weigh the achievements of these and many more fine workers the one against the other. They have all of them the defects of their very great virtues: we all do have the defects of our virtues; and I do not think that any of us has yet found or will find a total answer.

Even our mistakes, it seems, go according to the fashion. In my apprentice days, the great mistake which was being pioneered against by my master Arnold Dolmetsch was regarding the romantic orchestra as so inherently superior to the baroque orchestra that you could do no better than give Bach and Handel the full benefit of it. And they did. To hear the Sixth Brandenburg with viola and cello sections not merely complete but specially augmented for the occasion was something to be remembered across all my years of playing gamba in it, one to a part in chamber-music style; and the Third Brandenburg pounded along with similarly augmented strings. To hear the big brass coming in on Bach nights at the Proms was even more memorable: and I am not going to pretend that I did not enormously enjoy it all, young schoolboy as I was; but that was before I got to enjoy Bach more congruously in the Dolmetsch way.

The old Prom way was magnificent, but it was not Bach. It is the same now with Switched-on Bach; but that is an electronic red-herring and not a musicological one. The musicological mistake of which our own times stand most in danger is at the opposite swing of the pendulum. It is history for history's sake. It is performing Bach as he is supposed to have had to put up with being performed at Leipzig, rather than as he sought to be performed and would have been performed by bigger and better baroque (but N.B. baroque) forces at the time. Above all (and this is by far the worst of our fashionable musicological temptations) it is scaling down our baroque performances under the almost puritanical misconception that reticence, quite unconditional and general reticence, is a necessary part of authenticity.

My final plea, therefore, is to keep our interpretation of early music full-bodied. That is indeed a necessary part of authenticity.

BOOK ONE
STYLE

CHAPTER I

The Approach to Early Music

1. PREVIEW OF AN 'EARLY' STYLE

Between 1948, when I planted the very first seeds of this book about a quarter of a century ago, and 1963, when the first edition of its original version appeared, the change in our attitude to early music and its interpretation was already remarkable. In the dozen years since I completed that first manuscript it has become phenomenal. The young generation so active in baroque and earlier music today will find it quite hard to believe that their own parents a quarter of a century ago were mostly indifferent to music of the age of Bach and Handel, apart from those two acknowledged giants, and to almost everything before. But so it was, and this is one side of the change. The money the recording industry must have made out of Vivaldi alone would show it; and indeed, it is not in doubt.

The other side of the change concerns the desirability, admitted probably by a majority now but only by a small minority then, of interpreting early music on its own terms rather than on ours: that is to say, on the instruments for which it was originally composed and in a style congruous with that in which it was originally performed. This is a viewpoint, however, not yet so generally accepted as the former. Hardly anyone now doubts the broad value of early music; many excellent musicians still doubt the value of its original instruments and performing styles. Since I take this dissenting opinion very seriously, and consider that it deserves a careful answer, I am retaining here the case much as I first worked it out a dozen years ago. Those who are already in agreement with its arguments may nevertheless find it convenient to have them set out systematically; while newcomers to the idea of a substantially authentic approach to early music may be well advised to cover this ground before moving to the levels of ever greater detail by which this book proceeds.

There is a place for transcriptions which are a genuine marriage of two musical personalities across the generations: the product is a new and often interesting work. But in ordinary performance, music of whatever generation will sound more effective and more moving when we make every reasonable attempt to present it under its original conditions of performance. If we want to share in a composer's experience, we have to carry out his intentions. If we find his experience somewhat strange, we have to remember that it may be more rewarding to come to terms with an unfamiliar experience than to recapitulate a familiar one in a less telling form. It may be more rewarding to make the most of the unfamiliarity than to dilute that unfamiliarity in the doubtful hope of adapting it to modern ears.

Modern ears are no more than ordinary ears in a modern setting. Our response to music is fundamentally intuitive, and our human faculty of intuition can have changed very little during the longest period considered in this book. The fundamentals of interpretation are the same for us as they were for Bach or Monteverdi, or indeed for Josquin or Perotin le Grand. We not only can but must rely on our intuitive response to the expressive implications of early music. But this does not mean that we have nothing to learn which the music itself cannot teach us. On the contrary, we have a great deal to learn.

It is unrealistic to think that we can give an adequate rendering of any music in the absence of a detailed acquaintance with its relevant conventions. Musical notation is a wonderful invention, but it is not as wonderful as all that. We need a vast amount of traditional working knowledge in order to bring even the most cunning and thorough of these notated marks on paper into living performance. With baroque music and earlier, the tradition has been much distorted and partly forgotten; the marks may be cunning but we have to be still more cunning to know what some of them mean; while notation in general was of deliberate intention a great deal less thorough than we are nowadays accustomed to finding it.

To recover something of what direct tradition can no longer convey to us, our best and indeed almost our only recourse is to read what the actual contemporaries of the music had to say about it. Almost exactly half the words in my first version consisted of quotations from the early authorities and other witnesses themselves. I do most earnestly commend these quotations to the careful attention of the reader. It is not only that they have an inherent authenticity with which no mere summary or discussion of them can compete; it is also that they convey so much more than merely factual information. That they are unreliable in varying degrees, self-contradictory or contradictory with one another in many respects, and tiresomely repetitive in others I shall be the first to admit. I almost feel inclined to suggest that this is just why they are so valuable. They add up to such a very human picture. They evoke the original atmosphere of interpretation more faithfully than any systematically consistent account could do. The reality was neither systematic nor consistent, and no amount of learned historical after-thought can make it so.

What we are trying to find out is not the exact interpretation such-and-such a composer intended for such-and-such a passage. There is no such thing as an exact interpretation. No one, not even the composer, plays a passage in exactly the same way twice running. It would be a much duller world if music would not tolerate more than one interpretation; we should miss the intensely personal contribution which different performers have to offer, or even the same performer when in a different mood. What we are trying to find out is partly the kind of detail which did not and should not depend on mood at all, and partly the outside limits within which the performer's mood can suitably operate. We want him to illuminate different aspects of the music in accordance with whatever is individual in his response to it; we do not want him to impose his individuality on the much greater element in the music which is common to us all, and to which there is fundamentally only one way of responding. We do not want him to go outside the boundaries of the style.

In the case of early music, this is tantamount to saying that we need to know, not exactly how the composer would have taken his music, but broadly how any good performer of his day might have taken it. That leaves a very wide field for personal taste and individuality; it even opens the way to performances which I personally, or the reader, or any other given person might happen to dislike. But it does set a boundary to positive incongruities of style, because while a bad contemporary performer might all too easily have committed them (and indeed there is plenty of evidence for this at all times and places), a good contemporary performer could not have done so, unless, of course, the style in question was outside his experience even though contemporary in time.

Every piece of music carries implications with regard to performance which can be differently interpreted: but not beyond certain limits, because so soon as those limits are overstepped we feel a contradiction between the style of the music and the style of the interpretation. We may not, it is true, feel this contradiction explicitly; we may feel vaguely uneasy without knowing quite what is wrong or what to do about it; or we may notice nothing wrong, and merely fail to be moved by the music as in a more understanding performance it could be moving us. But whether we are directly aware of it or not, there will still be something missing which need not be missing.

A performer contemporary with the music had opportunities for becoming familiar with the style which we are denied at this distance of time. A single satisfactory sound-recording might tell us more about baroque methods of performance than all our painstaking researches; but we have not got that recording, and must do the best we can without it. The best we can do is to start from such contemporary evidence as does survive.

This does not imply idealising the contemporary performers, who so far as we can make out must have been much worse than ourselves in some branches of the art, much better in other branches, and perhaps as an overall average very much the same. It is simply that whatever else may or may not have been wrong with a contemporary performance, under ordinary circumstances it would at least have been within the style, whereas under ordinary circumstances a modern performance, whatever its other merits, is likely to be partly at odds with the style. It is only fair to add that extraordinary circumstances, in which great specialised knowledge has been successfully brought to bear, are becoming so much more frequent nowadays that we may in a few years' time be able to regard this as no longer the exception but the rule. I wrote these words in 1963. They read still truer today.

There are now, and to some extent always will be, limits to the authenticity we can hope to achieve. Anyone specialising in the interpretation of early music needs not only a sufficiently scholarly grasp but sufficient competence and experience as a practising musician. He must be able to get inside the problems as they actually come up in rehearsal; he must be able to envisage solutions which can come off in performance. His scholarship can only be helpful if it is used musically; yet at the same time it can only be used musically if he has plenty of it. He must be in a position to weigh one piece of evidence against another. An isolated statement, out of context and perhaps untypical, can lead to devastatingly unmusical results; and that after all is the last thing we want our scholarship to end in. We are trying to be authentic not because there is anything sacrosanct in historical reproduction, but because our best chance of matching the interpretation to the music lies in matching it to the original intentions. We are trying to be better scholars in order to make better music.

Ultimately it is our personal responsibility as performing musicians to make historical authenticity a living thing. It seems unlikely that we shall ever make so close a match that it would deceive any visiting seventeenth-century or eighteenth-century ghost into thinking that he was listening to a performance of his own day; but at least we may hope that he would recognise the general style—and enjoy the music. We may hope to be, not ideally, but reasonably authentic.

As a corollary to being as authentic as we reasonably can, I think we should still accept it that under modern conditions of performance some aspects of authenticity are more important than others, and that it may often be worth letting the less important aspects go, provided we can get the more important aspects established. It is, for example, worth a great deal to get really good performers who are willing to co-operate to the best of their ability, but who may have neither the time nor the temperament to undergo a prolonged training in early style. On the other hand, performers who are not willing to co-operate to the best of their ability with regard to the essential points of style are unsuitable for the purpose.

Some modern musicians, again, seem to have a greater natural affinity with the stylistic requirements of early music than others. In any more or less permanent chamber ensemble or other organisation which wants to give special attention to early music, it is wisest to choose members with as much of this natural affinity as possible, and then to concentrate and go on concentrating on essentials, with as many inessentials added as the circumstances of the case permit. The same considerations apply to performers brought together only for a particular performance or series of performances, except that the necessity to concentrate on essentials is then still more obviously pressing. We can expect more now than a dozen years ago.

The question as to what are the essentials can only be answered in concrete detail, as this book proceeds. But it is perhaps worth asking here whether there can in principle be any such thing as might be described as an 'early' style of interpretation. If we press that question too hard, it is plain that the answer must be 'no'; but in very loose terms, it may be possible to give a more positive reply. The contemporary quotations of which this book so largely consists have the effect of building up cumulatively a picture of our predecessors in their music-rooms and auditoriums, not as stiff historical figures but as very human beings with all our own human diversity of tastes and abilities. Behind all this diversity, however, we see also what is still more illuminating: a certain common denominator of tacit assumptions and habitual attitudes which may give us our first and most general indications of such an 'early' style of interpretation.

I have fallen back on this non-committal word 'early' whenever I have wanted to leave my chronological boundaries deliberately undefined. I am mainly though not by any means exclusively concerned in this book with baroque music, *i.e.* approximately from Monteverdi to J. S. Bach. There is diversity enough here on any showing; but we find throughout a general disposition to join the composer and the performer in a more equal partnership than our present custom is. Even when the two were not, as they so frequently were, one and the same person, the performer was expected to make the music his own with much less respect for the written text and much more reliance on spontaneous expression and improvisation than we expect now except in avant-garde and dance music. It was not that composers were lazier or performers were prouder, but that both parties set an overriding value on the freshness and immediacy which are among the most positive results of such an attitude. They valued spontaneity.

To recapture this sense of spontaneity is the most important single factor in our search for an adequately authentic rendering. Trills and appoggiaturas; conventions of rhythm, tempo and dynamics; small forces and original instrumentation: such matters are valuable contributions to the style; but they are not the style. The whole is greater than the parts.

The style most widely appropriate to baroque music is less massive but more incisive than that in which my generation grew up. It is vivid yet relaxed; glowing yet transparent. It sparkles and it dances, alive with natural ease and unforced conviction. It charms like a smile, and it cuts like a knife. The less we inflate it the stronger it sounds. Even the best baroque music can be made ponderous by overweighting it, but its true nature is mostly as volatile as its performers can possibly conceive of it in their most impulsive moods.

Contrary to some recent opinion, there is nothing unimpulsive, and nothing dry, about an authentic rendering of early music. That such an opinion should have arisen was understandable and valuable earlier in the twentieth century when the most pressing necessity was to escape from the incongruous influence of post-Wagnerian weight, sonority and smoothness. But this escape has now virtually been accomplished, and one mistake now may be not too little austerity but too much. We are then in danger of depriving early music of the sheer animal vitality which carries all genuine musical performance along as nature always needs to carry along and underwrite the achievements of culture.

There is a magnificence of storm and stress which is part of Wagner's musical language. But there is also a poise and a crispness and a crystalline translucency shared by composers as unlike in other respects as Monteverdi and Vivaldi, as Purcell and Couperin, as Bach and Handel. This baroque brand of eloquence is not less impassioned than the romantic variety. To match up to the baroque intentions in our interpretation does not, as is sometimes mistakenly suggested, mean renouncing all our warmest feelings and all our richest colourings of tone. It does mean applying them appropriately to the matter in hand, keeping the style sharply etched and the mood unaffected and direct, and reconciling the complementary requirements of passion and serenity. This is now much better known than a dozen years ago.

Ignoring the passion in early music is a mere escape into fantasies of unbroken serenity in some past golden age: fantasies just as comfortable and illusory as our by now untenable and discarded Victorian fantasies of unbroken progress. There has never been an age of unqualified serenity or unqualified passion; these are two extremes of human experience which the art of living consists in more or less successfully reconciling. And the art of music, like the visual and literary arts, has its own ways of showing how they can be reconciled.

It is this reconciliation of opposites achieved by the composer in his music which it is so necessary for our interpretation to carry faithfully into effect. All great music achieves it, but not all in the same way. The differences do not lie simply along chronological divisions. It is personality rather than period which separates the other-worldliness of Palestrina from the earthy immediacy of Monteverdi, the rich homeliness of Haydn from the profound lucidity of Mozart, the lyricism of Schubert from the indomitability of Beethoven. Some are outgoing like Vivaldi or Handel, others inturned like Purcell or J. S. Bach, in any age. Brahms and Wagner and Debussy are all of the nineteenth century; Stravinsky and Schoenberg and Vaughan Williams and Bartók are all of the twentieth. Their solutions to the equation are various in the extreme; but not the elements in the equation. Pain and joy, suffering and delight, adversity and triumph, and more particularly the bitter-sweet triumph of accepting adversity as part of our human lot: these are the ingredients, and we all mix them differently according to our manner of experience.

Nevertheless there are some styles which seem able to balance them up better than others. What we call the baroque period of music had such balance, and the remarkable hold which this period has now gained on our affections is certainly not due to its having run away from one end of our human paradox by divorcing passion from serenity or keeping music unemotional. Not even Stravinsky (least of all Stravinsky) did this, although he seemed to think he did. The hold which baroque music has gained over our affections may well be due to the fact that its most typical composers, from the supreme case of J. S. Bach downwards, had each in their degree the secret of not only balancing the passion and serenity, but balancing them at a high level of intensity. Bach's music is very passionate and very serene, not in mere alternation, but as an integrated whole. If ever there was a case of transcending the opposites in a reconciliation which is more than the sum of its parts, that case is Bach's music. This is the measure of our problem in doing justice to him with our interpretation.

Because the question of how emotional our interpretation of early music ought to be is a primary question which takes precedence even over the more complex question of how to apply the right kind of emotion in the right kind of way, I have collected a small sampling of evidence demonstrating contemporary responses to music at various moments of history before and during the baroque period. These demonstrations are intended particularly to correct any impression which the reader may have that early music was or should be a less intense experience than later music, or that a scaled-down interpretation could possibly be justified on historical grounds, as it certainly is not on artistic grounds.

2. THE ELEMENT OF PASSION IN EARLY MUSIC

(1) Charles Butler, *Principles of Musik*, London, 1636, p. 109, citing the fifth-century St. Augustine:

'O how I wept at thy Hymns and Songs, being vehemently moved with the voices of thy sweet-sounding Church. Those Voices did pierce mine ears, and thy truth distilled into mine heart; and thereby was inflamed in me a love of Piety: the tears trickled down, and with them I was in happy case.'

(2) William Prynne, *Histriomastix*, London, 1633, Ch. XX, citing the twelfth-century Bishop Ethelred:

'Whence hath the Church so many Organs and Musicall Instruments? To what purpose, I pray you, is that terrible blowing of Belloes, expressing rather the crakes of Thunder, than the sweetnesse of a voyce? To what purpose serves that contraction and inflection of the voyce? This man sings a base, that a small meane, another a treble, a fourth divides and cuts asunder, as it were, certaine middle notes. One while the voyce is strained, anon it is remitted, now it is dashed, and then againe it is inlarged with a lowder sound. Sometimes, which is a shame to speake, it is enforced into a horse's neighings; sometimes, the masculine vigour being laid aside, it is sharpened into the shrilnesse of a woman's voyce; now and then it is writhed, and retorted with a certaine artificiall circumvolution. Sometimes thou may'st see a man with an open mouth, not to sing, but, as it were, to breathe out his last gaspe, by shutting in his breath, and by a certaine ridiculous interception of his voyce, as it were to threaten silence, and now again to imitate the agonies of a dying man, or the extasies of such as suffer.'

(3) Baldassare Castiglione, *The Courtyer*, Venice, 1528, transl. Sir Thomas Hoby, London, 1561, Everyman ed. 1928, p. 61:

'Marke me musicke, wherein are harmonies sometime of a base sound and slow, and otherwhile verie quicke and of new devises, yet doe they all recreate a man, but for sundrie causes, as a man may perceive in the manner of singing that Bido useth, which is so artificall, cunning, vehement, stirred, and such sundrie melodies, that the spirites of the hearers move all and are inflamed, and so listing, a man would weene they were lift up into heaven.

'And no lesse doth our Marchetto Cara move in his singing, but with a more soft harmony, that by a delectable way and full of mourning sweetenes maketh tender and perceth the mind, and sweetly imprinteth in it a passion full of great delite.'

(4) Myles Coverdale, *Goostly Psalmes*, London, [? 1539], preface 'Unto the Christen reader':

'Yf yonge men also that have the gyfte of syngynge, toke theyr pleasure in soch wholsome balettes . . . it were a token, both that they felt some sparks of Gods love in theyr hertes, and that they also had some love unto hym, for truly as we love, so synge we: and where our affeccyon is, thence commeth our myrth and joye . . .'

(5) Charles Butler, *Principles of Musik*, London, 1636, p. 92:

'[Good composing is impossible] unless the Author, at the time of Composing, be transported as it were with some Musical fury; so that himself scarce knoweth what he doth, nor can presently give a reason for his doing.'

(6) Samuel Pepys, *Diary*, 27 Feb., 1667/8:

'That which did please me beyond any thing in the whole world was the wind-musick when the angel comes down, which is so sweet that it ravished me, and indeed, in a word, did wrap up my soul so that it made me really sick, just as I have formerly been when in love with my wife; that neither then, nor all the evening going home, and at home, I was able to think of any thing, but remained all night transported.'

(7) Angelo Berardi, *Ragionamenti Musicali*, Bologna, 1681, p. 87:

'Music is the ruler of the passions of the soul.'

(8) François Raguenet, *Comparison between the French and Italian Music*, 1702, transl. ? J. E. Galliard, 1709, ed. O. Strunk, *Mus. Quart.*, XXXII, 3, July, 1946, p. 422:

'[Music is] transport, enchantment and extasy of pleasure . . .'
[Translator's *f.n.*, p. 419:] 'I never met with any man that suffered his passions to hurry him away so much whilst he was playing on the violin as the famous Arcangelo Corelli, whose eyes will sometimes turn as red as fire; his countenance will be distorted, his eyeballs roll as in an agony, and he gives in so much to what he is doing that he doth not look like the same man.'

(9) Dr. Charles Burney, *Present State of Music in Germany*, London, 1773, II, p. 269:

'[C.P.E. Bach at the clavichord] grew so animated and *possessed*, that he not only played, but looked like one inspired. His eyes were fixed, his underlip fell, and drops of effervescence distilled from his countenance.

He said, if he were to be set to work frequently, in this manner, he should grow young again.'

(10) C. H. Blainville, *L'Esprit de l'Art Musical*, Geneva, 1754, p. 14:

'A musician falls into inspiration at the moment when he least thinks of it; his imagination is fired, his heart swells, his blood pulses rapidly without his volition; a luminous cloud surrounds him, he is transported into a vast space; it is that which has reality, all his senses lend him their mutual aid, and are transformed piece by piece into passion, the image which he desires to paint; it all comes pressing upon him, he guides and selects. Exalted above himself, he traces, without knowing it, the beauties which he scarcely understands: like a second Pythian, he falls into a frenzy, he speaks the language of the Gods; he is drained at last, the forces fail him; he returns to himself . . .'

(11) [J. Mainwaring] *Memoirs of . . . Handel*, London, 1760, p. 52:

'The audience was so enchanted with this performance, that a stranger who should have seen the manner in which they were affected, would have imagined they had all been distracted.'

3. THE ELEMENT OF SERENITY IN EARLY MUSIC

(12) Richard Allison, *Howres Recreation in Musicke*, London, 1606, foreword, citing the early sixteenth-century founder of the Reformation:

'Musicke, saith he [Martin Luther] to Divels we know is hateful and intolerable, and I plainely thinke, neither am I ashamed to averr it, that next Theologie, there is no Arte comparable with Musicke: for it alone next to Theologie doth affect that, which otherwise only Theologie can performe, that is a quiet and a cheareful minde.'

(13) Thomas Sternhold, *Psalter*, London, 1560, title-page:

'Very mete to be used of all sorts of people privately for their godly solace and comfort, laiying aparte all ungodly songues and ballades which tende only to the nourishing of vice, and corrupting of youth . . .'

(14) John Milton, *Of Education*, London, 1644, ed. of 1836, p. 162:

'The solemn and divine harmonies of Music . . . have a great power over dispositions and manners, to smoothe and make them gentle from rustic harshness and distempered passions.'

(15) Jean-Jacques Rousseau, *Dictionnaire de Musique*, Paris, 1768, *s.v.* 'Imitation':

'Night, sleep, solitude and silence are among the great pictures of music.'

4. RECONCILING THE PASSION WITH THE SERENITY

(16) Sir Thomas Browne, *Religio Medici*, London, 1642, Everyman ed., p. 79:

'It is my temper, and I like it the better, to affect all harmony, and sure there is musick even in the beauty, and the silent note which Cupid strikes, far sweeter than the sound of an instrument. For there is a musick where ever there is a harmony, order or proportion . . .

'Whosoever is harmonically composed delights in harmony; which makes me much distrust the symmetry of those heads which declaim against all Church-Musick. For my self, not only from my obedience, but my particular Genius, I do embrace it: for even that vulgar and Tavern-Musick, which makes one man merry, another mad, strikes in me a deep fit of devotion, and a profound contemplation of the First Composer. There is something in it of Divinity more than the ear discovers: it is an Hieroglyphical and shadowed lesson of the whole World, and creatures of God; such a melody to the ear, as the whole World, well understood, would afford the understanding. In brief, it is a sensible fit of that harmony which intellectually sounds in the ears of God.'

(17) Thomas Mace, *Musick's Monument*, London, 1676, p. 19:

'But when *That Vast-Conchording-Unity* of the whole *Congregational-Chorus*, came (as I may say) *Thundering in*, even so, as it made the very *Ground shake* under us; (*Oh the unutterable ravishing Soul's delight!*) In the which I was so *transported*, and *wrapt* up into *High Contemplations*, that there was no room left in my *whole Man*, viz. *Body*, *Soul* and *Spirit*, for any thing below *Divine* and *Heavenly Raptures* . . .

[p. 118] '. . . *Musick* speaks so transcendently, and Communicates Its Notions so Intelligibly to the Internal, Intellectual, and Incomprehensible Faculties of the Soul; so far beyond all *Language* of *Words*, that I confess, and most solemnly affirm, I have been more *Sensibly*, *Fervently*, and *Zealously Captivated*, and drawn into *Divine Raptures*, and *Contemplations*, by Those *Unexpressible*, *Rhetorical*, *Uncontroulable Persuasions*, and *Instructions* of *Musicks Divine Language*, than ever yet I have been, by the best *Verbal Rhetorick*, that came from any Mans Mouth, either in *Pulpit*, or elsewhere.

'Those *Influences*, which come along with It, may aptly be compar'd, to *Emanations*, *Communications*, or *Distillations*, of some *Sweet*, and *Heavenly Genius*, or *Spirit*; *Mystically*, and *Unapprehensibly* (yet *Effectually*) *Dispossessing the Soul*, and *Mind*, of *All Irregular Disturbing*, *and Unquiet Motions*; and *Stills*, and *Fills It*, with *Quietness*, *Joy*, and *Peace*; *Absolute Tranquillity*, and *Unexpressible Satisfaction*.'

CHAPTER II

The Interplay of Styles

1. A BASIC BAROQUE PROBLEM

With sixteenth-century polyphony, one basic problem is to keep the seamless tapestry of the counterpoint intact while bringing out the themes and entries with sufficient light and shade. In early baroque opera, one basic problem is to mould a single expressive monody to each fluctuation of feeling, words and drama, with the support of simple but extraordinarily intense and significant harmony. In the main baroque period, one basic problem of this same general order is not quite either of these; it is something between the two.

We have to build up a tremendously strong, balanced tension between a melody less fluid than early opera, and a bass less static. The middle is usually the least important, or at any rate the least well defined. Even the favourite trio-sonata form, with its twin melodies and its strongly melodic bass-line figured for the accompanist's improvisations, has more the nature of an upper part going into duplicate than of fully spaced-out counterpoint. The fugal form itself is no longer equal-voiced polyphony in quite the old sixteenth-century meaning; it, too, consists of progressions on a harmonic bass, however skilfully embodied in a contrapuntal texture. And in spite of the opposition of solo and ripieno in concertos, in spite of the fashionable echo-effects inherited from the brilliant Gabrieli tradition, the contrasts of baroque music are not characteristically within the movement. They are between movements.

That is the principle of the suite. Most baroque 'sonatas' are really suites, with movements which are either monothematic or thematically homogeneous. Even opera lost much of its dramatic flexibility as the first stage of fluid music-drama waned; a late baroque opera has something of the quality of a dramatised vocal suite. In music constructed, in this characteristic baroque fashion, on the suite principle, we have to build up a further tension, by every variety of expressive resource, between the contrasting movements.

We have here, then, two fairly general guides to baroque interpretation: the strong balance between the top and bottom of the music, which implies keeping the bass-line nearly or quite as telling as the upper melody or melodies; and the strong opposition between movements, which implies somewhat sustained moods not unnecessarily diversified within the movement.

This is, of course, the merest starting-point.

2. THE FACTOR OF DATE

(18) J. S. Bach, memorandum to Leipzig Town Council, 1730 (in Spitta's *Bach*, transl. Bell and Fuller-Maitland, 1889):

'The present *status musices* is quite different to what it used to be formerly—the art being much advanced and taste marvellously changed, so that the old-fashioned kind of music no longer sounds well in our ears.'

(19) Joachim Quantz, *Essay*, Berlin, 1752, XVIII, 6:

'The old musicians complain of the melodic extravagances of the young, and the young mock the dryness of the old.'

(20) Dr. Charles Burney, *Present State of Music in Germany*, London, 1773, II, p. 156:

'Quantz' music is simple and natural; his taste is that of forty years ago.'

Thus J. S. Bach regarded himself as a modernist; and his music shows that he was in cordial sympathy with the then modern 'galant' tendencies in general, and with French idioms in particular. Quantz, who was also in sympathy with French music, was something of a conservative; Burney (*op. cit.*, p. 82), called his great *Essay* of 1752 'classical'. Though this *Essay* was not actually published in J. S. Bach's lifetime, its contents are largely applicable to J. S. Bach's music. (I have sometimes followed the French edition.)

J. S. Bach's most famous son, C. P. E. Bach, published the first part of his still more distinguished *Essay* in 1753, only a year later. He too, like his father, was a modernist, but there is a great difference. The foundation of J. S. Bach's art was traditional in a degree in which C. P. E. Bach's was not. Looking beneath the surface, and with two centuries of historical perspective to help us, we might say that both men were beyond their time, but the father in a different direction from that in which their time was then moving, and the son in the same direction. In C. P. E. Bach's own time, it merely appeared that the father was old-fashioned, and the son a leader of fashion. The son himself acknowledged his father's greatness and his own immeasurable debt to him; yet the tendency of C. P. E. Bach's *Essay* is somewhat further from J. S. Bach than Quantz' *Essay*, and its contents, though still largely applicable to J. S. Bach's music, are somewhat less generally so. Somewhat more caution is needed in arguing from C. P. E. Bach to J. S. Bach than in arguing from Quantz to J. S. Bach.

This is a characteristic situation. We cannot always count on finding evidence as close in time or place as we should wish, and slightly distant evidence may be better than a purely modern guess. The evidence leaves surprisingly few major uncertainties about the substance of the conventions for baroque music, but it is often extraordinarily hard to discover how widely they apply. We are not helped by the fact that no baroque authority displays a very sound or well-informed historical sense; most of them display none at all. On the other hand, their interest in national differences was unbounded, and here we have at least no dearth of evidence.

POSTSCRIPT TO NEW VERSION

The warning given above, to use caution when applying information from treatises to music a little distant from them, but to apply it judiciously none the less, was sufficient at the time of the first and second editions of my original version. But Frederick Neumann (*Music and Letters*, XLVIII, 4, 1967, pp. 315–324) has called in question, for example, the relevance of Quantz to the music of J. S. Bach, where I and others, though not unaware of the need for caution, have certainly made good use of him, together with other members of what we have come to think of as the Berlin school.

How far distant is Quantz actually from J. S. Bach? Since Quantz was born in 1697, just under twelve years after J. S. Bach, he was a member, though a younger member, of the same generation. Quantz worked his way up the hard way through town bands, and a brief study in the old school under a pupil of Fux, to twenty-five active years at Dresden, where J. S. Bach sometimes played, and where Quantz absorbed much the same mixture of native German and imported French and Italian music which J. S. Bach had elsewhere imbibed: a Lully-style orchestra, for example, with Corelli and Vivaldi in its repertoire; Italian opera increasingly in the foreground; German organ-music always in the background; and harpsichord idioms more French than German—it is the world of J. S. Bach with no great local or chronological difference. There follows Quantz' instructive Italian, French and English journey, such as J. S. Bach never made; the profitable move to Berlin in 1741; and the great *Essay* at age 55 in 1752, but Burney called it 'classical' and in 1773 described Quantz' taste as 'forty years' behind the times: see (20) above. I can hardly imagine our being lucky enough to get any closer to J. S. Bach than that with a great pedagogical treatise, replete in fine detail and broad insight alike.

Unless, indeed, we count as closer J. S. Bach's own son and best pupil, C. P. E. Bach. Here, however, we are into the next generation, for though C. P. E. Bach's *Essay* (Part I) came, in 1753, only a year after Quantz, he was the younger man by 17 years. That their books are so largely similar is a testimony to how traditional a pedagogue C. P. E. Bach was, with his proudly acknowledged debt to his father's teaching and all the family taste for French-style harpsichord idioms, ornaments and fingerings. Marpurg, four years younger again, formed his tastes as much as anywhere in Paris, where he seems to have been associated with Rameau and others. All three authors spent important years, but not all their working years, in Berlin: hence the convenience (but it is only a convenience) of thinking of them as members of a 'Berlin school'.

Indeed tastes were on the change at J. S. Bach's death in 1750; they had been on the change for a generation or more, and J. S. Bach when in his modern vein had been a part of the change, rebuked as he was for making even his church music too *galant*, too much like a modern opera. We saw, at (18) above, how little liking J. S. Bach had for 'the old-fashioned kind of music'. There was, in short, no abrupt shift from baroque to classical; merely the usual cumulative transition, much more gradual and less dramatic than historians once romantically supposed. Some of C. P. E. Bach's own fantasies actually sound so like his father's toccatas that one quite blinks and looks again.

Suppose in imagination that we could hear a performance of J. S. Bach's very *galant* trio-sonata from the *Musical Offering* (1747), with Quantz taking the flute part and C. P. E. Bach sitting down at the harpsichord. Should we not expect to hear a more authentically stylish performance, one nearer to J. S. Bach's own expectations, than any of our own painstaking reconstructions from another two hundred years farther away? Is it not our own distant modern inferences about J. S. Bach that need the greater caution?

Some of Frederick Neumann's own modern inferences seem right to me, as my revisions will show, and others seem wrong; for it really is a very difficult and uncertain field. But in that uncertainty, Quantz and C. P. E. Bach stand out for us like clear beacons, and we cannot afford to underestimate their value for many areas of late baroque musicianship.

3. THE FACTOR OF NATIONALITY: MAIN CURRENTS

(a) We may think of Italy as the radiating centre of baroque music. The foreign influences returning to that country were comparatively slight. Her exports included the operatic forms which spread at different rates in different directions, but were paramount all over Europe by the eighteenth century. The Italian violinist-composers, like the Italian singers, gained a supremacy seriously challenged only in France. The highest extent of the Italian leadership lasted a full three-quarters of a century, from about 1675 to about 1750, and it was not much lower in the decades before and after. In other fields, however, particularly keyboard music and orchestral suites, the French, too, were an internationally exporting nation over much of the same period, especially the latter part of it.

(b) It is the paradox of the French national style that its most classical exponent, Lully, was himself an Italian-born immigrant. Lully made few concessions to the Italian taste. It was French-born composers, among them Couperin the Great himself early in the eighteenth century, who added to their output of French-style suites a number of sonatas on the Italian model—to which, therefore, Italian and not French conventions of interpretation should largely be applied.

(c) Germany was hardly a musically exporting country at all during the baroque period, though the German violinist-composers, with their typical predilection for solo polyphony such as culminated in Bach's six astonishing unaccompanied suites, were a partial exception from an early date in the seventeenth century onwards. For the rest, the Italian trio-sonata was accepted, but with an interesting and markedly transforming disposition to replace two violins and a bass by a violin, a gamba and a bass, which not only deepens the sonority but distributes the part-writing more evenly in pitch.

Late in the seventeenth century, French orchestral, chamber and solo suites were imported into Germany with growing enthusiasm, and at the same time many of the French conventions of interpretation, for which, therefore, we have to watch from this time onwards. J. S. Bach himself, though very open to the Italian influence (above all of Vivaldi) was also a profound admirer of the French idioms, however much he modified both influences in adapting them to his Germanic background and his own unique personality. His keyboard music other than for organ is mainly, though not entirely, founded on French models and in need of a French style of interpretation. His organ music is basically indigenous, with that solid power combined with rich poetic feeling which was the peculiar inheritance of Protestant German music—a deeply religious inheritance in which the Lutheran chorale played a crucial role, not only as a symbol but also in conditioning the forms.

(d) England in the first half of the seventeenth century had already imported the Italian madrigal, and some elements of the Italian string fantasia, out of both of which she proceeded to manufacture highly indigenous products. None of this, however, was exported in turn, although the very expressive and brilliant keyboard music of the beginning of the century passed into the continental tradition which led eventually to Bach—and with it some advanced elements of fingering technique. There was some mutual interchange with France, mainly in lute music, *airs de cour*, and light dance forms: English lute ornamentation is thought to have inspired the French lutenists and through them the French keyboard school; but none of this was on a very substantial scale.

At the Restoration, French influence was cultivated in England both deliberately and extensively. This is very markedly the case with Purcell, whose sacred and secular music alike is conspicuous for its French idioms—or rather for what would be French idioms if they were not so astonishingly transmuted by that most individual of English composers. Their performance needs French elements, at any rate, particularly with regard to rhythm. In his youthful string fantasies, Purcell is wholly English; in his trio-sonatas, he is deliberately using Italian models and half-unconsciously including French models, so that conventions from both of those national traditions are needed in the interpretation.

(e) This whole problem of national styles in the interpretation of baroque music is the subject of a valuable discussion by Thurston Dart in his short but brilliant *Interpretation of Music* (London, 1954, pp. 77 *ff.*), where among other suggestions he gives a simple hint remarkably effectual in nine cases out of ten. He points out that we have usually a clue to the national style in question, if we notice what language is used for any title or expression mark given to the piece. Thus suite, ordre, allemande, courante, gigue, sarabande, vivement, vite, lentement, *etc.* normally imply a French idiom. Partita, sonata, allemanda, coranto, giga, sarabanda, allegro, presto, grave, adagio, *etc.*, normally imply an Italian idiom.

In the case of the courante, the name is a less reliable guide than usual, partly because different spellings confuse the issue of language (this does occur with other titles also) and partly because the Italian form is found quite frequently with the French name. But here the form itself is readily distinguishable: the French in a characteristic alternation of simple and compound triple rhythms (*e.g.*, 3–2 and 6–4); the Italian in simple triple rhythm throughout or almost throughout, and a more smoothly flowing movement. Couperin sometimes pairs the two kinds by way of contrast. The saraband is another interesting case: there is a very light and rapid English seventeenth-century variety; a more lyrical Italian variety much favoured by Corelli; and a still more lingering and tender French variety, adopted and carried often to great lengths of embellishment by J. S. Bach. The dance itself was thought to come from Spain, and perhaps before that from the Near East; but such attributions are notoriously uncertain. It must be remembered, too, that as musical structures, dance-forms are apt to develop very far from their folk or ballroom origins. It is their nationality as music, not as dances, which affects their interpretation in the developed state.

THE INTERPLAY OF STYLES

4. THE FACTOR OF NATIONALITY: MUSICAL EFFECTS

(21) M. Mersenne, *Harmonie Universelle*, Paris, 1636–7, II, vi, 356:

'As to the Italians, they . . . represent as much as they can the passions and the affects of the soul and the spirit; for example, anger, fury, spleen, rage, faintheartedness, and many other passions, with a violence so strange, that one judges them as if they were touched with the same affects as they represent in singing; in place of which our Frenchmen are content to caress the ear, and use nothing but a perpetual sweetness in their songs; which hinders their energy [a detailed study of the means employed by composers follows].'

(22) Georg Muffat, *Florilegium I*, Augsburg, 1695, preface:

'[The French style is now catching on in Germany and Muffat himself is a pupil of Lully; this style has] natural melody, with an easy, and smooth tune, quite devoid of superfluous artifices, extravagant divisions [improvisatory embellishments], and too frequent and harsh leaps.'

(23) François Raguenet, *Comparison Between the French and Italian Music*, Paris, 1702, transl. ? Galliard, London, 1709, ed. Strunk, *Musical Quarterly*, XXXII, 3, pp. 417 *ff.*:

'The French, in their airs, aim at the soft, the easy, the flowing and coherent. . . . The Italians venture at everything that is harsh and out of the way, but then they do it like people that have a right to venture and are sure of success . . . as the Italians are naturally much more brisk than the French, so are they more sensible of the passions and consequently express 'em more lively in all their productions. If a storm or rage is to be described in a symphony, their notes give us so natural an idea of it that our souls can hardly receive a stronger impression from the reality than they do from the description; everything is so brisk and piercing, so impetuous and affecting, that the imagination, the senses, the soul and the body itself are all betrayed into a general transport; 'tis impossible not to be borne down with the rapidity of these movements. A symphony of furies shakes the soul; it undermines and overthrows it in spite of all its care; the artist himself, whilst he is performing it, is seized with an unavoidable agony; he tortures his violin; he racks his body; he is no longer master of himself, but is agitated like one possessed with an irresistible motion.

[p. 415] 'our masters [in France] touch the violin much finer and with a greater nicety than they do in Italy.'

(24) Le Cerf de la Viéville, in *Histoire de la Musique* of 1725, II, p. 61:

'Our violins [in France] are more tranquil than there in Italy . . . [the same work, IV, p. 149]: The Italian instrumentalists, as much for accompaniment as in their pieces, have no other merit than that of drawing plenty of sound from their instruments.'

(25) Roger North, *Autobiography*, c. 1695, ed. Jessopp, London, 1887, sect. 114:

'The court [of Charles II] about this time [later 17th century England] entertained only the theatrical music and French air in song, but that somewhat softened and variegated; so also was the instrumental more vague and with a mixture of caprice. . . . At length the time came off the French way and fell in with the Italian, and now that holds the ear. But still the English singularity will come in and have a share.'

(26) Joachim Quantz, *Essay*, Berlin, 1752, X, 19:

'After the pupil has gained also a general idea of the difference of taste in Music, he must recognise distinctive pieces of different nations and provinces, and learn to play them each according to its kind. . . . The diversity of distinctive pieces is commoner in French and German music, than in the Italian and in that of the other nations. Italian music is less restrained than any other; but the French is almost too much so, whence it comes about perhaps that in French Music the new always seems like the old. Nevertheless the French method of playing is not at all to be despised, above all an Apprentice should be recommended to mix the propriety and the clarity of the French with the chiaroscuro of the Italian instrumentalists. It is mainly a question of bow-strokes and the use of ornaments, of which last the Italian instrumentalists make too many, and the French in general too few [he is presumably speaking here of improvised free embellishments, not of specific ornaments, of which the French often wrote, and performed, a maximum].

'[XVIII, 53: There are two leading musical nations.] These are the Italians and the French. Other nations are ruled in their taste by these two. . . . [76: Italian instrumentalists are decadent and eccentric, but skilful. Italian singing is supreme]. In a word: Italian music is arbitrary and French is limited: so that if the effect is to be good, the French depends more on the composition than on the performance, the Italian almost as much, and in some pieces almost more, on the performance than on the composition.

'[XVII, vii, 14: it is disastrous] to make up an orchestra of people some of whom play in the Italian style, others in the French, and others again in another style.'

(27) [J. Cazotte] *Observations sur la lettre de J.-J. Rousseau* [? Paris], 1753, p. 11:

'[The French airs de Ballet are] full of fire, of variety, of gaiety, and of expression.'

(28) [E. C. Fréron] *Lettre sur la Musique Françoise* [Paris, 1753]:

'The extreme vitality [of the Italians inclines them] even to an excess of imagination. . . . But we [French] who are used to serious, tender and sustained passions . . . are moved by the same things in a different way from the Italians.'

(29) [C. C. de Rulhière] *Jugement de l'Orchestre de l'Opéra* [? Paris, not before 1753], p. 5:

'Italian music is full of epigrams; French music is more noble.'

(30) [L'Abbé Laugier] *Apologie de la Musique Françoise* [Paris] 1754, p. 5:

'The character of a national music does not depend at all on the quality of the language; but on the amount of genius. It is genius, and genius alone which gives birth to whatever music has that is most pleasant and moving. Its tender sweetness, its light vivacities, its sad and sombre langors, its harshnesses, its furies, its swiftnesses, its confusions, are the fruit, not of a language more or less favourable to the charms of melody; but of a spirit which flows freely into inventions full of fire, and which subordinates the harmony to its ideas. . . . Every nation where genius can light its flame, can have true music.'

To recognise the main varieties of national style, even when found elsewhere than in their countries of origin, is not, perhaps, so difficult as it sounds. Once, for example, the salient characteristics of the French overture style are grasped at all, with its notated dots all meant to be double-dotted and its typical up-beat scales all delayed, quickened and taken at the rush, these characteristics are very recognisable whether they are found in the German-born Handel, the English Purcell, or even on occasion the Italian Vivaldi; and it soon becomes second nature to interpret them in the pointed French style (for which see Ch. XLIV below). Similarly with the four-square Italian opening allegro style; once it is known, there is no risk of confusing it with the jerkier French movement. There are, indeed, other national characteristics much less clearly distinguished than these—but then they are also less important to distinguish. Styles were largely international.

5. THE FACTOR OF PURPOSE CUTTING ACROSS BOTH TIME AND PLACE

(31) John Cosyn, *Psalmes*, London, 1585, Dedication:

'. . . for the private use and comfort of the godlie, in place of many other Songs neither tending to the praise of God, nor conteining any thing fit for Christian eares.'

(32) The brothers Lawes, *Choice Psalmes*, London, 1648, preface:

'. . . having been often heard, and well approv'd of, chiefly by such as desire to joyne Musick with Devotion . . .'

(33) John Playford, *Introduction*, London, 1654, eds. of 1672 on, preface 'Of Musick in General':

'The first and chief Use of *Musick* is for the Service and praise of God, whose gift it is. The second Use is for the Solace of Men, which as it is agreeable unto nature, so is it allowed by God as a Temporal blessing to recreate and Chear men after long study and weary labour in their vocations . . .'

(34) Thomas Mace, *Musick's Monument*, London, 1676, pp. 233–35:

'Know, That in my *Younger Time*, we had *Musick* most *Excellently Choice*, and most *Eminently Rare*; both for *Its Excellency in Composition*, *Rare Fancy*, and *Sprightly Ayre*; as also for *Its Proper*, and *Fit Performances* . . .

'We had for our *Grave Musick*, *Fancies* of 3, 4, 5, and 6 *Parts* [for viols] to the *Organ*; Interpos'd (now and then) with some *Pavins*, *Allmaines*, *Solemn*, and *Sweet Delightful Ayres*; all which were (as it were) so many *Pathettical Stories*, *Rhetorical*, and *Sublime Discourses*; *Subtil*, and *Accute Argumentations*; so *Suitable*, and *Agreeing to the Inward*, *Secret*, and *Intellectual Faculties of the Soul and Mind*; that to set *Them* forth according to their *True Praise*, there are no *Words Sufficient in Language*; yet what I can best speak of *Them*, shall be only to say, *That They have been to my self*, (*and many others*) *as Divine Raptures*, *Powerfully Captivating all our unruly Faculties*, and *Affections*, (*for the Time*) *and disposing us to Solidity*, *Gravity*, *and a Good Temper*, *making us capable of Heavenly*, *and Divine Influences* . . .

'And *These Things* were *Performed*, upon so many *Equal*, *and Truly-Sciz'd Viols*; and so *Exactly Strung*, *Tun'd*, *and Play'd upon*, as no one *Part* was any *Impediment* to the *Other*; but still (as the *Composition* required) by *Intervals*, each *Part Amplified*, and *Heightned the Other*; *The Organ Evenly*, *Softly*, *and Sweetly Acchording to All* . . .

'But when we would be most *Ayrey*, *Jocond*, *Lively*, and *Spruce*; Then we had *Choice*, and *Singular Consorts*, either for 2, 3, or 4 *Parts*, but not to the *Organ* (as many (now a days) *Improperly*, and *Unadvisedly* perform such like *Consorts* with) but to the *Harpsicon* . . .'

(35) P. F. Tosi, *Observations on the Florid Song*, Bologna, 1723, transl. Galliard, London, 1742, p. 92:

'By the *Ancients* . . . *Airs* were sung in three different Manners; for the Theatre, the Stile was lively and various; for the Chamber, delicate and finish'd; and for the Church, moving and grave. This Difference, to very many *Moderns*, is quite unknown.

107

(36) Joachim Quantz, *Essay*, Berlin, 1752, XVII, vii, 53:

'With Church music . . . the expression as well as the tempo should be more moderate than in opera . . .

[XVII, vii, 12] 'Church music requires a grander and more serious air than theatre music, and this last allows more liberty.'

(37) [De Rochement] *Réflexions sur l'Opéra François et . . . Italien*, Lausanne, 1754, p. 90:

'The language of music is very vague, and very indeterminate, we have already said: the most powerful, vehement, excessive image, the most highly charged, if you like, with passion, will be better, more just, more perfect, more pleasing, more free from musical defect, than the image of a moderate passion which seems too restricted and always a little cool. That is the true reason for the decided superiority of the Italians in instrumental music of a grand character. The same principle applied to vocal music gives a different result. It is unsuitable then to charge the image too much with passion, because it is necessary to have regard to the relative congruities, and to confine oneself to them.'

(38) J. P. Kirnberger, *Kunst des reinen Satzes*, Berlin, Part I, 2nd ed., 1774, Sect. V, p. 80:

'The former, or strict, style is chiefly used in church music, which is always of a serious or solemn character; but the latter is chiefly proper to the stage and to concerted music, of which the purpose is to please the ear rather than to arouse serious or solemn feelings. It is therefore generally known as the *galant* style, and a number of elegant licenses and various departures from the rules are allowed to it.'

6. THE GALANT STYLE

Like all antipathies, the musical antipathy of Italy and France had its undercurrent of sympathy, from which presently a new synthesis arose. This took the form of what became known, loosely enough, as the 'galant style'. The word 'galant' here really means 'polite', in the sense of 'polite conversation', and for much of the music this description could not be bettered. In polite conversation, the deeper emotions, when they are mentioned at all, are brought in with a light touch. The best of such music glows with a genuine radiance; but it is the radiance of sensibility and not of passion (Fr. *sensibilité*; Ger. *Empfindsamkeit* —recurrent terms in this connection). Sensibility is feeling rendered elegant. Yet it is still feeling, and potentially capable of burning through its polite conventions.

The easy-going Telemann, who made both Lully and the Italian operatic melody his models, may stand very well for the shallower forms of galant music. Domenico Scarlatti, born though he was like

J. S. Bach and Handel in 1685, was an altogether galant composer whose elegance adorns but does not conceal his depth of feeling. J. S. Bach himself shows far more of the galant influence than is generally realised, and the quotation from Heinichen at (40) below could easily apply to him. This and the following quotation from Quantz at (41) below almost make us feel as if the long hidden ideals of Monteverdi were re-emerging, to lead on to Gluck, Mozart and that classical Viennese tradition to which we are still the heirs. For all its facile aspects, it was galant music which achieved the crucial transition between baroque music and classical music. At the end of that road stood Beethoven.

(39) Gabriel Guillemain, sonatas, Paris, 1743:

'Six sonatas of four parts or Galant and Witty conversations between a Transverse Flute, a Violin, a Bass Viol and the Thorough Bass.'

(40) J. D. Heinichen, *General-Bass*, Dresden, 1728, Introd., p. 24:

'And, oh, how wonderfully it pleases the ear, when, in an exquisite piece of church music or other composition, we hear how a master musician has tried from time to time, by his *galant* idioms and the closeness of his expression to the verbal text, to move the feelings of his hearers and thus to achieve successfully the true aim of music.

[Note:] 'Whence practical modern musicians are rightly inclined to depart from the unseasoned character of a too antique church style.'

(41) Joachim Quantz, *Essay*, Berlin, 1752, XI, 16:

'The performer should, so to speak, change to a different emotion in every bar.'

7. THE TRANSITION TO THE CLASSICAL PERIOD

This last quotation from Quantz at (41) above would suggest a certain risk of chaos if we did not know that the galant composers were also insistent on clarity of form, and were, in fact, engaged in pioneering what became the most strong yet balanced form of all those which the nineteenth century inherited: sonata form.

A suite-form movement is essentially a monad; but a sonata-form movement is a duad. Its themes, though not necessarily two in number, are organised in two fields of force. They are first expounded in opposing keys; next developed, often in relation to each other, through a whole drama of modulations; then recapitulated with their keys and their opposition reconciled. It is a perfect microcosm of common human experience. Tension, relationship, resolution are elements of life itself, and as such, of course, no innovations of the post-baroque period. It is the way in which sonata form deploys these elements which was in some genuine degree a novelty. Essentially this novelty consists in a greater acceptance of conflict within the movement, and not merely, suite-fashion, between the movements. In terms made famous in another context by Hans Keller, to the 'unity of contrasting movements' there was added a greatly increased 'unity of contrasting themes'.

In sonata form, and indeed in post-baroque music generally, the expression is conditioned to a greater extent by dramatic contrasts within the movement; in suite form, and baroque music generally, it is conditioned to a greater extent by dramatic contrasts between the movements. This is one of the practical differences which the interpreter does well to bear in mind. There are, of course, dynamic and other contrasts which can properly be made, and should be made thoroughly, within the normal baroque movement; any unnatural restraint in this respect can only be harmful. But it is a mistake to work up more internal contrasts of expression than the music itself genuinely suggests. Where the music itself remains emotionally on one level, we should be content to remain on one level of expression without seeking an artificial variety. This is a situation which can occur in music of any period, but which is much more frequent in baroque than in post-baroque music. Slighter fluctuations, within the main levels, are never excluded

It should be noticed, however, that the operative principle is the same in either case. Whether the main contrasts in the structure of the music fall within or between the movements, it is still the structure which conditions the expression. In working out the expression for a baroque composition, where the composer will have left a far greater share in the responsibility for it to the performer than is nowadays the case, it is particularly important to refrain from building up big effects for their own sake. It is particularly important to listen quietly for the implications of the music to make its own requirements plain. But this is, of course, only a more extreme case of what any good interpreter will do even in music where the main lines of the expression have been laid down beforehand, as they are not laid down in baroque music, by the composer himself through a systematic use of expression marks. Matching the expression to the music is an axiom of interpretation under whatever circumstances.

CHAPTER III

Music as Expression

1. THE THEORY OF AFFECTS

The belief, common to the galant composers, that music expresses not only emotion but specific emotions, was elaborated into a regular 'theory of affects' at the time; but it was not a new belief (indeed it is at least as old as Plato). See also Ch. XXXIII below.

(42) Sir Thomas More, *Utopia*, Louvain, 1516, *etc.*, Bk. II, Everyman ed., p. 109:

'For all their musike bothe that they [the Utopians] playe upon instrumentes, and that they singe with mannes voyce dothe so resemble and expresse naturall affections, the sound and tune is so applied and made agreable to the thinge, that whether it bee a prayer, or els a dytty of gladnes, of patience, of trouble, of mournynge, or of anger: the fassion of the melodye dothe so represente the meaning of the thing, that it doth wonderfullye move, stirre, pearce, and enflame the hearers myndes.'

(43) R. Hooker, *Lawes*, London, V, 1597, Everyman ed., p. 146:

'An admirable faculty which music hath to express and represent to the mind, more inwardly than any other sensible mean, the very standing, rising, and falling, the very steps and inflections every way, the turns and varieties of all passions whereunto the mind is subject; yea so to imitate them, that whether it resemble unto us the same state wherein our minds already are, or a clean contrary, we are not more contentedly by the one confirmed, than changed and led away by the other. In harmony the very image and character even of virtue and vice is perceived, the mind delighted with their resemblances, and brought by having them often iterated into a love of the things themselves. For which cause there is nothing more contagious and pestilent than some kinds of harmony; than some nothing more strong and potent unto good. And that there is such a difference of one kind from another we need no proof but our own experience, inasmuch as we are at the hearing of some more inclined unto sorrow and heaviness, of some, more mollified and softened in mind; one kind apter to stay and settle us, another to move and stir our affections; there is that draweth to a marvellous and sober mediocrity, there is also that carrieth as it were into ecstasies, filling the mind with an heavenly joy and for the time in a manner severing it from the body.'

111

(44) Thomas Morley, *Plaine and Easie Introduction*, London, 1597, p. 177 (an adaptation of Zarlino):

'It followeth to shew you how to dispose your musicke according to the nature of the words which you are therein to expresse, as whatsoever matter it be which you have in hand, such a kind of musicke must you frame to it. You must therefore if you have a grave matter, applie a grave kinde of musicke to it, if a merrie subject you must make your musicke also merrie. For it will be a great absurditie to use a sad harmonie to a merrie matter, or a merrie harmonie to a sad lamentable or tragical dittie. You must then when you would expresse any word signifying hardnesse, crueltie, bitternesse, and other such like, make the harmonie like unto it, that is somewhat harsh and hard but yet so it offend not. Likewise, when any of your words shall expresse complaint, dolor, repentance, sighs, teares, and such like, let your harmonie be sad and dolefull. so that if you would have your musicke signifie hardness, cruelty or other such affects, you must cause the partes proceede in their motions without the halfe note . . . but when you woulde expresse a lamentable passion, then must you use motions proceeding by halfe notes.'

(45) William Byrd, *Gradualia*, I, London, 1605, transl. Fellowes, *Byrd*, London, 1936, p. 85:

'. . . There is a certain hidden power, as I learnt by experience, in the thoughts underlying the words themselves; so that, as one meditates upon the sacred words and constantly and seriously considers them, the right notes, in some inexplicable manner, suggest themselves quite spontaneously.'

(46) Charles Butler, *Principles of Musik*, London, 1636, p. 1:

'Music . . . having a great power over the affections of the mind, by its various Modes produceth in the hearers various affects.'

(47) Thomas Mace, *Musick's Monument*, London, 1676, p. 118:

'And as in *Language*, various *Humours*, *Conceits*, and *Passions*, (of All sorts) may be Exprest; so likewise in Musick, may any *Humour*, *Conceit*, or *Passion* (never so various) be Exprest; and so significantly, as any *Rhetorical Words*, or *Expressions* are able to do.'

(48) Johann Mattheson, *Neu-Eröffnete Orchestre*, Hamburg, 1713, p. 161 and p. 167, transl. Cannon, *Johann Mattheson*, New Haven and London, 1947, p. 129:

'[Opera is the best medium of all for expressing] each and every *Affectus* [since] there the composer has the grand opportunity to give free rein to his invention. With many surprises and with as much grace he there can, most naturally and diversely, portray love, jealousy, hatred, gentleness,

112

impatience, lust, indifference, fear, vengeance, fortitude, timidity, magnanimity, horror, dignity, baseness, splendour, indigence, pride, humility, joy, laughter, weeping, mirth, pain, happiness, despair, storm, tranquillity, even heaven and earth, sea and hell, together with all the actions in which men participate . . .

'Through the skill of composer and singer each and every Affectus can be expressed beautifully and naturally better than in an Oratorio, better than in painting or sculpture, for not only are Operas expressed in words, but they are helped along by appropriate actions and above all interpreted by heart-moving music.'

(49) Joachim Quantz, *Essay*, Berlin, 1752, XVIII, 24:

'To judge operatic music reliably, it must be examined if the symphony or the overture has a true correspondence with the subject of the entire piece or the first act, or at least the first scene, and if it is capable of putting the hearers into the passion which prevails in the first act, whatever it be, tender or sad, gay, heroic, furious, *etc.*, . . . if the composer has expressed the passions well in the way the subject requires; if he has distinguished them from one another well, and set each in its suitable context . . . if he has kept up the main character of the piece from start to finish . . . finally if most of the audience are moved by the music and put into the passions represented . . .'

(50) F. W. Marpurg, *Der critische Musicus an der Spree*, Berlin, 2 Sept. 1749:

'All musical expression has an affect or emotion for its foundation. A philosopher when expounding or demonstrating will try to enlighten our understanding, to bring it lucidity and order. The orator, the poet, the musician attempt rather to inflame than to enlighten. The philosopher deals in combustible matter capable of glowing or yielding a temperate and moderate warmth. But in music there is only the distilled essence of this matter, the most refined part of it, which throws out thousands of the most beautiful flames, always with rapidity, sometimes with violence. The musician has therefore a thousand parts to play, a thousand characters to assume at the composer's bidding. To what extraordinary undertakings our passions carry us! He who has the good fortune at all to experience the inspiration which lends greatness to poets, orators, artists, will be aware how vehemently and diversely our soul responds when it is given over to the emotions. Thus to interpret rightly every composition which is put in front of him a musician needs the utmost sensibility and the most felicitous powers of intuition.'

(51) C. P. E. Bach, *Essay*, Berlin, 1753, III, 13:

'A musician cannot move others without himself being moved. He will have to feel all the emotions he hopes to call up in his audience, since by showing his own mood he will rouse a similar mood in the listener. Where the passage is languishing and sad, the performer must languish and grow sad. When it is lively and joyful, the performer must likewise put himself into the mood in question. He must especially perform this duty in music of which the nature is highly expressive, whether it is by him or another composer. In the latter event he must be sure to take on the feeling which the composer intended in writing it. . . .

'It will be realised from the many emotions which music depicts that the expert musician has need of special talents and the ability to use them judiciously. He must sum up his audience carefully, their response to the feelings expressed in his programme, the actual place and other added considerations. Nature has wisely endowed music with all manner of attractions so that everyone may share in enjoying it. Hence it falls to the performer to please to the best of his power every last manner of listener.'

(52) Joachim Quantz, *Essay*, Berlin, 1752, XVIII, 28:

'And since instrumental music has, without words, to express different passions and to carry the hearer from one to another, as well as vocal music; we can readily see that to do that, and supply it in the absence of word or human voice, the composer and he who performs the music must alike have a feeling soul, and one capable of being moved.'

(53) C. H. Blainville, *L'Esprit de l'Art Musical*, Geneva, 1754, p. 86:

'There are also purely instrumental pieces pursued with such truth that they seem to suggest words, notions of passion, imagery or painting; such seems to me the language of Tartini [Locatelli, Geminiani, Leclair, Corelli and Senaillé are subsequently mentioned in the same connection], a true language of sounds . . .'

(54) John Trydell, *Two Essays*, Dublin, 1766, p. 97:

'Musical Sounds do of themselves, that is to say, merely by the Sound, suggest our Ideas. Chiefly those of the Passions, as Desire, Aversion, Joy, Sorrow and the like.'

(55) Jean-Jacques Rousseau, *Dictionnaire de Musique*, Paris, 1768, *s.v.* 'Imitation':

'The art of music consists in substituting for the insensible image of the object that of the emotions which its presence excites in the heart of the contemplator. Not only does it agitate the sea, animate the flame of conflagration, make the streams to flow, the rain to fall and the torrents to swell; but it paints the horror of a terrible desert, darkens the walls of a subterranean prison, renders the air tranquil and serene, and sheds from the orchestra a new freshness through the groves. It will not represent these things directly, but it will excite in the soul the same emotions as one experiences in seeing them.

'[*s.v.* 'Genie'] It paints pictures by sounds; it makes even silence speak; it renders ideas by feelings, feelings by accents; and the passions which it expresses, it stirs from the bottom of the heart.'

(56) Joachim Quantz, *Essay*, Berlin, 1752, Introd., 17:

'[But] if anyone wants to know, what ought to be the object of our researches and our reflections, here is our answer. After a new Composer shall have solidly learnt the rules of Harmony, which are only a matter of what is least and most convenient in Composition, although again many people are found without this knowledge; it is necessary that according to the purpose of each piece, he tries to make a just choice and a happy blend of his thoughts from start to finish; that he expresses properly the movements of the soul; that he sustains a flowing melody; that he applies himself to being original,`and yet always natural in his modulation and just in his measure; that he sets above all light and shade; that he knows how to confine his inventions within reasonable bounds; that he does not make his melody stand still too much, and that he does not repeat the same thoughts too often; that he only composes in a manner suitable both to the voice and to the instruments; that in vocal Music he does not write against the scansion of the syllables, and still less against the sense of the words; and finally that he tries to acquire a sufficient knowledge, both of the manner of singing, and of the different qualities of each instrument . . .

'He who would be a Composer must have a spirit lively and full of fire, a soul open to tender feelings; a happy blend of what Philosophers call *Temperament*, in which not too much melancholy is found; much imagination, invention, judgment and discernment; a good memory; a sensitive and keen ear; an outlook good and shrewd and full of humility . . .'

(57) [De Rochement] *Réflexions sur l'Opéra François et sur l'Opéra Italien*, Lausanne, 1754, p. 27:

'Music only makes such a pleasant impression because it awakens the image of the passions.'

(58) C. H. Blainville, *L'Esprit de l'Art Musical*, Geneva, 1754, p. 39:

'A certain disorder which pleases . . .'

(59) J. F. Marmontel, *Essai sur les Revolutions de la Musique en France* [Paris, 1777], p. 22:

'The object of the arts which move the soul is not only emotion, but the pleasure which accompanies it. It is not enough for the emotion to be strong, it must also be agreeable.'

(60) W. A. Mozart, *Letter* to his father, 26 Sept., 1781 (transl. E. Anderson, London, 1938):

'For just as a man in such a towering rage [as Osmin in *Die Entführung aus dem Serail*] oversteps all the bounds of order, moderation and propriety, and completely forgets himself, so must the music too forget itself. But as passions, whether violent or not, must never be expressed in such a way as to excite disgust, so music, even in the most terrible situations, must never offend the ear, but must please the hearer, or in other words must never cease to be *music*.'

2. THE FACTOR OF TECHNIQUE

An illusion which can be very misleading to the modern performer, because it makes him think that he can improve on the original methods and puts him generally into a closed, patronising and sentimentalising state of mind, is the illusion that modern standards of technique are higher than early standards. That appears to be largely true in some departments, but the reverse of true in others. Our singers are sadly taxed by the virtuoso baroque parts. We have considerable trouble with early trumpet and horn parts, or again with J. S. Bach's unaccompanied violin music (and he was not the man, nor was that the age, to have composed so much of it without adequate prospects of performance). We have too few masters of the difficult baroque techniques of improvising continuo accompaniments or ornamental figuration. No doubt we read severe criticisms of contemporary performances in the early authorities; but so we do in the *Times* or the *Telegraph* today, the inference being not that our standards of performance are low but that our standards of criticism are high. Here, at any rate, are two baroque criticisms which cancel out (my italics).

(61) Joachim Quantz, *Essay*, Berlin, 1752, Introd., 8:

'[In the last century] how many changes have there not been in music in Germany? At how many courts, and in how many towns did it not flourish *in the past*, in a manner which brought up a good number of skilful people, and at present nothing but ignorance reigns in this respect. At the majority of courts which were once provided with skilful people, of whom a proportion were actually excellent, the custom is introduced at present, of giving the first places in the music, to people who would not deserve the last in a good orchestra . . .'

(62) Dr. Burney, *Present State of Music in Germany*, London, 1773, ed. of 1775, II, p. 202:

'I must observe that the musicians of many parts of Europe have discovered and adopted certain refinements, in the manner of executing even old music, which are *not yet* received in the Berlin school, where pianos and fortes are but little attended to, and where each performer seems trying to surpass his neighbour, in nothing so much as loudness . . . when a piece is executed with such unremitting fury, as I have sometimes heard, it ceases to be music.'

3. DIFFERENCES OF AMATEUR STANDARD

(63) Sir Thomas Elyot, *The Governour*, London, 1531, Everyman ed., p. 25:

'. . . some pleasaunt lernynge and exercise, as playenge on instruments of musicke, whiche moderately used and without diminution of honour . . . is not to be contemned.'

(64) John Marston, *The Malcontent*, London, 1604, I, iii:

'*Malevole* Fool, most happily encountered: canst sing, fool?
Passarello Yes, I can sing, fool, if you'll bear the burden; and I can play upon instruments, scurvily, as gentlemen do.'

(65) Gervase Markham, *Countrey Contentments*, London, 1615, I, xi:

'[A gentleman] shou'd not be unskilful in Musick, that whensoever either melancholy, heaviness of his thoughts, or the perturbations of his own fancies, stirreth up sadness in him, he may remove the same with some godly Hymn or Anthem, of which *David* gives him ample examples.'

(66) William Byrd, *Psalmes, Songs and Sonnets*, London, 1611, preface:

'Only this I desire; that you will be but as carefull to heare them well expressed, as I have beene both in the Composing and correcting of them. Otherwise the best Song that ever was made will seeme harsh and unpleasant, for that the well expressing of them, either by Voyces, or Instruments, is the life of our labours, which is seldom or never well performed at the first singing or playing. Besides a song that is well and artifically made cannot be well perceived nor understood at the first hearing, but the oftener you shall heare it, the better cause of liking you will discover: and commonly that Song is best esteemed with which our eares are most acquainted.'

(67) Orlando Gibbons, *Madrigals and Mottets*, London, 1612, preface:

'Experience tels us that Songs of this Nature are usually esteemed as they are well or ill performed.'

(68) Roger North, *Autobiography*, c. 1695, ed. Jessopp, London, 1887, sect. 103:

'Whereas in the country, where there is not such variety of gay things to call young folks away, it is incredible what application and industry will grow up in some active spirits, and this voluntarily, without being incited, as where there is an inlet to music, having time and a fancy to it, some will be wonderfully resigned to master a reasonable performance in it . . . I would not have families discouraged for want of a perfection, which, to say truth, is not to be had out of a trade.'

(69) Joachim Quantz, *Essay*, Berlin, 1752, Introd., 2:

'[Rules must first be given for would-be musicians] by which they can discern, whether they are provided with the qualities necessary to a perfect musician . . . I speak here only of those who wish to make a profession of Music, and who count on excelling in it with time. Not so much is asked of those who only wish to take their pleasure in it [provided that being amateurs they do not give themselves the airs of professionals].'

4. DIFFERENCES OF PROFESSIONAL STANDARD

(70) Giulio Caccini, *Nuove Musiche*, Florence, 1602, preface, transl. Playford, *Introduction*, London, 1654; ed. of 1674, p. 41:

'*Art* admitteth no Mediocrity, and how much the more curiosities are in it, by reason of the excellence thereof, with so much the more labour and love ought we, the Professors thereof, to find them out.'

(71) Robert Dowland, *Varietie of Lute-lessons*, London, 1610, preface:

'Perfection in any skill [in this case lute-playing] cannot be attained unto without the waste of many yeares, much cost, and excessive labour and industrie.'

(72) Roger North, MS notes in Brit. Mus., early 18th cent., Add. 32536, *f.* 14:

'Musick demands not only utmost spirit, and decorum in the composition, but little less than perfection in the performance, which is not alwaies found.'

(73) Joachim Quantz, *Essay*, Berlin, 1752, preface:

'A man who only aspires to become a good *Ripienist* has not need of such great talents . . . . But he whose soul is not open to any feeling, who has clumsy fingers, and no ear for music, will do better to apply himself to quite another science than Music . . .'
'To excell in music, it is necessary to have an insatiable ambition, love and desire, to spare no pains and labour, and to have the courage to support all the discomforts which meet one in this kind of life . . . a noble obstinacy . . . which inspires us to perfect ourselves more and more.'

5. THE FACTOR OF TASTE

It is only because we human beings are alike at bottom that composer, interpreter and listener (each with their own personal background, great or little familiarity with the art, *etc.*) can come together in the shared experience of music. Yet on a less archetypal plane we are full of divergencies. It is these divergencies which give our individual interpretations their intrinsic value, and make it worth listening not just to one good interpretation but to many.

(74) Joachim Quantz, *Essay*, Berlin, 1752, preface:

'I seem at times to speak rather like a Dictator, resting what I suggest on a simple: *it must*, without advancing other proofs.

'But it will be taken into account that it would be too long and at times impossible, to give demonstrative proofs on matters which nearly always look only to taste. Whoever does not want to trust mine, which I have endeavoured to purify by a long experience and by plenty of reflections that I have made thereon, will be at liberty to try the contrary, and to choose then that which appears to him the best . . .'

This means that it is unrealistic to ask: 'how exactly did the composer mean such-and-such a passage to be interpreted?' There are no exact interpretations, and there are no unchanging ones—not even from the same performer. There are only individual interpretations within the flexible though not indefinitely elastic boundaries of style. It is more realistic to ask: 'how approximately might the passage have been interpreted on some typical occasion by some good contemporary performer?' Since good performers varied even more widely in their interpretations in the baroque age than they do today, this should leave margin enough for any reasonable modern taste, whether leaning towards the driest and most correct or towards the warmest and most romantic rendering which the style will tolerate.

(75) Roger North, MS. notes in the Brit. Mus., early 18th cent., Add. 32536, *f.* 14:

'The taste of the audience is commonly prejudicate and Bizearre, some affect one kind, and will not hear another, and few allow any to be good that jumps not with their caprice.'

(76) Joachim Quantz, *Essay*, Berlin, 1752, XVIII, 7–8:

'Most people let themselves be ruled by ignorance, prejudice and passion. . . . Some like what is majestic and lively, others what is sad and sombre, and others what is tender and gay. The diversity of taste depends on the diversity of temperaments . . . one is not always in the same mood.'

119

BOOK TWO

THE NOTES

PART ONE

ACCIDENTALS

CHAPTER IV

Accidentals in Early Music

1. MODE AND KEY

We have a problem over the accidentals in early music inherited from the more fundamental and historic problem of adapting the originally melodic modes first to harmony (a medieval achievement) and then to modulation (the great late-renaissance contribution).

Western music since antiquity has virtually confined itself to the twelve semitones of the chromatic scale (crudely, the notes of the piano).

The modes further confined themselves to the five tones and two semitones of the diatonic scale (crudely, the white notes of the piano). Each mode distributes its two semitones in a *different* relationship to its centre of tonality ('final'): an absolute difference irrespective of context. Any chromatic modification of this distribution weakens the mode.

The keys take their choice of diatonic scale. But each key distributes its two semitones in the *same* relationship to its centre of tonality ('tonic'): its difference is established by context. The power of modulating fluidly from one centre of tonality to another comes from this fact, which is the meaning of key.

This fluidity was carried so far in twelve-tone music that key in its turn disappears. Here all twelve semitones of the chromatic scale are drawn upon equally and simultaneously. Like a temporary mode, a serial tone-row establishes the distribution of intervals, any departure from which reduces its distinctive character. Established centres of tonality are avoided; but the field of force is still the familiar tonal pull which is the fundamental acoustic reality of music.

Mixed systems are both possible and desirable. Our key system incorporates two modes (major and minor) and accommodates others. Yet the historic transition from mode to key during the late renaissance was crucial: it marked the advent of modulation.

2. MUSICA FICTA—'FEIGNED MUSIC'

There was one unavoidable exception to the diatonic character of the modes. This was the alternative of *B* natural (*B durum*, hard, from its supposed musical effect, or *quadratum*, square, from the use of the square form of the letter *B* to indicate it) and *B* flat (*B molle*, soft, or *rotundum*, round).

The exception was unavoidable because of the acoustic realities. A diatonic scale includes the augmented fourth or *tritonus* (as *F* to *B*) and its enharmonic equivalent, the diminished fifth or *quinta falsa* (as *B* to *F*). These intervals have a complex ratio between the vibration frequencies of the tones composing them, and produce much discordant beating among their upper harmonics and combination tones. They have, therefore, an inherently restless and inconclusive effect which was highly distasteful to the medieval musicians, with their preference for the simplest ('perfect') concords, namely the octave, fifth and fourth, and their only qualified acceptance even of the less simple ('imperfect') concords, namely the thirds and sixths, major and minor. Indeed, the medieval ear was more tolerant of plain discord than of the ambiguous augmented fourth and diminished fifth.

To escape them, chromatic alteration of *B* to *B* flat was admitted. This note was not then regarded as chromatic; it was regarded as a slightly irregular extension of the diatonic material. But another method was to leave the *B* natural while taking the *F* sharp. This further extension was evidently harder for the theorists to accept; and others followed. Their valid chromatic nature was still not fully recognised; but neither were they adopted, as *B* flat was adopted, into the material regarded as basically diatonic (*musica vera*). They were treated as a kind of falsification (*musica falsa*) or fiction (*musica ficta*). Once this concept of 'false music' or 'feigned music' was established, *B* flat also tended to be included within it.

(77) Anon. II, 'Tractatus de discantu', [13th cent.], Coussemaker, *Scriptorum*, I, 312:

'Now false music was invented for two reasons, namely by reason of necessity and by reason of beauty of melody for its own sake.'

The necessity was that of avoiding augmented fourths, diminished fifths, and imperfect or augmented octaves; the beauty was an ever-expanding conception, in practice largely connected with the growing disposition to sharpen leading notes at important closes. The theory of 'false' or 'feigned' music encouraged what would in any case have been the normal tendency of the period to leave chromaticisms unwritten for the performer to introduce at his own discretion. The terms *musica falsa* and *musica ficta* themselves, however, do not necessarily imply improvisation. They refer to chromatic alteration whether written in the text or introduced in performance.

3. THE HEXACHORD

The means by which the diatonic material was explained by medieval, renaissance and early baroque theorists was not a seven-note scale recurring at the octave, but a six-note scale of three overlapping hexachords. Table I (p. 64) will show the structure.

The point of the hexachordal system is that each hexachord contains only one semitone, and that one always in the same position: between *mi* and *fa*.

In the 'hard' hexachord starting on *G*, *mi* is *B* and *fa* is *C*. No difficulty here: they are a semitone apart anyhow in the 'white note' diatonic scale. The *B* stays natural.

In the 'natural' hexachord starting on *C*, *mi* is *E* and *fa* is *F*. Again no difficulty; these two are also a semitone apart in the 'white-note' diatonic scale. No *B* occurs in this hexachord.

In the 'soft' hexachord starting on *F*, *mi* is *A* and *fa* is—what? Not *B*, which would make it a tone instead of a semitone above *mi*; but *B* flat, regarded not as a chromatic alteration but as a different kind of diatonic *B*.

The letters signifying these two forms of *B* were written approximately in the shapes we have inherited as ♮ (square, *i.e.* natural *B*) and ♭ (round, *i.e.*, flat *B*). Originally notes in themselves, these symbols soon came into convenient use as signs for altering notes: at first only *B*s, but later, as genuine chromatic alteration grew, other notes as well. A further symbol approximating to our ♯ was never a note, but began as a sign cancelling a flat, and was subsequently extended to raising any note a semitone. The ♮ became partly disused for some time in later medieval and renaissance music, ♯ being the normal cancellation of ♭ and ♭ of ♯.

It will be noticed that the lowest hexachord starts on *G* under the Greek style of Gamma (Γ), regarded as the theoretical bottom of the system; and that it ascends to *e*ˡˡ, regarded as the theoretical top. The system as a whole was called the gamut (a compression of gamma ut). Its limits were exceeded in practice. Beware of a rare use of ♭ before *f*ˡˡ or *F* without influence on the pitch, apparently as a mere warning that these are notes *extra manum*, outside the compass of the Guidonian hand.

To learn your gamut meant training yourself in singing or thinking of the hexachordal names so that you always knew where to expect the semitone from *mi* to *fa*. As you ascend the hard hexachord, you find its fourth note, *C fa*, on a level with the first note of the natural

TABLE I

The Hexachordal System

Pitch in Helmholtz' notation	HARD HEX'D*	NAT'L HEX'D†	SOFT HEX'D‡	HARD HEX'D*	NAT'L HEX'D†	SOFT HEX'D‡	HARD HEX'D*	THE BASIC GAMUT
e''							E la	E la (Ela)
d''						D re	D sol	D re sol (Delasol)
Treble c''						C sol	C fa	C sol fa (Cesolfa)
b'						b fa B	B mi B	b fa B (Befa) mi or mi
								B (Bemi)
a'					A la	A mi	A re	A la mi re (Alamire)
g'					G sol	G re	G ut	G sol re ut (Gesolreut)
f'					F fa	F ut		F fa ut (Fefaut)
e'				E la	E mi			E la mi (Elami)
d'			D la	D sol	D re			D la sol re (Delasolre)
Middle c'			C sol	C fa	C ut			C sol fa ut (Cesolfaut)
b♭			b fa B					b fa B (Befa) mi or mi
b♮				B mi B				B (Bemi)
a		A la	A mi	A re				A la mi re (Alamire)
g		G sol	G re	G ut				G sol re ut (Gesolreut)
f		F fa	F ut					F fa ut (Fefaut)
e	E la	E mi						E la mi (Elami)
d	D sol	D re						D sol re (Desolre)
Tenor C	C fa	C ut						C fa ut (Cefaut)
B	B mi							B mi (Bemi)
A	A re							A re (Are)
G	Γ ut							Γ ut (Gamma Ut)

* *Hexachordum durum*, because it includes *b durum* or *quadration*, i.e. *B mi* (*B natural*).
† *Hexachordum naturale*, including no *B*.
‡ *Hexachordum molle*, because it includes *B molle* or *rotundum*, i.e. *b fa* (*B flat*).

hexachord, *C ut* (see Table I). The full name is thus *C fa ut*; and if the continuation of the melodic line makes it convenient, you can think yourself over into that overlapping hexachord—*i.e.* think of this *C* as its first note, *ut*, and carry on as before. This 'thinking yourself over' from one hexachord into another is called mutation; and actually the standard note on which to mutate is one higher, *i.e. D sol re*. The standard mutation from a natural into a soft hexachord is *G sol re ut*. The return journey is similarly made. Reference to Table I will show that for a semitone between *B* and *C* you need to think in terms of a hard hexachord; for a semitone between *E* and *F*, in terms of a natural hexachord; for a semitone between *A* and *B* flat, in terms of a soft hexachord. Thereafter *musica ficta* begins.

4. UNFAMILIAR CHROMATIC SIGNS

TABLE II: Baroque Chromatic Signs (mainly 17th cent.)

Flat:	♭ ♭
Sharp:	⨳ ⨳ ♯ ⨳ ✕
'Natural' (mainly to restore *B♮*)	♮ ♯
Double-flat:	♭♭
Double-sharp:	⨳ ⨳ ✠

TABLE III: Baroque Chromatic Signs (mainly 18th cent.)

Flat:	♭ ♭
Sharp:	⨳ ♯ ✕
Natural (in modern usage):	♮♮
Double-flat:	♭♭ β
Double-sharp:	⨳ ⨳ ⨳ ✠ ✕

It remained the normal baroque method to cancel ♭ by ♯ and ♯ by ♭.

The difference is that whereas in modern notation ♭, ♯ and ♮ give us fixed positions for their notes, in early notation ♭ and ♯ give us semitone alterations down and up respectively, but not fixed positions. Thus *D* ♭ may stand either for *D* flat, or for *D* natural restored after a previous *D* sharp; while *D* ♯ may stand either for *D* sharp, or for *D* natural restored after a previous *D* flat. Similarly in words: '*B* sharp' is the normal seventeenth-century English term for what we call *B* natural. A 'flat key' meant a minor key; a 'sharp key' meant a major key. The importance of remembering these differences of notation and terminology is obvious.

In the early baroque period we find ♮ at times used to cancel a flat against *B*, but not against other notes.

(78) Galeazzo Sabbatini, *Regola . . . per sonare sopra il Basso continuo*, Venice, 1628, Ch. XV:

'In the case of the aforesaid letter [the note *B*] one should, it is true, in place of ♯ set ♮, which is its proper sign . . . but . . . ♯ is commonly used.'

But generally ♮ is not even mentioned.

(79) Christopher Simpson, *Compendium*, London, 1665, ed. of 1732, p. 5 (all eds. have it):

'As for the ♭ Flat . . . [except in the key signature] it serves only for that particular Note before which it is placed . . . that ♭ takes away a *Semitone* from the Sound of the Note before which it is set, to make it more *grave* or *flat*: This ♯ doth add a semitone to the Note to make it more *acute* or *sharp* . . . [except in the key signature] it serves only for that particular Note before which it is applied.'

(Leclair actually uses ♮ to restore a sharp present in the key-signature: *e.g.* in *A* major, *C* natural is shown as *C*♭, and the subsequent restoration of *C* sharp is shown as *C* ♮! He sometimes restores a *B* flat, present in the signature, with ♮! In none of this is he in the least consistent, though he does appear, fortunately, to be unique.)

Not until the eighteenth century do we find our modern use of ♮ (as a general sign cancelling previous chromatic alteration by a semitone either down or up) becoming gradually standardised.

The sensible β for double flat never came into regular use. The modern × for double sharp was an early-eighteenth century improvement on ✲, of which the horizontal stroke tends to be obscured when it stands on a line. Beware of confusion with × used for ♯ by Penna, Leclair and some others, against figures of a figured bass; also with × used not as an accidental at all but as a frequent sign of ornamentation.

A note already sharp or flat in the signature might be made double sharp or double flat by ♯ or ♭.

Return from double sharp or double flat to single sharp or single flat might be shown by ♮♯ and ♮♭, by ♮, or (very commonly) not at all.

The use of, *e.g.*, G for F double sharp and D for C double sharp is surprisingly common, not only in the seventeenth century, but also in the eighteenth (as in Johann Philipp Treiber's little *Accurate Organist*, Jena, 1704—where, since G sharp is in the signature, F double sharp appears on the stave as ♭G!).

During the middle of the eighteenth century our modern chromatic signs became increasingly standardised, the transition being virtually completed by the end of that century. But see also Appendix V 1.

5. UNFAMILIAR MODAL SIGNATURES

The ordinary signature for a once-transposed mode (*i.e.* moved up bodily by a fourth) is one flat, and for the much rarer double transposition (*i.e.* two fourths up, totalling one tone down), two flats; or the same results may be shown by accidentals.

But the different parts of a polyphonic composition may be genuinely in different modes, and correctly bear different signatures (no flats against one flat, or even two), or show different accidentals.

It will be appreciated that if the mode is not to be altered but merely transposed, C sharp becomes F sharp and B flat becomes E flat (for single transposition), *etc.*

6. UNFAMILIAR KEY SIGNATURES

In baroque music, a key signature may often show one sharp or one flat short of the number required, the deficiency being subsequently made good by accidentals throughout the piece as required. This is a relic of modal notation, where what looks to us like a key signature was in fact a modal signature (*i.e.* showing transposition).

Thus D minor, which we notate with a signature of one flat, grew out of the Dorian mode when its leading note, C, became habitually sharpened by the workings of *musica ficta*. The distinctively minor form of the scale has a flat sixth as well as a flat seventh; and it is this flat sixth which we notate as the B flat in our signature for D minor, adding the sharp leading-note (C♯) and its concomitant the sharp sixth (B♮) by means of accidentals as required. But the B♮ is a distinctive element in the Dorian mode, for which the signature therefore showed no sharps or flats. Once-transposed Dorian likewise led to G minor with a signature of one flat (B flat), the second (E flat) being accidentally supplied; *etc.* The habit lingered after the tonal facts had changed; and other signatures, by analogy, also appeared a sharp or a flat too few. We find, for example, Handel's *Harmonious Blacksmith*, which is in E major, with a signature of three sharps instead of four.

Since in such cases the accidentals needed to make up the number required for the key are ordinarily present, unless left out by oversight, no problem of interpretation arises here.

Another discrepancy affecting only the eye is the not uncommon habit of duplicating the sharps or flats of a key signature at the octave, where that octave lies within the stave. This may give the appearance, at first glance, of at least one sharp or one flat *too many*—which is soon seen not to be the case. And where this duplication in the signature is not employed, a similar precaution may appear in the use of accidental sharps or flats against notes already shown thus sharpened or flattened in the signature, but at a different octave. None of this should be more than momentarily confusing.

7. WRITTEN AND UNWRITTEN ACCIDENTALS

Genuine problems of interpretation over accidentals arise in two main aspects: the range of influence of written accidentals; and the necessity of supplying unwritten accidentals under the conventions of *musica ficta*. Though the two aspects are intimately connected, they can be considered most conveniently in separate chapters.

Recent findings concerning baroque accidentals are presented in Appendix V.

CHAPTER V

Interpreting Written Accidentals

1. EARLY ACCIDENTALS APPLY BASICALLY TO SINGLE NOTES

The basic convention governing the influence of accidentals down to
the end of the baroque period remained that given by Simpson, at (79)
in Ch. IV, 4, above: each accidental affects only that note against
which it is placed.

Exceptions were extremely numerous, however, and were partly
guided by subsidiary conventions.

2. EFFECT OF THE BAR-LINE ON ACCIDENTALS

A convention which does *not* apply in early music is that governing
accidentals strictly by the bar. The reason for this will readily be
appreciated.

Bar-lines are found as occasional conveniences at very early periods,
but first became frequent in organ scores and tablatures of the late
sixteenth century, to make it easier to keep the place (*i.e.* when accompanying unbarred polyphonic parts). They serve the same practical
purpose of place-keeping in keyboard solos, where the notes themselves
may often be written considerably out of vertical alignment; and the
lutenists also employed them. But few of these early bar-lines occur at
regular and consistent intervals of time; nor do they always appear at
the same places in different copies of the same work. Except in dance
or dance-influenced music, there *were* no regular intervals of time.
There was no unit in the structure corresponding to our modern word
'measure' in its sense of bar.

In baroque music of the main period there was such a unit; but not
until late in the eighteenth century did advantage begin to be taken of
this change to build up our modern convention governing accidentals
by the bar. We have to watch for cases such as Ex. 1, and conversely
(but less frequently) Ex. 2.

Ex. 1. Uncancelled accidentals within the bar, assumed to be
cancelled:

131

Ex. 2. Accidental maintained across the bar-line:

In Ex. 2, however, we should be more likely to find a sharp written not only against the second *G* but also against the third.

By the middle of the eighteenth century, the force of an accidental was sometimes extended indefinitely until cancellation, the bar-line, however, still not being given a cancelling effect.

(80) C. P. E. Bach, *Essay*, II, Berlin, 1762, I, 38:

'Unless an accidental [in the figuring] is cancelled, it remains in force.'

The modern convention became fully established during the early nineteenth century: but there is no baroque music for which it was more than an incipient tendency, and no eighteenth-century music for which it is to be relied on unreservedly. For early music generally, it is necessary to ignore the bar-line when considering the scope intended for a written accidental. See Postscript at end of this chapter.

3. EFFECT OF THE HEXACHORD ON ACCIDENTALS

(a) In the hexachordal system, an accidental *B* flat implies mutation into a soft hexachord, and it was therefore a regular convention that the influence of this flat should persist until further mutation was necessitated, either by a written *B* natural intervening, or by the melodic line moving beyond the limits of the hexachord (see Ch. IV, 3, above).

By analogy, this convention also held good for flats other than *B*, but not for sharps, which have no place in the basic hexachordal system (though they were brought in by transposition, *F* sharp being *mi*, for example, where *D* is *ut*).

(b) As a loose consequence of this convention, we find in music at least down to the middle of the seventeenth century a general tendency, other things being equal, for flats to last but for sharps not to last.

4. EFFECT OF REPETITION ON ACCIDENTALS

In theory, the basic convention that a written accidental affects only the note against which it is placed covered even the special case of the same note repeated twice or more times in succession.

(81) Jacopo Peri, *Euridice*, Florence, 1600, *Avvertimento:*

'[An accidental] is never to be introduced except on that note alone on which it is shown, even though there may be several repetitions of that same note.'

In practice, great variability obtained. This is virtually admitted by Peri in this very work, since he several times, when repeating the same note in the bass, writes in a cancelling accidental which should not be necessary according to his own rule. We may infer that the rule might very easily be ignored by the performer in the absence of this precaution.

When a note shown with an accidental is repeated, but the accidental is not repeated, we can (according to the sense of the music) either regard that accidental as cancelled or regard it as influencing the repetition or repetitions of the note (including repetitions which are not quite immediate, *i.e.* where one or two other notes of brief duration intervene).

Where either a rest or the start of a new phrase intervenes, it is a virtual certainty that the accidental should be regarded as cancelled, except possibly in the case of flats where the compass of the hexachord has not been exceeded.

When neither rest nor new phrase intervenes, the choice depends on our judgment of the musical situation; but the tendency for the influence of the accidental to persist increased during the course of the seventeenth century, and still more in course of the eighteenth.

5. ACCIDENTALS SOMETIMES RETROSPECTIVE

(a) A particular instance of repetition occurs in the ornamental resolution of discords.

Ex. 3. Lodovico Grossi da Viadana, *Concerti*, Venice, 1602, IV, 'Laetare Hierusalem', bar 3 (of bass):

The *C* sharp shown a third above and slightly to the left of the bass note *A* tells the accompanist to play an *A* major triad against the dissonant *D* of Cantus I (to sound the note of resolution against the note of dissonance in this way would not have been approved later in the baroque period, but was quite favoured both in practice and in theory at the date here in question). Hence the first *C* in Cantus I will have to be taken sharp as well as the second, though the accidental is only marked before the second. That accidental, in other words, exerts a retrospective as well as a prospective influence.

For one case such as this which can be proved, there must be many hundreds which cannot be proved, but in which the same retrospective influence of a written accidental must, by analogy, be regarded as extremely probable. The probability is that most if not all cases of ornamental resolution written in this way, with an accidental marked against the main note of resolution but not against the previous ornamental notes of resolution, are to be interpreted on the lines of the example above: *i.e.* as if the previous ornamental note or notes of resolution were marked with the same accidental as the main note of resolution.

(b) The retrospective use of accidentals is not, however, confined to ornamental resolutions.

Ex. 4. Lodovico Grossi da Viadana, *Concerti*, Venice, 1602, II, 'Peccavi super numerum', bar 10 (of bass):

Here the ♭ marked before the first *D* of the cantus is a precautionary accidental, of a rather remarkable character. It warns us to take this *D* natural, and not, as the composer evidently expected that we should otherwise do, sharp. But why should we take it sharp? The only reason can be a retrospective influence exerted by the sharp marked against the second *D*.

Attention has already been drawn by Knud Jeppesen (*The Style of Palestrina*, 2nd ed., London, 1946, p. 36) to a case of the same general character in Palestrina's eight-part mass, 'Confitebor tibi Domine', where a theme beginning with two repeated notes enters without accidentals, and elsewhere a tone higher with the accidental which this transposition necessitates shown before the second, only, of these repeated notes, though it must certainly influence them both in order to keep the theme unchanged.

Ex. 5. Retrospective accidental in Palestrina.

The first of the two entries shown here, at Ex. 5 (a), is indistinguishable, in its notation, from a chromatic step (*F* natural to *F* sharp);

and it is only the lucky accident of its parallel appearance a tone lower at Ex. 5 (b) which enables Jeppesen to prove that both the first and the second *F* of Ex. 5 (a) are intended to be sharp.

(c) Although Jeppeson was not quite alone in noticing the retrospective influence exercised by written accidentals in certain cases, the extent of this really very troublesome ambiguity has not yet been altogether appreciated. I have made a recent study of the retrospective accidental in baroque passages where it appears to be either certain or probable, or at least optional; and of others where it might seem to be so on a casual glance, but cannot be so on closer examination. As with many other ambiguities of early notation, its existence, and indeed its frequency, can no longer be doubted; and it remained a factor which we shall have to take very seriously in much baroque music. But the difficulty lies precisely in knowing where to apply it and where not. My recent study will be found reported more fully in my *Performer's Guide to Baroque Music*, with numerous examples illustrated. A briefer survey will be found in this present book, at my Appendix V, 2 below.

6. ACCIDENTALS IN FIGURED BASS

See Ch. XXVII *ff*. But a warning may be given here that one of the most frequent misprints in early baroque editions is setting an accidental which should be above or below the bass note, *i.e.* as an indication of the accompanying harmony, in front of that bass note so that it looks like (but is not) a chromatic modification in the bass line itself.

POSTSCRIPT TO THE NEW VERSION

The following passages show the modern bar-line convention for accidentals in course of establishing itself. Notice, however, the reservation which occurs even into the nineteenth century.

(81a) Daniel Gottlob Türk, *Klavierschule*, Leipzig and Halle, 1789, p. 46:

'[Accidentals] are valid only through one bar; yet one must not wish to observe this rule too strictly, for such a modifying sign often remains valid through several bars, or indeed so long, until it is cancelled by a ♮. Above all . . . when the first note of the following [bar] and the last [note] of the previous bar stand on one degree [*i.e.* are the same note repeated].'

(81b) Anon., *New Instruction for Playing the Harpsichord, Piano-Forte or Spinnet . . .*, London, [*c.* 1790], p. 4:

'A Sharp or flat when put before any single Note accidentally affects only so many notes as follow on that line or space in that Bar.'

(81c) Domenico Corri, *The Singer's Preceptor*, London, 1810, p. 79:

'Placed before a Note [accidentals] affect only those [notes] within the same Bar, and which [*i.e.* their influence] continues if the last Note of a Bar is the same as the first Note of the following Bar.'

CHAPTER VI

Adding Unwritten Accidentals

1. UNWRITTEN ACCIDENTALS FOR NECESSITY AND BEAUTY

The convention that the performer should add unwritten accidentals where necessary, and might add them even where not necessary, is of importance for music down to the early seventeenth century, and in decreasing degree throughout the baroque period.

(82) Pietro Aaron, *Thoscanello de la Musica*, Venice, 1523, 2nd ed., 1529, on, p. 1 of adds. following Ch. 41:

'There are, among students of music, many arguments as to flats and sharps, that is whether composers should mark such accidentals . . . or whether the singer is supposed to perceive and know the unknown secret of the places where such accidentals are required. I myself, who always was, and am, in favour of those who like to make their wishes clear . . . shall with all possible brevity treat the subject [unlike those who think that marked accidentals are for] beginners with no mind of their own.'

(83) Stephano Vanneo, MS., 1531, tr. Vincentio Rosseto, *Recanetum de musica aurea*, Rome, 1533, III, 37:

'The ears are considered the best interpreters, which can help you most, if you observe the parts of an accomplished singer, who when he feels that he is producing a dissonant progression, at once little by little and so discretely, that it can scarcely be recognised and detected, either flattens or sharpens it, until a consonant and sweet progression strikes the ears.'

(84) Gioseffe Zarlino, *Istitutioni harmoniche*, Venice, 1558, but cited from complete ed. of 1589, III, 252 (a contrary view):

'There are some who in singing sharpen or flatten a melody in a case which the composer never intended—as when they sing a tone instead of a semitone or the other way about, and other such things. By this they not only offend the ear but also commit innumerable errors. Singers should therefore take care to sing only what is written according to the mind of the composer.'

(85) William Bathe, *Briefe Introduction*, London, *c.* 1590:

'Thappendancy of the flat by the sharp, and of the sharp by the Flat is taken away, though by negligence and ignorance of prickers, we are oft driven to gather thappendencie by the course of the song.'

(86) Thomas Morley, *Plaine and Easie Introduction*, London, 1597, p. 88:

'Because I thought it better flat then sharpe, I have set it flat. But if anie man like the other waie better, let him use his discretion.'

Theoretical recognition of *musica ficta* introduced more or less impromptu by performers was never as extensive as the practice of it; indeed it was at all times a controversial matter; but we find musical evidence for it well into the later seventeenth century, and its influence lingered indirectly in the general baroque attitude towards accidentals for some considerable period after it had become obsolete as a convention.

2. CORRECTING IMPERFECT INTERVALS

The most famous of ancient musical mnemonics is *mi contra fa est diabolus in musica: mi* against *fa* is the devil in music.

B mi against *F fa ut* gives a diminished fifth (*quinta falsa*) or an augmented fourth (*tritonus*). *B mi* against *B fa* gives a diminished or augmented octave.

(87) Pietro Aaron, *Thoscanello*, Venice, 1523, 2nd ed., 1529, on, p. 1 of adds. after Ch. 41:

'The softening and tempering of the tritone [is] either by raising or lowering.'

(88) Charles Butler, *Principles of Musik*, London, 1636, p. 49:

'But these harsh Discords, by the help of Flats and sharps, are reduced to their true Concords. For as the *Tritonus* [augmented fourth] either by flatting the sharp, or sharping the Flat, is made a true *Diatessaron* [fourth]; so the *Semidiapente* [diminished fifth], by the same means, is made a true *Diapente* [fifth].'

These intervals are not always, of course, to be eliminated by *musica ficta*; it is obvious that they were very frequently tolerated as elements in the harmony, and quite often as melody. But there are also a great many passages from which, at any rate as melody, they need to be eliminated. The standard corrections are as follows:

Ex. 6. Imperfect fourths and fifths corrected:

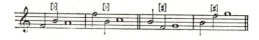

In each of these cases it will be seen that the note altered by *musica ficta* is the *second* of the two, which is obviously much easier to accomplish impromptu than altering the first.

3. THE DIMINISHED OR AUGMENTED OCTAVE CLASH

Diminished and augmented octaves would in principle be regarded as in need of correction to perfect octaves by *musica ficta*. But there is one form of diminished octave which involves the simultaneous use of different hexachords in different parts, and which became a favoured idiom, particularly in England from Byrd to Purcell.

In its milder, and presumably original shape, this idiom is a striking case of false relation, but produces no actually discordant harmony. In its more advanced and harsher shape, it is a clash of harmony, but produced by so natural a movement of its component melodies that its rightness and logic are really unassailable. Our English taste for it throughout the greatest period of our musical history is an instance of the emotional depth and poignancy so typical of our national character at the time. It is, indeed, extremely beautiful.

Ex. 7. The diminished octave clash:

Not only is it wrong to eliminate this form of *mi contra fa* by a misuse of *musica ficta*; it will normally be proper to introduce it even where not written, by taking the lower *C* (owing to its function as leading note) sharp even in the absence of a written accidental. Similarly in transposed positions: *e.g. B* flat in the upper part against *B* natural in the lower part. (See 6 below.)

A somewhat comparable use of the augmented octave, quite typical although not amounting to so definite an idiom, may be seen in the following passage. The *C* sharp is marked, but even if not marked could have been introduced by *musica ficta*. The bass is correctly shown as *C* natural.

Ex. 8. Nicholas Carleton, 'Gloria Tibi Trinitas', bar 26, *Mus. Brit.* I (Mulliner Book), ed. Denis Stevens, London, 1951, p. 5:

The first *F* in the bass (not the second) might optionally be taken sharp as an example of *musica ficta* introduced not 'for necessity' but 'for beautification': see 10 below.

4. THE PICARDY THIRD

The minor third differs acoustically from the major third in giving rise to much more dissonant beating among its upper harmonics and combination tones. Moreover, any single note includes a major third fairly prominently among its upper harmonics, so that if a minor third is sounded on voices or instruments, it is always in faint but disturbing conflict with a major third on the same bass sounding of its own accord among the overtones.

The medieval ear was just as sensitive to this inherently restless and inconclusive character of the minor third as it was to the ambivalent character of the augmented fourth and the diminished fifth. The minor third was therefore not felt to be a tolerable element in any important close, least of all a final close, until well into the baroque period. The original solution was to exclude both major and minor thirds, leaving a bare octave or an octave with fifth. During the sixteenth century, however, thirds were increasingly used in final closes; but with the understanding that if the prevailing modality or tonality would have made them minor, they must be altered to major whether so written by means of an accidental or not (the so-called *Tierce de Picardie* or Picardy Third). This understanding persisted in some degree, though it is hard to be certain in what degree, throughout the seventeenth century.

(89) Thomas Morley, *Plaine and Easie Introduction*, London, 1597, pp. 155–6:

'[Morley's *Master Gnorimus* corrects, with an absence of comment more eloquent than words, his pupil's final close in the minor by writing in a Picardy Third.]'

(90) Francesco Bianciardi, *Breve regola*, Siena, 1607, ninth rule:

'In the final closes, one always ends with the major Third.'

(91) Wolfgang Ebner, Germ. transl. Johann Andreas Herbst in his *Arte prattica e poëtica*, Frankfurt, 1653, Rule 8:

'But when it is a full cadence (vollkommliche Cadentia), the last note must always be taken with the sharp.'

(92) Lorenzo Penna, *Primi Albori Musicali*, Bologna, 1672, Bk. III, Ch. V, Second Rule:

'On the last note, a . . . major third.'

Penna's example to this rule shows that he has in mind a close which would otherwise be minor.

Ex. 8A. Penna, Picardy Third:

(93) Friedrich Erhard Niedt, *Musicalische Handleitung*, First Part, Hamburg, 1700, Ch. VIII, Rule 6:

'[The final chord must be major regardless of what goes before, except that] French composers do the opposite, but everything is not good merely because it comes from France or has a French name.'

Niedt's evidence is the first written statement of which I am aware casting doubt on the universality of the convention of the Picardy Third. As regards the French composers, Niedt's statement may well be too sweeping. As regards the general European practice, in spite of the categorical repetitions of the rule quoted above, it is hard to believe that the convention was so invariable as we are told. There are some French minor movements of the late seventeenth and early eighteenth centuries which have every appearance of being as well suited by a Picardy Third on their final closes as those of other nations. But on the other hand, there are very many minor movements of all nationalities at the same period which seem by no means well suited by a Picardy Third, but which are far more convincing musically when ending, as they have proceeded, in the minor mode. In practice I have very little doubt that they should be allowed to do so, and that whatever the nationality of the music, the Picardy Third should only be applied as late as this where the musical advantages of doing so are very evident.

It may be mentioned that with the sole exception of Morley all the treatises quoted above, in this section, are dealing with figured bass. It is one matter to introduce a Picardy Third into the accompaniment of a close in which the composer has brought all the written melodic parts to a unison, as baroque composers so often do; it is another matter to introduce it into the last chord, for example, of a harpsichord solo, where this is written minor. Closes *showing* the Picardy Third by a written accidental are common in seventeenth century music of all kinds, and not scarce in eighteenth century music. But Picardy Thirds as a performer's option may well have become almost confined to figured bass accompaniments at latest by the beginning of the eighteenth century, and a matter for considerable discretion even there.

141

5. THE LEADING-NOTE PRINCIPLE

(a) The principle of the leading-note depends on the fact that the semitone, being the smallest interval in Western use, draws the mind rather as an electric pole draws a spark when the opposite pole is brought near enough. As the word implies, we are led across this interval, and led more easily than across a larger interval. This fact is among the realities which constitute the field of force we call tonality.

(b) We find a very early tendency to make the third major when it is about to open out into a fifth but minor when it is about to close in to a unison; and to make a sixth major when it is about to open out into an octave but minor when it is about to fall to a fifth.

(c) The same economy of effort lies behind the traditional injunction *una nota super la Semper est canendum fa:* a single note above *la* always must be sung *fa*, that is to say at the interval of a semitone. The rule means that where the melody (particularly at the summit of a phrase) rises from a note to one note (*i.e.* a 'single note') above it, and at once returns, that one note, whether so written or not, shall be at the less effortful interval of a semitone, and not at the more effortful interval of a tone.

Reference to Table I (Ch. IV, 3) will show that where *la* is *E la mi*, the requisite semitone above it is hexachordally available as *F fa ut*; and that where *la* is *A la mi re*, the semitone is available as *B* (flat) *fa*; but that where *la* is *D la sol re*, there is no semitone *fa* available, so that an accidental *E* flat must be introduced. (Indeed in modern language, though not in hexachordal language, *B* (flat) *fa* is already an accidental.)

Thus *E* rising to *F* and at once falling again to *E* makes no problem: so it is written, and so performed.

A to *B* and back to *A* requires the *B* to be taken flat whether so written or not.

D to *E* and back to *D* requires the *E* to be taken flat whether so written or not.

There will be exceptions in practice; and both in theory and in practice none of this applies in the Phrygian and Aeolian modes and their transpositions (the final notes *B, E* or *A*, or with a transposing flat in the signature, *E, A* or *D*, or with two transposing flats in the signature, *A, D* or *G*, suggest a Phrygian or Aeolian disposition—see also Percy Scholes, *Oxford Companion to Music*, 9th ed., London, 1955, *s.v.* 'Mode', for a succinct guide).

(d) When the melody moves one note downwards and at once returns, there was again a certain tendency, but a far less clearly defined one, to make the interval a semitone, if not already so, by a written or unwritten use of *musica ficta*: thus *D, C, D* in some contexts *might* become *D, C* sharp, *D*; but only where the *C* is being treated strictly as a leading-note (see 6 below) is there any reason to suppose that it *must* be sharpened in this way.

Ex. 9. Una nota super *la* Semper est canendum *fa*:

at summit   not at summit
of phrase.   of phrase

6. THE LEADING-NOTE ITSELF

(a) By the leading-note is meant the note a semitone below (and pulling strongly towards) a tonic whether already established or newly reached. It is a fundamental element in tonality but not a prominent one in modality. Some modes have this semitone naturally, others can be given it by *musica ficta*. But the greater the insistence on a true leading-note, the greater the invasion of mode by key. The historical consequences of turning potential leading-notes (a tone distant) into actual ones (a semitone distant) by *musica ficta* were the advent of true modulation and the subordination of modality to key tonality.

This historical revolution began late in the middle ages but was mainly the work of the renaissance. The convention which came to govern the sharpening of notes not so written, in order to make them into true leading-notes, depends on one of the most important structural concepts of those periods: the concept of the cadence. The primary cadence, or tenor cadence, was a fall of a tone from the note above the final or tonic to that final or tonic (cadence means fall—'that strain again; it hath a dying fall', wrote Shakespeare). The secondary cadences were the progressions of the other parts joined with the tenor cadence. A close was established when a tenor cadence and a descant cadence appeared together; the others (including the bass cadence which later became so prominent in defining key and key modulations) were optional additions.

Ex. 10. Four-part 'close' with its 'cadences':

1 Descant cadence

2 Tenor cadence

3 Contratenor cadence

4 Bass cadence

143

It makes no difference in what inversions the cadences appear; if the tenor and descant cadences are present together in any parts, a close has been defined. The normal procedure is then to sharpen the lower note of the descant cadence so as to form a true leading-note, if (as in the Dorian, Mixolydian and Aeolian modes) it is not already such (*i.e.* as a modal *subsemitonium*). Where the necessary accidental is not marked, it should be supplied if the close is an important or final one, but not if the close is only taken in passing.

(94) Thomas Morley, *Plaine and Easie Introduction*, London, 1597, p. 94:

'The base being a [descant] *Cadence*, the nature thereof requireth a sharp.'

Ex. 11. Morley: 'descant cadence' in the bass:

[p. 144:] 'In your third note you have a flat [descant] *Cadence* in your counter Tenor, which is a thing against nature, for everie *Cadence* is sharpe [with exceptions described as] passing closes and not of the nature of yours, which is a kind of full or final close . . .'

(b) When the tenor cadence falls to *A*, its penultimate note *B* may be flattened accidentally to *B* flat, as an alternative to sharpening the penultimate note *G* of the descant cadence; and similarly in certain transpositions. This is the so-called Phrygian cadence (because it arises naturally in that mode, from which it should on no account be eliminated by *musica ficta*; the tenor cadence here being, exceptionally, a semitone fall which is sometimes called by a happy metaphor the 'leading-note' of the Phrygian mode).

Ex. 12. 'Phrygian cadence':

(95) Charles Butler, *Principles of Musik*, London, 1636, p. 83:

'In true Cadences, the Binding half-note must ever be sharp. . . . Nevertheless the *La Cadence* is sometimes admitted; as in these examples.'

Ex. 13. Butler, 'Phrygian cadences':

(c) In spite of the crucial part played by modal theory and practice in the historical evolution of the true leading-note, it is not only in modal music that the structure of the close gives us the clue to the accidentals required. Something corresponding to the medieval and renaissance descant cadence is found in a majority of baroque closes. The 'Phrygian cadence' still accounts for a proportion of baroque half-closes; otherwise, the sharp or sharpened leading-note is the invariable rule for every genuine close. It is the 'bass cadence' (bass rising a fourth or falling a fifth) rather than the 'tenor cadence' (fall of a tone to the tonic) which, in conjunction with the 'descant cadence' (suspension resolved on the leading-note) now pre-eminently defines the close: but the treatment remains the same; and while the accidentals are less likely to be left unwritten, cases occur. The following from Monteverdi's own madrigal transcription of his monody, 'Ariadne's Lament', is instructive in more ways than one.

Ex. 14. Monteverdi, leading-notes not marked but requiring to be sharp (Malipiero's ed., VI, 16):

In the first place, all the *F*'s are meant sharp (not only is this musically obvious, but in a previous entry a tone lower they are all *E* naturals, no accidental being required).

In the second place, bar two shows in effect a descant cadence (top line) with a tenor cadence (bottom line), and the leading-note *E* must be taken sharp although not written so (again musically obvious, but also proved, by the monodic version, Malipiero ed., XII, p. 165, where the corresponding passage has this leading-note *marked* sharp). We could have no clearer confirmation that accidentals have still to be supplied at need by the performer in the early seventeenth century.

Later in the baroque period, as with other varieties of *musica ficta*, the need to supply sharps on leading-notes where they are not already present in writing rapidly diminishes, until we really find it remaining only in the special case of figured bass.

(96) Agostino Agazzari, *Del sonare sopra 'l basso*, Siena, 1607, p. 6:

'All cadences, whether intermediate or final, demand the major Third; some people, therefore, do not mark it, but as an added precaution, I recommend using the sign [when figuring basses].'

(97) Francesco Bianciardi, *Breve regola*, Siena, 1607, second of the nine rules:

'When [the bass] rises a fourth [or falls a fifth] we give it the major Third, and if it is not naturally major, it is made so by adding the Sharp, because it is by this progression that the close is established.'

(98) Matthew Locke, *Melothesia*, London, 1673, Rule 3:

'A *Cadence* is a Fall or Binding, wherein after the taking of a *Discord* or *Discords*, there is a meeting or Closure of Concords [on two bass notes] the last of which two *Notes* generally riseth Four, or falleth five *Notes* from the former; by which it is known (for the most part) to be a *Cadence* . . . the Thirds are *Thirds Major*, and so are to be Play'd on all Bindings, and generally on all such bass *Notes* as the following *Notes* riseth four or falleth five *Notes*.'

The last statement is particularly to be noticed for its almost unrestricted scope. But we must also be prepared for passages in which the sharpening of the (apparent) leading-note by *musica ficta* is not intended, although the baroque criterion of a bass rising a fourth or falling a fifth is duly satisfied.

(99) Adriano Banchieri, *Dialogo Musicale*, in 2nd ed. of *L'Organo suonarino*, Venice, 1611:

'Here is an example of the freedom of the composer's mind in avoiding the accidental in leaps [by the bass] of a Fourth and Fifth.'

Ex. 15. Banchieri: apparent cadences not treated as such (until the last):

It would be a gross misuse of *musica ficta* to make the first *F* sharp; though if the first note of the second bar had been *G* or *B* natural in place of *B* flat, it would have been an equally gross negligence not to do so.

(d) It may be worth adding an early eighteenth century version of the formal cadences, to compare with the sixteenth century (and earlier) version given in Ex. 10 above.

(100) Andreas Werckmeister, *Harmonologia Musica*, Frankfurt and Leipzig, 1702, p. 48:

'These Cadences (Clausulae) take their name from the four principal parts, namely Treble, Alto, Tenor, and Bass; wherefore they are called "Discantisirend", "Altisirend", "Tenorisirend", and "Bassirend".'

Ex. 16. Werckmeister, formal cadences:

In a further example, Werckmeister shows the upper three cadences in different inversions, but retains the bass cadences in the bass part: it is hard to see why, since examples of both the descant cadence and the tenor cadence in the bass part are familiar enough in baroque music.

7. THE 'DOUBLE LEADING-NOTE'

The name 'double leading-note' has been appropriately suggested for the beautiful and characteristic formula of the late fourteenth and early fifteenth centuries, shown at Ex. 17A below.

But by the second half of the fifteenth century, the parallel perfect fourths which give this formula its special flavouring went out of fashion, and the penultimate note of the middle part was taken flat, as at Ex. 17B below. It is then no longer in double harness with the leading-note proper, but is a normal flat (or normally flattened) subdominant.

Ex. 17. (A) 'double leading-note'; (B) leading-note with flat subdominant:

Where this formula is encountered in transposed versions, the same results, if not written, must be produced by *musica ficta* as required.

8. THE 'LANDINI CADENCE'

The cadence named after Francesco Landini, the blind organist of early renaissance Florence, has the sixth degree of the scale inserted ornamentally between the leading-note and the final note, but is otherwise normal in its behaviour.

Ex. 18. 'Landini Cadence':

9. SHARP MEDIANTS ASSUMED NEXT TO SHARP LEADING-NOTES

Where the seventh degree of the scale, in its function of leading-note, is sharp or has been made so by *musica ficta*, its neighbouring mediant, the sixth degree of the scale, either is or must be made so too, if it takes part in the cadence; and this it often does, where the resolution of the dissonance in the descant cadence is ornamental. The augmented second occurs as a melodic interval in Monteverdi, but was not ordinarily acceptable. Being so obvious, therefore, the necessary sharp on the sixth degree is very commonly left unwritten, even when the sharp on the seventh degree is present. It must then be supplied by *musica ficta*, as in Ex. 19 below (in the original, the sharp sign in the bass stave indicating the major triad on the bass note *E* is misplaced against that *E* itself, by an obvious and indeed common misprint, instead of appearing in its proper place, the space above, where it stands, in the normal manner of Viadana's and some other very early Italian figured basses, for *G* sharp in the accompanying harmony).

Ex. 19. Lodovico Grossi da Viadana, *Concerti*, Venice, 1602, II, 'Peccavi super numerum', bar 19 (of bass):

10. ACCIDENTALS SUGGESTED BY THE PERFORMER'S TASTE

It was understood that accidentals might be introduced not merely for necessity's sake (*causa necessitatis*) but also for beauty's sake (*causa pulchritudinis*). See (77) in Ch. IV, Sect. 2 above.

How widely this should be taken we do not know; but it seems highly probable that most of what a contemporary performer would have thought beautiful would have been covered by one or other of the specific conventions already considered in this chapter, and that there is little scope for further unspecified alterations of the accidentals.

In *applying* the conventions, we should be much bolder than some modern editors have dared to be since the reaction against the reckless liberties taken a generation ago; Edward Lowinsky has given us a good model in his recent editing.

Outside the conventions, an occasional chromatic alteration may certainly suggest itself, which while difficult to bring under any particular heading, has the stamp of authenticity and makes a pleasing improvement; but we have to be extremely careful not to spoil a good thing by insinuating an anachronistic flavouring which dilutes instead of enriching the original effect. (See Ex. 8 above, the? *F* sharp.)

All in all, the main difficulty with *musica ficta* is in deciding how far to go. Some of the most successful of modern treatments of the problem will be found in Volumes I and IV of *Musica Britannica*, and in Helen Hewitt's edition, with its valuable prefatory remarks on this subject, of *Odhekaton A*. The reader is strongly recommended to compare the detailed solutions shown in these editions with the statements made in the present Chapter.

11. DIFFERENT 'MUSICA FICTA' SHOWN IN DIFFERENT TABLATURES OF THE SAME PIECE

(a) Tablature which shows, not notes directly, but fingerings implying notes (*e.g.* lute tablature showing the strings and frets to be fingered), needs no signs for accidentals, and cannot be unclear about them, though it can be mistaken. A comparison of such tablatures one with another, or with staff notation, can therefore be particularly instructive, provided we are not under any illusions as to its being infallible.

(b) I am indebted to Alan Fen-Taylor for the following Ex. 19A, where the chromatic alterations, though equally clear in each version, are not the same. Are they equally correct? They may be so, in the sense of not having mistakes; but in that case, they certainly show how wide a range of correct possibilities lies open to the performer. We are not, therefore, so much concerned with correct or incorrect solutions as with better or worse solutions, and even with different solutions of equal merit. We are sent back in the end to our own musical judgement, after absorbing as much guidance as we can from available comparisons.

Ex. 19A. Cipriano de Rore (1516–65), (a) madrigal 'Ancor che col partire', with keyboard intabulations: (b) by Antonio de Cabezón, posthumously published in *Obras de música para tecla, arpa y vihuela*, Madrid, 1578; (c) by Bernhard Schmid, *Zwey Bücher*, Strassburg 1577; (d) by Andrea Gabrieli, *Terzo libro de Ricercari*, Venice, 1596

(c) The following Ex. 19B illustrates the limitations of the help to be got on accidentals from tablature comparisons.

In the first measure, two string parts and the tablature agree on *G* natural. This is correct, since the harmonic progression is quite evidently a normal Phrygian cadence on *B* flat dropping to *A* in the bass. To sharpen both *G*'s as clumsily doubled leading notes, and make the *B* natural to fit, would be so perverse that it would have occurred to nobody.

In the second measure, the top string part shows *G* sharp, the tablature shows *G* natural. Because lute tablature needs no separate signs for accidentals, we expect it to be more reliable in the matter of chromatic changes than staff notation, which does. But the argument can just as well be turned the other way round. Someone must deliberately have inserted the sharp in the top string part: someone might inadvertently have put the fingering for *G* natural instead of *G* sharp in the lute tablature; therefore the (deliberate) insertion in staff notation, we can argue, is more likely to be reliable than the (perhaps inadvertent and mistaken) fingering in tablature.

This ambiguity in the argument sends us back to the music for our choice of solution. A *G* sharp slightly worsens the melody here, but improves the harmony, since it progresses in effect to A minor (awkwardly enough, because of the *C* sharp in the alto part). My previous choice in this second measure was for the lute tablature, and *G* natural as a passing note. My present inclination is towards the written accidental in the string part, and *G* sharp as a momentary leading-note. The only certainty is that one or the other part will have to be changed. Both together make simple nonsense; and we really have to decide in rehearsal, as no doubt the original performers decided, more or less by trial and error.

Ex. 19B. John Dowland, *Lachrimae*, London, [1604], 'M. Giles Hobies Galiard', bars 20–21, accidental in string part conflicting with lute tablature:

PART TWO

EMBELLISHMENT

CHAPTER VII

The Place of Embellishment

1. THE PERFORMER'S SHARE IN THE FIGURATION

Music hardly ever, if at all, consists only of its basic progressions. It is embellished. This may mean far more than mere decoration.

The embellishment is everything in the music which can be changed without affecting the basic progressions. It is partly a matter of rhythmic and harmonic detail, but mainly of melodic outline. It is, in fact, what we normally call the figuration.

We are so accustomed in the modern West to the composer providing his own figuration in its entirety that we may not realise how different the situation has been at other periods. There have been whole schools depending on spontaneous invention within a traditional framework. Even when formal composition became more important than improvisation, it continued to benefit from the same source; the improvisation of the performer continued to pour over into the resources of the composer. Our present instrumental music largely derives from the spontaneous adaptation of vocal and dance material to the idiomatic requirements of renaissance organists, lutenists, viol-players and others. Renaissance and baroque singers made a crucial contribution to florid vocal music. Even in the nineteenth century, composer-pianists like Chopin and Liszt were still enriching keyboard figuration at their finger ends; but this time-honoured flow of impromptu invention from performer to composer (whether in the same or different persons) must have thereafter largely dried up until its enthusiastic re-invention in the present generation.

It is the wealth of passing detail, the felicity, unexpectedness and exuberance of the figuration which makes music out of its mere basic progressions. It may not ultimately matter where the figuration comes from, but it matters very much that it should be present. Our problem here is that even in the baroque period composers still left substantial proportions of their figuration to be supplied, more or less impromptu, by the performer. Not enough modern performers are yet capable of doing this. The main responsibility thus passes to the editor, who can, in a performing edition, provide a working version in writing. This is not an ideal solution, but it is greatly preferable to leaving the figuration in its incomplete state as originally composed and published.

2. THE PRIMARY ARGUMENT ABOUT EMBELLISHMENT ITSELF

(101) Desiderius Erasmus, note on Corinthians, XIX, 19, transl. J. A. Froude, *Life and Letters of Erasmus*, London, 1894, p. 116:

'Modern church music is so constructed that the congregation cannot hear one distinct word.'

(102) Archbishop Cranmer, letter to Henry VIII, 1544:

'In my opinion, the song that shall be made [as music to the Litany] would not be full of Notes, but as near as may be, for every syllable a note, so that it may be sung distinctly and devoutly.'

(103) Queen Elizabeth, 49th Injunction of 1559:

'. . . a modest distinct songe [for the body of the service] that the same may be as playnely understanded, as yf it were read without syngyng [but for the anthem] the best sort of melodie and music that may be conveniently devised, having respect that the sentence of the Hymne may be understanded and perceyved.'

(104) Pope Marcellus, address to the papal choir, 1555, cited *Grove's Dictionary*, 5th ed., London, 1954, *s.v.* 'Palestrina':

'[Church music must be sung] in a suitable manner, with properly modulated voices, so that everything could be both heard and properly understood.'

(105) Charles Butler, *Principles of Musik*, London, 1636, p. 116:

'Too much quaint Division, too much shaking [trilling] and quavering [breaking down into rapid variations: *cf* Cotgrave's *Dict.*, London, 1650, *s.v.* "quaver"] of the Notes, all harsh straining of the Voices beyond their natural pitch, as they are odious and offensive to the ear; so do they drown the right sound of the words . . .'

(106) Giulio Caccini, *Nuove Musiche*, Florence, 1602, Preface, transl.? Playford (from 2nd ed. of 1607), *Introduction to the Skill of Musick*, London, 1654 (1664 on), cited from ed. of 1674, p. 37:

'Hitherto I have not put forth to the view of the World, those Fruits of my Musick Studies employed about that Noble manner of Singing, which I learnt of my Master the famous *Scipione del Palla* in *Italy*; nor my

Compositions of *Ayres*, Composed by me, which I saw frequently practised by the most famous Singers in *Italy*, both Men and Women: But seeing many of them go about maimed and spoil'd, and that those long winding Points were ill performed, I therefore devis'd to avoid that old manner of running Division which has been hitherto used, being indeed more proper for Wind and Stringed Instruments than for the Voice. And seeing that there is made now a days an indifferent and confused use of those excellent Graces and Ornaments to the good manner of Singing, which we call *Trills, Grupps, Exclamations of Increasing and Abating* of the Voice, of which I do intend in this my Discourse to leave some footprints, that others may attain to this excellent manner of Singing: To which manner I have framed my last *Ayres* for one Voice to the *Theorbo*, not following that old way of *Composition* whose Musick not suffering the Words to be understood by the Hearers, for the multitude of Divisions made upon short and long Syllables, though by the Vulgar such Singers are cryed up for famous. But I have endeavoured in those my late Compositions, to bring in a kind of Musick, by which men might as it were Talk in Harmony, using in that kind of Singing a certain noble neglect of the Song (as I have often heard at *Florence* by the Actors in their Singing *Opera's*) in which I have endeavoured the Imitation of the Conceit of the Words, seeking out the Cords more or less passionate, according to the meaning of them, having concealed in them so much as I could the *Art of Descant*, and paused or stayed the Consonances or Cords upon long Syllables, avoiding the short, and observing the same Rule in making the passages of Division by some few *Quavers* to Notes and to Cadences, not exceeding the value of a quarter or half a *Semibreve* at most. But, as I said before, those long windings and turnings of the Voice are ill used, for I have observed that Divisions have been invented, not because they are necessary unto a good fashion of Singing, but rather for a certain tickling of the ears of those who do not well understand what it is to sing Passionately; for if they did undoubtedly Divisions would have been abhorr'd, there being nothing more contrary to Passion than they are; yet in some kind of Musick less Passionate or Affectuous, and upon long Syllables, not short, and in final Cadences, some short Points of Division may be used, but not at all adventures, but upon the practice of the Descant . . . certain it is, that an *Ayre* composed in this manner upon the conceit of the words, by one that hath a good fashion of singing, will work a better effect and delight, more than another made with all the Art of Descant, where the Humour or Conceit of the words is not minded.'

(107) **Chr. W. Gluck, dedication to** *Alceste* **Vienna, 1769:**

'When I undertook to compose *Alceste*, I set out to divest the music entirely of all those abuses with which the false vanity of singers, or the too great complacency of composers, has so long distinguished the Italian opera. . . . It was my intention to confine music to its true function of serving the poetry in the interests of the expression and situations of the story; without interrupting the action, or stifling it with useless and superfluous ornaments . . . my first and chief care, as a dramatic composer was to aim at a noble simplicity; and I have accordingly shunned all parade of unnatural difficulty, in favour of clearness.'

3. THE SECONDARY ARGUMENT ABOUT PERFORMER'S EMBELLISHMENTS

(108) Bénigne de Bacilly, *L'Art de bien chanter*, Paris, 1668, p. 135:

'A piece of music can be beautiful and please not, for want of being performed with the necessary embellishments, of which embellishments the most part are not marked at all on paper, whether because in fact they cannot be marked for lack of signs for that purpose, or whether it has been considered that too many marks encumber and take away the clearness of a melody, and would bring a kind of confusion; besides, it is useless to mark things, if you do not know how to fashion them with the appropriate refinements (former avec les circonstances necessaries), which makes all the difficulty.'

(109) Anthony Aston, *Brief Supplement to Colley Cibber, Esq.*, 1748, ed. R. W. Lowe in Cibber's *Apology*, II, London, 1889, p. 312:

'[The boy singer Jemmy Brown] when practicing a Song set by Mr. *Purcell*, some of the Music told him to grace and run a Division in such a Place. *O let him alone*, said Mr. *Purcell; he will grace it more naturally than you, or I, can teach him.*'

(110) *Gentleman's Journal*, London, Nov. 1692:

'[Counter-tenor solo in Purcell's "Ode on St. Cecilia's day"] was sung with incredible Graces by Mr. Purcell himself [actually by Pate].'

(111) Roger North, Brit. Mus. MS. Add. 32533, English early 18th cent., *f.* 106 *v.*:

'It is the hardest task that Can be to pen the Manner of artifical Gracing an upper part; It hath bin attempted, and in print, but with Woefull Effect . . . the Spirit of that art is Incommunicable by wrighting, therefore it is almost Inexcusable to attempt it.'

(112) Johann Adolf Scheibe, *Critische Musicus*, I, 12, Hamburg, 1737:

'To a good method belong the appoggiaturas, the grace-notes, the trills, the alteration or elaboration of the notes, certain small, agreeable additions and variations, and many other things which are better listened to than described.
[I, 6:] 'All embellishments, all little graces, and all that is understood by the method of playing, he [J. S. Bach] expresses in [written] notes, and not

only deprives his pieces of beauty and harmony but makes the melodic line utterly unclear.'

(113) J. A. Birnbaum in reply, repr. in Mizler's *Musikalische Biblio-thek*, Leipzig, April, 1738, I, iv:

'[J. S. Bach] is neither the first nor the only man to write thus . . . . It is certain that what is called the method of singing or playing is almost universally valued and thought desirable. It is further beyond doubt that this method can content the ear only when introduced in suitable places and that it is bound, on the other hand, to distress the ear markedly and destroy the fundamental melody if the performer introduces it at the wrong moment. Now we know from experience that its introduction is ordinarily left to the free choice of singers and players. If all such people were well enough brought up in all that is genuinely beautiful in the method; if they always knew how to introduce it where it may function as a genuine embellishment and special emphasisation of the fundamental melody; then there would be no point in the composer writing down in notes what they knew already. But only a minority have enough know-ledge, and the remainder destroy the fundamental melody by an unsuitable introduction of the method, and often actually introduce embellishments of a kind which could readily be ascribed by those unacquainted with the truth of the matter to a mistake by the composer. Thus every composer including [J. S. Bach], has the right to bring the erring back into the true way by indicating a proper method in accordance with his desires, thereby seeing to the safeguarding of his own reputation.'

(114) Louis Bollioud de Mermet, *De la corruption*, Lyon, 1746:

'[All sonatas sound alike now, being overladen with the same embel-lishments.] One could easily persuade oneself that he who plays music in such a complicated and unnatural manner is an evil-doer on whom this labour was imposed for punishment.'

(115) [John Hawkins] on Agostino Steffani, *Memoirs of the Life of A.S.* [? London, *c.* 1740], p. ii:

'. . . the exactness he required in the performance of his music, which was so remarkably great, that he would never admit of any divisions, or graces, even on the most plain and simple passages, except what he wrote himself: nor would he, with regard to his duets in particular, even suffer them to be performed by any of those luxuriant singers, who had not sense enough to see the folly of sacrificing to the idle vanity of displaying their extent, or power, of voice, not merely the air, but frequently the very harmony of an author's compositions.'

(116) [L'Abbé Laugier] *Apologie*, [Paris], 1754, p. 71:

'There ought to be a law preventing all singers and all those who make up the orchestra from changing anything in the melody of which the character is traced out for them, with orders to restrict themselves scrupulously to the notation before their eyes. There ought to be a like law obliging all masters who give instruction to instil in their pupils the habit of literal performance.'

(117) G. C. Weitzler, in Marpurg's *Historisch-Kritische Beyträge*, Berlin, III, 2, 1, 1756:

'With regard to the embellishments, I think it advisable to write them out in notes only when they are ordinary quick passages; with others which come partly from the natural facility of the fingers, partly from luxuriant invention, it is useless to do so. Either they cannot be indicated in notes, or else good taste will reject such embellishments so soon as one realises that they are supposed to be these and none others, thus and not otherwise at a given place; in short, as soon as one misses the fortuitousness so essential to them. [Such written-out embellishments do not sound natural; notation cannot always ensure a proper performance.] A musical person with good interpretative powers will never play in the same way but will always make modifications [in the notes] in accordance with the state of his feelings.'

Marpurg follows this letter with a biting and satirical attack on Weitzler for his championship of the 'fortuitous' element in musical inspiration. The word evidently exasperated him and he does less than justice to Weitzler's real argument. Even so he adds:

(118) Marpurg, *loc. cit.*, 1756:

'It is true that the larger embellishments . . . by which one modifies the repeat of a piece, are arbitrary. But are not some always better than others? . . . Moreover, must not these larger embellishments always reflect the content and emotions of a piece? If an ignorant keyboard player not gifted with judgement of feeling plunges fortuitously into an Adagio with embellishments better suited to an Allegro, will this embellishment be natural? The ear of a connoisseur will badly miss the performer's skill in such a case.'

Weitzler's reply (p. 357) was dignified. He had not wanted to overthrow the rules for good embellishment; but there are some kinds which cannot be satisfactorily written out in notes, because they should be spontaneous. A good teacher will play them in the right places, and a good pupil unconsciously pick them up; they sound fresher and express the personality of the performer better if they are his own invention. And so on at considerable length. His arguments were undoubtedly of a kind which many, perhaps most of his contemporaries would still have endorsed; even his immediate opponent in this wordy duel, Marpurg, shared with him the fundamental assumption that decorative embellishment was required and that much of it was best supplied by the performer—provided it was not done 'fortuitously'!

(119) F. W. Marpurg, *Anleitung*, Berlin, 1755, 2nd ed. 1765, I, 9, p. 36:

'It has been found that it is not enough to play off a number of pre-scribed notes according to their succession and time-values. It has been found necessary to render this succession agreeable to the ear, and to rid the composition of any roughness still adhering to it. From this have originated the performer's embellishments . . .'

(120) Dr. Charles Burney, *A General History of Music*, London, 1776, ed. of 1935, London, II, 443:

'Purcell, who composed for ignorant and clumsy performers[!] was obliged to write down all the fashionable graces and embellishments of the times, on which accounts, his Music soon became obsolete and old fashioned; whereas the plainness and simplicity of Corelli have given longevity to his works, which can always be modernised by a judicious performer, with very few changes or embellishments.'

(121) Dr. Burney, in Rees' *Cyclopaedia*, London, 1819, *s.v.* 'Adagio':

'An adagio in a song or solo is, generally, little more than an outline left to the performers abilities to colour . . . if not highly embellished, [slow notes] soon excite languor and disgust in the hearers.'

4. ALL ORNAMENTAL FIGURATION TO BE TAKEN LIGHTLY

When Scheibe, at (112) above, criticised J. S. Bach for writing out so much of the ornamental figuration which almost any other composer of the time would have left to be supplied more or less impromptu by the performer, he had in mind that a performer who sees only the main notes (chiefly the harmony notes) of the melody written down tends to give these main notes their natural weight and to festoon his own ornamental figuration in between with the requisite lightness and elegance. This makes everything clear and in proper balance. But if the ornamental figuration has been fully written out by the composer, it all looks equally important to the eye, and the performer tends to play or sing the ornamental notes as emphatically as the structural notes. He weights them too regularly and measures them too literally. The melody is indeed obscured, as Scheibe wrote, and the effect is very ponderous and unsatisfactory. *Cf.* also (108) above.

Bach's departure from baroque custom has the advantage of enabling us to learn from the Courante *avec deux Doubles* (First English Suite) or the Sarabands with *Les Agrémens de la même Sarabande* (Second and Third English Suites) how he varied his own figuration; from his Vivaldi transcriptions, how he varied another composer's figuration;

from the slow movements of his Violin Sonatas, how we should embellish such baroque slow movements when they survive only in the customary bare outlines. Handel's second slow movement to his A major Violin Sonata, which he altogether exceptionally wrote out in full, has quite the sound of a Bach slow movement, and it is obvious that this style was far more general than we used to suppose, though it was not generally committed to writing. But it is also necessary to realise that being essentially of the nature of improvisation, it must be made to sound impromptu even where it is in fact prepared beforehand by the composer, the performer, the editor, or a combination of these. How much of it is written, memorised or improvised is not important, provided that it has a genuine spontaneity in performance. As so often in baroque music, it is the freshness and incisiveness of the effect which really matters. Heaviness is the real danger; and this applies not only to ornamental figuration in slow movements, where it was so often left to the performer, but also in quick movements, where it was normally written out in adequate quantity, and impromptu variations, though usual, were in no way obligatory.

(122) James Grassineau, *A Musical Dictionary*, London, 1740, *s.v.* 'Fioretti':

'Canto Fioretti, is a song full of diminutions, graces, passages, *etc.*, and is indeed figurate counterpoint.'

(123) Jean-Jacques Rousseau, *Dictionnaire de Musique*, Paris, 1768, *s.v.* 'Passage':

'[Passage-work is music] composed of many notes or divisions which are sung or played very lightly.'

I can hardly emphasise enough the importance of those last two words.

5. EFFECT OF OMITTING OBLIGATORY ORNAMENTATION

The disastrous effect on a slow movement by Corelli, Vivaldi, Handel, in some cases Purcell, *etc.*, of failing to supply any ornamental figuration where only the bare framework has been provided by the composer in writing may be measured by reducing a familiar movement of 1801 to the notation in which it might have survived had it been composed half a century earlier (solution at the end of this chapter).

Ex. 20.:

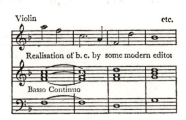

159

6. SOME EARLY TERMS FOR EMBELLISHMENT

'Ornamentation' can conveniently be kept for the longer, free embellishments, and 'ornaments' for the shorter, specific embellishments such as trill, appoggiatura, *etc.* They were not clearly distinguished at the time, but List A below *tends* to imply ornamentation, and List B ornaments.

TABLE IV
Terms for Embellishment

	List A	List B
English:	diminution	graces
	division	ornaments
	embellishment	
	flourish	
	ornamentation	
	variation	
Latin:	diminutio	lepores
	minuritio	
Italian:	coloratura	abbellimenti
	fioretti	effetti
	fioritura	
	gorgia	
	passaggio	
	vaghezzi	
Spanish:	diferencia	
	glosa	
French:	broderie	agrémens *or*
	diminution	agréments (du chant, de
	fredon	musique)
	passage	
	roullemens	
German:	Koloratur	Manieren
	Setzmanieren	Verzierungen

7. SOLUTION OF EX. 20

Ex. 21. Beethoven: Spring Sonata, Op. 24, *Movt.* I, as actually notated:

CHAPTER VIII

Sixteenth-Century Ornamentation

1. SIXTEENTH-CENTURY ORNAMENTATION A MELODIC ART

The sixteenth-century art of ornamentation, which was inherited from a much older tradition, was used on a variety of material. This included many kinds of *canto fermo* (plainchant, chorales and other hymns, popular melodies, *etc.*); ground-basses (traditional or taken from existing bass-parts or specially composed); and complete polyphonic works (mainly motets, chansons and madrigals) of which each part in turn, or even several together, might be involved in the ornamentation.

Each of these practices led incidentally towards new forms of composition, some of them of the greatest value and importance, such as the early baroque English music for harpsichord and organ (the 'virginalists') or the Lutheran German choral prelude.

The most characteristic common feature of sixteenth-century ornamentation is that it affects the melody but not the harmony, with the result that it can be, and frequently was, performed simultaneously with the original.

2. FIFTEENTH AND EARLY SIXTEENTH CENTURIES

Treatises such as Ganassi's *Fontegara* (Venice, 1535) give written instructions, with examples, on introducing more or less improvised ornamentation such as had previously been given by word of mouth.

(124) Adrianus Petit Coclico, *Compendium musices*, Nürnberg, 1552 (of his first example: N.B. the inference that Josquin approved):

Ex. 21A.

'This is the first embellishment which Josquin taught his own pupils.'

The examples are specimen runs, turns and similar small figurations filling in the intervals of notes at various intervals apart. The manner in which these figurations were combined into music can already be demonstrated for the fifteenth century. The type of Venetian song called *Justiniana* after its originator and chief exponent, Leonardo Giustiniani (*c.* 1383–1446), depended on the florid ornamentation of its upper melody in performance. W. H. Rubsamen (*Acta Musicologica*, XXIX, 4, Basel, 1957) has been able to compare one of these with a performing version as taken down from improvisation. He prints both versions complete; the opening is reproduced here by his kind permission and that of Bärenreiter-Verlag, Kassel and Basel.

Ex. 22. 15th-century ornamentation:

This is solo music, accompanied with a lute (which might be played by the singer) or viols. The ornamentation is therefore performed by itself, without the plain original.

3. THE LATER SIXTEENTH CENTURY

By the middle of the sixteenth century, we have much fuller treatises on improvisation, both in extemporising new compositions and in ornamenting existing ones.

(125) Diego Ortiz, *Trattado de Glosas sobre Clausulas*, Rome, 1553, Introduction:

'[Advice to viol players:] The first and most perfect manner consists of when one wants to pass from the passage or embellishment on any note found in the original to another succeeding note, the last note of the embellishment being the same as the note which was embellished, as these examples show.

Ex. 23:

'This is the most perfect way as the embellishment begins and ends on the same note, making the leap in the same way as the plain melody, so that it can have no imperfections [i.e. forbidden consecutives].

'The second manner is freer, since, at the moment of progressing from one note to the next, it does not move like the plain notes, but on the contrary as these examples show.'

Ex. 24–25:

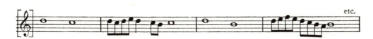

'This manner is necessary because with its freedom many pretty fancies and pleasant preluding can be made which cannot be made with the first alone; therefore I supply it in some parts of this book. It may be thought a fault that at the movement from one fourth note (*quarto punto*) to another, since it does not make the same leap as in the first manner, the other parts may form two perfect consonances [forbidden consecutives] with it; but this is unimportant since at that speed they cannot be heard.

'The third manner is: to deviate from the composition, going by ear without being certain of what you are playing. This is the habit of some who want to demonstrate whatever skill they have, but depart from the composition at the wrong time and without rhythm, landing up eventually on a cadence or on notes known to them. This is an objectionable process because it does not agree with the composition and can therefore have no perfection.

'[Part II gives three methods for a viol and a harpsichord.] First . . . I

cannot show the fantasy since everybody plays it in his own style; but
. . . on the harpsichord it should consist in well-ordered harmonies; the
viol enters with some graceful passages, and when it sustains some plain
notes, the harpsichord should answer it [with similar passages] at the
right time; you should do some fugues, the one waiting for the other in
the way in which you sing concerted [impromptu] counterpoint.

'[The second way of Part II is for the viol to improvise an embellished
version of a given plainchant; the harpsichord meanwhile playing the
original version but with a simple, mainly chordal, accompaniment
improvised above it: *i.e.* "with accompanying chords and some counterpoint fitting in with the Ricercada which the viol is playing". The same
is also given for two viols alone without harpsichord accompaniment,
when "the counterpoint will remain as perfect as if it had been written
for one part alone" in addition to the plainchant.]

'[The third is to:] Take a Madrigal or a Motet or any other piece and
adapt it to the harpsichord in the usual way; the viol player can now play
two, three or more variations over each given piece. When the soprano
part is the one which is being embellished it is more pleasing when the
harpsichord player does not play the soprano [*i.e.* its plain version at the
same time as the embellished version, though otherwise Ortiz treats it as
standard to sound the plain part and the embellished part at the same
time]. . . .

'He who uses this [third] manner should note that it is different from
what we treat in the first book, namely to play together on four or five
viols; there, it is necessary for good effect to suit the counterpoint [*i.e.* the
embellishment] to the part [*i.e.* the particular line of the original polyphonic composition] being played, holding on firmly to it . . . but in
this manner here, it is not necessary to follow one and the same part; for
though the bass must be the main argument, yet the player may leave it
and pass over into the tenor, alto or treble as he pleases, taking the most
suitable of each part. The reason is that the harpsichord plays the work
completely in all its parts; the viol accompanies and gives grace to what
the harpsichord plays, the changing sound of the strings giving pleasure
to the listener.'

The many beautiful examples of this style which follow are accessible
in the modern reprint, for which see my Bibliography.

(126) Hermann Finck, *Practica Musica*, Wittenberg, 1556, Lib. V,
[p. 8]:

'[Advice to singers:] Truly in my opinion embellishments both can and
ought to be scattered through all the voices [parts], but not all the time,
and indeed in appropriate places, and not simultaneously in all voices, but
let them be embellished in a fitting situation, remaining in their own
places, so that one embellishment can be heard and picked out expressly
and distinctly from another, yet with the composition whole and
unharmed.'

(127) Lodovico Zacconi, *Prattica di Musica*, Venice, 1592, LXVI, p. 58:

'Nimble minds are continually discovering new embellishments . . . even to works previously embellished . . . like so many well-trained birds . . .

'[Must be taught by ear] because it is not possible to give in an example the exact measure for performing them . . . it must be done to perfection, or left alone . . .

'Perfection and beauty lie in the measure and tempo . . . this is the greatest difficulty in ornamentation, requiring more care and study than the ambition to make long strings of figures together. Indeed, the singer who with a little ornamentation in good time goes not too far afield will always be better appreciated than another who digresses far too much, whether in good time or not . . .

'At the start of a [polyphonic] vocal composition, where the other voices are silent, you should not begin with an embellishment, nor immediately after the start . . . the beauty of an embellishment arises from the enchanting and graceful movement of the parts when one of them moves faster [than the other: *i.e.* from their mutual contrast]. Thus opening passages unless they are in [homophonic] part-writing should always be set forth simply and clearly so that the entry of each part may be the better heard.

'[Moreover, until you know what the other singers are keeping in reserve, you should go cautiously] and then gradually unfold your own ornamentation [yet do not] save up everything for the end, having left the middle dry and empty.

'[Crochets are too short to be generally suitable for ornamentation. Minims may be treated more freely, and still more semibreves and breves] but care should invariably be taken not to obscure the words.'

4. ORNAMENTING POLYPHONIC WORKS TODAY

The 'unaccompanied' polyphony of the sixteenth century has been such a bye-word for purity that it comes as something of a surprise to learn that it was not only quite often accompanied by instruments, but actually embellished in performance with ornamental figuration, even when sung unaccompanied. This does not mean that unaccompanied and unornamented Josquin or Palestrina is unhistoric: on the contrary, all these methods of performance are authentic, and the choice rests with the performers.

Where there are more performers than one to a part, either there was careful rehearsal to secure harmonious results, or the ornamentation was left to soloists with the others holding the plain original. A high degree of passing dissonance and a certain degree of 'incorrect' progression was tolerated, because disguised by the speed at which the ornamentation proceeded. It was for the ear to decide how much. We must remember that the finest choirs were in very regular practice indeed, and that they were schooled to the last subtleties of disciplined musicianship.

In modern performance, it would be difficult to recover the art of improvising this kind of ornamentation, even where the choir itself approaches sixteenth-century standards, because the training in extemporising counterpoint at sight which was normal at the time, and from which the immense facility required for such improvisation was derived, is no longer given. It would be possible for a modern musician to acquire it from treatises such as Morley's *Plaine and Easie Introduction* (London, 1597); but without doing that, he may wish to make some experiments in writing out ornamentations and performing them. He should then work from the models of sixteenth and early seventeenth century polyphonic ornamentation which survive. See also Appendix III.

Two shorter illustrations may be given here. The first shows a selection of the figures suggested by Ortiz for ornamenting a given cadence. The second is a combination according to his directions of the opening of two of his full workings, one in the treble (not accompanied by the plain part) and the other in the bass (accompanied by the plain part). Viols were the medium primarily intended here; but 'brass' (cornetts, trombones), wood-wind (recorders, crumhorns) or voices (to the words of the original chanson) would have been contemporary alternatives. Readers interested in doing so can readily complete the piece from the modern reprint of Ortiz (see Bibliography).

Ex. 26. Ortiz, specimen figurations:

Ex. 27. Ortiz, ornamentation of chanson, 'O felice mei':

CHAPTER IX

Early Baroque Ornamentation

1. EARLY BAROQUE ORNAMENTATION STILL MAINLY MELODIC

Renaissance methods of ornamentation were carried into early baroque music with very little change other than the general disposition to restraint due to the expressive ideals of the new Italian monodists. The effect of the ornamentation remained essentially melodic.

It is the long appoggiatura which gives later baroque embellishment its special character. This had its source in the suspensions of sixteenth-century harmony; and its beginnings can be traced at least as far back as Ortiz. But they were very small beginnings, and they were not much bigger in early baroque music, during the first decades of the seventeenth century. They were not yet big enough to produce essential changes in the harmony.

On the other hand, there was no intention in the new monody, at any rate, of sounding the plain original simultaneously with its ornamentation. There was no harmonic obstacle to prevent it; but a monody is one actor's cry from the heart. Doubling in any form is inconceivable.

2. VOCAL ORNAMENTATION IN EARLY BAROQUE MUSIC

(a) The concerted vocal music of the Gabrieli school, with its strong element of showmanship, is particularly well suited by a thorough

Ex. 28. Caccini, *Euridice*:

Ex. 29. Monteverdi, *Orfeo*:

168

Exs. 30–31. Peri, 'Funeste piaggie':

display of normal ornamentation, as described in Ch. VIII above.

(b) The new monody of Caccini, Peri or Monteverdi calls for greater reticence. But vocal ornamentations are found written out, mainly at important closes; others may be added, as the following confirms.

(127a) Jacopo Peri, *L'Euridice*, Florence, 1600, Preface:

'. . . Vettoria [*sic*] Archilei, who has always made my compositions worthy of her singing, adorning them not only with those ornaments (*gruppi*) and those long turns of the voice (*lunghi giri di voce*), simple and double, which from the liveliness of her talent are found again at every moment, more to obey the fashion of our times than because she considers the beauty and strength of our singing to consist of them; but also [she adorns my compositions] with those pretty and graceful [things] which cannot be written, and writing them, cannot be learned from writings.'

(c) The solo songs of the English Elizabethan and Jacobean lutenist composers such as Dowland, Campion and Rosseter, and of their Caroline and Commonwealth successors, were ornamented freely in performance, and some of the ornamentations more or less improvised in them were written down in MS. copies. See Appendix III.

The imitations of Italian monody produced in fair numbers, though mostly by minor composers, towards the middle of the seventeenth century and subsequently in England can be treated like their models in regard to ornamentation.

3. INSTRUMENTAL ORNAMENTATION IN EARLY BAROQUE MUSIC

(a) The written-out instrumental parts in Monteverdi and other early baroque composers invite ornamentation of the same kind as the vocal parts, but only where they can indulge in it without getting in the way of the vocal parts. Where there are no vocal parts, the character of the music must be the guiding factor. A symphonia or ritornello in Monteverdi may often be in too direct and simple a mood to admit elaborate or indeed any ornamentation, except that the closes can carry one of the ornamentations approximating to what later became the regular baroque trill. Others can be more freely ornamented.

(b) The problem is altogether different in the case of instrumental parts not written out but needing to be supplied.

There are very numerous renaissance descriptions and pictorial representations of instrumentalists in combinations sometimes including voices and sometimes not. In the former they may be doubling the voices, with or without ornamentation; in the latter they may be borrowing and probably ornamenting a vocal polyphonic composition, they may be playing a composed canzona or ricercare, or they may be elaborating their own version of a popular song or dance. The early baroque musicians continued all these practices; but they had an added problem in providing instrumental parts for the new monodies, written out only with their thinly-figured continuo basses (*i.e. without* any polyphonic inner parts on which to elaborate), even the choice of instruments being, as usual, left to the performers.

(128) [? Alessandro Guidotti] preface to Emilio de' Cavalieri's *Rappresentatione di Anima, e di Corpo* (Rome, 1600):

'A Lyra da Gamba (Lira doppia), a Harpsichord, an Archlute (Chitarone), or Theorbo as it is called, make an excellent effect together; as also a smooth Organ [*i.e.* a small "organo da legno", not a regal with its snarling reeds] with an Archlute . . .

'Signor Emilio [Cavalieri: the composer] would recommend changing the instruments about to suit the feelings of the singer.

'[Avvertimenti:] The [written–out] Symphonies and Ritornelli may be performed with a great many instruments.

'A violin may double the upper part note for note with excellent effect . . .'

Forty different instruments are listed or mentioned by Monteverdi for his *Orfeo*; but only intermittently are their names set against an actual passage, and only in a few brief but extraordinarily suggestive passages are they given written-out parts other than for the straight-forward symphonias and ritornelli. These few passages are remarkable both for their beauty and their virtuosity, and they afford us a sudden glimpse into the tradition of virtuoso improvisation which lay behind them. The score of Monteverdi's *Combattimento di Tancredi e Clorinda* is another guide; here the virtuosity is less in evidence, but the writing for strings is highly idiomatic.

Where nothing was provided in writing, the instrumentalists partly prepared during rehearsal and partly improvised in performance the necessary material, which included fully independent melodies as well as chords to fill up the harmony. The only authorities, apparently, who tell us in any detail how (and throw light on the previous period, since there is clearly no novelty in what they are describing) are Agazzari and Praetorius, of whom the latter merely translates the former's instructions with some concurring comments of his own. But there are many indications through the seventeenth century. Doni in about 1635 and Pietro della Valle in 1640 complained of its difficulties (see Appendix IV and Epilogue).

(129) A. Agazzari, *Del sonare sopra 'l basso*, Siena, 1607, pp. 3, 6, 8, 9:

'As foundation, we have the instruments which hold together and support the whole consort of voices and instruments in the aforesaid Consort, as Organ, Harpsichord *etc.*, and, likewise, in the case of few or single Voices, Lute, Theorbo, Harp *etc.*

'As ornamentation, we have those which make playful melodies (scherzando) and counterpoints (contraponteggiando), thereby rendering the harmony more pleasant and resounding; as the Lute, Theorbo, Harp, Lirone [bass lyra or lyra da gamba] Cither, Spinet, Chitarrina [small Chitarone], Violin, Pandora, and such-like . . .

'When playing an instrument which functions as foundation, you must perform with great discretion, keeping your attention on the body of the voices; for if these are numerous, you must play full chords and draw more stops, but if they are few, you must reduce the stops and use few notes [*i.e.* in each chord], sounding the work as purely and correctly as possible, without indulging much in passage-work or florid movement (non passeggiando, ò rompendo molto); but on the contrary, sustaining the voices by sometimes reduplicating the bass in the double-bass register, and keeping out of the upper registers when the voices, especially the sopranos and the Falsettos, are employing them; at such times you must so far as possible try to keep off the same note which the Soprano sings, and avoid making florid divisions on it, so as not to reduplicate the voice part and cover the quality of that voice or the florid divisions which the good singer is making up there; whence it is desirable to play compact chords in a lower register (assai stretto, e grave) . . .

'[Of the instruments of ornamentation:] The instruments which blend in with the voices in a variety of ways, blend in with them for no other purpose, I think, than to add spice to (condire) the aforesaid consort: a harder matter, because as the foundation [instrumentalist] has to play [with mainly chordal harmony] the Bass as it stands in front of him, he does not need a great skill in counterpoint, whereas [the ornamenting instrumentalist] does need it, for he has to compose original parts, and original and diverse divisions and counterpoints upon that given bass.

'Thus whoever performs on the Lute, the noblest instrument of any, must perform nobly, with great fertility and diversity, yet not, like some who have an agile hand, making continual runs and divisions from

171

start to finish, particularly in combination with other instruments all doing the same, which leaves nothing to be heard but noise and confusion, distasteful and distressing to the hearer.

'Chords should be struck at times, with restrained reiterations; at other times, florid passages both slow and fast should be executed, besides [thematic or canonic] points of imitation at different intervals of pitch and of time (in diverse corde, e lochi), together with ornaments such as *gruppi*, *trilli* and *accenti*.

'And what we say of the Lute, as chief of instruments, we want applied to the remainder each according to its kind, since it would be too long a matter to take each individually.

'Yet since each instrument has its own limitations, the player must appreciate them and adapt himself accordingly, in order to succeed. Thus: bowed instruments have a different idiom from those sounded by a quill or by a finger. Thus he who plays on the Lirone [lira da gamba] must take long bows, clear and resonant, bringing out the middle notes [in his chords] well, and paying particular attention to the [places requiring respectively] Thirds and Sixths: an exacting business, and one which is important on this instrument.

'The violin requires fine passages, long and clear, lively sections (scherzi), little replies, and fugal imitations repeated in several places, affecting appoggiaturas (accenti), nuances of bowing (?—arcate mute), gruppi, trilli, *etc.*

'The [great bass-viol, the Italian] *Violone*, proceeds gravely, as befits its position in the lowest register, supporting the harmony of the other parts with its mellow sonority, keeping on its thick strings as far as possible, and frequently doubling the Bass at the Octave below.

'[Among foundation instruments which can also serve for ornamentation are the Theorbo, the Double Harp—"as useful in the Soprano register as in the Bass"—and the Cither and Bass Cither.] But every instrument must be used with discretion; since if the instruments are by themselves in the Consort, they must take everything on themselves and be the leaders of the Consort; if they are in combination, they must have consideration for one another, and not get in each other's way; if they are numerous, they must wait for their own good time and not be like the sparrows, all playing at once, and each trying to make the greatest noise.'

See also the Postscript on p. 179; and App. IV. The following direct confirmation of Agazzari may be noted here:

(129a) Scipione Cerreto, *Dell'arbore musicale*, Naples, 1608, p. 41:

'The good and perfect player of the cornett must have a good knowledge of the art of counterpoint, so that he can make up varied [ornamental] passages at his ease, still more extemporaneously. . . . It is equally necessary for the trumpet player to know how to make up counterpoint.'

172

CHAPTER X

Later Baroque Ornamentation

1. LATER BAROQUE ORNAMENTATION HARMONIC AS WELL AS MELODIC

In its melodic aspect, baroque ornamentation continued to develop in direct descent from renaissance ornamentation. We merely find an extension of the same little runs, changing-notes, turns and other figures of the kind. But with the emergence of genuine long appoggiaturas, a harmonic aspect arose, of which the most obvious consequence is that the ornamentation cannot any longer be accompanied by the plain original, on account of the harmonic disagreement which would result.

It is true that Christopher Simpson (*Division-Violist*, London, 1659) still gives instructions in extemporising variations on a reiterated ground-bass, with specimens of outstanding virtuosity and poetic beauty; while Friedrich Erhard Niedt (*Handleitung zur Variation*, Hamburg, 1706) applies similar methods to a thorough-bass on the keyboard. The normal variation form, on the other hand, does not reiterate the theme with the variations, even where the same harmonic progressions recur. And in the closely related art of more or less improvised ornamentation, the plain original was no longer now in any ordinary circumstances intended to support its own ornamental elaboration. It was intended to be replaced by it.

2. VOCAL ORNAMENTATION IN LATER BAROQUE MUSIC

(a) There is no true monody in late baroque music, with the possible exception of much French recitative based consciously on verbal prosody; but there is a considerable amount of declamatory song or arioso which is not quite recitative and not quite aria, and is the nearest equivalent to monody then common. Purcell's famous *Expostulation to the Blessed Virgin* is a splendid example. There is a great deal of florid ornamentation in this piece, but it is written out by the composer, and there is little if any scope for additional ornamentation from the performer. There are also arioso sections in the same piece, but here the simplicity of the style precludes florid ornamentation: their point is their contrast with the ornate declamatory sections.

In other examples of the species, the declamatory ornamentation is not always as well worked out in writing, so that there are opportunities for the performer to elaborate it in the same style on his own initiative.

(b) In simple strophic songs, or songs with straightforward repeats, the principle is to build up interest by gradually increased ornamentation. So too with songs in rondo form, and *da capo* arias.

(130) B. de Bacilly, *L'Art de Bien Chanter*, Paris, 1668, p. 224:

'Everyone agrees that the less one can make passages in the first verse, the better, because assuredly they prevent the melody being heard in its pure form [thereafter in moderation].'

(131) Francesco Tosi, *Opinioni*, Bologna, 1723, transl. Galliard, as *Observations on the Florid Song*, London, 1742, p. 93:

'The manner in which all *Airs* divided into three Parts [*da capo* arias] are to be sung. In the first they require nothing but the simplest Ornaments, of a good Taste and few, that the Composition may remain simple, plain and pure; in the second they expect, that to this Purity some artful Graces be added, by which the Judicious may hear, that the Ability of the Singer is greater; and in repeating the *Air* [*i.e.* in the "*da capo*"], he that does not vary it for the better, is no great Master.'

(132) Dr. Burney, *Hist. of Music*, London, 1776, ed. of 1935, II, p. 545:

'This triffling and monotonous rondo, in which the *motivo*, or single passage upon which it is built, is repeated so often, that nothing can prevent the hearer of taste and knowledge from fatigue and languor during the performance, but such new and ingenious embellishments as, in Italy, every singer of abilities would be expected to produce each night it was performed . . .'

Of the two main functions of embellishment, sustaining the musical interest and offering scope for the performer's virtuosity, the first is well suggested by the quotation above, and the second by the quotation below.

(133) Dr. Burney, *Hist. of Music*, London, 1776, ed. 1935, II, p. 545:

'Of [Farinelli's] execution the musical reader will be enabled to judge by a view of the most difficult [written] divisions of his bravura songs. Of his taste [in the technical sense] and embellishments we shall now be able to form but an imperfect idea, even if they had been preserved in writing, as mere notes would only show his invention, and science, without enabling us to discover that expression and neatness which rendered his execution so perfect and surprising. Of his shake, great use seems to have been made in the melodies and divisions assigned [ascribed] to him; and his taste and fancy in varying passages were thought by his contemporaries inexhaustible.'

Ex. 32. Farinelli: bravura ornamentation of the opening of *Quell'* *usignolo* from Giacamelli's *Merope*, Venice, 1734, as shown in Vienna, Österreichische Nationalbibliothek, Cod. 19111, f. 7 v-r (this, it may be added, is a very mild, brief and unelaborate cadenza on Farinelli's standards—there are much more formidable ones later in this song):

3. INSTRUMENTAL ORNAMENTATION IN LATER BAROQUE MUSIC

(a) Slow movements (often referred to as 'the adagio' whether actually so marked or otherwise) require ornamentation mainly for enrichment and diversification; quick movements ('the allegro'), if at all, mainly for additional virtuosity.

(134) Joachim Quantz, *Essay*, Berlin, 1752, partial Engl. transl. as *Instructions . . . how to introduce Extempore Embellishments*, London, [*c.* 1790], p. 3:

'It is a principal Rule with regard to Variations [in the sense of more or less improvised ornamentation], that they must have a just reference to the plain Air . . .
'Brisk and lively Variations must not be introduced in an Air that is soft, tender and mournful . . .
'[Variations are] for no other end, than to render an Air in the Cantabile Stile more melodious, and [brilliant] Divisions in general more brilliant.
'[Variations] are only to be introduced after the simple Air has been heard first.
'[For a cumulative effect in sequences:] in the Repetition of one and the same [sequential] Passage the Variations ought to be different; which is to be observ'd [apart form the special case of sequences] as a general Rule [for the avoidance of anticlimax and the gradual building-up of the ornamentation].

[p. 19:] 'All those instructions concerning Variations are chiefly calculated for the Adagio, the most proper and convenient Stile for that purpose, where in general most room is left for Embellishments; yet there are many among the Examples above, which with equal Propriety may also be introduced in the Allegro, the proper choice, however, is entirely left to the Discretion of the Performer.

[Fr. ed., p. 119:] 'The plain melody ought in Allegro as in Adagio to be ornamented and made more pleasing by appoggiaturas, and other small essential ornaments, according to the demands of the emotion found there.

'The Allegro does not admit many arbitrary variations [in the sense of more or less improvised ornamentation, as opposed to specific ornaments], because it is most often composed of a melody and passages where there is no room for embellishments. But if it is desired to make some variations, that must only be in the repeat . . . when by the inadvertence of the composer there are too frequent repeats which might easily cause tedium; then the player is obliged to correct them by his talent. I say correct; but not disfigure.'

Ornamentation in quick movements was not, however, confined to repeats, though often best so treated. Ex. 33 shows plain and performing versions from a Corelli slow movement (grave). Ex. 34 shows the *opening* of a Corelli quick movement (gavotte).

Ex. 33. Corelli: Op. V, No. 1, (a) in first ed., (b) ornamentation from Roger's ed. of ?1715:

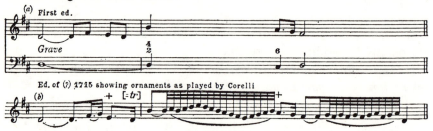

Ex. 34. Corelli: versions collated by Sol Babitz and privately communicated:

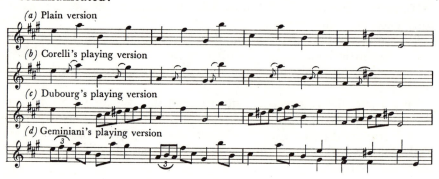

(135) C. P. E. Bach, *Essay*, Berlin, 1753, III, 31:

'Not everything should be varied, since if it is the repeat will become a new composition. There are many instances, particularly expressive or declamatory passages, which cannot well be varied. Moreover, music in the galant style is written with so many new turns and phrases that it is not often possible even to understand it at once. All variations must accord with the expressive intention of the music, and be as good as the original, if not better.'

(136) Dr. Charles Burney, *Hist. of Music*, London, 1776, ed. of 1935, II, p. 10:

'It was formerly more easy to compose than to play an *adagio*, which generally consisted of a few notes that were left to the taste and abilities of the performer; but as the composer seldom found his ideas fulfilled by the player, *adagios* are now made more *chantant* and the performer is less put to the torture for embellishments [but see (121) in Ch. VII, 3 above].'

The deeper reason was that galant music grew more *chantant* with the changing artistic climate of the second half of the eighteenth century.

(b) Of the following two quotations, the first shows the melodic treatment which was still the foundation of later baroque ornamentation. If the plain notes are sounded in their original places as here described, or if the only liberty taken is to postpone them by some other note from the same harmony, bringing in the postponed plain note immediately afterwards, it is obvious that the plain and ornamental versions will not conflict harmonically, and could in theory still be performed simultaneously, although in practice (with such possible exceptions as soloists in the *tutti* passages of *concerti grossi*) they were not.

The second quotation shows what happens when on this melodic foundation a harmonic modification is also introduced: chiefly by the use of long appoggiaturas.

(137) Joachim Quantz, *Essay*, Berlin, 1752, Eng. transl. *c.* 1790, p. 3:

'The original Notes may be heard at proper Intervals of Time, as for Instance: in varying Notes equal to the Value of a Crochet, the first Note of the Variation must for the most Part be the same with the original or plain Note, and thus one proceeds with all other Notes of equal Proportion; or any other Note may be chosen instead of it from the Harmony of the Bass, provided the Principal or plain Note be heard immediately after it.'

(138) C. P. E. Bach, *Essay*, II, Berlin, 1762, XXXII, 5:

'An intelligent soloist will [make modifications to the harmony] when he knows he has an able accompanist . . . in introducing embellishments . . . The accompanist must modify his harmony accordingly. In addition to such substitutions, the accompanist must be attentive and give way when embellishments introduced into the solo part lead to a later entrance of chords than is actually shown by the figuring.'

4. CONCERTED ORNAMENTATION IN CHAMBER AND ORCHESTRAL MUSIC

(139) Joachim Quantz, *Essay*, Berlin, 1752, XVI, 24:

'In a trio [sonata], little ornamentation must be used, and the second part must not be deprived [by excessive ornamentation in the first part] of the chance of displaying himself too on his side. The ornamentation ought to be such, that it not only suits the subject, but can also be imitated by the second part. It should only be used in passages which consist in imitations, whether at the fifth above, or at the fourth below, or at the same pitch. If the two parts have the same melody one against the other, in sixth or in thirds; nothing should be added, unless it has been agreed beforehand to make the same variations.

[25:] 'If in a trio one of the parts starts to make a variation, the other must make it in the same manner; and where the latter is in a position to add something further which is suitable and pleasing, it can do so. However, it must do it at the end of the variation, so as to show that it is capable of imitating simply, as well as of varying further. It is easier to make a variation in the first place than to imitate it in the second.

[26:] '[In a quartet] there is still less liberty than in a trio to add arbitrary variations.

[27:] 'There is more freedom in a concerto with regard to ornamentation than in a trio, especially in the Adagio; nevertheless attention must be paid to whether the accompanying parts make tuneful progressions, or whether they are only the plain harmony. In the first case, the melody [of the soloist] must be played quite plainly; but in the second all kinds of ornamentation can be made; provided the rules of harmony, taste and reason are not violated.'

5. NATIONAL DIFFERENCES IN EMBELLISHMENT

While we have every reason to believe that all the baroque national schools included a tradition of free embellishment, they did not cultivate it in the same degree or altogether in the same form.

(140) Joachim Quantz, *Essay*, Berlin, 1752, X, 13:

'[For learning to play "with a sustained melody"] the French pieces, or those composed in this style, are more advantageous than the Italian. For the pieces in the French style are mostly pieces characterized and composed with appoggiaturas and trills, in such a way that hardly anything can be added to what the Composer has written; whereas in Music composed in the Italian style, a great deal is left to the wishes and capacity of the player. In this respect the performance of French music, as written in its simple melody complete with its ornaments except for the free embellishments, is more servile and more difficult than that of the Italian Music, as it is written today. However, because for the performance of French Music there is no need to know Thorough Bass, nor to understand the art of Composition; whereas on the contrary these skills are essential for Italian Music; and this because of certain passages which are written in a very plain and dry way, to leave the performer the freedom to vary them more than once, according to his capacity and judgement, so as continually to surprise the hearers by new inventions; for these reasons the Pupil ought to be advised, not on any account to undertake to play solos in the Italian style before it is time, and before having acquired certain skills in harmony.'

6. GENERAL ADVICE

(141) Engl. translator's *f.n.*, London, 1742, p. 159 to Tosi's *Opinioni*, Bologna, 1723, IX, sect. 48:

'Many Graces may be good and proper for a Violin, that would be very improper for a Hautboy [*etc.*; likewise it is wrong] for the Voice, (which should serve as a Standard to be imitated by Instruments,) to copy all the Tricks practised on the several Instruments.

(142) P. F. Tosi, *Opinioni*, Bologna, 1723, Engl. transl. London, 1742, p. 93:

'The finest Graces [are] confin'd to the most exact Time of the Movement of the Bass.
'[13:] Seek for what is easy and natural.'

(143) Joachim Quantz, *Essay*, Berlin, 1752, XI, 6:

'[It is mere bad taste] to load the Adagio with a quantity of ornamentation, and to disguise it in such a way that often among ten notes there is scarcely one which is in harmony with the fundamental part, and the principal melody of the piece can hardly be heard any longer.'

POSTSCRIPT TO SECOND EDITION

The following passages were written fairly early in the seventeenth century, but have a general bearing on baroque practice as a whole. The distinction between those performers with a bent for ornamentation, and those without much, if any, bent for ornamentation, is suggestive. The basic assumption was that ornamentation was ordinarily needed. If the performer was willing and able to produce his own, so much the better; if not, someone would have to provide it for him—even if it had to be the composer himself! Nowadays, it will normally have to be the editor. But this emphasises once more how necessary it is that a modern editor *should* provide sample ornamentation where needed, except in the somewhat rare instances in which the composer has already performed that service for us.

(144) Bartolomeo Barbarino, *Il secondo libro delli motetti . . . da cantarsi à una voce sola . . .* , Venice, 1614, Preface:

'Because I have heard from many people that in my first book of motets . . . some of them are difficult to sing for those who do not have the bent to add ornamental passages (*passaggiare*). Therefore, in this second [book] I wanted to write the vocal part in two ways, simple and ornamented (*passaggiata*). The simple for those who do not have the bent, and for those who have [a knowledge of] counterpoint and the bent, who will be able by themselves to make up ornamental passages and the other refinements required for the good manner of singing. The ornamented, then, for those who, having the bent, do not have counterpoint to be able to make up diminutions, as properly one must.'

(144a) Enrico Radesca, *Il quinto libro delle canzonette, madrigali et arie, a tre, a una, et a due voci*, Venice, 1617, Preface:

'[These compositions] are not given ornamental passages, in order that those who by nature are not endowed with the bent may not at all be deprived of the work; all the more in that it is clearly seen that, however skilful the singer may be, he will never extemporaneously perform that ornamental passage exactly as it is written down. . . . So those who do not have the bent may sing them as they are notated, for which I am sure they will not be ungrateful; and those who do have it [the bent] will be able to add the ornamental passages to their taste, according to their views.'

(144b) Giovanni Battista Doni, 'Trattato della musica scenica' [ca. 1635], in his *Trattati di musica*, ed. A. F. Gori, Florence, 1763, II, 69:

'Nevertheless, if they [ornaments of all kinds] can be allowed in any place, this would seem truly to be (contrary to common opinion) in theatres, where all sorts of people come together, and the ignorant always in greater number than the intelligent; they [ornaments] are better adapted to theatrical music than to any other kind. . . . In chambers, similarly, where somewhat delicate music is accustomed to be sung, and in gatherings of people who understand music, they [ornaments] are not required to be used abundantly, but more sparingly.' [For fuller quotation see App. IX.]

CHAPTER XI

Post-Baroque Ornamentation

1. THE DECLINING IMPORTANCE OF FREE ORNAMENTATION

Free ornamentation began to lose its status as a primary element of interpretation during the second half of the eighteenth century. Its decline was one symptom of a profoundly changing attitude, of which another symptom was the decline of more or less improvised accompaniment on a figured bass. There can be no doubt of the growing desire of that age to have the figuration of the composition decided beforehand by the composer.

Mozart, Beethoven and even Chopin still varied their ornamental figuration (particularly of their slow movements) in performance. Liszt's variations on the music of other composers, above all of Chopin, were legendary, but are perhaps across the narrow boundary between ornamentation and transcription. The art of public improvisation was a very flourishing one throughout the nineteenth century, but closely allied though it is to the art of freely ornamenting existing music in the ordinary course of performance, it is not the same. As a problem of normal interpretation, free ornamentation ceases to be of importance to us in music of the classical Viennese school. There is scope for it in Mozart's operas, but its absence will not leave the music incomplete as baroque opera is left incomplete without it. There is scope for it in almost all Italian opera in the grand tradition, and here an enterprising modern singer might well make some successful experiments. But from Haydn and Mozart onwards, if no attempt at all is made to vary the notated text beyond the indispensable specific ornaments (chiefly appoggiaturas and cadential trills), our interpretation will in no way be vitiated. The case is far otherwise with earlier music.

(145) C. P. E. Bach, *Sonatas with Varied Repeats*, Berlin, 1760:

'Nowadays varied repeats are essential, being taken for granted from every performer. . . . Often it is nothing but the variations, particularly when joined to prolonged and over-curiously ornamented cadenzas, which arouse the loudest applause from the audience. And what abuses of these two resources occur! . . . Yet in spite of the difficulties and abuses, there is always a value in good variation.'

(146) John Hoyle, *Complete Dictionary of Music*, London, 1770, ed. of 1791:

[*s.v.* 'Adagio':] 'It is a prevailing custom amongst many performers, when they come to an Adagio (as it is slow and consequently easy), to throw out favourite passages, which entirely destroy the true harmony and intention of the composer.

'COLORATURA, denotes all manner [*i.e.* not necessarily improvised] of Variations, Trillos, Diminutions, *etc.*, serving to make the Music agreeable.

[*s.v.* 'Expression':] 'What is commonly called good taste in playing or singing, has been thought, for some years past, to destroy the true Melody, and the intention of the composer. It is supposed by many, that a real good taste cannot be acquired by any rules of art; it being a peculiar gift of nature, indulged only to those who have naturally a good ear; and as most flatter themselves to have this perfection, hence it happens that he, who sings or plays, thinks of nothing so much as to make continually some favourite passages; but in expressing with strength and delicacy the intention of the composer, should his thoughts be most taken up with. [This article is repeated *s.v.* 'Taste.']

(147) Thomas Busby, *Complete Dictionary of Music*, London [1786], *s.v.* 'Flourish':

'An appellation sometimes given to the decorative notes which a singer or instrumental performer adds to a passage [he wants caution but takes the practice for granted].'

(148) A. E. Müller, *Fortepiano-Schule*, ed. Czerny, Leipzig, 1825:

[Advice to pianists:] 'Arbitrary embellishments are those of which the performance is left more to the feeling and taste of the performers. . . . To bring them in impromptu is only allowed to those who understand composition and have already been trained to this art.'

(149) Louis Spohr, *Violin School*, Vienna, 1832, Ch. XXIV:

[Advice to string quartets:] 'In passages, *decidedly solo*, the usual embellishments may be allowed. [cf. Scholes' statement, *Oxford Companion to Music*, *s.v.* "Fioritura", that the violinist David elaborated the recapitulations of Haydn's string quartets when leading them.]

[Ch. XXV] 'Further rules for Orchestra playing are: to avoid every addition of turns, doubleturns, shakes, *etc.* . . . . in short, every embellishment properly belonging to the Solo.'

(150) Nicola Vaccai, *Metodo Pratico per il Canto Italiano*, Florence, *c.* 1840, Lesson IX:

[Advice to singers:] 'All the ornaments or so-called embellishments which singers are so apt to add to the original melody and accent, are out of place and bad.'

(151) Manuel Garcia, *Traité . . . du chant*, Paris, 1840, Ch. III, p. 56, of Engl. ed. of 1911:

[Advice to singers:] 'When there is no accent to give colour to melody, recourse is had to embellishments (or *fioriture*). This is the case with almost all Italian music prior to the present [*i.e.* the nineteenth] century; for authors formerly, in sketching out their ideas, reckoned on the talent of a singer to add at pleasure, accent and ornamental accessories. [But many of Garcia's musical examples of additional embellishment are applied to nineteenth century composers: Rossini, Bellini, *etc.*] There are different kinds of pieces, too, which, from their very nature, must be entrusted to the free and skilful inspiration of their executants—as, for instance, variations, rondos, polaccas, *etc.*'

(152) Henry F. Chorley, *Thirty Years' Musical Recollections*, London, 1862, ed. E. Newman, New York and London, 1926, p. 195:

[Of Jenny Lind:] 'Her shake (a grace ridiculously despised of late) was true and brilliant—her taste in ornament was altogether original.'

Chorley was music critic of *The Athaeneum* for some forty years till his death in 1872. The concert reviews, notices of singers and so on in this, the *Quarterly Magazine of Music* and other nineteenth century periodicals often refer to the improvisatory embellishments used by singers, and to a lesser extent by instrumentalists.

(153) *The Athaeneum*, London, obituary of the violinist, W. Ernst, d. 1865:

'He was not above the virtuoso habit of introducing his own embellishments into the works of the great masters.'

(154) F. de Courcy, *Art of Singing*, London, *c.* 1868, p. 93:

[Advice to singers:] 'Embellishments . . . are used to give a finish to a song; if not found in the music, they should be introduced very cautiously and sparingly. . . . In Bravura airs alone should the voice be allowed freely to use embellishments. [But throughout the book the practice is taken entirely for granted.] . . . They depend upon tone, accent, and velocity, and their being executed rather sotto voce, and with exquisite precision; for though highly elaborated embellishments may surprise the ear, yet they never affect the heart.

[p. 95:] 'In encores . . . change the embellishments, for an artist must be barren of invention, indeed, or possess a very poor memory not to be ready with a second equally excellent set of graces, *etc.*'

(154a) Stewart Deas, *Music and Letters*, London, Jan. 1953, p. 8:

'[On Corelli—in apparent unawareness of the incompleteness of his slow movements if left unembellished; though the article as a whole is very good:] Oddly unconvincing, on the other hand, are most of the Sarabands. . . .'

(154b) Dyneley Hussey, *Musical Times*, London, May 1958, p. 259:

'A great singer [Zinka Milanov] even if not always note-accurate so that some of her phrases do not correspond with the text.'

CHAPTER XII

The Cadenza

1. THE TYPICAL BAROQUE CADENZA AN ELABORATION OF A CLOSE

A cadenza is an extension of the embellishment outside the time of the movement. It occurs at a point where the remaining parts can reasonably wait (except in the case of accompanied cadenzas, which are written out, and are not in the strictest sense cadenzas at all). Since it usually occurs at or towards the end of a movement or section, it can be regarded as a special case of the familiar principle of saving up the most striking embellishment for the concluding passage.

We find incipient cadenzas written out on or around the dominant penultimate note of closes in Caccini, Monteverdi and others of their school; and similar passages were freely improvised. This remained a favourite position, both for voices and for instruments.

(155) P. F. Tosi, *Opinioni*, 1723, tr. Galliard as *Observations on the Florid Song*, 1742, p. 128 (with irony):

'Every *Air* [da capo aria] has (at least) three *Cadences*, that are all three final. Generally speaking, the Study of the Singers of the present Times consists in terminating the *Cadence* of the first Part with an overflowing of *Passages* and *Divisions* at Pleasure, and the *Orchestre* waits; in that of the second the Dose is encreased, and the *Orchestre* grows tired; but on the last *Cadence*, the Throat is set a going, like a Weather-cock in a Whirlwind, and the *Orchestre* yawns.'

(156) F. W. Marpurg, *Beyträge*, Berlin, 1754, p. 15:

'. . . but before she dies, she gathers all her strength in a cadenza, by means of which her heart recovers from its faintness, thus enabling her to repeat to her lover, in the *Da Capo* recapitulation, the first forebodings of her just fears.'

(157) Joachim Quantz, *Essay*, Berlin, 1752, partial Engl. transl. as *Instructions, etc.*, c. 1790, p. 22:

'The Cadences [cadenzas] to be treated of in this place are properly those Embellishments commonly introduced at the End of a Solo Part or Air on the last Note but one, mostly on the Fifth of the Key, and are the productions of the momentary Invention of the Performer.'

(158) C. P. E. Bach, *Essay*, Berlin, 1753, II, ix, 2 *ff.*:

'[Of Pauses (fermate):] Their sign is a slur with a dot under it [⌒], which means that a note is to be held as long as required by the character of the music. [3:] A note without the sign may sometimes be held for reasons of expression . . . [Pauses are used] on the penultimate note, the last note, or the rest after the last [bass] note. In correct usage the sign ought to be marked at the beginning and again at the end of an ornamented pause [cadenza]. [4:] Pauses over rests occur most often in allegro movements and are not ornamented. The other two kinds are usually found in slow, expressive movements and must be ornamented if only so as to avoid artlessness. In any case, [*i.e.* even in the absence of a sign] elaborate ornamentation is more needed here than in other portions of movements.'

2. THE LATER CADENZA PART OF THE STRUCTURE OF THE MOVEMENT

In the Turin MSS. of Vivaldi's violin concertos we find some lengthy cadenzas written out, which are not in the printed editions (either because Vivaldi wished to keep them for himself, or because he did not trust violinists other than his own pupils to meet their formidable difficulties—including exceedingly high passage-work).

These violin cadenzas are normally not at the close, but in or before the last recapitulation of the thematic material. Coming in such a position they contribute strikingly not only to the brilliance but to the structure of the movement, especially in their occasional use of thematic reminiscences.

For wind soloists Vivaldi wrote simpler cadenzas, within the traditional stipulation that they shall be able to be taken in a single breath —for which see (159) and (160) in 4 below.

This position within the final recapitulation became standard for the classical period, when the structural function of the cadenza became still more developed.

3. ENTIRE MOVEMENTS REPLACED BY CADENZA-LIKE IMPROVISATION

Exceptional examples occur (*e.g.* Bach's third Brandenburg concerto, Handel's organ concertos) where with the least hint from the written music (in the third Brandenburg, a pair of chords forming a half-close) the leader or soloist was required to improvise an entire movement, or the solo portions of one. This sets a problem for editor, conductor or performer which cannot be evaded; for the effect, for example, of playing the two Brandenburg chords *molto espressivo* instead of elaborating them at least to some reasonable duration is quite inadequate. A suitable movement, however short, must be supplied.

4. THE STYLE OF BAROQUE CADENZAS

The following is a brief instrumental example (for a vocal example see Ex. 32 in Ch. X, 2, above).

Ex. 35. J.-B. Loeillet, Sonata F major for flute, violin or oboe, Largo, last bars, brief written out cadenza (ed. Hinnenthal, Berlin, 1945):

The performance of such a passage as the above requires all the incisive lightness usual in this style of free ornamentation. A baroque cadenza, whether vocal or instrumental, should always sound as if improvised, whether it is so in fact or not. It is there not to add weight to the music, but a last touch of exhilaration.

(159) Joachim Quantz, *Essay*, Berlin, 1752, partial Engl. transl. as *Instructions, etc.*, c. 1790, p. 25:

'Regular Time is seldom to be observ'd in Cadences. . . . Those for Voice or Wind Instruments ought to be short and so managed that they may be perform'd in one Breath, but those for String Instruments are not limited, but the Performer has as much Latitude given him, as his own Skill and fruitfulness of Invention will permit, but notwithstanding will gain more Applause from the Judicious by a moderate length than otherwise.

[Fr. ed. p. 162:] 'If it is easy to invent cadences in two parts and write them down; it is nevertheless very hard to make them on the spot without having agreed beforehand. However if the advantages offered by imitation and the practice of dissonance are familiar, these difficulties can be overcome.'

(160) Dr. Burney, *Music in Germany*, London, 1773, II, p. 153:

'The cadences which his majesty [Frederick of Prussia, Quantz's employer] made, were good, but very long and studied. It is easy to discover that these concertos were composed at a time when he did not so frequently require an opportunity of breathing as at present; for in some of the divisions, which were very long and difficult, as well as in the closes [cadenzas], he was obliged to take his breath, contrary to rule, before the passages were finished.

[p. 233:] 'if any of his Italian troops dare to deviate from strict discipline, by adding, altering or diminishing a single passage in the parts they have to perform, an order is sent, *de par le Roi*, for them to adhere strictly to the notes written by the composer, at their peril. This, when compositions are good, and a singer is licentious, may be an excellent method; but certainly shuts out all taste and refinement.'

(161) William Jackson, *Observations on the Present State of Music in London*, London, 1791, pp. 20–23:

'The Performer, no doubt, ought to be able to run from the bottom to the top of the keys in semitones; but let him be satisfied with having the power, without exerting it. . . . Cadences with, for ever, a concluding shake [trill]—though sometimes it seems as if it would *never* conclude. . .'

(162) Dr. Burney, *Commemoration of Handel*, London, 1785:

'One night, while Handel was [at the harpsichord] in Dublin, Dubourg having a solo [violin] part in a song, and a close to make *ad libitum*, he wandered about in different keys a great while, and seemed indeed a little bewildered, and uncertain of his original key; but at length, coming to the shake [trill] which was to terminate this long close, Handel, to the great delight of the audience, and augmentation of the applause, cried out, loud enough to be heard in the most remote parts of the theatre, "You are welcome home, Mr. Dubourg".'

Gerhardt Krapf kindly showed me how many places he finds in baroque organ music (including that of J. S. Bach) where brief connecting passages or actual short cadenzas are habitually supplied by him in performance with excellent effect. He is also in the habit, where a chorale melody begins with notated ornamentation but is continued in plain notation, of supplying suitable ornamentation to prevent the unintended anti-climax which otherwise results.

CHAPTER XIII

Ornaments

1. THE PROLIFERATION OF ORNAMENTS IN BAROQUE MUSIC

An ornament is a short melodic formula which has formed in the tradition of free ornamentation as a crystal forms in a saturated solution.

Oriental music is full of ornaments. They were common in medieval music, where signs for them existed. They are not very conspicuous in renaissance music, though several sixteenth century treatises describe a few rather fluctuating ones, not sharply defined. They reached a peak in baroque music, when an immense vocabulary of signs developed. These signs, the names attached to them and the interpretation allotted to them all show *an extreme inconsistency*, and the reader is warned that the same sign or the same name may have many different meanings in different sources, indeed often in the same source. Much of this inconsistency cancels itself out, however, and it is not impossible to trace certain principles fundamental enough to give the musician what he chiefly needs: a clear account of the standard practices underlying the countless variations of detail.

These standard practices are adequate to ninety-nine situations out of a hundred. In the hundredth situation, the ordinary rules may make intolerably bad grammar or excessive harshness, and we have to reach the best compromise we can. In certain styles a knowledge of some of the more exotic ornaments is necessary. But in most baroque music it is the few plain and relatively straightforward ornaments, not the many complicated variants, which are needed and ordinarily suffice.

2. SOME WORKING RULES FOR BAROQUE ORNAMENTS

(a) *There are obligatory and optional ornaments.*

(163) Jean Rousseau, *Traité de la viole*, Paris, 1687, p. 72:

'You must practice all the ornaments in all their fullness, especially the prepared trill and the appoggiatura.'

The cadential trill, with its preparation (accented upper-note start), and the (long) appoggiatura are the only baroque ornaments of which it would be true to say that in normal contexts they are obligatory, as is seen in Ch. XX and Ch. XIV below. Hotteterre's list (*Principes de la Flute*, 1707, p. 21) of 'ornaments which are absolutely necessary to the perfecting of the performance' also includes these two, among others whose necessity is in fact less unconditional.

(164) F. W. Marpurg, (a) *Historisch-kritische Beyträge*, Berlin, 1756, III, 2 and (b) *Anleitung*, 2nd ed., Berlin, 1765, I, ix, 3, p. 44:

[a:] 'Regarding the smaller ornaments, they are so essential at most places that without their strict observance no composition can please the more refined ears.

[b:] But where does one learn what notes are given ornaments or at which point of the melody this or that ornament ought to be introduced? One should hear persons who are reputed to play elegantly, and one should hear them in pieces one already knows. In this way one may form one's taste, and do likewise. For it is impossible to devise rules to meet all possible cases, so long as music remains an inexhaustible ocean of options, and one man differs from the next in his appreciation. One should try to give a piece of music in which ornaments have not yet been marked to ten different people, each playing in the good style of the day, and ask them for their ornaments. In certain cases, perhaps, many will agree; in the rest, they will all be different.'

(b) *The absence of a sign does not preclude an ornament.*

If the context implies an obligatory ornament, the mere absence of a sign does not absolve the performer from the necessity of introducing it. Indeed, the very fact that the ornament is obligatory made its presence so obvious that the sign is more likely to be absent.

If the context suggests an optional ornament, the mere absence of a sign is no reason for not introducing it. A baroque performer did not wait to be told when he could put in an ornament. See the previous quotation (164b).

(c) *The presence of a sign does not enforce an ornament.*

The corollary of the above is that if a sign is present but the performer does not wish to put in an ornament, he is not compelled to do so unless the ornament in question is in any case an obligatory one. This also is implied in (164b).

If, however, he does wish to put in an ornament, and the sign is specific, he is still not compelled to put in that particular ornament, although he will normally give it preferential consideration.

It may also happen that the sign is not specific. It is most probable that the single and double strokes used by the English virginalists from the turn of the sixteenth and seventeenth centuries were not specific, or at any rate not wholly so. The common + and × of the main baroque period were certainly not very specific. The + is used in the violin part of Mondonville's Op. III, of which the harpsichord part carries more differentiated signs, the significant instruction being added: 'ornament like the harpsichord'. The inference is that a violinist, even in France, would not have understood the more differentiated signs, which were, in fact, mainly developed by harpsichordists.

The best general approach to the baroque signs for ornaments is to treat them not as commands but as hints.

(d) *But certain schools require a stricter treatment of the ornaments.*

(165) Fr. Couperin, *Pièces*, Liv. III, Paris, 1722, preface:

'I am always surprised (after the pains I gave myself to mark the ornaments which suit my Pieces, of which I have given, incidentally, a clear enough explanation in my special Treatise, known under the title of The Art of playing the Harpsichord) to hear of people who treat them without respecting them. This is an unpardonable neglect, in view of the fact that it is not at all an optional matter to take such ornaments as one wishes. I declare then that my pieces must be performed as I have marked them, and that they will make a certain impression on people of good taste only if everything which I have marked is observed to the letter, without addition or subtraction.'

Yet Couperin himself marked, for example, his first (string) version of 'Les Pellerines' only with a few crosses, but his second (harpsichord) version with all his customary explicitness. No doubt it was on the harpsichord that he regarded his exact ornaments as so particularly integral to the music. It is worth trying them all, even if a few are subsequently dropped. The crystalline sparkle with which they invest not only the harpsichord music but also the vocal and the chamber music of this fascinating school is so characteristic that it well rewards the initial effort. But his complaint itself shows that his signs were not necessarily followed at the time.

(166) C. P. E. Bach, *Essay*, Berlin, 1753, II, i, 4:

'In justice to the French it should be said that they mark their ornaments with scrupulous exactness. So too do the masters of the harpsichord in Germany, yet without carrying their ornaments to excess. Who can tell but that our restraint both in the quantity and in the quality of our ornaments has been the influence which caused the French to leave their earlier way of putting an ornament on almost every note, to the detriment of clarity and of noble directness?

[25:] 'Since our present taste, to which the Italian *bel canto* has contributed so much, requires other ornaments in addition to the French, I have had to draw on the ornaments of various countries. I have added some new ones to these. I believe that the best style of performance, on whatever instrument, is the one which skilfully unites the accuracy and brilliance of the French ornaments with the smoothness of Italian singing. Germans are in an excellent position to accomplish such a union . . .'

(167) F. W. Marpurg, *Beyträge*, Berlin, 1754, p. 27:

'Many of our most famous players admit that they have learnt the nicety of their execution from the French. In the notation of the ornaments with which a piece is to be played, they prove more careful than other nations. Among the Germans, next to the famous Georg Muffat [*c.* 1645–1704], it seems to have been the able harpsichordist Joh. Casp. Ferdin. Fischer [*c.* 1665–1746] who first spread this kind of music among us. He has ornamented in the French manner all his keyboard scores, *e.g.* those in the *musikalischen Blumenbüchlein* which appeared at the beginning of this century, and one sees from the explanations prefacing the pieces that these notations must have been fairly unknown then.'

(e) *Ornaments must suit their contexts.*

(168) Jean Rousseau, *Traité de la Viole*, Paris, 1687, p. 73:

'Avoid a profusion of ornamental figures, which only confuse the melody and obscure its beauty.'

(169) F. W. Marpurg, *Critische Musicus*, Berlin, 1750:

'[The Berlin School] makes restrained use of ornaments and ornamentation, but what is used is the more choice and the more beautifully and clearly performed.'

(170) Joachim Quantz, *Essay*, Berlin, 1752, VIII, 19:

'It is true that the ornaments of which we have spoken are absolutely necessary for good expression. All the same they must be used in moderation, it never being right to go to excess in what is good.'

(171) C. P. E. Bach, *Essay*, Berlin, 1753, II, i, 9:

'Above all, the extravagant use of ornaments is to be avoided. They are to be looked upon as details which may ruin the most admirable building, or as spices which can spoil the best dish. Many notes, because they have no distinction, must remain exempt; many notes which have enough brilliance, likewise do not permit [ornaments], because these should only enhance the importance and impact of such notes'.

(172) C. P. E. Bach, *Essay*, Berlin, 1753, II, i, 8:

'The expression of simplicity or of sadness admits of fewer ornaments than other feelings. [10:] Many passages permit of more than one kind of ornament. In such cases, the art of contrast may well be brought into play; use first a tender ornament, next a brilliant one, or even . . . play the notes simply as written. [19:] All ornaments are in a proportionate relationship to the length of the main note, the measure, and the content of the piece . . . the more notes there are in an ornament, the longer the main note must be . . . [avoid] ornaments of too many notes [or] excessive embellishment of rapid notes.'

(f) *Ornaments are influenced by the instrument in use.*

(173) C. P. E. Bach, *Essay*, Berlin, 1753, III, 7:

'The ear accepts more movement from the harpsichord than from other instruments.'

This implies, what experience confirms, that more frequent and more brilliant ornaments can be successfully used on the harpsichord than on most other instruments, including, for example, the piano; and to some extent, they are more needed to keep up the sound.

(g) *In fugal entries, etc., the use of ornaments must be consistent.*

(174) C. P. E. Bach, *Essay*, Berlin, 1753, II, i, 28:

'All imitations must be exact down to the last detail. Hence the left hand must practice ornaments until it can imitate them efficiently.'

If J. S. Bach, for example, marks one sign over one fugal entry and another over another fugal entry in the same composition, this is not a distinction subtly intended, but simply casual notation of the common baroque kind. The *same* ornament should be played.

Even in imitations, it may be enough to reproduce the general contour of the ornament first heard: *e.g.*, a short trill in an upper part may be echoed by a turn to avoid clumsiness in a bass imitation of it.

(h) *The ornaments on sequences should often be cumulative.*

(175) Joachim Quantz, *Essay*, Berlin, 1752, XIII, 29:

'In passages which resemble one another, the [ornamental] variations ought not always to be the same.'

This is to avoid anticlimax, and is the corollary of the above: see (134) in Ch. X, 3 above.

(i) *Ornaments in ensemble music should be concerted.*

(176) J. A. Scheibe, *Critische Musicus*, 2nd ed., Leipzig, 1745, art. 78:

'The conductor must see to it that all the violins use the same ornaments as their leader.'

(j) *Ornaments must be supplied with accidentals at discretion.*

(177) C. P. E. Bach, *Essay*, Berlin, 1753, II, i, 17:

'The notes of an ornament adapt themselves to the sharps and flats of the key signature [with exceptions and modifications] which the trained ear at once recognises.'

(k) *Obligatory ornaments never anticipate the beat.*

The cadential trill and the long appoggiatura are obligatory chiefly for harmonic reasons which *require* them to take the beat. We may also *prefer* to bring optional ornaments (other than those falling between beats, like some turns and all passing or changing notes) on the beat. (See Postscript to this chapter.)

(178) C. P. E. Bach, *Essay*, Berlin, 1753, II, i, 23:

'All ornaments written in little notes relate to the following note. Thus while the previous note is never curtailed, the following note loses as much of its duration as the little notes take away from it . . .

[24:] 'Following this rule, the little notes rather than the main note are sounded with the bass and the other parts. The performer should carry them over smoothly into the following note. It is a mistake to arrive with an accent on the main note . . .

[Ed. of 1787 adds:] 'It might be thought unnecessary to repeat that the remaining parts including the bass must be sounded with the first note of the ornament. But as often as this rule is invoked, so often is it broken.'

3. THREE PRIMARY FUNCTIONS SERVED BY BAROQUE ORNAMENTS

(179) C. P. E. Bach, *Essay*, Berlin, 1753, II, i, 1:

'[Ornaments] join notes; they enliven them . . . they give them emphasis and accentuation . . . they bring out their expression.'

These functions clearly overlap; but there is a distinction implied here which is valuable for interpretation. For if we know what an ornament is put there to do, we begin to know what to do with it.

(a) There are primarily *melodic* ornaments whose natural function is to 'join notes' and 'enliven them'. Turns are an excellent example; so are the little scale-wise passages sometimes treated as a specific ornament under the name tirata. Such ornaments tend to be characteristically between beats; little accented; long and smooth enough to fill much or all of the duration of their main notes.

(b) There are primarily *rhythmic* ornaments whose natural function is to 'give emphasis and accentuation'. Mordents, slides and acciaccaturas are typical examples. Such ornaments are characteristically on the beat (or on a syncopation displacing the beat); highly accented; crisp and short, or prolonged to take little of their main notes.

(c) There are primarily *harmonic* ornaments whose natural function is to 'bring out the expression'. Cadential trills and long appoggiaturas are the main examples. Such ornaments are necessarily on the beat; firmly accented or with a languishing stress, according to the feeling of the passage; long enough to delay their resolution on to their main notes expressively, and at times to push those main notes right off their own beat and into the space afforded by an ensuing rest.

(d) Where more than one of these functions is in evidence, the disposition of each has to be reconciled. A long mordent, for example, must start with enough incisiveness to fulfil its rhythmic function, but continue with enough grace to fulfil its melodic function; a long trill must have its initial upper note stressed and prolonged enough to fulfil its harmonic function, but its continuation smooth enough to fulfil its melodic function. And so with other combinations of function.

4. TABLE V: THE MAIN BAROQUE ORNAMENTS GROUPED BY FAMILIES

(See also the Index of Signs on pages 571–578.)

A: the Appoggiatura Family

A (i): The Appoggiatura proper
    (a) early baroque (indeterminate length)
    (b) long
    (c) short

A (ii): The Compound Appoggiatura (or disjunct double appoggiatura)

A (iii): The Slide (or conjunct double appoggiatura)

A (iv): The Acciaccatura (crushed appoggiatura)
    (a) simultaneous
    (b) passing

A (v): The Passing Appoggiatura

B: the Shake Family

B (i): The Tremolo (or organ shake)

B (ii): The Vibrato (or close shake)

B (iii): The Trill (or shake proper)

B (iv): The Mordent (or open shake)

C: the Division Family

C (i): Passing Notes

C (ii): Changing Notes

C (iii): Turns

C (iv): Broken Chords

C (v): Broken Notes

C (vi): Broken Time

195

D: Compound Ornaments

    D (i):   Appoggiatura with

          (a) trill
          (b) half-shake
          (c) mordent
          (d) arpeggio
          (e) turn

    D (ii):   Ascending turn (slide with turn)
    D (iii):   Trill with

          (a) mordent
          (b) turn

    D (iv):   Ascending trill (slide with trill)
    D (v):   Descending trill (turn with trill)
    D (vi):   Double Cadence
    D (vii): Double Relish
    D (viii): Truncated Note with other ornaments

POSTSCRIPT TO NEW VERSION

Other groupings of baroque ornaments are possible. Frederick Neumann, who has so kindly let me see the still (1973) not quite finalised typescript of his forthcoming *Baroque and Post Baroque Ornamentation*, prefers four groups which he calls in effect: (a) before-beat; (b) after-beat; (c) between-beat; (d) middle-beat. This is chiefly because he views the behaviour of several ornaments differently. I have taken his views very carefully into consideration, and the reader will find them reflected in a number of the revisions in this third edition; but I have not always found his arguments convincing. I have done my best to sum up, in Appendix VI below, the position in regard to baroque ornaments as I think the most recent discussions and investigations by my colleagues and myself now leave it.

CHAPTER XIV

A (i): The Appoggiatura Proper

English:	Appoggiatura
	Beat
	Forefall, Backfall, Half-fall
	Lead
	Prepare
Latin:	Accentus
Italian:	Accento
	Appoggiatura
	Exclamatio
	Portamento
French:	Accent
	Appoggiature
	Appuy
	Cheute *or* Chute
	Coulé
	Port-de-voix
German:	Accent
	Accentuation
	Vorschlag

1. WHAT THE NAME APPOGGIATURA IMPLIES

The Italian verb *appoggiare* means 'to lean' and implies an ornamental note expressively emphasised and drawn out before being more gently resolved on to its ensuing main note. This is the true appoggiatura.

There is no appoggiatura so characteristic of this family of ornaments as the long appoggiatura, and no ornament more characteristic of its age. Its influence on the history of music surpasses that of any other ornament, and it is an outstanding instance of the principle: the impromptu ornamentation of today becomes the written figuration of tomorrow. Long appoggiaturas fully written out in the notated text are so indispensable to nineteenth-century melody and still more harmony that their origin in more or less impromptu ornamentation is apt to be forgotten. The harmonic progressions with which *Tristan* opens—certainly the most revolutionary passage in music since Beethoven, and the most decisive for future developments—are not merely conditioned but created by the bold and original handling of written-out long appoggiaturas. Mahler without his written-out long appoggiaturas would be deprived indeed. No one who has absorbed these realities into his musical consciousness will ever again wish to deprive baroque

197

music of its long appoggiaturas merely because they were not written down. They were intended, they were familiar to contemporary composers and performers alike, and they add profoundly to the expressiveness of the passages which demand them. There are very few details of authentic interpretation which are so important as the correct and imaginative use of long appoggiaturas.

2. THE MOVEMENT OF APPOGGIATURAS

(a) The name appoggiatura itself does not carry any implication as to the direction of movement of the appoggiatura.

We use the descriptions 'upper' or 'superior' or 'descending appoggiatura' for a stepwise downwards movement from the tone or semitone above (Old Eng. *backfall*; Fr. *coulé, chute, port-de-voix, etc., en descendant, coulement*; Ger. *Accent fallend*).

And we use the descriptions 'lower' or 'inferior' or 'ascending appoggiatura' for a stepwise upwards movement from the tone or semitone below (Old Engl. *forefall*; Fr. *coulé, etc., etc., en montant*; Ger. *Accent steigend*).

(b) Except in connection with recitative, it is most usual now to think of appoggiaturas as moving by step; but this was less so in the baroque period.

Ex. 36. Johann Mattheson, *Vollkommene Capellmeister*, Hamburg, 1739, II, iii, 24 and 25, appoggiaturas by leap:

(c) Rules are found for the movement of appoggiaturas, but they are far from reliable, and the performer has in practice to judge each context on its merits.

(180) Joachim Quantz, *Essay*, Berlin, 1752, VIII, iii:

'[An appoggiatura, when] a retardation from a previous note . . . may be taken from above or below. . . . When the previous note is one or two steps higher than the following note . . . this must be taken from above. When the previous note is lower, this must be taken from below.'

(181) C. P. E. Bach, *Essay*, Berlin, 1753, II, ii, 6:

'An appoggiatura may be a repetition of the note before or otherwise . . . [it may proceed by step, ascending or descending, or by leap].'

Ex. 37. C. P. E. Bach, appoggiatura by leap (my interpretation):

This last, like most appoggiaturas which move by leap, is a note of retardation (in exactly the complementary sense to a note of anticipation). But stepwise appoggiaturas show much less predilection for being notes of retardation (*i.e.* prepared). Nor do they necessarily approach their main note from the same side as the previous note, though they usually do so.

(182) F. Tomeoni, *Théorie de la Musique Vocale*, Paris, 1799, Ex. 6.

Ex. 38:

(d) The movement of appoggiaturas should be grammatical (but see App. VI, 49 below).

(183) F. W. Marpurg, *Anleitung*, 2nd ed., Berlin, 1765, I, ix, 9, p. 49:

'One must no more introduce faulty progressions with an appoggiatura than one may count on an appoggiatura to save consecutive fifths' [N.B. they are not faulty if taken as accented passing notes].

3. ALL TRUE APPOGGIATURAS TAKE THE BEAT

(184) François Couperin, *L'Art de toucher le Clavecin*, Paris, 1716, ed. of 1717, p. 22 [N.B. the influence of Couperin *e.g.* on J. S. Bach]:

'Strike [appoggiaturas] with the harmony, that is to say in the time which would [otherwise] be given to the ensuing [main] note.'

(185) F. W. Marpurg, *Anleitung*, 2nd ed., Berlin, 1765, I, ix, 4, p. 48:

'All appoggiaturas . . . must come exactly on the beat . . .
[8] 'If several parts are present with an appoggiatura, the accompanying parts must not be delayed by that, but should be played at once with the appoggiatura, only the main note to which the appoggiatura is the accessory being delayed.'

4. ALL TRUE APPOGGIATURAS ARE JOINED TO THE ENSUING BUT NOT TO THE PREVIOUS NOTE

(185a) Joachim Quantz, *Essay*, Berlin, 1752, VI, i, 8:

'It is a general rule, that one must make a small [N.B.] separation [silence of articulation] between the appoggiatura and the note which preceeds it, above all if the two notes are at the same pitch; so that one can make the appoggiatura distinctly heard.'

(186) C. P. E. Bach, *Essay*, Berlin, 1753, II, ii, 7:

'All appoggiaturas are performed more loudly than the ensuing note, including any ornaments which it [the ensuing note] may carry, and are joined with it, whether slurs are written or not.'

See also (195) and (196) in 6 below.

5. THE EARLY BAROQUE APPOGGIATURA

The appoggiatura occurs, as one of a group of similar little figures crystallizing out of the main tradition of free ornamentation and together called *accenti*, early in the baroque period.

Ex. 39. M. Praetorius, *Syntagma*, III, Wolfenbüttel, 1619, p. 233:

The following in Frescobaldi are written out:

Ex. 40. G. Frescobaldi, 'Partite sopra l'aria della Romanesca', appoggiaturas:

'Fiori musicali' "Avanti il recercar"

We have here, then, a genuine appoggiatura of moderate length: *i.e.* taking a third of dotted notes and a quarter of undotted notes (no doubt with some variability in performance).

Such an appoggiatura is long enough to be heard as a momentary diversion of the harmony, and has the effect of an accented passing note. It does not actually change the harmonic progression. It will be accented and louder than its ensuing main note. It will be taken on the beat, whenever it is a true appoggiatura. But see Chapter XVIII.

Through most of the seventeenth century the evidence suggests that this was then a standard length for the true appoggiatura.

When ascending it is called beat by Playford (*Introd.*, 1660 on) and Simpson (*Division-Violist*, 1659); half-fall ('ever from a Half-Note beneath') by Mace (*Musick's Monument*, 1676); forefall by Locke (*Melothesia*, 1673) and Purcell or Purcell's editor (posthumous *Lessons*, 1696): forefall becoming the standard English term. When descending it was called backfall.

Ex. 41. J. Playford, *Introduction*, London, 1654 (1660 on), appoggiaturas:

Ex. 42. Appoggiaturas in H. Purcell's posthumous *Lessons*, London, 1696:

This appoggiatura of moderate length did not disappear from later baroque music, and in some contexts it is the obvious solution, as either melodic or more probably harmonic considerations will suggest. But it ceased to be standard, and was increasingly over-shadowed by two other appoggiaturas never moderate or indefinite in length, but in the one case decidedly long, and in the other case, decidedly short.

6. THE LONG APPOGGIATURA

(a) From the last years of the seventeenth century onwards, we meet evidence to suggest that the standard appoggiatura now took half the length of an undotted main note; two-thirds of the length of a dotted main-note; all the first of two tied notes in compound triple time; and all of a note before a rest. (N.B. the standard position on the beat.)

Ex. 43. D'Anglebert, *Pièces de Clavecin*, Paris, 1689, appoggiaturas (cheute ou port de voix):

Ex. 44. J. M. Hotteterre, *Principes*, Paris, 1707, p. 28, appoggiaturas at (a) necessarily, at (b) probably not, on the beat:

The length of the little notes at (b) is misleading as so often.

Ex. 45. Dieupart, *Suites de Clavecin*, Paris, *c.* 1720, appoggiaturas:

Ex. 46. J. S. Bach, *Clavier-Büchlein*, begun Cöthen, 1720:

Frederick Neumann speculates extensively on J. S. Bach's appoggiaturas, which he assumes to have been before the beat in a majority of cases, and in most other cases, short. There is nothing in the known facts to support this view, or to indicate that J. S. Bach's own explanation, above, is contrary to his own practice. The following gives the standard practice of the first half of the eighteenth century, conforms with J. S. Bach's own table so far as that goes, and may be applied with all reasonable confidence to standard situations. See also App. VI.

(187) Joachim Quantz, *Essay*, Berlin, 1752, VIII, 7 *ff.*:

'Hold the appoggiatura half the length of the main note. [But] if the appoggiatura has to ornament a dotted note, that note is divided into three parts, of which the appoggiatura takes two, and the main note one only: that is to say, the length of the dot . . .

'When in six-four or six-eight time two notes are found tied together, and the first is dotted . . . the appoggiaturas should be held for the length of the first note including its dot. . . . When there is an appoggiatura before a note, and after it a rest; the appoggiatura . . . is given the length of the note, and the note the length of the rest.'

Ex. 47:

(188) C. P. E. Bach, *Essay*, Berlin, 1753, II, ii, 11:

'The general rule for the length of the appoggiaturas is to take from the following note, if duple, half its length; and if triple, two-thirds of its length.'

(b) Appoggiaturas of more than standard length also became fashionable during the first half of the eighteenth century.

(189) Fr. Geminiani, *Art of Playing on the Violin*, London, 1751, p. 7:

'The Superior Apogiatura is supposed to express Love, Affection, Pleasure, *etc.* It should be made pretty long, giving it more than half the Length or Time of the Note it belongs to. . . . If it be made short, it will lose much of the aforesaid qualities; but will always have a pleasing Effect, and it may be added to any note you will.

'The Inferior Apogiatura has the same Qualities with the preceding . . .'

(190) Galliard, *f.n.* to Tosi's *Opinioni*, 1723, tr. as *Observations on the Florid Song*, London, 1742, p. 32:

'You dwell longer on the Preparation [*i.e.* the appoggiatura] than on the [main] Note for which the Preparation is made.'

(191) C. P. E. Bach, *Essay*, Berlin, 1753, II, ii, 16:

'There are cases in which [the appoggiatura] must be prolonged beyond its normal length for the sake of the expressive feeling conveyed. Thus it may take more than half the length of the following note. Sometimes the length is determined by the harmony.'

(c) The last sentence in the above quotation is important.

The likeliest interpretation of an eighteenth century appoggiatura, and the one to try first when in doubt, is long. It may alternatively be genuinely short. But if it is long, its length must ultimately be decided by context rather than by rule. It may need shortening.

Arnold Dolmetsch (*Interpretation of the Music of the* 17th *and* 18th *Centuries*, London, 1915, 115–116) gives an instructive instance in J. S.

203

Bach's Prelude XVIII from Vol. II of the 'Forty-Eight'. The rule would put the first pair of appoggiaturas at a crotchet length, their main notes being pushed over into the ensuing rest. That makes nonsense of the harmony. The next pair, having no ensuing rest, *must* be of quaver length; later, in bars 44–45, the same 'appoggiaturas' are *written out* as quavers. The solution throughout is therefore a quaver length.

Ex. 48. J. S. Bach, appoggiaturas:

(d) A long appoggiatura on an exceptionally long main note may need shortening a little; but it is generally desirable to make long appoggiaturas *as long as the context makes feasible*. Long appoggiaturas at *less* than (*e.g.* half of) the standard length are sometimes imposed by the harmonic progression.

(e) Appoggiaturas taking three-quarters of the length of an ordinary duple note were beginning to be regarded as regular by the middle of the eighteenth century, though the standard continued to be half.

Ex. 49. Leopold Mozart, *Violinschule*, Augsburg, 1756, IX, 4, very long appoggiaturas:

(f) Dotted figures in baroque music tend to have their dotted notes prolonged (see Ch. XLIII below); this has the effect of prolonging an appoggiatura on such notes.

(192) Joachim Quantz, *Essay*, Berlin, 1752, Eng. tr. *c.* 1790, p. 18:

'The short note after the Point [dot] is always to be play'd very quick. An Apogiatura prefix'd to a pointed Note, must be play'd exactly to the time of the larger or principal Note, and the latter to the time of the Point, and be play'd softer than the former.'

C. P. E. Bach prints an interesting example of this.

Ex. 50. C. P. E. Bach, *Essay*, Berlin, 1753, II, ii, 11, appoggiatura on a dotted note:

(g) The last words in the last quotation above refer to the stress on the appoggiatura, and the diminution of volume into and upon its ensuing main note, which were characteristic of long appoggiaturas. This is in conformity with the normal baroque (and indeed intrinsic) diminuendo from discord on to resolution, and is both natural and expressive. Some writers describe a crescendo on the appoggiatura itself, if long enough; the effect in practice is a mild and somewhat gradual sforzando, but the least exaggeration will be fatal here.

(193) Galliard, *f.n.* to Tosi's *Opinioni*, 1723, Eng. tr. as *Observations on the Florid Song*, London, 1742, p. 32:

'You lean on the first [*i.e.* the appoggiatura] to arrive at the [main] Note intended.'

(194) Fr. Geminiani, *Art of Playing on the Violin*, London, 1751, p. 7:

'Swell the Sound [of the long appoggiatura] by Degrees.'

(195) F. W. Marpurg, *Anleitung*, 2nd ed., Berlin, 1765, p. 48:

'The note with which the [appoggiatura] is made should always be sounded a little louder than the main or essential note, and should be gently slurred towards it.'

(196) Joachim Quantz, *Essay*, Berlin, 1752, VIII, iii:

'Swell [the appoggiaturas] if time permits and slur the ensuing note to them somewhat more softly.'

7. THE FUNCTION OF THE LONG APPOGGIATURA PRIMARILY HARMONIC

(197) Joachim Quantz, *Essay*, Berlin, 1752, VIII, i:

'Ports de voix, in Italian Appoggiaturas, are not only ornaments, but necessary elements. Without them the tune would often be very dry and very plain. For a melody to have a stylish air, it must always have more consonances than dissonances. However, when there are several consonances in succession, and after some quick notes there comes a long consonance, the ear can easily get tired of it. Dissonances are sometimes needed then to stimulate and awaken it. This is where the appoggiaturas can make a great contribution; for they turn into dissonances, as fourths and sevenths, when they are before the third or sixth counting from the principal note [bass of the harmony], but are resolved by the following note.'

(198) C. P. E. Bach, *Essay*, Berlin, 1753, II, ii, 1:

'Appoggiaturas are among the most necessary ornaments. They enrich the harmony as well as the melody. They enhance the appeal of the melody by joining notes smoothly together, and with notes which might be found tedious on account of their length, by making them shorter while satisfying the ear with sound. At the same time they make other notes longer by repeating, on occasion, the note before. . . . Appoggiaturas change chords which in their absence would be too straightforward. All syncopations and dissonances can be attributed to them. Where would the art of harmony be without these ingredients?'

(199) F. W. Marpurg, *Anleitung zum Clavierspielen*, 2nd ed., Berlin, 1765, I, ix, 1, p. 46:

'The appoggiatura (Vorschlag) is also called suspension (Vorhalt), and consists, as implied, in suspending a note by a previous one. It is notated either by certain signs or by little subsidiary notes, or properly written out. The first notation is no longer usual, or can only be used with the very shortest appoggiaturas. Formerly, we used for it a simple cross, a hook before the note, or a small, slanting line. When, later on, long appoggiaturas occurred, we began to introduce the small, subsidiary notes, and with them the second notation of this ornament.'

It is only long appoggiaturas which behave like true suspensions and change the progression of the harmony.

8. THE SHORT APPOGGIATURA

(a) The short appoggiatura varies in length from the shortest performable, at the minimum, to a quarter or more of its main note according to the context, the maximum being, however, always shorter than would sound like a long appoggiatura in that context.

(200) Joachim Quantz, *Essay*, Berlin, 1752, VIII, ii:

'Appoggiaturas are marked with little added notes, so as not to confuse them with the ordinary notes, and they take their value from the notes before which they are found. It does not much matter whether they have more than one tail, or whether they have none. It is, however, usual to give them only one tail. And those with two tails are only made use of before notes which cannot be deprived of any [*sic*] of their value; *e.g.* before two or more long notes, whether they are crotchets or minims, if they are at the same pitch. . . . These little notes with double tail are rendered very briefly in whatever manner they come to be taken, from below or from above; and they are played on the beat of the main note.'

Observe that Quantz does not say that all short appoggiaturas will be found written with the little semiquaver symbol; he merely says that any appoggiatura which is found so written is certain to be short. When he says 'notes which cannot be deprived of any of their value' he is exaggerating; he means, no doubt, any measurable part of their value. The only appoggiatura which takes literally no value away from the main note, because it actually coincides with it, is the simultaneous acciacatura (crushed appoggiatura), for which see Ch. XVII below.

(201) C. P. E. Bach, *Essay*, Berlin, 1753, II, ii, 13:

'It is only natural that the invariable short appoggiatura should most often appear before quick notes. It is written with one, two, three or more tails and played so fast that the ensuing note loses hardly any of its length. It also appears before long notes when a note is repeated [or] with syncopations.

[14:] 'When the appoggiaturas fill in leaps of a third, they are also taken short. But in an Adagio the feeling is more expressive if they are taken as the first quavers of triplets and not as semiquavers. . . . The appoggiaturas before [actual] triplets are taken short to avoid obscuring the rhythm. . . . When the appoggiatura forms an octave with the bass it is taken short. . . . [15:] If a note rises a second and at once returns . . . a short appoggiatura may well occur on the middle note.'

Ex. 51. C. P. E. Bach, short appoggiaturas:

The above are the most interesting of C. P. E. Bach's numerous examples. The rule that appoggiaturas filling in leaps of a third are taken short must obviously be accepted with reservations; C. P. E. Bach himself gives many instances to the contrary, and it is only a certain type of passage which he has in mind here. His example is this (the interpretations are mine, but carry out his instructions).

Ex. 52. C. P. E. Bach, *Essay*, Berlin, 1753, II, ii, 15, appoggiaturas filling in leaps of a third:

It will once again be realised that the notation with tails suggestive of the timing is not even consistently applied by C. P. E. Bach (the last example should have double tails on his own principle) and was never in standard use.

The term 'invariable' applied to the short appoggiatura at the beginning of the above quotation also requires a warning. The length of short appoggiaturas varies within narrower limits than the length of long appoggiaturas, and in view of this C. P. E. Bach called the former 'invariable' and the latter 'variable'. Yet he does not in practice treat the short appoggiatura as invariable; and, of course, it is not. Nor does the variability of a long appoggiatura extend indefinitely. It does not (as has sometimes been wrongly inferred) extend to the point of turning a long appoggiatura into a short one. C. P. E. Bach's terminology here, though understandable, is unfortunate.

(b) The following is a particularly typical use of a short (semiquaver) appoggiatura in a context which would equally admit of a long (quaver) one. Notice how much better, however, the short appoggiatura carries on the rhythmic pattern of the first part of the bar.

Ex. 53. F. W. Marpurg, *Anleitung zum Clavierspielen*, 2nd ed., Berlin, 1765, I, ix, Tab. III, Exx. 43–44:

(c) The following are four different ways of notating the standard short appoggiatura, in its position between notes a third apart.

Ex. 54. F. W. Marpurg, *Anleitung zum Clavierspielen*, 2nd ed., Berlin, 1765, Table III, Figs. 11–13:

(d) The use of ♪ to indicate a short appoggiatura occurs in Manfredini's *Regole* (Venice, 1775) Tab. VI (I am indebted to Eva Badura-Skoda for showing me this); I have seen it in an Italian cantata MS of about 1750 (Brussels Bibl. du Conservatoire Royal de Musique, *ff.* 90v to 91v and 96v to 99v); and in another dated 1776 (London, RCM, MS 181 (2), *f.* lv and *f.* 84v); it becomes familiar in the nineteenth century. Full-size and not as an ornament, it is merely one common baroque way of notating the second tail of an ordinary semiquaver.

THE APPOGGIATURA PROPER

9. WHERE TO INTRODUCE UNWRITTEN APPOGGIATURAS

(202) Joachim Quantz, *Essay*, Berlin, 1752, VIII, 12:

'It is not enough to know how to perform the appoggiaturas according to their nature and difference, when they are marked; it is also necessary to know how to put them in suitably when they are not written. Here is a rule which can be used for understanding them. When after one or more short notes on the down or up beat of the bar a long note comes, and remains in consonant harmony; an appoggiatura must be put before the long note, to keep the melody continuously agreeable; the preceding note will show whether the appoggiatura should be taken from above or below.'

In reality the harmony will gain even more than the melody in the context here envisaged. Such a context also implies that the appoggiatura should be long.

(203) C. P. E. Bach, *Essay*, Berlin, 1753, II, ii, 8:

'Because the sign for the appoggiatura with that of the trill is almost the only one familiar everywhere, we furthermore generally find it written down. Yet since this cannot always be depended on, it is necessary to decide on the proper contexts of the variable [*i.e.* long] appoggiatura, so far as this can be done.

[9:] 'The variable [long] appoggiatura in duple time frequently appears either on the down beat (Fig. II, Ex. *a*) or the up beat (*b*); but in triple time only on the down beat (Fig. III) and that always before a comparatively long note. It is also found before closing trills (Fig. IV, Ex. *a*); half-closes (*b*), caesuras (*c*), fermatas (*d*) and closing notes with (*e*) or without (*f*) a previous trill. We see from Ex. *e* that the ascending appoggiatura is better than the descending after a trill; thus the instance (*g*) is weak. Slow dotted notes also bear the variable [long] appoggiatura (*h*). When such notes have tails, the tempo must be such as to be suitable.'

Ex. 55. C. P. E. Bach, contexts inviting unwritten appoggiaturas:

It will be realised that in the above examples, the little notes represent the appoggiaturas which C. P. E. Bach suggests should be put in by the performer in cases where no indication of them appears in the written text. The examples are all found in Tab. III.

10. APPOGGIATURAS IN RECITATIVE

(a) In late baroque Italianate recitative, at phrase endings (especially when falling a fourth or a third) an appoggiatura is obligatory.

(203a) J. F. Agricola, *Anleitung*, Berlin, 1757, p. 154:

'One sings [at endings falling a fourth] the next to last note a fourth higher [than notated].'

(204) J. A. Scheibe in F. W. Marpurg's *Kritische-Briefe*, Berlin, for 1760–62, letter 109, p. 352:

'Regarding the notation of the feminine cadence with the falling fourth, we must observe that the last two notes are written by some composers differently from what is sung, *e.g.*:'

Ex. 56. Scheibe, misleading notation of feminine endings:

'This notation is undoubtedly regrettable because in the nature of things we should not write differently from what is sung, and because many untutored singers can be led astray by this, especially in the middle of a recitative.'

(b) By a feminine cadence is meant a close (whether passing or final) in which the last syllable falls not on the beat (which is the masculine ending) but off the beat. It will be noticed that Agricola and Scheibe speak of this not as a matter of optional ornaments, but as a definite misnotation of which the performer has to know, and apply, the intended interpretation. Some conductors oppose it on the grounds of wanting only what the composer wrote. As so often in baroque music, this gives them what the composer wrote at the expense of what he meant by what he wrote. There are few rules so unambiguous as this rule concerning appoggiaturas in recitative, and its consistent application is very strongly to be recommended.

Ex. 57. G. P. Telemann, *Cantatas*, Leipzig, 1725, preface, feminine and masculine endings in recitative:

(c) Of the above, the first two are examples of feminine endings, the last two of masculine endings. Telemann treats both alike, and makes no suggestion of any possible exceptions in either case. J. F. Agricola's translation, cited at (203a) above, of Tosi's *Opinioni* includes his own examples, one a masculine ending, likewise given normal appoggiaturas. On the other hand, Scheibe's rule was given specifically for feminine endings, and he does not mention masculine ones at all. Thus we are not categorically precluded by his evidence from making an exception in a masculine ending where there seems a strong musical reason for doing so. Both the following endings from J. S. Bach's *St. Matthew Passion* are masculine: (a) implies the normal appoggiatura; but the phrase at (b), which is one of peculiar forthrightness and power, sounds stronger if the second *A* balances the first *A* exactly, without being complicated by an appoggiatura. We have no evidence suggesting that an exception would, even so, have been made at the time; but it is exactly the sort of rare case where we might just possibly make an exception now. And, of course, outside recitative or near-recitative the situation is much more fluid.

Ex. 58. J. S. Bach, masculine endings (*St. Matthew Passion*, recit. No. 4 in Novello's ed., last two bars):

Ex. 59: the same (recit. No. 32, bar 26):

Ex. 60. G. P. Telemann, *Cantatas*, Leipzig, 1725, preface, mixed masculine and feminine endings:

(d) That this convention was itself subject to further ornamentation by the performer is suggested by the following written-out example, though it should only be imitated with considerable discretion and restraint, in carefully selected contexts.

Ex. 61. J. S. Bach, *Christmas Oratorio* (B.-G., V, 2, p. 236, bar 9), written-out ornament:

dass ich ach kom-me und es an- be – – te

11. THE POST-BAROQUE APPOGGIATURA

(a) Both the long and the short appoggiatura continued to be taught by the treatises of the late eighteenth century. The long appoggiatura tended to grow not shorter, but longer still.

(205) D. G. Türk, *Klavierschule*, Leipzig and Halle, 1789, nine rules for appoggiaturas, including:

Ex. 62. Türk, very long appoggiaturas:

'Every long appoggiatura to be played with more emphasis then the ensuing note.'

(206) G. F. Wolf, *Unterricht*, 3rd ed., Halle, 1789, p. 69, includes:

Ex. 63:

'[Short appoggiaturas appear only before short notes, when] the main note itself loses almost nothing at all.'

Hoyle's *Dictionary of Music*, 1770, pirates Geminiani's description of the long and short appoggiatura—for which see (189) in 6 above—almost word for word.

Ex. 64. J. C. F. Rellstab, *C. P. E. Bach's Anfangsgründe mit einer Anleitung*, Berlin, 1790, VIII, very long appoggiatura:

(207) Thomas Busby, *Complete Dictionary of Music*, London, [1786], *s.v.* 'Appoggiatura or *Leaning Note*':

'The appoggiatura not being always in consonance with the bass and other parts, to avoid a *visible* breach of the laws of harmony, it is generally written in a small note.'

(b) Cramer, Pleyel, Czerny and Hummel in the early nineteenth century taught similar rules for the appoggiatura. J. D. Andersch's *Musikalisches Woerterbuch* (1829) makes the standard distinction between long and short appoggiaturas.

(208) Louis Spohr, *Violinschule*, 1832, *etc.*, rules for appoggiaturas:

'If the appoggiatura stands before a note which can be divided into equal parts, it obtains the half of its value. . . . Before a note with a dot it obtains the value of the note, which then begins only at the dot. . . . Where there are two dots the appoggiatura obtains the value of the note and this then begins with the first dot.'

(c) Nineteenth-century appoggiaturas continued to be normal:
(209) F. de Courcy, *Art of Singing*, London, *c.* 1868:

'[Appoggiaturas are] generally half the succeeding or principle note.'

(d) In the twentieth century, the more traditional schools of Italianate singing retained the standard long and short appoggiaturas, and there are still a few circles in which they are not forgotten. It must be remembered that Manuel Garcia's *Traité complet de l'art du chant* (Paris, 1840) is still in use: an edition of 1911 is very sound on ornaments. The following is unequivocal:
(209a) Manuel Garcia, *Hints on Singing*, London, 1894, p. 67:

'Of two identical notes ending a phrase or a section of a phrase, the first always bears the prosodic accent, and therefore must be turned into an appoggiatura. Though Mozart had not marked the appoggiatura it must be introduced.'
[p. 73: in recitative] 'when a sentence ends with two equal notes, in the Italian style, we raise the first [as] an appoggiatura.'

(e) Indeed, in Mozart's operas, for example, many appoggiaturas (particularly long appoggiaturas) are so plainly implied that their neglect amounts to a disregard of the composer's intention. Charles Mackerras ('Sense about the Appoggiatura', *Opera*, Oct. 1963) quotes orchestral parts having written-out appoggiaturas in unison with vocal parts not showing (but certainly meaning) these appoggiaturas. The next suggestions are mine:

Ex. 65. Mozart, *Così Fan Tutte* (recit. and aria No. 11 in Novello's ed.):

A typical appoggiatura problem appears in the slow movement of Beethoven's posthumous quartet, Op. 127. In view of Beethoven's admiration for C. P. E. Bach's *Essay*, which according to Czerny's autobiographical notes (cited L. Nohl, *Beethoven Depicted by his Contemporaries*, 1877, tr. E. Hill, 1880, Ch. VII) Beethoven recommended to his pupils, and in view of the generally continued currency of the rules for appoggiaturas as given by C. P. E. Bach, there can be no real doubt that the appoggiaturas in this movement are not short (as played even by so traditional a quartet as the Flonzaley, which is as far back as my memory goes) but long. They should be performed as dotted crotchets. The effect sounds somewhat revolutionary at first, but when its novelty has worn off becomes most convincing, both melodically, and still more harmonically. It is, in fact, what Beethoven intended.

In Mozart's Piano Concerto K. 459, second movement, the appoggiaturas in the orchestral parts at bar 67, *etc.*, are nowadays, but incorrectly, taken short (and often, still more incorrectly, before the beat as well). They should be long (*i.e.* half the length of the quavers on which they stand) as is proved by their having to match the piano part at bar 71, *etc.* This again is a typical case of modern misunderstanding. For one such case where proof positive is afforded (in this case by the precisely notated piano part) there must be many hundreds of others where there is no specific proof, but where the standard rules make the correct interpretation virtually certain.

As an instance of a modern on-the-beat short appoggiatura, it may be mentioned that Mahler, whose use of very numerous, very long appoggiaturas is a feature of his style, but who writes these long appoggiaturas out, also writes a few ornamental appoggiaturas in little notes. These were taken by Bruno Walter, who directly inherited his tradition, definitely short but with a lingering expression, and firmly on the beat. To anticipate the beat with them would spoil the whole effect.

CHAPTER XV

A (ii): The Double Appoggiatura

French: Port-de-voix double
German: Anschlag, Doppelvorschlag

1. WHAT THE NAME DOUBLE APPOGGIATURA IMPLIES

The clearest name for this ornament is Putnam Aldrich's in the *Harvard Dictionary of Music* (1944): disjunct double appoggiatura. This distinguishes it from the Slide, well called by him: conjunct double appoggiatura. But even these names are not ideal, since double, triple appoggiatura, *etc.*, have also the meaning of two, three or more appoggiaturas going on in different parts of a chord at the same time.

The reason for calling the ornament here under consideration a double appoggiatura at all was that two notes behave in some respects like the one note of which the appoggiatura proper consists. These two notes are always disjunct with each other. The second is always conjunct with and nearly always superior to the ensuing main note.

This ornament is not of widespread importance nor much to be used outside the galant school.

2. VARIETIES OF DOUBLE APPOGGIATURA

(210) Joachim Quantz, *Essay*, Berlin, 1752, XIII, 41:

'[The double appoggiatura] must be joined very quickly, but softly, to the [main] note. The [main] note must be slightly louder than the accessory notes.'

Ex. 66. Quantz, double appoggiaturas:

Ex. 67. F. W. Marpurg, *Principes du clavecin*, Berlin, 1756, double appoggiaturas (interpretations below each):

Notice the curious effect of the dotted double appoggiaturas in the last but one of the above examples. C. P. E. Bach (*Essay*, 1753, II, ii, 20) confirms this dotted form, but not in rapid passages. He gives three general rules.

(211) C. P. E. Bach, *Essay*, Berlin, 1753, II, vi, 3:

'[The accessory notes] comprising a double appoggiatura are played more softly than the main note. [7:] the [main] note yields as much of its length as the ornament requires. [10:] all three notes are slurred.'

The second of these rules shows that his double appoggiatura is taken on (and not before) the beat, in spite of its far from appoggiatura-like behaviour in being softer than its main note. Its function is more rhythmic than melodic or harmonic; it is not itself accented, but displaces the accent of its main note to an irregular position just after the beat.

But in view of the technical and musical difficulty of carrying out these instructions literally, there is some reason to suppose that it may also have been used as a normal rhythmic ornament taking the accent as well as the beat; or even as a melodic ornament, unaccented but before the beat. It is not, in any case, an ornament of much baroque importance.

3. THE POST-BAROQUE DOUBLE APPOGGIATURA

When encountered in composers of the Romantic school, such as Chopin, the double appoggiatura is to be taken on the same principles as in the baroque period.

CHAPTER XVI

A (iii): The Slide

English:	Elevation
	Double backfall
	Slide
	Slur
	Whole-fall
French:	Coulé
	Coulé sur une tierce
	Flatté
German:	Schleifer
	Schleiffung
	Überschlag
Latin:	Superjectio

1. WHAT THE NAME SLIDE IMPLIES

The name slide is admirably fitted to this ornament, which slides rapidly and smoothly through its two conjunct accessory notes to its main note—whence its alternative description as a conjunct double appoggiatura. It is a very widespread ornament in different ages and is of value in all baroque music. N.B.: see Chapter XVII for the very close connection between the slide and the acciaccatura.

2. VARIETIES OF SLIDE

(212) G. Caccini, *Nuove musiche*, Florence, 1602, tr. Playford, *Introduction*, London, 1654, ed. of 1674, p. 42:

'There are some therefore that in the *Tuning* of the first *Note*, Tune it a Third under . . . it agrees not in many cords, although in such places as it may be used, it is now so ordinary, that instead of being a Grace (because some stay too long in the third Note under, whereas it should be but lightly touched) it is rather tedious to the Ear.'

No mention is made here of the intervening note, but in other respects the description fits the slide, and this seems to be intended. Bovicelli (*Regole*, 1594) and Praetorius (*Syntagma*, III, 1619) include the ascending slide, in the form evidently disliked by Caccini, in which its first note is dotted. Praetorius also shows it undotted.

Being undoubtedly a very common ornament at the turn of the sixteenth and the seventeenth centuries, the slide has been suggested by Thurston Dart (*The Interpretation of Music*, London, 1954, p. 120) for the single-stroke ornament of the English Virginalists. This suggestion gains weight from the fact that a slanting stroke (though not normally across the stem) is found later in the seventeenth century for ascending notes forming or resembling slides, among other meanings. In many contexts, a quick slide makes a musically convincing solution for this single-stroke Virginalists' ornament; on the other hand, there are other contexts where it does not serve so well, if at all. It may therefore be better to confine ourselves to regarding the slide as one of the two or three possible solutions at a choice of which this sign hints, perhaps in common with the double-stroke so often associated with it or substituted for it: the other possibilities being a rapid lower mordent and a (usually brief) half-trill. Occasionally a full trill with turned termination may be the right solution.

Ex. 68. Playford, *Introduction*, London, 1654 (1660 on), descending and ascending slides:

Simpson (*Division-Violist*, 1659) agrees; Mace (*Musick's Monument*, 1676) gives (p. 105) an ascending slide under the name of whole-fall, and (p. 102) its sign as +. Purcell or his editor of 1696 (*Lessons*) gives an ascending slide under the name of slur, probably as a translation of the French *coulé*.

Ex. 69. Chambonnières, *Pièces*, Paris, 1670, on the beat slide:

Ex. 70. D'Anglebert, *Pièces*, Paris, 1689, on the beat slides:

J. G. Walther shows slides taken, not on the beat, but before it, and slurred to it. He therefore regarded it as a before-the-beat ornament, for which he used the same sign (see Ex. 71 below) as J. S. Bach and other used to show the slide as an on-the-beat ornament. But just as a before-the-beat appoggiatura is really a contradiction in terms, so a before-the-beat slide is really a confusion in terms. Both these should most properly be described as passing-note ornaments: their function is melodic rather than harmonic or rhythmic.

Ex. 71. J. G. Walther, 'Praecepta', 1708, slides anticipating the beat:

The slide is most properly an on-the-beat, accented ornament. When J. S. Bach wanted a before-the-beat, unaccented ornament using the same notes as a slide, I think he was inclined to write these notes out in ordinary values. When he wrote the sign for a slide, I think he was inclined to mean it on-the-beat and accented. Cases of both methods in the same piece may be found in the solo violin obbligato of the aria 'Erbarme dich' from the *St. Matthew Passion*, discussed also in Chapter XX, 4.

Ex. 71A. J. S. Bach, *St. Matthew Passion*, 'Erbarme dich', old BG. p. 168, violin obbligato showing sign for slide, on the beat, and ordinary notation for the same notes before the beat:

The following Ex. 71B shows this same sign for a slide in a voice part of J. S. Bach's *Trauer-Ode*, and a unison oboe d'amore doubling part with the ornament written out in ordinary values, confirming an accented on-the-beat interpretation.

Ex. 71B. J. S. Bach, *Trauer-Ode*, I, NBG, I, 38, 186–87, accented interpretation of slide confirmed by unison doubling in ordinary note-values:

(213) Joachim Quantz, *Essay*, Berlin, 1752, XVII, ii, 21:

'When, in a slow movement, one finds added small quavers, the first of which is dotted, they take the time of the succeeding main note, and the main note takes only the time of the dot. They must be played caressingly.

'[23: undotted slide] belongs to the French style rather than the Italian [and] must not be played so slowly [but] with rapidity.'

The first example next to follow is an extreme case; the remainder are normal variants.

Ex. 72. C. P. E. Bach, *Essay*, Berlin, 1753, II, vii, very extended slide:

Ex. 73. *ibid.*, normal slides:

Ex. 74. F. W. Marpurg, *Clavier zu spielen*, Berlin, 1750, slides:

3. POST-BAROQUE SLIDES

Hummel, a modernist in matters of ornamentation, nevertheless shows (1828) slides on the beat in the traditional baroque fashion.

The slides with which Beethoven's last quartet, Op. 135, opens should take both the accent and the beat, or the figure is greatly weakened.

THE SLIDE

Frederick Neumann, in his book now (1973) in preparation*, demonstrates the very extensive French use of a pair of ambiguously notated little notes often found slurred to the ensuing main note. He classifies these as unaccented slides, anticipating the beat, and has I think shown that they often do this. On the other hand, both Chambonnières and D'Anglebert notate their slides unambiguously on the beat (see Exx. 69–70), as do German sources such as Gottlieb Muffat's *Componimenti per il Cembalo* (Augsburg, ? 1735) and his *Toccatas* (Vienna, 1726) where he advances the authority of the great Fux himself. Not only harpsichordists took the slide thus accented and on the beat; for example, it is the same in the table of ornaments (in a different but contemporary hand) at the end of the English MS Harley 1270 mainly of Italian cantatas, with some English songs. Then as now, it was perhaps more a matter of temperament than of rule; but a slide on the beat is always much stronger and was probably much commoner.

* *Baroque and Post Baroque Ornamentation.*

CHAPTER XVII

A (iv): The Acciaccatura

English:	Acciaccatura
	Crushed appoggiatura
Italian:	Acciaccatura
	Tasto
French:	Pincé étouffé
German:	Zusammenschlag

1. WHAT THE NAME ACCIACCATURA IMPLIES

(a) The Italian (and borrowed English) name acciaccatura means a 'crushed stroke'; the German equivalent means a 'together stroke'. Both are descriptive of the manner of performing the primary ornament, which is to strike simultaneously the main note and an accessory note a semitone or tone below, but to release the accessory as soon as possible.

The French name means a 'smothered mordent', which indicates the lines on which some authorities, such as Marpurg and C. P. E. Bach, explained the ornament.

(b) The name was also extended secondarily by Geminiani and others to indicate a little ornamental note foreign to the harmony and interpolated momentarily in chords, particularly if arpeggiated.

(c) We may distinguish the first of these two forms (the one now ordinarily associated with the name) as the simultaneous acciaccatura; the second as the passing acciaccatura.

(d) It will be evident that both forms of the acciaccatura are feasible only on keyboard instruments. Both are valuable, but the second was of much more importance than the first, being a regular impromptu resource of keyboard players though not very frequently notated.

2. THE SIMULTANEOUS ACCIACCATURA

(214) Francesco Geminiani, *Treatise of Good Taste*, London, 1749:

'*Tatto* [simultaneous acciaccatura] which has a very great and singular Effect in Harmony, and which is perform'd by touching the key lightly, and quitting it with such a Spring as if it was Fire.'

222

THE ACCIACCATURA

(215) C. P. E. Bach, *Essay*, Berlin, 1753, II, v, 3:

'. . . an unusual manner of executing a very short mordent [simultaneous acciaccatura]. Of the two notes struck together, only the upper one is held, the lower one being at once released. . . . It is only used abruptly, that is to say in detached passages.'

Ex. 75. C. P. E. Bach, *Essay*, Berlin, 1753, II, v, 3, simultaneous acciaccatura:

(216) F. W. Marpurg, *Principes du Clavecin*, Berlin, 1756, XIX, 2:

'Instead of playing the two keys successively, they are often struck both together, but the accessory note is held for only half its value, so that the main note may be heard by itself afterwards. . . . This kind of mordent is called *Pincé étouffé*, in Italian *Acciaccatura*, and it is frequently used in the bass. In transitions from soft to loud it can be effectively used to emphasise the harmony.'

3. THE PASSING ACCIACCATURA

(217) Fr. Geminiani, *Treatise of Good Taste*, London, 1749:

'The *Acciaccatura* is a Composition of such Chords as are dissonant with respect to the fundamental Laws of Harmony; yet when disposed in their proper place produce that very Effect which it might be expected they would destroy.'

Ex. 76. C. P. E. Bach. *Essay*, Berlin, 1753, III, 26, 'an arpeggio with an *acciaccatura*':

The acciaccatura in the above example, giving as it does two notes a third apart which are held down while the dissonant note between is released, has precisely the form of one of the varieties of the slide; and it is here notated with the same sign. This sign is also used for an acciaccatura which does not join notes a third apart, and is therefore different from a slide.

Ex. 76a. J. S. Bach, Partita VI, Sarabande, acciaccaturas ornamentally notated by slanting strokes and by a little note:

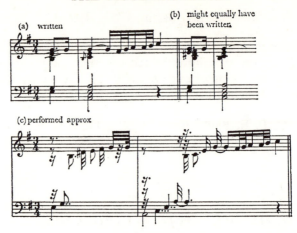

The notation used by J. S. Bach was as at (a). The alternative notation shown at (b) illustrates a still commoner method of writing down the passing acciaccaturas with which a chord may be enriched, particularly if, as here, it is full enough to be well arpeggiated. Domenico Scarlatti was especially fond of introducing thick chords which look on paper impossibly discordant for the period, because they include their passing acciaccaturas fully written out in the manner of (b) above. However slightly such chords are to be arpeggiated, there is always time to raise the interpolated discords while holding down the essential notes of the chord; the distinction may be very momentary indeed, but the ear will pick it out immediately, hearing the acciaccaturas as fleeting disturbances of an intelligible harmony. The effect can be extraordinarily subtle, rich and beautiful; and it can be very freely introduced in suitable contexts, when not written (as, of course, it usually is not). Indeed, in those passages of accompaniment which are best served by freely arpeggiated chords (figured arpeggios), the passing acciaccatura is of almost continuous utility. This subject will be treated partly in Ch. XXIV, 1, as a branch of ornament, and partly in Ch. XXX as a branch of accompaniment. In solo passages of a certain type, particularly the unmeasured preludes of the French school, the passing acciaccatura is equally of value. See also Chapter XXXII, 2.

(217a) Vincenzo Manfredini, *Regole armoniche*, Venice, 1775, p. 62:

'These Acciaccature make a better effect when the Chords are executed in Arpeggio form, as one is accustomed to do when accompanying Recitatives.'

4. THE POST-BAROQUE ACCIACCATURA

(a) The crushed acciaccatura remained in limited but accepted use in the late eighteenth century, and also, since it is very effective on the piano, in the nineteenth century.

In the twentieth century it is not entirely obsolete, being correctly taught by some; but by the majority it has become confused with the ordinary short appoggiatura whether correctly performed on the beat, or (as more often) incorrectly before the beat. Even if the short appoggiatura is correctly performed, however, it is a regrettable substitution, since the true acciaccatura remains a splendidly virile ornament whose displacement is to be deplored.

(b) The passing acciaccatura did not remain a standard nineteenth century ornament. In the twentieth century, effects of fleeting dissonance somewhat resembling it are found written out in certain styles, but the device of holding the essential notes while releasing the dissonant interpolators is not so typical now that our familiarity with such inessential dissonances makes it less necessary to remove them as quickly as possible from the harmony.

POSTSCRIPT TO NEW VERSION

The close relationship of the simultaneous acciaccatura, the passing acciaccatura and the slide comes out in tables of ornaments, of which Ex. 76b below is from the table of ornaments (in a different hand of about the same date) at the end of an English manuscript (Brit. Mus. Harley MS. 1270, f. 64v.) of about 1690 or 1700, containing Italian and English vocal solos; while Ex. 76c is from a table by Gottlieb Muffat (*Toccatas*, Vienna, 1726) influential enough to have been copied entire by P. Pantaleon Roskovsky in his 'Museum Pantaleonianum' (MS. mus. 749, f. 240r, c. 1750); Ex. 77d shows variant rhythms in Gottlieb Muffat's *Componimenti*, Augsburg, ? 1735.

CHAPTER XVIII

A (v): The Passing Appoggiatura

French: Coulé
German: Nachschlag
              Durchgehender Vorschlag

1. WHAT THE NAME PASSING APPOGGIATURA IMPLIES

This name is the translation of the second and more explicit of the two German names above, which means literally: through-going fore-stroke. As that indicates, it was regarded as an appoggiatura, not as a mere passing note. Its claim to be so regarded rests, however, only on a confused terminology in the baroque period itself, and on a single fact: it was often slurred to the following and not to the previous note, which would have been its natural behaviour as a passing note.

The fashion for this ornament appears to have been of substantial duration, and it is important partly because it looks in notation like a normal appoggiatura, so that it is not very obvious at first sight which is intended; and partly for reasons given in the Postscript below.

2. EVIDENCE FOR THE PASSING APPOGGIATURA

(218) Joachim Quantz, *Essay*, Berlin, 1752, VIII, 5:

'There are two sorts of appoggiaturas. One is taken, like accented notes, on the down-beat; the other like [unaccented] passing notes, on the up-beat of the bar. The first could be called striking [Ger. ed: *anschlagende*; Fr. ed.: *frappant*], and the other passing [*durchgehende*; *passagers*] appoggiaturas.

[6:] 'Passing appoggiaturas are found when several notes of the same value descend by leaps of a third [Ex. (a)]. They are rendered in practice as [Ex. (b)]. It is necessary to sustain the dots, and give a stroke of the tongue [*i.e.* on the flute, concerning which Quantz is ostensibly writing] on the notes where the slur begins, that is to say on the second, the fourth and the sixth note. This sort must not be confused with the notes where there is a dot after the second, and which yield almost the same melody [Ex. (c)]. In this latter figure the second, the fourth, and the subsequent short notes come [as normal accented appoggiaturas] on the beat of the bar, as dissonances against the bass; moreover they are rendered with boldness and liveliness. The appoggiaturas with which we are here concerned, on the contrary, require a flattering expression. If then, the little notes at [Ex. (a)] were taken long and given a stroke of the tongue on the beat which follows, the melody would be completely changed [from] the French style of performing, from which these appoggiaturas are derived. . . One must hold the dots long and stress the notes on which the slurs start.

[7:] 'Striking appoggiaturas, or those which come on the beat of the bar, are found before a long note on the down-beat, following a short one on the up-beat [and are] held for half the following main note.'

Ex. 77. Joachim Quantz, *Essay*, Berlin, 1752, VIII, 5:

(219) Leopold Mozart, *Violinschule*, Augsburg, 1756, IX, 17:

'Passing appoggiaturas . . . do not belong to the time of the main note on to which they fall but must be taken from the time of the note before. . . . The semiquaver is taken quite smoothly and quietly, the accent always coming on the quaver.'

Ex. 78. Leopold Mozart, *Violinschule*, 1756, IX, 17, passing appoggiaturas:

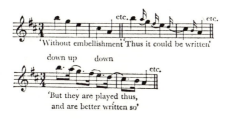

Ex. 79. Jean-Jacques Rousseau, *Dictionnaire de musique*, Paris, 1768, Plate B, passing appoggiatura:

227

3. OPPOSITION TO THE PASSING APPOGGIATURA

(220) F. W. Marpurg, *Anleitung*, 2nd ed., Berlin, 1765, I, ix, 4:

'All appoggiaturas . . . in whatever progression they occur, must fall exactly on the beat. Therefore it is wrong if [Ex. (a) is] performed as at [Ex. (b)] or even as at [Ex. (c)]. They must be played as at Ex. (d).'

Ex. 80. F. W. Marpurg, *Anleitung*, 2nd ed., Berlin, 1765, Tab. III, examples of passing appoggiaturas condemned:

POSTSCRIPT TO NEW VERSION

(a) The unfortunately mis-named 'passing appoggiatura' will be found fully discussed in Frederick Neumann's forthcoming *Baroque and Post Baroque Ornaments*; and I had certainly underestimated though I was not unaware of it in the typically French form shown at Ex. 79 in Sect. 2 above. It is really a passing grace-note which the French frequently and other nationalities sometimes slurred to the ensuing mainnote; and Frederick Neumann has earned my gratitude by refusing to call it an appoggiatura at all. For as he rightly says (footnote 1 to his Part III) 'the commonly used term appoggiatura is unsatisfactory because its connotation of "leaning" is too specific' and he therefore limits it to '*Vorschläge* that fall on the beat'. I think that meets the situation very well.

See also Appendix VI below. The prevalent eighteenth-century appoggiatura (more or less long; accented; on-the-beat) can be seen in Exx. 43–46 in Ch. XIV, 6 above, J. S. Bach's included.

(b) The similarity in notation and in name but not in execution between the appoggiatura proper and the so-called passing appoggiatura is seen, for once unambiguously, in the following French example:

Ex. 80a. Étienne Loulié, *Elemente*, Paris, 1696, S. V. PORT DE VOIX:

CHAPTER XIX

B (i): Tremolo and B (ii): Vibrato

B (i): TREMOLO

Old English:	Organ shake
	Shake
	Trill
Italian:	Tremolo
	Tremoletto
	Trillo
	Mordente fresco
French:	Balancement
	Martèlement
	Souspir
	Verre Cassé
German:	Bebung

1. WHAT THE NAMES TREMOLO AND VIBRATO IMPLY

There is great confusion of terms here. But the clearest terminology is to reserve the word tremolo for a fluctuation of intensity, often but not necessarily amounting to a reiteration of the note; and the word vibrato for a fluctuation of pitch not amounting to a change of note.

When two notes a tone or semitone apart alternate, we speak of a trill in the normal modern sense. When the notes are more than a tone apart, we again speak of a tremolo or tremolando, whether these notes are reiterated simultaneously or alternately.

But at the beginning of the baroque period, the Italian word *trillo,* and its abbreviations *t, tr, tri, etc.,* usually meant not trill, in the modern sense, but what is here called tremolo (on one note at a time).

All the above were regarded as specific ornaments in the baroque period.

2. THE VOCAL TREMOLO

(a) It is mainly tremolo, not vibrato, with which a good singer brings his tone to life. It is essential that he should.

(b) The following refers to a particular development of the tremolo, carried to the point at which the fluctuations of intensity are just but only just slow enough, and distinct enough, to sound like a reiteration of the note. In this form, the tremolo is treated as an ornament: *i.e.* the early baroque Italian vocal *trillo.* (See Postscript at end of Chapter XIX.)

(221) Playford, *Introd.*, London, 1654 (1664 on), cited from ed. of 1674, on Caccini's Preface, *Nuove Musiche*, Florence, 1602:

'The *Trill* [here meaning tremolo] is by a beating in the Throat . . . rather the shaking of the Ovula or Pallate on the Throat, in one sound, upon a Note. . . . I have heard of some that have attained it by this manner, in singing a plain song, of 6 Notes up and 6 down, they have in the midst of every Note beat or shaked with their finger upon their throat, which by often practice came to do the same Notes exactly without. . . . The *Trill*, or *Shake* of the Voice, being the most usual Grace, is made in *Closes*, *Cadences*, and other places, where by a long note an *Exclamation* or *Passion* is expressed, there the Trill is made in the latter part of any such Note; but most usually upon binding Notes in *Cadences* and *Closes*, and on that Note that precedes the closing Note. Those who once attain to the perfect use of the Trill, other Graces will become easie.'

Ex. 81. M. Praetorius, *Syntagma*, III, Wolfenbüttel, 1619, p. 237, *trillo* (original lacks one tail on last four):

As Praetorius rightly adds, 'this kind is found in Claudio Monteverdi'. The ornament was correctly described by Michel L'Affillard in his *Principes* of 1694, and by Brossard, who indicates (i) its free and somewhat hesitant (not mathematical) acceleration, to which notation can only approximate; (ii) its extreme 'lightness and rapidity', to which the heavy and measured pulsation sometimes heard today is quite opposite. The sound must not break too much.

(222) Brossard, *Dictionaire*, Paris, 1703, *s.v.* 'Trillo':

'*Tr* . . . is very often, in Italian music, the sign that one must beat several times on the same note, at first somewhat slowly, then ending with as much lightness and rapidity as the throat can make . . . [but] our example can give only a very crude idea of it, compared with the quickness with which it can be done.'

Ex. 82 lacks the third note of bar two (needed if the two bars are meant to match) in the 1703 edition; later editions have mistakes or changes replacing irregular by regular acceleration. The entire notation is no more than a suggestion for this most subtle and elusive ornament.

Ex. 82. Brossard, *Dictionaire*, 'the true Italian "Trillo" ':

But Tosi in his *Opinioni* of 1723 disapproved of the ornament, as *mordente fresco*. It is possible that the ornament survived considerably longer.

(c) There is every reason for giving baroque music a moderate use of the ordinary tremolo not as an ornament but as the means by which singing tone is kept alive and vibrant, just as string tone is kept alive by the vibrato, for which see 4 below.

(223) Praetorius, *Syntagma*, III, Wolfenbüttel, 1619, p. 231:

'A singer must have a fine, pleasing, trembling and shaking (zittern und bebende) voice, yet not used as in some schools, but with especial moderation.'

3. INSTRUMENTAL TREMOLO

(a) Tremolo in the sense of rapidly reiterated notes was written for the violins by Monteverdi in his *Combattimento di Tancredi e Clorinda* (1624): probably meant measured, *i.e.* as written, not as a free tremolando. This was no novelty in music, but the peculiarly expressive purpose to which the device is there put may well have been. Unmeasured tremolando is, however, a possible interpretation.

(224) Christopher Simpson, *Division-Violist*, London, 1659, p. 10:

'Some also affect a Shake or Tremble with the Bow, like the Shaking-Stop of an Organ, but the frequent use thereof is not (in my opinion) much commendable.'

This free (unmeasured) tremolando is a feasible interpretation of the wavy lines in the frost scene, Act III, Sc. 2, of Purcell's *King Arthur* but they may merely mean measured tremolo in quavers, as they certainly do in Act IV, Sc. 3 of Cesti's *Pomo d'oro*.

(b) Instruments plucked with fingers or plectrum are amenable to thrumming, which is a species of tremolo; not part of classical lute technique.

(c) The clavichord has a species of vibrato which if intensified produces a genuine tremolo. The general names for this technique are It. *tremolo*, Fr. *balancement*, and Ger. *Bebung*. The second aspect is sometimes distinguished as *Tragen der Tone*. But the two things are so closely allied that their names also tend to be confused.

B (ii): VIBRATO

Old English:	Close shake
	Sting
Latin:	Tremor Pressus
Italian:	Vibrato

VIBRATO

French: Aspiration
             Balancement
             Battement
             Flattement
             Langueur
             Pincé
             Plainte
             Souspir
             Tremblement mineur
             Verre cassé

German: Bebung
             Schwebung

4. VIBRATO ON INSTRUMENTS

From the middle of the baroque period until the generation of Kreisler, there was controversy whether the instrumental vibrato should be used (in the modern way) more or less continuously as a means of enlivening the tone, or intermittently as a specific ornament. But that it was used throughout the baroque period, there can be no doubt at all; nor have we any reason to suppose that it was then a novelty. Both Martin Agricola (*Musica Instrumentalis Deutsch*, ed. of 1545, 42–3) and Ganassi (*Regola Rubertina*, 1542, Ch. II) mention a "trembling" of the fingers which is almost certainly vibrato.

(224a) M. Mersenne, *Harmonie Universelle*, Paris, 1636–37, tr. R. E. Chapman, The Hague, 1957, Book II, sect. on Lute ornaments, p. 24:

'The tone of the violin is the most ravishing [when the players] sweeten it . . . by certain tremblings [here meaning vibrato] which delight the mind.

[p. 109:] 'The verre cassé [here meaning vibrato] is not used so much now [on the lute] as it was in the past [partly in reaction] because the older ones used it almost all the time. But [it cannot be dispensed with and] must be used in moderation . . . the left hand must swing with great violence [the thumb being free of the neck].

Ex. 83. Playford, *Introduction*, London, 1654 (1960 on), Table of Ornaments, vibrato:

'a close shake'   'Explan'

(225) Christopher Simpson, *Division-Violist*, London, 1659, sect. 16:

'*Close-shake* is that when we shake the Finger as close and near the sounding Note as possible may be, touching the String with the Shaking finger so softly and nicely that it make no variation of tone. This may be used where no other Grace is concerned.'

Two fingers are used for this form of vibrato. By 'no variation of tone' Simpson evidently means (as an American though not an English

232

writer would now) 'no change of note'. There is, however, a distinct fluctuation of pitch, and the result is a vibrato rather more prominent than usual.

(226) Thomas Mace, *Musick's Monument*, London, 1676, p. 109:

'The *Sting* [vibrato], is another very *Neat, and Pritty Grace;* (But not *Modish* [on the lute] in *These Days*) . . . first strike your *Note,* and so soon as It is struck, *hold your Finger (but not too Hard) stopt upon the Place,* (letting your *Thumb loose*) and *wave your Hand (Exactly) downwards, and upwards, several Times, from the Nut, to the Bridge;* by which *Motion,* your *Finger will draw, or stretch the String a little upwards, and downwards, so,* as to make the Sound seem to *Swell.'*

This too results in a fluctuation of pitch rather than of intensity, and is a normal (one finger) vibrato.

(227) Jean Rousseau, *Traité de la Viole*, Paris, 1687, pp. 100–101:

'The *Batement* [here meaning the extreme form of vibrato] is made when two fingers being pressed one against the other, the one is held on the string, and the next strikes it very lightly . . . [it] imitates a certain sweet agitation of the Voice . . . is used in all contexts where the length of the Note permits, and should last as long as the note.

'The *Langueur* [here meaning the normal vibrato] is made by varying the finger on the Fret. It is ordinarily used when it is necessary to take a Note with the little finger, and time permits; it should last as long as the Note. This ornament is to replace the *Batement* which is unavailable when the little finger is held down.'

Marin Marais (*Pièces de viole*, Paris, 1686) gives *Pincé ou flattement* for the two-finger vibrato and *Plainte* for the one-finger vibrato. In his music the sign for the former is a thin, horizontal wavy line, for the latter a similar line but vertical; the absence of either sign does not, of course, preclude vibrato—he merely marks them where he wants to make particularly sure of them. (But Jean Rousseau means by *Plainte* a *portamento*.)

(228) Fr. Geminiani, *Art of Playing on the Violin*, London, 1751, p. 8:

'Of the Close SHAKE . . . you must press the Finger strongly upon the String of the Instrument, and move the Wrist in and out slowly and equally. When it is long continued, swelling the sound by degrees, drawing the bow nearer to the bridge, and ending it very strong, it may express majesty, dignity, *etc.* But making it shorter, lower, and softer, it may denote affliction, fear, *etc.*, and when it is made on short Notes, it only contributes to make their Sound more agreeable and for this Reason it should be made use of as often as possible.'

(229) Leopold Mozart, *Violinschule*, Augsburg, 1756, XI, i *ff.*:

'The Tremolo [here meaning vibrato] is an adornment which arises from Nature herself . . . if we strike a slack string or a bell sharply, we hear after the stroke a certain undulation. . . . Take pains to imitate this natural quivering on the violin, when the finger is pressed strongly on the string, and one makes a small movement with the whole hand . . . forward and backward . . .

'Now because the tremolo is not purely on one note but sounds undulating, so it would be a mistake to give every note the tremolo. There are performers who tremble [make vibrato] on every note without exception as if they had the palsy . . .

'There is also a slow, an increasing, and a rapid undulation.'

Whether or not vibrato 'arises from Nature herself', it certainly arises from the nature of bowed string instruments. It should be used with sufficient restraint to keep it in style; but it should certainly be used. String tone can sound very dead without it. (Like so much about ornaments in Leopold Mozart, the above is lifted, without acknowledgement, from Tartini's MS. *Traité*, p. 84 in Jacobi's ed.—see Bibl.)

(c) Vibrato is a regular part of clavichord technique.

(230) C. P. E. Bach, *Essay*, Berlin, 1753, III, 20:

'A long, expressive note [on the clavichord] may be performed with a vibrato. The finger holds down the key and rocks it, so to speak.'

(231) Dr. Ch. Burney, *Present State of Music in Germany*, London, 1773, II, 268 (of C. P. E. Bach):

'In the pathetic and slow movements, whenever he had a long note to express, he absolutely contrived to produce, from his instruments, a cry of sorrow and complaint, such as can only be effected upon the clavichord, and perhaps by himself.'

(d) A very reticent approach to vibrato on the violin, not at all to our modern taste, is suggested by the following nineteenth-century recommendation.

(231a) Louis Spohr, *Violinschule*, Vienna, 1832, II, 20:

'[In the vibrato—called oddly by its singer's name of tremolo] the deviation from the perfect intonation of the note, should hardly be perceptible to the ear. . . . Avoid however its frequent use, or in improper places.' [Even in the twentieth century, some hesitation remains as to the continuous vibrato.]

(231b) Carl Flesch, *The Art of Violin Playing*, transl. F. H. Martens, Boston, 1924, ed. of 1939, II, 40:

'From a purely theoretic standpoint, the vibrato, as a means for securing a heightened urge for expression, should only be employed when it is musically justifiable [but in practice the continuous vibrato is to be approved].'

A curiously roundabout way of putting it, but one sees what he means. In truth a continuous vibrato always is musically justifiable provided it is adapted to the degree of intensity which the music momentarily requires. Totally vibrato-less string tone sounds dead in any music. It is just as much an illusion to think that early performers preferred it as to think that early singers preferred a 'white' tone. Sensitive vibrato not only can but should be a normal ingredient in performing early music.

POSTSCRIPT TO NEW VERSION

We have difficulty with the early baroque *trillo*, actually a tremolo, for which see 2(b) above: also App. IX, last par. of (784). Caccini's famous description is mostly even vaguer than the Playford commentary on it at (221) above where 'a beating in the throat' stands for Caccini's 'begin with the crotchet and re-beat each note with the throat' (*ribattere ciascuna nota con la gola*). Caccini's music example is identical with that of Praetorius as I have printed it at Ex. 81 above, except in lacking the tie and the underlayed word; in Praetorius (but not in Caccini) the third tail is lacking (I think by inadvertence) from each of the four notes which I have printed as demi-semiquavers (thirty-second notes).

In the Playford explanation, the clue is: 'in one sound, upon a Note'. The 'note' is not changed (as it would be in what we ordinarily call a trill): moreover, there is only 'one sound' (so that we are not meant to repeat the note in any ordinary sense); yet there is a 'beating' (which must therefore mean a sort of light repercussion not amounting to repetition).

It is common today (*e.g.* in Raymond Leppard's mainly excellent Monteverdi and Cavalli) to caricature the *trillo* by repeating the same note with exaggerated emphasis and in strongly measured rhythm. Caccini includes it in 'the good manner of singing', as a thing written one way but sung another way 'for more grace' and 'refinement' (*squisitezza*). It seems to need only the slightest unmeasured pulsation of intensity within a note otherwise continuous and sustained, as Brossard confirms at (222) above. If it is conspicuous, it is wrong. Its subtlety, its *squisitezza*, is the whole point of it.

CHAPTER XX

B (iii): The Trill

English:	Shake
	Trill
Latin:	Crispatio
	Trepidatio
Italian:	Groppo
	Tremoletto
	Trillo
French:	Cadence
	Pincé renversé
	Tremblement
	Trille
German:	Triller

1. WHAT THE NAME TRILL IMPLIES

By a trill is meant a more or less free and rapid alternation of the main note with an upper accessory note a tone or semitone above it.

Trills are as indispensable to baroque music as appoggiaturas, and even commoner. Few cadences apart from plagal cadences are complete without the conventional trill at least in one of the parts. Cadences are an inescapable feature of baroque style, and rather than trying to escape them, it is better to carry them off with conviction, including the almost inevitable trill. That means not only starting the trill in standard baroque manner with its upper note, but accenting, and often prolonging, that upper note with great assurance and emphasis. Many modern performers who are aware of the need to start baroque trills with the upper note still do not realise that the chief stress should go to it, the remainder of the trill functioning as the merest resolution of the strong suspension thus introduced. The effect is closely related to that of the appoggiatura, and is standard practice. See Appendix VI for another view of baroque trills proposed though not I think established by Frederick Neumann.

2. PRE-BAROQUE AND EARLY BAROQUE TRILLS

(a) Figures resembling trills occur in the earliest sixteenth-century treatises on ornamentation.

236

Ex. 84. Sylvestro di Ganassi, *Fontegara*, Venice, 1535, specimen divisions showing the notes of trills:

Ex. 85. Diego Ortiz, *Trattado*, Rome, 1553, division showing notes of a trill [slur understood; see (612) in Ch. XLVIII, 6 below]:

(b) Shortly after the middle of the sixteenth century we find several specific ornaments taking shape which became prominent in the baroque period, among them genuine trills, of which the notation is still measured in appearance, but the performance is free and unmeasured, as the following implies.

(232) Fray Tomás de Santa María, *Arte de tañer fantasia*, Valladolid, 1565, sect. 8:

'Take care not to make the redoble too long with the effect of making the music clumsy.'

The *redoble* is a trill with special preparation; normal trills, under the name of *quiebro*, are also shown with the same implication.

Ex. 86. Fray Tomás de Santa María, *Arte de tañer fantasia*, Valladolid, 1565, sect. 8, special trill and normal trill:

Written-out trills apparently measured but meant to be free occur in manuscripts and editions not only of the sixteenth but of the seventeenth century. The number of repercussions *shown* is usually but not always what the measure requires; it is not always the same in different copies of the same passage; some copies may have a sign instead. The *intention* may usually be to leave the number of repercussions to the discretion of the performer: in other words, to indicate not a measured division, but some kind of trill, still occasionally with lower-note start (as a melodic, not a harmonic ornament) even into the eighteenth century.

(233) Girolamo Frescobaldi, *Toccate*, Rome, 1615–16, Preface, 6:

'You must not divide the trill [exactly] note for note, but only try to make it rapid.'

(233a) J. A. Herbst, *Musica Moderna Prattica*, Nuremberg, 1642, ed. of 1652/3, p. 59:

'You beat as many [repercussions] in the trill as you desire [*i.e.* regardless of the notation].'

Ex. 87. Giovanni Luca Conforti, *Breve et facile maniera d'essercitarsi a far passaggi*, Rome, 1593, written-out trill:

Groppo di sopra

Ex. 88. Giulio Caccini, *Euridice*, 1600, divisions ending (a) with written-out trill; (b) with implied trill (called by Caccini *groppo*) or *trillo* (ornamental tremolo, for which see Ch. XIX, 2 above):

Written-out trills occur in the manuscripts of the English Virginalists, as well as the double and single strokes, 𝄍 and 𝄌, of which certainly the first and perhaps the second includes the trill (usually a short half-trill) among its possible interpretations. It is further a possibility, though by no means a certainty, that the double stroke suggests an ornament (not necessarily restricted to one kind) made with more repercussions than the single stroke suggests. It does not seem to me very probable that either of these signs was meant as a specific indication of one ornament only, though this too is by no means impossible. The chief arguments against it are first the difficulty of finding two separate ornaments to fit equally well all the contexts in which this pair of signs are used, and second the inconsistency with which the signs appear. See my article 'Ornaments' in Grove's *Dictionary*.

(234) Girolamo Diruta, *Il Transilvano*, II, Venice, 1610, iv, 18:

'Tremolos [here meaning trills] are to be played at the beginning of a Ricercare, or song, or any other composition and again when one hand plays several parts and the other only one, you should play tremolos in the latter, and then at the organist's convenience and discretion, observing always that the tremolo, if played lightly and gracefully and appropriately, makes the music live and sound beautiful.

[p. 19:] 'You should take care to play tremolos with extreme lightness and agility [alternating not] with the note below [*i.e.* as mordents, but] with the note above [*i.e.* as trills], and if you have ever observed players of the viol, violin, lute and other string instruments, and even wind instruments, you must have noticed that they accompany [the main note] of the tremolo with the note above and not with the note below.'

Ex. 89. Girolamo Diruta, *Il Transilvano*, II, Venice, 1610, accelerating trill (for date see Bibliography):

The intention in the above example is evidently a gradually accelerating trill, as it also is in the following.

Ex. 90. Claudio Monteverdi, *Orfeo*, 1607, Act III, accelerating trill:

(c) The trills so far considered, being primarily melodic in their function, start indifferently from their lower (main) note or from their upper (accessory) note. The latter have slightly more harmonic influence, but only by way of coloration. They do not modify the progressions.

(d) The termination which predominates in the trills so far considered is a turn, a characteristic and melodically graceful ending which retains its association with many trills to the present day.

3. BAROQUE TRILLS OF THE MAIN PERIOD

(a) The baroque trill proper is a harmonic ornament, and consequently starts, in all standard cases, from its upper (accessory) note, well accented to mark the ensuing modification of the harmony, and often to a greater or lesser extent prolonged so as to give this modification still greater prominence. The start takes the beat. See Appendix VI.

A typical late renaissance ornamental resolution of a suspended discord might be as follows.

Ex. 91. Typical late renaissance resolution by way of a trill:

Here the discord is present in the written progression. But by an easy transition, trills became used very early in the baroque period to introduce a discord (prepared or otherwise) which is not present in the written progression. This discord is the upper accessory of the trill itself, which may change a plain dominant 5-3 to tonic 5-3 progression into a much more interesting dominant 5-4, through dominant 5-3, to tonic 5-3. Here the 4 is the upper note of a trill on the 3. A trill on the 5 gives dominant 6-3, through dominant 5-3, to tonic 5-3. A double trill in thirds on both 5 and 3 gives dominant 6-4, through dominant 5-3, to tonic 5-3. In each case the resolution is the main note of the trill. An accent on the upper-note start brings out the discord.

Ex. 92. Typical baroque trills modifying the written harmony:

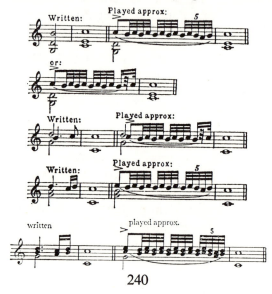

It is because of their modification of the harmony, and particularly of cadential harmony, that baroque trills are so often obligatory and not merely optional ornaments.

(235) B. de Bacilly, *L'Art de Bien Chanter*, Paris, 1668, p. 164:

'[The trill is] one of the most important ornaments, without which the melody is very imperfect.'

We see above that the melodic function was not altogether forgotten; and indeed as late as 1676 we find Mace (*Musick's Monument*, London, p. 103) describing a genuinely lower-note trill for the lute, as well as the normal upper-note trill of his period.

The cadential function, essentially a harmonic function, is, however, stressed in the following.

(236) Tosi, *Opinioni*, Bologna, 1723, tr. Galliard, London, 1742, p. 42:

'Whoever has a fine *shake*, tho' wanting in every other Grace, always enjoys the Advantage of conducting himself without giving Distaste to the End or Cadence, where for the most part it is very essential.'

(237) Joachim Quantz, *Essay*, Berlin, 1752, IX, i:

'Trills infinitely enhance the rendering of music, give it a great brilliance, and just like appoggiaturas are indispensably necessary to it.'

(b) The necessity for the cadential trill must be recognised by the performer regardless of whether any sign or other hint is present in the notation or not; and if a sign is present, regardless of what that sign may be, since there are many possible signs misleading or otherwise, but there is only one basic species of cadential trill.

(238) J. M. Hotteterre, *Principes de la flûte traversière*, Paris, 1707, p. 18:

'It is necessary to point out that the trills (Cadences ou tremblements) are not always marked in musical pieces.'

A masterly understatement.

4. THE PREPARATION OF BAROQUE TRILLS

(a) From our modern point of view, all standard baroque trills are 'prepared' trills, beginning as they do on their upper notes; but in baroque terminology, the upper-note start was taken for granted, and the trill was called 'unprepared' if this initial upper note was not especially prolonged, 'prepared' only if it was very decidedly prolonged.

Ex. 93. Playford, *Introduction*, London, 1654 (1660 on), table of ornaments, trill:

A Backfall
shaked

The above trill is 'unprepared' unless the preceding crotchet *G* is tied to it, in which case it is 'prepared', the crotchet *G* constituting the preparation (a very common method of performance).

Ex. 94. Purcell (or his ed.), posthumous *Lessons*, London, 1696, unprepared and prepared trills (in the baroque sense):

Jean Rousseau (*Traité de la Viole*, Paris, 1687, p. 76) makes this same very usual baroque distinction between trills 'with leaning' (*avec appuy*) and 'without leaning' (*sans appuy*), *i.e.* 'prepared', 'unprepared'.

Ex. 95. D'Anglebert, *Pièces de Clavecin*, Paris, 1689:

Tremblement
simple

Tremblement
appuyé

(238a) Loulié, *Elements*, Paris, 1696, p. 70:

'The trill is an Appoggiatura (*Coulé*) repeated two or more times from a little [*i.e.* ornamental] sound (*petit Son*) to an ordinary [*i.e.* main] note, one degree lower . . .

'When the Voice remains appreciably (*demeure sensiblement*) on the little sound of the first Appoggiatura (*coulé*), this is called preparing the Trill (*appuyer le Tremblement*) . . .

[p. 71]: The preparation [*appuy*] of the trill should be longer or shorter in proportion to the duration of the Note trilled. The Trill [after being prepared] should begin within the Beat (*dans le Temps*) on which the trilled Note begins . . .

'When the Voice does not remain appreciably on the first Note [consisting] of the first Appoggiatura, the Trill is called unprepared Trill (*non appuyé*), or without Preparation (*sans Appuy*).

'The Appoggiaturas of the Trill ought not to be jerked (*secoüez*) . . . but slurred (*liez* [my suggested emendation for corrupt *licez*]) as much as possible as if there were only one sound.'

242

THE TRILL

(239) J. M. Hotteterre, *Principes de la flûte traversière*, Paris, 1707, pp. 11 *ff.*:

'[Trills begin] on the sound above [and are slurred] without taking breath or giving further strokes of the tongue . . . [the preparation may extend to] about half the duration of the [main] note, especially in grave movements.'

(b) The rule that the preparation of the trill shall be slurred to it (the slur including the whole trill) is a further link between the trill and the appoggiatura. Some baroque authorities actually explain the trill as a series of reiterated appoggiaturas from above: see (238a) just quoted. Others call the preparation of the trill an appoggiatura, which is exactly its musical effect. All trills are to be slurred.

(240) Joachim Quantz, *Essay*, Berlin, 1752, IX, 7:

'Each trill starts with the appoggiatura . . . [8:] The appoggiatura is often as quick as the other notes which form the trill; for example when after a rest there comes a new idea with a trill [*i.e.* a new entry actually starting with a trill]. However this appoggiatura, whether it is long or short, ought always to be attacked with a stroke of the tongue [on the flute]; but the trill and its termination ought to be slurred.' [N.B. 'slurred'.]

(241) C. P. E. Bach, *Essay*, Berlin, 1753, II, ii, 9:

['The appoggiatura] is found before cadential trills (*Schluss-Trillern*)'.

(242) Leopold Mozart, *Violinschule*, Augsburg, 1756, X, 11:

'If a trill occurs in the middle of a passage [as at Ex. 96 (a)] then not only is an appoggiatura made before the trill, but the appoggiatura is held throughout half the duration of the note, while the trill is not started till the remaining half [as at Ex. (b): t. transcribed as tr throughout].
'But if a passage begins with a trill an appoggiatura is hardly heard, and is in such a case nothing but a strong attack on the trill [as at Ex. (c)].'

Ex. 96. Leopold Mozart, *Violinschule*, Augsburg, 1756, X, 11:

The preparation is not always called appoggiatura.

(243) Tosi, *Opinioni*, Bologna, 1723, tr. Galliard, London, 1742, p. 48 [see also App. VI, 4–5]:

'The *Shake* [Trill], to be beautiful, requires to be prepared [in the baroque sense], though on some Occasions, Time or Taste will not permit it. But on final Cadences, it [the preparation] is always necessary.'

(c) The following examples from Couperin are ambiguously notated, but can be interpreted, as shown, from the other evidence.

Ex. 97. Fr. Couperin, *Pièces de clavecin*, Paris, 1713, trills: (for *appuyer*, see (586) in Ch. XLV, 7; also Appendix VI, 5):

(243a) F. W. Marpurg, *Principes*, Berlin, 1756, p. 66:

'The trill . . . starts on the accessory [*i.e.* upper] note'. [p. 68]: 'the leant-upon (*appuyé*) or prepared (*préparé*) trill [is] when one remains a little time on the accessory note before making the beating, or when one starts with a slow beating and increases the speed by a kind of gradation' [see (247) below].

Ex. 98. J.-J. Rousseau, *Dict.*, Paris, 1768, Plate B, trill with very long preparation (his interpretation followed by mine):

(d) When a baroque trill is preceded by a note which is the same note as its own accessory note, the accessory (*i.e.* upper) note begins the trill, as usual, whether by repeating the previous note, or by being tied to it: either interpretation being equally correct and the choice between them depending on taste and context. The example concerned is given by C. P. E. Bach in illustration of his rule, quoted at (241) above, that cadential trills need preparation.

Ex. 99. C. P. E. Bach, *Essay*, Berlin, 1753, II, ii, 9, trill prepared even when preceded by the same note as its own accessory note (my interpretations):

The correctness of the two alternative interpretations here suggested is confirmed by the following, which mentions them both.

(244) F. W. Marpurg, *Anleitung*, 2nd ed., Berlin, 1765, I, ix, 7, p. 55:

'A trill, wherever it may stand, must begin with its accessory note . . . [annotation on p. 56:] If the upper note with which a trill should begin, immediately precedes the note to be trilled, it has either to be renewed by an ordinary attack, or has, before one starts trilling, to be connected, without a new attack, by means of a tie, to the previous note.'

(e) For ornamental preparations see Ch. XXV, 3 below.

(f) So general was the baroque view of the initial upper note of the trill as in normal circumstances the actual equivalent of an appoggiatura that the little note commonly used to indicate an appoggiatura was sometimes used as a sign for a (well prepared) trill. Thus at bar 26 of J. S. Bach's Cantata 1, *Wie schön leuchtet* . . . , the second oboe da caccia has this appoggiatura sign against *tr* in the second violin, with which it is playing in unison; and the same thing happens to the first oboe da caccia and the first violin. The little quaver *C* sharp in bar 1 of the aria 'Erbarme dich' from J. S. Bach's *St. Matthew Passion* can be taken as a prepared trill in this way, the semiquaver *A* sharp being delayed and shortened to a demi-semiquaver in the usual manner. (The first ornament is a Slide, for which see Ch. XVI. It is best taken on the beat. The appoggiatura in bar 2, not shown here, lasts a dotted crotchet; those in bar 3 last a semiquaver. None of these can be trilled.)

Ex. 99a. J. S. Bach, appoggiatura sign indicating trill:

5. THE SPEED OF BAROQUE TRILLS

(244a) Loulié, *Elements*, Paris, 1696, p. 71:

'[Trill] quicker or slower, in proportion to the quickness or slowness of the piece [and] longer or shorter, in proportion to the length of the Note trilled.'

(245) J. M. Hotteterre, *Principes*, Paris, 1707, p. 11:

'The number of repercussions is governed solely by the length of the note.'

(246) Fr. Couperin, *Pièces de Clavecin*, Premier Livre, Paris, 1713, note on table of ornaments:

'It is the length of the note which should decide the duration of mordents, of appoggiaturas, and of trills. You must understand by the word duration the greater or lesser number of strokes, or repercussions.'

(247) Fr. Couperin, *L'Art de toucher*, Paris, 1716, ed. of 1717, p. 23:

'Although the trills are marked as regular in the table of ornaments in my first book, they are nevertheless to begin more slowly than they finish.'

This accelerating trill is confirmed by other evidence, as at (243a) above, but was probably much less usual than the following.

(248) Joachim Quantz, *Essay*, Berlin, 1752, IX, 5:

'For trills to be perfectly beautiful, they must be made equal, that is to say, of an equal speed and one kept to the same rapidity.'

As usual, it is the musical context which determines the performance of any given trill. But the speed of repercussion is never measured.

(249) Joachim Quantz, *Essay*, Berlin, 1752, IX, 2:

'There is no need to make all trills with the same speed. It is necessary to adapt yourself not only to the place where you play, but also to the piece itself which you have to play. If the place where you play is large, and if it reverberates, a rather slow trill will make a better effect than a quick trill [and *vice versa*] . . . In addition you must know how to distinguish what sort of piece you are playing, so as not to confuse one thing with another, which is what happens with a lot of people. In sad pieces the trills are made slowly; but in gay pieces they ought to be made more quickly.

[3:] 'With regard to the slowness and quickness, you must not fall into any excess. The completely slow trill, only used in French singing, is worth as little as the completely quick trill, which the French call bleating (chevroté).'

(250) Leopold Mozart, *Violinschule*, Augsburg, 1756, X, 7:

'The slow [trill] is used in sad and slow pieces; the medium in pieces which have a lively but yet a moderate and restrained tempo, the rapid in pieces which are very lively and full of spirit and movement, and finally the accelerating trill is used mostly in cadenzas and with gradual crescendo . . . . The trill must above all else not be played too rapidly.'

6. THE TERMINATION OF BAROQUE TRILLS

(a) Every standard baroque trill (as opposed to half trills) requires a termination, which can only be one of two kinds, unless it is complicated by further ornamentation, for which see Ch. XXV, 3 below.

(b) The oldest termination was the turned ending to which attention has already been drawn in the sixteenth-century examples in 2 above. It appears in Playford (*Introduction*, London, 1654, *etc.*), in Purcell's posthumous *Lessons* (London, 1696), in Tosi (*Opinioni*, 1723), in Gottlieb Muffat (*Componimenti*, ?1735) and many other sources, and has in fact never gone out of use.

(251) Joachim Quantz, *Essay*, Berlin, 1752, IX, 7:

'The end of each trill consists of two little notes, which follow the note of the trill and which are made at the same speed. . . . Sometimes these little notes are written . . . but when there is only the plain note . . . both the appoggiatura [preparation] and the termination must be understood.'

When the little notes are written, we have to remember that they are not necessarily to be taken at their written time value, but as a continuation of the trill itself, a point on which Quantz, above, is confirmed by other authorities.

(252) C. P. E. Bach, *Essay*, Berlin, 1753, II, iii, 13:

'Trills on notes of a certain length are played with a termination . . . [15:] The termination must be played as quickly as the trill itself.'

Even when the turned termination of a trill is supplied in ordinary notes of seemingly slower value (as at Ex. 97b and c above) it is almost always best to assimilate the termination to the trill by taking it without a break, and at the same speed as the repercussions of the trill, with which it imperceptibly merges. This is a very important and valuable rule, to which occasional exceptions can (but need not) occur:

Ex. 100. Purcell (or his editor), *Lessons*, 1696, table of ornaments, trill with termination in unusual rhythm:

Ex. 101. Leopold Mozart, *Violinschule*, Augsburg, 1756, X, 6, trill with termination in most unusual and unattractive rhythm:

(253) J. C. F. Rellstab, *C. P. E. Bach's Anfangsgründe mit einer Anleitung*, Berlin, 1790, p. ix:

'Present fashion has brought it in that the termination shall be slower than the trill; and that a little embellishment is added to the termination. Formerly this was thought absurd; true connoisseurs may still think so.'

Ex. 102. Leopold Mozart, *Violinschule*, Augsburg, 1756, X, 13, trill with ornamented turn:

(254) C. P. E. Bach, *Essay*, Berlin, 1753, II, iii, 13:

'Although in rather slow tempos the trills [at Ex. 103] may be given a termination (in spite of the fact that the short notes following the dot can serve instead) . . . it is not absolutely necessary to insert the termination, provided that the dotted notes are trilled for their full duration.'

Ex. 103. C. P. E. Bach, *Essay*, Berlin, 1753, II, iii, 13, short notes, after trills, which may serve as their terminations·

The following, according to Quantz, requires a turned ending.

Ex. 104. Joachim Quantz, *Essay*, Berlin, 1752, Engl. tr. *c.* 1790, Ex. 21 (a), trill followed by rest but requiring termination:

(c) The alternative termination, which, for the baroque period itself, was as important as the turned ending just described, is a little note of anticipation inserted just before the note succeeding to that on which the trill is made.

(255) B. de Bacilly, *L'Art de Bien Chanter*, Paris, 1668, p. 164:

'The termination . . . is a join made between the trill and the note on which it is desired to arrive, by means of another note touched very delicately.

[p. 183:] 'Although the composer has not marked on paper the joins after the trills . . . it is a general rule to assume them, and never to suppress them, otherwise the trill will be maimed, and will not be complete.'

Where, on the other hand, the composer has written down the note of anticipation, it may appear misleadingly, at a greater length than it must be given in performance. The normal baroque principles of rhythmic alteration (for which see Ch. XLIII below) come into operation here, by which a dotted figure may have its dot prolonged and its shorter note delayed and shortened, usually with a silence of articulation taking part of the value of the prolonged dot. The following would be a typical example.

Ex. 105. Conventional notation implying a trill with termination by a short note of anticipation:

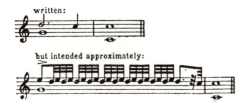

In the above example, the main note of the trill is shown held to a length of a dotted quaver before the demisemiquaver silence of articulation and the demi-semiquaver note of anticipation. This holding of the main note, which cannot arise when the trill is terminated by a turned ending taken normally at the speed of the trill itself, is the meaning of the following rule.

(256) T. B., *Compleat Musick-Master*, 3rd ed., London, 1722, ch. III:

'Always let the Proper Note [*i.e.* the main note of the trill] be distinctly hear'd at the last.'

(257) F. W. Marpurg, *Anleitung*, 2nd ed., Berlin, 1765, I, ix, 7, p. 55:

'A trill . . . must finish, with a certain emphasis, on its main note, for this to be properly felt.'

Ex. 105a. Leopold Mozart, *Violinschule*, Augsburg, 1756, X, 6, trill terminated with note of anticipation:

Ex. 106 (b) following is the end of a passage which balances that ending at Ex. 106 (a); they are meant to sound the same (except for any flourish added impromptu by the player). The inconsistency in their notation is revealing because it shows that a cadential ♩♩ may normally be taken for ♩.♩, and, of course, given the cadential trill which this latter figure invites.

Ex. 106: G. F. Handel, *Deutsche Arien*, No. 4, Vn. Obbligato:

7. THE SO-CALLED 'CORELLI CLASH' RESOLVED BY THE CONVENTIONAL TRILL?

Ex. 107. 'Corelli clash' (a) as written and (b), (c), as perhaps intended to be performed (approximately) but see App. VI, 6 (i) for trills in consecutive seconds, also possible here:

8. HALF-TRILLS

(a) The standard baroque half-trill is prepared in the modern but not in the baroque sense of the word: that is to say, it starts with its upper note, but this initial upper note is not, as a rule, substantially prolonged. There is no termination; the trill ends on its main note, held long enough to make a distinct effect (but subject to the total time available). The function of the half-trill is scarcely harmonic; it is partly melodic; but it is, when short, primarily rhythmic.

(b) The least number of repercussions to constitute a trill at all is two, giving four notes (one repercussion is an appoggiatura). This double repercussion is the half-trill at its purest, in which form its correct German name is *Pralltriller* ('compact trill'). The *Pralltriller* occurs most typically in passages descending by step: the opposite of the mordent, for reasons given at Sect. 4(a) below.

(c) The theoretical interpretation of the following *Pralltriller*, which is also the practical interpretation except at too rapid a speed, is as follows. It is on the beat, though tied. (N.B.: no Ex. 108.)

Ex. 109. C. P. E. Bach, *Essay*, Berlin, 1753, II, iii, 30, half-trill (Der halbe oder Prall-Triller) TAB. IV, Fig. XLV:

At a rapid speed, this cannot be executed, and becomes in practice the following, which is not theoretically a trill at all, but an upper (*i.e.* inverted) mordent. One German name for this is *Schneller* ('jerk'); and this and the *Pralltriller* became very confused both in theory and in practice during late baroque and post-baroque times. It is quite probable that the methods first shown as Ex. 110B below, by which the slurring of the ornament to the note before it produces this transformation of a *Pralltriller* (half-trill) into a *Schneller* (inverted mordent) with or without the compulsion of rapid speed, were already coming into fashion when C. P. E. Bach wrote in 1753, although he does not himself recognise them. But in the generation of J. S. Bach, no general recognition seems to have been accorded to the inverted mordent, and the only cases (if any) may have been those produced by a rapid speed as at Ex. 110A or Ex. 111 below.

Ex. 110. Mixed gathering of MSS in part (but not in this part) associated with J. L. Krebs (J. S. Bach's pupil around 1735), Deutsche Staatsbibliothek, E. Berlin, Mus. MS. Bach P803; anon. table of ornaments, *ff.* 22v–23, copied probably not very much before 1800, '*Pralltriller oder Abzug*' ('off-pull'):

Pralltriller oder Abzug

---

[1] Tie omitted in original, but shown correctly in the identical illustration (presumably borrowed from C. P. E. Bach) by his brother, J. C. F. Bach, in the *Musikalische Neben-stunden*, I, Rinteln, 1787.

Ex. 110A. *Pralltriller* becoming *Schneller* at speed (my Ex.):

(d) The same half-trill may be taken without the tie; but it is just as subject to the effect of great speed. It is on the beat, struck instead of tied.

Ex. 111. (a) half-trill not tied, (b) as performed at moderate speed, (c) and (d) as transformed into an upper mordent by increasing speed (my Ex.):

The German terms *Pralltriller* for (b) and *Schneller* for (c) or (d) are equally applicable to these untied versions, where they have, however, been equally subject to confusion.

(e) Whether tied or not, the short half-trill (*Pralltriller*) is always performed (even in slow movements) with the greatest attainable sharpness.

(258) C. P. E. Bach, *Essay*, Berlin, 1753, II, iii, 30–32:

'The half-trill or *Pralltriller* (der halbe oder Prall-Triller) . . . must really bounce [*prallen*] . . . with such extreme speed that the [separate notes] will only be heard with difficulty . . .

[34:] 'The half trill or *Pralltriller* only occurs on a descending step of a second regardless of whether the interval is produced by an appoggiatura or by large [*i.e.* main or written] notes . . . when it occurs over a note prolonged by a pause, the appoggiatura is held rather long and the trill is then quite briefly snapped as the fingers draw away from the keys.'

Where the written notes are short, the following example shows with what extreme velocity the ornament has to be carried off, and how inevitably it becomes changed into the upper (inverted) mordent or *Schneller* as soon as the tempo becomes rapid.

Ex. 112. C. P. E. Bach, *Essay*, Berlin, 1753, II, iii, 35, (a) half-trill, (b) changed into an inverted mordent by the effect of speed, (c) as performed if the speed permits (my interpretations):

Of the following examples, the first should be taken as normal half-trills (*Pralltriller*), but the second, not only on account of the speed but also from the presence of the slur, can in practice only be satisfactorily executed as inverted mordents (*Schneller*). (Leopold Mozart states in a footnote to the edition of 1787 that 'all these trills are without turns'.)

Ex. 113. Leopold Mozart, *Violinschule*, Augsburg, 1756, X, 16–17, (a) half-trills and (b) inverted mordents (my interpretations).

(f) But while it is both necessary and correct to allow the fastest half-trills to be transformed into inverted mordents by the effects of speed, it is neither correct nor musically desirable under any circumstances to allow them to anticipate the beat.

(g) Half-trills can also be used in a more leisurely manner than the Berlin school of C. P. E. Bach preferred. They can, moreover, on sufficiently long notes, be allowed more repercussions, provided time is still left to dwell on the last appearance of the main note sufficiently to prevent their turning into hybrid, unterminated full trills. The following is a typical half-trill of greater length.

Ex. 114. Long half-trill:

9. CONTINUOUS TRILLS

(a) A special case arises when trills are found, or are placed by the performer, over a number of notes in succession. We may call them continuous trills.

(b) The continuous trill may be of any length from very short to very long; but whatever its length, it normally fills out the entire duration of the note on which it is placed. We therefore cannot regard it, even in its shortest examples, as a half-trill. It is a full trill of which the behaviour is in some respects irregular.

(c) The purpose of the continuous trill is essentially to add brilliance. Its shortest examples serve primarily a rhythmic function; its longer examples might be called melodic, although their primary effect is one of coloration. In no case does the continuous trill serve a primarily harmonic function. Thus it may but does not have to start with the upper note, accented in the shortest examples, but much less accented in the longer examples. And however long the trill, the initial upper note is not prolonged, but is taken at the same speed as the remaining repercussions.

(d) In spite of the fact that the continuous trill fills out the entire duration of the note, there is no necessity for a termination, though under some circumstances a turned ending may be supplied at the performer's option.

(259) Leopold Mozart, *Violinschule*, Augsburg, 1756, X, 22:

'These rising and falling [continuous] trills [may be fingered 1, which makes them without a turn: Ex. 115 (a) and (b)].

[25:] 'With notes [not taken stepwise but] lying some distance apart, continuous trills may be used, but this is seldom feasible in a quick allegro, and then normally only in cadenzas. [Ex. 115 (c)].

[Added in ed. of 1787:] 'These continuous trills used on notes lying some distance apart are best taken with turned ending. Also the rising and falling trills shown [at Ex. 115 (a), (b) and (c)] can be taken with turns if the tempo is very slow . . . but the turn must be rapid and fierce.

[26:] 'There is a species of rising and falling trill each of whose [main] notes [has instead of the turn] a quick leap to the open string below. [Ex. 115 (d)]. In such cases the trill should be held on [virtually] as long as if there were only one note, and the leap down should be delayed so as to be scarcely heard.'

Ex. 115. Leopold Mozart, *Violinschule*, Augsburg, 1756, X, 22 *ff*., continuous trills:

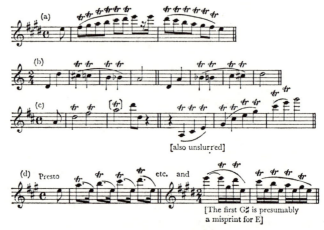

[also unslurred]

[The first G♯ is presumably a misprint for E]

(e) The longest continuous trills are those found primarily in harpsichord music on notes so long that they would die away unduly if the sound were not kept in being in this way. Similar trills are also found for wind and string instruments, either to match a harpsichord part which includes them, or purely as an effect of colour. They do, moreover, considerably intensify the melodic line, wherever they are found.

THE TRILL

(260) C. P. E. Bach, *Essay*, Berlin, 1753, I, ii, 5:

'The sign [a wavy line] is extended when it appears over long notes. [The trill] always begins on the note above the main note . . . [6:] Sometimes two little notes from below [*i.e.* the turned ending] are added. . . .'

A series of very long trills (perhaps each a full bar in length) may either be given turned endings (at the same speed as the trill, and therefore not very conspicuous), or they may be run straight into one another. But if the last trill ends with the bar (or half-bar) it is generally better to give at least this trill a turned ending before passing on to the continuation of the melodic line. If, on the other hand, the trill is tied over to the first beat of the next bar, it is generally the most effective solution to dispense with a termination, ending the trill with this beat, and holding the beat itself as a plain note: in other words, to treat the trill as a greatly prolonged half-trill.

It is also possible to treat all the trills in the series as prolonged half-trills, dispensing with a termination, and holding the main note plain for perhaps the last third or quarter of its length.

10. THE RIBATTUTA

The ribattuta (*Ger.* Zurückschlag) is an ornament of the Caccini-Monteverdi school which remained in some use at least to the end of the baroque period. It is in effect a slowly accelerating trill of which the rhythm is uneven until the repercussions reach a certain speed, by which time they have gradually become even and take the form of an ordinary trill—either in the old Italian sense of tremolo, or in the later sense in which we use the word trill. Originally a singer's ornament, but subsequently borrowed by instrumentalists, the ribattuta always served a melodic function, and it begins on its lower note. It is really effective only for the voice; yet C. P. E. Bach (*Essay*, Berlin, 1753, II, iii, 25) shows it for the harpsichord, and Leopold Mozart (*Violinschule*, Augsburg, 1756, X, 5) for the violin. Mattheson gives it only for the voice, and says (in 1739) that he has not found it in the published treatises.

Ex. 116. Johann Mattheson, *Vollkommene Capellmeister*, Hamburg, 1739, Pt. II, Ch. 3, 48, ribattuta, leading to trill (the whole described as a species of 'tenuta'):

[performed as a gradual acceleration]

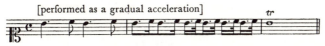

11. THE POST-BAROQUE TRILL

(a) The typical and intrinsically powerful baroque cadence by dominant suspension-resolution passed at last into transition and eventual decline in the subsequent period; and with it the operative purpose of the harmonic trill. As early as Daniel Gottlob Türk (*Klavierschule*, 1789) we find a hint that exceptions to the upper-note start occurred, though he does not show any such exceptions in his examples. J. A. Hiller (*Anweisung zum Violinspielen*, 1792) neither mentions nor shows any exception to the baroque rule; J.-B. Cartier makes one exception, and for a very interesting reason:

(261) J.-B. Cartier, *L'Art du Violon*, Paris [1798], ch. on ornaments:

'It is necessary to use it often, for if we made continual mordents and trills, without ever perceiving the main note, the melody would be too obscured.'

Ex. 117. J.-B. Cartier, *L'Art du Violon*, Paris [1798], delayed trill:

Tenue sur la Note   Ou de même

This somewhat illogical example appears to give first a form of main-note start (but when the trill really arrives it does so with an upper-note start), and second a normal upper-note start as an alternative rendering.

Louis Adam (*Méthode*, 1798) gives a lower-note start only on a long cadence of special type. Clementi (*Introduction*, c. 1803) makes several exceptions, but otherwise respects the baroque rule. Pollini (*Metodo* used at Milan Conservatory, 2nd ed. 1811); Cramer (84 *Studies*, c. 1810); Rode, Kreutzer (to whom Beethoven dedicated the Kreutzer sonata) and Baillot with their famous *Méthode de violon* (drawn up for the Paris Conservatoire, chiefly by Baillot, whose own *Art du violon* was published in 1834): all these retained the upper-note start without exceptions.

Hummel (*Anweisung*, 1828—not 1827; see Bibliography), Spohr (*Violinschule*, 1832) and Czerny (*Pianoforte School*, 1839), argued in favour of a lower-note start to all trills, on the same reasonable grounds already used by Cartier at (261) above to justify his single case: *i.e.* that for melodic purposes the main note ought to be more strongly impressed on the ear than the accessory note.

The trill was now again, in short, what it had previously been in the sixteenth century: a primarily melodic ornament. As such, it should perhaps more logically have a main-note start; but this is not a pressing necessity, as the upper-note start is for a harmonic trill. Even in the second half of the nineteenth century we can still find evidence for the upper-note start as an equally recognised alternative to the main-note start.

(262) F. de Courcy, *Art of Singing*, London, c. 1868, p. 95:

'[In trills, the main] note itself, or the [accessory] note above, may be begun with and given the accent to. . . .'

It must be clearly understood that the upper-note start remained standard at least until the second quarter of the nineteenth century. Hummel, for example, was proposing to standardise the main-note start *as an innovation* in 1828, a year after Beethoven's death. The interpretation, then, which Haydn and Mozart, Beethoven and Schubert mainly gave their trills, and which their contemporary performers gave them, may be an upper-note start. Our present interpretation with a main-note start may be contrary to the composer's intention.

On the other hand, while the initial upper-note will always take the accent normal to its position in the bar, and may frequently be given added accentuation, it will not ordinarily be prolonged. Such prolongation is only associated with trills used primarily for harmonic purposes; and that was only exceptionally the case in nineteenth century music.

In the adagio of Beethoven's quartet Op. 127 (bar 55, Vn. II) a single appoggiatura appears which may be taken as confirming a normal initial upper note to the trill; but the same treatment must be given to the many corresponding trills which are not thus marked. The following example supports such a treatment.

Ex. 118. I. Pleyel, *Méthode de pfte.*, early 19th cent., trill with prolonged initial upper note shown as appoggiatura:

(b) The body of the trill remained what it still is: the same as in the baroque period.

(c) The termination of standard trills of the late-eighteenth century and the nineteenth century was the turned ending. There seems to be a rare unanimity among the authorities on this point, including all those so far cited in the present section. It will be sufficient to quote three passages, the first two because they are so plainly put, the third for its late date.

(263) Türk, *Klavierschule*, Leipzig and Halle, 1789, ed. of 1802, p. 27:

'The Turn is made to the Shake trill even without a Mark, when the length of the Note admits of it.'

(264) Hummel, *Anweisung*, Vienna, 1828, III, p. 387:

'Every trill must end with a turned ending, whether this is marked or not. . . . Except for rare and special effect it is at the same speed as the trill.'

(265) F. de Courcy, *Art of Singing*, London, *c.* 1868, p. 95:

'Shakes [trills] generally conclude with a turn. . . .'

The alternative ending by a little note of anticipation was still described by the notoriously conservative J.-B. Cartier (*L'Art du*

Violon, Paris [1798]) as 'how one ordinarily and most naturally finishes' a trill; but the balance of evidence suggests that this was now the exception, and the turned ending the rule. Hummel (*Anweisung*, 1828, III, 387) certainly treats it so (N.B. not 1827: see Bibliography).

It thus appears that all the hundreds upon hundreds of standard trills in Haydn, Mozart, Schubert or Beethoven are meant to be taken with a turned ending (performed at the same speed as the rest of the trill) in spite of the fact that some are so marked while others are not. A typical instance occurs in the opening phrase of Beethoven's violin sonata Op. 96. His fourth violin sonata, last movement, second subject shows a trill marked with a turn in the recapitulation, but without at its first appearance; they should both be the same, *i.e.* with the turn. The scherzo of his posthumous quartet Op. 127 has numerous trills of which some but not others are shown with turned endings; but they all require turned endings, while some additional trills not marked at all may be supplied to complete the pattern (*e.g.* Vn. II, bar 10, *cf.* bar 281; Viola, bar 20, *cf.* bar 291). Later in the nineteenth century, it remains by far the strongest probability that trills shown without any marked termination should be given a turned ending by the performer. The unterminated trill appears to be an entirely modern innovation. There is no such thing as an unterminated standard trill either in baroque or in classical music.

(d) The half-trill, on the other hand, continued to be unterminated; it also continued to start on its upper-note (ordinarily unprolonged), with much the same exceptions due to speed.

The distinction between the half-trill and the full trill could not be more clearly shown than in the following examples.

Ex. 119. Busby, *Complete Dictionary of Music*, London, [1786], *s.v.* 'Shake', (a) half-trill, (b) full trill:

C. P. E. Bach's rather subtle tied *Pralltriller* (Ex. 109 above), besides being impossible at a rapid speed, is by no means easy to keep intact even at a slower speed; and his treatment tended to be replaced by the following.

Ex. 120. L'Abbé le fils, *Principes du Violon*, Paris, c. 1761, (a) *Schneller*, (b) *Pralltriller*:

In both cases the ornament falls on the beat, as usual. But at (a), the effect of the slur is to make the ornament sound as if it already had an upper-note preparation in the first note of the bar, and did not need another. Its transformation into what is actually a slurred *Schneller* (inverted mordent) has therefore a natural and satisfactory effect. At (b), on the other hand, the first note of the bar, not being slurred to the ornament, does not sound like a preparation for it, and it is therefore natural to supply one in the ordinary way. This keeps the *Pralltriller* (half-trill) intact.

D. G. Türk (*Klavierschule*, 1789) still shows C. P. E. Bach's tied *Pralltriller* as the correct interpretation of the sign ⁓ in adagio; for andante he shows the *Schneller*, but includes it under *Pralltriller* instead of giving it its own proper name. Subsequent authorities confused both these and other names, as well as a variety of signs, to a quite remarkable extent, and it is not surprising that this confusion has persisted, and somewhat thickened, in modern times. We have no such excuse for taking these ornaments before the beat, or for beginning them before the beat, since all the authorities appear to assume that they fall on the beat, and a number of them including J. A. Hiller (*Anweisung zum Violinspielen*, 1792), J. H. Knecht (*Methodenbuch*, early 19th century) and I. Pleyel (*Méthode de pfte.*, early 19th cent.) actually state the fact or make it clear from their examples.

The inverted mordent in its own right (and not merely as a *Pralltriller* transformed into a *Schneller*) is treated in Chapter XXI, 3 below.

The half-trill in its special aspect as a *Pralltriller* may be treated either as at Exx. 109 and 111 in 8 above, or as at Ex. 120 above in the present section: this remains true for any music in which it makes a genuine appearance.

The half-trill in its more genuine aspect as a trill of two or more repercussions but ending, without termination, on its own main note held long enough to be distinctly heard, should normally be treated in classical music in the same way as in baroque music. It is not unknown with a main-note start (*e.g.* in J. H. Knecht, *Methodenbuch*, early 19th century), but in this form it loses much of its true character as a curtailed trill, and becomes in effect a more or less prolonged inverted mordent.

(e) The continuous trill remained as in baroque times in so far as it was still used by virtuoso singers, violinists and others.

(f) The ribattuta was still described by J. D. Andersch (*Musikalisches Woerterbuch*, 1829), on baroque lines.

(g) The regular trills in Manuel Garcia's *Hints on Singing* (London, 1894), perhaps the last will and testament of traditional *bel canto*, are all given upper-note, on-the-beat starts.

CHAPTER XXI

B (iv): The Mordent

English:	Beat
	Mordent
	Open Shake
	Sweetening
Latin:	Tremulus
Italian:	Mordente
French:	Battement
	Martellement
	Mordant
	Pincé
	Pincement
	Tiret
German:	Beisser
	Mordant, Mordent

1. WHAT THE NAME MORDENT IMPLIES

By a mordent is meant a more or less free and rapid alternation of the main note with a lower accessory note a tone or semitone below it.

The name means 'biting' and a certain ferocity is normally associated with the shorter mordents, of which the function is essentially rhythmic, while the longer mordents, which have some melodic influence, tend to be a little smoother. The ornament is extremely valuable throughout baroque music.

2. SINGLE, DOUBLE AND CONTINUED MORDENTS

(a) A single mordent has only one repercussion, and is the sharpest of rhythmic ornaments except for the acciaccatura.

(b) A double mordent has two repercussions, and is still primarily a rhythmic ornament.

(c) A continued mordent may have any number of repercussions, lasting up to several bars, and like the longest trills, sustains and intensifies the melodic line and adds colour to the texture.

Ex. 121. Fr. Couperin, *Pièces de clavecin*, Paris, 1713, (a) single (b) double, (c) continued mordents:

260

(c) written

performed

3. THE INVERTED MORDENT

(a) A single mordent may occur inverted: *i.e.* alternating with an upper instead of with a lower accessory note. But see 6(a) below.

These are the notes of a trill rather than of a mordent; but being so short, the ornament sounds like a mordent and not like a trill.

The correct German name for this is *Schneller* (called by C. P. E. Bach, II, viii, 1, a 'short inverted mordent'); the French name is *pincé renversé* (inverted or reversed mordent). We have seen in Ch. XX, 8 and 11 (d) above, that if circumstances rob a *Pralltriller* of its initial note, it becomes a *Schneller*. Nevertheless the *Pralltriller* is not an inverted mordent; it is long enough to sound like a prepared half-trill, and that is what it is. The two ornaments are distinct, but since they only differ by one brief note and the *Schneller* may under certain circumstances replace the *Pralltriller* in practice, it is not surprising that they became, as they still are, seriously confused.

(b) There are in practice no other inverted mordents, since to invert a double or continued mordent is to turn it into a half-trill or a trill.

4. THE POSITION OF MORDENTS

(a) Mordents may be used in many positions, always on the beat, as (278) below confirms; but the following are pointers.

(266) C. P. E. Bach, *Essay*, Berlin, 1753, II, v, 4:

'The mordent is particularly effective in an ascent by step or by leap. It appears seldom in a descent by leap, and never on descending steps of a second.

[14:] 'The mordent is the opposite of the half-trill. This latter may be used on a step only in descent, which is just where a mordent is unsuitable.'

This rule (*i.e.* that a mordent is effective on a step only in ascent) is reliable for pre-baroque as well as for baroque music, and if the reader will make the experiment of trying it in reverse, he will see why; for the ornament thus used weakly anticipates the following note. An inverted mordent, however, behaves like a half-trill in this respect (*i.e.* it is effective on a step only in descent).

(b) The following are more hints than rules, but as such are widely applicable.

THE MORDENT

(267) C. P. E. Bach, *Essay*, Berlin, 1753, II, v, 9:

'Mordents, especially short ones, lend brilliance to leaping, detached notes.

[10:] 'The mordent is of all ornaments the most freely introduced by the performer into the bass, especially on notes at the highest point of a phrase, reached either by step or by leap, at cadences and other places, especially when the next note stands at an octave below.'

5. PRE-BAROQUE MORDENTS

Ex. 122. Fray Tomás de Santa María, *Arte de tañer fantasia*, Valladolid, 1565, sect. 8, (a) inverted (upper) and (b) standard (lower) mordents ('single quiebro'):

Ex. 123. E. N. Ammerbach, *Tabulatur*, Leipzig, 1571, double mordents:

6. BAROQUE MORDENTS

(a) The inverted mordent, which appears on equal terms with the standard mordent in 5, Ex. 122 above, disappears from baroque music, except as the result of a certain speed in descending steps, *i.e.* as the *Schneller* of C. P. E. Bach and others, for which see Ch. XX, 8 and 11 (d) above.

(268) F. W. Marpurg (ed.), *Kritische Briefe*, Berlin, 30 May, 1759, letter 2:

'Ask your honest Mr. Amisallos whether anyone knew anything of the Pralltriller or Schneller in his youth.'

This means that the not uncommon modern practice of relying on the inverted (upper) mordent as the chief ornament for baroque music is incorrect. The standard baroque mordent is the lower mordent.

(b) Mordents are among the probable renderings for the English Virginalists' ♪ from the turn of the sixteenth and seventeenth centuries, and perhaps also for ♪ (see Ch. XX, 2 for the possibility that the double stroke may suggest more repercussions than the single stroke; but the most useful mordent in this music is the single mordent, just as the most useful trill, except at cadences, is the half-trill).

(c) Later in the baroque period, mordents are among the ornaments suggested by the ubiquitous + and ×.

THE MORDENT

(d) At any stage in the baroque period, mordents are among the ornaments most freely at the disposal of the performer when not marked. This applies as much to singers as to instrumentalists; but see (277) in 9 below.

7. DIATONIC AND CHROMATIC MORDENTS

(a) A mordent is diatonic when its accessory (lower) note is taken at the interval of a tone or of a semitone from its main (upper) note in accordance with the key in which the passage stands.

If this key is not the main key of the piece, as shown in the key signature, an accidental may have to be supplied, which may or may not be shown in writing: most usually not. If it is not shown, the performer must make the implied modification.

(b) A mordent is chromatic when its accessory (lower) note is taken at the interval of a semitone from its main (upper) note although the key of the passage would make this interval a tone.

Here, too, the requisite accidental may or may not be shown, but is most usually not. If it is not shown, the choice between a diatonic and a chromatic mordent rests with the performer.

(c) Both diatonic and chromatic mordents were freely used in baroque music, though different authorities state somewhat differing views.

(269) Thomas Mace, *Musick's Monument*, London, 1676, p. 105:

'Continued mordent always into a *Half-Note beneath*.'

(270) Jean Rousseau, *Traité de la Viole*, Paris, 1687, p. 88:

'The Mordent is ordinarily [but not invariably] made on the second Note of an ascending Semitone.'

(271) Georg Muffat, *Apparatus musico-organisticus*, 1690, preface:

'A mordent [is made with] the lower accessory note, which is often (if the ear does not forbid it) a whole tone below.'

(272) T. B., *Compleat Musick-Master*, 3rd ed., London, 1722, Ch. II:

'A Beat [mordent] . . . is always from the half Note below.'
'[But Ch. III:] A *Beat* . . . proceeds from the Note, or half Note next below.'

Ex. 124. Gottlieb (Theophil) Muffat, *Componimenti*, Augsburg, ?1735, semitone mordents, diatonic and chromatic:

263

Ex. 125. Johann Mattheson, *Vollkommene Capellmeister*, Hamburg, 1739, Pt. II, Ch. 3, 56, chromatic mordent:

'So it is written'   'So, more or less, it is sung'.

The notation above is not mathematically logical, but the intention is clear. The semitone is here effected by an accidental sharp; but though not in the key-signature, it is diatonic to the key of G in which the example evidently stands.

(273) Johann Mattheson, *Vollkommene Capellmeister*, Hamburg, 1739, Pt. II, Ch. 3, 55:

'The lower tone or semitone (according to the key) must be touched.'

(274) C. P. E. Bach, *Essay*, Berlin, 1753, II, v, 11:

'With regard to accidentals this ornament adapts itself to its context in the same way as the trill. Its brilliance is frequently enhanced by raising its lower [*i.e.* accessory] note, as [at Ex. 126].'

Ex. 126. C. P. E. Bach, *Essay*, Berlin, 1753, II, v, 11, chromatic mordents:

C. P. E. Bach's fingering here shows that the notes of all three mordents above are the same: *i.e.* single, standard (lower) mordents. The sharp, though it stands above the sign, indicates *D* sharp. In the ordinary course of events we should not expect to see the accidental marked at all—even if the mordent was. The performer is intended to use his own judgment.

(274a) Leopold Mozart, *Violinschule*, Augsburg, 1756, XI, 16:

'The continued mordent [is] always from the semitone.'

Ex. 127. L. Mozart, *Violinschule*, Augsburg, 1756, XI, 9, 16:

(a) unprepared single mordent; (b) unprepared double mordent; (c) prepared continued mordent:

264

8. THE PREPARATION OF MORDENTS

(a) The normal situation with regard to the standard mordent of any period (and the inverted mordent at such periods as have used it) is that it starts unprepared, on its main (upper) note, which thus takes the accent. This accent may often be considerably stressed, particularly with the shorter mordents; but the note itself is not prolonged.

(b) Occasionally, however, a mordent may be prepared by its accessory (lower) note, which then receives the accent, but without being prolonged: see Ex. 127 (c) above.

(c) When, on the other hand, this initial lower note is not only accented but also prolonged, it was treated by the baroque authorities not as the preparation to the mordent, but as an appoggiatura from below with a mordent added to its resolution—just as a trill with its initial upper note prolonged was sometimes treated as an appoggiatura from above with a trill added to its resolution. But whereas preparation (whether prolonged or otherwise) is an integral part of the baroque trill, it has never been an integral part of the mordent. For this reason, the combination of appogiatura and mordent will be treated here on the baroque precedent as a compound ornament, for which see Ch. XXV, 2.

9. THE SPEED OF MORDENTS

A long continued mordent is not a rhythmic ornament, but an intensification and coloration of the texture. Like the long trill which it so much resembles, it may be taken at a very steady rate of repercussion. But the shorter mordents, and above all the single mordent, are rhythmic ornaments, and their repercussions are normally taken at a very rapid speed.

(275) Le Sieur de Machy, *Pièces de violle*, Paris, 1685:

'[To make a mordent,] lift the finger from the [main] note as soon as sounded, and replace it at the same time.'

(276) Jean Rousseau, *Traité de la viole*, Paris, 1687, p. 87:

'[To make a mordent,] the finger stopping a Note first makes two or three little repercussions more brilliantly and rapidly than a trill, and then remains on the Fret.'

(277) Johann Mattheson, *Vollkommene Capellmeister*, Hamburg, 1739, Pt. II, Ch. 3, 55:

'In playing, [mordents] can be variously used, in singing only in one way [*i.e.* as a single mordent]. First, the written main note is sounded; then the tone or semitone below (according to the key) must be touched upon, and left for the main note with such speed that these three notes make one sound which, as it were, hesitates a little, is delayed by something, gently collides with something. From which it should be obvious that the Mordent has not to divide or break anything, but rather joins and unites the sounds.'

10. THE TERMINATION OF MORDENTS

There is no termination to any normal mordent. The ornament ends on its own main note, out of which the single mordent takes very little time, and the double mordent not much more, but the continued mordent the greater part.

(278) Couperin, *L'Art de toucher*, Paris, 1716, ed. of 1717, 'Agrémens':

'Every mordent must be set on the [main] note on which it stands . . . the repercussions and the note on which one stops must all be included within the [total] time-value of the main note.'

(279) C. P. E. Bach, *Essay*, Berlin, 1753, II, v, 8:

'When mordents are continued to fill out a note, a small portion of its original duration must still be left plain, since even the best used mordent sounds wretched when carried like a trill straight into the next note.'

11. THE POST-BAROQUE MORDENT

(a) Apart from confusing the *Pralltriller* and the *Schneller* in a manner subsequently very common, Türk (*Klavierschule*, 1789) gives normal mordents on the baroque pattern. He includes prepared mordents. He calls the upper mordent *Pincé renversé* (inverted).

Ex. 128. D. G. Türk, *Klavierschule*, 1789, prepared mordents:

Clementi (*Introduction to the Pianoforte*, 1801) contrasts with his normal trills (upper-note start) a 'short shake beginning by the note itself . . . transient or passing shakes', which are in fact inverted mordents; but he also gives under the name of 'beat' normal lower mordents both prepared and unprepared. On an ascending step he recommends taking the accessory (lower) note of the mordent at the same pitch (usually diatonic) as the preceding note; but on leaps or first notes of passage, he recommends taking a semitone interval whether diatonically or chromatically. Hummel (*Anweisung zum Pianofortespiel*, 1828), Spohr (*Violinschule*, 1832) and Czerny (*Pianoforte*

School, 1839) all give inverted (upper) mordents under a variety of names and signs. From the second quarter of the nineteenth century onwards, the normal assumption appears to be that an inverted (upper) mordent and not a standard (lower) mordent is intended.

(b) Passages occur in the nineteenth century romantics where an upper mordent appears written out in little notes before a main note bearing a sign of accentuation, or immediately before a bar-line. On the assumption that this notation is authentic, the intention is presumably to take the mordent before the beat. But this is not natural to the ornament; nor was it so in classical any more than in baroque music.

POSTSCRIPT TO NEW VERSION

Just as it is the nature of an appoggiatura to lean (that nature being literally expressed in its name of 'leaning' note); so it is the nature of a mordent to bite (this nature likewise being literally expressed in its name of 'biting' notes).

And just as there are ornamental passing notes of which the notation may be indistinguishable from that of an appoggiatura, causing us to rely on the context (especially if French) and our own musicianship to tell the one from the other; so there are ornaments using the same succession of notes as a mordent without being mordents.

And just as appoggiatura is a misnomer for such passing notes, which Frederick Neumann very properly will not use (and I use only because of eighteenth-century precedent); so mordent is, for such notes resembling but not behaving like a mordent, a misnomer which it would be proper not to use.

Nor is it proper to describe as written-out mordents any melodic figures using the same succession of notes: for example, the figure so prominent in the first movement of J. S. Bach's Sixth Brandenburg. That is not an *ornament* at all: it is a *structural* element of the theme; for it is performed not free but measured.

By virtue of leaning, an appoggiatura properly so-called takes the beat, and if long is mainly for melodic and harmonic poignancy. By virtue of biting, a mordent properly so-called takes the beat (including, very characteristically, a syncopated beat), and if short is mainly for rhythmic sharpness.

CHAPTER XXII

C (i): Passing Notes and
C (ii): Changing Notes

C (i): PASSING NOTES

1. WHICH ORNAMENTS ARE HERE CLASSED AS PASSING NOTES

The ornaments here grouped together under the loose heading of passing notes are those which connect two disjunct main notes by a more or less conjunct movement. See also Chapter XVIII.

2. THE PASSING NOTE PROPER

We saw in Ch. XVIII that an ornament arose from slurring an otherwise ordinary passing note to the following main note instead of to the previous one; and that late authorities recommending it treated it under the self-contradictory heading of Passing Appoggiatura.

When a similar passing note is slurred, as it is much more natural for it to be slurred, to the previous note, it is and behaves in every way like an ordinary passing note. This ornament is so normal that it does not even possess a specific name, being merely one of the most obvious of the figures by which disjunct notes a third apart are connected in free ornamentation. It became in effect, however, if not in name, a specific ornament, and one very commonly introduced by the performer without indication in the written text.

Ex. 129. Passing notes introduced as ornaments:

3. THE TIRATA

English: Run
Italian: Tirata
French: Cascata
              Tirade
              Coulade

The above are names more or less specifically applied to a series of passing notes connecting two disjunct notes more than a third apart. When the series is itself conjunct, these are strictly passing notes; when it is partially disjunct, the passing notes are called irregular or free.

Ex. 130. Johann Mattheson, *Vollkommene Capellmeister*, Hamburg, 1739, Pt. II, Ch. 3, 44, strict tirata:

A few further examples are given below; but it is obvious that we are here on the very borders of free ornamentation.

Ex. 131. Leopold Mozart, *Violinschule*, Augsburg, 1756, XI, 20–21, tiratas, (a), (b), (d) strict, (c) free, (e) strict but chromatic:

C (ii): CHANGING NOTES

4. WHICH ORNAMENTS ARE HERE CLASSED AS CHANGING NOTES

The ornaments here grouped together under the equally loose heading of changing notes are those which move in a variety of patterns around or between main notes which may be the same, or conjunct, or disjunct.

5. THE NOTE OF ANTICIPATION

An ordinary note of anticipation, slurred to the previous note, and taken very lightly, was commonly used and sometimes described as a specific ornament (Old English *cadent*).

Ex. 132. Playford, *Introduction*, London, 1654 (1660 on), note of anticipation used as an ornament:

Ex. 133. F. W. Marpurg, *Principes du Clavecin*, 1756, Tab. IV, notes of anticipation used as ornaments:

6. THE SPRINGER

English:	Acute
	Sigh
	Springer, Spinger
French:	Accent
	Aspiration
	Plainte
German:	Nachschlag

This ornament, the simplest of true changing notes, is among the various *accenti* given by M. Praetorius (*Syntagma*, III, 1619), and remained popular throughout the baroque period. It is included by Playford (*Introduction*, 1654), Simpson (*Division-Violist*, 1659), Mace (*Musick's Monument*, 1676), Jean Rousseau (*Traité de la viole*, 1687), Georg Muffat (*Florilegium I*, 1695), Couperin (*Pièces*, 1713), Marpurg (*Principes du clavecin*, 1756), Jean-Jacques Rousseau (*Dictionnaire*, 1768) and others.

Ex. 134. Playford, *Introduction*, 1654 (1660 on), springer:

Ex. 135. F. W. Marpurg, *Principes*, 1756, Tab. IV, springers:

7. THE GROPPO

This name was applied to an even wider variety of ornaments than most, including some forms of trills and turns: it means a 'cluster' of notes. By the end of the baroque period, however, it had acquired a slightly more definite meaning of which the following is representative.

Ex. 136. Leopold Mozart, *Violinschule*, 1756, XI, 18, *groppi*:

8. POST-BAROQUE PASSING AND CHANGING NOTES

These never very distinct groups of ornaments (to which others equally ill-defined might be added) soon lost what specific status they possessed, and in post-baroque music appear mostly as ordinary written-out figuration—as indeed they often do in baroque music also.

CHAPTER XXIII

C (iii): The Turn

English:	Single Relish
	Turn
Italian:	Circolo mezzo
	Groppo
	Gruppetto
French:	Brisée
	Cadence
	Doublé
	Double-cadence
	Tour de gosier
German:	Doppelschlag
	Halbzirkel

1. WHAT THE NAME TURN IMPLIES

(a) The turn is an alternation of the main note with both an upper and a lower subsidiary. It is thus a group of changing notes, or groppo (see Ch. XXII, 7), which acquired independence as a specific ornament.

(b) The turn, a most beautiful ornament, has always been subject to variations of form and rhythm; but it has not significantly varied between different periods.

By the middle of the nineteenth century it began to decline as a specific ornament, but remained just as important as an ingredient in the written-out melodic line. Wagner used the sign for it in early life, but later wrote it out (as in Brynhilde's main theme in the *Ring*). Mahler made it almost as much a feature of his idiom as the long appoggiatura (see the last movement of his ninth symphony).

(c) The main distinction is between accented turns and unaccented turns. The former take the beat; the latter fall between beats. The difference is sometimes shown by the exact vertical placing of the sign, but this cannot be relied upon; and, of course, the ornament may be freely used where no sign exists to give any such assistance.

(d) The upper or standard turn begins on its upper auxiliary, passes through its main note, touches its lower auxiliary, and returns to its main note.

The lower or inverted turn begins on its lower auxiliary, passes through its main note, touches its upper auxiliary, and returns to its main note.

There is also a main-note or five-note turn, which begins on its main note, touches its upper auxiliary, passes through its main note, touches its lower auxiliary, and returns to its main note.

The theoretically possible inverted main-note turn does not seem to occur.

Upper, lower and main-note turns can all of them occur either in accented or in unaccented form.

2. THE ACCENTED TURN

Ex. 137. Diego Ortiz, *Trattado de glosas*, Rome, 1553, accented upper turn:

Ex. 138. Etienne Loulié, *Principes de musique*, Paris, 1696, Amsterdam ed. of 1698, accented upper turn:

Ex. 139. Fr. Couperin, *Pièces de clavecin*, I, Paris, 1713, accented upper turn:

Ex. 140. J. S. Bach, *Clavier-Büchlein*, 1720, accented upper turn:

Ex. 141. C. P. E. Bach, *Essay*, Berlin, 1753, II, iv, 1, 34 and 36, (a) accented upper turns and (b), (c), accented main-note turns:

273

Ex. 142. F. W. Marpurg, *Principes*, Berlin, 1756, (a) accented upper turns, (b) accented lower turns, (c) tied upper turn, (d) accented main-note turns:

3. THE UNACCENTED TURN

Ex. 143. Diego Ortiz, *Trattado de glosas*, Rome, 1553, (a) unaccented lower note turn, (b) unaccented upper turn:

Ex. 144. Fray Tomás de Santa María, *Arte de tañer fantasia*, Valladolid, 1565, unaccented upper turn:

Ex. 145. Henry Purcell (or his ed.), posthumous *Lessons*, London, 1696, unaccented upper turn:

Ex. 146. C. P. E. Bach, *Essay*, 1753, II, iv, 23, (a) unaccented

upper turns on dotted notes (N.B. for rhythm) and at 36, (b) unaccented upper turn on undotted note (Ex. is from ed. of 1787).

Ex. 147. D. G. Türk, *Klavierschule*, 1789, unaccented upper turns
(N.B. for rhythm):

4. INTERPRETATION OF TURNS

(a) The accented upper turn and the accented lower turn both serve
a harmonic as well as a melodic function, because their initial note,
which receives the accent, is foreign to the harmony given by their
main note, and often discordant with it. The case is therefore similar

to that of the normally prepared baroque trill. A firm attack is thus indicated, though its firmness will be proportionate to the prevailing mood.

It will be noticed from the examples given above that the accented upper turn is the most usual through the greater part of the baroque period.

(b) The accented main-note turn and all the unaccented turns are primarily melodic, and are more or less unstressed.

(c) The speed and the rhythm of the turn are both governed entirely by circumstances, at the discretion of the performer.

(d) On dotted notes, the unaccented turn has a strong tendency to delay and shorten the note after the dot, unless the tempo is such as to make this undesirable.

(e) A slur, if not written, is implied over the entire ornament, including its main note; except that with unaccented turns on dotted notes, the note after the dot may (though it need not) be preceded by a brief silence of articulation.

(f) Accidentals will be found in some of the above examples; but their presence in writing cannot be counted upon, even when a sign for the turn is marked. Both upper and lower auxiliary notes may be diatonic to the key of the passage; either may be chromatic; they will seldom both be chromatic at the same time. Nor will they usually both be at a semitone interval from their main note at the same time, which puts them only a diminished third apart; but this is by no means unknown in baroque music, and became less unusual at a later date.

It will be noticed that an accidental placed above the sign for the turn may affect either the upper or the lower auxiliary note. The convention by which an accidental above the sign affects only the upper auxiliary and an accidental below the sign only the lower auxiliary did not become established until well into the nineteenth century.

(g) The interpretation of turns remained unchanged down to and including the generation of Beethoven, and very little changed from then until the present time. The following remarks are in many respects as relevant to the nineteenth century as they are to the baroque period at the close of which they were written.

(280) C. P. E. Bach, *Essay*, Berlin, 1753, II, iv, 3 *ff.*:

'The turn is used in slow as well as in quick pieces . . . it is not very effective over a short note . . . for the most part the turn is performed rapidly . . . the turn is better when the next note ascends rather than descends . . . its sign is little known except on the keyboard. It is often marked with the signs of the trill or even the mordent, which two are also often confused . . . in slow, expressive pieces the turn may give up its brilliance and become deliberately languid.'

CHAPTER XXIV

C (iv): Broken Chords, C (v): Broken Notes and C (vi): Broken Time

C (iv): THE BROKEN CHORD

English:	Arpeggio
	Battery
Italian:	Arpeggio
	Battimento
	Harpeggiato
French:	Arpégé, harpégé
	Arpègement, harpègement
	Batterie
German:	Brechung
	Harpeggio

1. IN WHAT RESPECT THE BROKEN CHORD IS AN ORNAMENT

(a) The arpeggio as we now understand it is not regarded as an ornament. On keyboard instruments and above all on the harp, it is a device for spreading the sound, usually beginning with the bass (which should normally take the beat) and continuing upwards through one hand, or both hands either successively or simultaneously.

This degree of spreading was so general on the harpsichord, the clavichord or the lute in renaissance and baroque music as to have needed no special mention. There were also other varieties of spreading taken for granted then which did not occur later unless written into the notation: from the top downwards (the treble note, especially if it is the melody note, taking the beat); from the bottom completely up to the top and down again (both this and the former may well occur when the melodic line itself continues in the bass); up, down, and up again, or up and down twice or more (especially where a long chord needs to be sonorously filled out); once up and partly down (to end on an inner note from which the melodic line continues); and other patterns more elaborate still. Some of the above patterns receive special mention in the baroque authorities under the heading of ornaments. However elaborate, such patterns are all varieties of the plain arpeggio.

(b) Where, in addition to spreading the chord in more or less elaborate patterns, the performer gives these patterns a melodic value, he makes not a plain arpeggio but a figurate arpeggio. He may do so exclusively from the notes proper to the chord; or he may diversify the chord by momentarily introducing notes which are foreign to it. The notes thus momentarily introduced are acciaccaturas, for which see Ch. XVII above. See also Ch. XXXII, 2 below.

2. THE ORIGINS OF THE BROKEN CHORD IN PRE-BAROQUE MUSIC

In so far as the broken chord is a mere spreading (whether slight or considerable) for the sake of enriching the texture and increasing the sonority, it arose from the natural technique of such instruments as the harpsichord (where an absolutely simultaneous full chord sounds intolerably harsh), the lute (where the fingers available may not allow it) or the lyra da braccio (which is specially designed for partially arpeggiated chords).

In so far as the broken chord achieves a truly melodic pattern, it arose as part of the general tradition of free ornamentation, selected figures from which became to some extent stabilised here as specific ornaments in the usual way.

3. THE BROKEN CHORD AS AN ORNAMENT IN BAROQUE MUSIC

(a) The toccata in its late renaissance and early baroque sense as a 'touch-piece' for loosening the fingers, establishing the tonality and preparing the listener for the more formal music to come was largely constructed from improvised arpeggiation. So, too, was the prelude of the same periods, before the two forms diverged. The unmeasured preludes of the French school of D'Anglebert and others continued to be written in a very incomplete form of notation, for the interpretation of which some experience with baroque methods of breaking the chord is necessary. J. S. Bach's first prelude of the 'Forty-Eight' is a written-out example of a series of broken chords such as a majority of baroque composers would have notated as plain chords, leaving it to the performer to invent his own figuration. For this reason it was certainly meant to be played fast enough and freely enough to give the impression of an improvisation, and not in the portentous manner preferred by some modern interpreters. On the other hand, it is equally deprived of its natural effect if it is played too fast. Between the two extremes there lies a rendering which is at the same time relaxed and full of feeling.

(281) G. Frescobaldi, *Toccate*, Rome, 1615–16, Preface, 3:

'The openings of the toccatas are to be taken adagio and arpeggiando; it is the same with suspensions or discords, even in the middle of the work, one breaks them together, so as not to leave the instrument empty: which breaking is to be performed at the discretion of the performer.'

Ex. 148. G. Frescobaldi, '*Toccata ottava*', opening bars as interpreted by Arnold Dolmetsch, *Interpretation*, London [1915] p. 261:

Ex. 149. Mace, *Musick's Monument*, 1676, arpeggiation of chords, transcribed by A. Dolmetsch, *Interpretation*, London [1915] p. 264:

Ex. 150. Jacques Champion de Chambonnières, *Pièces*, Paris, 1670, broken chords:

Ex. 151. Jean-Henri D'Anglebert, *Pièces de Clavecin*, Paris [1689], broken chords:

Ex. 152. J. S. Bach, *Forty-Eight*, II, Prelude XXI, bar 17, as inter-preted by Arnold Dolmetsch, *Interpretation*, London [1915], pp. 273–4:

Ex. 153. C. P. E. Bach, *Essay*, Berlin, 1753, III, 26, broken chords:

(b) In virtuoso violin music of the late baroque schools, passages occur which are written as chords but intended as arpeggiation. Where the composer has not shown the figuration by writing out a bar or two in full, the performer has full liberty to introduce what figures he prefers, in any variety of rhythm suitable to the context, and with any variety of bowing. He is not even obliged to confine himself to the notes written in the chords, provided he keeps to the harmony together with such extraneous notes as can be momentarily introduced as passing acciaccaturas (simultaneous acciaccaturas are confined to keyboard instruments).

4. THE BROKEN CHORD IN POST-BAROQUE MUSIC

D. G. Türk (*Klavierschule*, 1789) includes arpeggios starting from the top as well as from the bottom, with a variety of the usual baroque signs for each. But the piano is much less well suited by arpeggiation of the baroque kind than the harpsichord. Arpeggio-like written-out figuration, meant to be performed with the damper-raising pedal down, took its place.

As late as 1790, however, J. C. F. Rellstab (*C. P. E. Bach's Angfangs-gründe mit einer Anleitung*) published workings of C. P. E. Bach's chord passages, with which he took the most striking liberties (examples in Dolmetsch, *Interpretation* [1915] pp. 271–2).

And as late as the first decades of the nineteenth century, J.-B. Cartier (1765–1841) was teaching the breaking of violin chords on the baroque method, such as the following taken by him from Geminiani's *Art of Playing on the Violin:*

Ex. 154. Jean-Baptiste Cartier, *L'Art du violon*, Paris [1798], broken chords (with a variety of bowings):

C (v): THE BROKEN NOTE

5. THE BROKEN NOTE TREATED AS AN ORNAMENT

A note deliberately brought in late for expressive effect (the rest of the harmony arriving punctually) was regarded as an ornament by some composers of the French school, under the name of *suspension* or *demi soupir* (compare the medieval hocket). A convenient English term for this is truncated note. The Italian word *mezzo-sospiro* given in the following suggests that it may have been originally an Italian singers' ornament.

(282) S. de Brossard, *Dictionaire*, Paris, 1703, *s.v.* 'Mezzo-Sospiro':

'The figure 𝄼 . . . marks that one is silent for the eighth part of a bar [or less or more in proportion].'

A note of which the latter part is replaced by a silence of articulation was similarly regarded as an ornament by some, though in fact this is one of the commonest effects of ordinary expression. Its French names were *aspiration, coup sec, demi soupir, détaché, son coupé, suspension, tacté,* and we can conveniently call it in English a curtailed note.

Ex. 155. Jean-Philippe Rameau, *Pièces de clavecin*, Paris, [1724], (a) curtailed note, (b) truncated note:

281

I have not noticed any post-baroque evidence for either of the above regarded as a specific ornament.

C (vi): BROKEN TIME

6. BROKEN TIME TREATED AS AN ORNAMENT

Tempo rubato, besides its normal modern meaning of liberties taken with the tempo, had for many baroque authorities the further meaning of a displacement of note-values within the bar, or even merely of a displacement of the accentuation. There was some tendency to regard this as an ornament, and in extreme instances it has certainly an effect of free ornamentation; but fundamentally it is a matter of rhythmic alteration, for which see Ch. XLI below.

CHAPTER XXV

D. Compound Ornaments

1. WHAT IS MEANT BY THE TERM COMPOUND ORNAMENT

Two or more ornaments were frequently run together in baroque music. When these combinations appear with sufficient regularity to become specific ornaments in their own right, it is convenient to call them compound ornaments. There is no sharp dividing line between these and many others which could be regarded as such with almost as much justification; but the following are the commonest combinations.

2. COMBINATIONS WITH THE APPOGGIATURA

(a) We have seen in Ch. XX, 4 above that while all standard baroque trills start with their upper (accessory) note, some have this initial note so prolonged that it is in fact a long appoggiatura (and was often so regarded). There is nothing to be added here except the warning that where such an appoggiatura is written out in ordinary notation, it should be tied over to include the initial upper note of the trill itself. See Ex. 97 in Ch. XX, 4 above, where at (a) and (d) the first note is in effect an appoggiatura to the ensuing trill, as opposed to (e), where it is not.

(b) The long appoggiatura from below was so often rounded off with a mordent that some authorities made a rule of this, which was certainly an exaggeration.

(283) Jean Rousseau, *Traité de la viole*, Paris, 1687, p. 87:

'The Mordent is always inseparable from the Appoggiatura, for the Appoggiatura must always be terminated by a Mordent.'

(284) J. M. Hotteterre, *Principes de la flûte*, Paris, 1707, Ch. VIII:

'Often one links mordents with appoggiaturas.'

(284a) Johann Mattheson, *Vollkommene Capellmeister*, Hamburg, 1739, Pt. II, Ch. 3, 56:

'In singing, there is hardly an ascending Appoggiatura without a Mordent.'

(285) C. P. E. Bach, *Essay*, Berlin, 1753, II, v, 6:

'When it follows an appoggiatura, the mordent is taken lightly, in accordance with the rule governing the performance of appoggiaturas by which they diminuendo on to their resolutions].'

Ex. 156. Henry Purcell (or his ed.), *Lessons*, London, 1696, 'beat' (meaning short appoggiatura with mordent):

Ex. 157. G. T. Muffat, *Componimenti*, ?1736, appoggiaturas with and without mordents:

3. COMBINATIONS WITH THE TRILL OR TURN

(a) The ordinary turned ending which is one of the two standard endings of the baroque trill (Ch. XX, 6) was sometimes regarded as a trill rounded off with a turn, which is fairly plausible; sometimes as a trill rounded off with a mordent, which (because of the rhythm) is not. In any case, this is not a genuine compound ornament.

(b) The ascending trill (Fr. *tremblement coulé en montant*; Ger. *Triller von unten, Doppelt Cadence*) is a genuine compound of ascending slide leading to trill; the descending trill (Fr. *tremblement coulé en descendant*; Ger. *Triller von oben, Doppelt Cadence*) is the exact reverse, but produced by a turn leading to a trill.

Ex. 158. J. S. Bach, *Clavier-Büchlein*, 1720, ascending and descending trills:

Ex. 159. F. W. Marpurg, *Principes*, 1756, Tab. V, ascending and descending trills:

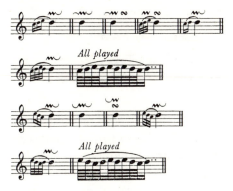

(c) The following are on the borders of the trill and the turn.

Ex. 160. C. P. E. Bach, *Essay*, II, iv, 27 and 37, (a) trilled turn (*prallende Doppelschlag*); (b) ascending turn (*Doppelschlag von unten*):

(d) There is a more developed form of the ascending trill to which it is convenient to reserve the name double cadence, although this served for both in different baroque sources. The ornament became a very common cadential formula in the eighteenth century.

Ex. 161. L'Affillard, *Principes*, 1694, double cadence ('double cadence coupée')—(a) as written; (b) as explained; (c) as presumably intended:

Ex. 162. Georg Muffat, *Florilegium I*, 1695, double cadence:

Ex. 163. Other possible rhythms for the double cadence:

(e) Playford (*Introd.*, 1654, 1660 on), Simpson (*Division-Violist*, 1659) and Mace (*Musick's Monument*, 1676) agree substantially on an English seventeenth century ornament called the double relish, a combination of two trills and an appoggiatura from below, on the main note or resolution of which a mordent may well be added. The primary form is as follows.

Ex. 164. Chr. Simpson, *Division-Violist*, London, 1659, p. 12 double relish:

(f) J. S. Bach wrote out in ordinary notation the following rather beautiful double cadence, as at Ex. 164A (a). Those who really like to go the whole way may care to introduce a still more elaborate double cadence into such passages as Ex. 164A (b).

Ex. 164A. J. S. Bach, (a) E major Violin Sonata, end of first movt., written out double cadence in harpsichord against ordinary cadential trill in violin; (b) D major Fugue, Bk. I of the 48, as the end of it might be ornamented with a particularly elaborate double cadence:

COMPOUND ORNAMENTS

PART THREE

ACCOMPANIMENT

CHAPTER XXVI

Figured Bass

1. IMPROMPTU ACCOMPANIMENT

Until the end of the baroque period it was normal for accompaniment to be more or less improvised. From a remote antiquity, the necessary understanding between the performers was facilitated by traditional modes (in the wide Oriental sense) or other conventions. More recently, some partial indication in writing was provided.

Renaissance accompanists were trained to fill out the harmonies from a bass part alone. With polyphonic music, this was not entirely reliable. In spite of some useful working rules, it was difficult to see quickly enough whether a triad or a chord of the sixth was required, whether the third or sixth was major or minor, whether the concord was delayed by a suspension and so forth. Many organists went to the trouble of copying the parts in score: an early known printed example of such a score is *Tutti i Madrigali di Cipriano di Rore a 4 voci, spartiti* ('divided', *i.e.* barred) *et accommodati per sonar d'ogni sorte d'istrumento perfetto* . . ., Venice, 1577. At this time, the ideal standard accompaniment was regarded as one which reduplicated the written vocal parts; and this the score made easy. A close approximation could also be effected where the bass line was copied or printed with the top line of the polyphony shown above it.

Where the polyphony is distributed among more choirs than one, each has its own bass line, but only one of these can form the true bass of the harmony at any given moment. In some organ parts of the late sixteenth century, the several bass lines are printed, it being left to the organist to pick out the true bass; in others, not the bass lines but the true bass extracted from them is printed. This came to be called a Thorough or Through Bass, *Basso Continuo*, *Generalbass* or their equivalents, meaning a bass continued throughout the music by taking whatever happened to be the lowest part for the time being. And presently (perhaps first in Viadana's *Cento concerti ecclesiastici*, Venice, 1602) portions or all of this continued bass were not merely extracted from the parts to be accompanied, but added to them.

A few particularly ambiguous bass notes now had ♯ or ♭ above them to show the major or minor third. These are the 'sigma' or signs, which soon included 'numeri' or figures (the first being a 6); from these developed the baroque system of Figured Bass, *Basso numerato*, *Basse chiffrée*, *bezifferter Bass* or their equivalents.

2. THE GENERAL CHARACTER OF FIGURED BASS

A figured bass is thus a thorough-bass or continuo to which accidentals and figures have been added showing the main intervals required. But the distribution of the intervals, the conduct of the parts and the melodic figuration are not shown. The performer is told, with very varying degrees of thoroughness and accuracy, what harmonies to produce; how he produces them is his own affair.

There are some obvious practical advantages in this ingenious form of musical shorthand. There is first the great saving in composing and copying time and printing costs; there is next the flexibility of an arrangement which enables each performer to adapt his accompaniment to the requirements of his own instrument. A lutenist can employ his typically thin and widely spaced distribution of notes: sketchy to the eye; unexpectedly sonorous in performance, and suggestive of more complex part-writing than is actually present. A harpsichordist can fill out his instrument with resounding arpeggios and acciaccaturas; an organist can sustain counterpoint pure enough and sparse enough not to overload the texture. Any fully written-out part which suited one could only hamper the others; but a figured bass part hampers nobody. It leaves the crucial decisions of sonority and spacing to the circumstances of the moment: the instrument; the resonance of the hall; the balance of the ensemble as a whole.

There was also a more fundamental consideration. It was not from mere casualness that baroque composers preferred to trust their performers with figured bass, as they also trusted them with free ornamentation. It was from the high value they set on spontaneity. They believed, and modern experience confirms, that it is better to be accompanied with buoyancy than with polished workmanship. An accompanist who can give rhythmic impetus to his part, adapt it to the momentary requirements of balance and sonority, thicken it here and thin it there, and keep every bar alive, can stimulate his colleagues and help to carry the entire ensemble along. This is not merely to fill in the harmony; nor is it merely to make the harmony into an interesting part; it is to share in the creative urgency of the actual performance.

As with free ornamentation, it hardly matters how much is actually improvised, and how much is memorised or written out by the performer or the editor. It only matters that it should have the fresh and flexible feeling of an improvisation. Some movements lend themselves readily to an improvised realisation; others present opportunities of which the fullest advantage can only be taken by working out a part on paper. Such a worked-out part, however, can itself often be improved in performance, and may not reach its best until it has been played many times.

Almost all the more old-fashioned modern editions have realisations of the figured bass which are so bad that they really spoil the music—heavy, pianistic, and with a strangely nineteenth-century flavour to the harmonisation even when they are not palpably contravening the figuring. Recent editions are generally quite usable, but they still suffer from two very common faults: the part may frequently be too thick and need to have a great many notes thinned out before it will take on a natural, easy flow; and at the same time the real musical interest is too slight. There is too much sound for a clear texture, but too little musical significance to match up to the solo melody. Alternatively, the part itself is far two thin. The present tendency is a great relief from the previous romantic over-elaboration, but it has on the whole swung too far in the direction of dull correctness and austerity. The balance, indeed, is not an easy one to strike; and it must also be remembered that there is no one right solution. The essence of the system is that it leaves the performer free to find his own solution within the given indications and the general boundaries of the style.

All this points to the desirability, for any accompanist seriously interested in baroque music, of learning figured bass: if possible to the extent of realising his own parts; and at least to the extent of being able to modify an editor's parts to his own taste, which makes a very good start. No realisation, after all, is sacrosanct: whoever made it, and however well, it is only one working version out of the unlimited possibilities. That is the best of figured bass.

The following treatment is confined to the essentials, but F. T. Arnold's lengthy *Art of Accompaniment from a Thorough-Bass* (London, 1931) is one of the most entirely satisfactory modern studies in early interpretation, and anyone going far into the subject will certainly turn to it for its mass of detailed and accurate information. Some knowledge of harmony and counterpoint is a necessary prerequisite; I know of no better introduction to these than H. K. Andrews' articles on them in *Grove's Dictionary* (5th ed., London, 1954).

CHAPTER XXVII

The Figuring

1. UNFIGURED BASSES

It is in the nature of baroque music to rest on a bass of which the outline is firmly melodic. This bass is the foundation on which the continuo player will construct his accompaniment, and is always given in his part complete.

A minority of baroque musicians continued to regard this bass line as a sufficient indication in itself, without figures, either because they expected the accompanist to make a short score or tablature and play from that, or because they thought figures were an unnecessary complication for a competent accompanist.

(286) Lodovico Viadana, *Concerti Ecclesiastici*, Venice, 1602, preface, rule 6:

'I hope that the Organists will be able to make the said tablature at their own convenience, which, to tell the truth, is much better.'

(287) Giovanni Piccioni, *Concerti Ecclesiastici*, Venice, 1610, preface:

'I have prefered not to set any sort of signs, such as sharps, flats, and figures, over the notes, as many do, since to unskilful Organists, they are confusing rather than otherwise, while to the knowledgable and expert, such signs are unnecessary, for they play them correctly by ear and by art.'

A similar attitude persisted in some quarters even into the eighteenth century. Figures are especially scarce in opera continuo.

(288) Andreas Werckmeister, *Harmonologia Musica*, Frankfurt and Leipzig, 1702, sect. 120, p. 65:

'Those, again, who say that the signs above the notes in a continuo bass are perfectly useless and unnecessary, show no little ignorance and stupidity: for it is plainly impossible even for an expert who knows the natural movement of harmony and composition to perform everything correctly in accordance with another man's ideas, since the progressions and the resolutions may take many different courses.'

(289) C. P. E. Bach, *Essay*, II, Berlin, 1762, XXXV, 2:

'Some people have been at great pains to elaborate a system for realising unfigured basses, and I must confess that I have made experiments of the kind. But the more thought I have given to it, the more richness I have found in the turns of harmony . . . it is impossible to devise fixed rules. [3:] an accompaniment made from an unfigured part can only be inadequate. . . . He who is too lazy or too ignorant to figure his own basses as a good performance requires should get it done for him by an expert accompanist.'

It must be admitted that the necessity for figures is somewhat less pressing when the progressions are very regular and largely comprised of sequences. It is interesting that the Turin MSS. of Vivaldi's music often give no figuring where the printed editions have figuring supplied, not very well and presumably by the publishers. Moreover, when at least one melodic part is printed above the bass, the need for figuring is much reduced. But though rare exceptions occur in which more than one melodic part is shown in this way, it is ordinarily only in the case of solos that this is done.

The best course for a modern accompanist who wants to realise an unfigured bass at sight (especially where no melodic part is shown above the bass) is to look at the other parts and put in sufficient figuring for his own information.

2. THE SIGNS USED IN FIGURED BASS

(a) Ordinary numerals show the intervals of the required harmony, as reckoned from the bass. These intervals are shown simple, without regard to octave transposition. Thus 3 implies the interval of a third, a tenth or any further octave transposition required. The 'position' of each chord is, of course, defined by which note of it forms the bass; but above that, its notes may be spaced in any order desired.

This rule applies to all figured basses after Peri, Caccini, and Cavalieri, with only one partial exception of any importance: 2 and 9 are figured separately, because of the different progressions to which the intervals of a second and of a ninth incline. The distinction, however, was not always kept free from confusion. Moreover, it must be realised that even with these two intervals, octave transposition is still taken for granted. An interval correctly figured 2 may still be taken an octave and a tone, or even two octaves and a tone, above its bass note.

(b) The numerals shown are normally those regarded as sufficient to define the chord in question. Further intervals needed to complete the chord were assumed, and were only figured for some special reason, usually a desire to indicate the actual progressions between the chords (*i.e.* the 'voice-leading').

This is a very important point in practice. Any unnecessary figures make the part much harder to read. Complete figuring would merely be a less efficient way of writing out the realisation; the whole point of figured bass is that, being a form of shorthand, it makes a fully written-out part superfluous.

The art of reading from a figured bass largely depends on having memorised all the combinations of figures normally encountered, together with the unfigured intervals which these combinations imply to complete the chord in question. This memory becomes so quick that it almost appears to be localised in the fingers themselves, which can be trained to take up the spacing required by the pattern of each chord without the need for conscious thought—for which there is no time.

Circumstances may call for any feasible amount of doubling. Not all intervals in a chord can be doubled with equally satisfactory effect, and there were a number of rules and conventions to give the accompanist guidance in this matter. These varied in detail in different periods, schools and authorities, but were basically in accordance with the ordinary grammar of composition as it is taught in our better colleges of music and university music departments today. For a thorough treatment both of the basic principles and of the variations of detail, the reader is referred to Arnold (*op. cit.*). The same applies to the principles and details of 'voice-leading' by which the progression from chord to chord is actually effected: the basis is our normal academic basis, and the variations are best studied in Arnold.

Not only doubling of intervals but thinning out may be called for by circumstances. Three-part or even two-part harmony sometimes meets the momentary requirements of sonority and texture better than four-part; very light movements may benefit from such thinness of harmony throughout. The choice of the best interval or intervals to omit is less subject to rule than the choice of intervals for doubling, but some brief guidance is given below, and more will be found in Arnold (*op. cit.*).

The intervals which, subject to any deliberate doubling or thinning, the figures imply in addition to those which they themselves indicate, are the subject of very definite conventions, to which attention will be drawn here under each chord in turn.

(c) Accidental signs have the same effect on the intervals shown by the figures against which they appear as they have on ordinary notes in the stave.

But it is important to remember the differences between baroque and modern conventions with regard to accidentals, for which see Ch. IV, 4, Ch. V generally and Ch. VI, 4, 6 and 9.

In particular, the need to sharpen leading notes and to make major (Picardy) thirds on important closes, whether so written or not, must be taken into account; individual cases are not always easy to judge, especially at sight, but both these are conventions which an accompanist cannot altogether ignore in baroque music of any date.

As usual in baroque music, accidental signs sometimes show a specific pitch, as they do in modern times, but sometimes state a chromatic modification, or merely a chromatic situation, irrespective of specific pitch. Thus, for example, a ♭ 5 is often used to indicate a diminished fifth even where diatonic to the key. This does not mean that the 5 is to be chromatically flattened; it merely warns the reader that he must play a fifth which is flatter by a semitone than the one he might otherwise assume: *i.e.* a perfect fifth (see 4 below). On a B ♮ bass he would normally play F ♯ if the D were shown sharp, and might do so even if it were not; hence the figuring for an F natural, even in the key of C where it is diatonic, might either be 5 (as we should nowadays expect) or ♭ 5 (as a precautionary measure to make sure of it). No baroque performer could mistake that for an F flat, which a modern performer might conceivably do for a moment.

(d) The figures themselves may appear in special forms indicative of chromatic modification and cancellation.

TABLE VI

A. Figures in a form equivalent to an added sharp

$$+\ \ 2\ 4\ 5\ 6\ 7\ 8\ 9$$
$$\ \ \ 2\ \ \ \ 5\ \ \ \ \ \ \ \ \ 9$$

B. Figures in a form equivalent to an added natural

$$5̵7$$
$$5̵9$$

C. Figures in a form equivalent to an added flat

$$4̶\ 5̶\ 6̶\ 7̶7\ 7̶\ 9$$
$$\ \ 5̶$$
$$\ \ 5̶7$$
$$\ \ 5̶9$$

(e) A sign ⌒ placed over the figures is occasionally met. It was the invention of G. P. Telemann, and excludes some interval from the chord which the figures would normally imply.

(f) A more or less horizontal dash or line following a figure prolongs the note given by this figure until the dash or line ends; unfortunately this only became established in the latter part of the baroque period.

(g) Most composers were to some extent illogical and inconsistent in their notation of figures and other signs, and the performer must not be deceived by apparent absurdities but use his intelligence to infer the actual meaning. Some (*e.g.* Abel, Leclair) were definitely idiosyncratic on occasion: Arnold gives examples (*op. cit.*).

3. THE POSITION OF THE FIGURES

(a) When a bass is figured, the figures are normally placed above the stave carrying the bass line. But they may also be placed below, with identical effect.

(b) When an accidental is added to a figure, it may be placed either before or after the figure, with identical effect. There was little consistency in this matter, except that the accidental might tend to be placed on the side where there was most room for it when space was short.

(c) When more harmonies than one are to be played in succession on a single bass note, the exact horizontal spacing of figures is supposed in theory to give some indication of the timing of the subsequent harmonies; but in practice it hardly ever does. It is very common to find all the figures bunched together towards the left side of the bar at the beginning of the bass note, with no means of seeing what is meant to be the duration of the harmonies thus figured. Even if the figures are spaced out, the spacing is only approximate—no copyist or compositor could be expected to do more than that, if as much.

The earliest figured basses of the monodic school (Peri, Caccini, Cavalieri) met this difficulty by dividing a long bass note into as many shorter notes as there are changes of harmony, each such short note being of the exact duration required, and bearing its own figures; and a tie being placed over the whole to show that these short notes are not played themselves as separate notes, but are one long note notated in this way to give the necessary information. This method was apparently regarded as too clumsy to be continued; but it had the advantage of complete unambiguity. Incidentally, to a string player this notation is misleading in another way: it looks like a *portato*, *i.e.* a slight reiteration of emphasis within one bow. He must be warned that there was no such intention here.

(290) Giulio Caccini, *Nuove Musiche*, Florence, 1602:

'I have used the ties in the bass part because, after the consonance [or other interval figured] only the interval figured is to be struck again [and not the bass note].'

Ex. 165. Caccini, method of showing time values of figures:

Here the bass note *A* is held for a semibreve; but the chords are held for the time values which the tied subdivisions of the *A* depict: *i.e.* three crotchets and two quavers.

In the main baroque period, conventions grew up which, though less reliable, gave some assistance.

(291) C. P. E. Bach, *Essay*, II, Berlin, 1762, I, 43–7:

'Figures placed over the dots which prolong notes are played at the time when the dot comes into effect, though they relate to the previous note. . . . Figures placed over short rests are played at the rest, but relate to the following note. . . . Figures over long rests are also played at the rest, but relate to the previous note. . . . A trained musician can readily decide which is in question by looking at the context.

'Figures placed after a [duple] note are played on its second half . . . if two figures are placed over a duple bass note, each figure is given half of its duration. . . .

'If three figures in succession are placed over such a note, the first figure, immediately above the note, is given half its length and the others take half each of the remaining half. . . . If two figures in succession are placed over a dotted note . . . the first figure is given two-thirds . . . and the second the remaining third. . . . If there are three figures in succession, each is given a third of the duration.'

It was also possible to mark a short dash after a figure to prolong it at the expense of the others. But in practice, it is most often necessary for the performer to discover the requisite distribution with little or no visual aid; and this is, in fact, one of the chief details to look out for if it is possible to take a brief, but only a brief glance at the music before realising the part at sight.

(d) The normal vertical arrangement of the figures is to place those of higher denomination above those of lower denomination. When they are disposed in a different order, this may be to show a particular spacing of the harmony, or it may be without notational significance.

(e) In very early figured basses, an accidental set a little to the left of a bass note, and a third above, was intended to show a modification of the third to major or minor as the case may be. An accidental similarly set a sixth above or (more likely) a third *below*, was intended to show a like modification of the sixth. These accidentals are very frequently misplaced by copyist or printer. When, in this music, an improbable accidental appears at the same pitch as the bass note, and with apparent reference to that note, it is worth asking whether the intention was to modify not the bass note but either the third or the sixth of the chord, according to circumstances.

Later in the seventeenth century, cases occur of accidentals placed above or below the figures to which they apply, instead of before or after.

(f) A rare convention, but troublesome enough to be worth noting, can only be called (as it is by Arnold, *op. cit.*, p. 880) retrospective figuring. It occurs on a bass moving by a step, the second note of which bears figures reckoned not from that note, but from the previous note.

Ex. 166. H. Purcell, *Sonnata's of III Parts*, 1683, Sonata VII, 1st movt., bar 9, retrospective figuring as realised by Arnold, *Thorough-Bass*, London, 1931, p. 880:

It will be seen that the figures are as if the bass had been a semibreve *F* sharp, and that this would have made a conventional cadential formula of which the actual notes are merely a slight variant. This is the best explanation I can see; but it is more understandable than logical, and is an excellent example of the perennial need to pick out the correct solution from the literal absurdity. The logical and proper figuring of the *E* bass note is, of course, ♯ 4–2.

4. PERFECT TRIADS (COMMON CHORDS)

(a) If a bass note is essential (and not, *e.g.*, merely a passing note, for which see 14 below), it will normally be given fresh harmony whether figured or not.

In the absence of any figure, this harmony is normally assumed to be a diatonic triad.

(b) But in all except the most amply figured basses, this assumption is subject to exceptions. Any bass note chromatically sharpened to become a leading note is assumed, in the absence of figuring, to bear not a triad but a chord of the sixth. This is often extended to leading notes in the bass even when diatonic. And in general, in any context in which to a trained accompanist the choice would be fairly obvious, we are liable to find that an unfigured bass note requires not a triad but a chord of the sixth. This is one of the many matters in which a good accompanist needs an extra sense to guide him; and it must be admitted that in this respect it is not particularly difficult to acquire. Genuine ambiguity, even when sight-reading, between triads and chords of the sixth in the absence of figuring is much less frequent than might be expected. Generally the progression speaks for itself, given familiarity with the style.

(c) In very ambivalent cases, the correct figuring to prevent mistakes is 3. This states that the third is present.

The presence of the third, whether assumed or indicated, implies the fifth to complete the triad, in the absence of any further assumption or indication to the contrary.

The figure 3 also occurs to indicate the resolution of a 4 preceding it on the previous portion of the same bass note (or its octave), or in other situations where it is desired to draw particular attention to the third. Other intervals may also be figured for similar reasons (*i.e.* the 5 and the 8) either above or in combination.

But where a third requires chromatic modification, the necessary ♯ or ♭ or ♮ is normally set in the position which the 3 would otherwise occupy, the 3 itself being omitted. Much less commonly, both accidental and figure are shown, as ♯ 3 or ♭ 3 or ♮ 3.

The sign ♮, however, remained comparatively infrequent in the figuring of basses (more so than in the rest of the text) and the reader must be prepared to find ♯ as the cancellation of ♭ and ♭ as the cancellation of ♯ (see Ch. IV, 6 above).

When the 5 but not the 3 is to be accidentally sharpened, the figuring 5̗ (or ♯ 5, *etc.*) is necessary (for variants, see Tables II and III in Ch. IV, 4 above).

When both 3 and 5 are to be accidentally sharpened, the figuring ♯ or ♮ is necessary, there being no need to indicate the sharpened fifth, because in the absence of indication the 5 with a major 3 is normally assumed to be perfect, not diminished. Nevertheless the sharpened 5 is sometimes shown, the figuring then being $\frac{5̗}{♯}$ or $\frac{5̗}{♮}$ as the case may be.

The same assumption (that 5 with major 3 is perfect) operates when the bass is accidentally flattened, so that no figuring is then needed.

(d) It is normally desirable (except in sequences) to avoid doubling the major third in any context which makes it function as a leading note (especially if it has been chromatically altered to serve that function).

It must be realised that for a leading-note acting as such (in whatever inversion or part, of whatever chord) there is only one alternative to its natural progression by a semitone upwards. This alternative is a drop of a major third to the fifth of the ensuing tonic, which is allowable provided the leading-note is not in the top part (cases abound in J. S. Bach's four-part chorales). Even in a free style, these rules should command respect; they are deeply rooted in acoustic reality.

Otherwise, any intervals in a diatonic triad, major or minor, can be doubled in any suitable way.

(e) When thinning the chord to three parts, the most natural note to drop is the 8, and thereafter the 5. In two parts, the 3 itself must sometimes be dropped in the interests of good part-writing, and also of harmonic variety.

5. DIMINISHED TRIADS

(a) No figuring is needed for diatonic diminished triads (comprised of minor 3 plus diminished 5), but 5 or $\overset{\frown}{5}$ or $\overset{\frown}{5\flat}$ may be found. The semicircle over the figure is to exclude the 6 which might otherwise be assumed, although not figured, since a diminished triad and a 6–5 chord are in very many contexts interchangeable, and the fuller chord would generally be preferred by most accompanists, other things being equal.

$\overset{\frown}{5\flat}$ or $\overset{\frown}{5\natural}$ is usually a sufficient indication for a chromatically reached diminished triad, unless the third is also modified, when it should be shown.

The semicircle, being rare except in text-books, may not be present: ♭5 or ♮5 is the standard indication.

It will be noticed that the ♭ or ♮ to the 5, if found with diatonic diminished triads, merely indicates a diminished fifth, but if found with chromatic diminished triads, indicates the chromatic flattening of the fifth.

(b) The best interval to double depends on circumstances. When the chord stands on the seventh degree of a major scale or the sharpened seventh degree of a minor scale, the best (and in pure style, the only correct) interval to double is the 3. In its only other standard situation, which is on the second degree of a minor scale, the 3 is better than the 8 to double, and the 8 is better than the (diminished) 5; but the part-writing will be the main consideration. The truth is that this is essentially a three-part chord, which is never at its best in four-part writing.

(c) Thinning to two parts can only be by dropping the 3, since the diminished 5 is essential to the chord.

6. AUGMENTED TRIADS

(a) Augmented triads (comprised of major 3 plus augmented 5) are figured $\overset{\diagup}{5}$ (or ♯5, *etc.*) or ♮5 as the case may be.

(b) It is most inadvisable (and in pure style, impossible) to double the augmented 5, which needs to progress by a semitone upwards and cannot properly take any other course. This chord, like the diminished triad, is at its most natural in three parts, as C. P. E. Bach points out (*Essay*, Part II, 1762, Ch. 5, 6).

(c) Thinning to two parts can only be by dropping the 3; but the chord is most unsuited to two-part writing.

7. SIX-THREE CHORDS (CHORDS OF THE SIXTH)

(a) Six-three chords are the first inversions of triads. The figuring is 6 if diatonic; $\overset{\diagup}{6}$ (or ♯6, *etc.*), ♮6, or ♭6, as the case may be, if chromatic.

The 3 is implied, but not normally figured unless requiring accidental modification, when the ♯ or ♮ or ♭ is shown, but not usually the 3 itself.

Fuller figuring is sometimes given to show the progression from the previous harmony.

(b) When the bass (representing the 3 of the triad) functions as a leading note (especially if accidentally modified for the purpose) it is frequently left unfigured, the 6 being assumed.

(c) When serving as leading note (especially if accidentally sharpened), the bass is not normally a desirable interval to double (except in sequences).

If the triad inverted is either diminished or augmented, the note now representing the leading note is unsuitable for doubling (and so is that now representing the augmented 5).

(d) The 3 can be dropped in two-parts, but the chord, as such, ceases to exist.

(e) Sequences of six-three chords are natural and admirable in three-part writing. In four-part writing, they need some care to make the progressions reasonably correct (see Arnold, *op. cit.*, pp. 525 *ff.*). The fourth part can best leap, alternately by contrary and direct motion.

The 3 should not be above the 6 in consecutive six-three chords, or parallel fifths will result. These may be tolerable, however, if one of them is diminished.

8. SIX-FOUR CHORDS

(a) Six-four chords are the second inversions of triads. The figuring is $^6_4$ if diatonic, with the appropriate accidentals for any chromatic modifications required by modulation, or by any diminished or augmented interval in the triad inverted.

(b) The 4 is strongly inclined (and in pure style compelled) to progress by step downwards (in pure style, it also requires preparation if on a strong beat).

But if the 4 remains stationary from the previous chord and into the next chord, or if the previous chord was another inversion of the same chord, or if the chord is taken as a passing chord on the same bass, the above does not apply.

(c) Doubling is reasonably free except for the inverted leading note when the triad inverted is an augmented one.

(d) In two parts the 4 must be dropped; but the chord, as such, ceases to exist.

9. CHORDS OF THE AUGMENTED SIXTH

(a) Chords of the augmented sixth consist of an augmented sixth with a major third ('Italian sixth'); with a major third and an augmented fourth ('French sixth'); or a major third and a perfect fifth ('German sixth').

(b) The 'Italian sixth' is figured ₆̷ (♯ 6, *etc.*). The proper figuring for the 'French sixth' is $\frac{6}{4}$ and for the 'German sixth' $\frac{6}{5}$.

(c) The augmented 6 requires no preparation, but should resolve by the step of a semitone upwards. The bass moves a semitone downwards, and the 3 should do likewise. The 4 of the 'French sixth' remains stationary into the next chord. The 5 of the 'German sixth' is better if prepared; it should resolve a semitone downwards with the bass, the resultant parallel fifths being acceptable in a free style (though some authorities both contemporary and modern would deny this) provided they are neither between outer parts, nor between tenor and bass—in other words, provided only one of them is on the outside, and they are also separated from one another by an intervening part.

In most cases, however, these parallel fifths will have been averted by the composer. He will have figured a $\frac{6}{4}$ suspension on the note to which the bass moves, followed by a $\frac{5}{3}$ resolution on the same bass note.

(d) No notes can be doubled without some risk of introducing either consecutives or faulty progressions.

(e) No notes can be dropped without changing the identity of these chords, except that in theory the 'Italian sixth' might exist in two parts without its 3—if ever occasion for it arose in practice.

10. CHORDS OF THE SEVENTH

(a) Chords of the seventh are normally indicated by 7 alone, except when the third needs accidental modification, and this is shown as usual. Fuller figuring occurs when the progressions are to be indicated, or when the presence of the 5 or the 8 is to be indicated. The presence of a 3 not accidentally modified may indicate that the 5 is to be omitted.

The 7 is a discord, whose normal resolution is by step downwards. In the pure style, it needs preparation; and even in a freer style, it should be prepared in most ordinary contexts unless there is a good musical reason to the contrary. But except in the pure style dominant sevenths and diminished sevenths may be taken unprepared without hesitation, and so may chains of sevenths resolving from one on to the next. The resolution of the seventh may also be suppressed or omitted in the free style, if there is good musical reason, particularly when the 7 remains stationary into the next chord, or when the bass moves to the first inversion of the same chord, or when the bass moves to what would have been the note of resolution (transferred resolution), or the whole chord moves to one of its own inversions.

Though there are plenty of exceptions, it is generally undesirable to sound the note on which any discord is going to resolve in the same chord in which the discord itself is sounded (but see Ch. XXIX, 5 (*f*)). The effect is not only apt to be muddy, but tends to anticlimax.

(b) The 3 as leading note should not normally be doubled, except in sequences. Nor, in general, should the 7.

(c) The most natural interval to drop when thinning chords of the seventh to three parts is the 5, whose presence is not by any means always desirable even in four parts (it may be better to include the 8 instead, which keeps the chord considerably less weighty).

In two parts, the 5 and the 3 must be dropped; but though quite possible in this form, the chord of the seventh becomes too empty for very much use in two-part writing.

11. SIX-FIVE CHORDS

(a) Six-five chords are first inversions of chords of the seventh. The figuring is $^6_5$, together with any necessary accidental modification to the 3, shown as usual by accidentals normally without the figure 3 itself.

The dissonance here is the 5, which is the 7 inverted, and is subject to similar stipulations with regard to preparation and resolution.

(b) The bass as leading note should not normally be doubled, except in sequences.

(c) In thinning to three parts, the 3 should be dropped. The chord cannot exist in two parts.

12. FOUR-THREE CHORDS

(a) Four-three chords are second inversions of chords of the seventh. The figuring is $^4_3$, the 6 being added only when accidentally modified, or when it is inserted to show the progression.

On the supertonic of a prevailing major or minor key, and on the submediant of a major and sometimes of a minor key, the single figure 6 was conventionally held to imply 4 as well as 3 at the discretion of the performer—*i.e.* a four-three chord in place of a six-three.

The dissonance here is the 3, which is the 7 of the uninverted chord, and is subject to similar stipulations with regard to preparation and resolution.

(b) The 6 as leading note should not normally be doubled, except in sequences.

(c) The note to be dropped in three parts is either the 6, or when the 6 cannot be spared because it is functioning as leading-note, the 4, though this unfortunately robs the discord of actuality. The chord cannot exist in two parts.

13. FOUR-TWO CHORDS

(a) Four-two chords are third inversions of chords of the seventh. The figuring is normally $\frac{4}{2}$, which is frequently abbreviated to 2, and sometimes expanded to include the 6.

On the subdominant of a prevailing major or minor key, the 4 is augmented, and a frequent figuring is 4 (or ♯4, *etc.*) or ♮4 as the case may be.

When the second is augmented, the most frequent figuring is ♯2 or ♮2, as the case may be, or 2 serving as the equivalent of either. The fourth is then augmented too, but is nevertheless not usually shown in the figuring, even when accidental, the presence of the augmented 2 being normally regarded as implying the augmented 4.

The dissonance here is the bass note, so that its preparation, if any, and its resolution, which is normally indispensable, are the responsibility of the composer and not of the performer.

(b) The augmented fourth as leading note should not normally be doubled, except in sequences.

(c) In thinning to three parts, the 6 should be dropped; in two parts, the 6 and the 4.

14. 'PASSING NOTES' IN THE BASS

(a) Passing notes in the normal sense are notes joining harmony notes by step; but from the viewpoint of figured bass any note which is passed over, in the sense of not bearing harmony of its own, can be called a 'passing note' even if it leaps (and in whatever direction).

To distinguish 'passing notes' in the bass, which merely require the previous harmony to be held on, from harmony notes in the bass, which require their own appropriate chord to be struck whether shown by figures or not, is one of the chief practical problems in realising a figured bass at sight. When no upper part is given, the problem cannot invariably be solved with certainty; even with a good knowledge of the style (which is the main help here) mistakes are virtually unavoidable unless the composer has gone to unusual lengths to impart the necessary information. But in working on paper with the other parts available to refer to, the problem is no longer troublesome, since it is always possible and seldom difficult to find a realisation which fits the existing parts.

(b) When the passing note in the bass is unaccented, the harmony of the previous note is continued. This may be shown by the very simple and satisfactory device of a dash over the passing note. The same applies when there are more passing notes than one, in which case the dash is prolonged across all of them. But unfortunately the dash did not come into common use until the end of the seventeenth century, and even then was not employed with the regularity it deserved. Occasionally the passing note is itself figured to show the harmony carried over from the previous note (rather than struck again). The cases, however, in which no direct indication is given are by far the most frequent.

A special case of a 'passing' note in the bass which requires knowing is shown by the following example. The crotchet *F*, being unfigured but approached by leap, looks as if it should have its own harmony, *i.e.* a triad, but is in fact treated as though it were a passing note from a (non-existent) *E*.

Ex. 167. J. D. Heinichen, *General-Bass*, Dresden, 1728, Part I, Ch. IV, sect. 33, p. 323, irregular passing note in the bass (the *F* in bar 2):

(c) When the passing note in the bass is accented, it carries the harmony of the next note, and is in effect a measured appoggiatura (or unprepared suspension) in the bass. Perhaps the commonest way of showing this is to place the figuring over the second, unaccented note, leaving it to the performer to understand that he has to strike it over the first, accented note. An improvement on this by no means self-evident method was to place a dash over the first note, connecting it with the figures shown over the second note. Better still, but by no means as common as it should have been, is the correct figuring for the passing note placed over that note, and held on through the next (and actual harmony) note. Here, too, it is common to find no direct indication at all. One indirect indication of the harmony intended may be the necessity for it in order to prepare an ensuing discord. Another moderately dependable clue is the presence of a leap following the short notes in question.

(d) With both unaccented and accented passing notes in the bass, the most decisive factor is their speed. In common $\frac{4}{4}$ time, the crotchet is the standard unit of harmony; shorter notes in the bass are apt to be passing notes unless otherwise figured. In allabreve $\frac{2}{2}$ time, the minim is the standard unit of harmony, or under some circumstances in the pure style, even the semibreve; shorter notes in the bass again tending to be passing notes. But in what was sometimes called the semi-allabreve time (in effect a rapid $\frac{4}{4}$, not a steady $\frac{2}{2}$) the crotchet is the standard unit; and there are other complications: in $\frac{3}{2}$ the minim, in $\frac{3}{4}$ the crotchet, in $\frac{3}{8}$ the quaver is the unit, but either one or two of these may go to a single harmony.

No great reliance, however, should be placed on these and other baroque rules of the kind. Still less reliance should be placed on the various non-numerical signs, C, ₵, *etc.*, since these were in a state of utter confusion throughout the baroque period, as the best authorities of that period unhesitatingly admitted (Ch. XXXVIII below). The performer should allow his own musicianship to tell him, irrespective of the signs, what is the main harmonic pulse of the piece in question. Notes in the bass shorter than this pulse will tend to be passing notes unless otherwise figured. There will be very numerous exceptions, many of them undetectable except by the instinct born of long experience or by reference to the other written parts.

When an accompanist who is realising a figured bass at sight feels completely doubtful, he has a choice of evils. He can evade the difficulty by a momentary gap in his harmony. He can treat the ambiguous bass note as a passing note in the knowledge that if this is a mistake, it will be a less conspicuous one than the opposite mistake of striking a fresh harmony on what was meant to be a passing note. He can, very often, thin his part down to tenths moving in parallel with the bass, which will in many cases sound right on either basis.

On the other hand, if he is experienced, the occasions on which he is seriously in doubt will be far less frequent than might be expected in theory. The harmonic movement is much more foreseeable in some styles than it is in others, but even in the least foreseeable there are grades of probability to which an experienced accompanist becomes remarkably sensitive, not only over this particular problem, but over many others. It is only an occasional situation which should be capable of defeating him completely.

It must be admitted that such situations do occur.

CHAPTER XXVIII

Going Beyond the Figures

1. WHAT THE FIGURES SHOW

Figurings, like signs for ornaments, are not commands but hints. They give information about the harmonies going on in the written parts to which the accompanist has to fit. They may also impart the composer's wishes; but this is not usually their main function.

So long as polyphonic parts were regarded as best accompanied by doubling them, the two functions coincided.

(292) Bernardo Strozzi, 'Concerti Ecclesiastici', III, preface (quoted with approval by Praetorius, *Syntagma*, III, 1619, Ch. VI):

'A great deal of discordance was heard [with unfigured basses] because everyone applies the rules of music according to his own methods, whim, disposition and fancy . . . [Figures were invented as a means by which] a man might play it correctly, in such a way that no mistakes were heard, and might handle it as far as possible in the manner intended by the composer.

'With the help and use of the said figures, they handled and performed the Motets of Palestrina . . . in such a way that it appeared to the listeners exactly as if the whole had been set out in full Tablature.'

The Italian monodists, who took up the use of figured bass on its first appearance and were certainly among the pioneers in developing it, by their use of compound figuring controlled the progression of their harmonies to an extent impossible so soon as compound figuring was dropped in favour of simple figuring regardless of octave transposition. This change itself is evidence of a change of policy. Before many years had passed, we have clear evidence for what became the accepted ideal of standard figured bass accompaniment: a more or less chordal texture against which the written parts can stand out, as opposed to being doubled. Ironically enough, the basis of this ideal was the part-writing of the great polyphonists, which is the starting point for good harmonic progression in the chordal style.

(293) Johann Staden, *Kurzer Bericht*, Nuremberg, 1626:

'[It is] good authors such as Orlando [di Lasso], Luca Marenzio, Claudio Merulo, Pierluigi Palestrina, Andrea and Giovanni Gabrieli, Horatio Vecchi, Giovanni Paulo Cima, Johann Leo Hassler, Gregor Aichinger, Christian Erbach, Agostino Agazzari, Flaminius Comanedus, *etc.*, especially in their four-part writing, from whom a beginner can best learn how the harmony is to be conducted to suit the Organ Bass. For if a man were to turn himself to the present much ornamented (*zierliche*) vocal style and use it at the keyboard without first knowing what is conformable with the rules of music, he would certainly not learn from the new style in question to tell good from bad, far from it, he would go in quite the opposite direction, since it continually requires an absolutely different pattern of harmony from the existing parts.'

At this stage, information as to the harmonies going on in the written parts and instructions as to the composer's wishes are no longer necessarily the same thing. The accompanist has no obvious means of knowing which is which; all he sees is figures. But there is sometimes a certain abnormal fullness in the figuring which suggests that the composer has special wishes to impart, over and above the harmony already imposed by the written parts. Even these special wishes do not absolutely bind the performer, which would be contrary to the spirit of baroque music in general and of figured bass in particular; but he will obviously give them his respectful attention. In some of J. S. Bach's fullest figurings, which are really quite exceptional and stretch the system almost beyond its useful capacity, a strict rendering leaves little choice, not merely in the harmony, but in the part-writing needed to embody it.

(294) A. Werckmeister, *Anmerckungen*, Aschersleben, 1698, sect. 70:

'Furthermore it is not desirable just to play blindly with the singers and instrumentalists the discords shown in the continuo, or to double them: for when the singer is conveying an agreeable feeling by the written discord, an unthinking accompanist, if he does not go carefully, may ruin all the beauty by the same discord: hence the figures and the discords are not always written in with a view to being blindly reproduced; but a performer skilled in composition can see from them what is the composer's intention, and how to avoid conflicting with them with any matter which would be injurious to the harmony.'

(295) Friedrich Erhard Niedt, *Musicalische Handleitung*, Hamburg, 1700, Ch. V, rule 8:

'If the singer or instrumentalist sings or plays the figures which are set above the continuo, it is not necessary for the Organist to play them; he can just play Thirds instead if that seems suitable; or, again, it is at his own discretion if he chooses to put in something more highly elaborated.'

(296) C. P. E. Bach, *Essay*, II, Berlin, 1762, I, 4:

'I am no supporter of great quantities of figures. I am against everything which makes needless trouble and kills enjoyment. [XXV, 17:] Accompanists of experience capable and courageous enough to improvise small corrections in a piece of music should be given praise for what they do.'

2. DEPARTING FROM THE FIGURES

(a) There are many occasions on which it is possible, and has an excellent effect, to add to the harmonies shown by the figuring.

(297) Lorenzo Penna, *Albori Musicali*, Bologna, 1672, III, Ch. 14:

'The discords can be accompanied (if so desired) by the consonances of the note written.'

This is a late date to find the sounding of the chord of resolution with the note of dissonance unrestrictedly accepted as a desirable enrichment of the harmony; but see 4 (c) below for a restricted permission, and Ch. XXIX, 5, below for a wider permission under the special circumstances of a very full accompaniment.

(298) Michel de Saint-Lambert, *Traité*, Paris, 1707, Ch. VI, p. 71:

'On a bass note of substantial duration, one can put in two or three different chords one after the other, although the text only asks for one, provided that one senses that these chords go with the melodic part. . . .

'[p. 89: With two rising minor sixths the second of which is in effect a leading note in the bass] one can take . . . on the second, the diminished Fifth [although not figured].'

Ex. 168. Saint-Lambert, *loc. cit.*, added dissonance:

[Ch. IX, p. 133:] 'One can sometimes add a fourth note to the chords indicated by the regular Rules, either in order to soften the hardness of a discord, or on the contrary in order to make it more piquant, so as to increase the pleasure of its resolving concord. What interval from the Bass this fourth note should comprise . . . let your ear decide as occasion arises, and if you cannot decide, leave it out.'

The example above is connected with a very general convention by which certain sixths, figured merely 6, could have the 4 added to the already implied 3. The most important is the major sixth on the supertonic of the prevailing key (major or minor). Here the 3 is minor, and the chord as figured is the first inversion of the imperfect triad on the seventh degree of the scale. The addition of the 4 turns it into the second inversion of the dominant seventh.

(299) J. D. Heinichen, *General-Bass*, Dresden, 1728, Part I, Ch. III, sect. 7, p. 150:

'In the case of the major 6th combined with a minor 3rd . . . one may take the 4, holding it on from the previous chord, provided it can remain as a stationary note into the next.'

The first of Heinichen's two conditions (the presence of the 4 in the previous chord) was not indispensable; but if the 4 is not thus prepared, the 3 should be.

(300) J. D. Heinichen, *General-Bass*, Dresden, 1728, Part I, Ch. III, sect. 7, p. 151:

'The same thing is allowed in certain cases with the augmented 4th, which, however, is then combined with the major 3rd.'

When the sixth as well as the fourth is augmented, the result is a 'French Sixth' (see Ch. XXII, 9); the figuring may still be only the ♭6 (♯6, *etc.*).

(301) C. P. E. Bach, *Essay*, II, Berlin, 1762, VII, i, 11:

♭6

'Many people figure [the 5] insufficiently with only 6 and its accidental.'

3

Instead of a $\frac{4}{3}$ chord, a ♭6 may occasionally be taken as a $\frac{6}{5}$, provided there is no 4 in the existing parts to conflict with it.

(302) G. P. Telemann, *Generalbass-Übungen*, Hamburg, 1733–35, p. 9:

'It is, in fact, a useful attribute of the diminished 5 that one can bring it in on all sorts of occasions. . . .

[p. 11:] 'The 5 is not always figured, but it is always in keeping when the movement [of the bass] is upwards to a minor chord, and the composer has not put the 4, unfigured, in place of it; a good ear, which listens ahead, is needed. A 3 completes the chord.'

But the main authorities do not describe this particular possibility, probably because it is very liable to go wrong in sight-reading, when the presence of the 4 in the existing parts may well not be foreseen.

Telemann (*op. cit.*, 16 *f* and 18 *h, i*) also allows a $\frac{6}{5}$ on the subdominant in the absence of figures: *i.e.* a 6 added to a perfect triad. Here, of course, the 5 is perfect. There are more occasions for this addition than for the one last mentioned, and it will often be found valuable.

Ex. 169. G. P. Telemann, *Generalbass-Übungen*, Hamburg, 1733–35, (unfigured) $\frac{5}{3}$ with unfigured 6 added (on second chord):

A dominant major triad may have a 7 added, though not shown in the figuring. This is always justifiable as a passing note. Struck as part of the chord it requires more discretion.

(303) A. Scarlatti, *Regole*, Brit. Mus. MS. Add. 14244, *f*. 13a, Rule 1:

'On a $\frac{5}{4}$ to $\frac{5}{3}$ cadence in resolving on to the 3rd one strikes the 7th as well.'

(304) C. P. E. Bach, *Essay*, II, Berlin, 1762, XIII, ii, 1:

'When the bass, whether in a cadence or not, either rises one degree or leaps to the 4th above or the 5th below, the chord of the 7th, even when not figured, may be taken with the penultimate note, provided that the next note bears a triad.'

C. P. E. Bach also gives an example in which a 6 is figured but he prefers to take a suspended 7 resolving on to the 6, for the sake of a better progression (*op. cit.*, Ch. 34, Sect. 2, Ex. a).

(305) G. M. Telemann, *Unterricht im Generalbass-Spielen*, Hamburg, 1773, III, 8, p. 104:

'In final dominant cadences in root position one commonly strikes the 7th after the 5th or 8th of the penultimate chord, even when not figured. . . . There is, however, no obligation.'

Cases of incomplete figuring also occur, however, in which there is an obligation, because the figuring is left incomplete not merely to give the performer the option, but on the assumption that he would know the intention. This assumption is often most unreasonable. The inadequacy of much continuo figuring is eloquent testimony to the skill of most accompaniments in making do with the most scanty hints, or none at all in the case of the numerous totally unfigured basses in operatic and other music of the period. In a sense it increases our liberty; but it also adds heavily to our responsibility. Typical instances which are not merely incomplete but highly misleading are $\frac{6}{4}$ for $\frac{6}{4}_{2}$ or $\frac{3}{4}_{6}$, and $\frac{7}{4}$ for $\frac{7}{5}_{4}$; but many others are found, often quite unpredictable.

A more comprehensible economy occurs when a figure is omitted because the progression implies the interval in question if it is to be grammatically correct. Thus a note required either for the preparation or for the resolution of a discord is quite commonly left unfigured on the assumption that the need for it will be self-evident. A special case of this is 9 used by itself for a chord which, besides the obvious 5 and 3, must also include the 7 to prepare a following discord. And, of course, such added elements are often desirable merely to complete a harmony, or to enrich it, even without the further compulsion of securing a correct progression. The whole matter lies wide open to the intelligence and enterprise of the accompanist, provided that he knows what he is doing and can therefore keep within the boundaries of the style.

(b) There are equally occasions when the accompanist may not wish to sound all the notes shown in the figuring. He is just as much within his rights in leaving out part of what is figured as he is in adding to what is figured. The only condition is again that just mentioned: that he shall know what he is doing and why he is doing it.

Adding to the figures naturally increases the sonority; but mere sonority can be as effectively increased by simply doubling the intervals already present. The primary reason for adding further intervals is to increase the interest and the sophistication of the harmony.

Subtracting from the figuring is at the same time for decreasing the sonority and for decreasing the harmonic sophistication. There are many quick and airy movements where three-part writing, or indeed two-part writing, is the obvious recourse, not necessarily or not only because the dynamic balance requires no more, but primarily because the character of the music required the lightest possible mood in the accompaniment. It is as much a matter of simplifying the harmonies as of thinning the texture. But, of course, beyond the point at which all unnecessary doubling is avoided the only further direct recourse for decreasing the sonority is thinning the chords themselves. Thus here the two things go together.

(306) Michel de Saint-Lambert, *Traité*, Paris, 1707, Ch. VI, p. 71:

'On the other hand one can avoid sounding all the intervals marked in the text, when one finds that the notes are too heavily loaded.

[Ch. IX, sect. 1, p. 128:] 'This taste consists chiefly in managing the harmony well, so that you do not draw so much sound from the harpsichord that it stifles the melodic part entirely, or on the contrary so little that it does not sufficiently support it. . . . For very light voices . . . you can even reduce the accompaniment to two parts.

[Ch. IX, p. 133:] 'One is not always obliged to include three different parts in a chord, having the option of doubling [including unisons which on a keyboard suppress a part] some of them at pleasure, or even of dispensing with one of the three when that seems necessary.'

(307) F. E. Niedt, *Musicalische Handleitung*, Hamburg, 1700, Ch. VIII, rule 8:

'When there are rapid notes or notes with tails in the continuo, one must not take the Third and Fifth with each note, nor play all the figures (when there are many of them over the Bass).'

(308) C. P. E. Bach, *Essay*, Berlin, II, 1762, XXXII, 6 (see Ch. XXIX, 4 (328), below for the continuation of this passage):

'One of the main refinements of the accompaniment is parallel movement in thirds [tenths, *etc.*] with the Bass. The right hand is never obliged here to maintain a consistent fulness of harmony [whatever the figuring].'

(c) It is occasionally desirable not merely to add to or subtract from the intervals shown by the figuring, but actually to contravene them in order to improve an awkward corner, such as may occur by oversight even in the best composers.

Copyist's or printer's errors in the figuring are very common indeed; and, of course, if such an error is suspected, an intelligent performer will do his best not to be misled.

(309) C. P. E. Bach, *Essay*, II, Berlin, 1762, Introd., 27:

'In defective and awkward passages, where there can often be no proper middle part owing to the faultiness of the Bass from which such parts should flow, one hides the deficiencies as far as possible with a thin accompaniment; one is sparing with the harmony; at need, one introduces a [contravening] figure.

[XXXII, 5:] 'Sensitive accompaniment means, moreover, making modifications to match certain liberties sometimes taken by the soloist, who may at his own option to some extent contradict the written notes when bringing in embellishments and variations. A skilled soloist will do this when he knows that he has a competent accompanist, so that he lets himself go with complete abandon to the feeling of the music. . . . The accompanist must modify his harmony to suit.

[Part I, 1753, Foreword:] 'The keyboard player . . . must have at his command a thorough knowledge of thorough bass, which he must perform with judgement, often departing from the written text.'

Finally, there is nothing in baroque theory or practice to forbid an accompanist from changing the harmony shown by the figures purely for his own pleasure, provided that he keeps within the style and does not clash with the written parts. It need hardly be added that a modern performer has to be very sensitive in doing this, so as to avoid artistic incongruity whether anachronistic or otherwise.

(309a) Michel de Saint-Lambert, *Traité*, Paris, 1707, Ch. VI, p. 71:

'You can sometimes change the chords marked on the notes [*i.e.* figured], when you judge that others will suit better.'

3. DEPARTING FROM THE BASS

(a) The liberties regarded as legitimately open to the accompanist included altering the bass line itself if he felt that it was really unsatisfactory at any point.

(310) C. P. E. Bach, *Essay*, II, Berlin, 1762, Introd., 27:

'When the continuo is not doubled by other instruments, and the nature of the piece permits it, the accompanist may make impromptu modifications in the bass line with a view to securing correct and smooth progressions of the inner parts, just as he would modify faulty figuring. And how often has this to be done!'

(b) Where the bass line is satisfactory in itself, but is either not very suitable to a keyboard instrument as it stands, or at any rate can be improved from that point of view, the accompanist is entitled to make appropriate modifications in it. He may simplify it; he may adapt it; or he may elaborate it with arpeggios or divisions.

(311) Michel de Saint-Lambert, *Traité*, Paris, 1707, Ch. VIII, p. 120:

'When the measure is so compressed that the accompanist cannot conveniently play all the notes, he can content himself with playing the first note of each bar, leaving the bass viol or violoncello to play all the notes.

[p. 121:] 'On the other hand if the Bass has too few notes, and drags too much for the liking of the accompanist, he may add other notes by way of pleasing figuration, provided he is sure that this will not interfere with the melody.'

(312) J. D. Heinichen, *General-Bass*, Dresden, 1728, p. 377:

'There is no need to be put out by a number of rapid repeated notes, but, so long as no fresh figuring occurs over the notes, the previous chord is repeated in slower notes, one or more times (according to the measure), and the playing of the rapid notes is left to the other accompanying bass instruments. . . . There are various other ways of treating such notes.'

Ex. 170. J. D. Heinichen, *loc. cit.* and I, vi, 39, methods of adapting rapid repeated notes to the idiom of the harpsichord:

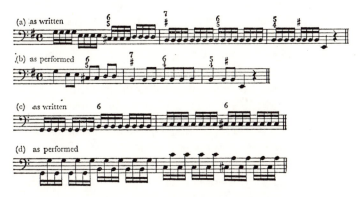

In the above examples, Heinichen shows right-hand chords taken with the same rhythm as the bass. He also gives the alternative of quavers consistently replacing semiquavers in the left hand, while the right hand takes over the semiquaver movement with 'Alberti bass' patterns resembling those in the left hand at (d) above. C. P. E. Bach (*Essay*, II, Berlin, 1762, Ch. 29, sect. 17) gives, for slow tempos only, the repeated semitones of the bass played literally and accompanied by their lower octaves in quavers (all in the left hand). For faster passages, he is prepared to sacrifice the added sonority of the octave doubling; and when a string bass is present, he is strongly opposed to letting the left hand drum out repeated semiquavers, which only serve to stiffen the player's hand without being really effectual. As a final resort, he allows chords to be struck on alternate semiquavers in either hand, when a real noise is wanted.

(313) C. P. E. Bach, *Essay*, Berlin, 1753, Introd., 9, *fn.*:

'It is best to let one, three or five such notes, according to the speed and measure, pass unstruck, those which are struck being taken with the octave, or in a *fortissimo*, even with full chords in either hand, with a heavy touch and rather sustained, so that the strings may sufficiently vibrate, and one note be joined to the next. Or if every note must and shall be heard on the harpsichord, there remains the following recourse, namely to reproduce the movement by striking the notes [in full chords] with alternate hands.

[II, 1762, XXXVI, 8:] 'When the bass has a continuous succession or at least a large number of demi-semiquavers or faster notes, the left hand may leave out one or more notes, provided a melodic bass accompaniment is present. [Some authors waive this last proviso.]'

(c) It is legitimate, and very often desirable, to introduce melodic 'leads' to take the music neatly back to the beginning of a repeated passage, at the first time through, and also (with the requisite modulation) on to the next section, at the second time through. If this is not done, the whole piece may hang fire, and the interest flag, for lack of the necessary movement to keep the last bar from falling empty. These 'leads' will frequently need to be added to the bass line as well as to the other parts. The following examples from C. P. E. Bach, like almost all that he gives, were shown for economy of printing on a single stave, of which the top line, however, was to be taken at any required octave transposition (*e.g.* at the tenth instead of at the third).

Ex. 171. C. P. E. Bach, *Essay*, II, Berlin, 1762, XXXI, 6, 'leads' back to the beginning of repeated sections:

(314) C. P. E. Bach, *Essay*, II, Berlin, 1762, XXXVI, 13:

'When transitional passages [in the bass] cannot be accompanied in thirds [or tenths, as at Ex. 171 (a) above] or some pleasing variant [as at Ex. 171 (b)], they should be treated as passing notes.'

(d) Occasionally the bass has to be modified in order to accommodate ornamentation in the solo part.

(315) C. P. E. Bach, *Essay*, II, Berlin, 1762, XXX, 6:

'When a composer allows his bass to continue moving through a closing cadence, as at [Ex. 172], regardless of the possibility of ornamentation, the accompanist [if necessary] holds on the first *G* and repeats it under the [concluding] trill, after which he begins the following bar. Such a case, which often happens in allegros, wants careful listening.'

Ex. 172. C. P. E. Bach, bass needing modification if the soloist makes a cadenza at the point here indicated by the ⌒:

(e) An odd case of conventional mis-notation in recitative is mentioned by J. A. Scheibe. If figuring and bass appear as at Ex. 172 (a), the accompanist, unless somehow prevented, is almost bound to resolve the 2 of the $\frac{4}{2}$ as at Ex. 172 (b); some composers actually write it so— yet *still* mean the realisation to be as at Ex. 172 (a) (*i.e.* with the resolution transferred to the octave above, in the right hand, the bass being allowed to keep its rest as written at Ex. 172 (a)). The remedy suggested is to write the bass as at Ex. 172 (c); but it is not a very self-explanatory remedy, and certainly not one which shows any signs of having recommended itself to composers.

Ex. 172a, b, c: a tricky case shown by J. A. Scheibe in F. W. Marpurg's *Kritische Briefe*, Berlin, for 1760–62, 87 on pp. 354–55:

4. ACCOMMODATING HARMONIC ORNAMENTS

(a) Trills and long appoggiaturas have so pronounced an effect on the harmony that their presence has to be taken into account when realising the accompaniment. A few other ornaments have sufficient effect for it to be desirable to take them into account in some contexts.

(b) The best accompaniment to give to a trill depends on how prolonged the initial upper note (the preparation or 'appoggiatura' of the
trill) is made. This varies partly with the style; partly with the taste of
the soloist.

When the preparation is very long, the accompaniment should
normally consist of two chords, whether so figured or not. The first is
the chord implied by the preparation ($^5_4$ or $^6_3$, or with two simultaneous
trills $^6_4$, as the case may be). The second is the chord implied by the
resolution on to the main note of the trill (normally $^5_3$).

At Ex. 173 (a) below, we see a typical case of misleading figuring
which nevertheless gives the necessary hint to an accompanist familiar
enough with the style concerned, which is that of the French school of
gambists. The 4 by itself would tend to suggest a $^5_4$, but at least we can
be certain that it is not a $^5_3$, which follows on the second beat with the
♯ marked. We therefore know that the solo parts, which are notated to
give a $^5_3$ on both the first and the second beat, are not going to be
performed literally, but with a harmonic ornament of whose effect the
4 is meant to warn us. And in fact both solo parts have a trill shown,
by the sign normal to this school: a comma after the note on which the
trill is to be made (not to be confused with Couperin's phrasing comma,
which looks the same!). The harmonic effect of which the 4 is the
warning will therefore be due to the long preparations of these two
trills: and this in turn shows us that the 4 must stand not for $^5_3$ but for
$^6_4$. The interpretation will therefore have to be approximately as at Ex.
173 (b).

Ex. 173. Marin Marais, *Pièces à 1 et à 2 violes*, Paris, 1686, 2nd
Suite, Sarabande, bar 8: (a) as written; (b) approximately as intended
(my interpretation confirmed by Ex. 174, but see also App. VI):

At Ex. 174 (a) below we have a clearer instance of the same kind,
in which the figuring is correct and in no way misleading; it is realised
as it is figured, but this figuring takes into account the harmonic effect
of an ornament in the solo part. No sign for this ornament appears;
but that is not surprising, since the context is one in which, as both
soloist and accompanist would have been well aware at the time, a

cadential trill is not merely optional but obligatory. My interpretation, therefore, is approximately as at Ex. 174 (b).

Ex. 174. (a) G. P. Telemann, *Generalbass-Übungen*, Hamburg, 1733–35, No. 36, harmony figured to accommodate implied cadential trill; (b) my interpretation:

At Ex. 175 (a) below, we have a contrary case. Here, the figuring shows no warning of the presence of a harmonic ornament; nor is there any sign for an ornament in the solo part. But the realisation of the accompaniment (which is original, *i.e.* by Telemann) shows a harmony which contravenes the figuring; and this harmony does in fact take into account the presence of a harmonic ornament on the *F* sharp of the solo part. That again is not surprising; this context, too, is one in which a cadential trill is not merely optional but obligatory. Even without Telemann's explanation, this would all have been quite clear; but his explanation confirms it. The passage is one which suggests a less prolonged preparation to the trill than Ex. 174 above; but the change of harmony in the accompaniment comes at the same moment: namely on the second half of the dominant bass (*i.e.* on the second *D*). My interpretation is approximately as at Ex. 175 (b).

(316) G. P. Telemann, *Generalbass-Übungen*, Hamburg, 1733–35, No. 5, sect. 1:

'The $\frac{6}{4}$ intervals are taken for ornamentation, because, of course, the singer allows the *g*, that is to say the 4, to be strongly heard before the trill comes.'

Ex. 175. (a) G. P. Telemann, *loc. cit.*, his own figuring contravened in his realisation to accommodate the implied cadential trill; (b) my interpretation:

There are two other possible ways of accommodating a trill in the realisation. One is by ignoring its harmonic effect entirely: *e.g.* by taking Ex. 175 (a) above not as realised, but as figured, bringing the $\frac{5}{3}$ on the first *D* instead of on the second. This has the result of sounding the chord of resolution against the note of dissonance; but if the speed is fairly fast, and if the note of dissonance (*i.e.* the initial note, or preparation, of the trill) is not unduly prolonged, this result is often surprisingly good—at worst inconspicuous, at best piquant. To sound a dissonance against its own resolution was not normally regarded as good workmanship in the latter part of the baroque period; yet J. D. Heinichen (*General-Bass*, 1728, Part I, Ch. II, Sect. 54 *ff.*, pp. 202 *ff.*) allows some instances (9 against 8 and variants of this); and even C. P. E. Bach, the strictest of the great late baroque authorities, permits it in accommodating harmonic ornaments under certain circumstances —see (c) in this section, below.

The other remaining way of accommodating a trill in the realisation is by leaving out of the accompaniment any note or notes which would clash with it harmonically. This recourse is chiefly valuable in dealing with a slow expressive trill, when it is desired to give the greatest freedom to the soloist, and where any duplication of his ornamental notes, however well contrived, might sound clumsy. If, for example, his trill is prepared on 4 and resolves on 3, a bare fifth can be played in the accompaniment, including, of course, the 8, and if desired even the 7, but leaving out both the 4 and the 3. There are passages in which this method is by far the best, though they will always be in the minority.

(c) The problem of accommodating a long appoggiatura in the accompaniment is very similar to that of accommodating a well-prepared trill; and here we have the advantage of a very careful treatment of the subject by C. P. E. Bach.

(317) C. P. E. Bach, *Essay*, II, Berlin, 1762, XXV:

[2:] 'Appoggiaturas can seldom be ignored in the accompaniment; they have usually a great share in it.

[3:] 'Appoggiaturas retard the harmony which the bass note carries essentially. It is known that by the rules of good performance the appoggiatura is rendered loudly and its resolution softly. It is therefore doubly harmful to give no indication of it in the figuring; when this happens, the accompaniment is in most cases almost bound to be unsatisfactory.

[5:] 'When a bass note is figured without regard to an appoggiatura which goes with it, and this appoggiatura and its resolution is either compatible with the figures given, or the same as one of them, there is no necessity, even in four parts, to modify the accompaniment [*e.g.* where the appoggiatura is 4 and the figured chord $\frac{6}{3}$, in cases where this addition to the harmony is acceptable; or where the appoggiatura is the 6 and its resolution the 5 of a $^6_5$ chord].

[6:] 'But when the appoggiatura is not compatible with all the intervals with which its bass note is figured, because these belong to the harmony on to which it resolves, the appoggiatura should be played as part of the accompaniment, together with as many of the intervals shown by the figuring as are required by the loudness of the passage and are harmonically compatible with the appoggiatura. When the appoggiatura is performed with great feeling, and softly, at a length solely governed by the wishes of the soloist, the accompanist does not play it with him, but sounds one or at the most two of the remaining intervals of the harmony. The same is often done with appoggiaturas raised chromatically by a semitone. Appoggiaturas in two parts at once are played as parts of the accompaniment, and are thus treated in three parts [in all].

[18: Alternatively, appoggiaturas in two parts at once are omitted from the accompaniment.] 'One either plays the whole, or lets the right hand rest.

'. . . The short, [so-called] invariable appoggiatura is not included in the accompaniment. It does not, in fact, cause any modification of the accompaniment.'

Other treatments of the long appoggiatura which appear from C. P. E. Bach's examples include totally disregarding the appoggiatura and allowing it to clash with the harmony as figured; playing only part of the chord as the appoggiatura enters, and bringing in the remainder little by little, thus minimising the clash; doubling the appoggiatura, but resolving it in the opposite direction to the solo part; resting for the first half of the appoggiatura, but doubling its second half (especially useful in triple time—the resolution forming the third beat). All *short* appoggiaturas, as he says, can be ignored in the accompaniment. The final recourse where no other solution can be contrived is always, of course, the *tasto solo* (bass note alone without harmonisation).

C. P. E. Bach does not hesitate to alter the rhythm of the bass from even to dotted in order to avoid unpleasant or incorrect progressions to which the appoggiatura would otherwise give rise. Nor does he hesitate to *add* an interval to the harmony for the sake of improving it. (*Loc. cit.*, 18.)

As with trills, the best way of accompanying some slow and expressive appoggiaturas may well be to leave out of the accompaniment the intervals concerned: *e.g.* play a bare fifth if the appoggiatura is 4 and its resolution 3. But everything depends on the circumstances, and real subtlety is required to gain the maximum effect.

(d) C. P. E. Bach also discusses the effect on the harmony of certain other ornaments, but without introducing any further principles beyond those discussed above. (*Op. cit.*, Chs. XXV–XXVII.)

5. ADDING ACCENTED AND UNACCENTED PASSING NOTES

(a) However adventurous our approach to the subtler problems of figured bass, departures from the figuring or from the given bass line remain the exceptions and not the rule. But there is one common recourse which can have a profound influence both on the harmony and on the melody of an accompaniment, and which yet requires no exceptional circumstances to justify its free use. This is the recourse of introducing accented passing notes and (unprepared) appoggiaturas into the progressions without actual displacement of the figuring. There is no expedient more valuable both for enriching the harmony and for giving flexibility to the melodic outline.

The only limitations are the fundamental ones of keeping within the style and not conflicting with or in any other way detracting from the existing parts. It is naturally not possible to carry the use of accented passing notes and appoggiaturas so far when accompanying at sight as it is when preparing a realisation at leisure with all the existing parts accessible for comparison.

(b) Unaccented passing notes have little influence on the harmony, but for that very reason they are all the more freely available for increasing the melodic interest and fluency of the accompaniment.

(c) The following examples show passing notes (both accented and unaccented) and appoggiaturas. The first bar of Ex. 176 (b) shows two unaccented passing notes introduced as modifications of the bass line itself. The whole of this example was used by its author for a double purpose: to illustrate both passing notes and ornaments. So many ornaments in so short a space could not occur in normal practice. Ex. 177 shows a wealth of accented passing notes and appoggiaturas; here, too, it would be an exceptional context in which so many could be used without interference with or distraction from the existing parts. It is surprising, however, what can sometimes be done in this direction; and Ex. 179 shows the opening of my own realisation of an actual movement (by Handel) in which I have carried the accented passing notes to an unusual pitch of elaboration, since there seemed to be a good opening for doing so.

Ex. 176. J. D. Heinichen, *General-Bass*, Dresden, 1728, Part I, Ch. VI, sect. 6, passing notes added (b) to a mainly plain accompaniment (a):

Ex. 177. Fr. Geminiani, *Art of Accompaniament*, London [1755], Part II, Ex. xi, realisation with numerous accented passing notes and appoggiaturas:

(318) C. P. E. Bach, *Essay*, II, Berlin, 1762, XXXII, 12:

'In the use of these harmonic refinements, great care must be taken to avoid interfering with or covering up the solo part.'

Ex. 178. C. P. E. Bach, *loc. cit.*, passing notes (actual figuring above; theoretical figuring below; original an octave lower):

Ex. 179. Handel, Op. I, No. 5, 3rd movt., my realisation (*cf.* Ex. 177 above):

CHAPTER XXIX

The Texture of the Part

1. THE IMPORTANCE OF TEXTURE IN A GOOD ACCOMPANIMENT

An important factor in a good accompaniment is varying the texture
to suit the needs of different movements and passages. Some of the
most valuable resources for this purpose are mentioned in the present
chapter.

Variation in the texture ranges from broad contrasts to fine nuances.
It is an art akin to orchestration. At every bar and on every chord, a
slightly different situation may arise with regard to the needs of balance
and colouring. The success of an accompaniment very largely depends
on the sensitiveness with which it is adapted to these changing needs.
The fullness and the spacing of the chords, the degree of independent
melodic interest, the dynamics and the registration all have their part
to play in making an accompaniment which fits the music as the scoring
fits the orchestral piece. The timbre and the sonority of the realisation
have an influence only second to its actual harmony.

The reader is referred here to the long passage from Agazzari quoted
at (129) in Ch. IX, 3 above, and particularly to its third paragraph,
where the importance of adapting the volume, the spacing, the colouring
and the texture of a 'fundamental' accompaniment to the music
accompanied is brought out with great clarity and in considerable
detail. The date of the passage is 1607; yet it already covers all the
primary principles of baroque accompaniment.

2. NO ACCOMPANIMENT ('SENZA CEMBALO,' ETC.)

Provided a melodic bass instrument is present, it occasionally makes
an effective contrast to withdraw the harmonic continuo instrument.
This may be indicated by *senza cembalo* (without the harpsichord), *etc.*,
or be done at the accompanist's discretion. In practice, it nearly always
sounds too suddenly empty and unsonorous.

(319) C. P. E. Bach, *Essay*, II, Berlin, 1762, XXIII, 2:

'In Italian works, lightly-composed passages often bear the indication
senza cembalo over the bass-part by way of precaution. Entire arias may
sometimes have this indication.

[XXIX, 19:] 'When several parts including the bass are played pizzicato,
the accompanist falls silent, leaving the continuo to the violoncellos and

double-basses. If only the bass is pizzicato, however, the accompanist plays staccato, with his left hand [*i.e.* the bass line] only, unless the composer has seen fit to set figures over the notes, when the right hand completes the chords, also staccato.'

A rest in the continuo line implies, normally, a rest in the accompaniment, unless the rest is short and bears figures to an upper part. But in fugal openings where the bass has not yet entered (or later in the fugal movement if the bass drops out) it is open to the accompanist either to play the notes of the upper entries in unison, or to remain silent until the bass enters. In such passages, the entries themselves may be shown with the appropriate clefs in the continuo part, or only the lowest part which has already entered, with figures supposed to show the higher part or parts; these methods are interchangeable and both mean playing in unison with the entries, if at all.

3. UNHARMONISED ACCOMPANIMENT ('TASTO SOLO'; 'ALL' UNISONO')

(a) The strict meaning of *tasto solo* (single touch) or *tasto* or the abbreviation *t. s.* is: play only the bass line till the next figures occur (or a change of clef).

(320) J. D. Heinichen, *General-Bass*, Dresden, 1728, Part I, Ch. V, Sect. 18, p. 515:

'The words *tasto solo* indicate that one is to go on playing the notes concerned with one key or finger at a time, without other accompaniment, until another part, or another clef appears.

'In some instances, two parts only are to be seen, one above the other, meaning that in these instances no more is to be played than what is there shown [*e.g.* at the opening entries of fugues].'

(321) Lodovico Viadana, *Concerti Ecclesiastici*, Venice, 1602, preface, rule 5:

'When a Concerto opens in fugal fashion, the Organist also begins with a single note (*con un Tasto solo*), and at the entry of the several parts, it is open to him to accompany them at his own discretion.'

The *tasto solo* is not always indicated where it can be introduced, and need not always be used where indicated. It may sound too thin.

(322) C. P. E. Bach, *Essay*, II, Berlin, 1762, XXIII, 3:

'We use the *tasto solo* with excellent effect [even where it is not marked] in suitable passages: *e.g.* where bass and soloists move in thirds and sixths with no further parts present [or where it is desired to avoid getting in the way of an appoggiatura, or] with a bass carrying a melody low in pitch with no accompanying instruments above it [or (XXV, 17) merely where] it is impossible to contrive an accompaniment.'

(b) An effect distinct from the *tasto solo* is the *unisoni* or *all' unisono*, where the bass line is played on the harpsichord and also doubled at the octave or octaves above, and if desired, also at the octave below. A strict *tasto solo* may easily be spoiled if treated *all'unisono*, and the accompanist must use good judgment in the matter; but to some extent the two effects are interchangeable, and they were very naturally subject to confusion. It will be realised that a strict *tasto solo* is best taken without bringing in 16 ft. or 4 ft. stops unless urgently required for volume, but that an *all'unisono* is free from this restriction.

Like the *tasto solo*, the *all'unisono* is not always indicated where it is intended, or where it can be desirably introduced.

(323) C. P. E. Bach, *Essay*, II, Berlin, 1762, Introd., 29:

'The indications [*tasto solo* and *all'unisono*] are often lacking.

[XXII, 3:] 'Yet it is a matter for surprise that some composers do not always indicate their desire for an *all'unisono* accompaniment when writing out the bass. Figures are sometimes found over the bass where none are intended to be played. . . . [The composer deliberately plans, for special effect] to renounce the beauties of harmony for a time; his phrase is to sound in unison, and to monopolise both the thoughts and the fingers of all the accompanists [*i.e.* including any *ripieno* strings. But his pleasurable anticipations] are disturbed by the accompaniment of the keyboard player, who prepares and resolves the intervals figured, with the utmost conscientiousness and accuracy. . . . Fortunately for him the composer now realises that he has made a mistake in his notation of the bass part, and is delighted when the accompanist, disgusted with his inappropriate accompaniment, leaves out the harmony of his own accord, takes no more notice of the figures, and joins in reinforcing the passage at the unison, [remembering] the first principle of accompaniment: an accompanist shall fit to the music accompanied its appropriate harmony, in the appropriate strength.'

(c) Pedal points over a held bass, even when figured, may always be treated *tasto solo*, or *all'unisono*.

(324) C. P. E. Bach, *Essay*, II, Berlin, 1762, XXIV, 4:

'It is not easy to figure pedal points, and they are therefore generally handled *tasto solo*. Those who do figure them must put up with their being performed *tasto solo* just the same [because of the extreme difficulty, if not impossibility, of reading the unusual figurings required].'

The difficulty varies, of course, with the complexity of the harmony composed above the pedal point. When this harmony changes frequently and rapidly, a *tasto solo* or *all'unisono* makes the best effect, quite apart from the difficulty of doing otherwise. When, however, the harmony is simple and changes not too frequently or rapidly, it may often be desirable to accompany with full chords, whether these are shown by figuring or not. It may often happen that the parts above the pedal point, though melodically in rapid motion, are mainly executing broken chords, and that the chords change infrequently enough for the accompaniment to keep up with them quite easily if it takes the chords plain and without figuration. Indeed, the chords themselves may be mere alterations of dominant and tonic harmony. But whatever they are, if they move slowly enough to sound well when supported by the harpsichord in plain harmony, this support may be given at the accompanist's discretion.

4. HOW THICK THE ACCOMPANIMENT SHOULD BE

(a) The unharmonised accompaniment is naturally the rare exception. In the normal circumstances requiring harmony, the question arises as to how thick or thin this harmony should be.

There is a range of choice here from two parts to as many as the fingers can manage. This entire range should be exploited to the full, not merely as a means of contrasting one movement with another, but also for internal contrasts within movements.

(b) There is evidence that some organists, at any rate, of the seventeenth century preferred a three-part accompaniment when the ensemble was small.

(325) Michael Praetorius, *Syntagma*, III, Wolfenbüttel, 1619, Ch. VI, sect. on Organ, App.:

'When there are few voices singing, few keys [notes] should be touched, as *c g e*¹, *d a f, c c*¹ *e*¹ etc., so that the voices can be heard clearly and distinctly above the organ; but when more voices begin to sing, more keys and fuller harmony should be used.'

On the other hand Praetorius' own example (*loc. cit.*) is in four parts, and we should be wrong to infer a *general* early baroque preference for three-part writing such as Heinichen seems to imply in his reference (1728) to the 'old musicians', at (354) in 8 (a) below.

(c) There are movements so light that the best harmonisation is in two-parts, or mainly so; others for which a mainly three-part accompaniment is the most satisfactory.

(326) C. P. E. Bach, *Essay*, II, Berlin, 1762, Introd., 26:

'Accompaniments in three or fewer parts are used in lightly-composed music where the style, the execution or the feeling of the piece suggests a sparing use of harmony.'

Another possible (but by no means necessary) reason for thinning the accompaniment is a bass which goes high.

(327) Johann Staden, *Kurzer Bericht*, in his *Kirchen Music*, II, Nuremberg, 1626:

'When the clef [of the continuo] is Soprano or Alto, few parts are required [in the accompaniment].'

We shall see at (g) below that mere decrease of volume is another reason for thinning the accompaniment, either momentarily or throughout, just as increase of volume may be a reason for thickening it.

A particular form of two-part or three-part accompaniment is that in which a running bass is accompanied mainly in tenths, *etc.*

(328) C. P. E. Bach, *Essay*, II, Berlin, 1762, XXXII, 6:

'One of the main refinements of accompaniment is parallel movement in thirds [tenths, *etc.*] with the bass. The right hand is never obliged here to maintain a consistent fullness of harmony. Four-part writing is seldom maintained, excepting with slow notes, since thirds cannot be clearly brought out in four-part writing at a rapid speed. Three-part writing, and indeed in most cases two-part writing, is more satisfactory.'

[7:] 'Plain chords should be played, and movement in thirds abandoned, when the solo part already has these thirds or other intervals moving in the rhythm of the bass. . . .

[8:] 'Sometimes sixths may be mixed in with the movement in thirds . . . [and if there are to be three parts, the whole may be bound together by the addition of] sustained notes.'

(d) Other considerations being equal, a mainly four-part accompaniment is the normal standard.

(328a) Michel de Saint-Lambert, *Traité*, Paris, 1707, Ch. III, p. 19:

'You play the bass with the left hand, and to each note of the bass which you touch, you add three others in the right hand, thus making a chord on each note [this is a general statement and is later subjected to many qualifications].'

(329) Joachim Quantz, *Essay*, Berlin, 1752, XVII, vi, 4:

'The standard rule for thorough-bass is to play regularly in four parts, though for really good accompaniment it is often better not to follow this too consistently, but instead to leave out some parts or even double the bass at the octave above in the right hand [*i.e.* play *all'unisono*].'

(330) C. P. E. Bach, *Essay*, II, Berlin, 1762, Introd., 24:

'Consistent four-part writing, or more, is used in music which is thickly composed, or is in the learned style with counterpoint, imitations and so forth, or particularly in music composed for the music's sake with little scope for taste [of the galant kind].

[25:] 'To keep the spacing of the parts satisfactory it is better to bring two parts to a unison than to insist on four awkwardly distinct parts at the cost of pointless leaps and clumsy progressions.

'[37: We should when necessary have recourse to] first, playing a middle part [as well as the bass] in the left hand; second, bringing two parts to a unison; third, adding a fifth part momentarily to avoid consecutive fifths while at the same time changing the spacing; fourth, changing the spacing by repeating the same chord [in a higher position] over a single bass note, with a view to getting back into a higher position if the accompaniment has got too low [the same may be done in reverse].

[Ch. II, i, 37:] 'If the hands get too close together, or the right hand gets too low down, the same chord may be repeated in a higher position over the same [bass] note, if this note is not too quick; if there is no time for that, an additional part may be taken in at the top, and the lowest one [not counting the bass dropped]. This recourse is to be used (1) only in case of need, since I believe that as a normal procedure four regular parts should be maintained without unnecessarily adding to them; (2) only with consonances, since discords impose their own limitations on the accompaniment.'

If it is desired to retain four-part writing rather than momentarily increase the number of parts to five, an almost identical effect may be obtained by supposing two of the parts to cross. None of the stricter authorities were prepared to admit this device as a means of avoiding forbidden consecutives which it leaves audible; but where no such forbidden consecutives are involved, it can be used to gain a higher position than could otherwise be taken without incorrectly resolving a discord.

Ex. 180. Momentarily taking in a fifth part to gain a higher register:

Ex. 181. Crossing of parts to gain a higher register:

(331) Johann Philipp Kirnberger, *Grundsätze des Generalbasses*, Berlin [1781], Sect. after 172:

'With a succession of ninths, instead of taking in a fifth part, we can also allow the parts to cross without interfering with the correctness of the part-writing.'

(e) The regularity of the part-writing is not disturbed by adding octaves in the bass for greater prominence and sonority.

(332) C. P. E. Bach, *Essay*, II, Berlin, 1762, XXIX, 7:

'Merely doubling the bass [at the octave] has also a penetrating effect, and is essential where the notes are not very quick and can readily be executed [in this way], yet have a definitely melodic character of some considerable duration. When there is a [bass] entry in a fugue, or any imitation which needs bringing out, this doubling of the bass is extremely effective. But if an entry or any other phrase needing special prominence includes ornamental figuration which cannot readily be played in octaves by one hand, the main notes at any rate should be doubled and the remainder played singly.'

(333) G. M. Telemann, *Unterricht im Generalbass-Spielen*, Hamburg, 1773, Introd., 8:

'If the bass lies too low to double at the octave below, we must either not double at all, or double at the octave above.'

It is also quite often useful to double intermittently at the octave, sometimes adding the fifth in the left hand, and sometimes alternating octaves and fifths.

(f) When great sonority or great weight is required in the accompaniment, both hands may play as many notes as their fingers can accommodate. This is known as the filled-in accompaniment, and is necessarily exempt from most of the rules of correct part-writing which apply to the normal accompaniment. It may be used for entire movements of a suitable character; for certain passages in a movement otherwise normally accompanied; or for single chords to which it is desired to give additional volume and emphasis. The two chief principles on which a filled-in accompaniment is based are: keep a good progression between the topmost part and the bass (*i.e.* between the two outer extremes); and keep the thumbs close together (*i.e.* leave as little space as possible between the chords taken by the two hands, so that there is no room for prohibited consecutives to become conspicuous in the middle of the harmony).

(g) It must be realised that the subtraction or addition of parts is one of the chief means by which the harpsichord, whose control of volume by touch is very slight, can make dynamic variations, either momentary or continued: see (306) in Ch. XXVIII, 2 above. The other chief means is by the registration, where the instrument possesses stops which can be brought on and off. This latter means has also, of course, a crucial effect on the colouring of the tone. On the simplest harpsichords it is not available.

(334) C. P. E. Bach, *Essay*, II, Berlin, 1762, XXIX, 5:

'Of all instruments used for continuo playing the harpsichord with one manual is the hardest to manage for forte and piano. To meet the deficiencies of the instrument in this matter, the number of parts must be increased or decreased. Yet care must be taken to include all necessary notes and to avoid any incorrect doublings. [A staccato touch is a bad solution;] it is better to decrease the volume [by striking fewer chords] in the right hand over passing notes [in the bass].

'[7: On two-manual harpsichords] the fortissimo and the forte are taken on the stronger manual. [For the fortissimo, the filled-in accompaniment can be used: *i.e.*] doubling in the left hand all the notes of consonant intervals, and the consonant intervals only of dissonant chords, so far as the playing of the bass permits. . . . In the mezzo forte the left hand may play the bass, undoubled, on the stronger manual, while the right hand accompanies on the softer. In the piano, both hands play on the softer manual. The pianissimo is taken on this latter manual, but with a decreased number of parts.

[10:] 'Modulations are brought out by reinforcing the accompaniment. Thus in a fortissimo, for example, both hands take a filled-in chord rapidly spread upwards, the bass and its octave, together with the notes in the right hand, being held on. . . . Distinguish the most important notes by reinforcing their chords, perhaps in both hands.

[13:] 'When the solo part has a long sustained note which by the conventions of good style should start pianissimo, swell gradually to fortissimo, and fall back in the same way to pianissimo, the accompanist must follow it with the greatest accuracy. Every recourse open to him must be used to make the forte and the piano. His crescendo and diminuendo must correspond with the solo part, neither more nor less.'

5. HOW STRICT THE ACCOMPANIMENT SHOULD BE

(a) The standard of grammatical correctness, in so far as this applies to accompaniment, should be about as strict as the composer's own standard, so that the two shall match in style. A composer of somewhat classical temperament such as Corelli needs to be accompanied rather more correctly than a composer such as Purcell whose own revolutionary boldness not merely invites but demands a comparable boldness in the accompaniment.

Within the boundaries of the style in question, the degree of strictness is a matter of individual preference. The baroque authorities themselves show a remarkable variability, and it must be remembered that the rules themselves are only generalisations about what experience shows will sound well in practice.

(335) Michel de Saint-Lambert, *Traité*, Paris, 1707, Ch. VIII ('On the Liberties which may be taken when accompanying'), sect. 13, p. 126:

'Since Music is made only for the ear, a fault which does not offend it is not a fault.'

(b) The rule forbidding consecutive octaves and fifths is fundamentally valid in accompaniment, but with important exceptions.

So long as the ideal of accompaniment in polyphonic music remained a literal reduplication of the parts, consecutive fifths were inevitable on the keyboard wherever these parts produced them correctly by crossing; for crossing of this kind has no audible reality on keyboard instruments.

(336) Lodovico Viadana, *Concerti Ecclesiastici*, Venice, 1602, rule 9:

'The organ accompaniment is never under any obligation to avoid two fifths or two octaves [consecutively], but the parts sung by the voices are.'

As the ideal of reduplicating the existing parts gave place to the typical concept of figured bass, which is a harmonic texture conforming to but not reduplicating the existing parts, we find a somewhat increasing tendency to strictness here.

(337) Lorenzo Penna, *Li Primi Albori*, Bologna, 1672, Book III, Ch. I, rule 10:

'Two consecutive octaves, and two fifths, together with their compounds, are to be avoided whether occurring by step or by leap; which rule is mainly applicable to the outside parts.'

(338) Matthew Locke, *Melothesia*, London, 1673, rule 1:

'But (for prevention of glutting or offending the Ear) never ascend or descend with two Fifts, or two Eights together between the *Treble* and *Bass*.'

Yet composers of Locke's period, and to some extent into the eighteenth century as well, regarded the retardation of one of the parts as quite sufficient to rectify consecutive fifths or octaves: for example in preparing a ninth (even in the top part) on the octave of the bass, and then resolving it also on the octave of the bass.

Ex. 182. Consecutive octaves justified by retardation:

(339) Michel de Saint-Lambert, *Traité*, Paris, 1707, Ch. VIII, p. 125:

'[Two consecutive octaves or fifths are harmless] when you are accompanying a big musical ensemble, where the noise of the other instruments [covers them]. . . . But when you are accompanying a single melody, you cannot attach too much importance to correctness, especially if you are the sole accompaniment; for then everything shows . . . [two consecutive fifths are correct] provided that the first is perfect, the second diminished or augmented [or *vice versa* if not to the bass].

'Finally, it would only be taking a slight license for one part to make even a perfect [as opposed to a diminished] fifth twice in succession with another part.

'I know that the greatest strictness would not have it; but since this fault (if it is one) does not show at all, I hold that one can make it unhesitatingly!'

(340) F. W. Marpurg, *Handbuch bey dem Generalbasse*, I, Berlin, 1755, 2nd ed. 1762, Sect. II, ix*a*, p. 99:

'[Progression from diminished to perfect fifths is allowed in three or more parts] but only in the middle parts, or between an outside and a middle part. On the other hand, whatever the scoring, and between whatever parts, one may always progress from a perfect to an imperfect [*i.e.* diminished] or an augmented fifth.'

(341) C. P. E. Bach, *Essay*, II, Berlin, 1762, Introd., 36:

'While awkward progressions may be tolerated, incorrect ones cannot . . . forbidden [consecutive] fifths and octaves must be strictly avoided.'

[38:] 'Unavoidably awkward progressions, hidden fifths and octaves, and certain permitted consecutive fifths with the bass must be kept in the middle parts. The top part must always flow and keep a correct relationship with the bass.

[II, i, 22:] 'A perfect fifth may fall to a diminished fifth between any two parts. But a diminished fifth may fall to a perfect fifth only in case of necessity, and not, if it can be avoided, between outside parts.

[II, i, 23:] 'In ascending . . . both progressions [*i.e.* perfect rising to diminished fifth or diminished rising to perfect fifth] are correct only between middle parts.'

It is to be observed that C. P. E. Bach was one of the strictest of all baroque authorities in matters of musical grammar, and was unusually sensitive to consecutives occurring even in the middle parts and under circumstances where almost any other authority would certainly have excused them. A more typical baroque attitude towards accompaniment was to excuse, without actually encouraging, any consecutives which are not conspicuous to the ear in practice. This attitude produces very satisfactory results, and I have no hesitation in recommending it, as did Saint-Lambert at (339) above, or Marpurg at (340) and again very sensibly as follows.

(342) F. W. Marpurg, *Handbuch*, I, Berlin, 1755, 2nd ed. 1762, II, ii:

'I would [merely] say that a disposition of the parts which is free from all those [consecutive] octaves and fifths which are excusable is preferable to one in which such excusable octaves and fifths occur.'

To pretend that two of the parts have crossed was one of the most accommodating excuses, but we have already seen how little reality this pretence usually possesses, and it was only accepted by the laxer authorities (*e.g.* Johann Mattheson, *Organisten-Probe*, Hamburg, 1719), and even by these it was not held to cover consecutives between the two outside parts. Others (*e.g.* F. W. Marpurg, *Handbuch*, I, Berlin, 1755, II, ii) admitted it only in the case of obviously acceptable consecutives.

In harmony of four or more parts, or of fewer parts at a rapid speed, consecutive fifths or (but less readily) octaves *in contrary motion* even between outside parts were tolerated (*e.g.* by F. W. Marpurg, *loc. cit.*, Figs. 27 to 29).

Consecutive octaves or unisons between the accompaniment and a solo part were regarded as legitimate doubling, and in no sense prohibited, although for reasons of taste, not connected with musical grammar, such doubling was not favoured as a continued recourse after the very early baroque period. It should, indeed, be used very sparingly, and either from positive necessity, or as a special effect of scoring.

Consecutive fifths between the accompaniment and a solo part, on the other hand, are apt to sound unpleasant, but may be impossible to avoid when sight-reading a continuo part printed without the solo part or parts above it, for the simple reason that there is nothing to forewarn the accompanist that they are about to occur.

(343) G. Ph. Telemann, *Generalbass-Übungen*, Hamburg, 1733–35, No. 23:

'For if the player were only guided by the figures, not having the score, he would play [such consecutive fifths], without being blameworthy.'

This last consideration is of the utmost general interest. Very many problems in the realisation (on paper) of a figured bass are solved in the best and most natural way simply by asking oneself the practical question: what would or could an accompanist make of the passage if he were reading it at sight? A great many clashes between accompaniment and solo parts which look most alarming on paper resolve themselves without even being noticed in performance. An editor may wrack his brains for a correct solution and produce a most tortuous and unconvincing result, whereas if he merely sets down what the figures allow him to know at sight in the absence of the score, he will find a straightforward progression which perfectly meets the case. It is a great mistake in figured bass accompaniment, as in other matters, to try to be too clever.

(c) One of the best and oldest hints for avoiding unacceptable consecutive fifths and octaves is to make great use of contrary motion. This hint appears in most treatises on figured bass throughout the baroque period.

(344) Matthew Locke, *Melothesia*, London, 1673, rule 10:

'For the prevention of successive Fifts and Eights in the Extream Parts . . . the certainest way for the Beginner, is, to move his Hands by contraries: That is, when one Hand ascends, let the other descend.'

(344a) Michel de Saint-Lambert, *Traité*, Paris, 1707, Ch. V, p. 65:

'The hands should [with various qualifications] always move in opposite directions [to prevent unwanted consecutives].

[p. 66:] 'When the bass makes a wide interval [a fourth or more] in the progression of the notes, the two hands can make similar movement [since this does not conduce to unwanted consecutives].'

(d) Other things being equal, the more correctly the discords are prepared and resolved, the more satisfactory the accompaniment will sound. The chief gain is in the smoothness of the effect. Proper preparation and resolution give a sense of logical inevitability and stability as nothing else can do. These qualities are essential for music in the learned style. For more relaxed and informal music they are by no means so necessary, and it was recognised throughout the baroque period that many more liberties could be taken outside the learned style. Towards the end of the baroque period this distinction crystallised in the differentiation of the learned or 'old' style from the galant or 'new' style. But, of course, not all earlier baroque music had been learned music, and the distinction itself was not a novelty.

In the less strict forms of music, the preparation of a discord may be either shortened (contrary to the strict rule by which the preparation must be at least as long as the discord) or dispensed with. Wholly unprepared discords are extremely common in many baroque styles of music, and the accompanist can allow himself great freedom in this respect wherever the musical context suggests doing so.

The resolution of a discord may be either transferred to another part (not necessarily in the same octave), or suppressed in such a way that the mind can in some sense supply it without its being heard. In the former case the resolution is still present, although not in its normal situation. In the latter case the resolution is not so much dispensed with as ellided. A substitute 'resolution' by an upwards instead of a downwards progression is also not uncommon. The freedom to dispense

333

entirely with the resolution of a discord in baroque music is noticeably less than the freedom to dispense with its preparation.

Ornamental resolutions are, of course, perfectly correct, within limits for the learned style, almost without limits for the free style.

The following excellent advice to accompanists can be confidently applied.

(345) G. M. Telemann, *Unterricht im Generalbass-Spielen*, Hamburg, 1773, I, ii, 9:

'All the rules just given with regard to preparation and resolution are to be observed with care so long as they can be observed. . . . For since, in compliance with the figures, discords are often not prepared, and often not resolved . . . and since, moreover, discords which ought strictly to resolve downwards have sometimes, in compliance with the figures, to resolve upwards, and the other way about, and so on and so forth . . . I say: prepare so long as you can prepare, and again, resolve so long as you can resolve . . . and for the rest leave the responsibility with the author of the figures and the composer.'

(e) Throughout the baroque treatises, rules are found forbidding the doubling of accidentally sharpened major thirds, or notes of the bass which are accidentally sharpened. These rules, which are often unclear or unsatisfactorily formulated, have as their foundation the undesirability of doubling the leading note of the prevailing key, whether diatonic or accidental, and in whatever part (including the bass) it may appear. It is the nature of a leading note to lead: *i.e.* to progress by a semitone upwards to its (temporary or permanent) tonic. If it is doubled, one of the parts to which it is given must progress wrongly if consecutive octaves are to be avoided. The only escape from this difficulty is by way of the licence permitting a leading note in an inner part to drop a major third to the fifth of the key. But in a normal four-part accompaniment it would sound extremely crude to use this license at the same time as the normal progression upwards by a semitone. The rule forbidding this doubling (which in any case sounds ugly in itself) is one which should be respected to the full in all ordinary circumstances.

The following statement of the rule, though late in date, is quoted because it is put clearly and accurately, and it may be taken as generally reliable for the baroque period as a whole. Some of the earlier formulations are unnecessarily wide, and if taken literally prevent some perfectly harmless doublings. The standard implied by the following will be found adequate in any typical baroque context.

(346) Johann Philipp Kirnberger, *Grundsätze des Generalbasses*, Berlin [1781], III, 154:

'Theorists agree in forbidding the doubling of the major third; but this rule is only applicable to the dominant chord, in which this third is the leading note to the following semitone above; hence it also must not be doubled when it comes by reason of an accidental chromatic to the prevailing key, since it then becomes the leading note of the note next following. In the triad of the main note or tonic, and the triad of the subdominant, it can be doubled unhesitatingly, unless special circumstances point to the contrary.'

There have always been some authorities who dislike the mere doubling of the major third in a triad, but while this is certainly not quite satisfactory to the ear in many contexts, it hardly amounts to a fault of grammar. It would not usually be one's first choice, but it need by no means be excluded in every instance.

(f) It has commonly been regarded as a fault of grammar to sound the note of resolution at the same time as the discord about to resolve on to it: or in other words, to anticipate the resolution of a discord in the harmony accompanying it. Yet this procedure was not merely sanctioned, but encouraged and practised, by some authorities and composers at all stages in the baroque period, and indeed subsequently.

(347) Lorenzo Penna, *Li Primi Albori*, Bologna, 1672, Ch. 14, end:

'To complete the accompaniment of the [bass] notes on which stand discords to be resolved on to the concords, let the student know that it is a general rule that one can or rather should add to the discords the thirds, fifths, octaves and their compounds of the [bass] note written, making them all sound at the same time [more particularly if the music is in many parts], for even the composer writes them so.'

In practice, it is only in a full accompaniment that a discord can be accompanied by the entire concord on to which it is about to resolve. Half a century after the above quotation, we find this recognised in theory also: see (349) in 6 (c) below. It became unusual, moreover, to make such full clashes, except in the case of some suspensions. It was usual at most to sound the note rather than the entire chord of resolution against the discord.

6. THE FILLED-IN ACCOMPANIMENT

(a) The degree to which grammatical correctness may be dispensed with in the filled-in accompaniment was viewed somewhat differently by different authorities, but from the nature of the case it is obvious that very little except the relationship of the outside parts can really be kept at all ordinarily strict. With so many notes going on, and no possibility of genuinely crossing the parts to avoid faulty progressions, part-writing in the ordinary sense is not in question, and we are dealing with something much more like the doublings in orchestration.

(b) The two main rules are:

First: keep a good progression between the outside parts. This is very important and should never be disregarded.

Second: keep the thumbs close together so as to avoid an awkward space between the hands in which conspicuous forbidden consecutives may occur. This is highly practical, and should only be disregarded for a definite reason. But for special effect the hands may occasionally be taken wide apart.

When this is done, the sonority of the left hand wants careful attention. If it is taken down to a low register, it should not under any normal circumstances be given full chords, but only octaves or octaves and fifths. This is simply because of the acoustic fact that close scoring at a low pitch makes a thick effect. This thickness is less marked on a harpsichord (with its clear tone, due to the high proportion of its tonal energy going into its upper harmonics), than on the modern piano (with its massive lower harmonics) or on the organ (with its sustained sound). Nevertheless, even on the harpsichord, a third is too narrow an interval to sound at all natural below a certain pitch, and full chords sound still more unnatural. The cases in which such an excess of bottom-heavy thickness could be effective must be rare indeed, if they exist at all.

Full chords at the top of the harpsichord, on the other hand, can sound most effective; but the effect is still a special effect, particularly if the left hand is some distance away instead of being close up to give support. Like most special effects, this one has its uses; but they will not be at all common.

A third rule, then, is that the filled-in accompaniment will normally sound best when the two hands are not only close together but somewhere within the middle register of the harpsichord.

A fourth rule concerns the treatment of discords. Most authorities allowed the dissonant notes as well as the concordant notes to be doubled in both hands alike; some allowed only consonant notes to be doubled in the left hand, and dissonant notes to be doubled in the right hand alone, but there is certainly no need for a modern accompanist to observe this restriction unless he so desires.

Any doubling of dissonant notes makes it impossible to resolve them correctly in each part alike, except by allowing the parts to move in consecutive octaves. This was, in fact, very generally permitted: sometimes only in the left hand, the discords in the right hand being expected to behave correctly; sometimes in either hand.

The alternative to allowing the doubled dissonant parts to progress correctly, but in consecutive octaves with one another, is to allow one of them to progress correctly, but the other freely. This, also, was very generally permitted: sometimes in both hands; sometimes in the right hand alone. The degree of freedom should not, however, be in excess of the need: *e.g.* there is no need for the doubled dissonance to move by leap if it can, with a much nearer approach to correctness, move upwards (instead of downwards) by step, *etc.*

For general modern purposes, the rule concerning the treatment of discords in a filled-in accompaniment may perhaps be stated in the following form: where discords are doubled, one part (normally the higher) should observe much the same standard of correct preparation and resolution as in an ordinary four-part accompaniment; the other part can be taken in either hand, and has the choice of moving in consecutive octaves or quite freely.

(c) Of the following authorities, the first, a pupil of J. S. Bach (whom he here describes), gives a remarkable confirmation of the length to which the filled-in accompaniment might be carried; and it is, indeed, one of the most important resources of a well-equipped accompanist. The second was about average for strictness; the third, stricter than average. We have to allow for all the usual baroque variability; but sonority rather than correctness is the primary consideration here.

(348) Johann Christian Kittel, *Der angehende praktische Organist*, Part III, Erfurt, 1808, p. 33:

'When Seb. Bach performed a piece of Church music, one of his most able pupils had always to accompany at the harpsichord. One can well imagine that one dare not put oneself forward with a sparse realisation of the continuo, in any case. Nevertheless one had always to hold oneself prepared frequently to find Bach's hands and fingers suddenly mixed with the player's hands and fingers, and, without further interfering with these, decking out the accompaniment with masses of harmony still more imposing than the unsuspected near proximity of the stern teacher.'

(349) J. D. Heinichen, *General-Bass*, Dresden, 1728, Part I, Ch. II, Sect. 30, p. 131:

'[Experienced accompanists] commonly, and particularly on such instruments as harpsichords, try to reinforce the harmony yet further, and to accompany in as many parts with the left hand as with the right, according to the lie of the two hands, in an accompaniment of from 6 or 7 to 8 parts.

[F.n.:] 'On such instruments as harpsichords, the fuller the accompaniment in either hand, the more satisfying [in suitable contexts] the result. With organs, however, especially in lightly-composed music, it is as well not to get too fascinated by an over-full accompaniment in the left hand, since the constant growling of so many low notes is distressing to the ear.

[32:] 'One has only to take care to devise the outside [upper] part of the right hand so skilfully that it moves with the bass without any fifths, octaves or other incorrect progressions.

[35:] 'The great art of a filled-in accompaniment consists in managing the two outside parts.

[38:] 'The closer the hands are kept to each other, so that no undue distance or empty space lies between the middle [adjacent] parts of the right and left hands, the more satisfying will be the resulting accompaniment.

[Ch. III, Sect. 54, p. 202:] 'All discords in the right hand should progress correctly [but those in the left hand may either double the right hand's progressions, or move freely].

[54:] 'In certain cases, the left hand may anticipate the resolutions of the discords taken in the right hand.

[55:] 'It is well known that with the 9 taken in full harmony among other middle parts, one can also strike the octave . . . on which the 9 must resolve.

[56:] 'But if the ear can accept the anticipation of the resolution of the nine, it must necessarily also be able to accept all other anticipations of resolutions which are produced merely by the inversion of this 9 in full harmony.

[61:] 'With double suspensions, one can also introduce double anticipations of the resolutions, but infrequently and with discretion, so that the cumulative dissonances shall not be unbearable to the ear.'

(350) C. P. E. Bach, *Essay*, II, Berlin, 1762, XXIX, 7:

'[The filled-in accompaniment consists in] doubling in the left hand all the notes of consonant intervals, and the consonant intervals only of dissonant chords, so far as the playing of the bass permits. This doubling must not be done low down, but close to the right hand, so that the chords of both hands adjoin, and that no space may be left between them, since otherwise the growling low notes will make a hateful confusion.'

7. HOW THE ACCOMPANIMENT SHOULD BE SPACED

(a) During the seventeenth century, no reliable generalisation can be inferred as to the spacing of accompaniments; but in the eighteenth we find a distinct tendency to regard as standard the playing of the bass alone in the left hand, and the remaining parts in the right hand.

(351) Friedrich Erhard Niedt, *Musicalische Handleitung*, Part I, Hamburg, 1700, Ch. VI, rule 1:

'The written-out continuo bass is played with the left hand alone, the remaining parts (whether shown by figuring or not) with the right hand.'

338

(352) J. D. Heinichen, *General-Bass*, Dresden, 1728, Part I, Ch. II, Sect. 29, p. 130:

'[Four part accompaniment came to be] divided unequally between the hands, that is to say three parts to the right hand, and only the bass part to the left.'
[30:] 'This kind is nowadays the most general and fundamental accompaniment, which every beginner is taught.'

(b) At the same period we find the more open scoring, by which the parts are divided fairly evenly between the two hands, regarded as a distinct kind of accompaniment under the name of the divided or extended accompaniment. This is the converse of the full or filled-in accompanied just described, and like that was no novelty at the time when it began to attract theoretical attention.

An extended spacing may be a momentary necessity to avoid awkward part-writing or forbidden consecutives; but primarily it is an effect of scoring used for its own sake, either in passing, or throughout a passage or a movement. As a resource of accompaniment, it is as valuable as its opposite, the filled-in accompaniment; but it requires no special consideration, being subject to the ordinary rules of four-part accompaniment.

(353) C. P. E. Bach, *Essay*, II, Berlin, 1762, XXXII, 10:

'An extended accompaniment . . . is often one of the most pleasing refinements. In previous chapters we have already shown the occasional necessity for using it [for the sake of the part-writing]. Apart from such necessity, it is a familiar fact how very pleasing extended harmony can sometimes be in contrast to close harmony.'

8. HOW HIGH AND HOW LOW THE ACCOMPANIMENT SHOULD GO

(a) It was generally agreed that the accompaniment should not persistently reach a very high or low register.

The following suggests a reason for not going high which may well have influenced those accompanists who (like many organists of the seventeenth century) preferred a thin accompaniment when the ensemble was small (see 4 (b) above; but, of course, full accompaniments were also frequent at the same period, and Heinichen's information is to that extent misleading, no doubt because he is not giving it at first hand).

(354) J. D. Heinichen, *General-Bass*, Dresden, 1728, Part I, Ch. VI, Sect. 28, note h, p. 548:

'When the old musicians gave the rule that the right hand should not readily go above c^{ll} [in the treble stave] and on no account above e^{ll} [top space of treble stave], they were trying in this way to avoid in their accompaniments, which were then very thin, and most often only in three parts, too large a distance, or empty space between the hands, and in this they were well advised.'

The reason for not carrying the harmony too low, as we have seen, is primarily acoustic: the narrower intervals, such as thirds, beat more roughly at low pitches, and therefore sound less pleasing to the ear, so that on the whole a scoring which keeps these narrower intervals moderately high in pitch is more satisfactory than the opposite. It is therefore a natural tendency, other things being equal, to give most of the harmony to the right hand, though low dispositions are also found. They were commoner in the seventeenth century, before this tendency to restrict the left hand to the bass alone became something of a convention—see 7 (a) above—but they occur at all periods.

For most baroque music, the following general limits for the right hand are characteristic enough, though possibly a little wide for some of the earlier schools.

Friedrich Erhard Niedt (*Musicalische Handleitung*, Part I, Hamburg, 1700, Ch. VI, rule 2): between c^l (middle *C*) and c^{ll} (the octave above middle *C*) in the main, and not below *a* or *g* (below the treble stave) or above e^{ll} or f^{ll} (at the top of the treble stave) at the outside.

Michel de Saint-Lambert (*Traité*, Paris, 1707, Ch. V): up to e^{ll} or the highest f^{ll} (*i.e.* the top space or top line of the treble clef: but higher when the bass is high, *i.e.* becomes a *bassetto*: see (e) below).

F. W. Marpurg (*Kunst das Clavier zu spielen*, Berlin, 1750, II, ii, 24, p. 36): not usually below *e* (in the bass stave) or above g^{ll} (note above the treble stave).

(b) It was also understood that these limits, particularly the upper one, might be exceeded for special effect, or for special reasons.

(355) C. P. E. Bach, *Essay*, II, Berlin, 1762, II, i, 24:

'The right hand should not ordinarily be taken above f^{ll}, unless the bass goes very high, or a special effect is to be made in the higher registers.

[25:] 'The right hand should not be taken below the middle of the tenor octave [c^l to c^{ll}], except under the opposite conditions to those mentioned in the previous paragraph [*i.e.* when accompanying a solo which itself is low in pitch, as on the violoncello, *etc.*].'

(c) The general preference was to keep the top part of the accompaniment below the solo part (or below the highest solo part in trio sonatas, *etc.*).

(356) Joachim Quantz, *Essay*, Berlin, 1752, XVII, vi, 21:

'It has long been a well-established rule, that in playing continuo, the hands should not move too far apart from one another, and consequently that one should not play too high with the right hand. This rule is reasonable and good, if only it could always be observed. It is a much better effect if the accompanying part on the keyboard (Flügel) is taken below the solo part, than if it is taken in unison with the top part, or actually above it.'

In this respect, too, exceptions can always be made for special effect. There is some evidence, moreover, that the preference for keeping the accompaniment below the solo was not as universal as Quantz implies. Walter Kolneder (*Aufführungspraxis bei Vivaldi*, Leipzig [1955], pp. 85–9) gives examples of accompaniments, actually written out by Vivaldi, which move well above the solo part, and he suggests, I think correctly, that the Italian taste was more adventurous in this matter than the German.

Ex. 183. Vivaldi, Concerto PV 311, Grave, solo violin accompanied by organ:

Among German composers, G. Ph. Telemann was somewhat exceptional in taking his accompaniments quite freely above the solo part (*cf.* his examples in his *Generalbass-Übungen*, Hamburg, 1733–35). He was also exceptional in having no objection to making a full close with the tonic 5 in the upper part of the accompaniment—a small point on which many German authorities (including C. P. E. Bach, *Essay*, II, Berlin, 1762, II, i, 36) were sensitive.

(d) When the solo part to be accompanied was itself at a low pitch, the accompaniment could freely move above it, but was expected to be in reasonable relationship to the solo.

(357) C. P. E. Bach, *Essay*, II, Berlin, 1762, XXIX, 22:

'When accompanying an instrument of low pitch, such as a bassoon, a violoncello *etc.*, or a low voice, Tenor or Bass, in a solo or aria, one must take care, in the matter of height, not to get too far from the solo part, but must pay attention to the register within which it moves. Here one seldom takes chords above the one-stroke octave [c^l to c^{ll}]. If it is necessary to take chords in a rather low register, the harmony should be thinned out, since a low pitch does not permit the harmony to be thick without losing its clearness.'

(e) When the continuo part is given a clef which shows that it is no longer literally a bass line, but is reproducing some higher part in the temporary role of bass, all restrictions as to the height permitted to the accompaniment are waived. The clef will normally be one of the *C* clefs; occasionally a *G* clef. Such a bass passage is known as *bassetto* (Ger. *Basset* or *Bassetgen*). Unfortunately, the appearance of a *C* clef is not quite a reliable indication of a *bassetto* passage, since it may be put merely for the convenience of avoiding ledger-lines when the normal bass-part goes somewhat high. But the effect is, with one exception, much the same: chords are necessarily taken higher up than usual. The exception is that a true *bassetto* passage is often the entry of an upper part in fugal music. Such an entry is not necessarily harmonised at all: it may be taken *senza cembalo*, or *tasto solo*, or *all'unisono* (see 2 above).

There was some variety of opinion as to whether a high bass part should have chords as full as usual, but higher up, or whether the chords themselves should be somewhat compressed to avoid an undue upward extension of the compass. It is obvious that either treatment, or a mixture of the two, may be most suitable to the passage in question, and that the accompanist should rely on his own discretion. If no figures are shown, or only a single line of figures, the probable intention is one or two parts at most (doubling one or two fugal entries without harmonising them).

(358) J. D. Heinichen, *General-Bass*, Dresden, 1728, Part I, Ch. V, Sect. 18, p. 516:

'*Bassetti* must never be doubled with the octave below . . .

'The chords over the *Bassetto* may, however, be played with both hands (yet with a sensible regard for the number of the voices and instruments taking part) in as many parts as there is room for in the space remaining at the top of the keyboard.'

(359) Joachim Quantz, *Essay*, Berlin, 1752, XVII, vi, 27:

'When the bass deserts its proper register and has something to play in the register of the tenor . . . the accompaniment should be kept in few parts and quite close to the left hand.'

(f) Both in general and in relation to the other parts, the accompanist can allow himself considerable discretion as to the compass of his part, provided that he respects the principle behind these rules, which is that the solo shall not be obscured but set off to the best advantage. The danger of going unusually high is that this is very likely to confuse the solo melody or melodies; if it does not do that, and if it makes a convincing effect of scoring, there is no objection. Like any other special effect, however, it should not become habitual.

9. TEXTURE FURTHER TO BE CONSIDERED IN THE FOLLOWING CHAPTER

The remaining, more structural aspects of the texture of the accompaniment will be considered in the following chapter.

POSTSCRIPT TO NEW VERSION

I mention here a standard rule at all periods of our ordinary harmonic counterpoint, as practised from the baroque period onwards, because it has apparently been unknown to some modern authorities, including Erwin Bodky and Frederick Neumann: I was taught it, in the very strict school at Oxford, by R. O. Morris and H. K. Andrewes alike, and it seems to be part of the main tradition. It can, in fact, be confirmed for the baroque period by such accepted examples as that by G. P. Telemann, given below in App. VI, 6 (b); moreover, it is often exemplified in baroque compositions as part of their notated text. In accompaniment, it eases many situations, sounds well, and is in fact an ordinary recourse. It may be expressed as follows:

When of two notes moving in parallel consecutive fifths, one is an accented passing note resolving by step (in the same direction) before the other note has changed, the note of resolution is accepted grammatically in place of the passing note, and the progression is correct.

Ex. 183a. Correct progressions produced by the stepwise resolution of accented passing notes whose movement is itself in parallel consecutive fifths with another part:

CHAPTER XXX

The Structure of the Part

1. THE STRUCTURAL ASPECT OF THE ACCOMPANIMENT

This chapter continues the discussion of the texture, but in its more structural aspects: the smoothness or otherwise of the part-writing; varieties of broken chords and other figuration; the degree of melodic independence and contrapuntal workmanship.

2. HOW SMOOTH THE ACCOMPANIMENT SHOULD BE

(a) Just as four parts are the standard number on which other textures are variants, so the smooth style is the foundation for the other varieties of structure.

The rules for the smooth style of accompaniment are two: any notes which can be held over into the next chord are held over, preferably without repercussion; and the position of each chord is taken as near to the position of the previous chord, and with as few and narrow leaps, as possible.

(360) Michel de Saint-Lambert, *Traité*, Paris, 1707, Ch. III, p. 19:

'What decides the arrangement of the parts is the position of the accompanying [*i.e.* right] hand. The rule is, that when you have once placed the hand on the keyboard, to play the first chord of the melody you are going to accompany, you must take all the subsequent chords in the nearest possible place [with the result that] the parts change their arrangement with each chord you play.

[Ch. V, Sect. 21, p. 86:] 'When one moves from one chord to another, one should see if any notes of the chord which one is leaving can be used in the chord which one is approaching; when that can be done, one should not change these notes.

[Ch. V, Sect. 2, p. 66:] 'The right hand ought always to take its chords in the nearest position in which they are to be found, and never go far away in search of them . . . thus the accompanist always makes the chords progress by the smallest intervals possible.'

Both for technical and for musical reasons, these rules are valuable.

For technical reasons: because the right hand must be trained to take groups of figures as physical patterns of the fingers, this being the only way in which it can possibly get there in time, when one is sight-reading; and the less the hand jumps about the keyboard, the more readily it will find the positions into which these patterns fit.

For musical reasons: because one of the primary functions of a continuo part is to cement the harmony and bind the melodic parts together, by providing a steady flow of sound in the middle registers; and if it is jerkily realised, it will lose much of this binding influence. A part which offers the technical convenience of lying comfortably under the hands is also likely to be a part well designed for the musical purpose of supporting the existing melodies with a sustained sonority.

(361) C. P. E. Bach, *Essay*, II, Berlin, 1762, Introd., 25:

'I shall treat of good construction and the smooth progression of the harmonies . . . avoiding unnecessary leaps and clumsy part-writing.
[XXIX, 3:] 'A noble simplicity in the calm accompaniment . . .
[14:] 'When playing chords over a bass not marked staccato, there is no need to make a fresh repercussion on each note. Notes which are already part of the previous chord and can be carried into the next are sustained; for this method, together with flowing progressions well layed out, gives the part a singing quality.
[XXXII, 8:] 'Sustained notes . . . connect chords, help a cantabile style, are easier and less risky than repeated notes, which in four parts and at a rapid speed are nearly impracticable and in any case ineffectual.'

(b) For the smooth style of accompaniment, it will be appreciated that the touch itself should be smooth.

(362) Lorenzo Penna, *Li Primi Albori*, Bologna, 1672, Ch. XX, rule 8:

'It is always excellent to play legato, so as not to distract from the vocal part.'

(363) C. P. E. Bach, *Essay*, II, Berlin, 1762, XXIX, 5:

'Some people fall back on a very staccato touch when they want to achieve a piano [on a single-manual harpsichord without pedals, which cannot achieve it by change of stops in the middle of the piece], but this has a most harmful effect on the performance . . . it is better to decrease the volume by striking right-hand chords less frequently over passing notes [in the bass].'

(c) Even in the smoothest style, of course, the smoothness of the touch is always subject to the requirements of good phrasing and good articulation. The relatively short duration of harpsichord or lute tone (as opposed to the organ, or even the modern piano) has also to be born in mind, together with the need for rhythmic sharpness at certain points in the music, or as a help to good ensemble when there are many players.

For the bass ties mentioned by Caccini in (364) below, see Ch. XXVII, 3 (c) above.

(364) Giulio Caccini, *Euridice*, 1600, preface:

'I have used the ties in the bass part because, after the consonance [or other interval figured] only the interval figured is to be struck again [and not the bass note itself] . . . for the rest, I leave it to the discretion of the more intelligent class of performer [on the lute] to strike again, with their bass, such notes as they judge to need it, or as will the better accompany the solo singer.'

(365) Heinrich Albert, *Arias*, Part II, Königsberg, 1640, preface, rule 5:

'[Tied notes should be sustained on the organ; but on the] harpsichord, as likewise on the lute or the bandora, since the sound of a string, once touched, soon fades and becomes weak, the fingers should be lifted, and both the suspensions and the consonances often repeated and struck, [not all at once but] so that now the top part, now an inner part and now the bass moves and serves its function.'

(366) C. P. E. Bach, *Essay*, Berlin, 1753, Introd., 9, *f.n.*:

'It is thought quite proper and desirable for the accompanist to repeat chords which are held on by the other performers with a view to keeping up a clear indication of the measure.

[II, 1762, XXIX, 18:] 'In a concerto or other thickly scored music, when the bass and ripieno parts sustain a note [chord] during which the solo part continues with its own movement, perhaps varying it occasionally with syncopation, it is advisable for the accompanist to keep the beat going and give a lead to the other performers by striking a chord in the right hand at the bar-lines even though the harmony does not change. If only the bass sustains the note, then the accompanist may repeat the bass note only just as it fades away; but this must not be done across the beat, as the saying goes. In a duple-time bar, the repetitions may come at the beginning and in the middle, according to time-unit and speed. In a triple-time bar, only the first beat is to be played. [Or at a sudden forte on any beat.]

'[XXXVI, 14: Repeated pairs of bass notes of which the first is dotted] sometimes, for a particular kind of expression, require a [repeated] chord on each, instead of the more customary continuance of the same chord [unrepeated] over the short notes [after the dot].'

3. HOW THE SMOOTH ACCOMPANIMENT MAY BE BROKEN

(a) One very important way of breaking the smooth style of accompaniment is by arpeggiating: taking the notes of the chord in a free rhythm and any desired order and pattern. This, on the lute or the harpsichord, has the effect of keeping the sound going, and can thus actually be more sonorous than the smooth style itself.

When the rhythm is not free but measured, the effect can be used in many contexts where free arpeggiation would be distracting. This measured effect is what we usually call broken chords.

In both methods, as many notes are held on as the harmony, the phrasing and the available fingers permit. This gives the harpsichord some of the build-up of tone which the piano gets from its sustaining (damper-raising or 'loud') pedal, and is a crucial element in its technique. Within smaller limits of volume, the same applies to the lute; and the name of 'lute-play' was often given to the arpeggiated style, even on the harpsichord.

(367) Lorenzo Penna, *Li Primi Albori*, Bologna, 1672, Ch. XX, rule 19:

'Take care to arpeggiate the chords so as not to leave empty spaces on the instrument [here used, as quite often at this date, to mean "plucked keyboard instrument"].'

(368) Michel de Saint-Lambert, *Traité*, Paris, 1707, Ch. IX, Sect. 14, p. 132:

'On the organ one does not repeat the chords, and one uses scarcely any arpeggiation: on the contrary one ties the sounds a great deal.'

(369) Michel de Saint-Lambert, *Traité*, Paris, 1707, Ch. IX, Sect. 8, p. 130:

'[Chords may be arpeggiated one or more times, upwards, downwards, *etc.*] But this reiteration, which wants to be very well managed, cannot be taught by book; it must be observed in practice.

'[Unmeasured] arpeggiation is only suitable in [unmeasured] preludes, where there is no strict measure; for in airs with [measured] movement (Airs de mouvement) it is necessary to strike the chords definitely in time with the bass, except that when all the notes of the bass are crochets, in triple measure, one separates the notes of each chord in such a way as always to keep back one to sound between two beats.'

Ex. 184. Saint-Lambert, *loc. cit.*, broken chords:

There is actually no reason to restrict this technique to any one time or measure, and it is at once one of the simplest and one of the most useful forms of broken chord. It does not need to be the top note which is held back; an inner note can be equally effectual. Again, more notes than one can be held back. In a fuller accompaniment, part of the chord, or even the whole of it, can be brought on the beat by the left hand, and the remainder of the chord, or a reduplication of some

347

or all of it can be held back. Indeed, the varieties are only limited by the necessity of sounding the bass note itself on its proper beat.

Other typical methods of breaking the chords are shown in the following examples.

Ex. 185. Johann Mattheson, *Organisten-Probe*, Hamburg, 1719, broken chords:

In Ex. 185 (c) above the mixture of melodic notes with harmonic ones will be observed. On the analogy of figurate arpeggios, we may call this figurate broken chords. Ex. 186 (a) below shows a fuller handling with the harmony sounded in plain left-hand chords against broken right-hand chords; Ex. 186 (b) shows the bass itself broken (where the rule must be observed to *start* the arpeggio on the actual bass note); Ex. 186 (c) shows broken chords in either hand.

Ex. 186. J. D. Heinichen, *General-Bass*, Dresden, 1728, Part I, Ch. VI, Sect. 31 *ff.*, p. 556, broken chords:

Whether the broken chords are actually written into the bass part, or whether they are introduced there by the player, there is no need to put into the right-hand (unbroken) chord an interval both figured and present in the left-hand broken chord. Some authorities, ignoring the near approach to consecutive octaves which results, encouraged this doubling; others disallowed it. The choice depends partly on taste, partly on the fullness of the accompaniment.

(370) David Kellner, *General-Bass*, Hamburg, 1732, I, xvi:

'Sometimes the bass makes a sort of invasion into a middle part; but the accompanist should keep to his normal accompaniment without taking any notice.'

(371) G. P. Telemann, *Generalbass-Übungen*, Hamburg, 1733–35 No. 21:

'In the case of broken notes, that is to say where the bass includes one or more intervals which really fall within the province of the right hand . . . these may, indeed, be taken in one of the middle parts with the same progression [*i.e.* in consecutive octaves with the bass, concealed only by slight retardation], but we can scarcely allow this in the upper part; in view of this, we have preferred to leave out the 7 which in any case is sounded in the bass, rather than introduce two 8ves, namely *b* and ♯*a*.'

Ex. 187. G. P. Telemann, *loc. cit.*, 7 figured (but present in left-hand broken chord) not doubled in right hand:

(372) C. P. E. Bach, *Essay*, II, Berlin, 1762, XXXIV, 2:

'Where dissonances are resolved by a broken bass, the accompaniment [as figured] must be altered to avoid the disgusting retarded octaves. The dissonances included in the figures may therefore be unhesitatingly omitted [as so often, C. P. E. Bach is stricter here than most].'

4. THE BROKEN ACCOMPANIMENT IN RECITATIVE

(373) Michel de Saint-Lambert, *Traité*, Paris, 1707, Ch. IX, p. 131:

'When accompanying a long recitative, it is sometimes good to dwell for a long time on one chord, when the bass allows, and to let many notes be sung by the voice without [audible] harpsichord accompaniment, then strike again a second chord, and next stop again, and thus only make an accompaniment at long intervals, assuming that as I have said the bass only has long notes, which is normally the case in recitative.

'At other times, after striking a full chord on which you dwell for a long time, you strike one note again here and there, but with such good management that it seems as if the harpsichord had done it by itself, without the consent of the accompanist.

'At other times again, doubling the intervals, you strike all the notes again one after the other, producing from the harpsichord a crackling almost like musketry fire; but having made this agreeable display for three or four bars, you stop quite short on some big harmonious chord (that is to say, without a dissonance) as though to recover from the effort of making such a noise.'

(374) Nicolo Pasquali, *Thorough-Bass Made Easy*, Edinburgh, 1757, p. 47:

'[The art of accompanying recitative] consists in filling up the harmony as much as possible; and therefore the left hand strikes the chords in it as well as the right.

'Care must be taken not to strike abruptly, but in the harpeggio way laying down the fingers in the chords harp–like, *i.e.* one after another, sometimes slow, other times quick, according as the words express either common, tender, or passionate matters:

'For example; for common speech a quick harpeggio; for the tender a slow one; and, for any thing of passion, where anger, surprise, *etc.*, is expressed, little or no harpeggio, but rather dry strokes, playing with both hands almost [but, N.B., not quite] at once.

'The abrupt way is also used at a *punctum* or full stop, where the sense is at an end.'

For a full illustration of Pasquali's recommendations, see App. II below.

(375) C. P. E. Bach, *Essay*, II, Berlin, 1762, XXXVIII, 3:

'Arpeggiation is to be avoided in rapid declamation, especially when there are frequent changes of harmony. . . . [It should be kept for] slow recitative and sustained chords.'

For other aspects of recitative accompaniment, see Ch. XXXII, 2 below, where the above passage will be found quoted at length.

5. HOW FAR THE ACCOMPANIMENT SHOULD DOUBLE THE EXISTING MELODY

(a) A further variety of accompaniment is that in which the top part is not merely melodious in the sense of being flowing, but is an actual melody. This can happen in either of two ways, or a combination of both. The accompaniment can double the existing melody; or it can introduce an independent melodic interest of its own.

(b) The early baroque method of accompanying polyphonic music by a reduplication of the existing polyphonic parts (see Ch. XXVII, 1 above) gives the accompaniment melodic interest, but not independent melodic interest.

This method, which is really the continuation of a renaissance tradition into the early baroque period, was still favoured by a minority of accompanists for some generations longer. The German organists of the seventeenth century, who in some respects were unusually conservative, often insisted on an old-fashioned tablature from which they could follow and largely reduplicate the movement of the polyphony. The English chamber music of the viols during the greater part of the seventeenth century was an almost complete survival of sixteenth century polyphony in its construction, though abreast of its times in the warmth and often in the boldness of its harmony; its written-out organ accompaniments are usually somewhat thinned reduplications of the string parts.

In more progressive circles the method went rapidly out of fashion. It was never applicable to the monody of Caccini, Peri, Cavalieri or Monteverdi, as their use of compound figures makes it possible for us to be certain. Elsewhere, it was soon rejected, at first as unnecessary, and then as undesirable, by the leading theorists.

(376) Agostino Agazzari, *Del sonare sopra 'l basso*, Siena, 1607, end:

'In conclusion, there is no necessity for the accompanist to play the parts in their existing form, so long as accompaniment is his purpose, and not a performance [*i.e.* an organ transcription] of the music itself, which is quite another subject.'

(377) Michael Praetorius, *Syntagma*, III, Wolfenbüttel, 1619, Ch. VI, App.:

'It is not necessary for the organist in his accompaniment to follow the vocal parts as sung, but only for him to play his own version of the harmonies on the continuo.'

(378) Andreas Werckmeister, *Anmerckungen*, Aschersleben, 1698, ed. of 1715, Sect. 69:

'One must avoid continuous movement in octaves with the singers and instrumentalists.'

(379) Francesco Gasparini, *L'Armonico Pratico*, Venice, 1708, Ch. X:

'One must never accompany note for note as in the voice part or any other top part composed for the violin, *etc.*, since it is enough that the consonance or dissonance composed, or required by the bass, shall appear in the body of the harmony according to the rules of accompaniment.'

It must be clearly understood, therefore, that the accompaniment should not ordinarily reproduce the melody accompanied.

Apart from the exceptions mentioned above, there are a few situations which can best be met by such reduplication, though not usually for long at a time. In other situations, the effect is dull and ponderous, and should be avoided. But reduplicating the lower of two solo parts in the middle of the accompaniment, either at the unison or at the octave below, is not so conspicuous, and may often be useful and not easy to avoid.

(380) C. P. E. Bach, *Essay*, II, Berlin, 1762, XXIX, 24:

'Objectionable as is the accompaniment in which the upper line continuously reduplicates the melody of the main part, it is nevertheless sometimes necessary, and therefore permissible, at the start of a rapid piece, particularly if this is in two parts. By this means the performers join hands over the tempo, and the listeners will miss no part of the opening, which will be kept unanimous and in good order. And generally speaking, unreliable musicians whether accompanists [here meaning *ripienists*] or leaders are allowed this assistance even apart from the opening, if they can thereby be helped to regain a lost steadiness of tempo.'

6. HOW FAR THE ACCOMPANIMENT SHOULD POSSESS AN INDEPENDENT MELODIC INTEREST

(a) If the reduplication of the existing upper melody is to be avoided, the question remains how much independent melody is to be given to the accompaniment in place of it.

The answer to this question depends largely but not entirely on circumstances. The remaining factors are, of course, the individual taste and talents of the performers. But it is only by adapting himself ungrudgingly to the circumstances of the case that the performer can indulge his taste and his talents without spoiling both the parts which he is accompanying and his own accompaniment.

(b) The principle, as usual, is to put the interests of the existing melodies first.

(381) Lodovico Viadana, *Concerti Ecclesiastici*, Venice, 1602, preface, rule 2:

'The organist is obliged to play the organ part in a straightforward manner, especially in the left hand; if he wants, however, to introduce some movement into the right hand, for example by embellishing the cadences, or by some suitable free ornamentation, he must perform this in such a way that the singer or singers shall not be covered or confused by too much movement.'

The reader is again referred back to the third paragraph of (129) in Ch. IX, 3 above, where Agazzari in 1607 develops this theme at somewhat greater length.

(c) The most obvious application of this principle of putting the interests of the existing melodies first is that the accompanist should find the chief outlet for his own impulses towards elaboration at precisely those points in the music where there is least elaboration in the solo parts.

In passages where the continuo is playing alone, the accompanist not only may but must produce his own elaboration to fill the gap. Such passages may occur at introductions before the solo entry, or as interludes when no soloist is for the moment being heard.

(382) Lorenzo Penna, *Li Primi Albori*, Bologna, 1672, Ch. 14:

'In the Ritornelli, or in the pauses intended to rest the singer, the organist must perform something of his own invention, in imitation of the Arietta or other lively matter which has just been sung.'

(383) Friedrich Erhard Niedt, *Musicalische Handleitung*, Hamburg, 1700, Ch. VIII, rule 8:

'[Quick basses ordinarily need a chord] only with the first note of a half-bar or crotchet: the remaining [bass notes] are called passing notes . . .

'But if it should chance that [an opportunity for] a solo passage were written into the continuo, then the organist must play in a more florid manner.'

The same kind of opportunity also occurs, though not quite so freely, when the solo part comes to any long sustained note against which the accompaniment can and should move more rapidly and elaborately.

(384) J. D. Heinichen, *General-Bass,* Dresden, 1728, Part I, Ch. VI, Sect. 28, p. 547:

'[An ornate accompaniment,] for which the cantabile solo and the unaccompanied ritornello of arias without [ripieno] instruments afford the best opportunity, [which can be fully exploited] so long as no harm is done thereby to the composed parts.'

We see from this that not merely isolated long notes, but entire pieces in a cantabile style (*i.e.* with a preponderance of sustained notes, not necessarily all of them particularly long) admitted a suitably ornate accompaniment. Experience confirms this, though not necessarily in the form of independent melody: broken chords and figurate arpeggios, for which see 3 and 4 above, may often provide the necessary movement and interest in a less distracting form.

(385) C. P. E. Bach, *Essay*, II, Berlin, 1762, XXIX, 3:

'Where the opportunity arises and the nature of the music allows, when the solo part is resting or is performing plain notes, the accompanist may relax the control on his held-back fire. But this needs great ability and an understanding of the true feeling of the music.

[4:] 'It is sometimes a necessary and indeed a perfectly proper course for the accompanist to discuss the music with the soloist before performing it, and let him decide how much liberty is to be taken with the accompaniment. Some prefer their accompanist to be very restrained; others the opposite.

[XXXII, 11:] 'Transitional passages offer a challenging invitation to the inventiveness of an accompanist. But his inventiveness must be in sympathy with the feeling and substance of the music. If some reminiscence of a previous phrase can be introduced, even at the cost of slightly altering the bass part and modifying the transition, so much the better . . . so long as the solo part is not subjected to interference.'

A small but very important variety of the transitional passages referred to in the last paragraph above occurs at the joins between sections, where two workings of the transition are often required: one leading back to the original key of the section for the repeat, the other leading to the key in which the next section opens. For examples, see Ch. XXVIII, 3 (c) above.

(d) When the bass itself is florid, it is most unlikely that the remainder of the accompaniment should be florid too, except where the continuo is on its own.

(386) Johann Mattheson, *Organisten-Probe*, Hamburg, 1719, Mittel-Classe Prob-Stück 9, Erläuterungen, Sect. 1:

'There is seldom opportunity for ornamental and florid playing when the bass itself is purposely written in an ornamental and florid style. If, however, the bass is without particular embellishment, and one is playing alone, either in the introduction to an Aria, in the middle, or wherever else there may be a rest [for the soloist], then and there it is that these adornments, these figurations, these inventions, these embellishments find their proper, indeed one might almost say their necessary place.'

(e) Among the embellishments which may be introduced into any part of the accompaniment, including the bass, are the specific ornaments.

(387) Michel de Saint-Lambert, *Traité*, Paris, 1707, Ch. IX, Sect. 15, p. 132:

'One can on the organ, as well as on the harpsichord, make from time to time certain trills or other ornaments, in the bass as well as in the other parts.'

(388) J. D. Heinichen, *General-Bass*, Dresden, 1728, Part I, Ch. VI, Sect. 2, p. 521:

'The art of a properly embellished continuo [includes] sometimes introducing an ornament in all the parts (particularly the outside part of the right hand, which is the most conspicuous).'

(f) The extent to which opportunities can be found for independent melody in the accompaniment without detriment to the existing parts is not entirely predetermined, since it depends to some extent on the performer's ability to invent a counter-melody so exquisitely adapted to the existing melody as to enhance it rather than draw attention away from it.

The following gives us some account of J. S. Bach's abilities in this direction.

(389) Lorenz Mizler, *Musikalische Bibliothek*, Leipzig, I, Part 4, 1738, p. 48:

'Whoever wishes to form a real conception of refinement in continuo, and of what good accompaniment means, has only to put himself to the trouble of hearing our Capellmeister [J. S.] Bach here, who performs any continuo to a solo so that one imagines that it is a concerted piece, and as if the melody which he plays in the right hand had been composed beforehand. I can bring living witness to this, since I have heard it myself.'

7. HOW CONTRAPUNTAL THE ACCOMPANIMENT SHOULD BE

(a) The independent melodic interest of the accompaniment may occasionally extend to taking equal part in the existing structure by way of imitation.

(390) Michel de Saint-Lambert, *Traité*, Paris, 1707, Ch. IX:

'When one is accompanying a single voice which is singing some air with [measured] movement (Air de mouvement) in which there are a number of melodic imitations, such as the Italian arias, one can imitate on the harpsichord the subject and the points of imitation of the song, making the parts enter one after the other. But this demands a supreme skill and it must be of the first excellence to be of any value.'

(391) J. D. Heinichen, *General-Bass*, Dresden, 1728, Ch. IV, Sect. 40, p. 578:

'Imitation does not depend on your own invention, but must be taken from the written composition itself. Thus what is here called imitation is when the accompanist tries to copy the beginning of a phrase or an invention of the composer in passages into which the composer himself has not introduced it. But since we have never to interfere with the singer or player with this phrase, where he has it himself, and since, on the other

355

hand, the composer himself must be imagined to have put it into the passages where the beginning of an imitation is in keeping, and thus to have left the accompanist little room for imitation, from all this it is evident that this kind of embellishment on the harpsichord is the most wretched of all.

'But since a few cases may be found here or there, in some piece where (especially in Cantatas and Arias without [ripieno or obbligato] instruments) there is room left for a skilful accompanist to imitate a phrase occurring in the continuo or the solo part, more frequently than the composer has done himself, the following example may serve by way of illustration; here a further feature is to be observed, in that the right hand tends to want to accompany the solo part in 3rds and 6ths, and in this way to form a sort of concerted duet with it. This kind of imitation is particularly successful in vocal pieces, and is the easier to achieve [impromptu] in that with [solo] chamber music and with operatic music the [solo] part ordinarily written above [the bass] makes it possible to watch the singer closely, to keep out of his way, and to follow his lead.'

Heinichen's example to the above, which is a beautiful piece of neat and telling workmanship, will be found complete in App. II below. There is no doubt that imitation can be a most attractive enrichment of the accompaniment in the not very frequent instances in which it can be brought in easily and naturally and without any forcing of the overall effect. It is obviously much harder to improvise than to prepare beforehand, and it is, on the whole, one of those recourses over which it should be possible to work a prepared part more closely than a more or less impromptu one. Nevertheless, a quick enough accompanist can sometimes seize his chance at sight.

(392) Johann Friedrich Daube, *General-Bass*, Leipzig, 1756, Ch. XI, Sect. 12, *f.n.*:

'The admirable [J. S.] Bach commanded [the elaborate style] of accompaniment in the highest measure; when he was the accompanist, the solo was bound to shine. He gave it life, where it had none, by his abundantly skilled accompaniment. He knew how to imitate it so cunningly in either right or left hand, and again how to introduce so unexpected a counter-melody, that the hearer would have sworn that it had all been composed in that manner with the greatest care. At the same time, the regular accompaniment [*i.e.* chords realising the figuring] was very little cut down. All in all, his accompanying was always like a concerted part worked out most elaborately, and matching up to the solo part, so that at the right time the solo part was bound to shine. This privilege was also granted even to the bass, without interference to the solo part. Suffice it to say that anyone who did not hear him missed a great deal.'

(b) Daube's reference to imitations introduced into the left hand as well as into the right is accounted for by the passage to which the quotation above is a footnote. This distinctly states that the bass itself may be altered if a successful point of imitation can be gained by so doing.

(393) Johann Friedrich Daube, *General-Bass*, Leipzig, 1756, Ch. XI, Sect. 12:

'[The elaborate style of accompaniment] arises: (1) When, in masterful alternation with [the simple style] one tries from time to time to introduce suspensions where the composer has not written them nor shown them in the figuring. (2) When the solo part has a rest: here one can sometimes bring in some melodic passages. (3) One may also move in 3rds or 6ths with the solo part. (4) When one tries to imitate the theme of the solo part, or further, at one's discretion, to let a countermelody be heard. (5) As it may sometimes happen, moreover, that even with a good solo part the bass is badly constructed, either because it could have brought in an imitation, but this has been left out from carelessness or inadvertence, or because where it might have moved [better] in quick notes or slow notes, the opposite has been done; in such cases the accompanist may be allowed the liberty of attempting a correction while his accompaniment proceeds.'

Changing the bass so as to introduce an imitation presupposes either the absence of any other bass instrument with which the change might conflict, or harmonic compatibility between the written bass and the improvised point of imitation. In the second case we have an opposite method to the characteristic seventeenth century method of keeping the fundamental bass on the keyboard and letting the melodic bass instrument make any improvised divisions.

(c) Imitations both strict and free between the solo part and the bass are, of course, often introduced in writing by the composer. Where the soloist makes either an ornament or some impromptu variation in one of his entries, the accompanist must be quick to imitate this ornament or variation in his next answer. He may also be the one to instigate such a variation, if his own entry precedes that of the soloist.

(394) C. P. E. Bach, *Essay*, II, Berlin, 1762, XXXIII, 1:

'Imitation often occurs in passages of which the repeat is varied [impromptu]. The accompanist must take part in the variation so that his imitation shall remain recognisable and shall not fall short in beauty. The accompaniment must follow the pattern of the solo part as closely as possible. [2:] In [Ex. 188] the bass leads the imitation.

[5:] 'A keyboard player who has other bass players doubling him must refrain from variations if he is doubtful whether the others will follow him.

'[6: Of imitation added to the accompaniment by the performer, in addition to that given by the composer; sometimes] neither the bass nor

357

the accompaniment can imitate the solo part exactly. In such cases it is sufficient to invent an imitation of which the [rhythmic] outline matches that of the solo part, while the bass is left with its notes as they are or slightly varied.

[7:] 'Those with good knowledge of part-writing can furthermore bring into a middle part an ornamental imitation of the solo part instead of the ordinary accompaniment. . . . The speed must not be very fast, however, or the effect will be confused.'

Ex. 188. C. P. E. Bach, *loc. cit.*, (a) imitation started by the bass; (b) the same imitation with a variation, also started by the bass, as it might be improvised in performance during the repeat:

(d) Apart from imitation of any kind, a certain amount of neat contrapuntal workmanship is often very effective in the right context. The more formal the music, the more likely such contrapuntal workmanship is to suit it well; but in all cases, it will be appreciated that this workmanship should not sound stiff or self-conscious. There can, indeed, be a very light and delicate counterpoint, often in no more than two parts (including the bass), which can give a more exhilirating effect in a crisp and rapid movement than any succession of chords no matter how thin. At the opposite extreme there stands the solid craftsmanship of a movement in the 'learned' style. There is, in short, counterpoint to suit all calls and all situations, and while by no means all movements will tolerate any kind of counterpoint, it is surprising how frequently the more informal kinds can add a certain cleanness to the technique and a certain definiteness to the idiom. The part will gain in tautness and the accompanist will sound as if he knew exactly where he was going. When he relaxes into a fanciful and casual passage, he will gain all the more effect from the contrast. Such variety is the life of good accompaniment.

This recommendation to keep a certain amount of informal but workmanlike imitation going in the inner parts, wherever suitable, is confirmed by a marked disposition of surviving baroque realisations, or fragments of realisation, to do exactly this. See the addition made in this new version to App. II.

CHAPTER XXXI

Instruments of Accompaniment

1. EARLY BAROQUE INSTRUMENTS OF ACCOMPANIMENT

(a) At the start of the baroque period, the choice of accompanying instruments was wide and flexible.

In church music, the organ had pre-eminence; many performances of music once thought to have been always unaccompanied evidently included it, but as a reduplication of the polyphony, not as an independent texture. The range of melodic instruments which might be introduced was also extensive. These, too, doubled the polyphony; but as the monodic style came into sacred use, they required parts of their own, which were not at first always provided by the composer.

In secular song, the lute was pre-eminent during the late renaissance, and remained so at the beginning of the baroque period: particularly Caccini's favourite, the large accompanying arch-lute or chitarrone, which took a conspicuous share in the early monody. It could be used alone; but many options were open to the performers, and here again a number of melodic accompanying instruments might be assembled, the parts for which had normally to be more or less improvised in performance in so far as they had not already been preconcerted in rehearsal.

These conditions of performance fall somewhat outside the main problem of baroque accompaniment as here understood, and have already been discussed, as a problem in free ornamentation, in Ch. IX, 3 above. The reader is particularly referred to the long quotation given there at (129), showing Agazzari's mention of various accompanying instruments.

(b) It is, however, worth noting here that such contemporary lute accompaniments to early monodic songs as have survived in fully written-out form (*e.g.* Caccini's famous 'Amarilli' in Robert Dowland's *Musicall Banquet*, London, 1610) are conspicuously simple: much more so, for example, than John Dowland's characteristically contrapuntal settings of his own songs (Robert Dowland was the son of John). This is in full accordance with the insistence of the Italian monodists and their imitators that nothing in the music should be allowed to detract from the direct dramatic impact of the words; but in view of the complexity of melodic accompaniment described by Agazzari and Praetorius (see Ch. IX, 3, above) it is impossible to believe that lutenists and keyboard players, even when accompanying monody, were always reticent, and we may allow something for the usual diversity of individual practice.

(c) In the early baroque period, the harpsichord, though carried to great lengths of virtuosity as a solo instrument, was not yet exploited with the same virtuosity as an instrument of accompaniment. It will be remembered that in Diego Ortiz' *Tratado* of 1553 it is the viol which makes the elaborate divisions, the harpsichord which sustains the solid part-writing of the original motet or chanson; and the roles are not yet reversed in early baroque music. A few momentary points of imitation, an occasional ornamental flourish and a considerable recourse to broken chords are the only relief to straightforward part-writing which should ordinarily diversify an early baroque accompaniment on the harpsichord.

(d) The organ, apart from its massive share in church music, was during the renaissance, and remained into the baroque period, an important instrument in chamber music: not in its larger representatives, but in the smaller positives and portatives, and in the little regal with its surprisingly telling and incisive tone, produced by beating reeds with very short tubes.

The evidence suggests that an organ part for accompaniment would be still more regular in its part-writing than a harpsichord part, and still more subject to the accepted ideal of reduplicating the polyphony, when present, and otherwise of replacing it by a similar texture.

2. SUPPORTING THE HARMONIC ACCOMPANIMENT WITH A MELODIC BASS INSTRUMENT

(a) At the very beginning of the baroque period, and at the same time, therefore, as the colourful ensembles in the traditions of the renaissance mentioned by Agazzari, the emergence of music supported by a true 'general bass' was laying down the pattern for the most characteristic of all baroque combinations for accompaniment: an instrument (or instruments) of harmony in conjunction with a melodic bass instrument (or instruments) to reinforce the bass line itself.

(395) Michael Praetorius, *Syntagma*, III, Wolfenbüttel, 1619, Ch. VI, Sect. on Organ, App.:

'It is further specially to be noticed that when 2 or 3 voices sing accompanied by the General Bass which the Organist or Lutenist has in front of him and from which he plays, it is very good, and indeed almost essential, to have this same General Bass played in addition by some bass instrument, such as a bassoon, a dolcian [a form of bassoon], or a trombone, or best of all, on a violone [probably meaning here a bass, rather than double-bass viol].'

The entire structural tendency of baroque music encouraged this disposition of forces. However important the middle parts, it is rare, in a characteristic piece of baroque music, for them to equal the outer parts in importance. It is this fact which makes the system of figured bass so eminently suitable for its purpose. The composer establishes the upper melody or melodies; he supports them with an equally strong melodic bass; but what lies between these outer extremes is of a different texture, and is not meant to be so sharply defined. These requirements can only be met with complete satisfactoriness when the bass line is itself outlined by an instrument or instruments of melody.

Voice and lute, recorder or violin with harpsichord can be perfectly satisfactory. Trio sonatas without a melodic bass are apt to be much less so. The bass should, moreover, be played with about as much volume and significance as the solo parts, actually standing out above them for fugal entries and other prominent matter. It will not serve its function if it is played in a discreet and retiring manner.

J. S. Bach's sonatas for violin and obbligato harpsichord are, in effect, trios with one melodic line on the violin and one in each hand on the harpsichord, with frequent interchange of themes. A partially autograph MS. calls them 'Six Sonatas for Harpsichord Obbligato and Violin Solo, with Bass accompanied on the Viola da Gamba at will'; but here the effect is somewhat to unbalance the fine distribution of the parts, and is hardly desirable.

Titles such as 'Thorough-Bass for the Harpsichord or Violoncello', *etc.*, are to be taken in the sense of 'and/or': cases occur (*e.g.* Vivaldi's Op. I) with 'or' in the title but 'and' in the parts. Two bass parts are usual, both figured, but only because they are printed from the same plates to save expense: one is for the melodic bass. No doubt the 'or' was for commercial reasons; it encouraged amateur buyers who might not muster the complete complement of instruments. In the same way they were often given the choice of violins, flutes, recorders or oboes as solo instruments.

(396–7) [Peter Prelleur] *Modern Musick-Master*, London, 1730, ed. of 1731, in 'A Dictionary':

'Organo, signifies properly an Organ, but when it is written over any Piece of Musick, then it signifies the Thorough Bass.'

(398) Sébastien de Brossard, *Dictionaire de musique*, Paris, 1703, *etc.*, s.v. 'Basso-Continuo':

'We also often play it [the continuo] simply, and without figures [harmonies] on the *Bass Viol* [gamba] or the *Bass Violin* [violoncello], together with the *Bassoon*, the *Serpent*, *etc.* [as alternatives], whence the Italians also call it *Basso Viola*, *Violone*, *Fagotto*, *etc.*'

(399) Fr. Couperin, *Leçons de Ténèbres*, Paris, 1714, Avertissement:

'Although their melody is notated in the treble clef, all other kinds of voice can sing them, seeing that most present-day accompanists know how to transpose. . . . If one can join a Bass Viol [gamba] or Bass Violin [violoncello] to the accompaniment of the Organ or the Harpsichord, that will be good.'

(400) C. P. E. Bach, *Essay*, II, Berlin, 1762, Introduction, 8:

'Some people have themselves accompanied in a solo on the viola, or even on the violin, with no keyboard instrument. If this is done from necessity, for lack of a good keyboard player, they must be excused [but not otherwise].

[9:] 'The most complete accompaniment to a Solo, and the one to which no possible exception can be taken, is a keyboard instrument in combination with the Violoncello.'

The effect of a melodic bass instrument with no instrument of harmony is more successful in trio sonatas, where there are three real parts, than in solos, where there are two. It sometimes sounds surprisingly complete and beautiful.

As a substitute for the full continuo with both melodic and harmonic continuo instruments present, either alone is quite justified on baroque precedents, but neither is nearly as satisfactory as the two together.

3. GAMBA OR CELLO

For orchestral music, the cello was and is the obvious choice, except that as the *concertante* bass in a concerto grosso the gamba makes an attractive variant.

For chamber music, Italy was probably the first country to develop a preference for the cello, and France the last—not until more than half-way through the eighteenth century. The gamba led in Purcell's England, and was still quite active in J. S. Bach's Germany. The following is a somewhat late reference.

(401) Dr. Charles Burney, *Present State of Music in Germany*, London, 1773, I, p. 139:

'[The Elector of Bavaria] played [the bass of] one of Schwindl's trios [trio sonatas] on his *Viol da gamba*, charmingly: except Mr Abel, I never heard so fine a player on that instrument.'

(402) [J. S. Sainsbury] *A Dictionary of Musicians*, London, 1824, 2nd ed. 1827 [N.B. the date], *s.v.* 'Abel':

'The viol da gamba, now hardly used.'

(b) The gamba, being more lightly constructed and strung than the cello, has a less massive but more transparent tone, with its own peculiar warmth and beauty of colouring. It is nearer to violin tone than the cello; and the blend of two violins and gamba in a baroque trio sonata, with the harpsichord to give a crystalline edge and sparkle, is one of the best sonorities in music.

The cello also makes a magnificent effect here, but a more bottom-heavy one. There is not so close a blend of tone. Care should be taken to avoid its more ponderous colourings.

(c) A second main difference between gamba and violoncello is their technique of bowing, which was originally the same (underhand) but was changed by Italian violoncellists of the early eighteenth century (and subsequently elsewhere) into an approximation to the (overhand) bowing of the violin. The resultant technique is more forceful, and better suited to the violoncello; the gamba technique gives, however, a pointed articulation characteristic of this instrument, and in its different style equally effective. This difference should be retained, and not obliterated by using violoncello bowing on the gamba. Here, too, there is a noticeable distinction between the effect of giving the continuo line to a gamba and giving it to a violoncello. Like so many such distinctions, it is valuable for its own sake, and adds to the subtle possibilities of varying the accompaniment.

4. ADDING A DOUBLE-BASS

In larger chamber groupings, the gamba as a continuo bass is at its best when supported at the octave below by a double-bass instrument. Its own double-bass, the violone, which has the same relative lightness of construction and the same six relatively thin strings, makes with it a combined sonority of remarkable silkiness and tranquil depth. A normal modern double-bass (which is a double-bass violin modified by some refining influence from the double-bass viol) is also extremely satisfactory if it is played purely; the smaller 'chamber' basses being the most suitable for this purpose.

In orchestral music, gambas on the bass line can be multiplied in the same way as cellos, and given the same support from the double-basses. (They can also be used as tenor instruments.)

5. OTHER EFFECTS OF SHARING RESPONSIBILITY FOR THE ACCOMPANIMENT

(a) A harpsichordist supported by a melodic bass instrument is relieved of the responsibility for making special efforts to bring out the bass line in sufficient strength.

(b) The less support from other instruments, the more need for correctness in the harpsichord part.

(403) Michel de Saint-Lambert, *Traité*, Paris, 1707, Ch. VIII:

'[Forbidden consecutives do not matter when disguised by the presence of many voices or instruments.] But in accompanying a single voice, particular when unsupported [by a melodic bass instrument], it is impossible to be too strictly correct; for in that case everything shows clearly, and the Critics will tolerate no fault.'

(c) The bass-line can be simplified on the harpsichord by leaving florid divisions to the melodic bass instrument: see (311) in Ch. XXVIII, 3 (b) above. Indeed, in Purcell's trio sonatas of 1685 and 1697 we actually find the continuo bass part separately printed; it is a slightly plainer version of the string bass part, lacking some of the detailed figuration and exact fugal imitation. The discrepancies sound better when the harmonic instrument is a chamber organ, less convincing when it is a harpsichord.

When, as is normal, the two bass parts are printed in duplicate from the same plates, the choice in this matter rests with the player. In spite of the historical justification for sometimes doing otherwise, it is ordinarily by far the most satisfactory course for the harpsichord to double all the notes of the melodic bass instrument with the sole exception of rapid repeated notes—for which see Ch. XXVIII, 3 (b) above.

6. THE CHOICE OF HARMONIC INSTRUMENT

(a) The choice of instrument greatly affects the nature of the part.

(404) C. P. E. Bach, *Essay*, II, Berlin, 1762, Introd., 1:

'The organ, the harpsichord, the pianoforte, and the clavichord are the keyboard instruments most commonly used for accompaniment.

[3:] 'The organ is indispensable in church music on account of the fugues, loud choruses, and more generally, on account of the binding effect. It adds to the grandness and it preserves order.

[4:] 'But whenever Recitatives and Arias are used in church, especially those whose inner parts [on *ripieno* instruments] accompany simply so as to leave the voice free to make ornamental variations, there must be a harpsichord.

'Unfortunately we all too often hear how bare the performance of such music sounds without the accompaniment of the harpsichord.

[5:] 'This instrument is also essential in the theatre or in a room, on account of such Arias and Recitatives.

[6:] 'The pianoforte and the clavichord make the best accompaniment in a performance associated with the greatest refinements of [galant] taste.

However, some singers would rather be accompanied on the clavichord or the harpsichord than on the first-mentioned.

[7:] 'No piece, therefore, can be adequately performed without the accompaniment of a keyboard instrument. Even with music on the grandest scale, in opera—indeed, even in the open air, when it would be confidently supposed that the harpsichord could not be heard at all, it is missed if it is not present. A listener who is above the performers can clearly distinguish every note. I speak from experience, and anyone can try the same experiment.'

(b) The organ is an instrument which can take such very different forms that it is hardly possible to generalise about its uses for accompaniment. However, two main aspects may be mentioned.

As an accompaniment to large-scale church music we are, of course, familiar with the organ, and the only comment required here is that baroque organs are markedly different from modern organs (other than deliberate replicas) in their scaling and registers. Wind pressure is low, but voicing is very positive. The attack is sharp, the tone unforced but colourful, and employed more for strong contrasts than for smooth gradations. Pungent mixtures are another characteristic feature. Some excellent baroque church organs survive, mainly on the Continent; of many modern replicas, the baroque department of the Royal Festival Hall organ, London, designer Ralph Downes, was of early interest.

Small and often portable organs were used for chamber music. Some had a single rank, usually wide open wooden diapasons; others had several stops. Like the harpsichord, the chamber organ blends with other instruments, but without the sharp edge and brilliance: its effect with strings is well described by Thomas Mace in 1676—see (34) in Ch. II, 5 above—'the Organ Evenly, and Softly, and Sweetly Acchording to All'. The same passage makes it clear that in late seventeenth century England the chamber organ was at least as common an accompanying instrument as the harpsichord: Mace performed livelier music, e.g. violin as opposed to viol music, 'not to the Organ (as many (nowadays) Improperly, and Unadvisedly perform such like Consorts with) but to the Harpsicon'. The evidence of part-books suggests that it may have been more common, unless the word 'organ' is there used loosely for 'continuo instrument' as Prelleur stated that 'organo' was, in 1731 —see (397) in 2 above.

The titles of Corelli's 'church sonatas', Op. I and III specify *Basso per l'Organo* and of his 'chamber sonatas' Op. II and IV *Violone o Cembalo* ('big viol and/or harpsichord'): a useful hint, but the choice is at the performer's discretion. See also (348) in Ch. XXIX, 6 above.

(c) The harpsichord, large or small, was the standard baroque instrument of accompaniment. Even the smaller forms provide a satisfactory continuo if there is a melodic instrument on the bass line as well. With the larger harpsichords, it should be remembered that hand-stops, not pedals, were the normal means of changing registers on baroque instruments, and that this greatly limited the player's ability to change the registration in the middle of a passage. The pedals found on many modern harpsichords are slightly more convenient, and in view of C. P. E. Bach's insistence at (326) in Ch. XXIX, 4 above on adapting the volume to that of the solo parts, we need not hesitate, when they are present, to make good use of them for this purpose: see (743) in Ch. LXIV, 1 below for his praise of one of the rare pedal harpsichords of his period, and (742) for Mace's praise of another in 1676. On the other hand, there is undoubtedly some temptation to use the pedals too much. The best modern makers (often basing their instruments on particular historical varieties, of which the best taken all round is probably 18th-century French) do not now usually fit pedals, but a sliding coupler and hand-shifts. On balance, this is very advantageous indeed, saving both expensive complication and artistic temptation. Changes of registration imposed on the music where it does not really lend itself to them can become very restless, and are against the basic nature of the instrument.

In the same way, many big modern harpsichords have a 16-foot register of striking colouring and apparent massiveness; but the added tension overloads the instrument, reducing both clarity and volume. When in addition the frame is too heavy, the soundboard too thick and the ribbing too rigid and extensive, the entire resonance of the instrument is catastrophically diminished: it costs too much to buy; it weighs too much to carry; and in return it yields a sound both too harsh and too feeble, metallic in attack and inferior in sustaining power. It has only the superficial attraction of strongly contrasted colourings to recommend it, and these are harmful (because unblending) in chamber music and not ultimately satisfying in solos. Many though not all commercially produced harpsichords show these misconceptions of design in some degree, and some though not many good players prefer them.

But there are now numerous good craftsmen making and many players using an excellent 18th-century French-style instrument of light construction, two keyboards, no pedals, push-pull coupler, two 8-foot registers and one 4-foot, sometimes having but not needing a harp (buff) stop and perhaps a lute (plucking one 8-foot closer to the string-end). With a proper touch, the volume then meets all normal requirements. Recording engineers should be warned *not to balance the harpsichord down:* it wants to be well heard. For big halls or weak instruments or players, electrical amplification may be essential.

A harpsichord concerto needs the solo to be heard easily, but a continuo harpsichord in the orchestra has only to make its presence felt by the clarity and sharpness it imparts. Even so, it may have to be electrically amplified for a large hall and orchestra. Or double the continuo with two or more harpsichords, or with several lutes.

(d) The mid-eighteenth century piano included by C. P. E. Bach in his list of accompanying instruments at (404) above had a tone, though not an attack, nearer to the harpsichord than to the modern piano, which is unsuited to baroque accompaniment, not being a sufficiently blending instrument. Throwing most of its acoustic energy into its lowest few partials, it has a solid neutrality of tone which tends to obscure the colouring of the instruments it is accompanying, unless the dampers are raised by using the 'loud pedal', when the upper partials come surging in to brighten and colour the tone, but at the expense of the clarity so necessary in baroque music.

(e) C. P. E. Bach's own clavichord was a Silbermann of exceptional quality and power (J. H. Reichardt, cited by W. J. Mitchell, trans. of C. P. E. Bach's *Essay*, New York, 1949, p. 36n); even so it is surprising and interesting, to find him at (404) above taking the clavichord for granted as an accompanying instrument. Its dynamic range is wide, because of its extreme pianissimo; but it has a very small absolute volume for its fortissimo.

(f) The lute, not being a keyboard instrument, was not included in C. P. E. Bach's list, but is mentioned elsewhere as an accompanying instrument at a considerably later date.

(405) John Hoyle, *Dictionary of Music*, ed. of 1791, *s.v.* 'Arcileuto':

'An Arch Lute, or very long and large Lute, with Bass Strings, like a Theorbo Lute. . . . and is much used by the Italians for playing a Thorough Bass.
[*s.v.* 'Bass (Thorough)':] 'Is the harmony made by the Bass Viols, or Theorboes, continuing to play, both while the Voices sing, and the other instruments perform their parts . . .'

Hoyle's dictionary is a mere popular compilation from Grassineau and Geminiani, and of little evidential value in itself. This point is, however, made again by Busby, a rather better authority.

(406) T. Busby, *Complete Dictionary*, ed. of [1801], *s.v.* 'Arch-Lute':

'A Theorbo, or Large Lute. . . . It is still used in Italy.'

A lute is louder than a clavichord, less loud than a harpsichord. It is capable of the greatest refinement of expression and tone-colouring and is an especially satisfying accompaniment for a solo voice, with or without a gamba to double the melodic bass-line. Its carrying-power varies remarkably with the skill of the player in producing that easy, free vibration which is so much more telling than violence on any musical instrument (the voice included). But in a fairly large hall, electrical amplification is the only recourse. In early baroque orchestral music, on the other hand, twelve or more lutes might be assembled together: that should dispense with any need for electricity.

CHAPTER XXXII

The Good Accompanist

1. WHAT MAKES A GOOD ACCOMPANIST

The best of accompanists need not be too proud to make as much preparation as the situation allows and as he feels that it calls for.

(407) Lodovico Viadana, *Concerti Ecclesiastici*, Venice, 1602, preface, rule 3:

'It will further be desirable for the Organist to take a preliminary look at the Concerto which is to be sung, since he will always make his accompaniments better for understanding the music.'

(408) Lorenzo Penna, *Li Primi Albori*, Bologna, 1672, Book III, Ch. XX, rule 1:

'Make sure, so soon as you are given the part from which you are to play, that you understand its character, so that you may accompany properly.'

(409) Le Cerf de La Viéville, 'Comparaison', in *Histoire*, Amsterdam, 1725, I, p. 297 (a prejudiced account but none the less a warning):

'All that is generally heard in the Italian music is a thorough-bass accompaniment unceasingly varied (doublée), this variation being often a kind of breaking of chords, and an arpeggiation, which throws dust in the eyes of those who know no better, and which, reduced to its elements, comes back to the same as ours. These thorough-basses are good only for showing off the quickness of hand of those who accompany on the harpsichord or the [bass] viol [gamba] or again, to go one better (rencherir) on these basses, already varied in themselves, they vary them further, and it goes to him who will vary them the most; in such sort, that you cannot hear the melody any more, which would seem too naked after so much brilliance, and vanishes buried (demeure enseveli) beneath a chaos of embroidered (tricottez) and rattling (pétillans) sounds, which pass so lightly that they cannot make any harmony against the melody. There then have to be two instruments, one to play the plain version of the bass, and the other the variation. These thorough-bass accompaniments pass rather for solos for the viol, than for an accompaniment, which ought to be subordinate to the melody, and not overpower it. The voice ought to stand out and attract the main attention; just the opposite happens here: you only hear the thorough-bass accompaniment, which rattles so loudly, that the voice is smothered. An awkwardness arises in basses with broken chords and variations [improvised] on the spot (sur le champ): this is that it is difficult for a harpsichord, a [bass] viol and a theorbo [arch-lute] to contrive to come together correctly, in the same kind of variation, not to mention other string or wind instruments; the one takes one turning, the other another, and the result is a remarkable cacophony such that the composer can no longer recognise his own work, which comes forth totally disfigured. You are supposed, in the midst of all this, to take pleasure in admiring the quickness of hand of the performers. There you have, at any rate, the modern taste in performance of the Italian music, so greatly vaunted.'

(410) C. P. E. Bach, *Essay*, II, Berlin, 1762, XXIX, 2:

'The accompanist is usually given much less time [than the soloist]; he is only allowed a brief examination of the music [of which he should make the best use he can].

[XXXII, 3:] 'The commonest phrase to describe a good accompanist is: "he accompanies with judgment". Such praise covers a multitude of qualities. It amounts to saying that the accompanist can discriminate, and therefore realise his part to suit the character of a piece, the number of parts, the remaining performers and especially the soloist, the instruments and voices concerned, the auditorium and the audience. . . . He puts himself into sympathy with the intentions both of performer and of composer, and he tries to help and back up these intentions. He uses every refinement of execution and realisation—provided it is in keeping with the emotional requirements of the music. But in using such refinements he takes the greatest care that they shall not interfere with anyone. With this aim in view he does not make extravagant use of his accomplishments, but spends them economically and only where they can be of good effect. He does not always have to know best, and he never forgets that he is an accompanist, and not a soloist. . . . In short, an accompanist of judgment needs a soul full of fine musicianship, including great understanding and great good will.'

2. ACCOMPANYING RECITATIVE

(411) C. P. E. Bach, *Essay*, II, Berlin, 1762, XXXVIII, 2:

'Some recitatives, in which the bass, and possibly other instruments as well, perform a well-defined melodic line or continuous progression which does not share in the singer's pauses, are to be taken in strict time so as to keep them in order. The rest are declaimed according to their content, now slow, now fast, without regard to the measure, even though they are written with bars. In both cases, above all the latter, an accompanist must be attentive. He must listen constantly to the soloist, and when there is dramatic action, watch him too, so as to be always punctual with his accompaniment, for he must never desert his singer.

[3:] 'When the declamation is rapid, the chords must be ready in the instant, particularly at pauses in the solo part where the chord precedes a subsequent entry. When the chord ends, the next one must be played promptly. In this way the singer will not be held back in his expression or in the rapid delivery needed for it; for he will always be warned in good time of the progression and nature of the harmony. If it is necessary to choose between evils, rather hurry than hold back; but indeed better is always better. Arpeggiation is to be avoided in rapid declamation, especially when there are frequent changes of harmony. For one thing, there is no time for it, and even if there were time, it might very easily throw accompanist, singer and audience into confusion. Moreover, arpeggiation is not needed here; its natural use is in quite different contexts, namely slow recitative and sustained chords. In such contexts it helps to remind the singer that he is to remain in the given harmony, and prevents him from losing his pitch through the length of the chord, or from concluding that the chord has changed.

[4:] 'The rapidity with which a chord is arpeggiated depends on the speed and character of the recitative. The slower and more expressive the recitative, the slower the arpeggiation. Recitatives in which the accompanying [ripieno] instruments have sustained parts are well suited by arpeggiation. But so soon as the accompaniment changes from sustained notes to short, detached notes, the accompanist must play short, firm chords, without arpeggiation, and grasped entire in both hands. Even if tied white notes are written in the score, resort must still be had to short, detached playing.

[5:] 'The organ holds only the bass of recitatives accompanied by instruments with sustained parts; it takes off its chords soon after playing them . . . arpeggiation is not used on the organ. Apart from arpeggiation, the other keyboard instruments bring in no ornaments or elaborations when accompanying recitatives.

[7:] 'When a singer departs from the written notes, it is better to play repetitions of a full chord rather than single notes. The right harmony is the main factor in recitative; singers should not be expected to sing nothing but the written notes, especially in passages carelessly composed. It is sufficient if they keep their declamation within the right harmony. . . The reason may be a wish to keep in a comfortable register, or merely a failure of memory.

[8:] 'When completing the arpeggiation of a preparatory chord it is as well to reach the top of the arpeggio with the note on which the singer is to begin [even if this means irregularities in the progressions; but] generally this can be achieved quite easily without any such liberties by means of a rapid arpeggio.'

3. ACCOMPANIMENT AS COMPOSITION

Whether committed to paper or not, the realisation of figured bass is a branch of composition, and one with the very interesting condition attached to it of working to a given pattern and with partly given material. An accompanist who finds himself making small, half-instinctive changes in an editor's part as he goes along, who thins a chord here or changes a detail of figuration there, has already set foot on a fascinating path. He is co-operating with genius, in the person of the composer; in however small a way, he is contributing to a master-piece. He should go further, and learn more or less to improvise his own part.

It is a principle of composition that material should be used economically. If a counter-melody is needed, it is uneconomical and distracting to use entirely new thematic material; something not necessarily imitated from the existing melodies, but at least derived from them, is more concise and effectual. If a good and suitable figure of accompaniment has been established, we shall not change it unnecessarily before it has had time to make its proper effect. One thing must grow out of another; the contrasts must contribute to the underlying unity; the part must sound consistent both with itself and with the written melodies. The less the material, the more inventively we are compelled to develop it; and it is wealth of development, not wealth of material, which enriches a work of art. In these and other ways, we need a composer's ear for what has gone before and his quick grasp of what can most naturally develop out of it.

Francesco Gasparini (*L'Armonico pratico al cimbalo*, Venice, 1708, Engl. tr. p. 42) calls figured bass accompaniment 'improvised composition'; and it ought to sound so. Hence it ought also to sound complete in itself, and not to depend for its completeness on the existing parts which it is accompanying. This is a most useful principle, which experience over and over again substantiates. Good 'voice-leading' can make even the simplest accompaniment sound a convincing and satisfactory entity in its own right. It can then give adequate *musical* support to the existing parts. If it depends upon their presence to make it sound complete, it cannot.

(412) Roger North, Brit. Mus. MS. Add. 32531, *c.* 1710, *f.* 29:

'Altho a man may attain the art to strike the accords true to a thro-base prescribed him according as it is figured, yet he may not pretend to be master of his part, without being a master of composition in general, for there is occasion of so much management in ye manner of play, sometimes striking only by accords, sometimes arpeggiando, sometimes touching ye air, and perpetually observing the emphatick places, to fill, forbear, or adorne, with a just favour, that a thro-base master, and not an ayerist, is but an abecedarian, besides that which is called voluntary, which is a ready touching an air, and perfection of Musick (as is expected) upon every key, will not be done without a mastery of composition.'

BOOK THREE
THE EXPRESSION

PART ONE

GENERAL

CHAPTER XXXIII

Expression in Early Music

1. EXPRESSION A SPONTANEOUS IMPULSE

Expression is the reaction between what a performer brings to the music and what he finds there. If he brings too untrained a conception of the style, he is bound to inflict any number of ingenious wrong interpretations on to it, simply because he does not know the right ones. If he has some training, he can put his knowledge out of his mind and let his own musicianship produce the right expression exactly as it does in the later styles with which he has grown up from childhood. But indeed a generation is already growing up which can take many of the early styles as much for granted as we take the nineteenth-century classics. (See also Chapter III.)

Marks of expression, as opposed to expression, seem (like signs for ornaments) to have been characteristically few in renaissance music; nor did they (as the signs for ornaments did) proliferate during the baroque period. They became gradually commoner through the eighteenth century, plentiful in the nineteenth, almost exaggeratedly so in, for example, Mahler, yet they can never notate more than a fraction of the expression latent in the music and inviting the performer's intuitive response. As in other directions, the baroque musicians preferred to trust to the performer's instincts not as little but as much as possible, and we must always keep the principle in sight: there are fewer expression marks in early music, but there was not less expression.

(413) Giulio Caccini, *Nuove Musiche*, Florence, 1602, Introd., transl. John Playford, *Introduction*, London, 1654, ed. of 1674, p. 40:

'In Encreasing and Abating the Voice, and in Exclamations, is the foundation of Passion. . . . [p. 46:] We see how necessary a certain judgement is for a Musician. . . . [p. 47:] But because there are many things which are used in a good fashion of Singing . . . we use to say of a man that he sings with much Grace, or little Grace.'

375

(414) François Couperin, *L'Art de Toucher le Clavecin*, Paris, 1716, ed. of 1717, preface:

'Experience has taught me that powerful hands capable of performing whatever is most rapid and light are not always those which show to best advantage in tender and expressive pieces, and I declare in all good faith that I am more pleased with what moves me than with what astonishes me.'

(415) Francesco Geminiani, *Treatise of Good Taste*, London, 1749, p. 4:

'And I would besides advise, as well the Composer as the Performer, who is ambitious to inspire his Audience to be first inspired himself, which he cannot fail to be if he chuses a Work of Genius, if he makes himself Thoroughly acquainted with all its Beauties; and if while his Imagination is warm and glowing he pours the same exalted Spirit into his own Performance.'

(416) Charles Avison, *Essay on Musical Expression*, London, 1752, p. 89:

'For, as *Musicall Expression* in the Composer, is succeeding in the Attempt to express some particular Passion; so in the *Performer*, it is to do a *Composition* Justice, by playing it in a *Taste* and *Stile* so exactly corresponding with the Intention of the Composer, as to preserve and illustrate *all* the Beauties of his Work.'

(417) Joachim Quantz, *Essay*, Berlin, 1752, XI, 5:

'The good effect of the music depends almost as much on the performers as on the composers.

[9:] 'Almost every musician has a different expression from that of others. It is not always the different teaching that they have received which causes this variety; the difference of temperament and character also contribute.

[15:] 'The performer of a piece ought to seek out and arouse in himself not only the main feeling but the others which occur. And since in most pieces there is a perpetual interchange of feelings; the performer should know how to judge which is the feeling in each idea, and to govern his expression accordingly.'

(418) C. P. E. Bach, *Essay*, Berlin, 1753, III, 13:

'A musician cannot move others unless he too is moved. He has to feel in himself all the feelings he hopes to rouse in his hearers, for it is the showing of his own emotion which calls up a similar emotion in the hearer.'

CHAPTER XXXIV

Repeats and Omissions

1. REPEATS AND OMISSIONS WITHIN THE PERFORMER'S OPTION

A practical point of some importance to decide before the performance begins is what repeats are to be made, and in the case of suites, which movements are to be included. As we should expect under the free conditions of baroque performance, both these decisions are within the option of the performer, though conventions existed which will influence his choice.

2. REGULAR REPEAT SIGNS A BAROQUE DEVELOPMENT

At the beginning of the baroque period, the dots on one or both sides of a bar-line, single or double, which now indicate a repeat, had not yet acquired this meaning. They were decorative in origin: we find them between double bar-lines or beside them, often more numerous than our customary pair, and in a variety of pleasing patterns. But standing, as they did, at the division between sections which in many instances were regularly repeated as a matter of convention, they took on the function of repeat marks by gradual stages, and by the latter part of the seventeenth century they were established more or less in their normal modern use.

(419) Charles Butler, *Principles of Musik*, London, 1636, p. 37:

'A Repete is either of the same notes and ditty words together, having this mark ˙j˙; or of ditty with other Notes having this mark; :||:, or this, ij: before which the first word of the Repeated ditty is commonly placed under his note or notes: or of a whole Strain [section]; having at the ende thereof 2 prickt Bars bars with dots, through all the Rules [lines].'

In vocal part-books of this period we find Butler's signs, including the double bar with dots to either side, between staves, in the senses he indicates.

(420) John Playford, *Introduction to the Skill of Musick*, London, 1654, ed. of 1674, p. 35:

'2. *Bars* are of two sorts, *single* and *double*. The single Bars serve to divide the Time, according to the Measure of the Semibreve: the double

Bars are set to divide the several Strains or Stanzas of the Songs or Lessons [pieces], and are thus made,

'3. A *Repeat* is thus marked S, and is used to signifie that such a part of a Song or Lesson must be Played or Sung over again from that Note over which it is placed.'

Here the sign which looks most like our modern repeat sign has no such meaning, and a quite different sign is used for the repeat. Other signs of this period which may bear the meaning of repeat signs are various clusters of dots such as ∴ and ⁛ together with a few other patterns; but these may also be the equivalent of ⌒ in its modern sense of a pause (not with its common baroque implication of an ornamental cadenza). We also find 𝄋 and allied forms, both in the modern meaning of the 'segno' (sign) from which a repeat (usually less than a full section in length) is to be made; and as the equivalent of ⌒ meaning a pause with or without ornamentation.

Georg Muffat (*Florilegium I*, Augsburg, 1695, preface) gives ⌐‾‾‾‾‾¬ ⌊_____⌋ for 'first-time' bars.

The next quotation states clearly what most authorities evidently regarded as too obvious and elementary to need stating at all: *i.e.* that in music falling into regular sections, the double bar itself implies a repeat even in the absence of dots before or after it. This confirms what has been said above, that it was not originally the dots which indicated a repeat, but the double bar—or more accurately, the sectional construction itself which the double bars merely helped to make clear, while the dots, in turn, merely ornamented the double bar.

(421) Benjamin Hely, *The Compleat Violist*, London [*c.* 1700], p. 3:

'When you meet with double Bars these show that you are at ye end of the part or Strain, which is to be play'd twice and then to proceed.'

Brossard (*Dictionaire de musique*, Paris, 1703, *s.v.* 'Ripresa'), gives a variety of repeat marks recognisably identifiable with the modern sign, and also two signs not unlike Playford's repeat sign, but in the special sense of the French *Petite Reprise*. This occurs over the last few bars of a section which has already been repeated in its entirety (*Grande Reprise*), when these few bars only are given an additional repeat conventionally taken very softly as an echo effect.

Ex. 189. Sébastien de Brossard, *loc. cit.*, marks (a) for Grande Reprise and (b) for Petite Reprise:

Montéclair (*Petite Methode*, Paris, *c.* 1730, p. 36) gives the following for 'first-time' and 'second-time' bars.

Ex. 190: Michel de Montéclair, *loc. cit.*, repeat sign and continuation:

(422) Joachim Quantz, *Essay*, Berlin, 1752, V, 27:

[Ex. 191 (a)] 'means that the piece has in truth two parts, and that the first ought to be repeated; but that the first should not be repeated, until after having played all the piece from one end to the other. For then one repeats the first part up to the double bar; or what comes to the same thing, up to the note which precedes it, and on which one finds an arc with a dot [*i.e.* ⌒].

[Ex. 191 (b) means] 'that it is necessary to play twice the notes which follow up to another Bar which has the same dots before it [often *Bis* is written].

[Ex. 191 (c) means] 'that the piece has two parts, and that each part must be played twice. But when at the end there are one or two arcs with two dots [Ex. 191 (d)] that signifies that the piece finishes at this point.'

Ex. 191. Quantz, *loc. cit.*, repeat signs, *etc.*:

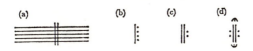

The first paragraph of the above quotation describes the normal *da capo* procedure. The word *bis* in the second paragraph is the Latin for 'twice'. There is nothing in Quantz' account which is any longer inconsistent with modern practice and notation.

3. REPEATS IN DANCES

It was standard practice to repeat the sections of dances, whether so indicated or not.

(423) Thomas Morley, *Plaine and Easie Introduction*, London, 1597, p. 181:

'A pavane . . . most commonly made of three strains, whereof every straine is plaid or sung twice.'

This convention appears to have been universal in renaissance court dancing, and to have continued throughout the baroque period. The convenience of a regular understanding on the point is obvious. The musicians know what to do without being told; the dancers arrange their figures on the same assumption. But in addition there is a natural symmetry in the regular repeats which is as satisfying to the ear as the symmetry of the dance figures is to the eye.

In accompanying renaissance and baroque dances, the repeats must be correctly made. In playing such music purely for its own sake, the same course should be followed. There is no good artistic reason for departing from it.

See also (421) in 2 above.

4. REPEATS IN SECTIONAL MUSIC

Music composed in dance form, but meant to be enjoyed for its own sake and not primarily, if at all, for dancing, may be less symmetrical, in which case the repeats may not so obviously impose themselves as they do where the symmetry of the music conditions our minds to expect a corresponding symmetry in the repeats. But even in long suites it is usually better to make every repeat which the structure of the music itself suggests. The sectional form is part of the effect, and the repeats which belong to it should be treated as emphasising the sectional form. It is usually better to cut movements than to cut repeats, if the total length is felt to be excessive. On the other hand, in many cases the first section in binary form is shorter than the second section: it may then work very well to repeat the first but not the second section.

5. VARIED REPEATS

We have seen in Ch. X, 3 (a) above that more or less impromptu variations were especially favoured at the repeat of a section. It is almost certain that the ornamented versions of the sarabandes in J. S. Bach's English Suites were meant to be used as varied repeats rather than in their entirety after the plain versions.

6. OMITTING MOVEMENTS OR SECTIONS

Suites, sets of variations and even sonatas, were not necessarily meant to be performed complete: many 'suites', indeed, are mere convenient collections of pieces in the same key.

(424) François Couperin, *Concerts Royaux*, Paris, 1722, preface:

'I have composed them [at different times] for the little chamber concerts where Louis Quatorze made me come every Sunday in the year [but for publication] I have arranged them by keys.'

(425) Girolamo Frescobaldi, *Toccate*, Rome, 1615–16, preface, 2:

'In the Toccatas, I have tried not only to provide plenty of diverse passages and expressive effects, but also to arrange the different passages so that they can be performed separately from one another, in such a way that the performer, without being compelled to finish all of them, can stop wherever he prefers.

[Ed. of 1637, 9:] 'The Passacaglias [*i.e.* the variations severally, as seen by the use of the plural *Passachagli* for each set in the Tavola] can be played separately, according as you best wish, adjusting the tempo of the one to the other part (*parte*) [and] likewise with the Chaconnes.'

(426) Francesco Maria Veracini, *Sonate Accademiche*, London and Florence [1744], 'Intentions of the author':

'Each of these 12 sonatas consists of 4 or 5 movements: take notice, that this is done for the enrichment, and adornment of the work, and for the greater entertainment of lovers and connoisseurs of music. Nevertheless 2 or 3 movements chosen at pleasure from each sonata will be sufficient to make up a sonata of satisfactory proportions.'

To insist on every movement of a lengthy suite or every variation of an interminable set is to show a misplaced respect for the composer which would have seemed quite meaningless under baroque conditions. The gain in force and compactness from leaving out the least interesting matter, or indeed simply from reducing the length irrespective of the degree of interest, may make all the difference between losing the attention of the audience and holding it.

POSTSCRIPT TO NEW VERSION

The optional character of repeats and omissions in baroque music is again confirmed, for example, by Loulié's suggestion (*Elements*, Paris, 1696, tr. Albert Cohen, New York, 1965, p. 34) that when a double bar has dots before it, the previous section should (he does not say it must) be repeated; when no dots appear, the previous section need not (he does not say it must not) be repeated.

The only obligation, therefore, comes from the nature of the music as judged by the performer. Considerations both of symmetry and of length may be taken into account; and there is no necessity to make the same choice on different occasions. Good program-building will also affect the choice (*e.g.* not getting too long). A shorter selection, a longer selection, or the entire work may be used at discretion and convenience, whether in suites, in suite-like sonatas, or in sets of variations. Similar liberties may be taken with repeats, whether or not these are marked in the notation, though the natural disposition of dance or dance-like sections (especially if about of the same length) to repeat should not be overlooked.

A good sense of musical balance and proportion is the main guide.

PART TWO

TEMPO

CHAPTER XXXV

Tempo in Early Music

1. TEMPO A VARIABLE QUANTITY

To set a good tempo; to maintain it, flexibly, yet so that the piece ends at the same tempo at which it started; to remember this tempo so as to be able to set it again, within a reasonable margin, at the next performance: these are some of the hardest things in music.

Notation is at its least helpful here. This is not because tempo cannot be recorded in writing, but because, in practice, it is not an absolute but a relative quantity.

The familiar story of Beethoven's irascible inability to believe his own previous metronome markings illustrates very well the fallaciousness of assuming that a good tempo at one performance is a good tempo for every performance. It is not so; there are too many variables which affect the case.

Some of these variables are physical. A room, hall or church with resonant acoustics imposes a slower tempo than one with little echo. Large choirs and orchestras make for a slower tempo than small forces in the same music.

The most important variables, however, are the temperament and the passing mood of the performer. Fine music has depths and shades of meaning which cannot all be fully brought out in the same performance. We can make the most of its brilliant side, of its tender side and so forth, but not all at the same time. Not only may different performers find different affinities in the same music; the same performer may do so at different times. And one of the main changes involved in such changes of interpretation is a change of tempo—as Beethoven discovered.

We have often the impression that a tempo is so exactly right that the least change could only be for the worse. But this is really a compressed statement. What we mean is that the interpretation pleases us so well that none could please us better; and that for this interpretation the tempo is exactly right.

A fast movement taken steadily may gain a breadth of interpretation for which no mere speed can compensate; it may even sound more brilliant. A slow movement may gain more poignancy from being kept well in motion than from being dragged under the illusion of making the most of it. No slow movement should make us *think* of it as slow, nor fast movement as fast. A certain pulse should keep the slow movement alive; a certain ampleness should keep the fast movement from sounding hurried. Yet if these conditions can be met, some very slow speeds can be made to pay dividends by sheer intensity of feeling, and some very fast ones by breath-taking poise and rhythm.

Some movements allow a much narrower margin of tempo than others. Perhaps there is always just one interpretation, and therefore just one tempo, which most musicians will find more convincing than any other; or perhaps interpretation is always relative. In either case, the only way of finding the tempo is by responding to the music itself, with a sensitiveness not given to every musician alike nor to any metronome at all.

2. EARLY TEMPOS ONLY TO BE JUDGED BY GOOD MUSICIANSHIP

(a) Attempts have been made to establish an agreed standard of tempo by relating, for example, the crotchet to the pulse-rate of the human heart (Mersenne, *Harmonie Universelle*, Paris, 1636–7; Simpson, *Compendium*, London, 1665; Quantz, *Essay*, Berlin, 1752), to the tick of a watch (Simpson, *loc. cit.*), to the swing of a pendulum (Galileo, 16th cent.; Mace, *Musick's Monument*, London, 1676; Loulié, *Principes de musique*, Paris, 1696; Tans'ur, *New Musical Grammar*, London, 1746), or merely to time in the abstract ([l'Abbé Laugier] *Apologie de la Musique Françoise* [Paris], 1754). The Maelzel metronome (a compound pendulum of manageable size, actually invented or developed by Winkel) was perfected by 1816, since when we have possessed a reliable and agreed means of notating tempo. But for the reasons given above it is of limited value in practice, and can be misleading if this limitation is not understood.

(427) Anton Bemetzrieder, *Leçons de Clavecin*, Paris, 1771, p. 68:

'Taste is the true metronome.'

For the same reasons, time-words and time-signatures, besides being much vaguer, can be equally misleading. The evidence concerning these in the contemporary authorities is very extensive, and we cannot afford to ignore it; but it is also very contradictory and on the whole very out of touch with practical realities. Indeed, having aired the theories of tempo which seem to have been conventionally expected of them, most authorities warn us that these have not much resemblance to the practice of musicians, and tell us to judge our tempos from the music itself. It is most important to remember this whenever we are puzzled by a time-word or a time-signature, or any other problem of early tempo. We must be guided by the music and not by the notation.

(b) For a seventeenth-century warning of the perpetual tendency of notated time-values to slow down, thus seriously misleading later users, see (564) in Ch. XLII, 2 below. Many modern editors, including some of the best, prefer to halve or even to quarter the note-values of much early music in order to protect the performer from playing what appear to be long notes far too slowly. When the discrepancy between appearance and reality is very wide, this course is desirable in spite of the fact that it can also be misleading, chiefly on the natural pulse of the music. Performers are nearly always to some extent hypnotised by what they see in notation. Ideally they should be able to grasp that a minim in renaissance music was still very nearly what its name (minima nota, 'the smallest note') describes—and play accordingly. Actually the mere sight of breves, semibreves and minims does slow most people down to a funeral pace, which for a gay dance or part-song of the sixteenth century is very damaging. But where, as in much seventeenth-century music, the discrepancy between the apparent and the real note-values is not very wide, to halve the original note-values may easily result in too fast a speed, and it may be better not to make this change.

3. J. S. BACH'S TEMPOS

The following is interesting, since both authors were pupils of J. S. Bach, and one was his most gifted son.

(428) C. P. E. Bach and Johann Friedrich Agricola, joint article in Lorenz Mizler's *Musikalische Bibliothek*, Leipzig, 1739–54, V, iii:

'[J. S. Bach] was very accurate in his conducting and very sure of his tempo, which he usually made very lively.'

That does not, of course, tell us how lively, or when. It does not justify empty speed; but it does tell us not to be afraid of a virtuoso tempo in movements which suggest it. We may set against it J. S. Bach's mention of a 'slow time' in Italy and Germany in the only document directly recording his own teaching on tempo—which seems both brief and perfunctory, as if he had decided that there is not much to be said about tempo; the only way to learn it is through your ears.

(429) J. S. Bach, ? lecture notes taken at dictation in the handwriting of his pupil, Johann Peter Kellner, in a MS. entitled 'Instructions and rules for the playing of a Thorough-Bass . . . by Master John

Sebastian Bach', and most of it copied, presumably with approval, from F. E. Niedt's *Musicalische Handleitung* (Hamburg, 1700); printed complete in Philipp Spitta's *J. S. Bach* (Leipzig, 1873–80, transl. Clara Bell and J. A. Fuller-Maitland, London, 1884–85):

CAP. IV.
OF TIME OR MEASUREMENT

'Of this much need not here be said for it is presupposed that a person wishing to learn figured-bass will not only have learnt the notes but also the intervals before doing so, whether by previous practice of music or from some other cause, and also the differences of time. For no one can inculcate a knowledge of time all at once. This must, however, be noticed, that in the present day one single kind of time is indicated in two ways, thus: **C2**, the second way being used by the French in pieces that are to be played quickly or briskly, and the Germans adopting it from the French. But the Germans and Italians abide for the most part by the first method, and adopt a slow time. If the piece is to be played fast the composer expressly adds *Allegro* or *Presto* to it; if slowly, the pace is indicated by the word *Adagio* or *Lento*.'

(430) Joachim Quantz, *Essay*, Berlin, 1752, XVII, vii, 52:

'The sense of the words should be taken into account, the movement of the notes, especially the fastest, and in quick arias the skill and the voice of the singer. A singer who pushes his quick passages with his chest can scarcely take them as fast as one who only sings them from his throat, though the first will always excel the second in clarity, particularly in a large place. . . .

[53:] 'It is the same with church music as it is with arias; except that both expression and tempo should be more restrained than in opera, to show respect for the sacredness of the place.'

CHAPTER XXXVI

Time-Words

1. TIME-WORDS IMPLY BOTH MOOD AND TEMPO

Time-words are notoriously vague. They often relate strictly to mood, not to tempo: *e.g.* largo (broadly), grave (gravely), adagio (at ease), maestoso (with majesty), allegro (cheerfully), *etc.* Tempo is a function of mood, rather than the other way about.

(431) A. Malcolm, *Treatise of Musick*, Edinburgh, 1721, p. 394:

'Time . . . is a various and undetermined thing . . . tho' the same Notes of *Time* are of the same Measure in any one Piece, yet in different Pieces they differ very much, and the Differences are in general marked by the Words *slow, brisk, swift, etc.*, written at the Beginning; but these are still uncertain Measures, since there are different Degrees of *slow* and *swift*; and indeed the true Determination of them must be learnt by Experience from the Practice of Musicians.'

(432) Joachim Quantz, *Essay*, Berlin, 1752, XI, 15:

'There are indeed various degrees of liveliness and sadness, for example in a furious mood an expression is needed which has more fire than in a witty piece, although both the one and the other ought to be lively.

'[16: The prevailing mood can be judged (1) by the mode—major or minor; (2) by the intervals—close or leaping; (3) by the discords—mild or harsh; (4) by] the word found at the beginning of the piece, such as: Allegro, Allegro non tanto . . . *etc.* All these words, provided they are not put without reason, demand each the use of a particular expression and moreover, as we have already said, since each piece of the kinds described can include a mixture of pathetic, tender, gay, sublime and witty thoughts, each must therefore be given, so to speak, another mood, to be sometimes sad, sometimes gay, sometimes serious, *etc.*, the which interplay is absolutely necessary in music.

[17:] 'Each [performer] ought in this respect to conform to his temperament and know how to guide it suitably.

[XII, 2:] 'Since many composers put these words above mentioned more from habit than to characterise well the true movement of the pieces, and to assist the knowledge of their true time for those who render them; there are many cases where they cannot be used for guidance, and where it is necessary to divine the intention of the composer more from the content of the piece than from the word which is found at the head to indicate its movement.

[11:] 'Whatever speed an Allegro demands, it ought never to depart from a controlled and reasonable movement. For everything that is hurried, causes the ear more pain than satisfaction. The object must always be the feeling which is to be expressed, never only to play fast.

[24:] 'The mood often changes as much in Allegro as in Adagio.

'[XVII, i, 6: it is for the composer] to leave it to the player of the principal part to take the time which he judges suitable.'

(433) C. P. E. Bach, *Essay*, Berlin, 1753, III, 10:

'The tempo of a piece, which is usually indicated by a variety of familiar Italian terms, is derived from its general mood together with the fastest notes and passages which it includes. Proper attention to these considerations will prevent an allegro from being hurried and an adagio from being dragged.'

(434) Leopold Mozart, *Violinschule*, Augsburg, 1756, I, ii, 7:

'It is true that special words are written at the start of each piece which are supposed to give its character, such as Allegro (lively), Adagio (slow) and so forth. But both slow and fast have their gradations, and even if the composer tries to describe more plainly the speed required by adding further adjectives and other words, it still remains impossible for him to describe accurately the speeds he wants for the performance of the music. Thus it must be inferred from the music itself, and this is what infallibly shows the true quality of a musician. Every melodic piece includes one phrase at least from which the variety of tempo needed by the music can be clearly recognised. This phrase, if other considerations are taken into account, often compels one into its own natural speed. Bear this in mind, but also realise that for this sort of intuition long experience and fine sensibility are required. Who will contradict me if I regard this as among the highest accomplishments in the art of music?'

The above quotations confirm that we should let the music suggest its own tempo even if this appears to be contradicted by the time-word.

They also warn us at (432, 11) and (433) against one of the commonest mistakes in the interpretation of early music: taking slow movements too slow and fast movements too fast. *Most baroque slow movements need to go faster and most baroque fast movements need to go slower than first thoughts may suggest.*

2. EARLY BAROQUE TIME-WORDS

We find tardo (slow), presto (fast) in Biagio Marini (*Sonatas, etc.*, Venice, 1626) and others; 'long', 'slow', 'away' in Orlando Gibbons (fantasies, Christ Church, Oxford, MSS. 732–5, early 17th cent.) and subsequent English sources. The number of such words increased later in the seventeenth century, until our familiar vocabulary became developed—particularly in Italian and French.

3. LATER BAROQUE TIME-WORDS

Considerable discrepancies will be noticed in the order of speed given in the following lists. We find, too, inconsistent time-words in different contemporary copies of the same piece, and even in different part-books of the same edition. This was not because tempo was regarded as unimportant, but because, as usual, the performer was expected to use his judgment with a minimum of textual help.

The entries from Brossard and Grassineau occur, of course, in their alphabetical positions in the dictionaries concerned. For ease of comparison, they are shown here, like the others, in ascending order of speed so far as this is shown by the descriptions. Leopold Mozart's list, with its valuable hints on style, is also shown here in ascending order of speed, for the same reason; but unlike most such lists, his is shown by the original edition in descending order of speed. The reader who wishes to read this list in its original order should therefore start with the last entry as shown here, and work his way backwards to the beginning. The same applies to Rellstab's list.

(435) Henry Purcell, *Sonnata's of III Parts*, London, 1683, preface:

'Adagio and Grave . . . import nothing but a very slow movement: *Presto Largo*, *Poco Largo*, or *Largo* by it Self, a middle movement.'

(436) Sébastien de Brossard, *Dictionaire de musique*, Paris, 1703:

'LARGO . . . VERY SLOW, as if *enlarging* the measure and making the main beats often unequal, *etc.*

'ADAGIO ADAGIO means very slow.

'ADAGIO . . . COMFORTABLY, *at your ease, without pressing on*, thus almost always *slow* and dragging the speed a little.

'LENTO means SLOWLY, *heavily*, not at all *lively* or *animated*.

'AFFETTO, or *con Affetto*. This is the same as *Affettuosò* or *Affettuosamente*, which means FEELINGLY *tenderly* and thus nearly always *Slow*.

'ANDANTE . . . *to stroll with even steps*, means above all for Basso Continuos, that all the Notes must be made equal, and the Sounds well separated.

'ALLEGRETTO diminutive of *Allegro*, means RATHER GAILY, but with a gracious, pretty, blithe gaiety.

'ALLEGRO . . . always GAY, and *decidedly lively*; very often quick and light; but also at times with a *moderate* speed, yet *gay*, and *lively*.

'ALLEGRO ALLEGRO marks an intensification of *gaiety* or of *liveliness, etc.*

'PRESTO means, FAST. That is to say the speed must be pressed on, by making the beats very short.

'PRESTO PRESTO or *Prestissimo*. Means, very quick.'

(437) Alexander Malcolm, *Treatise of Musick*, Edinburgh, 1721, p. 395:

'*Grave, adagio, largo, vivace, allegro, presto*, and sometimes *prestissimo*. The first expresses the slowest Movement, and the rest gradually quicker; but indeed they leave it altogether to Practice to determine the precise Quantity.'

(438) James Grassineau, *Musical Dictionary*, London, 1740 (the following entries are not, like most of this work, taken from Brossard's *Dictionaire*, Paris, 1703, for which see above):

'ADAGIO . . . expresses a slow time, slowest of any except grave [British Museum copy corrected in ink by Dr. Burney to "the slowest of any"].
'ALLEGRO . . . brisk, lively, gay and pleasant . . . yet without precipitation.
'LARGO, a slow movement, *i.e.* one degree quicker than grave, and two than adagio.
'LENTE, or LENTAMENTE, signifies a slow movement, much the same as *largo*.
'LENTO, the same as *lente*.
'CANZONE, in general signifies a song, wherein some little fugues are introduced. . . . If played in any part of a Sonata, it signifies much the same as Allegro, and only denotes that the part to which it is prefixed is to play or sing in a brisk and lively manner.
'PRESTO, *fast* or *quick, gayly yet not with rapidity*. PRESTISSIMO, is extreamly quick, hastily, with fury.'

(439) Leopold Mozart, *Violinschule*, Augsburg, 1756, I, iii, 27:

'GRAVE, sadly and earnestly, hence very slow indeed.
'LARGO, a still slower tempo [than Adagio Pesante], must be played with long bow-strokes and with much tranquillity.
'ADAGIO PESANTE, a sad Adagio, must be played somewhat slower [than Adagio], and dragging.
'ADAGIO, slow.
'ANDANTE, going (gehend). This word itself tells us that one must give the piece its natural gait (Gang); especially when MA UN POCO ALLEGRETTO occurs with it.
'MAESTOSO, with majesty, deliberately, not hurried.
'SOSTENUTO means sustained, or rather held back and the melody not exaggerated. One must also make use of earnest, long and sustained bow-strokes in such cases, and hold on to the melody in a very legato manner (den Gesang wohl aneinanderhängen).
'TEMPO COMMODO and TEMPO GIUSTO lead us in the same way [as

Moderato] back to the piece itself. They tell us that we must play the piece neither too fast nor too slow, but in a suitable, convenient and natural tempo. We must therefore look for the true pace of such a piece in the piece itself.

'MODERATO, moderately, temperately; not too quick and not too slow. This again the piece itself must show us, we must become sensible of the moderation during the course of it.

'VIVACE means lively, and SPIRITOSO says that we should play with intelligence and spirit, and ANIMOSO is almost the same. All three kinds stand midway between fast and slow, as to which the piece of music bearing these words must itself show us more.

'ALLEGRETTO is somewhat slower than ALLEGRO, has usually something agreeable, something pretty and playful, and has much in common with ANDANTE. It must therefore be performed prettily, lightly and playfully: which prettiness and playfulness can be as clearly indicated, in this as in other tempos, by the word GUSTOSO.

'ALLEGRO, MA NON TANTO, or NON TANTO, or MODERATO, which is to say that one must not exaggerate the speed. For this a lighter and more lively, yet at the same time somewhat more earnest and broader bowing is required than in a quicker tempo.

'ALLEGRO which indeed shows a gay, but not hurried tempo; especially when it is moderated by adjectives and adverbs [as above].

'MOLTO ALLEGRO is somewhat less than ALLEGRO ASSAI, but is still faster than [the foregoing].

'PRESTO means fast, and ALLEGRO ASSAI is very little different.

'PRESTISSIMO shows the fastest tempo, and PRESTO ASSAI is almost the same. For this rapid time a light and somewhat shorter stroke is needed.'

(440) J.-B. Cartier, *L'Art du Violon*, Paris [1798], list of speeds in ascending order:

'Largo, Larghetto, Adagio, Grave, Andante, Andantino, Grazioso, Affectuoso, Amoroso, Moderato, Tempo Giusto, Maestoso, Allegro, Allegretto, Allegro Molto, Allegro con moto, Allegro Agitato, Allegro Spiritoso, Allegro assai, Vivace, Presto, Presto assai, Prestissimo.'

The following requires special attention.

(441) Sébastien de Brossard, *Dictionaire de Musique*, Paris, 1703:

'ASSAI . . . which the Italians often join with *Allegro, Adagio, Presto etc.*, means, according to some, MUCH; and according to others that neither the measure nor the tempo should be carried to excess, but that a judicious *mean* of slowness, and of rapidity should be preserved, according to the different impressions it is necessary to convey.'

4. METRONOME EQUIVALENT FOR TIME-WORDS

Quantz (*Essay*, Berlin, 1752, Ch. XVII, Sect. vii, 49 *ff.*) illustrates his scheme for measuring tempo by the human pulse (treated as averaging

80 per minute) by giving four, later increased to five groups of time-words. These are not actual tempos, but averages for teaching purposes. They do not seem altogether realistic.

TABLE VII

M.M. numbers based on Quantz

I: Allegro assai (including Allegro molto, Presto, *etc.*)   ♩ = 160

II: Allegro (including Poco Allegro, Vivace, *etc.*)   ♩ = 120

III: Allegretto (including Allegro ma non tanto, non troppo, non presto, moderato, *etc.*)   ♩ = 80

IV: Adagio cantabile (including Cantabile, Arioso, Larghetto, Soave, Dolce, Poco Andante, Affettuoso, Pomposo, Maestoso, Alla Siciliana, Adagio spiritoso, *etc.*)   ♩ = 40

V: Adagio assai (including Adagio pesante, Lento, Largo assai, Mesto, Grave, *etc.*)   ♩ = 20

The above values are 'in Common time'.
Double the speed 'in Alla breve time'.

Quantz (*loc. cit.*) gives the same theoretical but unreal distinction of 'full time or alla breve' for triple time, where it corresponds to C or ₵ set before numerical triple-time signatures: see Chapter XXXVIII, 5 below.

POSTSCRIPT TO NEW VERSION

French time-words were equally inconsistent, but likewise meant in the main to have significance for tempo as well as for mood.

(442) Michael de Saint-Lambert, *Accompagnement*, Paris, 1707, p. 25:

'The Signs [time-signatures], then, only indicate the tempo (*mouvement*) of the Pieces very imperfectly; and Musicians [therefore often add] certain of these words, *lentement, gravement, legereement* [*sic*], *gayement, vite, forte vite,* and the like, to supplement thereby the powerlessness of the Sign, to express their intention.'

But Jean-Jacques Rousseau (*Dictionnaire*, Paris, 1768, 'Chaconne') also spoke of passing 'from *grave* to *gai*, or from *tendre* to *vif*, without increasing or decreasing the speed of the beat'. Thus, for example, Couperin's wonderfully poetical *Les Baricades Mistérieuses* (*Pièces*, [1717]) need not be taken faster than the very steady tempo to which the music points, merely because it is headed *vivement*.

CHAPTER XXXVII

Dance Tempos

1. DANCE-TITLES AS GUIDES TO TEMPO

(a) Dance steps can only be performed correctly within narrow margins of speed. It is thus possible to discover the tempo of a dance by actually reconstructing it and dancing it. For pioneer work in this direction, see my Bibliography under Mabel Dolmetsch and John Guthrie. See also Imogen Holst, George Houle.

It must, however, be remembered that both the steps and the figures of a dance may have varied widely, sometimes almost unrecognisably, at different times and places; and with them, the tempo.

It must further be remembered that dances which have once left the dance-floor and become musical forms in their own right almost inevitably undergo some modification, and usually a considerable transformation. They tend to slow down as well as growing more flexible in rhythm. Their style may be more sophisticated, their figuration more elaborate, their mood more introspective. A Sarabande by J. S. Bach must clearly be interpreted in the light of its own context, not as it might be if it were a mere background for dancing.

(443) Ch. Burney, *Music in Germany*, London, 1773, I, p. 162:

'[This Polish nobleman] would gladly give me a specimen of the [violin] music of his country, as it depended so much on the *coup d'archet*, that seeing it on paper, without hearing it performed, would afford but a very imperfect idea of it.

'[The Pole added that] the kind of music which we call Polonaise, is played quicker for dancing than at other times.'

(b) The fluctuations of the commoner dances and dance-forms can be followed to some extent in the following quotations, which are taken from Thomas Morley (*Plaine and Easie Introduction*, London, 1597, ed. of 1952, pp. 296 *ff*; Thomas Mace, *Musick's Monument*, London, 1676, pp. 129 *ff*.); James Talbot (manuscript notes, Christ Church, Oxford, MS. 1187, *c*. 1690); Ch. Masson (*Nouveau Traité*, 2nd ed., Paris, 1699, pp. 7 *ff*.); Sébastien de Brossard (*Dictionaire de Musique*, Paris, 1703); Johann Gottfried Walther (*Musicalisches Lexicon*, Leipzig, 1732); Jean-Jacques Rousseau (in the Encyclopedia of Diderot and d'Alembert, Paris. 1751–65, *s.v.* 'Minuet', repeated almost verbatim in his own *Dictionnaire de Musique*, Paris, 1768, *s.v.* 'Minuet'); Joachim Quantz (*Essay*, Berlin, 1752, XVII, vii, 58).

See also Ch. XXXVIII below for further references to dance tempos.

2. THE ALMAIN (ALLEMANDE, ETC.)

Two main forms, an earlier and more rapid, and a later and more steady (as in J. S. Bach).

(444) Morley, *loc. cit.*, 1597:

'The Alman is a more heavie daunce than [the Galliard] (fitlie representing the nature of the [German] people, whose name it carrieth), so that no extraordinarie motions are used in dauncing of it.'

(445) Mace, *loc. cit.*, 1676:

'*Allmaines*, are *Lessons* very *Ayrey*, and *Lively*; and Generally of Two Strains, of the *Common*, or *Plain-Time*.'

(446) Talbot, *loc. cit.*, *c.* 1690:

'Almain so called from Almaine or Germany from whence it came, this is sett in Common the same time as the Pavan, but its movement is somewhat quicker and more Airy.'

(447) Brossard, *op. cit.*, 1703, 3rd ed. [1707?]:

'Allemanda grave symphony, usually in two time, often in four.'

(448) Walther, *loc. cit.*, 1732:

'Allemanda . . . is a serious and dignified movement and should be so performed.'

3. THE AYRE

Not a dance-form, but very like one in seventeenth-century England: also developed to a serious polyphonic movement associated with the fantasy for viols, and in this shape often profoundly beautiful, yet always with an 'ayery', *i.e.* a lyrical quality.

(449) Mace, *loc. cit.*, 1676:

'*Ayres*, are, or should be, of the *same Time* [as Allmaines] . . . only they differ from *Allmaines*, by being commonly *Shorter*, and of a more *Quick, and Nimble* Performance [but some Ayres are slow].'

4. THE BRAWL (BRANLE, BRANDO, ETC.)

A generic name for a large species of renaissance round dances, with stamping of the feet.

(450) Morley, *loc. cit.*, 1597:

'Like unto [the Alman] is the French Bransle (which they call *branle simple*) which goes somewhat rounder in time than this, otherwise the measure is all one.

'The bransle de Poictou or bransle double is more quick in time.'

5. THE BOURRÉE

A dance of which the movement resembles the gavotte, but with a pronounced pulse of two in the bar, whereas the gavotte has four.

(451) Talbot, *loc. cit.*, c. 1690:

'Borée [one of five] French Measures of a very quick and rapid Movement.'

(452) Masson, *loc. cit.*, 1699:

'Bourée and Rigaudon, quicker [than Gavotte].'

(453) Quantz, *loc. cit.*, 1752:

'Bourrée and Rigaudon played gayly and with a short and light bow-stroke. Each bar has one beat of the [human] pulse.'

6. THE CANARIES

A quick dance with a forthright dotted rhythm like an English jig.
(454) Talbot, *loc. cit.*, c. 1690:

'[Same as for Borée, above] very quick and rapid movement.'

(455) Masson, *loc. cit.*, 1699:

'Canaries a little quicker than Gigue.'

(456) Quantz, *loc. cit.*, 1752:

'The Gigue and the Canarie have the same movement. If written in 6-8 time, each bar has one [human] pulse beat. . . . In the Canarie, which consists always of dotted notes, the bowing is short and sharp.'

7. THE COURANTE (CORANTO, ETC.)

A dance with both duple-time and triple-time variants, of which the former did not persist.

Of the triple-time variants, there are two sub-variants whose differences are important.

The Italian coranto is quick, and normally straightforward in rhythm: literally 'running'.

The French courante has a much more sophisticated rhythm, with a very characteristic alternation of simple with compound triple time (mainly 3–2 and 6–4). To make this rhythm effective, a steady tempo and a pointed style are needed: no longer 'running' in the literal sense.

(457) Morley, *loc. cit.*, 1597:

'Like unto [the bransle double] be the voltes and courantes which being both of a measure, are notwithstanding daunced after sundrie fashions . . . the courante travising [traversing, *i.e.* crossing] and running [whence the name].'

(458) Mace, *loc. cit.*, 1676:

'*Corantoes*, are *Lessons* of a *Shorter Cut* [than Galliards], and of a *Quicker Triple-Time*; commonly of 2 *Strains*, and full of *Sprightfulness*, and *Vigour, Lively, Brisk*, and *Cheerful*.'

(459) Masson, *loc. cit.*, 1699:

'Courante [is taken] steadily (gravement).'

(460) Walther, *loc. cit.*, 1732:

'The measure of the Courante or rather the rhythm of the Courante dance is the most solemn of any [an exaggeration; but the contrast of this slow French courante with the quick Italian coranto is instructive].'

(461) Quantz, *loc. cit.*, 1752:

'The Courante [is] performed with majesty, and the bow is detached at each crotchet, whether there is a dot or not. Count one beat of the [human] pulse for each crotchet.'

8. THE CHACONNE

Not consistently differentiated from the Passacaille, and indeed works are found which bear one heading in one source and the other in another source. Bibliothèque Nationale, Paris, Rés. Vm⁷. 675, *ff.* 57v has 'Chaconne or Passacaille of Mr. [Louis] Couperin'. A lilting triple time is common to both (except for a very rare and untypical duple-time variant); but the actual tempo required not only differs in different specimens, but in some of the more freely-worked and elaborate specimens, *if not meant to be danced*, may need to be varied in course of the work. See below under Passacaille.

(462) Masson, *loc. cit.*, 1699:

'The Chaconne [is taken] lightly (legerement).'

(463) Quantz, *loc. cit.*, 1752:

'A Chaconne is also [like the Sarabande] performed with majesty. One beat of the [human] pulse goes for two crotchets.'

9. THE ENTRÉE

Besides its more general meaning of introduction, the word was used as follows.

(464) Walther, *loc. cit.*, 1732:

'The Entrée is a serious melody with two strains, for instruments only . . . taken with two beats in the bar and used for dance or theatre music.'

(465) Quantz, *loc. cit.*, 1752:

'[Same as for Courante above.]'

10. THE FURY

(466) Quantz, *loc. cit.*, 1752:

'A Furie is played with great fire. Count one beat of the [human] pulse for two crotchets, whether in Common or in Triple Time.'

(467) John Hoyle, *Dictionary of Music*, London, 1770:

'FURIA, or CON FURIA, is with fury and violence, and is to be understood not so much with respect to the loudness of the sound, as to the quickness of the time or movement.'

11. THE GALLIARD (SALTARELLO, CINQUE-PAS, ETC.)

In the ballroom, the Galliard was paired with the Pavan, and it often is so paired as a musical form.

The Pavan was the main ceremonial entry of the ball during the sixteenth century. It is a processional dance in which the entire company took part, with dignified, slightly swaying steps in a stately rhythm of four in a bar. But the Galliard which followed was intended only, as a display of agility and skill, for the younger and more energetic members of the party. Its steps are vigorous, and may be elaborated almost to the virtuosity of a ballet solo (including *entrechats*). It is therefore commonly described as more brisk and lively than the Pavan.

This description has given rise to a misconception. Modern writers have frequently stated that the tempo of the Galliard is faster than the tempo of the Pavan; but ordinarily the tempo remains nearly or quite the same, each of the four time-units in one bar of the Pavan being similar to each of the three time-units in one bar of the Galliard: *i.e.* the pulse keeps nearly the same speed as before, in triple time. What changes is the dance, not the pulse. The dancer moves faster though the music does not. He has now to fit many complex movements into the same time which in the Pavan was occupied with one simple movement, and if the music were much increased in speed he would not be able to perform them at all. The Galliard, in fact, is a rapid dance with a moderate pulse.

Even away from the ballroom these considerations apply: no Galliard is intended for a rapid tempo. Indeed, when there is no dancer and no steps to fit in, there may still be musical variations of such rapidity that any increase in speed would make them an absurdity if not an impossibility.

(468) Morley, *loc. cit.*, 1597:

'After every pavan we usually set a Galliard . . . This is a lighter and more stirring kinde of dauncing than the pavane.'

(469) Mace, *loc. cit.*, 1676:

'*Galliards*, are *Lessons* of 2 or 3 *Strains*, but are perform'd in a *Slow, and Large Triple-Time*; and (commonly) *Grave, and Sober.*'

(470) Talbot, *loc. cit.*, c. 1690:

'Galiard so called from Gallia or France, where it was first used [this etymology is incorrect; the derivation is from Fr. gaillard, "a young gallant"], a lofty Frolic Movement suitable to the gay temper of the Nation, is properly set in a pretty brisk Triple [but see my explanation above].'

(471) Masson, *loc. cit.*, 1699:

'Galliards [are taken] lightly (legerement).'

12. THE GAVOTTE

The pulse of the gavotte is a fairly rapid four in a bar.
(472) Talbot, *loc. cit.*, c. 1690:

'[Same as for Borée, above] very quick and rapid movement.'

(473) Masson, *loc. cit.*, 1699:

'Gavottes [are taken] lightly (legerement).'

(474) Quantz, *loc. cit.*, 1762:

'A Gavotte is almost equal to a Rigaudon; it has, however, a steadier movement.'

13. THE HORNPIPE

Another dance of which the musical pulse is steadier than the steps.
(475) Talbot, *loc. cit.*, c. 1690:

'Horn-pipe, [one of] two very nimble Movements peculiar to the English race . . .'

14. THE JIG (GIGUE, ETC.)

(476) Talbot, *loc. cit.*, *c.* 1690:

'[Same as for Horn-pipe, above.]'

(477) Walther, *loc. cit.*, 1732:

'Giga . . . a rapid English dance.'

(478) Quantz, *loc. cit.*, 1752:

'The Gigue and the Canarie have the same movement. If written in 6–8 time, each bar as one [human] pulse beat. . . . The Gigue is played with a short and crisp bow–stroke.'

15. THE LOURE

(479) Brossard, *op. cit.*, 1703, 3rd ed. [1707?]:

'Loure . . . ordinarily written under the measure of 6–4 and beaten *slowly* and *gravely* and marking the first beat of each bar more perceptibly than the second.'

(480) Walther, *loc. cit.*, 1732:

'Loure . . . a piece or dance, usually set in 6–4, to be taken in a dignified and slow fashion. The first note of each half bar has a dot, which is to be well prolonged.'

(481) Quantz, *loc. cit.*, 1752:

'[Same as for Courante, above.]'

16. THE MARCH

(482) Talbot, *loc. cit.*, *c.* 1690:

'March, a lively martial Movement.'

(483) Quantz, *loc. cit.*, 1752:

'A March is played seriously.'

17. THE MINUET

The Minuet has little in common with the Branle de Poitou, from which it has been derived by writers from Praetorius onwards, but a great deal in common with the Galliard, of which it is more likely to be a development (in the mid-seventeenth century). For no very clear reason it is often thought, especially by theatrical producers, to have been a vague, mincing, ceremonious and over-refined dance of courtly decadence; but none of this is true. The Minuet has very well-defined steps and figures, and is by no means lethargic. Its earlier versions were more vigorous than its later versions, but it never resembled the bowing and scraping and aimless shifting with which the modern stage has seen fit to caricature it.

Where two minuets are placed in succession, the direction '[First] Menuet da capo' is sometimes found; and this is normally the intention, even when the direction does not appear. The second minuet may be in the minor of the same key of which the first minuet is in the major; and in any case, the *da capo* is part of the design.

(484) Talbot, *loc. cit., c.* 1690:

'[Same as for Borée, above] very quick and rapid movement.'

(485) Brossard, *loc. cit.*, 1703:

'Minuet . . . a very lively dance; which comes originally from Poitou [but see above]. One ought in imitation of the Italians to use the sign 3–8 or 6–8 to mark the movement, which is always *very gay* and *very fast*; but the custom of marking it by a simple 3 or *triple crotchet* time has prevailed.'

(486) Masson, *loc. cit.*, 1699:

'The Minuet [is] quick.'

(487) Jean-Jacques Rousseau, *loc. cit.*, 1751–65 (but cited from *op. cit.*, 1768):

'According to [Brossard] this dance is very gay and its movement is very quick. But on the contrary the character of the Minuet is grave and a noble simplicity; the movement of it is rather moderate than quick, and one might say that the least gay of all the kinds of dance used in our balls is the Minuet. It is another matter in the theatre.'

(488) Quantz, *loc. cit.*, 1752:

'The Menuet is played in such a fashion that it almost carries or lifts the dancer up, and one marks the crotchets with a somewhat heavy, yet short, stroke of the bow. Count one [human] pulse beat for two crotchets.'

18. THE MUSETTE

This dance undoubledly derives its character from the beautiful species of bagpipe known by the same name, and extremely fashionable at the French court and in French polite society generally during the seventeenth and eighteenth centuries. The most conspicuous feature of the Musette as a musical form is its drone harmony.

(489) Quantz, *loc. cit.*, 1752:

'A Musette is given a very caressing expression. Count one beat of the [human] pulse for each crotchet in 3–4 but for each quaver in 3–8. Sometimes certain dancers take it into their heads to have it played so fast that there is only one beat of the [human] pulse to a whole bar.'

19. THE PASSACAILLE (PASSACAGLIA)

See above under Chaconne; the two were often confused in theory and sometimes interchangeable in musical practice, and the evidence *contrasting* them is therefore to be viewed with considerable caution.

(490) Talbot, *loc. cit.*, c. 1690:

'The Passacaille [is taken] gravely (gravement). The Chaconne [is taken] lightly (legerement) [but see my remark above].'

(491) Walther, *loc. cit.*, 1732:

'Passacaglio . . . actually is a Chaconne. The sole difference lies in its being played more slowly . . . and with a less vigorous expression [A translation of Brossard's entry, *loc. cit.*].'

(492) Quantz, *loc. cit.*, 1752:

'A Passecaille is equivalent to a Chaconne, but is played a little faster [the opposite view].' [See Postscript to New Version at end of Chapter.]

20. THE PASSEPIED (PASPY)

As a dance, this is virtually a Minuet taken at a faster speed, as a result of which it is easier to dance (because balance is easier).

(493) Talbot, *loc. cit.*, c. 1690:

'[Same as for Borée, above] very quick and rapid movement.'

(494) Masson, *loc. cit.*, 1699:

'The Passepied [is taken] very quick.'

(495) Quantz, *loc. cit.*, 1752:

'A Passepied is played a little more lightly and quickly than a Menuet.'

21. THE PAVAN

See under Galliard, above. The pulse of a Pavan is a very steady four in a bar. The dance scarcely survived, at least in fashionable circles, into the baroque period, but the form did, and a great many attractive specimens appear in the manuscripts of the English chamber music of the viols during the first half of the seventeenth century. The quiet polyphony of the best of these is among the most beautiful work of the school.

The spellings of the word are very various (pavan, paven, pavin, pavane, *etc.*), but, in English, the correct pronunciation is always păvn. The pronunciation pavāne is French.

(496) Morley, *loc. cit.*, 1597:

'A pavane, a kind of staide musicke, ordained for grave dauncing.'

(497) Mace, *loc. cit.*, 1676:

'*Pavines*, are *Lessons* of 2, 3 or 4 *Strains*, very *Grave*, and *Sober*; *Full of Art, and Profundity*, but seldom us'd, in These our *Light Days*.'

(498) Talbot, *loc. cit., c.* 1690:

'Pavan . . . a grave and stately Movement sett in common time, and consisting of 3 strains, this is not now so much in use as formerly.'

22. THE RIGAUDON (RIGADOON)

A dance of very characteristic quality with a swinging pulse of two in a bar; often the melody is less jerky than a bourrée and has a longer span.

(499) Masson, *loc. cit.*, 1699:

'Bourée and Rigaudon [are] quicker than [Gavottes and Galliards].'

(500) Quantz, *loc. cit.*, 1752:

'A Bourrée and a Rigaudon are played gayly and with a short and light stroke of the bow. Each bar has one beat of the [human] pulse.'

23. THE RONDEAU (RONDO)

The pulse of the baroque Rondeau may be two or three in a bar.
(501) Quantz, *loc. cit.*, 1752:

'A Rondeau is played with a certain serenity, and one beat of the [human] pulse makes almost two crotchets, either in the Allabreve or in the 3–4.'

24. THE SARABAND

The original dance has sinuous and complicated movements, and had a general reputation for lasciviousness. As a musical form, the slow Saraband requires considerable intensity of feeling, often of a sensuous variety. The quick Saraband is piquant and virile. J. S. Bach's Sarabandes, which are slow, include some of his most impassioned harmony combined with a contemplative inwardness which is perhaps unique; but some of the French Sarabandes approach them very nearly, and in the same mood. The very quick English Sarabands of the mid-seventeenth century, with their taut rhythm and nervous energy, are so different as to be for all practical purposes another form; they have one pulse to each triple-time bar. The following quotations refer to Sarabands of different speeds.

(501a) Phillips, *et al.* eds., *The New World of Words*, London, 1658, *s.v.* 'Saraband':

[Eds. 1–4:] 'Lesson or Air in Musick going with a quick time.
'[Fifth Ed. of 1696, partly revised by Purcell, leaves out the tempo definition. The B.M. copy of the 1st ed., owned by Rd. Kendall in 1719, has a hand-written correction of "a quick time" to "a slow time"— particularly interesting evidence of a changing usage.]'

(502) Mace, *loc. cit.*, 1676:

'*Serabands*, are of the *Shortest Triple-Time*; but are more *Toyish*, and *Light*, than *Corantoes*; and commonly of Two *Strains*.'

(503) Talbot, *loc. cit.*, c. 1690:

'Saraband a soft passionate Movement, always set in a slow Triple . . . apt to move the Passions and to disturb the tranquillity of the Mind.'

(504) Masson, *loc. cit.*, 1699:

'The Saraband [is taken] gravely (gravement).'

(505) Quantz, *loc. cit.*, 1752:

'The Sarabande has the same tempo [as the Entrée, the Loure and the Courante], but is played with a rather more flattering expression.'

25. THE TAMBOURIN

The name derives from *Tambour* or tabor (drum), since in its Provençal origins the dance was accompanied by a pipe and tabor. Its characteristic feature is a certain remorseless ferocity of rhythm, in which the beats of a drum partake when the music is orchestrated, and must be counterfeited when no drum is present. The pulse is a quick two in a bar.

(506) Quantz, *loc. cit.*, 1752:

'A Tambourin is played like a Bourrée or Rigaudon, only a little faster.'

26. THE VOLTA

A late sixteenth-century dance particularly fashionable at the court of Elizabeth in England; she was portrayed dancing it with Robert Dudley, Earl of Leicester, who died in 1588. The painting is at Penshurst

Place, Kent. It shows the typical movement of the dance, by which the woman leaps with a turning motion, assisted by the man's hands on her waist, at each climax of the tune. To do this properly requires perfect timing from the dancers, and a very exact tempo from the musicians. This tempo is, in effect, a two-pulse 6–4 rhythm of a very steady speed, but with a crotchet unit, and therefore faster than the galliard, which has a minim unit (3–2). But there is the same impression of an unexpectedly slow pulse supporting a very energetic dance.

(507) Morley, *loc. cit.*, 1597:

'Like unto [the bransle double] (but more light) be the voltes and courantes which being both of a measure, are notwithstanding daunced after sundrie fashions, the volte rising and leaping . . .'

27. METRONOME EQUIVALENTS FOR DANCE TEMPOS

Quantz' speeds for dance tempos are less hypothetical and more actual than his speeds for time-words (see Ch. XXXVI, 4 above); but the variable tempos of dances at different times and places, or when they have become musical forms in their own right, are a factor which no such table can take into account. The equivalent metronome markings are as follows.

TABLE VIII: Quantz' dance tempos

Bourrée [₵ or 2]:	♩ = 160
Canarie:	♩. = 160
Chaconne:	♩ = 160
Courante:	♩ = 80
Entrée:	♩ = 80
Furie:	♩ = 160
Gavotte:	about ♩ = 120
Gigue:	♩. = 160
Loure:	♩ = 80
Marche [₵ or 2]:	♩ = 160
Menuet:	♩ = 160
Musette [3–4]:	♩ = 80
[3–8]:	♪ = 80
Passecaille:	about ♩ = 180
Passepied [3–4]:	about ♩ = 180
[3–8]:	about ♪ = 180
Rigaudon [₵ or 2]:	♩ = 160
Rondeau [₵ or 3–4]:	about ♩ = 140
Sarabande:	♩ = 80
Tambourin:	about ♩ = 180

DANCE TEMPOS

The above table looks more useful than it really is. Wilfrid Mellers (*Couperin*, London, 1950, App. D) prints several similar tables, also based on eighteenth-century sources, but giving quite different results. Ralph Kirkpatrick has much the best discussion, in his article on 'Eighteenth-Century Metronomic Indications' (see my Bibl.). But he is not able to reach any definitive conclusions.

John Guthrie, from his experienced dancer's angle, suggests for the Minuet of about 1650–1710 a crotchet pulse of MM. 160; thereafter, about double that speed, though the change was presumably quite gradual (*Historical Dances for the Theatre*, Worthing, 1949, p. 27).

POSTSCRIPT TO SECOND EDITION

The following is worth noting, especially for its description of Galliard speed as 'very slow', as in my explanation in Sect. 11 above.

(507a) Giovanni Lorenzo Gregori, *Arie in stil francese a una e due voci*, Lucca, 1698, Preface:

'For whoever does not have some knowledge of dances, we mention that Gagliards are usually sung *in tempo assai largo*. The Minuet *allegro e vivace*. The Borè *presto* and *alla Breve*.'

POSTSCRIPT TO NEW VERSION

Neal Zaslaw has very kindly shown me portions of his dissertation, 'Materials for the Life and Works of Jean-Marie Leclair l'aîné' (Columbia, 1970), in which he makes a most sustained attempt at collating our scattered and somewhat inconsistent information on baroque French dance tempos. He there corrected me in a slip made in my comment on the Brossard-Walther entry on *passacaglio* (see 19 above). He warns us that Quantz gives bourrée, canarie, gigue, gavotte and passacaille faster, and loure and passepied slower than usual French sources, which also give chaconne faster than passacaille (the reverse of Quantz). He thinks moderate tempos altogether to have been to the French taste. And taste, of course, is the operative word.

It was Brahms who wrote in a letter to George Henschel (George Henschel, *Personal Recollections of Johannes Brahms*, Boston, 1907, pp. 78–79) that: 'the metronome is of no value. As far at least as my experience goes, everybody has, sooner or later, withdrawn his metronome marks'.

CHAPTER XXXVIII

Time-Signatures

1. ORIGIN OF OUR TIME-SIGNATURES IN MENSURAL (SO-CALLED PROPORTIONAL) NOTATION

(a) Our time-signatures originated in renaissance notation as a means of indicating the duration allotted to each note-value in proportion to the others.

This was necessary because the proportions were variable. In modern notation, we assume a standard proportion of one to two between each successive note-value: one semibreve to two minims; one minim to two crotchets; *etc.* But in renaissance notation, one long might contain two or three breves; one breve might contain two or three semibreves; one semibreve might contain two or three minims. Any smaller values, however, were in duple proportion only.

The relation of long to breve became known as 'mood' (modus—a word also used for the 'time-signature' itself); the relation of breve to semibreve became known as 'time' (tempus—this word is also used for a unit of time); the relation of semibreve to minim became known as 'prolation' (prolatio).

A triple relationship between any two of these is known as 'perfect', and a duple relationship is known as 'imperfect'.

The breve-unit measure of 'time' may also be referred to as the 'more' and the semibreve unit measure of 'prolation' as the 'less'. During the renaissance period, 'mood' became obsolete in practice, because of the perpetual tendency for long notes to grow slower as shorter notes are added at the other end of the scale.

One name for this system of mensuration as a whole is proportional notation. For English readers, the best and most accessible contemporary account of it, written just as it was becoming obsolescent, is in Morley's *Plaine and Easie Introduction* (London, 1597) in the annotated modern edition mentioned in my Bibliography. The best short account by a modern English authority will be found in two articles by Thurston Dart (*Grove's Dictionary of Music and Musicians*, London, 1954, Vol. VI, *s.v.* 'Notation' and 'Proportions'). See also App. VII, 3.

(b) At no period were the signs and symbols of proportional notation brought to a consistent or systematic condition; but a few of the best entrenched around 1600 were as follows.

TABLE IX: Signs of Mensuration *c.* 1600

SIGN	TIME		PROLATION	
⊙	Perfect:	|○| = ○ ○ ○	Perfect:	○ = ♩ ♩ ♩
○	Perfect:	|○| = ○ ○ ○	Imperfect:	○ = ♩ ♩
₵	Imperfect:	|○| = ○ ○	Perfect:	○ = ♩ ♩ ♩
C	Imperfect:	|○| = ○ ○	Imperfect:	○ = ♩ ♩

DIMINUTION AND AUGMENTATION

₵⃓	Note values become half those of					○
₵ or Ɔ	,,	,,	,,	,,		C
₵ or ꝯ⃓	,,	,,	,,	,,		₵
$\frac{2}{1}$	Dupla (diminution): ♩ = previous ○					
$\frac{1}{2}$	Dupla (augmentation): ○ = previous ♩					
$\frac{3}{1}$ or ⅜	Tripla (diminution): ○ ○ ○ = previous ○					
$\frac{3}{2}$ or 3	Sesquialtera (diminution): ♩ ♩ ♩ = previous ○					

(c) For all duple relationships, our modern system, with its one standard proportion, is on grounds of simplicity an obvious improvement.

For triple relationships, the improvement is by no means so obvious. In order to provide a note containing three notes of the next shortest value, we have to fall back on one of the complications of the old proportional system: the dot of augmentation. We have to say: let a dotted crotchet, *etc.*, contain three quavers, *etc.*

But for combining duple with triple relationships, we need two kinds of quavers, *etc.*: our standard kind, of which two go to a crotchet; and a further kind, of which three go to a crotchet. We have to say: let three quavers, *etc.*, written where there is apparently only time for two, be this further kind of quaver, of which three go to a crotchet. We call this triplets. But when we write triplets in duple time, or duplets or quadruplets in triple time, or quintuplets or sextolets or septuplets, *etc.*, we are no longer using our modern uni-proportional notation at all. We are using a remnant of the old multi-proportional notation, and using it very sensibly.

To indicate the proportion, we commonly write 3 against the triplet, *etc.*, often adding a square bracket to make the grouping clear if there are no connecting beams to make it clear already. But the proportion required may be so obvious that even this indication may not be necessary.

(d) In renaissance music, however, the proportion might not be obvious at all, especially where different parts in the same polyphonic composition were using different proportions, or where the proportion changed in course of a composition. It was therefore necessary to use symbols or numerical signs of mensuration, or both.

These are the symbols and signs which we have inherited under the name of time-signatures.

From what has been said, it will be realised that this name is somewhat misleading. The true function of these signatures was not to indicate time in our modern sense of tempo, but to indicate time in the old sense of mensuration. The only information which they impart directly is the relative time allotted to each note-value in proportion to the others. Any information which they may incidentally impart about time in the absolute is indirect information, and neither exact nor reliable.

The only reason why the signatures can impart even indirect information about the absolute time in which the music proceeds is that for certain stable forms of late renaissance polyphony a conception seems to have been current of a roughly uniform or standard pulse (tactus) of which the remaining note-values were either multiples or subdivisions. It will be appreciated that this was not a means of dictating tempo, which would be a musical absurdity, but of teaching it, and that it would not have been practicable if it had not been kept quite flexible in its actual application.

(508) Thomas Morley, *Plaine and Easie Introduction*, London, 1597, p. 9:

'[A stroke] *is a successive motion of the hand, directing the quantitie of every note and rest in the song, with equall measure, according to the varietie of signes and proportions. . . . The More stroke they call, when the stroke comprehendeth the time of a Briefe. The lesse, when the time of a Semibriefe: and proportionat where it comprehendeth three Semibriefes,* as in triple or three Minoms, as in the more prolation. . . .

'[The timing of a note] *is a certayne space or length, wherein a note may be holden in singing.*

[p. 23:] '*The signe of this Moode set with a stroke parting it thus* ₵ *causeth the song before, which it is set, to be so song as a breefe or the value of a breefe in other notes, make but one ful stroke, and is proper to motetes specially when the song is prickt in great notes.* . . . Although that rule bee not so generally kept: but that the composers set the same signe before songs of the *semibriefe* time.'

It would, of course, be for the hand to accommodate itself to the natural tempo of the music, not the music to the hand. But when the notation is, throughout all the parts, in note-values which look longer than they are meant to be performed, Morley tells us that a ₵ will warn the singers to read them as if they were notes of half the written value: *i.e.* to treat each of their parts as they would if some of those parts were notated in notes of half the written value under the signature C. The result is, at least in theory, that they all sing faster than they would if all their parts were written in the same values but under the signature C. This is the same result as we might secure by adding 'allegro' or 'non troppo lento'; but it has been reached by an entirely different process of thought.

In practice, as opposed to theory, the singers would have produced the same result by trained musicianship and good judgment of tempo, whether they saw C or ₵ or neither. That is why, as Morley at once adds, composers did not always trouble to distinguish C from ₵ in such cases: *i.e.* where all the parts are in the same proportions, and remain so. The matter is quite otherwise where C appears in some parts but ₵ in other parts, or where there is a change in course of the composition. There the signatures are necessary in order to keep the relative time-values in correct proportion; but then there is not even an indirect influence on tempo in the absolute.

2. THE FUNDAMENTAL CONFUSION BETWEEN MEASURE AND TEMPO

(a) During the early baroque the multi-proportional system declined. Its place was taken by our present uni-proportional system, of which the normal basis is duple. For this reason, it no longer requires the signs of imperfection (duple relationship) such as C and ₵: for this is assumed except where perfection (triple relationship) is shown or implied.

(509) Pierre Maillart, *Les Tons*, Tournai, 1610, p. 349:

'When there is no sign of perfection, the usage has established itself that to signify a general imperfection, a half circle is ordinarily used, as a mark or sign of imperfection: in that, just as the round figure, or the perfect circle, is the true hieroglyphic, and the essential mark of perfection, so the imperfect circle, is the mark of imperfection. . . . It follows from what we have said, that the signs of imperfection dealt with above, are superfluous and useless, seeing that the absence of signs of perfection suffices to declare the imperfection, as has been said.'

(b) Unfortunately the superfluous signs remained in use, but became subject to a fundamental confusion.

This is the confusion of relative time-values with tempo in the absolute.

It was remembered, for example, that the stroke of ₵ stands for diminution of C by one half.

This had meant: take two notes in the time-value of one, relative to a previous C or to a C continuing in another voice of the same composition.

It was now explained by the more pedantic theorists as meaning: take an entire composition at twice the absolute speed. The less pedantic, knowing that this did not happen in practice, compromised with some such evasion as: take a somewhat faster absolute speed. Only the really learned, however, could put the matter as realistically as the following.

(510) Athanasius Kircher, *Musurgia*, Rome, 1650, p. 676:

'There is nothing in music more confused . . . [p. 679] this most confused subject . . . this utter muddle (tota haec farrago). [p. 679:] an upright line [through the sign means that] the notes must be halved, that is to say, all the voices must sing twice as fast in those parts which are so marked. [p. 684: but we could nowadays show this] by the rapidity of our notes, such as minims, crotchets, quavers, semiquavers; hence we too judge it superfluous to use those signs; indeed I have found that a majority of the most excellent musicians and the most expert in theory of the present time have deliberately omitted them, and taken them for one and the same sign (pro unico signo).'

Zarlino (*Institutioni Harmoniche*, Venice, 1558, ed. of 1562, p. 278) had already made an almost identical attack. Where such great authorities agreed, who are we to expect reliable tempo indications from C, ₵, *etc.*? See also quotations (518) to (519) below; and App. VII.

3. THE SUBSIDIARY CONFUSION OVER TIME-SIGNATURES IN THE FORM OF FRACTIONS

A figure standing as a proportional time-signature shows the number of units to be taken *in the time of one previous unit*. Where there are two figures, the first or the top figure (numerator) shows the number of units to be taken in the time of the number shown by the second or the bottom figure (denominator).

Thus 3 or $\frac{3}{1}$ or $\frac{3}{1}$ means take three units in the time of one: *i.e.* in the proportion of 3:1 ('Tripla'). $\frac{3}{2}$ means take three units in the time of two: *i.e.* in the proportion of 3:2 ('Sesquialtera'); *etc.* This, in its context, was self-explanatory.

As the context became forgotten, so did the explanation. It came to be assumed that the top figure gives the number of units to a bar, and the bottom figure the size of these units in relation to the semibreve.

Thus $\frac{4}{4}$ now means four quarters of a semibreve, *i.e.* crotchets, to a bar; $\frac{2}{4}$ two crotchets to a bar; $\frac{4}{8}$ four quavers; $\frac{3}{4}$ three crotchets; $\frac{3}{8}$ three quavers, *etc.*

By the time this changed theory was recognised, perhaps first in G. M. Bononcini, *Musico prattico*, Bologna (1673), the facts themselves, by one of the pleasanter ironies of history, had changed to fit it.

(511) Leopold Mozart, *Violinschule*, Augsburg, 1756, I, ii, 5:

'Among the time-measures, common time is the chief measure, into relationship with which all the remainder are brought: for the top number is the numerator while the bottom number is the denominator. We may therefore say that of those notes of which four go to a bar of common time, two go to a bar of $\frac{2}{4}$ time. From this we see that $\frac{2}{4}$ time has only two parts, the up beat and the down beat, and since four black notes or crotchets go to common time, therefore two of the same value go to $\frac{2}{4}$ time. In this manner all time measures are calculated.'

4. CONTRADICTORY USES OF C AND ¢, etc.

(512) John Playford, *Introduction to the Skill of Musick*, London, 1654, p. 15:

'[Recent composers] make use onely of . . . the Triple Time [and] the duple, or Common Time . . . [p. 17:] thus marked ¢, and is usuall in Songs, Fantasies, Pavins, Almans, and the like. [Not pre-1672:] Note, *That when this* Common Mood *is reversed thus ₰, it is to signifie, that the* Time *of that Lesson or Song, before which it is so set, is to be Play'd or Sung as swift again as the usual Measure.*

'[1694 on, *"Corrected and Amended by Mr.* Henry Purcell", p. 25:] First, I shall speak of Common-Time, which may be reckond three several sorts; the first and slowest of all is marked thus C: 'Tis measured by a Semibreve, which you must divide into four equal Parts, telling *one, two, three, four,* distinctly, putting your Hand or Foot down when you tell *one,* and taking it up when you tell *three,* so that you are as long down as up. Stand by a large Chamber-Clock, and beat your Hand or Foot (as I have before observed) to the slow Motions of the Pendulum . . .

'The second sort of *Common Time* is a little faster, which is known by the *Mood,* having a stroak drawn through it, thus ¢.

'The third sort of *Common Time* is quickest of all, and then the *Mood* is retorted thus ₰; you may tell *one, two, three, four* in a Bar, almost as fast as the regular Motions of a Watch. The *French Mark* for this retorted *Time,* is a large Figure of 2.'

(513) Henry Purcell (or his editor), *Lessons,* 1696, preface:

'There being nothing more difficult in Musick then playing of true time, 'tis therefore necessary to be observ'd by all practitioners, of which there are two sorts, Common time and Triple time, & is distinguish'd by this C this ¢ or this ₰ mark, ye first is a very slow movement, ye next a little faster, and ye last a brisk & airry time, & each of them has allways to ye length of one Semibrief in a barr, which is to be held in playing as long as you can moderately tell four, by saying one, two, three, four.'

(514) Anon, *Compleat Flute Master,* London [c. 1700], cited A. Dolmetsch, *Interpretation,* London [1915], p. 34:

'C very slow motion. ¢ somewhat faster. ₰ Brisk and light Ayres.'

(515) — Dean, *Complete Tutor for the Violin*, London, 1707, cited A. Dolmetsch, *Interpretation*, London [1915], p. 34:

'C Very solid or slow movement. ₵ Quicker. 𝇍 or 𝟤 as quick again as the first, and are call'd Retorted Time.'

(516) Christopher Simpson, *Compendium of Music* (London, 1665, as *Principles of Practical Musick*), p. 19:

'The *Signe* of [the Common] Mood is a *Semicircle*, thus, C, sometimes with a Stroke through it thus ₵.

[Ed. of 1706, p. 12:] 'The Sign of [the Common] *Mood* is a *Semicircle*, thus, C, which denotes the slowest Time, and is generally set before grave Songs or Lessons; the next is this ₵ which is a Degree faster, the next mark thus 𝇍 or, thus 2, and is very Fast, and denotes the Quickest Movement in this Measure of *Common Time*. [Likewise to 9th ed. of ?1775.]

[p. 22:] 'The motion of the Hand is *Down*, and *Up*, successively and equally divided. Every *Down* and *Up*, being called a *Time*, or *Measure*. And by this we measure the length of a *Semibreve* [and from it compute the other note–values] . . .

'But you may say: I have told you that a *Semibreve* is the length of a *Time*, and a *Time* the length of a *Semibreve*, and still you are ignorant what that *Length* is.

'To which I answer, (in case you have none to guide your Hand at the first measuring of Notes) I would have you pronounce these words (*One*, *Two*, *Three*, *Four*) in an equal length, as you would (leisurely) read them. Then fancy those four words to be four *Crotchets*, which make up the quantity or length of a *Semibreve*, and consequently of a *Time* or *Measure*: In which, let those two words (*One*, *Two*) be pronounced with the Hand *Down*; and (*Three*, *Four*,) with it *Up*. In the continuation of this motion you will be able to measure, and compute all your other Notes.

'Some speak of having recourse to the motion of a lively pulse for the measure of *Crotchets*; or to the little Minutes of a steddy going Watch for Quavers; but this which I have delivered, will (I think) be most useful to you.'

Like Quantz' and other early instructions for turning relative time-values into absolute tempos, the above was not meant to limit the beginner's choice of tempo, but to give him an average starting-point 'in case you have none to guide your hand at the first measuring of notes'. Arnold Dolmetsch (*Interpretation*, London [1915], p. 31), taking the mean pulse rate at 75 since that 'makes the quavers agree with the "little minutes" or strokes of a watch, which usually beat five times a second or 300 times a minute', makes this MM ♩ = 75: reasonable enough as an ordinary allegro, but it *is* only a starting-point.

(517) Georg Muffat, *Florilegium I*, Augsburg, 1695, preface (here translated mainly from his parallel text in French):

'The measure marked thus 2 [or] ₵, being given in two beats, it is clear that in general it goes as fast again, as this C which is given in four. It is however understood that this measure 2 ought to go very slow in Overtures, Preludes, and Symphonies, a little more lively in Ballets, and for the rest on my advice almost always more moderate than this ₵, which itself ought to be less pressed on in Gavottes, than in Bourrées. However when this measure 2 is given very slowly, and (as has been said) in two beats, the notes are almost of the same value, as with the Italians under this measure C given in four beats with speed under the word *presto*.'

(518) Charles Masson, *Nouveau Traité*, Paris, 2nd ed., 1699, p. 6:

'Measure is the soul of music, since it excites with such truthfulness of emotion (fait agir avec tant de justesse) a great many people, and by the variety of its times (mouvemens) can again stimulate so many different feelings, being able to calm these and arise those, as has always been observed.

'Although there appear to be a quantity of different measures, I believe that it is useful to point out that it is only the number two or three which divides them, and that it is by the quickness or by the slowness of these two times (mouvemens) that the difference between melodies is effected.'

(518a) Étienne Loulié, *Elements . . . de musique*, Paris, 1696, p. 69:

'All these time-signatures were in use among the ancients . . . foreigners have retained some in their works, but the practice of them is not very certain, some use them in one way, some in another.'

(519) Michel de Montéclair, *Petite Methode*, Paris, [c. 1730], p. 48:

'There is a time-signature marked by ₵, of which the usage is no longer well defined; it is used in different manners for lack of willingness to recognise its character.'

(520) Le Cerf de La Viéville, 'Comparaison', in *Histoire de la Musique*, Amsterdam, 1725, I, p. 307 (also reprinted and translated in Mattheson's *Critica Musica*, III, pp. 222 *ff.*):

'[The Italians] find no music good, if it is not difficult, they can scarcely bring themselves to look at it when there are only minims, or crotchets in two- or three-time; as if all the Italian measures did not come down to these two measures, as if one could not reduce them to two- or four-time, and include two measures in one, as if the 4–8 did not come down to our light two-time? and the 6–8 measures, the 3–8 and the 12–8 did not come down to our three-time measure? when they are beaten more or less quickly, whether they are beaten in two-time or in four-time, of which each beat makes up one of our measures in three-time? This is nothing but a different manner of expressing what is good in itself, and gives the character of the piece, for slowness and quickness, and has more convenience for beating; for as there are in general only two different modes, the minor and the major, so there are in general only two measures, that in two-time, and that in three; in vain would you wish to imagine others.'

(521) J. D. Heinichen, *General-Bass*, Dresden, 1728, Part I, Ch. IV, Sect. 48, p. 348:

'The Overture Time is generally indicated by a 2 . . .
[49:] 'Its measure is properly slow and expressive . . .
[50:] 'But if in certain pieces the Overture Time is meant to have a rapid movement, then, instead of the slow measure just mentioned, a stroked 2 or ¢ is shown, or rather, with a few people it would be shown, in distinction from the slower measure. But since such correctness is not always found, and since the signs 2, 2, C or ¢ are used without discrimination, sometimes for a naturally rapid piece and sometimes for a slow one, [¢ may often serve for the slow introduction of the overture as well as for its succeeding quick movements].'

(522) Alexander Malcolm, *A Treatise of Musick*, Edinburgh, 1721, p. 394:

'COMMON TIME is of two Species, the *1st* where every *Measure* is equal to a Semibreve . . . the *2d*, where every Measure is equal to a Minim. . . . The *Movements* of this Kind of *Measure* are very various; but there are Three common Distinctions, the first is *slow*, signified at the Beginning by this Mark C, the *2d* is *brisk*, signified by this ¢, the *3d* is very *quick*, signified by this 𝄵; but what that *slow*, *brisk*, and *quick* is, is very uncertain, and, as I have said already, must be learned by Practice. [The usual references to a watch, or to counting One, Two, Three, Four, or to a pendulum, are then given for what they are worth.]'

(523) William Turner, *Philosophical Essay on Musick*, London, 1724, p. 20:

'C which denotes the slowest *Movement* . . .
'¢ which denotes the *Movement* to be somewhat faster than the former.
'𝄵 which is the quickest of all; the Crotchets being counted as fast as the regular Motions of a *Watch*.
[p. 27:] 'out of all these eight *Moods* I have been speaking of, there is, in reality, but *One* . . . the Reasons for the others, I cannot well understand . . .'

(524) Joachim Quantz, *Essay*, Berlin, 1752, V, 13:

'In four-crotchet time it must be carefully observed that when a stroke goes through the C . . . such a stroke signifies, that all the notes, so to speak, become of a different value, and must be played as fast again, than is the case when the C has no stroke through it. This measure is called: allabreve, or alla capella. But since with regard to the aforesaid measure many have fallen into error through ignorance: it is most desirable that everyone should become acquainted with this difference. This measure is more frequent in the galant style, than it used to be in former times.'

(525) Leopold Mozart, *Violinschule*, Augsburg, 1756, I, ii, 3:

'In the old music [of the time of Glareanus and Artusi, *i.e.* 16th cent.] there were conflicting views [as to notation], and everything was in great confusion.

[4:] 'Nowadays time is divided into equal [simple or common] and unequal [triple] measure [of which the equal are:]

'The Equal Time-Measure

C	2 or $\frac{2}{4}$	C
The straight or four-crotchet time	The two-crotchet time	The Allabreve

[7:] 'This is only the ordinary mathematical division of the bars, however, which we call the time-measure and the beat. Now comes a major issue, namely the source of the speed. Not only have we to beat time correctly and steadily, but also to be able to divine from the music itself whether it needs a slow or a somewhat faster speed.'

5. TIME-SIGNATURES IN TRIPLE TIME

Triple time-signatures tend to be diminutions rather than augmentations.

Baroque triple time-signatures therefore tend to make time-values shorter in relation to common time: hence to increase the speed.

This tendency of triple-time movements or passages to move faster than their written note-values suggest, though not reliable, is nearer to being reliable than the tendency of C to move faster than C, *etc.* It grew less reliable, however, in course of the baroque period.

The inconsistencies in the following evidence will again be noticed.

(526) John Playford, *Introduction*, London, 1654, p. 16:

'*The Imperfect of the More* . . . is thus signed C, and this is called the *Triple Time*. This Mood is much used in *Ayery Songs* and *Galliards*, and is usually called *Galliard* or *Triple time* and this *Triple time* is in some Lessons, as *Coranto's, Sarabands,* and *Jigs* brought into a Measure, as swift again [eds. of 1662 to 1687 have 'to another swifter motion'], for as before three Minims or Sembriefs [*sic*] with a prick [dot] made a Time, in this three Crochets [*sic*] makes a Time, or one Minim with a prick, and this measure is knowne by this signe or mark 𝄵 [3–1] which is usually called *Three to one*.

[1694 (p. 26) on:] 'There are two other sorts of *Time* which may be reckoned amongst *Common-Time* for the equal division of the Bar with the Hand or Foot up and down: The first of which is called *Six to four*, each Bar containing six *Crotchets*, or six *Quavers*, three to be sung with the Hand down, and three up, and is marked thus $\frac{6}{4}$, but very brisk, and is always used in *Jigs*.

'The other sort is called *Twelve to eight*, each Bar containing twelve *Quavers*, six with the Hand down, and six up, and marked thus $\frac{12}{8}$ . . .

'*Tripla-Time*, that you may understand it right, I will distinguish into two sorts: The first and slowest of which is measured by three *Minims* in each Bar, or such a quantity of lesser *Notes* as amount to the value of three *Minims*, or one *Pointed* [dotted] *Semibreve*, telling *one*, *two*, with your Hand down, and up with it at the *third*; so that you are as long again with your Hand or Foot down as up. This sort of Time is marked thus $\frac{3}{2}$.

'The second sort is faster, and the *Minims* become *Crotchets*, so that a Bar contains three Crotchets, or one Pointed Minim; 'tis marked thus 3 or thus 𝄵 [3–1]. Sometimes you will meet with three *Quavers* in a Bar, which is marked as the *Crotchets*, only Sung as fast again.

'There is another sort of *Time* which is used in *Instrumental Musick*, called *Nine to six*, marked thus $\frac{9}{6}$, each Bar containing Nine *Quavers* or *Crotchets*, six to be Play'd with the Foot down, and three up: This I also reckon amongst *Tripla-Time*, because there is as many more down as up.'

These explanations are given as proportions. By the next (thirteenth) edition of 1697, the signature $\frac{9}{6}$ (as 9:6) has been replaced by $\frac{9}{8}$ (as nine quavers) in tacit acknowledgement of the later reckoning by fractions of the semibreve.

(527) Christopher Simpson, *Compendium*, London, 1665, I, 10, Of Tripla Time:

'When you see this Figure [3] set at the beginning of a Song or Lesson, it signifies that the Time or Measure must be compted by *Threes*, as we formerly did it by *Fours*.

'Sometimes the *Tripla* consists of *three Semibreves* to a Measure, each *Semibreve* being shorter than a *Minim* in Common Time . . .

'The more *Common Tripla* is three *Minims* to a *Measure*, each *Minim* about the length of a *Crotchet* in *Common Time* . . .

'In these two sorts of *Tripla*, we compt or imagin these two words [*One*, *Two*] with the Hand *down*, and this word [*Three*] with it *up* . . .

[1706 (p. 23) on:] 'Sometimes the *Tripla* consists of three *Minims* to a Measure. The more *common Tripla* is three *Crotchets* to a Measure . . .

[p. 37:] 'There are divers *Tripla's* of a shorter Measure; which by reason of their quick motion, are usually measured by compting *three down* and three up with the Hand. [1706 (p. 25) on:] and those quick

415

Tripla's are prick't sometimes with *Crotchets* and *Minums*; and sometimes with *Quavers* and *Crotchets*.'

(528) Jean Rousseau, *Methode Claire*, Paris, 1678, ed. of Amsterdam, 1691, p. 31:

'With the ternary signature (au Signe Trinaire) [C3, the bar is beaten] in three slow beats, two down, and the other up.

'With the plain triple signature (au Signe de Triple simple) [3] in three quick beats, two down, and the other up.

'With the double-triple signature (au Signe de Triple double) [$\frac{3}{2}$], in three slow beats, two down and one up; [also called] Three to Two . . .

'With the signature of three to four, so called because in place of the bar composed of four crotchets, this has only three, the bar is beaten in three beats quicker than simple triple . . .

'With the signature of three to eight composed of three quavers, where the major has eight, the bar is beaten like that of three to four, but very much faster.

'With the signature of six to four [six crotchets] . . . the bar may be beaten in two . . .

'With the signature of six to eight [six quavers] . . . like the six to four but quicker, or like the three to eight, making two bars of one.

'With the signature of four to eight [four quavers] the bar is beaten in a very quick two.'

Grassineau is interesting for his retention of C and ₵ in front of the numerical signatures: *e.g.* C $\frac{3}{2}$ giving three beats to a dotted semibreve, but ₵ $\frac{3}{2}$ giving three beats to a dotted breve. His most important contribution, however, is the following, with which we may compare Simpson, second and third paragraphs at (527) above.

(529) J. Grassineau, *Musical Dictionary*, London, 1740, 'Allegro':

'It is to be observed, the movements of the same name as Adagio, or Allegro, are swifter in triple than in common Time.'

The following, very possibly by Purcell, is disappointingly incomplete even for his own music, since his sonatas include Largos in $\frac{3}{2}$ for which the 'very slow' tempo stated below is musically too slow, as well as conflicting with his own statement given at (435), Ch. XXXVI, 3 above that Largo is 'a middle movement' (*i.e.* neither fast nor slow); while some of his Hornpipes, marked $\frac{3}{2}$, are certainly fast. (See (533) below for a vivace $\frac{3}{2}$.)

(530) Henry Purcell (or his editor), *Lessons*, London, 1696, preface:

'Triple time consists of either three or six Crotchets in a barr, and is to be known by this $\frac{3}{2}$, this $\frac{3}{1}$ [3–1], this 3 or this $\frac{6}{4}$ marke, to the first there is three Minums in a barr, and is commonly play'd very slow, the second has three Crotchets in a barr, and they are to be play'd slow, the third has ye same as ye former but is play'd faster, ye last has six Crotchets in a barr & is Commonly to brisk tunes as Jiggs and Paspys [passepieds].'

(531) Anon, *Compleat Flute Master*, London [*c.* 1700], cited A. Dolmetsch, *Interpretation*, London [1915], p. 34:

'$\frac{3}{2}$ Grave movement. 3 Slow. $\frac{6}{4}$ Fast, for Jiggs, Paspies, &.'

(532) — Dean, *Complete Tutor for the Violin*, London, 1707, cited A. Dolmetsch, *Interpretation*, London [1915], p. 34:

'$\frac{3}{C}$ Very slow. $\frac{3}{2} \frac{3}{4}$ Much Quicker.'

(533) A. Malcolm, *Treatise of Musick*, Edinburgh, 1721, p. 394:

'Movements of the same Name, as *adagio* or *allegro, etc.* are swifter in triple than in common time [the same as Grassineau at (529) above] . . . in the *triple*, there are some species that are more ordinarily [N.B. not exclusively] of one Kind of Movement than another: Thus the triple $\frac{3}{2}$ is ordinarily *adagio*, sometimes *vivace*; the $\frac{3}{4}$ is of any Kind from *adagio* to *allegro*; the $\frac{3}{8}$ is *allegro*, or *vivace*; the $\frac{6}{4} \frac{8}{6} \frac{9}{8}$ are more frequently *allegro*; the $\frac{12}{8}$ is sometimes *adagio* but oftener *allegro*. Yet after all, the *allegro* of one Species of *triple* is a quicker Movement than that of another, so very uncertain these Things are.'

(534) W. Turner, *Philosophical Essay on Musick*, London, 1724, p. 22:

'[$\frac{3}{2}$] differs from [$\frac{3}{4}$] no otherwise than in being measured by different *Notes*: For in the former *Mood, Minims* are sometimes, as fast as *Crotchets*; and in this, the *Crotchets* are often as slow as *Minims* [while $\frac{3}{8}$] is exactly the same with the others: For in this *Mood*, the *Quavers* are sometimes, as slow as *Minims* are in the first.'

Leopold Mozart's list is very modern, as was his list of common times. In a footnote, he adds that he would have spared us $\frac{3}{1}$ if it did not occasionally appear in an old church piece. He calls $\frac{8}{4}, \frac{2}{8}, \frac{9}{8}, \frac{9}{16}, \frac{12}{16}, \frac{12}{24}, \frac{12}{4}$ all 'worthless stuff' because everything necessary can be expressed without them. He advocates $\frac{12}{8}$ in preference to $\frac{3}{8}$ for rapid melodies solely because it is easier to beat.

(535) Leopold Mozart, *Violinschule*, Augsburg, 1756, I, ii, 4:

'The Unequal Time Measure

3	3	3	3
1	2	4	8
The Semibreve Triple time	The minim triple time	The three-crotchet time	The three-quaver time

	6	6	12	
	4	8	8	
	The six-crotchet time	The six-quaver time	The twelve-quaver time'	

6. DISCREPANT TIME-SIGNATURES

Discrepancies often occur in the time-signatures given by different contemporary copies of the same music, or even between different parts in the same copy, *etc.* See Walter Emery (*Music and Letters*, XXXIV, iii, July, 1953, review) for a revealing study of such discrepancies in J. S. Bach. The inference, as usual, is not that tempo was disregarded, but that the performer must find it in any case; while the time-signature, being at best of little help, received only casual attention.

7. CONCURRENT TIME-SIGNATURES

In addition to inadvertent discrepancies, we find a few genuine survivals of proportional notation.

A melody may be in $\frac{9}{8}$ against a bass in $\frac{3}{4}$, or a melody in $\frac{12}{8}$ against a bass in C, *i.e.* $\frac{4}{4}$, *etc.* One crotchet of the bass then goes to three quavers of the melody, as if that melody were notated in triplets. If the bass presently requires shorter notes, these may actually be notated as (unmarked) triplets, or alternatively with dots intended to be softened into triplet rhythm. In spite of various illogicalities here, no real obscurity usually arises if the appropriate conventions are known, for which see Ch. XLVI below.

J. S. Bach's Chorale Prelude 'Herr Gott, nun schleuss' as printed in the Bach-Gesellschaft (25, ii, p. 26) has C on the top stave, C $\frac{24}{16}$ on the middle stave and C $\frac{12}{8}$ on the bottom stave. This looks formidable; but it merely states that the middle line has sextolets while the bottom line has triplets against the melody in the top line. If it were printed C in all three parts, or nothing at all, this would still have been obvious. It could then, as a precaution, have printed 6 against the first few sextolets and 3 against the first few triplets, though this precaution would not actually have been needed.

Walter Emery pointed out to me, however, that Bach himself wrote this music, like most of his organ music, not on three staves but on two. The top has C $\frac{24}{16}$ and the bottom has C $\frac{12}{8}$. The upper melody proceeds, in minims, crotchets, *etc.*, exactly as if its time-signature had been C, which in fact it is not. The tenor counter-melody, in sextolet relationship to the upper melody, wanders from stave to stave with a sublime disregard for their having different time-signatures. The bass, in triplet relationship to the upper melody, goes on unperturbed; but at bar 19 the alto part is written as duplet quavers. From their harmony these can only be played unevenly, in a triplet rhythm to fit the bass (see Ch. XLVI below).

In the third verse of J. S. Bach's Chorale Prelude 'O Lamm Gottes unschuldig' (B.G. 25, ii, p. 106) the top stave is changed from $\frac{3}{2}$ to $\frac{9}{4}$

while the bottom stave remains in $\frac{3}{2}$. This puts the crotchets of the top two parts into triplet relationship with the minims of the bass: once again the $\frac{9}{4}$ part wanders regardless between the two staves.

A more tortuous case occurs in Prelude XV from J. S. Bach's 'Forty-Eight'. Here we start with what in effect are semiquaver triplets in the treble accompanied by quavers in the bass. This J. S. Bach announces in the grand manner by setting $\frac{24}{16}$ in the treble stave and C in the bass stave. Presently he wants, very reasonably, to reverse his counterpoint by putting the triplet semiquavers in the bass and the quavers in the treble. He does so; the musical effect is excellent. But what about the effect on the notation?

There is no effect on the notation. The time-signatures remain unchanged. The semi-quavers in the bass are now unmarked triplets in theory as well as in practice; the quavers in the treble (still, remember, in $\frac{12}{16}$) are proportional quavers which it would be quite complicated to work out mathematically, but for the fact that it is totally unnecessary to do so. The performer knows at once that they are the same quavers as he has had previously in the bass. We could not have a more striking instance of the unimportance of notational detail, provided the sense is clear to an ordinary musical intelligence. And ordinary musical intelligence was precisely the quality most taken for granted in baroque notation.

8. BAROQUE TIME-SIGNATURES IN PRACTICE

To sum up:

(a) Different time-signatures used concurrently can give exact information, but only on the relative time-values in the concurrent parts.

(b) A sign or a number crossed or retorted suggests a faster absolute tempo; but this suggestion is vague and unreliable.

Smaller denominators suggest faster tempos; but this suggestion is equally vague and unreliable.

Any triple-time signature suggests a faster tempo; and this suggestion, though still as vague, is not quite so unreliable as the foregoing. It generally works. Often a very much faster tempo is required.

(c) A change of signature in course of the composition is much more likely to be of significance for tempo than the choice of signature at the beginning. Every attempt should be made to understand this change of tempo and to try applying it strictly in the proportion shown, when the result seems musically acceptable.

(d) Besides tempo, time-signatures have a bearing on pulse, which will be considered in the next chapter.

CHAPTER XXXIX

Pulse

1. PULSE NOT DELIBERATELY MADE AUDIBLE

(a) Pulse is not the same as accent, though the two may often coincide.

In renaissance polyphony, the accentuation follows only the natural shape of the phrase, not the underlying pulse. The accents in the different parts seldom come together, and there is no such thing as a regular accented beat. 'Follow the rhythm of the words, not the barring' is usually good practical advice. Yet the pulse, though not made audible, is somehow present at the back of one's mind as the groundwork against which the irregular accentuation takes its meaning. This is very like what happens so frequently in poetry: the regular stresses of the metre, once established, are present in one's mind; the actual stresses of the words partly conflict with them; and in this tacit 'counterpoint' lies much of the beauty.

In baroque music, the accentuation is likely to coincide with the pulse much more frequently; yet there are a great many passages in which this appears to be the case, but is not. The accentuation still goes by the phrase and not merely by the bar; and to find the actual peak-note to which the phrase is leading is often most difficult and subtle where the notes present a regular appearance.

(536) Francesco Geminiani, *Art of Playing on the Violin*, London, 1751, p. 9:

'If by your manner of bowing you lay a particular Stress on the Note at the Beginning of every Bar, so as to render it predominant over the rest, you alter and spoil the true Air of the Piece, and except where the Composer intended it, and where it is always marked, there are very few Instances in which it is not very disagreeable.'

2. THE FOUR-TIME PULSE AND THE TWO-TIME PULSE

There are no sharp distinctions; but if the harmony changes often enough for us most naturally to count four in a unit, we feel a four-square pulse; if the harmony changes infrequently enough for us most naturally to count two in a unit we feel a swinging pulse like a pendulum.

The unit may be a bar, or two bars thrown into one, or half a bar: this affects only the notation, not the music. Similarly we may for convenience of conducting beat a fast four-pulse unit in two, *etc.*

420

(537) Michel Corrette, *Methode de la Flûte Traversière*, Paris-Lyons, *c.* 1730, p. 4:

'The measure of 4 beats . . . is beaten in two different ways; to wit, in the Allegro always once [up and down]: and in the Adagio, or other slow pieces, twice if you so desire.'

₵ or 2 in place of C, *etc.*, could be used to indicate a two-pulse unit in place of a four-pulse unit; so could the terms *alla breve, alla capella, mesure à deux temps, etc.*; but the fatal confusion into which the system fell in practice can be seen below.

(538) Jean Rousseau, *Methode Claire . . . pour apprendre à chanter*, Paris, 1678, ed. of Amsterdam, 1691, p. 30:

'With the major signature [C] the bar is beaten in four steady beats, two down and two up.

'With the minor signature [₵], it is beaten in two slow beats, one down, and the other up.

'With the binary signature [2], in two quick beats, one down, and the other up.'

(539) Sébastien de Brossard, *Dictionaire de Musique*, Paris, 1703, *s.v.* 'Tempo':

'The *plain* C appears in two ways; 1°. turned from left to right, thus C, and then the Italians call it *Tempo ordinario*, because it is in more ordinary use than any other; or again *Tempo alla Semibreve*, because under this signature a *Semibreve* or *Ronde* ○ is worth one bar or four beats and the other notes in proportion. 2°. But it is sometimes found turned from right to left thus Ɔ, when all the figures are diminished by half their value. Thus a *Ronde* [Semibreve] is only worth two beats, a *Minim* or *Blanche* is only worth one beat, and so with the others.

'The *stroked* C is found, also either turned from left to right thus ₵, or from right to left thus ₫. When it is turned to the *right* the Italians, again, call it *Tempo alla breve*, because in earlier times all the notes were diminished under this signature by half their value; but now it indicates that the bar should be beaten in *two steady beats*, or in *four extremely quick beats*; at least if it has not got *Largo, Adagio, Lento* or some other term which tells us that we must beat the bar *extremely slowly*. And when the words *Da Capella*, and *alla breve*, are seen with this signature, this indicates *two very quick beats*.

'Finally others again of the more modern [musicians] divide time into only two varieties, The first is *Tempo Maggiore*, or *Major Time* which is indicated by a ₵ stroked and signifies that all the Notes can be sung *alla breve*, that is to say by making them last only half their ordinary value. The second is *Tempo minore* or *Minor Time* which is indicated by a plain C and under which all the notes have their natural value.'

J. G. Walther (*Musicalische Lexicon*, Leipzig, 1732, *s.v.* 'Tempo') and Quantz (*Essay*, Berlin, 1752, XVII, vii, 50) give the same names, signatures and descriptions as the last paragraph above; it will be noticed that Brossard at (539) above reverses the names given by Jean Rousseau at (538), but his signs and descriptions are the same. Leopold Mozart, on the other hand, at (540) below, gives the same names as Brossard.

(540) Leopold Mozart, *Violinschule*, Augsburg, 1756, I, ii, 6:

'Allabreve is a diminution of even time. It has only two pulses, and is no more than $\frac{4}{4}$ time divided into two. The signature for Allabreve is the letter C with a stroke drawn through it: ₵. In this measure only a few ornaments are introduced.

[F.n.:] 'The Italians call even time tempo minore; but allabreve tempo maggiore.'

3. THE TERMS 'ALLA BREVE' AND 'ALLA CAPELLA', *ETC.*

(a) A further complication is introduced by the terms *alla breve* and *alla capella* (or *da capella*, or *a capella*).

The term *alla breve* (It.) can be translated literally, 'in shortness', or technically, 'in connection with the breve'. It has two main meanings in baroque music: first, to indicate a style of composition; second, to indicate a variety of pulse.

The term *alla capella* (It.) can be translated 'in the church style', and also has two main meanings, of which the first does not concern us here: first, to indicate voices unaccompanied or only accompanied in unisons; second, as the equivalent of *alla breve*.

(b) The *alla breve* style was regarded in the eighteenth century as standing at the opposite extreme from the galant style. The following is an excellent description.

(541) J. D. Heinichen, *General-Bass*, Dresden, 1728, Part I, Ch. IV, Sect. 38, p. 333, *f.n.*:

'This antique, expressive style is surely the most beautiful and the most conducive, the one in which the composer can best reveal his profound science and correctness in composition. For the part-writing in this style must always be pure, its progressions and resolutions correct and far removed from all liberties, the melodic line sustained, with few leaps, in all the parts, these parts loaded with syncopations and beautiful suspensions both consonant and dissonant, and replete throughout with expressive thoughts, themes and imitations, to the exclusion of any fanciful characteristic. It is here that we should require a correct composer.

'[Text, Sect. 37: The *alla breve*] is marked either by C or ₵ and differs from all other measures in that its own movement always remains unaltered, and neither Adagio nor Allegro is attached to it.

[38:] 'Only crotchets can appear as quick notes in this measure, because shorter notes, namely quavers, are allowed either not at all or very sparingly, and barely two at a time.

[45: The *alla breve*] divides the harmony of each bar into 2 parts only, in that not less than 2 crotchets can go to a chord.'

The purpose of the chapter from which the above quotations are taken is to teach an accompanist to recognise passing notes in the bass, so that he does not introduce a change of harmony more often than is intended. By quick notes, therefore, Heinichen means notes so quick that they must normally be treated as passing notes when they appear in a figured bass. And the point of the last two paragraphs quoted is that in the *alla breve* style, these notes are crotchets, not less than two of which (and sometimes as many as four) should go to each change of harmony.

It is perhaps worth pointing out here that this chapter from Heinichen has been misinterpreted by Fritz Rothschild (*The Lost Tradition in Music*, London, 1953, pp. 132 *ff.*) in support of his theory that tempo in baroque music was regularly indicated and can now be discovered from the presence of C or ₵ respectively, in conjunction with the length of the quickest notes appearing substantially in the composition. All that Heinichen writes concerning which notes to take as quick for the purpose of detecting passing notes, Rothschild misreads as instructions for detecting tempo. He makes a similar misinterpretation of the extensive baroque evidence concerning which notes to take as quick for the purpose of making them expressively unequal in performance although written equal: for which see Ch. XLV below. He also believes (p. 3 and *passim*) that all notes on what he terms 'structural beats' should be audibly stressed and (p. 181) 'held slightly longer than other notes'. Those who have heard his demonstrations will realise that he means both these catastrophic recommendations literally. His book is sincere, but dogged by misfortune, and the reader is warned to approach it with the greatest caution.

We learn from Heinichen that the true *alla breve*, in addition to its 'antique, expressive style', has a rhythmic characteristic connected with its harmony. It is characterised by a harmonic pulse of two in the bar.

We also learn that 'its own movement always remains unaltered, and neither Adagio nor Allegro is attached to it'. In other words, its tempo is always moderate. At such a tempo, a pulse of four in the bar might otherwise be expected. Thus apart from its learned structure, the specific feature of the *alla breve* style is an unusually steady two in the bar. It has a gait like a pendulum swinging slowly.

Its signature, according to Heinichen, may be either C or ₵—a very helpful condition of affairs!

(c) Heinichen next informs us of certain varieties of *semi-allabreve* which may or may not retain something of the 'antique, expressive style'. These condense the harmonic pulse of two *alla breve* bars into one bar of *semi-allabreve*, by halving the written note-values. To the eye, this brings back a pulse of four crotchets in the bar. But since these crotchets, though moving faster than the minims of *alla breve*, will certainly move much less than twice as fast, the effect to the ear may still be that of a slightly faster *alla breve*. The ear does not perceive that two bars have been condensed into one and the written note-values halved; the ear merely perceives that something of the swinging, pendulum-like gait remains, although not at quite so moderate a tempo.

The signature shown by Heinichen for his *semi-allabreve* is C.

(d) From the above two usages we arrive at the general use of *alla breve, etc.*, to indicate not the 'antique expressive style' or any derivative of it, but simply a pulse of two in a bar with or without implication as to tempo. See Ch. XXXVIII, 4 (524)—Quantz, and (525)—Leopold Mozart; present chapter, 2, (539)—Brossard, middle paragraph, and (540)—Leopold Mozart.

4. THE 'ALLA BREVE' IN PRACTICE

In practice none of the possible indications for a two-pulse rhythm can be relied on, and it is the music and not the notation from which we must discover it; though a *change* from C to ₵, or the appearance of 'alla breve' *in the course of a piece*, may well be a valid hint.

5. THE HEMIOLA

When two bars of triple time unite to form, in effect, one bar of twice the duration, a change of pulse occurs to which the name hemiola (hemiole, hemiolia, lit. one and a half) is sometimes given (the implication is a proportion of 3:2).

This change of pulse is generally though not always quite visible in the notation, especially of the bass part, which tends to be tied across the bar-line in the middle of the hemiola. It is this bar-line which is in effect suppressed.

In performance, it is extremely important to make the change of pulse audible. Crudely: instead of *one* two three, *one* two three, the pulse becomes *one* two *three* one *two* three.

The hemiola is mainly but not only found at (passing or final) cadences.

CHAPTER XL

Variations of Tempo

1. THE NEED FOR EXPRESSIVE FLEXIBILITY IN BAROQUE TEMPO

Having decided on a basic tempo, we have to apply it with the necessary flexibility. Both evidence and experience confirm that the ordinary flexibility to which we are accustomed in later music is required for earlier music too, in a perfectly normal way. The next four quotations are quite general. The practical applications of this general principle will be treated under separate headings below, where further evidence in confirmation of the principle will be found.

(542) Thomas Mace, *Musick's Monument*, London, 1676, p. 147:

'*Many Drudge*, and take much *Pains* to Play their *Lessons very Perfectly*, (as they call It (that is, *Fast*) which when they can do, you will perceive *Little Life, or Spirit in Them, meerly for want of the Knowledge of This last Thing, I now mention, viz.* They do not labour to find out the *Humour, Life,* or *Spirit* of their *Lessons.*'

(543) Jean Rousseau, *Traité de la Viole*, Paris, 1687, p. 60:

'But genius and fine taste are gifts of nature, which cannot be learnt by rules, and it is with the help of these that the rules should be applied, and that liberties may be taken so fittingly as always to give pleasure, for to give pleasure means to have genius and fine taste.

[p. 66:] 'There are people who imagine that imparting the movement is to follow and keep time; but these are very different matters, for it is possible to keep time without entering into the movement, since time depends on the music, but the movement depends on genius and fine taste.'

(544) Fr. Couperin, *L'Art de toucher*, Paris, 1716, ed. of 1717, preface:

'Just as there is a difference between grammar and declamation, so there is an infinitely greater one between musical theory and the art of fine playing.

[p. 38:] 'I find we confuse time, or measure, with what is called cadence or movement. Measure defines the number and time-value of beats; cadence is properly the spirit, the soul that must be added to it.'

(545) Joachim Quantz, *Essay*, Berlin, 1752, XI, 13:

'The performance should be easy and flexible. However difficult the passage, it must be played without stiffness or constraint.'

2. FLEXIBILITY OF TEMPO IN UNMEASURED AND MEASURED PRELUDES

The prelude, like the toccata ('touch-piece'), was originally a free improvisation almost imperceptibly begun by the performer to check his tuning (on the lute, *etc.*), loosen his fingers, establish the tonality and prepare his own and his listeners' minds for the more formal music to follow. As it acquired some fluid artistic form of its own, so it came increasingly within the bounds of time and measure; yet in the seventeenth century, even preludes which were written down were sometimes written without bar-lines, and are in fact unmeasured, while those which have bar-lines and are measured may still require a greater freedom than ordinary measured music.

(546) Fr. Couperin, *L'Art de toucher le Clavecin*, Paris, 1716, ed. of 1717, eight illustrative preludes:

'[The player can choose one in the right key, in order] to loosen his fingers, or try the touch of an unfamiliar instrument.

[p. 60:] 'Although these preludes are written in measured time, there is nevertheless a conventional style to be followed. A prelude is a free composition, in which the fancy follows whatever occurs to it. But since it is exceptional to find talents able to create on the impulse of the moment, those who make use of these preludes should play them in a free manner, without confining themselves to strict time, except where I have purposely marked it by the word measured (mesuré).'

3. FLEXIBILITY OF TEMPO IN THE MONODIC STYLE, ETC.

Another style of composition in which an exceptional freedom of tempo is intended is the style which started as the *nuove musiche*, the 'new music' of the Italian monodists at the turn of the sixteenth and seventeenth centuries. This style did not continue for more than a generation in its first bold and uninhibited form; but it left a sequel of more or less declamatory idioms of which the most important later outcome was the recitative.

The following refers to the monodic style itself.

(547) Giulio Caccini, *Nuove Musiche*, Florence, 1602, freely transl. in Playford, *Introduction*, London, 1654:

'I call that the noble manner of singing, which is used without tying a mans self to the ordinary measure of time, making many times the value of the notes less by half, and sometime more, according to the conceit of the words; whence proceeds that kinde of singing with a graceful neglect, whereof I have spoken before.'

4. FLEXIBILITY OF TEMPO IN RECITATIVE

(a) Recitative continued to be true to its origins in depending for its effect on free tempo (see also App. VII, 2 for French recitative).

The name *recitativo secco* ('dry recitative') became attached to the most characteristic later Italianate variety, accompanied only by a continuo for harpsichord, organ or lute, with string bass. Since there are no melodic *ripieno* parts whose movement would impose a degree of measure, the singer is completely at liberty.

The name *recitativo stromentato* ('instrumented recitative') became attached to an alternative variety with orchestral parts, the presence of which keeps the rhythm within somewhat narrower bounds, though the tempo may still be more flexible than in most forms of measured composition.

There are other less clearly defined varieties of recitative, or of recitative-like melody, some of which (including, for example, much of Purcell's declamatory arioso for the solo voice) are more musically effective if they are taken in a measured tempo with not much more flexibility than any other expressive melody.

Only *recitativo secco* is recitative in the full meaning of the term. The less flexible varieties are declamatory music; but recitative in the full sense is declamation allied to music, and it is the declamation, not the music, which gives this style its character. And see App. VII.

(547a) Sébastien de Brossard, *Dictionaire de Musique*, Paris, 1703, *s.v.* 'Largo':

'[In Italian recitatives] we often do not make the beats very equal, because this is a kind of *declamation* where the Actor ought to follow the movement of the passion which inspires him or which he wants to express, rather than that of an equal and regulated measure.'

Jean-Jacques Rousseau went so far as to consider measured, accompanied recitative a contradiction in terms. He added:

(548) Jean-Jacques Rousseau, *Dictionnaire de musique*, Paris, 1768, *s.v.* 'Recitatif Mesuré':

'One measures the *Recitative* [only] when the accompaniment . . . obliges the Reciter to make his distribution of time-values conform to it.'

(549) John Hoyle, *Dictionary of Music*, London, 1770:

'RECITATIVO: Notwithstanding this sort of composition is noted in true time, the performer is at liberty to alter the Bars, or Measure, according as his subject requires; hence the Thorough Bass is to observe and follow the singer, and not the person that beats time.'

(b) But though the singer has such wide liberty with the tempo in true recitative, this liberty is more subject to conditions than might at first appear.

Declamation is not a mere matter of casual speech enlarged; it has a rhythm of its own. There is a symmetry even in its irregularity, and unless the singer can sense this symmetry, his liberties will sound not expressive, but formless. He hurries on regardless of intelligibility; his accompanists, having nothing intelligible to guide them, can only follow a fraction of a beat behind; the result is not merely ineffectual but untidy.

A recitative may move extremely fast provided that the singer keeps the rhythm of it intelligible and the enunciation clear. Recitative is an impassioned art; but it is not an impressionistic art. It has a melodic line to be drawn, freely, but with the greatest precision. It must be shaped to a pattern which the mind can grasp. An acceleration here is matched by a broadening there; an expressive pause in one place by a beat brought early in another place. Not only must the accompanists be able to keep in touch with all this; they must be in close enough sympathy to take much of the initiative. It is, at best, one of the most exacting skills; but there is nothing more telling than a harpsichordist and string bass player moving as one man, foreseeing every wish of their singer, and joining with him in making every irregularity sound not only natural but inevitable.

Suppose the singer has an up-beat phrase preceded by a little rest on the beat itself. He takes the phrase more rapidly than it is written: an excellent and dramatic effect. But he must not also take it early, by suppressing the rest: this does not sound dramatic, but merely hurried. On the contrary, he should take it late, by prolonging the rest, which restores the balance. There is now, however, a danger of sounding too cumbersome and literal. This is avoided if the accompanists, antici- pating his intention, bring the beat itself early, by playing their bass note and chord a little ahead of time. This allows the singer to press on without losing touch with the beat; for it is then the beat itself which presses on. There is a sense of urgency, but not a sense of being out of time. This urgency is balanced in its turn by an impression of breadth and power if the singer can draw out some corresponding phrase expressively. In particular, he will linger over his appoggiaturas as though he relished them and could hardly let them go. In these and other ways an overall proportion and relatedness can be built up out of the irregularities themselves.

It should be remembered that recitative has not necessarily to be forceful. It may also be quietly eloquent and contemplative, as so often in J. S. Bach. In these cases, the tempo, though still elastic, may need much less irregularity. The style, as always in recitative, should remain declamatory; but this is often more a matter of dramatic articulation than of irregular tempo. Crisp enunciation supported by warm, can- tabile sonority, the necessary declamatory ingredient being supplied by the sharpness of the consonants: this is a very satisfactory recipe for many kinds of recitative, even including some of the most theatrical.

VARIATIONS OF TEMPO

See also Ch. XXXII, 2 above, for the accompanist's point of view. See also App. VII for further discussion.

5. FLEXIBILITY OF TEMPO IN BAROQUE MUSIC GENERALLY

One of our most harmful reactions against over-romanticising early music has been the sewing-machine rhythm. No music, not even music based mainly on sequences, will stand a completely rigid tempo. Most baroque music needs considerable flexibility. See 1 above for general quotations on this point; those which follow are concerned with its application in music other than the special varieties already considered.

6. CHANGES OF TEMPO BETWEEN SECTIONS, *ETC.*

A change of tempo between sections or passages may sometimes be marked by a change of signature or by a time-word, but is more frequently left to the responsibility of the performer.

(550) Girolamo Frescobaldi, *Toccate*, Rome, 1615–16, preface, 7:

'When you find any passage of quavers and semiquavers to be played together for both hands, you must not play it too fast.

[9:] 'In the Partitas, when you find passages and expressive effects, it will be desirable to play slowly; the same consideration applies to the toccatas. The others not with passages may be played with a rather quicker beat, and it is left to the good taste and fine judgment of the performer to regulate the tempo, in which is found the spirit and perfection of this manner and style of playing.'

(551) Thomas Mace, *Musick's Monument*, London, 1676, p. 130:

'[If the music falls into sections or "short sentences", these may be] according as they best please your own *Fancy*, some very *Briskly*, and *Couragiously*, and some again *Gently*, *Lovingly*, *Tenderly*, and *Smoothly*.'

(552) C. P. E. Bach, *Essay*, I, [4th] ed., Leipzig, 1787, III, 28:

'Passages in music in the major mode which are repeated in the minor may be taken somewhat more slowly in this repetition, because of the expression.'

7. VARIATIONS OF TEMPO WITHIN THE PASSAGE

Apart from making sectional changes in the tempo, we may condense or stretch it in passing.

There are two ways of doing this: by borrowing time, and by stealing it. In the first case restitution for any extra time taken is made promptly enough for the mind to accept the underlying tempo as undisturbed: *i.e.* within the bar, or at most within a few bars. In the second case, restitution is not made at all: the underlying tempo may be resumed, but without any condensing to compensate for the previous stretching.

The name *tempo rubato* has been used for both these situations, though its literal meaning, 'stolen time', is strictly applicable only to the second.

8. BORROWED TIME

(a) We may first take certain technical meanings which *tempo rubato* had for baroque writers, but has not for ourselves. These meanings centred round the displacement of rhythm, or sometimes merely of accent, within an underlying tempo which is not disturbed. The following is really a form of that expressive inequalisation of rhythms written equally which was always open to the performer in appropriate situations: see Ch. XLII, 6 below, and Part III, Rhythm, generally. Caccini's notation of his explanation is no doubt approximate; the actual rhythm might be very flexible. But the bass would not be involved in the disturbance; it would continue with a steady pulse.

Ex. 192. G. Caccini, *Nuove Musiche*, 1602, tempo rubato in the old sense:

The following is a late reference to the same idiom, and to another in which the mere displacement of the accent serves to suggest an ambiguity of time.

(553) Daniel Gottlob Türk, *Klavierschule*, Leipzig and Halle, 1789, Engl. tr. [1804], p. 40:

'*Tempo rubato*, or *robbato*, signifies a stolen, or robbed Time, the application of which is likewise left to the judgment of the Performer. These words have several significations. Commonly they signify a manner of shortening, and lengthening Notes; that is to say, a part is taken from the length of one Note and given to the other . . . by an anticipation [or] by a retardation. Beside this signification, it is understood by *Tempo rubato*, that the Accent is put upon the inferior [off-beat] Notes instead of the superior [on-beat] ones.'

Ex. 193. D. G. Türk, *loc. cit.*, tempo rubato in old senses:

The following is yet another sense of *tempo rubato* to which we should not now apply the term.

(554) C. P. E. Bach, *Essay*, I, [4th] ed., Leipzig, 1787, III, 28:

'[This brings us to] the *Tempo rubato*. Its indication is simply the presence of more or less notes than are permitted in the measure of the bar. A whole bar, part of one or several bars may be distorted, so to speak, in this manner. The hardest but most important matter is to give all notes of the same value the same duration. When the performance is so managed that one hand seems to play across the measure and the other hand strictly with it, the performer may be said to be doing all that is required of him. It is only occasionally that all the parts come together. . . . A master of *Tempo* [*rubato*] need not be confined by the numbers [which divide notes into groups of] 5, 7, 11, *etc.* He sometimes adds or omits notes to taste . . . but always with fitting freedom.'

(b) The next quotation describes the normal form of borrowed time to which we commonly apply the term *tempo rubato*.

(555) Leopold Mozart, *Violinschule*, Augsburg, 1756, XII, 20:

'When it is a true virtuoso worthy to be so called whom you are accompanying, you must not let yourself be deceived by the ornamenting and drawing out of the notes, which he knows so well how to shape cleverly and expressively, into delaying or hurrying, but must go on playing throughout in the same manner of movement, or the effect which the soloist wished to build up would be destroyed by the accompaniment.'

Such descriptions of a timeless melody superimposed on a timed bass remind us of Chopin's famous explanation of his own ornamental figuration.

(556) Fryderyk Franciszek Chopin, cited by E. Dannreuther, *Musical Ornamentation*, II, London [1895], p. 161:

'The singing hand may deviate, the accompanist must keep time . . . . The graces are part of the text, and therefore part of the time. . . . Fancy a tree with its branches swayed by the wind; the stem represents the steady time, the moving leaves are the melodic inflections. This is what is meant by *Tempo* and *Tempo rubato*.'

But it is not all that is meant. As a corrective to undisciplined *rubato* in Chopin and elsewhere, the above passage is invaluable. The bass can far more often be kept perfectly steady than the undisciplined performer realises; but it must be admitted that there are also many passages in which the bass is inevitably involved. In such cases, if restitution is made either within the bar or shortly afterwards, the mind accepts the underlying tempo as undisturbed.

In a few exceptional passages, the structure lends itself to much longer accelerations compensated by subsequent de-accelerations (the opposite effect must be very rare, since normal ritardandos are not subsequently compensated).

(557) C. P. E. Bach, *Essay*, I, Berlin, 1753, III, 28:

'[Certain sequential passages] can be effectively performed by accelerating gradually and gently, and retarding immediately afterwards.'

All this still lies within the conception of time borrowed only to be subsequently restored. It is an important conception, and Leopold Mozart's advice at (555) above must be taken seriously.

9. STOLEN TIME

But time may also be stolen, with no intention of subsequently restoring it. This, which is now the most popular usage of the term *tempo rubato*, is, if not more important than the foregoing, at least more conspicuous.

The following passages refer both to borrowed and to stolen time, but perhaps more particularly to the latter. It will be appreciated that the distinction between them is by no means so sharp in practice as it has been made to seem here for the sake of clarity. It is, however, a valuable one to bear in mind. No *tempo rubato* should be without shape and reason; and it is not at all a bad guiding principle to make restitution where restitution can be made, but to have no hesitation over stealing time, where it cannot. The main point is to realise that *tempo rubato* in both these normal modern senses has a perfectly ordinary place in early music, in spite of the scarcity there of written indications for it.

(558) Girolamo Frescobaldi, *Toccate*, Rome, 1615–16, preface, 1:

'First, this kind of playing must not be subject to the beat, as we see done in modern Madrigals, which, in spite of their difficulties, are made easier by means of the beat, taking it now slowly, now quickly, and even held in the air, to match the expressive effects, or the sense of the words.

'[6: With trills in one hand and figuration in the other] let the passage flow less quickly, and with expression.'

(559) Thomas Mace, *Musick's Monument*, London, 1676, p. 81:

'[Beginners must learn strict time; but] when we come to be *Masters*, so that we can *command all manner of Time*, at our *own Pleasures*; we Then *take Liberty*, (and very often, for *Humour* [*i.e.* "mood", not "wit"], *and good Adornment-sake*, in certain Places), to *Break Time*; *sometimes Faster*, and *sometimes Slower*, as we perceive, the *Nature of the Thing Requires*.'

(560) C. P. E. Bach, *Essay*, I, Berlin, 1753, III, 8:

'Certain deliberate disturbances of the beat are extremely beautiful.
[28:] 'Certain notes and rests should be prolonged beyond their written length for reasons of expression.'

(561) Daniel Gottlob Türk, *Klavierschule*, Leipzig and Halle, 1789, Engl. tr. [1804], p. 40:

'[In addition to the special forms, ordinary] delaying, or hastening the time designedly, is likewise signified by *Tempo rubato*.'

10. RALLENTANDOS

Rallentandos are a case of stolen time, but so important that they need separate mention.

Cadences are extremely numerous in baroque music, and it is the nature of a cadence to be acknowledged by a rallentando. If we acknowledged them all, however, the music would fall to pieces. We have to distinguish cadences which pass on at once from cadences which bring some portion of the music to an end, or perhaps merely some thought. However slight the recognition which we grant the latter, they must not be completely over-ridden. A baroque movement taken with no internal rallentandos, and then jerked to an abrupt halt by putting on all the brakes within a bar or two of the finish, sounds ruthlessly insensitive and rigid: like the sewing-machine rhythm referred to in 5 above, this was part of a puritanical reaction which is not supported by the contemporary evidence.

The proper moment at which to start a rallentando is often suggested by the harmony, where it first gives unmistakable warning of the approaching close. Most long rallentandos are shallow, most steep rallentandos are short; but they must all be graded in a shapely proportion. No attempt should be made to conceal a weak cadence by unnaturally curtailing its rallentando: something may perhaps be done by added ornamentation; but in any case it is better to accept the inevitable with a show of conviction. The need for rallentandos should not, on the other hand, be exaggerated. It is a matter partly of temperament, but chiefly of a sensitive response to hints offered by the music.

(562) Girolamo Frescobaldi, *Toccate*, Rome, 1615–16, preface, 5:

'The cadences, although they may be written quickly, are properly to be very much drawn out; and in approaching the end of passages or cadences, one proceeds by drawing out the time more adagio.'

(563) C. P. E. Bach, *Essay*, I, Berlin, 1753, III, 28:

'In general, ritenutos are better suited to slow or comparatively moderate tempos than to very rapid ones.

[Ed. of 1787 adds:] 'In expressive playing, the performer should avoid numerous and exaggerated ritenutos, which are apt to cause the tempo to drag. The expression itself tends to bring this mistake about. In spite of beautiful details, the attempt should be made to hold the tempo at the end of a piece just as it was at the start, which is a very difficult achievement.

[II, 1762, XXIX, 20:] 'In slow or moderate tempos, pauses are usually prolonged beyond their strict length . . . this applies to [ornamental] pauses, closes, etc., as well as to [plain] pauses. It is usual to draw out somewhat and depart to some extent from the strict measure of the bar . . . the passage [thus] acquires an impressiveness which makes it stand out.

[XXXI, 3:] 'When the principal part draws out before coming to an [ornamented] pause, [the accompanist must do the same].'

The words 'drag' for rallentando and 'away' for *a tempo* appear in early seventeenth-century English MSS., and printed in Thomas Mace (*Musick's Monument*, London, 1676).

'Adagio' or 'grave' near the end of a baroque movement appears more likely to stand for molto rallentando (*i.e.* more drawing out than would in any case be assumed without indication) than for meno mosso or in tempo ritenuto (at a slower but constant speed): *e.g.* J. S. Bach, G major Prelude and Fugue for organ (B.G. 38, p. 12); B minor organ Fugue XIX (B.G. 38, p. 125); C minor organ Fugue XV (B.G. 38, p. 105), where the last section is Adagio but has 'adagio' again over the last half-bar, perhaps in the sense of più rallentando. This would be not unlike the well-established use of *p* . . . *mf* . . . *f* for crescendo and of *f* . . . *mf* . . . *p* for diminuendo, for which see Ch. XLIX below.

Ex. 194. F. W. Marpurg, *Clavierstücke*, Berlin, III, 1763, p. 19, rallentando suggested by the word adagio:

Allegro

Adagio piano

PART THREE

RHYTHM

CHAPTER XLI

Rhythm in Early Music

1. FLEXIBILITY THE KEY TO EARLY RHYTHM

Rhythm is second only to tempo in importance, and like tempo, depends eventually on the invisible clock which we carry inside us. But unlike tempo, it is sufficiently involved in the structure of the music to have an outward shape which can be, and since the middle ages normally has been notated.

The notation of rhythm, however, is necessarily mathematical, because our notated time-values go by fixed multiples. The inner vitality of rhythm is not mathematical; it is a variable reacting with other variables to embody the mood of a given performance. Every performer modifies the written rhythms to some extent, sharpening the dots in march-like music, softening them for lilting music, and so forth. Early performers carried these modifications to extremes some of which could at least approximately have been shown in notation. Since they were not, they were evidently left to the performer not from necessity but from policy: the usual early policy of making nothing in music rigid which can be left fluid and spontaneous. That fact is the key to the problem of rhythm in early music.

2. RHYTHMS LEFT ENTIRELY TO THE PERFORMER

Unmeasured preludes (see Ch. XXIV, 3, and Ch. XL, 2 above) and more or less improvised arpeggiation in figured bass accompaniment (Ch. XXX, 3 above) or in solos (especially for the violin) written as chords but meant to be broken into figurate rhythms at will (Ch. XXIV, 3b): these are among the rare examples of complete liberty of rhythm remaining in the baroque period.

3. RHYTHMS LEFT PARTLY TO THE PERFORMER

Liberty of rhythm within established conventions may be seen in the modification of certain kinds of dotted rhythm (Chs. XLIII–XLIV

435

below); and the expressive inequalisation of certain equally written rhythms (Ch. XLII below).

4. RHYTHMS LOOSELY NOTATED FOR MERE CONVENIENCE

(a) Certain difficulties in notating combinations of duple and triple rhythms were habitually evaded, not with any expressive intention, but as a mere matter of convenience: the performer is not here being trusted with a choice; he merely has to know what the loose notation means (see Ch. XLVI below).

(b) One particularly unpredictable convention concerning the placing of the bass note at cadences in recitative (luckily it is known to most modern musicians) will be described in Ch. XLII, 4 below. A different convention sometimes used for the same situation in opera is described in App. VII, 5.

CHAPTER XLII

Note-Values

1. METHODS OF SHOWING DIFFERENT NOTE-VALUES IN MENSURAL (PROPORTIONAL) NOTATION

In mensural (or proportional) notation, the factors governing the time-value of a note, *i.e.* its written rhythm, may include:

(a) The 'time-signature' (see Ch. XXXVIII above).

(b) The nominal value of the adjacent notes.

(c) The form of the note: round, square or oblong; with or without upward or downward tail or tails; *etc.*; also its grouping with other notes in ligatures, for which see App. I.

(d) The coloration: whether open red (or filled-in black) open black (= white), *etc.*

(e) A dot of augmentation (see Ch. XLIII below).

(f) A dot of division, grouping notes for purposes of mensuration.

See Thurston Dart (*Grove's Dictionary*, London, 1954, *s.v.* 'Notation') for a brief and Apel's *Notation* for a full account.

2. BAROQUE AND MODERN METHODS OF SHOWING DIFFERENT NOTE-VALUES

Of these methods, only (f) went quite out of use in baroque music, but the others were retained in varying degrees.

The use of connecting beams between groups of quavers, semi-quavers, *etc.*, in place of strokes to each separate tail, became established during the seventeenth century.

These beams often extended across more notes than is now custo-mary, or is very convenient to the eye. Moreover, the groups were not necessarily made up in units of a beat, or simple multiples or divisions of a beat; the number of notes included may be quite arbitrary, or governed more by calligraphy than by ease of reading. But otherwise they present no difficulty.

There may occasionally be a connection intended between the grouping by beams and the phrasing; but not ordinarily. Different contemporary manuscripts and editions of the same work are quite inconsistent in their arrangement of the beams. In particular, groupings by pairs and by fours seem indifferently interchangeable. On the

437

TABLE X: main baroque variants in showing note-values

RESTS	NAMES	FORMS	PROPORTIONS
	Large		equals two longs
	Long		,, breves
	Breve	or	,, semibreves
	Semibreve	or	,, minims
	Minim	or or	,, crotchets
	Crotchet	or or or	,, quavers
	Quaver	or or or or	,, semiquavers
	Semiquaver *etc.*	or or or or	,, demisemiquavers; *etc.*

occasions when a musical significance is intended, this is usually quite easy to see; elsewhere, the grouping is to be ignored for purposes of interpretation.

Notice the decorative forms of quaver and semiquaver, which look rather as if they had one more tail than is actually the case. White and black forms of the same shape are late instances of coloration: *e.g.* the black minim (*i.e.* the crotchet) may equal half the white minim; the black semibreve may equal half the white semibreve, and both may be encountered in seventeenth-century triple-time. White quavers may equal crotchets. But for other important possibilities, see App. VII, 4.

The longest notes went steadily into oblivion, the breve being the longest in normal baroque usage, as the semibreve is in modern usage.

(564) Christopher Simpson, *Compendium*, London, 1665, ed. of 1732, p. 13:

'The *Large* and *Long* are now of little use, being too long for any Voice, or Instrument (the Organ excepted) to hold out to their full length. But their *Rests* are still in frequent use, especially in grave Music, and Songs of many Parts.

'You will say, if those Notes you named be too long for the Voice to hold out, to what purpose were they used formerly? To which I answer; they were used in *Tripla Time* and in a quick Measure; quicker (perhaps) than we now make our *Semibreve* and Minum. For, as after-times added new Notes, so they (still) put back the former into something a slower Measure.'

See Ch. XXXV, 2 (b), above for the desirability of reducing the note-values in modern editions to protect the performer from being deceived into taking much too slow a tempo in music where the discrepancy between the apparent note-values in the original and their real speed is very wide.

The dot of augmentation, which now lengthens the note after which it is placed by one-half, had a more variable influence in baroque notation: see Chs. XLIII and XLVI below.

3. ARBITRARY NOTE-VALUES AT THE ENDS OF PHRASES, ETC.

(a) The last note of a piece or section, in all parts, may be written with a breve as a conventional indication to hold on to a natural but undetermined length—much like the pause sign often set there nowadays. That this is a mere convention is shown by the fact that some parts may be given a breve against a semibreve in other parts; and the same part may have different lengths notated in different contemporary copies of the same work. It is not intended that the full length should be held where the music does not require it; and sometimes, particularly at repeats, it is most undesirable to do so.

(b) At phrase-endings other than the end of a piece or section, the same convention applies, and it may be desirable to take the last note off very much shorter than it is written, in order to avoid fouling the next change of harmony or covering the next entry. Thus the autograph score of Henry Purcell's Golden Sonata (No. 9, 2nd set of ten trio sonatas, London, 1697) shows at bar six of the fourth movement a minim at the phrase end in the string bass-part; but the printed editions (just possibly benefiting from a lost intermediate copy corrected by Purcell himself, as Walter Emery shows in *Two Sonatas* by H. Purcell, ed. Robert Donington and Walter Emery, London, 1959) give a crotchet. The correction makes sure of what Purcell originally assumed that the performer would do of his own accord; but in countless other cases, both in Purcell and throughout baroque music, the notation was not corrected, and it was left to the performer to avoid an unmeaning dissonance or an unnecessary obscurity by adjusting the note-value according to the sense of the music.

Even where no actual dissonance or gross obscurity results from holding the literal value, the texture can often be lightened to very good effect by not doing so. Cases abound in which one part has a longer note-value written than another part which moves with it: there is no musical reason why they should differ, and we can again confirm that they were not meant to, from the casual discrepancies in different contemporary copies of the same works. In polyphonic motets, madrigals and fantasies this point will repay the most careful attention, and there is other music in which it is well worth watching.

(564a) Daniel Gottlob Türk, *Pflichten eines Organisten*, Halle, 1787:

'There are even occasions where one must not hold on to the full notated value of the note; if, for instance a long note [is notated] after a run in quick notes and is followed by a rest, the last note is generally cut short.'

4. A CONVENTIONAL MIS-NOTATION IN RECITATIVE

(565) J. A. Scheibe in F. W. Marpurg's *Kritische Briefe*, Berlin, for 1760–62, p. 352, letter 109:

'Further, some composers are in the habit of anticipating the penultimate note of the cadence, namely the dominant, without inserting a rest.'

Ex. 195. Scheibe, *loc. cit.*, miswritten basses in recitative (corrected notation mine, after Scheibe's instructions. In performance the two chords after the voice has stopped can be taken a little late, or at least not hurried. For a different convention of opera, see App. VII, 5).

CHAPTER XLIII

Dotted Notes

1. THE BAROQUE DOT A VARIABLE SYMBOL

(a) The dot which in our present notation prolongs the value of the notes before it by one half is the same dot which was called the dot of augmentation in proportional notation, where it had the same function.

(b) But in baroque notation, the dot of augmentation was also used to mean any convenient prolongation. Thus for example:

TABLE XI: the variable baroque dot

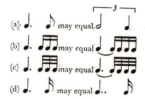

2. WHAT BAROQUE NOTES ARE 'OVER-DOTTED'

(a) The great majority of baroque dotted notes occur in the ordinary course of melody and are of approximately standard length.

(b) But when the dotted notes (i) are persistent enough to dominate the rhythm; or (ii) form a distinct rhythmic figure or formula; or more generally (iii), would sound sluggish if taken literally: then it was the convention to crispen them (Fr. *pointer*) by lengthening the dot, thereby delaying and shortening the note after the dot. This is often called 'double-dotting'; but an exacter term is 'over-dotting'. (iv) Over-dotting mainly occurs within the beat: see (565b) below.

3. 'OVER-DOTTING' ITSELF VARIABLE IN EXTENT

(a) The lengthening of the dot may greatly vary, and can be quite free and unmathematical, except when other parts move across the dot; then it is better to prolong it, if at all, in mathematical proportion.

(b) A dot followed by a pair or more of short notes may be similarly prolonged, and these short notes delayed and shortened: thus Ex. b Table XI in (1) b above may be performed as Ex. c.

TABLE XII: dots (a) unprolonged, or (b), (c), mathematically prolonged

Take (a) as written | or (b) as double-dotted | or (c) as triple-dotted

(c) When the short note or notes come before the dotted note, some recommended a similar sharpening, others a milder lilt.

(d) For dotted notes against triplet rhythm, see Ch. XLVI below.

4. BAROQUE INSTRUCTIONS FOR DOTTED NOTES

(565a) Michel L'Affillard, *Principes*, Paris, 1694, p. 30:

'One must delay the dotted Crochet, and pass quickly over the Quaver which follows it.'

(565b) Étienne Loulié, *Elements*, Paris, 1696, p. 16:

'When the Dot is in the same Beat as the Quaver which preceeds it, one must in singing hold this quaver a little longer, and pass quickly over the Semiquaver.'

(566) Joachim Quantz, *Essay*, Berlin, 1752, V, 21:

'In quavers, semiquavers and demi-semiquavers, the standard rule is altered, for the sake of the liveliness they ought to express . . . whether in slow or quick tempo.

'. . . it is not possible to determine exactly the time of the little note which follows the dot [but Quantz shows it as follows].'

Ex. 196. Quantz, *loc. cit.*, suggested lengths for 'double-dotting'

[23:] 'where the dot comes after the second note [the treatment is the same] for the length of the dot and the first note; only the order is reversed [as at (d)]. The same treatment is used with the two little notes at [(e) and (f);] the shorter we perform the first [note at (d)] the livelier and bolder the expression; and on the contrary the longer we make the dots [at (e) and (f)] the more flattering and agreeable the expression.'

DOTTED NOTES

(567) C. P. E. Bach, *Essay*, I, Berlin, 1753, III, 23:

'The short notes following dotted notes are always performed shorter than their written length. It is therefore superfluous to set dashes or dots [of articulation] over them. [The short notes at Ex. (a), (b), (c) and (d) would all be taken at the same speed *i.e.* as demi-semiquavers. The short notes of the two parts at Ex. (e) would be taken together. It may sometimes happen, especially at a quick tempo, that the note following the dot is best given its written value, to facilitate the movement of the remaining parts as at Ex. (f).]

[Ed. of 1787:] 'When four or more short notes follow a dot, they are rapidly disposed of, being so numerous. This also applies to [Ex. (h) to (l)], and when the tempo is not too slow, to [Ex. (m) to (q)].

[24:] 'The first notes of [a Scotch snap when] slurred, are not performed too rapidly, in a moderate or slow tempo; for that would leave too long a space after them with nothing happening. The first note is stressed with a gentle emphasis, but not by a sharp attack or by being prematurely left [the opposite of Quantz' advice at (566) above].

[II, 1762, XXIX, 15:] 'Since a proper accuracy is often lacking in the notation of dotted notes, a general rule of performance has become established which nevertheless shows many exceptions. According to this rule, the notes following the dot are to be performed with the greatest rapidity, and this is frequently the case. But sometimes notes in the remaining parts, against which these [dotted notes] have to come in, are so distributed that a modification of the rule is needed. Or again, a feeling of smoothness which would be disturbed by the inevitably challenging effect of dotted notes compels the performer to shorten the dotted note slightly. Thus if only one kind of interpretation is used as a starting point for performance, the other kinds will be lacking.'

Ex. 197. C. P. E. Bach, *op. cit.*, I, III, 23, dots of various lengths:

(568) Leopold Mozart, *Violinschule*, Augsburg, 1756, I, iii, 11:

'In slow pieces, there are certain passages where the dot should be held rather longer than the [strict] rule requires, to prevent the performance from sounding too sleepy . . . the time taken by this prolongation is so to speak robbed from the note which follows the dot.'

Ex. 198. Jean-Jacques Rousseau, *Dictionnaire de Musique*, Paris, 1768, *s.v.* 'Cadence', 'over-dotting' on trill (interpretation approximate only; N.B. the *E* functions as the *appuy*, the prolonged upper-note start of the trill):

(569) Johann Friedrich Reichhardt, *Über die Pflichten des Ripien-Violinisten*, Berlin and Leipzig, 1776, Sect. ii:

'When [notes] are dotted one after the other, the shorter notes should be taken as short as possible to give more emphasis to the longer.'

(570) D. G. Türk, *Klavierschule*, Leipzig and Halle, 1789, 48, p. 363:

'Figures in which the first note is short and the second is dotted are in all cases slurred smoothly and flattered. Admittedly the first note takes the accent, but the stress should be very mild.

'Note: it used to be the custom to give the first note of such a figure a greatly shortened length.'

5. DOTS AS SILENCES OF ARTICULATION

Dots followed or preceded by a pair of notes are normally slurred.

Dots followed (but not dots preceded) by a short note are very often taken in whole or part as silence of articulation. So are dots followed by more than two short notes.

(571) Joachim Quantz, *Essay*, Berlin, 1752, XVII, vii, 58:

'The dotted note must be accented and the bow must be stopped (Ger. *abgesetzet*, Fr. *détaché*) for the value of the dot.'

(572) C. P. E. Bach, *Essay*, I, Berlin, 1753, III, 23:

'Dots after long notes, or after short notes at a slow tempo, and dots occurring singly, are all held on [Ex. (g) above]. But at a fast tempo, continuing successions of dots are [often taken as rests] in spite of the contrary appearance of the notation. This contradiction should be avoided by a more exact notation. In the absence of that, however, the feeling of the music will throw light [on the proper way of performing it].'

(573) Leopold Mozart, *Violinschule*, Augsburg, 1756, I, iii, 9:

'In slow pieces . . . the dot has to be joined to its note with a diminuendo [and slurred to the subsequent short note].

[10:] 'In fast pieces the bow is lifted at every dot; hence each note is detached from the other, and performed in springing style.

'[IV, 13: After dots] demi-semiquavers are played very late and the next note is played immediately afterwards with a rapid change of bow.

'[15: When the dotted rhythm is reversed] the notes [*i.e.* the short note and the subsequent dotted note] are always slurred together in pairs, with one bow-stroke. However, the dotted note should not be allowed to die away too quickly, nor should it be accented, but held quite smoothly.'

(574) J. C. F. Rellstab, *Anleitung*, Berlin, 1790, p. 12:

'Dotted notes [written] as at [Ex. 198 (a)] are played as at [Ex. 198 (b)]. In most cases, the dot is regarded as a rest, and the last note taken shorter than its strict value. [In sostenuto passages] the dot is sustained conscientiously, although the last note is still played shorter than its strict value. Yet at other times, the short note must be kept at its strict value because of the speed or the synchronisation [with other moving parts]. A tender expression, or longer note values, again make exceptions here; the following passage [Ex. 198 (c)] is played with the notes fully sustained, and with the shorter notes taken at their strict value.'

Ex. 198a. Rellstab, *loc. cit.*, dotted notes (a), (b), articulated, (c) slurred:

6. GENERAL BAROQUE PREFERENCE FOR THE VARIABLE DOT

(a) Since the double-dot as a symbol of notation existed for several generations before being brought into general use in the later eighteenth century, the variable use of the single dot was evidently preferred; the transition begins to appear in the following two quotations.

(575) Leopold Mozart, *Violinschule*, Augsburg, 1756, I, iii, 11:

'It would be very good to decide and set down rightly this prolongation of the dot. I at least have often done so, and made clear my intended performance by writing a double dot followed by a shortened note.'

(576) F. W. Marpurg, *Anleitung zum Clavierspielen*, Berlin, 1755, I, x, p. 13, Anmerkung:

'If the dot is to be very sharp, *i.e.* if the succeeding short note is taken with more vivacity than its [written] value prescribes: then one should in the first place write *two dots one after the other*, and in the second place shorten the succeeding note by half.'

(b) In Ex. 199 (a) below Couperin has made certain of the 'doubledotting' by adding an extra tail to the short notes; yet he still does not use the double-dot, either because he was not aware of it, or because he saw no reason for it, being accustomed to using the dot for any required lengthening at will—*e.g.* as at Ex. 199 (b) below. The reason for the extra tail is that without it the dotted notes, so far from being 'double-dotted', might have been reduced to triplet rhythm, to fit the triplets which come against them (*e.g.* on the 2nd beat of bar 2), under the convention discussed in Ch. XLVI, below.

Ex. 199. (a) Couperin, *L'Apothéose de Corelli*, Mt. VI, dot used instead of double-dot; (b) Couperin, XIV Concert, Prelude, bar 1, dot used at convenience:

(c) The following is a rare exception: *i.e.* an accurate notation of 'double-dotting', complete with written-out silence of articulation. The explanation is obvious: it is an Italian composition in French overture style, which would not at that date be familiar to Italian performers.

Ex. 200. Arcangelo Corelli, Op. VI, No. 3, publ. posthumously, Amsterdam [1714] opening Largo:

(d) At Ex. 206 in Ch. XLV, 8 below, Handel has notated equal notes at the opening statement but unequal notes at its recapitulation. The intention is quite certainly that the inequality should be present from the start, since there can be no conceivable musical justification for performing the two passages in different rhythms from one another. Such cases abound.

7. POST-BAROQUE 'OVER-DOTTING'

The convention of 'over-dotting' certainly survived into the generation of Beethoven—see (574) in 5 above, and probably lost force quite gradually; it still survives to the extent to which every alert musician will sharpen a crisp rhythm without noticing that he is doing so. It is a natural instinct. It wants carrying much further in early music, however, than instinct alone will carry it; and it is, in fact, one of the reforms which make most difference to the vitality of baroque music. Passages which have seemed inexplicably sluggish leap into life and energy when the 'over-dotting' has been attended to with proper thoroughness.

Fuller instructions and suggestions for 'under-dotting' and 'over-dotting', *etc.*, will be found in my *Performer's Guide to Baroque Music*, London, 1973.

CHAPTER XLIV

Other Sharpened Rhythms

1. THE PIQUANT CONTRASTS OF FRENCH OVERTURE STYLE

(a) French Overture style is a convenient name for one of the most characteristically French contributions to baroque music. This is an idiom of composition which became typical of the slow introductory movement of the French Overture itself, and spread to many other contexts and countries. It can be recognised by its special feature, which is a remarkable contrast between a ground-swell of majestic rhythm and a surface turbulence of dotted notes and rushing scales.

This contrast is intended to be exaggerated in performance. The dots are strongly 'over-dotted'; and they are taken wholly or largely as silences of articulation. The scales, some three to seven notes long, are left as late as possible, taken very rapidly, detached. See Chapter XLIII, 4 for French and other evidence of 'over-dotting'.

When the scale-passage is written as the up-beat after a dotted note, it is a particular instance of ordinary 'over-dotting'. When it follows the beat after a short rest, it is this rest which is prolonged, and the result may be regarded as an extension of the 'over-dotting' principle.

The entire effect is one of ferocious flexibility on a foundation of strength and poise. In a literal performance, this effect is lost, and the music merely sounds heavy. French Overture style depends even more than most baroque music on the invigoration given it by conventional departures from the written rhythm. See Postscript at the end of this chapter.

(577) Joachim Quantz, *Essay*, Berlin, 1752, XVII, ii, 16:

'When some demi-semiquavers come after a long note and a short rest, they should always be taken very quickly, whether in Adagio or in Allegro. Before playing them, you should wait until the very end of the time allotted to them, so as to avoid getting out of [*i.e.* ahead of] time.'

Ex. 201. Quantz, *op. cit.*, runs in French Overture style (the interpretation is mine):

448

[Quantz, Ch. XII, 24:] 'The majestic style is conveyed by long notes, during which other parts have rapid passages, and also by dotted notes. These latter must be enforced with power and attack. The dot is prolonged and the following note thrown quickly away.

[vii, 58:] 'When there are three or more semiquavers after a dot, or a rest, they should not be given their strict value, particularly in slow pieces; but after waiting until the very end of the time allotted to them, you play them as fast as possible, in a style frequently found in Overtures, Introductions and Furies. Nevertheless you must give each one of these quick notes a separate bow, and you can hardly slur anything.

[iv, 10: The 'cellist] 'should play his dotted notes more gravely and weightily than the violins; but when it comes to the semiquavers which follow them, he must make them short and sharp [*i.e.* with the violins] whether in slow time or in quick.'

And see (567), 2nd par., in Chapter XLIII, 4.

(b) The following fugue by J. S. Bach is an excellent example of the wider influence of the French Overture style, and is given here in Arnold Dolmetsch's interpretation (*Interpretation*, London [1915], p. 65: *cf.* his historic recording on the clavichord for the Columbia 'Forty-Eight' Society).

Ex. 202. J. S. Bach, Fugue in D major, Bk. I of the 'Forty-Eight', interpretation by Arnold Dolmetsch, *loc. cit.*:

2. RESTS PROLONGED BEFORE DOTTED FIGURES, ETC.

(a) The following convention will be found of very wide application. (578) Joachim Quantz, *Essay*, Berlin, 1752, XVII, ii, 16:

'If in a slow allabreve or in normal common time there is a semiquaver rest on the accented beat followed by dotted notes, you must take the rest as if it had a dot attached to it, or [another] rest of half its value, and as if the note after it were a demisemiquaver.'

Ex. 203. Quantz, *loc. cit.*, shortening the note before a dotted rhythm (the interpretation is that given by Arnold Dolmetsch, *Interpretation*, London [1915], p. 58):

In Ex. 203a following, there is no distinction of rhythm intended; the conventional 𝄽 𝄾 𝅘𝅥𝅯𝅘𝅥𝅮 should be maintained throughout. Cases of this kind are exceedingly common and important to take correctly.

Ex. 203a. Handel, Op. I No. 1, 1st movt., Grave, sharpened rhythms not all correctly notated:

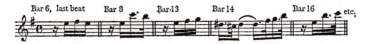

(b) A detail which falls under the same application of the principle of 'over-dotting' is the little preliminary note or pair of notes in certain dance movements such as allemandes, courantes and ayres.

Ex. 204 (a) below shows the normal 'over-dotting'. Ex. 204 (b) shows the single preliminary note delayed and shortened as if a hypothetical dotted note, or rather a hypothetical rest, were in front of it. (For the sharpening of the dotted rhythm specifically in courantes, see (592a) in Ch. XLV, 8 below. For the uneven rhythm in the interpretation of Ex. 204 (b), see Ch. XLV below.)

Ex. 204. Matthew Locke, Suite II for four viols, mid-17th cent., (a) Courante, (b) Ayre:

The Almand of Purcell's 2nd Suite for Harpsichord (G minor) has this little preliminary note shown as a semiquaver at the start of the first half, and as a quaver at the start of the second half. The following

Courante has the reverse of this. No distinctions are intended: the notation is casual, but a semiquaver is evidently intended throughout, there being no musical justification for any such inconsistency in the performance. These and other similar cases tend strongly to confirm the interpretation here suggested. It is so often these little inadvertent inconsistencies of notation which help to show the consistent intention at the back of them.

POSTSCRIPT TO NEW VERSION

Frederick Neumann ('La note pointée et la soi-disant "Manière Française" ', *Revue de Musicologie*, LI, 1965, No. 1, pp. 66–92) has expressed his disbelief in any such idiom as is here called the French Overture style, which he thinks my old master Arnold Dolmetsch 'was the first to proclaim' out of his own modern imagination. There has been a rebuttal by Michael Collins ('A Reconsideration of French Over-Dotting', *Music and Letters*, Jan., 1969, pp. 111–123), who shows, among other things, that the idiom was, on the contrary, sufficiently familiar in the eighteenth century for J. A. P. Schultz (*Allgemeine Theorie der Schönen Künste*, Leipzig, 1771, etc., 'Ouvertüre') to recall that 'in the previous [*i.e.* 17th] century one obtained the best overtures from France', whence they were later 'imitated elsewhere, particularly in Germany' by Handel, Telemann and others: the movement being slow but enlivened with many small notes 'fierily performed'; having its long notes 'usually dotted, and in performance held beyond their [notated] value', followed by little notes 'which must be played with the utmost rapidity and so far as possible, staccato'.

Thus great pioneer as he was, Dolmetsch did not invent the French Overture style. Indeed, we can (for once) trace the memory of it lingering down through William Crotch (1775–1847) notating Handel's *Messiah* overture and other movements with double-dotting in his early nineteenth-century organ arrangements; Sir Charles Stanford (1852–1924) recalling having heard the *Messiah* overture thus over-dotted, as a young boy in Dublin; William Cosins and Sterndale Bennett advocating a return to the correct over-dotted rendering in 1874; and Watkins Shaw documenting all this in his *Companion to Handel's Messiah* (London, 1965).

French Overture style is one of our best attested conventions of baroque interpretation.

CHAPTER XLV

Inequality

1. INEQUALITY AN ASPECT OF RHYTHMIC FREEDOM

(579) Michel de Saint-Lambert, *Principes du Clavecin*, Paris, 1702, p. 25:

'[We make certain notes unequal] because the inequality gives them more grace. . . . Taste judges of this as it does of tempo.'

2. WHICH NOTES SHOULD BE MADE UNEQUAL

(a) Inequality may be defined as the unequal performance of notes which are notated equally.

The degree of inequality may range from mild and lilting (much like triplet rhythm) on the one hand, to sharp and vigorous (much like dotted notes) on the other hand. It is not the difference of notation, but the musical effect required, which should determine the rhythm in performance. Dotted notes which are under-dotted in performance, and equal notes which are mildly unequalised in performance, sound the same: *i.e.* lilting.

This lilting, triplet-like rhythm is by far the most important and characteristic use of inequality.

(b) Inequality is nearly always out of place in mainly leaping melodies; it is highly suitable to mainly stepwise melodies.

(c) Only those notes which fall naturally into pairs are liable to inequality. If they are notated slurred in pairs, and are otherwise eligible, this is virtually an indication of inequality. They must in any case be slurred by pairs in performance if taken unequally. Notes slurred more than two at a time do not fall into pairs and are not eligible for inequality.

(d) Notes so slow that inequality would sound sluggish or so fast that inequality would sound restless are not eligible for inequality.

(e) Only the fastest notes appearing in substantial numbers are strictly eligible for inequality. Thus in quick time, the presence of semi-quavers in substantial numbers prevents inequality, since they are too fast themselves yet by their presence they make quavers ineligible. But if only a few are present, they can be ignored, and the quavers may then become eligible. At a slower time, semiquavers are eligible if demi-semiquavers are not present in substantial numbers; *etc.* See also (g) below.

452

(f) The notes ordinarily eligible for inequality are those which go either two or four to a beat, such as:

TABLE XIII: different time-signatures with typical note-values liable to inequality

3 1	4 3 2 2 2 2	6 4 3 2 4 4 4 4	12 9 6 4 3 8 8 8 8 8
Minims Crotchets	Crotchets Quavers	Quavers Semiquavers	Semiquavers Demi-semiquavers

(g) When such notes are mixed with substantial numbers of shorter notes not too fast to be eligible for inequality, either the shorter notes only, or both at the same time, may be taken unequally, in spite of what has been said at (e) above.

(h) Notes otherwise eligible for inequality, but bearing dots or dashes, are specifically precluded from being taken unequally.

The dot is not a regular baroque sign for staccato, though it sometimes has that meaning. It is a regular sign for equal notes.

The dash is one regular baroque sign for staccato; but since notes all staccato cannot be grouped in pairs, it incidentally precludes inequality.

(i) Notes otherwise eligible for inequality can also be specified as equal by such words as: également; notes égales; notes martelées; détachez; mouvement décidé; mouvement marqué; coups égaux; etc. See also (583) in 7 below.

Inequality can be specifically indicated by such words as: inégales; notes inégales; lourer; pointer; etc.

3. THE LILTING RHYTHM (LOURER)

Here the first note is lengthened and the second shortened, usually to about triplet rhythm, ♩♩ becoming ♩³♪ etc. A modern editor wanting to suggest the lilting lourer approximately in notation can often best do so by transcribing the entire piece from $\frac{4}{4}$ into $\frac{12}{8}$ or from $\frac{3}{4}$ into $\frac{9}{8}$, etc.

The actual proportioning, however, is at the performer's discretion.

Any dotted notes notated, in among the equal notes thus inequalised, should be sharply 'over-dotted' to distinguish them from the milder inequality. The term pointer is found for this—but also in the more general sense of 'point the rhythm 'in whatever degree.

Conversely, a passage notated consistently in dotted notes may, as an alternative to 'over-dotting' it, be softened to the lilting lourer rhythm. Many of the long dotted passages found so characteristically in Purcell and his contemporaries sound wonderfully well in this softer interpretation, though others need the brilliance of the sharper rhythm. It is a salutary shock to realise that this choice is freely trusted to the performer. We can do it in different ways, and still be in style.

4. THE SNAPPED RHYTHM (COULER)

Whereas the lilting rhythm helps the music along, the snapped rhythm sometimes known as couler (but this term, literally 'slur', has many other meanings) is inclined to hold it back with its limping gait. See Ch. XLIII, 4 above for the various degrees of jerkiness recommended by different writers for this rather jolting rhythm. It can be taken sharply, like a Scots snap, but can also be flattered into a gentle eloquence better suited, for example, to the typical Purcell passages in which it is written out. Here, the first note is shortened.

A pair of notes slurred without dot can mean the same.

The snapped rhythm, as opposed to the lilting rhythm more likely to be favoured by a baroque performer in the absence of other instructions, could be specifically indicated by a slur over pairs of notes and a dot over the second. Contrary to the modern significance, this meant: lengthen the note bearing the dot over it at the expense of the note before it, and thus introduce the snapped rhythm. See (586) in 7 below.

5. INEQUALITY IN PRE-BAROQUE MUSIC

(580) Fray Tomás de Santa María, *Arte de tañer fantasía*, Valladolid, 1565, '7th condition':

'Concerning performance in good style, which is our seventh condition, it is to be remembered that it is necessary for this to play the crotchets in one way, the quavers in three ways.

The method to be observed in playing crotchets is to linger on the first, to hurry on the second, to linger again neither more nor less on the third, and to hurry on the fourth, and treat thus all the crotchets. This is done as if the first crotchet were dotted, the second crotchet a quaver, and likewise as if the third crotchet had a dot, and the fourth crotchet were a quaver, and so on. And care must be taken that the hurried crotchet should not be too hurried but only moderately so.

'[The first method with quavers is] to linger on the first quaver and hurry on the second, to linger again neither more nor less on the third, and so on. This is done as if the first quaver were dotted, the second quaver a semiquaver, and likewise as if the third quaver had a dot, and the fourth quaver were a semiquaver, and so on. This method is used in works which are entirely contrapuntal, and for long and short passages of free ornamentation (glosas).

'In the second method, we hurry on the first quaver, linger on the second, hurry neither more nor less on the third, linger on the fourth, and so on. This is done as if the first quaver were a semiquaver, the second dotted, the third again a semiquaver, the fourth dotted, and so on. . . . This method is used in short passages of free ornamentation (glosas) which are made in [existing] works (obras) as well as in fantasies.

'Observe that this method is more graceful than the foregoing.

'In the third method, we hurry on three quavers, linger on the fourth, then hurry on the next three, linger on the fourth, remembering that we must linger long enough for the fifth quaver to arrive in its proper time mid-way in the measure, and so on, so that they move in groups of four and four. This is done as if the three quavers were semiquavers, and the fourth quaver dotted. This third method is the most graceful of all, and is used for long and short passages of free ornamentation (glosas).

'Care should be taken not to linger too long on the quavers, but just long enough to mark them, since long lingerings are the cause of great clumsiness and ugliness in music; and for the same reason, the three hurried quavers must not be hurried too much, but only moderately, to correspond to the amount of lingering on the fourth.'

We have here a vivid description of the lilting rhythm (paragraphs two and three) and of the snapped rhythm (paragraph four), though without the detailed conditions which later writers attached to them; and also of a third rhythm (paragraph six) which later writers do not seem to describe (but *cf.* the last of Caccini's modifications at Ex. 205 (c) in 6 below).

We may particularly notice the freedom of rhythm described: 'the hurried crotchet should not be too hurried, but only moderately', *etc.* The three semiquavers and dotted quaver in paragraph six do not even add up, mathematically, to the minim's length required. The whole account shows that mathematical subdivision is not what is intended. The inequality is not measured, but proportioned expressively at discretion.

This gives us incidental evidence that the dot was regarded in 1565 as a sign for unmeasured prolongation, as well as for measured prolongation by one half. The phrase 'somewhat dotted' used by Frescobaldi at (581) in 6 below is further confirmation; and so also is Couperin's use of the word 'dotted' in describing inequality at (586) in 7 below. Compare also the following: (580a) G. B. Bovicelli, *Regole*, Venice, 1594, p. 11: 'the more the first note is lengthened and the second shortened, the more graceful is the melody.'

6. INEQUALITY IN EARLY BAROQUE MUSIC

Ex. 205. Giulio Caccini, *Nuove Musiche*, Florence, 1602, preface, (a) lourer, (b) couler, (c) free rhythmic modifications:

(581) Girolamo Frescobaldi, *Toccate*, Rome, 1615–16, preface, 7:

'When you find any passage in quavers and semiquavers to be played together by both hands, you must not play it too fast; and the hand which has semiquavers should make them somewhat dotted; dotting not the first but the second, and so on with the others, one without dot, the other dotted.'

7. INEQUALITY IN LATER BAROQUE MUSIC

(581a) B. de Bacilly, *L'Art de bien chanter*, Paris, 1668, pp. 232–3:

'Although I say that alternate dots are implicit in divisions (that is to say that of two notes one is commonly dotted), it has been thought proper not to mark them for fear of getting used to performing them by jerks . . . these notes must be dotted with such restraint that it is not obvious (except in certain passages which require this manner of [jerky] performance). And it is even necessary in some passages entirely to avoid dotting.'

(582) Georg Muffat, *Florilegium I*, Augsburg, 1695, preface:

'All the difference [between a slow 2 with two in the bar and an ordinary C with four in the bar] consists, in that under the last, several quavers continued in succession ♩ ♩ ♪ ♪ *etc.*, cannot be alternately dotted ♩. ♪ ♪. ♪ *etc.* for elegance in performance, like the others; but should be expressly strictly the one equal to the other [because of the four-square character].'

(582a) Étienne Loulié, *Elements . . . de musique*, Paris, 1696, Amsterdam ed. of 1698, p. 38:

'In each measure but especially triple measure, the half-beats are performed in two different ways, although they are notated in the same way.
'1. They are sometimes made equally. This way is called detaching the notes, you use it in melodies of which the sounds move by leap, *and in all kinds of foreign music where you never inequalise (pointe) them except where marked* [but this latter remark, added to ed. of 1698, seems untrue or much exaggerated: see 8 below].
'2. Sometimes the first half-beats are made a little longer. This way is called *Lourer*. You use it in melodies of which the sounds move stepwise . . .

'There is further a third way, where the first half-beat is made much longer than the second, but [for this to be appropriate] the first half-beat ought to have [in the notation] a [written] dot.
'This kind is called *Piquer*, or *Pointer* [mention is made of the *couler*, though not by name].'

(583) Sébastien de Brossard, *Dictionaire*, Paris, 1703, *s.v.* 'Andante':

'Andante . . . means above all for Basso-continuos, that all the notes must be made equal, and the sounds well separated.'

(584) Jacques M. Hotteterre, *Principes*, Paris, 1707, p. 24:

'It will be observed that quavers are not always to be played equally, and that in some measures there should be a long one and a short one; this is governed by their number. When this is even, the first is to be taken long, the second short, and so on. When it is an odd number, the opposite arrangement is followed. This is called *pointer* [N.B. the confusion of names here—contrast (582a) above]. The measures in which this is most usual are two in a bar, $\frac{3}{4}$ and $\frac{6}{4}$.'

(584a) Michel de Montéclair, *Nouvelle Methode*, Paris, [1709], p. 15:

'[Notes are] equal in C, $\frac{2}{4}$ and $\frac{3}{8}$ [but] often unequal in ordinary Triple 3.
'It is very hard to give general principles as to the equality or inequality of notes, because it is the style of the pieces to be sung which decides it; however, you should observe that in whatsoever measure it may be, the notes of which four go to a beat are always to be uneven, the first a little longer than the second.'

(585) Michel de Montéclair, *Petite Methode*, Paris [*c.* 1730], p. 42:

'The length of the quavers, in the two-time measure marked simply by a 2, is unequal; the first quaver lasts almost as long as if it were followed by a dot, and the second almost as quickly as a semiquaver [unless marked "croches égales"].
'[The $\frac{2}{4}$ is beaten with two quick beats; the quavers are equal and the semiquavers unequal.]
'[Heavy three time is marked $\frac{3}{2}$, but gay three time is marked 3 or $\frac{3}{4}$ and in this] the quavers are unequal.
'[Quick three time is marked $\frac{3}{8}$ and in this] the quavers are equal. The semiquavers are unequal.
[p. 48:] 'The plain C marks the heavy four time measure, and the stroked ₵ marks the quick four time measure. However, when the movement is quick to the point of tiring the arm, this measure can be beaten with two beats, while retaining the equality of the quavers.
'[p. 50: In $\frac{6}{4}$ as in $\frac{3}{4}$] the quavers are unequal.
'[In $\frac{6}{8}$ there are] two equal beats; there are three equal quavers to each beat.' See also (519) in Chapter XXXVIII, 4.

(586) Fr. Couperin, *Pièces de clavecin*, Paris, 1713, table of ornaments:

'Slurs, of which the dots indicate that the second note of each beat must be more prolonged (*appuyée*)' [literally, 'leant upon'].

Ex. 205a. Fr. Couperin, *loc. cit.*, notation indicating stress on the second note of each pair: *i.e.* the *couler* (probable interpretation):

(587) Joachim Quantz, *Essay*, Berlin, 1752, XI, 12 (from both texts):

'A very necessary remark must be made, with regard to the time which is given to each note. A difference must be made in the rendering between capital notes, which are also called accented (*frappantes*), or among the Italians *good notes*, and those which pass, and which some foreigners call *bad notes*. The main notes ought always, if possible, to be brought more into relief than those which only pass. According to this rule it is necessary in pieces of a moderate speed and even in Adagio for the quickest notes to be played with a certain inequality, even though they appear at sight to be of the same value; so that at each figure the accented notes, to wit the first, third, fifth and seventh, must be pressed upon more than those which pass, to wit the second, fourth, sixth and eighth, though they must not be sustained as long as if they were dotted. By these very quick notes I mean the crotchets in triple-minim time, the quavers in triple-crotchet time, the semiquavers in that of quavers, the quavers in Allabreve, the semiquavers or the demisemiquavers in four-eight time or four time. This no longer occurs, however, as soon as these notes are found mixed with figures of notes yet quicker or half as short in the same time; for then these latter must be played [with] the first and the third of the four notes a little pressed upon, and their tone made a little louder than that of the second and fourth notes. But we except from this rule in the first place quick passages, in a very quick movement, in which time does not allow them to be performed unequally, and where it is thus only possible to use length and force on the first of the four. We further except all those passages which singers should render with speed, unless they ought to be slurred [in pairs]; for since each note of this sort of passage for the voice ought to be made distinct and marked by a little stroke of the chest [*sic!*—coup de poitrine], inequality has no place there. Lastly we should except notes on which there are dashes or dots. It is also necessary to make the same exception, when several notes follow at the same pitch, or when there is a slur over more notes than two, to wit four, six or eight; and lastly with regard to quavers in Gigues. All these notes ought to be rendered equally, the one no longer than the other.

'[XVII, 2: With semiquavers in a slow movement] give more emphasis, both for length and for volume, to the first of a pair than to the second [and take a quaver followed by two semiquavers] almost as though dotted.

[XII, 12:] 'When the first of four semiquavers is a rest, you must delay half as long again as the written value of the rest, because the second note [of each pair] should be shorter than the first.'

(588) C. P. E. Bach, *Essay*, II, Berlin, 1762, XXIX, 15:

'The semiquavers [at Ex. 205b] sound feeble in an adagio unless dots are placed between them [*i.e.* unless made unequal].'
    Ex. 205b.

(589) Dom Fr. Bedos de Celles, *L'Art du Facteur d'Orgues* [Paris] 1766–78, p. 600:

'Even notes of equal [written] value [are] more or less prolonged.

[p. 601:] 'In all movements in 2, 3 and 4 time, the quavers are articulated 2 by 2, and are distinguished as *first* and *second*: this distinction also sometimes takes place with crotchets . . .

'This distinction between *first* and *second*, can also occur in semiquavers of $\frac{2}{4}$ in a moderate movement . . .

'Almost always the *first* are longer, and the *second* shorter; I except however movements where they are articulated by 3 and 3, as in the $\frac{6}{4}$ and $\frac{6}{8}$: but in movements where they are articulated by 2 and 2, it is rare that they should be equal.

'This *inequality* should vary according to the kind of expression of the melody; in lively melodies, it should be more marked than in melodies which are gracious and of a tender expression, [more marked] in marches than in minuets; however, plenty of minuets are found in which the inequality is as marked as in a march [Dom Bedos evidently has in mind here inequality so extreme as to become equivalent to dotting—perhaps even to "over-dotting"].'

(590) M.-D.-J. Engramelle, *La Tonotechnie*, Paris, 1775, p. 32:

'There are cases in which this inequality is one-half, so that you should perform the *first* as if they were dotted quavers, and the *second* semi-quavers; other cases in which the inequality is one-third, as if the *first* were worth two-thirds of a quaver, and the *second* the remaining third; others again in which this inequality is less conspicuous and should be as 3 to 2, so that the *first* will be worth three-fifths of a quaver and the *second* two-fifths.

[p. 33:] 'There are many marches . . . in which the inequality between the *first* and the *second* is as 3 to 1. In certain minuets . . . the inequality is as 2 to 1; finally, in many minuets, the inequality is less conspicuous, *e.g.* as 3 to 2 or as 7 to 5.

[p. 230:] 'Inequalities . . . in many places vary in the same piece; it is left to fine taste to appreciate these variations of inequality . . . a little more or less inequality substantially changes the expression of a piece.'

8. HOW WIDELY OUGHT INEQUALITY TO BE APPLIED?

This is one of the most difficult questions in baroque interpretation. Some Frenchmen write almost as if they had a monopoly of inequality.

(591) Fr. Couperin, *L'Art de toucher*, Paris, 1716, ed. of 1717, p. 38:

'There are in my opinion defects in our notation of music comparable to those in the writing of our language. We notate otherwise than we perform, which is the reason why foreigners perform our music less well than we perform theirs. The Italians on the contrary, write music as they have conceived it. For example, we perform as dotted a succession of quavers moving by step; yet we notate them as equal.'

In spite of its distinguished author's experience in writing in the Italian as well as in the French style, this passage is unquestionably misleading. A truer picture emerges from the following.

(592) Michel Corrette, *Methode de la Flûte Traversière*, Paris-Lyons, [*c.* 1730], p. 4:

'The four-time C or ¢ is much used in Italian music, as in the Allemande, Adagio, Presto of sonatas and concertos.

'It is necessary to perform the quavers equal and to make unequal (pointer) the semiquavers two by two. These are also sometimes performed equal in Allegros and Prestos of sonatas and concertos.

'The 2 marks the measure of two beats. This measure is used for Rigaudons, Gavottes, Bourrées and Cotillons in French music; the Italians never use it. The quavers must be made unequal two by two, that is to say make the first long and the second short . . .

'The $\frac{2}{4}$ or $\frac{2}{8}$ is the 2-time of the Italians. This measure is often used in the Allegros and Prestos of sonatas and concertos. The quavers must be performed equal, and the semiquavers made unequal: they are also sometimes performed equal in sonatas.

'The $\frac{6}{8}$ is used for French and Italian Jigs. The quavers are performed equal, the first two are very often taken with one stroke of the tongue and sometimes three.

'The $\frac{3}{2}$ marks a slow movement. This measure is sometimes used for the Saraband.

'The crotchets must be made unequal two by two, and sometimes performed equal according to the character of the piece . . .

'The $\frac{3}{8}$ is used in French music for Passepieds. This measure of three beats is very often found in the Affetuoso, Minuets, and Allegros of sonatas.

'The quavers are taken equally except for the semiquavers which are made unequal.

'The ⁶₄ is a measure of two uneven beats [*i.e.* containing an uneven number of units, namely three crotchets to each beat]; it is used for the Loure in French music. The English compose many Vaudevilles, and Country-dances in this measure. . . . These airs ought to be played in a noble manner, marking the crotchets well; and making the quavers unequal two by two. This measure is very little found in Italian music.

'The ¹²₈ is found in Italian, German, French and English music, in 4-time Jigs.

'The quavers must be performed equal and the semiquavers made unequal.

'The first two quavers and sometimes three are taken with a single stroke of the tongue.

'[*Methode*, Paris, 1741: In the Courante] the quavers are performed equally in Italian music as for instance in the Courante of Corelli's Sonata Op. 5 No. 7. But in French music the second quaver in each beat is performed more quickly.'

(592a) Joachim Quantz, *Essay*, Berlin, 1752, XVII, vii, 58:

'In that measure [¢ two in a bar], as well as in the time of three crotchets in a bar, which is used for the Loure, the Saraband, the Courante, and the Chaconne, the quavers following the dotted crotchets are to be performed not in their strict [written] value but very shortly and sharply. . . . All dotted notes are to be performed in the same manner wherever there is time to do so.'

The musical situations in which the possibility of inequality arises are so numerous, and the possibilities themselves are so extensive, that a modern editor may have great difficulty in reaching suitable decisions. The following are comparatively simple cases. The Handel tune appears first in mainly equal notation, later in unequal notation. There can be no reason other than inadvertence; but though the notation was casual, the intention was not, and in spite of appearances the movement is to be taken consistently in unequal rhythm.

Ex. 206. G. F. Handel, Op. I, No. 1, *c.* 1724, opening slow movement:

In an earlier version of this sonata, there is a slur over the first E, D sharp and E in both bar one and bar twelve, the rhythm being even in both these bars; the next four notes are unslurred but uneven in both these bars. The two versions contain many similar discrepancies, which may be readily and valuably compared in the Urtext available as Lea Pocket Score No. 70.

It will be appreciated that slurs are among the details least likely to be carefully or consistently notated; and also that a phrase which appears equally notated in one contemporary edition will often appear unequally notated in another. No reliance can be placed on any of this; it is the convention, not the notation, which we have to take into account. It is true that the contemporary interpreters would have used various amounts and forms of inequality: so may we; but we must use, in general, enough.

A hint which we can sometimes take from the notation concerns the choice between the lilting rhythm and the snapped rhythm. Thus in the duet Domine Deus of the Gloria in J. S. Bach's B Minor Mass, the notation shows the snapped rhythm at the first appearance of a theme which returns in equal notation: the snapped rhythm should be maintained throughout. Again, in transcribing his own E major violin concerto for the harpsichord, J. S. Bach went to the trouble of changing the notation from equal to unequal, also in the snapped rhythm, and presumably with the object of securing this rhythm in preference to the lilting rhythm which the violin version perhaps most naturally suggested. It will be seen, incidentally, that whereas the steps of the melody are made unequal, the leaps are left equal: this is quite certainly intentional (see 2 (b) above). It will be remembered that J. S. Bach was notorious for including in his notation many elements of figuration which were normally left to the performer in his day: see Ch. VII, 3, (112) to (113) above. We can therefore often learn from his written text valuable lessons as to what other composers expected from the performer. Even J. S. Bach, however, did not by any means write down everything he intended and expected.

Ex. 207. J. S. Bach, written-out *couler* (a) in the Gloria of the B minor Mass, (b) in transcribing the E major Violin Concerto, Movt. II, for harpsichord:

(b) Vn. Concerto:

Rhythm changed in harpsichord concerto to:

9. POST-BAROQUE INEQUALITY

The generation of Beethoven appears to be the last in which contemporary authorities take inequality for granted.

A further discussion of inequality will be found in App. IX.

CHAPTER XLVI

Triplet Rhythm

1. TWO AGAINST THREE NOT A NORMAL BAROQUE RHYTHM

(a) Triplets, quadruplets, quintuplets, sextolets, septuplets, *etc.*, are all 'proportions' in the old sixteenth-century sense, and by sixteenth century musicians, may have been performed literally. But the seventeenth century lost interest in 'proportions', and through the baroque period, an appearance of 'two against three' or 'three against four' is deceptive. 'Three against four' as a genuine proportion *may* recur in the galant style, *e.g.* of G. P. Telemann; by the mid-eighteenth century, it is becoming difficult to be sure whether a real 'two against three' is intended. But neither of these proportions had an accepted place in true baroque rhythm.

Triplets as such are common. We find them written in the modern way as groups of three notes, with or without a 3 to make the grouping clear, at least from Petrucci's famous editions at the beginning of the sixteenth century. But the duple notes set against them in baroque music are not meant for cross rhythms; they are meant to accommodate themselves to, or be accommodated by, the rhythm of the triplet.

The notation is a mixture of half-remembered proportions and loose conventions. The convenient flexibility of the dot and the familiar practice of inequality were both pressed into service: ♩♪ was softened, and ♫ was sharpened, to produce the same result (*i.e.* ♩ ³ ♪).

(593) C. P. E. Bach, *Essay*, I, Berlin, 1753, III, 27:

'Now that triplets have come increasingly into use in common or ⁴₄ time, as well as in ²₄ and ³₄, many pieces have made their appearance which could with greater convenience be notated in ¹²₈, ⁹₈ or ⁶₈. The performance of other values against these [triplet] notes is shown [at Ex. 208].'

Ex. 208. C. P. E. Bach, *loc. cit.*, (a) dotted notes compressed and (b) equal notes expanded into triplet rhythm when set against triplets:

(b) Quantz, like C. P. E. Bach, treats the standard compression of dotted rhythm into triplet rhythm (bringing the little note after the dot into line with the last note of the triplet) as the strict meaning of the notation; he treats what to us is the strict meaning of the notation (bringing the little note after the last note of the triplet) as a case of 'over-dotting'—no doubt because if the dot is thus taken at all, it should be 'over-dotted' to emphasise the effect. He prefers this to the standard interpretation, which is that given by C. P. E. Bach.

(594) Joachim Quantz, *Essay*, Berlin, 1752, V, 22:

'This rule [of "over-dotting"] ought also to be observed, when one of the parts has triplets, against which the other part opposes dotted notes. It is then necessary to sound the little note which follows the dot, only after the third note of the triplet, and not at the same time with it. Otherwise we could confuse them with $\frac{6}{8}$ or $\frac{12}{8}$ time.' [But contrast (593) above.]

J. F. Agricola (in *Allgemeine deutsche Bibliothek*, 1769, I, 242–43) supported Quantz's preference, except for passages at high speed; he also stated that 'so J. S. Bach taught it to his pupils', but this would have to be interpreted in context (*e.g.* how high a speed?). F. W. Marpurg (*Anleitung*, Berlin, 1755, see facs. of ed. of 1765, p. 24) gives only the standard assimilations as at Ex. 208 above. See also Postscript to this Chapter at (c).

(c) The following movement starts with a correct use of proportional notation, and with the correct time-signatures to denote it: Ex. 209 (a). But by Ex. 209 (b) the notation has fallen back on mere common sense, and is no longer correct at all. The interpretation, however, is made quite certain by the imitation of rhythm between treble and bass: Ex. 209 (c).

Ex. 209. Arcangelo Corelli, Op. V, No. 3, Rome, 1700, Allegro, (a) correct proportional notation degenerating into (b) loose conventional notation meant for (c):

(d) The next is a case of perfectly correct proportional notation, interesting because its composer had evidently forgotten *why* it was 'customary to write thus'. Dolmetsch (*Interpretation*, London, [1915], p. 68) also mistook it for 'incorrect writing' conventionally accepted, as he did the opening of the previous example, though interpreting it rightly.

(595) Fr. Couperin, X Ordre, 'Fanfare', *II Livre de Pièces*, Paris [1717], note:

'Although the values of the treble do not seem to fit with those of the bass, it is customary to write thus.'

Ex. 210. Couperin, *loc. cit.*, proportional notation:

(e) The following, however, is rightly given by Dolmetsch (*loc. cit.*) as a case of conventional misnotation.

Ex. 211. Handel, Recorder Sonata No. 4, Larghetto, (a) original notation, (b) interpretation (mainly after Dolmetsch, *op. cit.*, p. 68):

Handel has here used the two contrary methods of loose notation within the space of a few bars: dotted rhythm condensed to triplet rhythm (bar 1, *etc.*, bass part); and equal rhythm expanded to triplet rhythm (bars 1 and 6, treble part, with the dot and quaver; bar 5, treble part, with the rest and quaver; bar 6, bass part, with the two quavers).

Handel's habitual casualness in details of notation (see Ex. 203a in Ch. XLIV, 2 (a), above) prevents us from concluding that he meant here literally what he wrote: dotted rhythm on the first two beats of bar 1, 'two against three' on the last beat and again on the first beat of bar 6, *etc.*; and indeed the musical result of all this confusion of rhythms is very unsatisfactory. Thus we have here an illustration of Quantz' tacit assumption at (594) above that whatever his own preference in the matter might be, the standard meaning of a dotted note in relation with triplets was triplet rhythm. It is the triplet on the last beat of bar 1 which tells the player to start in triplet rhythm. But the movement is also emphatically one of those which bear out C. P. E. Bach's contention that they would be better notated in compound triple time—in this case $\frac{9}{8}$.

(f) The next two cases are best taken together.

Ex. 212. J. S. Bach, Chorale Prelude for organ, 'In dulci jubilo' (B.G. 25, ii), misleading crochets expanded to triplet rhythm:

Ex. 213. J. S. Bach, Organ Sonata IV (B.G. 15, pp. 46 *ff.*) semi-quavers expanded and dotted notes condensed to triplet rhythm:

In Ex. 212, triplet rhythm is notated in the alto at bar 25, but not at bar 3 and bar 11, *etc.* In Ex. 213 (a) and (c) an exactly parallel mixture of different notations occurs. Even viewed as a phrase in itself, the middle part of bar 15 is eminently eligible for expressive inequality, *i.e.* for triplet rhythm; and the fact that the top melody is in triplets confirms that the performer would by now be taking triplet rhythm in both parts alike. But presently he runs into dotted semiquavers against the

467

same triplet melody. Does he here have second thoughts, and wonder whether he is meant to dot, or rather 'over-dot' this new passage? No: he just goes quietly on condensing the dotted rhythm to triplet rhythm as he was previously expanding the equal rhythm to triplet rhythm.

2. PRELIMINARY NOTES IN TRIPLET RHYTHM

When a movement has dotted rhythm in the notation but triplet rhythm in the interpretation, this includes any preliminary note.

Ex. 214. J. S. Bach, Partita I, Courante:

3. THE TRIPLET CONVENTION IN THE POST-BAROQUE PERIOD

F. W. Marpurg (*Anleitung*, 2nd ed., Berlin, 1765, p. 24) demanded a list of composers who meant the triplets to be taken as genuine 'two against three' and composers who did not. The first movement of Beethoven's 'Moonlight' Sonata is exceptional in following Quantz as at (594) above: Czerny makes this plain (*Piano-Schule*, Op. 500, IV, Vienna, 1842, ed. Paul Badura-Skoda, Vienna, 1963, p. 51). But even as late as Liszt the standard interpretation as shown by C. P. E. Bach at (593) is often necessary.

(596) Daniel Gottlob Türk, *Klavierschule*, ed. of 1802, p. 96:

'[Two against three] is a beauty to which one has to grow accustomed.'

Ex. 215. Louis Adam, *Méthode de Piano*, Paris [1804] p. 91:

POSTSCRIPT TO NEW VERSION

(a) New research by Michael Bruce Collins has suggested almost a disappearance from baroque music of simultaneous cross-proportions between binary and ternary rhythms.

In an unpublished dissertation and an article (see my Bibl.), Collins has given evidence from 1450 to 1750, when he believes that simultaneous ternary with binary rhythms were *never* practised.

Thus, for example, the famous mensuration canon 'Ex una voce tres' by Josquin des Prez ('Agnus Dei' from *Missa L'Homme armé*) shows in its notation a tricky combination of twos against threes and fours against threes. It is hard to sing so, but not at all impossible, and there is a strange tension and beauty in the effect. But if Collins is right, the triplets must be squared out to duple rhythm by lengthening each first note, and shortening each second and third note. He may not be right. His argument about renaissance music is not conclusive.

(b) For baroque music, Collins strongly supports the conventional assimilation of duple to triple rhythm, as in Sect. 1 above. But he also argues that triple may be assimilated to duple rhythm, notated triplet quavers being squared out to quaver, semiquaver, semiquaver (esp. French pre-1700), or to semiquaver, semiquaver, quaver (esp. Italian pre-1700, thereafter internationally).

In the second edition of my original version, I applied this squaring-out to the problematical 'Tempo di Gavotta' in J. S. Bach's E Minor Partita for harpsichord: but I now believe that its notated groups of two semiquavers and a quaver are no more than a written-out slide, to be taken quite normally on the beat, unmeasured, and a little quicker than notated; that its groups of four semiquavers are likewise to be taken ornamentally, unmeasured and a little quicker than they are notated; and that the rhythm of the movement throughout is that of the measured triplets as notated.

But there seem to be other baroque compositions in which Collins must be right.

(c) The following, noticed by Jacobi, Collins and others, has nine different measures (9, 17, 26, 42, 55, 63, 84, 90, 97) in which the last quaver of a triplet shares its note-head with the notated semiquaver following a dotted quaver. This compels us to play them together, and shows that J. S. Bach intended here the normal assimilation of dotted rhythm to triple rhythm. Notation in $\frac{12}{8}$ would have been better, as recommended at (593) in Sect. 1 above.

Ex. 215A. J. S. Bach, *Toccata*, BGA XXXVI, p. 571.

PART FOUR

PUNCTUATION

CHAPTER XLVII

Phrasing

1. PHRASING MUST BE AUDIBLE

Early music is very commonly under-phrased. This is not usually because the performer does not understand the phrasing, but because he does not realise how extremely articulate much early phrasing needs to be, especially in baroque music, in order to make the sense and structure really audible.

Phrases are moulded by various means, which may include a dynamic rise and fall, a suggestion of rallentando, *etc*. They are separated by a silence of phrasing which ranges from scarcely perceptible to very conspicuous. The silence may be taken out of the time of the note before, or if the separation in the music is sufficient to justify it, added to the time in the shape of a momentary pause.

A sense of phrasing is so intimate and incommunicable a part of interpretative musicianship that very little attempt is made to suggest it in notation. There are, however, a few exceptions.

2. PHRASING SIGNS

(a) The grouping of notes in ligatures partly indicated the phrasing under the proportional system of notation (see App. I for the more important effect of ligatures on note-values).

(b) Our 'corona' sign ⌒ when placed over a note means that it is to be held longer than strict time allows; the amount varies from very little to very much, and is for the performer to decide.

This sign when placed over a rest has the same effect, and may therefore be used to show an interval of silence added to the time.

It may also be used over a bar-line, particularly a double bar-line, with the same effect. Over the final bar-line it merely indicates, somewhat superfluously as a rule, that an indefinite silence is to follow the music; it may, however, serve the purpose of preventing too immediate an approach to an ensuing movement, in which case it is in effect the opposite of *attacca*.

These uses are all found in baroque music, but there may be a further implication that a note or pause thus marked should carry free ornamentation, perhaps amounting to a cadenza: for which see Ch. XII.

Other signs were occasionally used in place of ⌒ and some intelligence may be needed not to misinterpret them. The following, for example, shows an early baroque pause sign which became a repeat sign later in the baroque period.

(597) Emilio de' Cavalieri, *Rappresentatione di Anima, e di Corpo*, Rome, 1600, Avvertimenti:

'The sign 𝄋. indicates the incoronata, which is to serve for taking breath and to give time for making some gestures.'

(c) Couperin used a phrasing comma, which can easily be confused with the main contemporary French sign (he used it himself) for trill.

(598) Fr. Couperin, *Troisième Livre de Pièces*, Paris, 1722, preface:

'You will find a new sign of which the form is **'** ; this is to mark the ends of melodies (chants) or of our harmonic periods (de nos Phrases harmoniques), and to make it understood that it is necessary to separate the end of a melody (chant) before passing on to that which follows. That is almost imperceptible as a rule, though people of good taste will feel something lacking in the performance if this little silence is not observed; in a word, it is the difference between those who read aloud continuously (lisent de suite) and those who stop for full-stops and commas (aux points and aux virgules); these silences should make themselves felt without altering the time (sans altérer la mesure).'

Couperin uses his comma to show slight separations which might otherwise be missed, rather than long separations which he assumed no good performer could miss. Unlike the modern comma, therefore, which is used for separations added to the time, Couperin's comma is to be taken out of the note before, and should often be barely perceptible. It is frequently quite superfluous, occasionally very helpful.

3. PHRASING LEFT TO THE PERFORMER

(599) Girolamo Frescobaldi, *Toccate*, Rome, 1615–16, preface, 4:

'On the last note of the trills, or of passages [of figuration] by leap or by step, you must pause, even if this note is a quaver or a semiquaver, or different [in pitch] from the following [note], because such a pause prevents confusion between one passage and another.

[8:] 'Before performing double passages in semiquavers for both hands, you must pause on the note before, even if it is a black [*i.e.* short] one.'

(600) Thomas Mace, *Musick's Monument*, London, 1676, p. 109:

'(In proper Places) . . . make a kind of *Cessation, or standing still,* sometimes *Longer,* and sometimes *Shorter,* according to the *Nature,* or *Requiring* . . . of the *Musick.*'

(601) Joachim Quantz, *Essay*, Berlin, 1752, VII, 4:

'[Flautists should] take breath at the repeat of the subject, or at the start of a new thought; for the end of what goes before, and the start of what follows, should be well separated and distinguished one from the other.

[XI, 10:] 'Thoughts which belong together must not be separated; just as on the contrary, those where the musical sense is finished, and a new thought begins, without there being a rest [in the written text], must be separated; and this is something which must particularly be done, when the last note of the previous thought and the first note of the following thought are at the same pitch.'

(602) C. P. E. Bach, *Essay*, I, Berlin, 1753, III, 28:

'Certain notes and rests should be prolonged beyond their written length, for reasons of expression.

[II, 1762, XXIX, 20:] 'At slow or moderate tempos, breaks are often prolonged beyond their strict length . . . this applies to pauses, cadences *etc.,* as well as to breaks.'

(603) Daniel Gottlob Türk, *Klavierschule*, Engl. transl. [1804], p. 34:

'The end of a Period is best expressed by lifting the finger gently at the last Note, and by touching the first Note of the following Period stronger. By that means there arises a small Rest, which is taken from the last Note of the foregoing Period.'

CHAPTER XLVIII

Articulation

1. GROUPING BY LIGATURES

In proportional notation, the grouping of notes in ligatures (the equivalent of a modern slur) partly shows the points at which articulation occurs (*i.e.* between the ligatures—but see App. I for the more important effect of the ligatures on note-values).

2. WORDS OF ARTICULATION

Words such as cantabile and staccato, which indicate a general degree of articulation for the movement or passage as a whole, are not uncommon in the later stages of baroque music. Occasionally in the violinist-composers an instruction for a particular technique occurs, such as 'attacca alla corda', indicating an attack with the bow pressed on to the string, the result of which is a heavy staccato or marcato (*e.g.* Vivaldi, PV 419, PV 428).

Words giving a general indication have naturally to be applied with common sense, since the details of the articulation may vary very much within the general pattern.

3. SIGNS OF ARTICULATION

(a) The slur occurs in baroque music with increasing frequency. It may be used to tie notes; to show extreme legato (especially one bow or breath, or one word in singing); to show separate notes grouped in one phrase; and in conjunction with dots or dashes, to show separate notes taken in one bow.

(604) John Playford, *Introduction*, London, 1654, ed. of 1674, p. 36:

'A *Tye* is of two uses; first, when the Time is broken or struck in the middle of the Note, it is usual to Tye [notes across a bar-line, where earlier baroque notation would have divided the note-form with the bar-line, or put a dot after the bar-line].

'The second sort of Tye is, when two or more Notes are to be Sung to one Syllable, or two Notes or more to be plaid with once drawing the Bow on the *Viol* or *Violin*.'

In the mid-seventeenth century English manuscript Christ Church, Oxford, 732, which is the Canto part of fantasies for viols in two to

473

four parts by Giovanni Coperario (John Cooper) and Orlando Gibbons, long slurs occur which even pass across rests and are certainly not bowing marks. They may possibly indicate phrase-groupings, though if so, very casually and inconsistently. In later baroque music, we sometimes find (*e.g.* Vivaldi, PV 123, middle movement) long slurs which are clearly phrasing marks, not bowing marks: like the long slurs in Beethoven's string parts, which indicate a legato intention, although the bow will have to be changed inconspicuously within them.

A slur with dots or dashes is a standard sign of the later baroque period for notes articulated separately in one stroke of the bow.

(605) Marin Marais, *Pièces à ... Violes*, II, Paris, 1701, Avertissement:

'[A slur with dots means] to articulate all these notes, in one bow, as if they were played with different bowings.'

This gives, according to the speed, many varieties of articulation from a deliberate staccato to a brilliant spiccato. These were virtuoso resources, however, and not ordinarily appropriate in baroque orchestral and chamber parts.

Plain slurs abound, but they are seldom notated consistently enough to be taken literally. It is for the performer to work out a consistent scheme.

(606) Leopold Mozart, *Violinschule*, Augsburg, 1756, I, iii, 16:

'Among the signs of music the slur has considerable importance, although many pay small attention to it.'

In the more brilliant violin parts, sophisticated slurrings, as used and taught by Geminiani, Vivaldi and others, are appropriate. In the average orchestral or chamber part, most of the slurring should be simple and obvious, and most of the slurs quite short: *e.g.* on groups of two, three or four notes, and not as a rule against the beat. This simplicity in the slurring is an important element in the naturalness of most baroque idioms. The virtuoso idioms are a separate problem, in which a specialised knowledge of baroque violin technique is needed; the ordinary idioms should not be confused with them, since here the articulation, though crucial, should generally be as straightforward as possible. There are, of course, border-line cases.

Slurs are used on other instruments according to their respective techniques. They may indicate tonguing on wind instruments, and note-grouping on keyboard instruments. The harpsichord music of Couperin is particularly well served with short slurs, both with the beat and across the beat.

(b) Couperin also uses a slanting stroke or strokes joining notes which he wants grouped closely together.

(c) The beams connecting groups of quavers, semiquavers, *etc.*, in place of separate tails, while sometimes used as indications of phrasings, are not generally so used. They may sometimes give a useful and obvious hint, but they should never be assumed to have musical significance where this is not confirmed by the sense of the music itself. They show great inconsistency in different copies or different parts even of the same work.

(d) The standard baroque sign for staccato is the dash, of which the form is either | or ▼ (either way up) without distinction of meaning.

When the dot is used as a staccato sign, its meaning in the main baroque period is the same as that of the dash. At the end of the baroque period, however, the dot was beginning to be used to show a lighter, less abrupt staccato than the dash. Quantz and Leopold Mozart reflect this new tendency; C. P. E. Bach, however, regards the two signs as identical. Like slurs, the signs for staccato are seldom applied at all consistently, and the performer should work out his own scheme with or without their assistance. (See Ch. XLV, 2 (h), above for the dot used not for staccato but in connection with inequality.)

(607) Joachim Quantz, *Essay*, Berlin, 1752, XVII, ii, 5:

'It should be said in passing, that if there are several figures of the same sort of notes in sequence, and the first is marked with a slur, they must all be played in the same way until another kind of notes is met with. It is the same with notes above which there are dashes.

[12:] 'When the dash appears instead of the dot [under a slur] the notes must be strongly emphasised in one bow stroke. [When there is no slur] the notes with dashes must be cut short, but those with dots, merely made with a short bow-stroke, and held on.'

(608) C. P. E. Bach, *Essay*, I, Berlin, 1753, III, 17:

'When notes are to be separated one from the other dashes or dots are placed over them. . . . The latter sign has been used in the exercises so as to avoid a confusion between dashes [which look rather like the figure 1] and the numbers [showing the fingering].'

(609) Leopold Mozart, *Violinschule*, Augsburg, 1756, I, iii, 17:

'[Dots show] that the notes covered by the slur are not only to be taken in one bow-stroke but have also to be separated from each other by a slight pressure [of the bow] . . .
'If however small dashes are written in place of dots, the bow is lifted for each note, with the result that all these notes covered by the slur are to be taken in one bow-stroke yet have to be completely separated from each other.'

Ex. 216. Louis Adam, *Méthode . . . de piano*, Paris [1804], pp. 154–55, (a) the dash and (b) the dot distinguished:

(610) Daniel Gottlob Türk, *Klavierschule*, Engl. transl. [1804], p. 36:

'Lengthened, and Round Points [*i.e.* dashes and dots] have properly the same signification; but some Composers mean a shorter touch by the lengthened Points, than by the round ones.'

4. ARTICULATION IMPLIED BY KEYBOARD FINGERING

Modern fingerings are devised to assist velocity by being interchangeable in all keys; early fingerings were devised to assist phrasing and articulation by enforcing separations where they are musically desirable. They may often be used, and can always be studied, to advantage.

Two excellent examples from Couperin are cited by Wilfrid Mellers (*François Couperin*, London, 1950, p. 310). The slurs shown with dotted lines are not present in the original, but show the phrasing implied by the fingering. (The upper—unwritten—note is fingered in the two ornaments shown.) See also Ch. LXIV, 5, below.

Ex. 217. Couperin, (a) 'Le Moucheron', Livre II, Ordre 6, (b) 'La Passacaille', Livre II, Ordre 8, phrasing implied by the fingering:

(611) Fr. Couperin, *L'Art de toucher*, Paris, 1716, ed. of 1717, p. 10:

'It is certain that a certain melody, a certain passage, when taken in a certain manner [of fingering], produces to the ear of a person of taste (de la personne de goût), a different effect.'

5. ARTICULATION IMPLIED BY BOWINGS

The bowings shown in baroque violin treatises sometimes imply silences of articulation which a modern player would normally obliterate by avoiding the consecutive down-bows. Such bowings are occasionally useful.

Ex. 218. T. B., *Compleat Musick-Master*, London, 3rd ed. of 1722, Ch. III (but see note in my Bibliography), bowings implying silences of articulation (u = up; d = down):

Ex. 219. Leopold Mozart, *Violinschule*, Augsburg, 1756, IV, 9, bowings implying silences of articulation:

6. ARTICULATION LEFT TO THE PERFORMER

(a) Most problems of articulation in baroque music remain to be solved without assistance either direct or indirect from the notation.

(b) Actual slurs are a normal part of the technique of bowed instruments, and are to be used even in the music of periods at which it was not customary to show them at all.

(612) Diego Ortiz, *Trattado*, Rome, 1553, *f.* 3 r:

'When two or three crotchets occur in one example, only the first is to be defined and the others passed over without a fresh stroke of the bow.'

(613) Joachim Quantz, *Essay*, Berlin, 1752, XVII, i, 9:

'In case there is anyone among the ripienists whose expression does not yet equal that of the others, the first violin ought to take him aside and teach him by a separate practice the true method of performance, so that one musician, *e.g.* does not . . . make slurs where the others detach the notes . . .'

The equivalent of slurs on wind instruments and elsewhere should equally be introduced into the phrasing.

(c) The differentiation of legato from staccato is normal in any music. Girolamo Diruta (*Il Transilvano*, Venice, 1597) attaches great importance to distinguishing the smooth style proper to cantabile music for the organ from the detached style proper to dance music on the harpsichord. Late renaissance and early baroque keyboard fingerings (*e.g.* in E. Nicolaus Ammerbach, *Orgel oder Instrument Tabulatur*, Leipzig, 1571, in Diruta, *op. cit.*, and in some of the English pieces in the Fitzwilliam Virginal Book and elsewhere) enforce silences of phrasing and articulation like those of Couperin shown in 4 above.

The entire range from staccato to legato needs to be imaginatively used in giving baroque phrases their point and character.

(614) François Couperin, *L'Art de toucher le Clavecin*, Paris, 1716, ed. of 1717, p. 61:

'It is necessary [on the harpsichord] to sustain a perfect smoothness.'

(615) J. S. Bach, 'Inventionen und Sinfonien', 1723, title:

'An honest guide . . . to acquire a *cantabile* style of playing.'

(616) J. S. Bach, heading to Prelude and Fugue in G major for Organ (B.G. 38, p. 12):

'Fuga: Alla breve e staccato.'

The fugue thus headed is in a style highly similar to the fugal movements in J. S. Bach's violin sonatas and other works.

(617) [Riva], *Advice to the Composers and Performers of Vocal Musick, translated from the Italian*, London, 1727, p. 14:

'The Binding together or Stringing the Notes firm and distinct with the Voice, which the Italians express by the Terms (*Legare* and *Staccare la Voce*) are Graces equally agreable, although contrary to each other; and nothing but good Judgement can direct the Singer how to use them properly, (that is to say) according to the Nature and Design of the Composition.'

(618) Joachim Quantz, *Essay*, Berlin, 1752, VII, 10:

'It is necessary to study how to detect and understand well what makes musical sense, and what must be joined together. It is necessary to avoid, with equal care, separating what belongs together, and joining what comprises more than one thought and should therefore be separate. For it is on this that one element in true expression depends.

[XI, 10:] 'It is necessary to avoid slurring notes which ought to be detached and detaching notes which ought to be slurred.

[19:] 'Every instrumentalist ought to try to perform the *Cantabile* as a good singer performs it; and a good singer on his side ought to seek to acquire the fire of good instrumentalists with regard to liveliness, so far as the voice is capable of it.

[xii, 4:] 'It is the quick passages in Allegro which must above all be performed briskly, clearly, with liveliness, with articulation and distinctly.

[18:] 'Long notes ought to be given fulness in a manner characterised by the increase and diminution of the volume; and the quick notes which follow ought to be well separated in a lively idiom.

[20:] 'But when after quick notes there follow several slow and singing notes, the fire must at once be restrained, and the notes performed with the feeling which they require, in order that the hearer shall not experience any tedium.'

(619) C. P. E. Bach, *Essay*, I, Berlin, 1753, III, 5:

'In general, the liveliness of allegros is conveyed by detached notes, and the feeling of adagios by sustained, slurred notes . . . even when not so marked . . . I realise however that every style of performance may occur at any tempo.

[6:] 'There are many who perform stickily, as if they had glue between their fingers. Their touch is sluggish; they hold on to notes too long. Others, trying to remedy this, leave the keys too soon, as if they were red-hot. Both are mistaken. The mean between these extremes is best. Here too I speak generally, since every kind of touch has its place.

[22:] 'Notes which are neither detached, slurred nor fully sustained are sounded for half their value . . . Crotchets and quavers in moderate and slow tempos are generally performed in this half-detached style.'

(620) Leopold Mozart, *Violinschule*, Augsburg, 1756, IV, 38:

'[Lengthy passages in semiquavers should be practiced slowly to control their speed.] Then detach the notes with shorter strokes [at greater speed].'

(621) Giuseppe Tartini, *Letter to Signora Maddalena Lombardini*, Padua, 1760, transl. Dr. Burney, London, 1771, 2nd ed. 1779, reprint. London, 1913, p. 15:

'. . . practice, every day, one of the *allegros*, of which there are three in Corelli's solos, which entirely move in semiquavers. The first is in D . . . play the notes *staccato*, that is, separate and detached, with a little space between every two: for though they are written [as at Ex. 220 (a)] they should be played as if there was a rest after every note [as at Ex. 220 (b)].'

Ex. 220. Corelli, D major violin sonata, allegro semiquavers implying staccato in Tartini's opinion:

(622) F. W. Marpurg, *Anleitung*, Berlin, 1755, 2nd ed. 1765, I, vii, p. 29:

'Opposed to legato as well as to staccato is the ordinary movement which consists in lifting the finger from the last key shortly before touching the next note. This ordinary movement, which is always understood [in the absence of indications to the contrary] is never indicated.'

(623) M.-D.-J. Engramelle, *Tonotechnie*, Paris, 1775, p. 18:

'All notes in performance . . . have a certain proportion of sound and a certain proportion of silence which together make up the total value of the note. These silences at the end of each note determine its articulation.'

Engramelle's book, which is on organ-building, was seen and admired by the author next to be quoted, Dom Bedos, as he was finishing his own book, and the two have some passages almost exactly in common, including (623) above.

(624) Bedos de Celles, *L'Art du Facteur d'Orgues* [Paris] 1766–78, p. 599:

'These *silences* ought to vary according to the kind of expression which suits the piece; in lively melodies, they are ordinarily less considerable than in gracious ones.'

This does not imply that 'lively melodies' are less highly articulated than 'gracious ones', which would be contrary to experience and common sense; it implies that a silence of articulation, when present at all in 'gracious' melodies, will need to be longer, which is often true.

(625) J. C. Heck, *Art of Playing the Harpsicord*, London [1770], p. 5:

'The Gliding [*i.e.* legato] . . . more particularly used in an Adagio. . . . The Staccato . . . is properly to be applied in an Allegro.'

(626) Daniel Gottlob Türk, *Klavierschule*, Engl. transl. [1804], p. 36:

'In Notes which are to be played *staccato*, the fingers must be lifted, when almost half the Time of their length is expired, the other half is filled up by Rests . . .

'In Notes which are to be played *legato*, the finger must remain upon the Key, till the Time of the length of the Note is perfectly expired, so that not the least Separation or Rest may be heard . . .

'If Notes are to be played in the common way; that is to say, neither *staccato* nor *legato*, the fingers must be lifted a little sooner than the Time of the length of the Note is expired.'

7. BAROQUE 'ORDINARY MOVEMENT' SOMEWHAT ARTICULATE

In the aggregate, the above passages describe a degree of articulation, for ordinary passages of moderate speed, which is not legato (the ordinary basis today) but 'opposed to legato as well as to staccato', as Marpurg at (622) above calls his 'ordinary movement'.

Circumstances vary enormously; but we have the general impression of a very easy flow of sound, with no abrupt silence between the notes, yet with a certain distinctness. We tend today either to over-articulate baroque music, with too forceful a staccato and too little sense of line, or to under-articulate it, as in the modern violinist's 'détaché'—which is not detached at all.

The problem is high-lighted where we find, as in Handel's trio sonata Op. II, No. 8, 2nd movt., bar 11, parallel parts in tenths one of which has ♩. ♪ while the other has ♩ 𝄽 ♪; they must be meant to sound the same, but what they are meant to sound is so intermediate between a dot and a rest that Handel could casually notate one in one way and the other in the other way. It is a very characteristic and revealing piece of inadvertence. Comparable instances abound.

The technique of articulation differs on different instruments. But there is no doubt that if we can establish, particularly in the string department where it is most difficult, a satisfactory counterpart to Marpurg's 'ordinary movement', we have gone more than half way towards a vital performance of the average baroque allegro.

PART FIVE

DYNAMICS

CHAPTER XLIX

Volume

1. FITTING THE VOLUME TO THE MUSIC

Volume rises with rising emotion and relaxes with relaxing emotion. This happens in all music, and it is a complete misunderstanding to confine baroque music within a range of what has recently been called terrace dynamics: long stretches of loud or soft flatly sustained.

Baroque organs and harpsichords, in their dependence on hand-stops for changing the registration and with it the volume, lend themselves to terrace dynamics in some degree, owing to the difficulty of sparing a hand except at distinct breaks in the music; and indeed this treatment, within reason, brings out one of their characteristics, namely their imperturbable strength, very well. Other instruments have no such tendency; and while the structure of baroque music itself does often imply rather more terraced dynamics than a highly dramatic structure like sonata-form, it does so only on the assumption that a terrace need not be altogether flat.

Akin to terrace dynamics are the popular echo-effects, when a short phrase is echoed pianissimo.

But most fluctuations of loud and soft fall into neither of these set patterns. They have to be tailored individually to the music.

2. WORDS OF VOLUME

Words to indicate loud and soft or crescendo and decrescendo (diminuendo) occur in a considerable number of early baroque compositions. They may be written either in full, or in partial abbreviation, or abbreviated to their initial letters.

Claudio Monteverdi asks for a closing diminuendo to his *Combattimento* (first perf. Venice, 1624) in the words: questa ultima nota va in arcata morendo. Domenico Mazzocchi in his *Dialoghi e sonetti* of 1638 uses (No. 18) the series forte . . . piano . . . pianissimo to indicate the same effect; elsewhere he uses words and initial letters to indicate loud and soft, and crescendi and diminuendi of short extent, explaining in his Preface that 'P, F, E, t, understood for Piano, Forte, Echo and trill are certainly [standing for] common things, known to everyone'. His *Catena d'Adone* (Venice, 1626) had *e.g.* on p. 49 'Piano', 'forte', 'pianissimo'. Stefano Landi's *S. Alessio* (Rome, 1634) has *e.g.* on p. 34 'Piano', 'Forte'. The words 'loud' and 'soft', and their abbreviations 'lo.' and 'so.', appear in English seventeenth-century manuscripts and printed books (*e.g.* Orlando Gibbons' fantasies for viols, Christ Church, Oxford, MSS. 732–5, early seventeenth cent.; Thomas Mace, *Musick's Monument*, London, 1676). John Jenkins' probable autograph, British Museum Add. MS 31,423 has 'soft' on the last two measures of a section, followed by 'soft 2d tyme' at the start of the next (last) section. Matthew Locke uses the words 'lowder by degrees', 'violent', and 'soft and slow by degrees' in his music for *The Tempest* (London, 1675). *Fort* (F) and *Doux* (D) are common in Lully.

By the beginning of the eighteenth century, the Italian words forte and piano, *etc.*, with a long range of abbreviations, were internationally current. The abbreviations are graded from *ppp* to *fff*; but *pp* may mean più piano (*i.e.* more soft) as well as pianissimo. The words crescendo and decrescendo (or diminuendo) and their abbreviations *cresc* and *decresc* (or *dim*) came more gradually into use; but the words crescendo and decrescendo were included in Leopold Mozart's list of standard musical terms (*Violinschule*, Augsburg, 1756, I, iii, p. 27).

(627) Alessandro Scarlatti, Letter to Prince Ferdinando de' Medici, 29 May, 1706 (Archivio di Stato di Firenzi, *Mediceo*, Filza 5903, letter No. 204):

'I have marked . . . at suitable places, the pianos and fortes of the instruments [in Act I of *Il Gran Tamerlano*], which alone are the light and shade (*chiaroscuro*) that makes any singing and playing agreeable.'

3. SIGNS OF VOLUME

The letters *p*, *f*, *etc.*, are, in effect, used as signs of volume, and as we have seen in 2 above were so used in baroque music.

The signs ⟨ for crescendo and ⟩ for decrescendo (diminuendo) appear early in the eighteenth century (Giovanni Antonio Piani, *Violin Sonatas*, Paris, 1712; Francesco Geminiani, *Violin Sonatas*, London, 1739; Francesco Veracini, *Sonate accademiche a violino solo*, London and Florence [1744]). In some instances the hairpin is closed at the end: ⟨⟩ and ⟨⟩.

Where *f* is followed shortly afterwards by *p*, or *p* by *f*, the intention may be one of two alternatives, the choice between which can only be decided by the performer in the light of the music.

A *p* subito or a *f* subito may be intended.

Alternatively a diminuendo from the *f* to the *p*, or a crescendo from the *p* to the *f*, may be intended.

(628) W. M. Mylius, *Rudimenta Musices*, Gotha, 1686, p. 49:

'Yet with both [*p* and *f*] it is to be noted that one does not go so suddenly from *piano* to *forte*, but one should gradually strengthen the voice and again let it decrease so that at the beginning *piano* is heard, *forte* at the middle, and once again *piano* as one comes to the close.'

[Benedict] Lechler (*c.* 1640) has *p . . . pp . . . ppp . . . pppp*. Walter Kolneder (*Aufführungspraxis bei Vivaldi*, Leipzig, 1955, pp. 24 *ff.*) cites from Vivaldi *p . . . pp*, i.e. più piano *. . . pianissimo* (PV.182, V); *f . . . più f . . . ff* (PV.155, first movt.); *p . . .* un poco *f . . . f* (PV.428, last movt.); all these stand, not for a series of abrupt steps, but for gradual diminuendos or crescendos.

Kolneder (*loc. cit.*) then lists the following grades of dynamic volume all indicated in Vivaldi's music by words and their abbreviations:

TABLE XIV: original dynamic markings in Vivaldi

pianissimo	mezzo forte
piano molto	un poco forte
piano assai	*f*
mezzo *p*	*f* molto
pp più *p*	più *f*
p	*ff*
quasi *p*	

To this he adds the pleasing comment: welch Schreckensbild für einen Terrassendynamiker! ('What horror for a "terrace-dynamics-man"!')

A further confirmation of the use of an *f* or a *p* to indicate crescendo or diminuendo is found in Leopold Mozart (*Violinschule*, Augsburg, 1756, XII, 8), who writes of 'the sound then diminishing again in course of the melody' but in his example illustrating this sentence (Ex. 221 in 8 below) marks not a diminuendo but merely a *p*. The *p* here stands, apparently, at the *beginning* of the intended diminuendo and is thus literally equivalent to *dim.*

There is nothing in the notation to tell us whether an *f* or a *p*, *etc.*, in a baroque composition stands for an immediate contrast or a gradation. It is essential to take the context into consideration, holding an open mind until it is seen which interpretation makes the best and most natural effect. Cases of both kinds are numerous.

A further complication is the inaccuracy with which the signs are placed: sometimes obviously under the wrong note; sometimes inadvertently under a different note in different parts; sometimes present in only some of the parts; sometimes present in one copy of the same work but not in another copy; *etc.*

On the other hand, the presence of a series such as *p . . . f . . . ff*, *etc.*, may be taken with some confidence as an indication of a gradual crescendo, *etc.*

4. RANGE AND FLEXIBILITY OF EARLY DYNAMICS

Dr. Burney was so impressed by the disciplined gradation from extreme pianissimo to extreme fortissimo and back again which was the speciality of Stamitz' famous Mannheim orchestra in the middle of the eighteenth century that he started a legend of miraculous birth.

(629) Charles Burney, *Present State of Music in Germany*, London, 1773, I, p. 94:

'It was here [Schwetzingen, the summer resort of Mannheim] that *Crescendo* and *Dimimuendo* had their birth; and the *Piano*, which was before chiefly used as an echo, with which it was generally synonymous, as well as the *Forte*, were found to be musical *colours* which had their *shades*, as much as red or blue in painting.'

That this orchestra was exceptional we have no reason to doubt; its crescendos and diminuendos were evidently the finest of the day, and pushed to unusual limits; but they were not intrinsically novel. Ishak, son of Ibrahim, both famous musicians at the court of Harun-al-Rashid in the eighth century, had a similar reputation for passing gradually through an extreme range of volume (much Oriental music does the same today). See (2) in Ch. I, 2 for Bishop Ethelred's twelfth-century complaint that 'one while the voyce is strained, anon it is remitted, now it is dashed, and then againe it is inlarged with a lowder sound'.

Whether helped or not by dynamic markings, the performer has to produce a satisfactory range of louds and softs; of crescendos and diminuendos; and of fine shadings within the broader contrasts and gradations.

5. LOUDS AND SOFTS

(630) Christopher Simpson, *Division-Violist*, London, 1659, 2nd ed. (*Division Viol*), 1667, p. 10:

'We play Loud or Soft, according to our fancy, or the humour [mood] of the music.'

(631) Thomas Mace, *Musick's Monument*, London, 1676, p. 109:

'Play some part of the *Lesson Loud*, and some part *Soft*; which gives much more *Grace*, and *Lustre* to *Play*, than any other *Grace*, whatsoever.

[p. 130:] '*Humour a Lesson*, by Playing some *Sentences Loud*, and others again *Soft*, according as they best please your own *Fancy*.'

(632) Joachim Quantz, *Essay*, Berlin, 1752, XII, 23:

'And for repeats in general, the interchange of soft and loud gives much grace to the playing.'

(633) C. P. E. Bach, *Essay*, I, Berlin, 1753, III, 29:

'It is impossible to describe the contexts suitable to the forte or the piano, since for every case covered even by the best rule there will be an exception. The actual effect of these shadings depends on the passage, on the context and on the composer, who may introduce either a forte or a piano at a given point for reasons equally compelling. Indeed, entire passages, complete with all their concords and discords, may first of all be marked forte, and later on, piano.'

(a) It is important, either in rehearsal or beforehand or better still both, to work out a definite plan of louds and softs. If they are left too freely to a modern player's impulses, he tends to take them half-heartedly.

(b) The basis is the structure of the movement. For example, baroque allegros usually open with a straightforward exposition. Very few such openings are given a dynamic marking at all, whereas a piano sign at some point after the opening is not uncommon: evidently a loud opening was the normal assumption. In general, forte was the standard, piano (or pianissimo or fortissimo) the special effect.

Somewhere in the middle of the movement there is likely to be a more introverted section. The mood is quiet and contemplative, the modulations free and searching. A fairly consistent piano often suits this portion as well as a forte suits the extraverted opening. When the opening mood returns, the forte can return with it. These levels are subject to the finer shadings, but not to substantial crescendos and diminuendos unless the music quite definitely suggests them.

For repeats, the simplest dynamic plan is often the best. *E.g.*: first section loud, repeat soft; second section soft, repeat loud. Or first section loud, repeat soft; second section, first half soft but second half loud, repeat the same. Or with three sections: first section loud, repeat soft; second section soft, repeat soft; third section loud, repeat loud.

Da capo arias and slow movements have often a reflective middle section which may be taken softer on the whole than the outer sections.

Definite echo effects, even if not marked, should be treated as such. They are quite common at the ends of movements.

6. CRESCENDOS AND DIMINUENDOS

(634) G. Caccini, *Nuove Musiche*, Florence, 1602, preface, transl. in Playford, *Introduction*, London, 1654, ed. of 1674, p. 40:

'In Encreasing and Abating the Voyce, and in Exclamations is the foundation of Passion.'

(635) Christopher Simpson, *Division-Violist*, London, 1659, 2nd ed. (*Division-Viol*, 1667, p. 10):

'[Loud and soft sometimes occur] in one and the same Note.'

(636) M. Locke, *Observations upon a Late Book*, London, 1672, p. 36:

'The Viol and Violin [excell] in lowding, softing, and continuing a Note or Sound.'

(637) Roger North, *Autobiography*, c. 1695, ed. Jessopp, London, 1887, sect. 106:

'Learn to fill, and soften a sound, as shades in needlework, in sensation, so as to be like also a gust of wind, which begins with a soft air, and fills by degrees to a strength as makes all bend, and then softens away again into a temper [temperate strength], and so vanish.'

(638) François Raguenet, *Comparison between the French and Italian Music*, Paris, 1702, transl. ? J. E. Galliard, London, 1709, ed. O. Strunk, *Mus. Quart.*, XXXII, iii, p. 418:

'Sometimes we meet with a swelling to which the first notes of the thorough-bass jar so harshly as the ear is highly offended with it, but the bass, continuing to play on, returns at last to the swelling with such beautiful intervals that we quickly discover the composer's design, in the choice of these discords, was to give the hearer a more true and perfect relish of the ravishing notes that on a sudden restore the whole harmony.
[p. 420:] 'Every string of the bow is of an infinite length, lingering on a dying sound which decays gradually till at last it absolutely expires.
[p. 426:] 'Swellings of a prodigious length . . .
[p. 429:] 'In their tender airs [the Italian singers] soften the voice insensibly and at last let it die outright.'

(639) Scipione Maffei, 'Nuova Invenzione d'un Gravecembalo', *Giornale dei Letterati d'Italia*, V, Venice, 1711, p. 144:

'It is common knowledge among lovers of music that one of the chief methods by which the expert in that art contrive the secret of bringing particular delight to their listeners, is the piano and forte in subject and answer, or the gradual diminishing of the sound little by little, and the sudden return to the full volume of the instrument; which recourse is used frequently and with wonderful effect, in the great concerts of Rome [*i.e.* in the concertos, *etc.* of Corelli and others].'

(640) Joachim Quantz, *Essay*, Berlin, 1752, X, 3:

'Always keep the advantage of being able to produce, at need, after the *forte* a *fortissimo*, and after the *piano* a *pianissimo*.
[p. 108:] 'Increase or diminish the sound as required.'

(641) C. P. E. Bach, *Essay*, II, Berlin, 1762, XXIX, 12:

'Notes which lead up to closing cadences are performed loudly [*i.e.* presumably crescendo] whether they are so notated or not. In this way the leader is shown that an ornamental cadence [*i.e.* a cadenza] is to be expected, for which the accompanist will wait. This indication is particularly necessary in allegros, since ornamental cadences are more familiar in adagios.
[13:] 'When the solo part has a long sustained note which by the conventions of good performance should begin pianissimo, increase by degrees to a fortissimo, and return in the same way to a pianissimo, the accompanist must follow with the greatest exactitude.'

(a) Like the overall contrasts of loud and soft, the big crescendos and diminuendos are best worked out systematically.

(b) Again, the basis is the structure of the music. A crescendo or a diminuendo will sound meretricious unless it follows a genuine rise or fall in the emotional tension. On the other hand, if the genuine demands of the music are not followed merely because unmarked in an early text, the performance suffers from a serious loss of temperature.

(c) Pitch and emotion generally rise and fall together. Thus rising sequences tend to a crescendo, falling ones to a decrescendo. Taken on a flat dynamic level they are apt to be monotonous.

7. THE 'MESSA DI VOCE'

The effect of swelling a note and diminishing it again mentioned in several of the above quotations is the *messa di voce* of the virtuoso singers; but it was imitated by instrumentalists as well. It became a mannerism; but in really appropriate contexts it makes a beautiful effect. Thus the long g^{ll} with which the first violin opens J. S. Bach's C major trio sonata can build up to a forte, and drop to mezzo forte (piano would be too soft for the ensuing short notes); the second violin entry on c^{ll} can do the same; the accompaniment not being drawn into the *messa di voce*, but remaining mezzo forte.

8. THE FINER SHADINGS

(642) Jean Rousseau, *Traité de la Viole*, Paris, 1687, p. 23:

'The tenderness of his playing [Hautman on the gamba] came from those beautiful bowings which he brought to life and softened so skilfully and appropriately that he charmed all who heard him.

[p. 56:] 'The playing of melodic pieces should be simple, and thus requires much delicacy and tenderness, and it is in this style of playing that we should especially imitate all the expressive and delightful effects of which the voice is capable.'

(643) Roger North, *Autobiography*, c. 1695, ed. Jessopp, London, 1887, sect. 44 *ff* (musical reminiscences of the later 17th cent.):

'I was very much assisted [as a performer] by my knowledge of and acquaintance with the air [*i.e.* the art of composition]. It gave me courage as well as skill to fill and swell where the harmony required an emphasis.'

(644) Joachim Quantz, *Essay*, Berlin, 1752, XI, 14:

'Good expression ought nevertheless to be diversified. Light and shade must continually be kept up. For in truth you will never be touching, if you render all the notes at the same strength or the same weakness; if you perform, so to speak, always in the same colour, and do not know how to bring out and hold back the sound at the right time. Thus it is necessary to introduce a continual interchange of loud and soft.'

(645) C. P. E. Bach, *Essay*, I, Berlin, 1753, III, 29:

'It is broadly true that discords are performed loud and concords soft, since the former arouse our feelings and the latter quiet them. A special turn of thought designed to arouse a violent emotion must be performed loudly. The so-called deceptive [cadences], therefore, whose purpose is such, are usually performed loudly. A rule to be noticed, which is not without foundation, is that all those notes in a melody which are foreign to the key can well be emphasised regardless of whether they are consonant or dissonant, while the notes which are indigenous to the key are inclined to be performed softly, regardless of whether they are consonant or dissonant.' [But see also (633) in 5 above].

(646) Leopold Mozart, *Violinschule*, Augsburg, 1756, XII, 8:

'Indeed, you must know how to change from weak to strong of your own accord, each at its right time; for this, in the familiar language of painters, means *light* and *shade*. The notes raised by a sharp or a natural are always to be taken rather more loudly, the sound then diminishing again in course of the melody [as at Ex. 221 (a)]. In the same way a sudden lowering of a note by a flat or a natural should be brought out by a loud [as at Ex. 221 (b)].'

Ex. 221. Leopold Mozart, *loc. cit.*, fine dynamic shadings (the second *p* in each Ex. indicating *dim*):

489

(647) Carl Fr. Cramer, *Magazin der Musik*, Hamburg, 1783, p. 1217:

'All who have heard [C. P. E.] Bach playing the clavichord must have been struck by the continual refinement of shadow and light which he throws over his performance.'

(a) Unlike the overall contrasts and the big crescendos and diminuendos, the finer shadings hardly need to be premeditated. They are argely unconscious, and this has its dangers, since it can give rise to mannerisms such as the 'intrusive sforzando' with which a surprisingly large number of performers distort baroque music (and not only baroque music—but perhaps it shows more there). They are, however, an essential part of expression, and should grow naturally enough from the subtle promptings of the music.

(b) Several of the above quotations stress the importance of following the harmony intelligently in the dynamic shading. Quantz (*Essay*, Berlin, 1752, XVIII, vi, 12–17) elaborated a scheme for adjusting the volume of every chord by its degree of dissonance, with a long example showing markings from *pp* to *ff* on successive harmonies. Fortunately, he adds (*op. cit.*, 14) that 'good judgement and sensitiveness of soul must also play a large part'. They must indeed: taken literally, his example is absurd, though as an indication of his principle it is interesting enough. A year later, C. P. E. Bach (*Essay*, Berlin, 1753, see (633) in 5, above) is almost certainly voicing his low opinion of Quantz' scheme when he writes that 'it is impossible to describe the contexts suitable to the forte or the piano, since for every case covered even by the best rule there will be an exception'. But, he adds, 'it is broadly true that discords are performed loud and concords soft'.

Stated thus generally, this principle has almost the force of natural law. A discord should be perceptibly louder than its preparation, substantially louder than its resolution. If this is overlooked, as it commonly is by modern performers, the progression is deprived of its natural rise and fall. Even such fine dynamic shadings as this have something in the structure of the music for their origin.

(648) Roger North, [Notes on Music], Brit. Mus. Add. MS 32,532 (between 1695 and 1701), ff. 8v to 9:

'And this soft and lowd is discretionary' [but] 'binding notes or emphatical discords' [*i.e.* discords especially if suspended] 'should be prest hard' [and] 'when you come off into a sweeter calmer air, as to a cadence, which often follows such passages, then be soft and easy, as much as to say, Be content all is well.'

CHAPTER L

Balance

1. SUGGESTIONS FOR BALANCE SHOWN IN NOTATION

Balance is mainly a dynamic problem, though not entirely, since a part can be made to stand out by a certain significance in the manner of performing it, as well as by an actual predominance in volume.

2. WRITTEN INDICATIONS OF BALANCE

Indications of balance are occasionally found in baroque music. For example, in J. S. Bach's Chorale Prelude 'Christ lag in Todesbanden' (B.G. XL, p. 52), the melody is marked 'forte' and the counter subject 'piano'; his 'Jesu gütig', Var. X (B.G. XL, p. 133) has 'Choral *forte*'; his 'Liebster Jesu, wir sind hier', 2nd version (B.G. XXV, ii, p. 50) has 'forte' over the melody (in two-part canon) and 'piano' over the lower two staves; his 'An Wasserflüssen Babylon' (B.G. XXV, ii, p. 157) has 'piano' over the top stave, 'forte' over the chorale melody in the middle stave, and 'Pedale' over the bottom stave.

Other examples are found in orchestral scores. For example, Vivaldi (PV. 391, middle movement) has *f* and 'forte sempre' marked against a bass line of strong rhythmic outline, and *po* (piano) against the chords which accompany it on the remaining strings; and again (PV. 239, first movement) *p* followed by *f* (*i.e. p, cresc, f*) in the solo violin and *pianissimo* against the ripieno first and second violins which accompany it.

3. BALANCE LEFT TO THE PERFORMER

Normally it is left to the performer to bring out the most important matter in proportion to its significance. For this to be done without forcing, it is equally necessary to hold back the less important matter.

In polyphonic music, when the entries follow closely one upon another, it may be necessary to reduce the volume and significance of the part almost as soon as an entry has been made, in order to get out of the way of the next entry. This method is very effective in clarifying the more complex motets, madrigals and fantasies for viols.

In trio sonatas, the melodic parts (not excluding the bass) should sometimes be equal or almost equal, sometimes take precedence in turns.

Solo melodies should usually stand out from their accompaniment; but it is not always necessary to give them much, if any, dynamic prominence to secure this.

In baroque music, the bass part should nearly always be given very ample strength, in view of its supporting function; a point often overlooked in modern performance.

(649) Hermann Finck, *Practica Musica*, Wittenberg, 1556, Lib. V, [p. 7]:

'If in the beginning of the composition an elegant fugal subject occurs, this must be produced with a clearer and more decisive voice . . . and the succeeding voices, if they begin with the same fugal subject . . . are to be enunciated in the same way. This is to be observed in all the voices, when renewed fugal entries occur, so that the coherence and arrangement of all the fugal entries can be heard.'

(650) Lodovico Zacconi, *Prattica di Musica*, Venice, 1592, LXVI, p. 59:

'Entries should be emphasised a little so as to be instantly and clearly perceived by the hearer.'

(651) Charles Butler, *Principles of Musik*, London, 1636, p. 98:

'And in their great variety of Tones, to keep still an equal Sound [with one another] (except in a point [of imitation]): that one voice drown not another.'

(652) François Raguenet, *Comparison between the French and Italian Music*, Paris, 1702, transl. ? J. E. Galliard, London, 1709, ed. O. Strunk, *Mus. Quart.* XXXII, iii, p. 422:

'Sometimes the thorough-bass lays so fast hold of our ear that in listening to it we forget the subject; at other times the subject is so insinuating that we no longer regard the bass, when all of a sudden the violins become so ravishing that we mind neither the bass nor the subject.'

(653) Joachim Quantz, *Essay*, Berlin, 1752, XII, 23:

'When in an Allegro the subject returns several times, it is always necessary in the expression to distinguish well [from it] the less important thoughts. Whether it is majestic or caressing, gay or bold, it can always be made perceptible to the ear in a distinctive manner of performance . . . as also by loud and soft.

'[XVI, 24: In a trio sonata] with regard to soft and loud, one part must always adapt itself to the other, so that the increase and decrease of tone occurs at the same time. But if it happens that for a time one part makes a lower part, whose notes are only such as to fill in the harmony, it must be performed more softly than the other which makes the principal melody meanwhile, so that the less tuneful passages do not stand out unsuitably. If the parts imitate each other, or make passages which come together either in thirds or in sixths; the one and the other can play at the same strength.'

(654) Charles Avison, *Essay on Musical Expression*, London, 1752, p. 128:

'When the inner Parts are intended as Accompanyments only, great Care should be taken to touch them in such a Manner, that they may never predominate, but be always subservient to the principal Performer, who also should observe the same Method, whenever his Part becomes an Accompanyment; which generally happens in well-wrought Fugues and other full Pieces, where the Subject and Air are almost equally distributed. When the Attention of every Performer is thus employed by listening to the other Parts, without which he cannot do Justice to his own, it is then that we may expect to hear the proper Effect of the whole.'

(655) Jean-Jacques Rousseau, *Lettre sur la Musique Françoise* [Paris], 1753, p. 53:

'I am well aware that the bass, being the foundation of all the harmony, ought to dominate the rest of it, and that when the other parts stifle it or cover it, the result is a confusion which can obscure the harmony; and that is how I explain to myself why the Italians, sparing of their right hand in accompanying, usually double the bass at the octave in their left; why they put so many double basses in their orchestras; and why they so often make their tenors [violas] go with the bass, instead of giving them a separate part, as the French never fail to do.'

(656) [Laugier] *Apologie de la Musique Françoise* [Paris] 1754, p. 69:

'The first care which ought to be given is to arrange the consort in good order, to furnish all the parts sufficiently, to see that each makes its effect, that the chief parts, such as the treble and the bass, stand out to advantage, and that the subsidiary parts, such as the counter-tenor (Haute-contre) and the tenor (Taille) are less conspicuous, so that a harmony results in which nothing grows out of bounds, and which has unity. One cannot too strongly recommend furnishing the basses beyond the rest; for they are the foundation of the harmony, and from the nature of low-pitched sound, always less penetrating [a strong bass-line being especially necessary in recitatives].'

(657) Charles Burney, *Present State of Music in Germany*, London, 1773, I, p. 25:

'[A praiseworthy opera of which] the accompaniment is both rich, ingenious, and transparent, if I may be allowed the expression, by which I mean, that the air is not suffocated, but can be distinctly heard through them.'

(657a) J. F. Reichhardt, *Über die Pflichten des Ripien-Violinisten*, Berlin and Leipzig, 1776, Ch. II:

'In fugues . . . on long notes, the bow must be started somewhat more firmly, and a certain controlled stress of the notes is necessary here in order to keep the interpretation clear. This is the more necessary the more parts the fugue has. In particular the subject, at each new entry, has to be brought out with a certain pressure of the bow.'

CHAPTER LI

Accentuation

1. WORDS SUGGESTING ACCENTUATION

Accentuation was not shown directly in baroque notation; but instructions are sometimes found which indicate a well-accented style. Such instructions are not uncommonly attached to movements which might otherwise be taken as cases for expressive inequality, as discussed in Ch. XLV above: *e.g.* 'notes égales et marquées'; 'notes martelées' (hammered notes); 'détachez'; 'mouvement décidé'; 'mouvement marqué'; *etc.* Words such as staccato, spiccato or spiritoso, all suggestive of accentuation in some degree, are likewise found, especially in the Italian virtuoso violinist-composers.

2. ACCENTUATION SUGGESTED BY THE MUSIC

It is a universal necessity to respond with the appropriate accentuation to the implication of the music.

(658) René Descartes, *Musicae Compendium*, (1618) 1650, transl. William Viscount Brouncker, London, 1653, Ch. III, p. 5:

'Few have understood, how this Measure can be exhibited to the ears without a percussion, or stroke, in Musick, very diminute [florid] and of many voices. This we say is effected only by a certain intension of the *Spirit* or breath, in *Vocall* Musick; or of the *Touch*, in *Instrumental*: so as from the beginning of each stroke, the sound is emitted more distinctly. Which all Singers naturally observe, and those who play on Instruments; principally in Tunes, at whose numbers we are wont to dance and leap.'

In late renaissance and, less frequently, in early baroque music, we may find complete polyphonic freedom in the accentuation implied by the separate parts; and even in baroque music as a whole, where barring has become normal usage and mainly coincides with the prevailing measure, the requisite accentuation is often far more subtle and irregular than appearance suggests. The reader is referred to Geminiani's warning, quoted at (536) in Ch. XXXIX, 1 above, against crudely accenting the first beat of every bar. It is the shape of the phrase which implies the accentuation. Every case has to be judged on merits by ordinary good musicianship; but very often the highest note of a phrase is also its musical climax, and where this is so, the accent usually falls

495

in the same place too. A somewhat crude case of this is shown by Leopold Mozart below. Albert Schweitzer's discussion of the subject, in his *J. S. Bach* (Paris, 1905 and Leipzig, 1908) is worth consulting.

(659) Leopold Mozart, *Violinschule*, Augsburg, 1756, XII, 13:

'In lively pieces the accent is generally taken on the highest notes, so as to make the performance really cheerful.'

Ex. 222. Leopold Mozart, *loc. cit.*, accents on high notes off the beat:

3. THE AGOGIC ACCENT

The term 'agogic accent' has been adopted for a slight prolongation of a note by which it acquires a certain prominence, whether or not this agogic accent is combined (as it usually is) with an actual dynamic accent.

The agogic accent was familiar to baroque musicians, though not under that name. In so far as it required description at all, it was included under the principle of inequality. Quantz' account of inequality at (587) in Ch. XLV, 7 above, after mentioning the normal convention by which 'the first and third notes' of four are to be 'a little pressed upon, and their tone made a little louder than that of the second and fourth notes', adds: 'but we except from this rule in the first place quick passages, in a very quick movement, where it is only possible to press and use force upon the first note of the four', *etc., etc.* The term 'press upon' is here equivalent to 'prolong slightly'; the term 'use force upon' is equivalent to 'accent'. Quantz is thus describing what is actually a combination of agogic and dynamic accents.

4. THE WEIGHT ACCENT

On the violins, a weight accent is made literally with the weight of the arm as it presses or even drops the bow on the string. Other instruments can produce comparable effects.

There are many gradations of weight accent; but it tends to be too massive for most baroque contexts.

5. THE SFORZANDO

This is a slightly less abrupt access of weight just after the note has started. As a perpetual unconscious mannerism it is particularly harmful in baroque music, but as an intentional dynamic accent, particularly useful. Milder than the weight accent, it gives just the right emphasis for the peak of a phrase. It combines well with an agogic accent. It can be prepared by the slightest of deliberate hesitations. It is capable of fine gradations.

(660) Giulio Caccini, *Nuove Musiche*, Florence, 1602, preface, Eng. transl. in Playford, *Introduction*, London, 1654:

'There are some that in the *Tuning* of the first Note, Tune it a *Third* under: Others Tune the said first *Note* in his proper Tune, always increasing it in Lowdness, saying that this is a good way of putting forth the *Voyce* gracefully . . . I have found it a more affectuous way to *Tune* the *Voyce* by a contrary effect to the other, that is, to Tune the first *Note*, Diminishing it: Because Exclamation is the principal means to move the Affections; and Exclamation properly is no other thing, but in the slacking of the *Voyce* to reinforce it somewhat . . .
'*Exclaimations* may be used in all *Passionate* Musicks.'

(661) Joachim Quantz, *Essay*, Berlin, 1752, XII, 19:

'When after quick notes there suddenly comes a long note which holds up the melody, it must be marked with a special emphasis, and likewise in the following notes the volume can again be restrained a little.'

(662) Leopold Mozart, *Violinschule*, Augsburg, 1756, XII, 8:

'It is the custom always strongly to emphasise minims mingled with short notes, and to diminish the sound again [as at Ex. 223 (a)]. Indeed, many crotchets are performed in the same way [as at Ex. 223 (b)].'

Ex. 223. Leopold Mozart, *loc. cit.*, sforzandos:

6. THE ATTACK ACCENT

(a) The crystalline sharpness and transparency so characteristic of baroque music are well served by the attack accent, especially on string instruments. The player uses his forefinger to press the bow momentarily on to the string; as he releases it into motion, a beautifully crisp and clean attack should result. Wind instruments can do the same by tonguing.

This, too, can be finely graded. At its least, it is an incisive attack, but no more; in this form, it can be used on every note of a passage which needs to be sharply etched without being heavy. Taken more strongly, on selected notes, it is perceived not only as an attack, but as a subtle accent, so that any note or notes in the passage can be picked out with no sense of effort and no interruption of the flow. Combined with a certain weight borrowed from the weight accent, but in moderation, the attack accent can be given sufficient power for almost any baroque situation.

The effect of an attack accent can be greatly heightened by a little silence of articulation taken out of the time of the note before. The silence alone can give an impression of accentuation on the harpsichord, where there is scarcely any true dynamic accentuation, or on the organ, where there is none. The combination of preparatory silence and true attack accent can give the rhythm a quite intoxicating lift, and is the most generally valuable of all baroque methods of accentuation.

(663) Leopold Mozart, *Violinschule*, Augsburg, 1756, IV, 23:

'You must not forget to attack the middle [syncopated] note more strongly with the up bow-stroke; and to slur the third note to it with a gradual diminution of the volume.'

Ex. 224. Leopold Mozart, *op. cit.*, IV, 22, silence of articulation shown before (accented) syncopation:

BOOK FOUR
INSTRUMENTS

CHAPTER LII

Instruments in Early Music

1. MUSIC AND ITS INSTRUMENTS

There is an intimate connection between music and its instruments. The composer more or less consciously takes into account their sonority, the attack and decay of their sounds, their natural articulation and their range of technical resource. He also exerts more or less pressure on performers to extend their technique and on makers to develop or modify the instruments themselves; and performers and makers have their own urge to evolve in new directions, often advantageously, though not always without a loss to weigh against the gain.

The climate of the times may vary greatly. In the sixteenth century, there was a disposition towards polyphonic patterns which can be traced in different sonorities with no intrinsic difference of effect. This did not make sonority a matter of indifference; musicians took an almost extravagant delight in experimenting with rich and adventurous combinations of instruments. But, within appropriate limits, we can choose our own sonority for modern performance, provided only that we make it no less colourful and suitable than it would then have been.

A case, again, such as the Art of Fugue, the prodigious contrapuntal pattern on which J. S. Bach was working when he died, comes perhaps as near as music can come to abstract line; and it is not even known what instrumental sonority, if any, Bach conceived for it. Some writers have regarded it as music for the mind alone. But is music ever for the mind alone? Can mind and matter ever be divorced? The Art of Fugue can be made effective on the harpsichord, on a string quartet or a consort of viols, in a mixed scoring of strings and wind, and in other ways. It is only necessary to provide it with a sensitive reflection in sound of the thought and the pattern in the music. We are not confined to one sonority provided we keep our sonority appropriate.

Contrast with this the music written by J. S. Bach specifically for the keyboard instruments. Of these, the organ is in a class apart: works really well composed for the nature of this remarkable instrument are unmistakable. Harpsichord music is not quite so distinct; music designated for the *clavier* ('keyboard') in J. S. Bach's Germany was more or less interchangeable between the harpsichord and the clavichord, as becomes abundantly clear, for example, in C. P. E. Bach's great *Essay* of 1753. Yet the sonority of the two instruments, though similar, is not the same; while their attack and technique are not even very similar. The one excels in brilliance, the other in expressiveness. Of Bach's *clavier* music, some examples are far more effective on the harpsichord, other examples on the clavichord, others equally on either, but none are quite unsuitable on either, because the common qualities of the two instruments are more important musically than their differences.

Now consider the position of the piano with regard to baroque music. J. S. Bach was not favourably impressed by Silbermann's early pianos. They were, of course, imperfect instruments; but Bach would have been quick to see the possibilities behind the imperfections, if these possibilities had been of keen interest to him. They were not of keen interest, because they were quite foreign to his own keyboard idiom.

The possibilities latent in the piano were not merely its continuous gradations of dynamic control (the clavichord has these, though at a lower absolute volume) but its impressionistic surge of sound. The former possibilities were developed first: the pianos of Mozart's generation, though true pianos in dynamic control, are nearer to the harpsichord than to the modern piano in sonority, and also in clarity. The impressionistic surge is rather more developed in the pianos of Beethoven and Schubert; but not until Schumann and Brahms did composers, performers or makers exploit this aspect to its fullest extent. The contrast between Bach's clear counterpoint and Schumann's surging arpeggiation is precisely matched by the contrast between the mid-eighteenth century harpsichord and the mid-nineteenth century piano. There is no clearer instance in history of a change in the instruments of music evolving in mutual inter-reaction with a change in the prevailing aims and climate of music itself.

Thus while the choice of harpsichord or clavichord for Bach's *clavier* music is to a large extent a matter of taste or even of convenience, the use of the piano raises a nice point of artistic suitability. The profound integrity, the warmth and the intelligence of Harold Samuel's Bach playing will still be remembered by many; Myra Hess was just as memorable; Rosalyn Tureck, though too strict in her rhythm for me, is much enjoyed; and it is out of the question to dismiss such artists as despoilers of Bach's original intentions. Yet it is obvious that they are departing from the original. Music composed for the even flow and brilliant clarity of the harpsichord has to be mentally reconceived (transcribed would hardly be too strong a word) when interpreted in terms of the dynamic flexibility and massive impetus of the piano. It is probably better, at any rate in solo music, to treat the piano pianistically

502

and make the most of its own fine qualities, rather than try to make it sound like a harpsichord, which it can never do. To suppress its proper warmth is to spoil it and denature it, and does justice neither to the instrument nor to the music, both of which are so very excellent.

2. SUBSTITUTIONS MUST BE AS SUITABLE AS POSSIBLE

Substitutions were by no means foreign to the baroque mentality. Baroque title-pages do not usually specify quite the free choice of alternative instruments found regularly on renaissance title-pages; but the option is still often very wide. Solo and trio sonatas were commonly published for a choice of violin, flute or oboe. There was a fashion in operatic excerpts to be played on various instruments: *e.g.* Ballard's excerpts from Lully's operas 'suitable for singing and playing on the Flute, Violin and other instruments' (Paris, early eighteenth century). The same freedom extended to other vocal and instrumental music.

(664) Michel L'Affillard, *Principes tres-faciles*, Paris, 1694, ed. of 1722, p. 6:

'If people who play instruments wish to play the "Airs de mouvement" in this book, they have only to transpose them into the key which best suits the compass of their instruments.'

(665) François Couperin, *Concerts Royaux*, Paris, 1722, preface:

'They suit not only the harpsichord, but also the violin, the flute, the oboe, the viol and the bassoon.
'[*Troisième livre de pièces*, Paris, 1722, preface:] These pieces, indeed, are suitable for two flutes or oboes, as well as for two violins, two viols, and other instruments of equal pitch; it being understood that those who perform them adapt them to the range of theirs.'

(666) Jean-Philippe Rameau, *Pièces de clavecin en concerts*, with a violin or a flute and a [bass] viol or a second violin, Paris, 1741, preface:

'[When substituting the flute] if one finds chords, it is necessary to choose the note which makes the most beautiful melody, and which is ordinarily the highest.
'With regard to notes which pass beyond the compass at the bottom of the flute [take the passage an octave up, between the signs shown; but] in a rapid passage of several notes, it is sufficient to substitute for those which descend too low the neighbouring ones in the same harmony, or to repeat those which one deems fit.'

The motive behind such titles and instructions was only partly the obvious commercial one of increasing sales. There was also a genuine preference for leaving the choice open, for providing music in such a form that as many musicians as possible could use it, and for trusting them to do so with intelligent discrimination. If they made an undiscriminating choice, the loss was theirs. That remains true. Some pieces are extremely idiomatic, others are more accommodating. Some are for named instruments, and obviously require them. Where alternatives are stated, they do not necessarily all apply to the same piece. Often only one of them is really suitable. Conversely, where no alternatives are stated, this does not exclude them, provided that the same care is taken to suit the choice of instruments to the music in question.

There is no fundamental reason why the alternatives should be limited to the strict historical possibilities; though as most of the suitable ones already existed, this will ordinarily happen. The only fundamental issue is the issue of suitability. If a saxophonist finds a baroque sonata which makes an excellent musical effect on his instrument, which was invented in the nineteenth century, there is nothing in the baroque attitude to music which prevents him. On the other hand, if a small heckelphone (invented in the twentieth century) or a clarinet is used to replace a long D trumpet in a high and difficult baroque obbligato part, the musical effect is not adequately served: partly because it is in this context inferior as well as different; partly because we have here an instance not of optional timbres but of specific orchestration, so that the mere fact of sounding different is detrimental. If Bach's sixth Brandenburg concerto is taken with additional violas or cellos in place of gambas, its already dark colouring becomes disadvantageously sombre, and this imaginative experiment in chamber-music scoring (it is not really an orchestral work) suffers considerable loss of beauty. Yet such substitutions cannot always be avoided under prevailing conditions, and it is possible to minimise the disadvantages.

3. EARLY TECHNIQUE SHOULD BE TAKEN INTO ACCOUNT

We have also to consider the very substantial changes of technique found in many instruments whose basic form has not changed, and which are still in everyday use. These and other points will be briefly considered in the following chapters. For a fuller discussion the reader is referred to my shorter book, *A Performer's Guide to Baroque Music* (London, 1973); and beyond that to the special studies listed in my Bibliography, and others.

CHAPTER LIII

Pitch

1. THE EFFECT OF PITCH ON PERFORMANCE

The pitch at which music is performed makes a great difference to its effect.

Too high a pitch tends to a strident effect, too low a pitch to a sombre effect. Singers, indeed, can be pushed not only out of their best tessitura but out of their compass by a relatively small change in pitch. Instruments may be less obviously affected: but consider the difference in colouring between a B flat clarinet and an E flat clarinet!

2. ACTUAL PITCH AND NOMINAL PITCH

(a) Here we have to be careful not to confuse actual pitch with nominal pitch.

Our present international standard of pitch is $a^1 = 440$. This means that we assume for our nominal pitch a^1 an actual pitch given by 440 c.p.s. (double vibration-cycles per second).

No such assumption can be made for earlier periods, which related an astonishing variety of actual pitches to the nominal pitch a^1. We have abundant evidence on the nominal pitches of early instruments, *etc.*, but very little on the actual pitches, and much of what we have depends on calculations liable to error.

(b) We have also to allow for the effects of transposition, which was a common recourse to meet the numerous conflicting actual pitches in use. We may, for example, know the actual original pitch of a certain organ, at least approximately; yet the music performed with it may still have been performed at a quite different pitch, the organist transposing his part at sight. The same applies to woodwind or brass instruments.

When the three clefs (*G*, *C*, and *F*) are used on higher or lower positions of the stave than their usual S.A.T.B. positions, then in vocal polyphony of the late renaissance and early baroque periods, transposition may be implied—the commonest being a fourth or a fifth downwards (where the clefs stand high). Some authorities describe this as normal practice; others warn us against spoiling an intentionally low and sombre tessitura, or an intentionally high and brilliant tessitura, by such transposition. We are therefore thrown back on our musical

505

judgment of what the intended tessitura really is in any given case, except where a composer's preface specifies a transposition or a transposed organ part exists in writing; and even there, we are still dealing in nominal pitches, without necessarily knowing to what actual pitch they correspond. The problem (known since the later eighteenth century as that of the *chiavetti*, little clefs, or *chiavi trasportati*, transposed clefs, as opposed to *chiavi naturali*, natural clefs) has been studied with great thoroughness and insight by Arthur Mendel ('Pitch in the 16th and early 17th Centuries', *Mus. Quart.*, XXXIV, 1948, Nos. 3 and 4). His articles are essential reading for any musician directing vocal polyphony of the renaissance and early baroque periods. But they confirm only too clearly what has just been said: we must be prepared for extensive transposition, yet have usually to rely on purely musical considerations in deciding where, and by how wide an interval, to apply it.

Clefs also appear at other than their usual S.A.T.B. positions on the stave for convenience in avoiding ledger lines (to which early musicians cherished an exaggerated aversion) without any possible implication of transposition.

The *G* clef on the lowest (instead of the usual lowest but one) line of the treble stave ('French violin clef') was associated with French notation, and its presence is sometimes an indication that the music is in the French style (see Ch. II, 3, above).

(c) A remarkably painstaking attempt to clarify the situation with regard to early pitch was made by A. J. Ellis, culminating in a historic article ('History of Musical Pitch', *Journal of the [Royal] Society of Arts*, London, 5 March, 1880), which has been the foundation of all subsequent attempts. Ellis gave his results to one decimal place, in c.p.s.; and though he carefully explained the circumstances which made most of them subject to a margin of error, many writers who have since drawn on his article have ignored the explanation and copied the results, so that a mistaken assumption has become current that the pitch of some early organs, for example, can be stated with this degree of accuracy. Ellis himself worked largely on the pitch of actual organ pipes (which may have been changed at an intervening date) and on recorded measurements (but calculation of pitch from measurements is complicated by the need to make various corrections which cannot be exactly estimated, and of which even the theory was in one or two respects unknown to Ellis).

Not till the development of the tuning fork, early in the eighteenth century, did evidence of actual pitch appear which is both exact and dependable.

(d) The important series of articles by Mendel cited above, and 'On the Pitches in Use in J. S. Bach's Time', (*Mus. Quart.*, XLI, 3, 4) greatly added to our understanding of the problem. Two crucial points were clarified by Mendel's researches: the immense variety of nominal pitches of the late renaissance and baroque periods; and the narrow range of actual pitches after transposition has been taken into account. The practical importance of this is obvious.

(e) A brilliantly lucid account, both scientifically and musically reliable, was contributed by Ll. S. Lloyd to *Grove's Dictionary* (5th ed., London, 1954, *s.v.* 'Pitch, Standard'). This is now much the best introduction to the subject for the general reader.

3. PITCHES IN LATE RENAISSANCE AND EARLY BAROQUE MUSIC

(a) Michael Praetorius (*Syntagma*, II, Wolfenbüttel, 1619) records dimensions of a pipe in the Halberstadt organ, which he examined in the state in which it had been left when reconstructed in 1495. Ellis made a calculation which, taking into account the criticisms of his methods by Mendel and Lloyd, we may translate as meaning that the pitch of this organ stood at about $a^1 = 550$ to about 630. This is four to six semitones above our present $a^1 = 440$.

By a further calculation, based on information in Arnolt Schlick's *Spiegel der Orgelmacher*, [Speyer, 1511], but seriously questioned by Mendel, Ellis inferred an almost identical pitch which he took to be Schlick's high pitch, and another nearly three semitones below $a^1 = 440$, which he took to be Schlick's low pitch (particularly doubtful). Ellis further gives an organ at St. Catherine's, Hamburg, as a semitone and a half above $a^1 = 440$.

(b) Canon E. H. Fellowes (*English Madrigal Composers*, Oxford, 1921, pp. 70–74) argues the question of pitch in late Elizabethan and early Stuart England in a very practical and valuable manner. His chief evidence is the written compass and tessitura of voice parts; he also cites a little acoustic evidence (particularly Thomas Tomkins' mention of a 30-inch organ pipe at the nominal pitch of *F*, which might sound between *G* and *A* flat at $a^1 = 440$).

Fellowes concludes that Tudor church music was composed for an actual pitch just in excess of a tone above $a^1 = 440$, and should be transposed a tone up in performance to obtain the effect actually intended by the notation.

He concludes that secular music of the late sixteenth and early seventeenth centuries in England stood at a nominal pitch about equivalent to $a^1 = 440$, so that it requires no transposition, the actual standard of pitch being the same as ours.

He points out that these pitches would have been subject to considerable variation. There seems no reason to doubt the general correctness of his views.

He believes that there was another pitch a minor third below $a^1 = 440$, for virginals, of which the surviving specimens would not in his opinion stand being tuned higher. Here he was on much less secure ground: so much depends on condition, string-gauges and other variables.

(c) The instructions in tutors for the lute, the viol, *etc.*, are to tune up the gut top string to just short of breaking point. To find the point at which the string breaks in your face is in no way difficult; the point just short of it is, shall we say, less painfully obvious. But with good strings of the same gauge relative to their length it is more constant than might be thought. Michael Prynne (*Grove's Dictionary*, 5th ed., London, 1954, *s.v.* 'Lute') after experiments with the lute reached the tentative opinion that this instrument may ordinarily have been tuned no higher than three-quarters of a tone below $a^1 = 440$. But there are, again, too many variables for these experiments to be conclusive.

(d) Anthony Baines (*Woodwind Instruments and their History*, London, 1957, p. 242) in course of the most valuable study yet written of old and new woodwind, suggests from the examination of surviving instruments that some approach to a standard pitch of about $a^1 = 470$ or roughly a semitone above $a^1 = 440$ can be seen among the leading woodwind makers of the sixteenth century.

(e) Pitches given by Ellis for the first half of the seventeenth century include one for 'Mersenne's spinet, 1648', well over a semitone below $a^1 = 440$; an organ pitch recommended by Praetorius (1619), about half a semitone below $a^1 = 440$; another from the *Great Franciscan Organ*, Vienna (1640), nearly a semitone above $a^1 = 440$; two from Mersenne (1636), a *ton de chapelle* (or *Chorton*: church or choral pitch) well over a tone above $a^1 = 440$, and a *ton de chambre* (or *Kammerton*: chamber pitch) well over two tones above $a^1 = 440$.

4. PITCHES IN MUSIC OF THE MAIN BAROQUE PERIOD

(a) Ellis gives 'Euler's clavichord, 1739', a tone below $a^1 = 440$; a Silbermann organ at Dresden, 1754, a semitone below $a^1 = 440$; a Father Smith organ, 1690, at approximately $a^1 = 440$, and another, 1683, at well over a semitone above $a^1 = 440$; an organ at Rendsburg, 1700, just over a tone above $a^1 = 440$; *etc.* Varieties of *Chorton* and *Kammerton* high and low still abounded.

Lloyd states that many English organs were lowered in pitch, sometimes by as much as a tone, between 1650 and 1750, with the result, he says, that church pitch came down to secular pitch. This historical evidence of work actually done on organs is solid confirmation for Fellowes' assumption, mentioned in 3 (b) above, that church pitch was higher than secular pitch in Elizabethan and early Stuart England.

(b) By the end of the baroque period we begin to have the welcome evidence of tuning-forks (the older pitch-pipe is an inexact measure).

A tuning-fork said to be Handel's was examined by Ellis ('Handel's pitch, 1751') and found to give a pitch rather less than a semitone below $a^1 = 440$; and Lloyd concludes that one locally used pitch of Handel's time might be this or a little lower: in broad terms, let us say, a semitone below $a^1 = 440$. We have no evidence that the fork was Handel's.

(c) Anthony Baines (loc. cit.) believes from the examination of very large numbers of specimens that woodwind makers of the dominant French school of Hotteterre and others during the second half of the seventeenth century arrived at a moderately standard pitch of about $a^1 = 422$ or roughly a semitone below $a^1 = 440$, and that the influence of their famous instruments kept orchestral and chamber pitch reasonably constant for about a century or rather longer, at this 'low pitch' a semitone down on ours.

(d) Yet English recorders by Bressan are in existence, which were made between 1700 and 1730, and of which the pitch is in most cases nearly a tone below $a^1 = 440$.

5. PITCHES IN POST-BAROQUE MUSIC

(a) A copy of the tuning-fork to which Mozart's piano may have been tuned was seen by Ellis ('Mozart's pitch, 1780') and found to give rather less than a semitone below $a^1 = 440$. There is no evidence that this constituted a 'Viennese Classical Pitch'; but it may have been so, and it would make Beethoven's soprano $B\natural$'s more singable.

(b) Ellis further gives: 'Original Philharmonic Pitch, 1813', at just over half a semitone below $a^1 = 440$; 'Sir George Smart's fork, 1820–26', at rather less than a third of a semitone below $a^1 = 440$; 'Scheibler's Stuttgart Standard, 1834' at $a^1 = 440$; 'Madrid, 1858', 'San Carlo, Naples, 1857', 'Broadwood's Medium, 1849' and 'French opera, 1856', all at just over $a^1 = 440$; 'Highest Philharmonic, 1874', 'Broadwood, Érard and Steinway, England, 1879' and 'Vienna, high, 1859', all at just over half a semitone above $a^1 = 440$; 'St. James, Hamburg, 1879', at a tone above $a^1 = 440$.

(c) 'Scheibler's Stuttgart Standard, 1834' refers to a most interesting attempt by this notable pioneer to secure a standard pitch, which he proposed to a congress of physicists at Stuttgart in 1834. His suggestion of $a^1 = 440$, with its striking anticipation of our present level, was arrived at as the mean pitch of Viennese grand pianos taken at a variety of temperatures (because of the effect of rises of temperature in raising the pitch of most musical instruments), as they were tuned at that date.

(d) In 1858 the French Government appointed a commission of distinguished musicians, physicists and civil servants to consider the chaotic situation in which pitch still stood. Its report led in 1859 to two decrees giving legal force to a standard pitch of $a^1 = 435$, just below $a^1 = 440$. This is *diapason normal*.

This pitch was accepted to some extent in other Continental countries. In England, it was misunderstood, and the actual task of preparing a standard tuning-fork was incompetently handled; hence the Society of Arts, which had meant to establish $a^1 = 440$, found itself with a C fork giving 534·5 c.p.s., which produces (in equal temperament) an a^1 of 449·5 c.p.s.—about a quarter of a semitone above $a^1 = 440$.

The perennial fantasy of improving the brilliance by raising the pitch must have been particularly active in England at this date; for in May 1877, Wagner was enraged by the strain his singers were put to by being obliged to sing in London at a pitch much higher than usual, while in 1879 Patti actually refused to sing at Covent Garden at the pitch its orchestra had then reached, which was $a^1 = 455$, more than half a semitone above $a^1 = 440$. The orchestra came down to French pitch. The power of a great singer is not always misused.

(e) In 1885, an international conference on pitch was held at Vienna, at which, however, England was not represented. It accepted, in effect, $a^1 = 435$.

(f) In 1895, Robert Newman, the manager of Queen's Hall, and his young conductor Henry Wood, had the courage, regardless of the expense, to lower the pitch of the newly built organ. The Philharmonic Society responded with the admirable if belated decision to adapt the French pitch, the determinants of which they nevertheless still sufficiently misunderstood (by relating it to temperature, which had been deliberately avoided in France) to arrive, not at $a^1 = 435$, but at $a^1 = 439$. This is New Philharmonic Pitch: virtually $a^1 = 440$.

Any upward lead in pitch is all too readily followed, and the English mistake was unfortunate.

(g) In 1939, a fully representative international conference in London, organised, it is pleasant to record, by the British Standards Institution, adopted our present $a^1 = 440$, which had become standardised in America, and is a much more convenient frequency than $a^1 = 439$ for calculating mathematically and producing electronically. This is British Standard Pitch, and is generally accepted, though attempts to edge upwards again are reported. It is important that this pitch should be held, since there are real musical disadvantages in a higher one, and it is in any case a little on the high side.

Much the most exact and dependable standard by which to tune is an electronically produced tone such as that broadcast daily by the B.B.C. at $a^1 = 440$. A tuning-fork is sufficiently reliable in practice; an oboe A is not, though commonly relied upon for orchestral convenience.

6. PITCH IN PRACTICE

(a) The evidence as re-examined by Lloyd, and much more exhaustively by Mendel, does not permit us to believe that the pitch of about $a^1 = 422$, roughly a semitone below $a^1 = 440$, and nowadays known as 'low pitch', had any greater currency than other pitches during the baroque period. It was, indeed, a pitch in use, but only as one among a wide variety of others, and we have no grounds for giving it any general preference. It is sometimes a useful pitch, but no more than that.

(b) Any general statement that viols or harpsichords, *etc.*, were built to be tuned at 'low pitch' roughly a semitone below $a^1 = 440$ is thus against the evidence. In relation to the bulk of the repertoire, both classical and pre-classical, our present $a^1 = 440$ is a little too high to be ideal, but it is not far out, and the advantages of having at last secured an agreed standard are far too valuable to forego by adopting another pitch or pitches for early music. Under all ordinary circumstances, therefore, and except for special reasons, we should keep to $a^1 = 440$.

(c) We must, however, make use of transposition whenever this is necessary to bring the music within the compass of the human voice, or within the best tessitura having regard to the character of the music so far as we can judge it.

We may also make use of transposition if we suspect, even apart from vocal considerations, that the nominal pitch at which we find the music differs substantially from the actual pitch which its notation gives at $a^1 = 440$. This suspicion may often amount to no more than a conviction that the music sounds more its natural self when transposed, say, a fourth up, and we have to be careful then that we are not merely superimposing our own predilections at the expense of the composer's. But not too careful. His music is almost certain to have been performed at different pitches by different performers of his own day.

(d) Except where required to meet the needs of singers, small transpositions are sometimes to be avoided because of an adverse, or at least a transforming, effect on the sonority. Violins, viols or lutes lose some of their brightness when transposed, *e.g.*, from D major to E flat major, which has fewer notes enriched by sympathetic resonance from the open strings. On the other hand, transposition from F major to

G major makes less difference in this respect, and can therefore be used with less hesitation.

A lutenist accompanying a singer, and asked by him to transpose up or down by a small interval, may be better advised to change his tuning to a lower or higher actual pitch instead, in order to avoid this loss of resonance. But he cannot do this repeatedly in a single concert, because of the unsettling effect on the tuning—it will not hold its pitch if changed too frequently.

A larger transposition, for example by a fourth or a fifth, is not only more worth making, but has the further advantage that violins, *etc.*, can pass, *e.g.* from D major to A major without much affecting the number of open string giving support by sympathetic resonance.

A very simple and practical example of momentary transposition can be seen in the copy of Destouches' *Telemaque* (Paris, 1714) in the Bibliothèque de l'Opéra at Paris (A. 90a, p. xxii) where the bass line of a chorus is taken up an octave, for three bars, by the simple expedient of writing in 'en haut' and 'en bass' (at the high octave, at the low). The BC part goes with it; and on p. 3, some instrumental parts, while not only corrections but improvements are freely written in. Altogether an instructive example, and a typical one, of the free adaptation of detail as required in performance rather than rigidified by the original notation.

CHAPTER LIV

Temperament

1. WHY TEMPERAMENT IS NECESSARY

It is a surprising fact of nature, but true, that acoustically just intervals will not fit with one another.

If we pass a just fifth up from *C*, we reach *G*; from there a just fourth will take us down to *D*.

If we pass a just major sixth up from *C*, we reach *A*; and from here a just fifth will again take us down to *D*.

But not quite to the same *D*. It is a little flatter.

Again, twelve just fifths add up to the same as seven octaves—almost. They make, in fact, a little more.

Such discrepancies make 'perfect' intonation an impossibility. Good performers keep up a continual flexibility in their intonation, easing each interval into as just a relationship as they can, and paying no regard to where the sum-total of these instinctive adjustments may be leading them. That is why choirs (having no open strings, *etc.*, to limit their adjustments) so often end at a different pitch from their starting-point. Nature rather than the choir should take the blame for this.

These flexible adjustments are temperament—but temperament unconscious and in motion. Instruments rigidly pre-tuned, *i.e.* chiefly the keyboard instruments, cannot adjust flexibly and in motion. They have to be systematically tempered, in advance. *D* can only be one kind of tone's distance above *C*; twelve fifths have somehow to be condensed into seven octaves.

Temperament is thus a compromise for spreading the unavoidable adjustments as favourably as possible. Keyboard temperament is a static temperament, which if it flatters some tonalities, can only do so at the expense of others.

2. MEAN-TONE TEMPERAMENT

Late renaissance and baroque temperaments could flatter the 'near' keys because the 'remote' keys were not in common use.

A favourite was mean-tone temperament, in which the mean is struck between the tones *C* to *D* as reached by the different routes described in 1 above. Just thirds are possible, and sound beautiful; but where the cycle of fifths breaks (between *G* sharp and *A* flat, or

D sharp and *E* flat), the accumulated mistuning—the 'wolf'—is too much to be endured.

Hence mean-tone temperament is very good indeed in some tonalities, terrible in others.

3. MODIFICATIONS OF MEAN-TONE TEMPERAMENT

Among the comprehensive range of temperaments explored by late renaissance and baroque theorists and musicians, some of whose modulations pass through the entire cycle of keys, there were various modifications of mean-tone temperament. For example, by the slight sacrifice of sharpening the thirds to become a very little wide, the fifths can be widened too, and the gap in the cycle narrowed until the wolf howls much less noticeably. J. Murray Barbour ('Bach and *The Art of Temperament*', *Mus. Quart.*, XXXIII, January 1947, p. 64) has shown that this version of mean-tone temperament with sharp thirds (and not equal temperament as historians have assumed) is almost certainly the temperament for which J. S. Bach showed his practical enthusiasm by composing his Forty-Eight Preludes and Fugues—and much other music in tonalities too remote for normal mean-tone temperament.

4. EQUAL TEMPERAMENT

Equal temperament, a necessity now because of our unrestricted modulations of tonality, is reached by dividing the octave into twelve equal semitones regardless of all resulting mistunings. Every note can be taken enharmonically: we can reach the same note as *G* sharp and leave it as *A* flat, *etc.* No interval is really good, but none is really bad, and the howling of the wolf is for ever silenced.

5. TEMPERAMENT IN PRACTICE

(a) Experiments made by A. R. McClure (see *Galpin Soc. Jour.*, No. 1, London, March, 1948) and others show that mean-tone temperament brings very appreciable advantages for music in a sufficiently restricted range of tonalities.

A harpsichordist who keeps his own instrument in mean-tone temperament (no normal tuner at present would do so for him) is doing early music an interesting and valuable service by using this in solos. The difference, however, is not so marked as to be regarded as an interpretative necessity.

In ensemble music, the difference would not always be noticed. The melodic instruments would still pursue their own fluid compromise in the direction of just intonation, as they do now when playing with equally tempered keyboards.

(b) The case is somewhat different with the organ. Because of its sustained tone and its ranks of fifths and other mixtures, the organ beats very harshly in equal temperament, and because of its better common major chords, and better build-up of difference tones, is much purer, sweeter and more glowing in mean-tone temperament.

It is very greatly to the advantage of early organ music when the parts of any modern organ intended as baroque replicas are tuned to mean-tone temperament. Even with smaller organs the possibility of isolating some stops for this purpose is always worth considering. An organist prepared to forgo later organ music could insist on mean-tone through-out. The 'sharp' variety thought to have been used by J. S. Bach (see 3 above) would be another possibility, with the important advantage of being more versatile.

CHAPTER LV

The Voice

1. THE ITALIAN 'BEL CANTO'

Teachers of singing are legendary for their jealous conservatism. We find Stephen de la Madeleine's *Théorie du Chant* (Paris, 1864) frankly copying Tosi's *Opinioni* of 1723. We read nineteenth century accounts of vocal feats which remind us of Burney and the eighteenth. We hear the rare modern spokesmen of Italian tradition, such as Rupert Bruce Lockhart in London, talking like a page from Mersenne in 1636, de Bacilly in 1668 or Rameau in 1760.

There is only one fundamental technique of singing: what we now call the old Italian technique. But to Wagner, it did not seem either particularly old or exclusively Italian. It was simply good singing. The technique was in fact Italian; the resulting alliance with German interpretation lasted until the generation trained pre-1914 began to thin out. There are few singers of a generation younger than Ebe Stignani whose voice production carries full conviction. This does not only apply to Italian roles. It is becoming as hard to cast Wagner as Verdi or Bellini. The same basic requirements apply to Monteverdi or Bach.

Italian technique includes placing the vocal apparatus precisely; supporting the voice from the chest rather than directly from the diaphragm; using little rather than much breath; projecting vowel-sounds from the upper resonances in detachment from the voice; blending the so-called registers; preparing the placing for the next note before the last is left.

As we listen to the last generation of Italian singers on their primitive gramophone recordings, often made at an age when a faultily produced voice would have already disappeared and when even a superbly produced one is long past its best, we hear distantly through the mechanical barrier a limpid flow of incredible agility and accuracy, not one note of which is either forced or out of scale. No effort is made at volume; it is the placed voice which reaches the back of the hall, the forced voice which fails to carry. The line is moulded, the voice is placed, with almost superhuman control.

The interpretation is so intrinsically vocal that it cannot be conceived apart from its technique. The smooth, deep current of sound never falters, but its surface is a continual ripple of changing colours, modulations

516

of volume, flexibility of tempo. The imagination is pure singer's imagination. And not only each note, but each word is made to live. The vowels are exploited for their varied colourings, the consonants for their variety of articulation and their full declamatory value. Caressed in this way fiercely and gently by turns, the words add another dimension to the music.

There has been some, but not yet enough recovery. See my *Performer's Guide to Baroque Music* for much more detailed discussion of *bel canto*.

2. EARLY VOCAL TECHNIQUE

(a) The following descriptions record general impressions made by baroque singers on their contemporaries.

(667) M. Mersenne, *Harmonie Universelle*, Paris, 1636–7, II, vi, 353 *ff.*:

'[A solid sostenuto without pitch-wobble; flexibility in passage-work; accurate intonation;] sweetness and a certain harmoniousness, on which depends the charms which ravish the hearers, for voices which are hard do not please, however accurate they may be, and possessed of the other qualities I have mentioned, for they have too much sharpness (aigreur), and glitter (esclat), which hurts sensitive ears, and which hinders their gliding pleasantly enough into their hearers' spirit to win them, and to carry them whither so ever you desire.'

(668) Le Cerf de La Viéville, in *Histoire de la Musique*, Amsterdam, 1725, II, p. 305:

'A perfect voice should be sonorous, extensive, sweet, neat, lively, flexible. These six qualities which nature assembles but once in a century, are usually found bestowed by halves.'

(669) Charles Burney, citing a German correspondent, *Present State of Music in Germany*, London, 1773, II, p. 108:

'[Of the German singer Schmelling:] I never knew a voice so powerful and so sweet, at the same time: she could do with it just what she pleased. She sings from G to E *in altissimo*, with the greatest ease and force, and both her *portamento di voce*, and her volubility are, in my opinion, unrivalled; but when I heard her, she seemed to like nothing but difficult music. She sang at sight, what very good players could not play, at sight, on the violin; and nothing was too difficult to her execution, which was easy and neat. But, after this, she refined her taste, insomuch that she was able to perform the part of *Tisbe*, in Hasse's opera, which requires simplicity and expression, more than volubility of throat; and in this she perfectly succeeded, as Agricola, the translator of Tosi's *Arte de Canto*, and our best singing master in Germany, assures me.

'[Burney comments, p. 111:] Her voice was sweetly toned, and she sang perfectly well in tune. She has an excellent shake, a good expression,

517

and facility of executing and articulating rapid and difficult divisions, that is astonishing . . . she was by no means lavish of graces, but those she used, were perfectly suited to the style of the music, and idea of the poet.

'[p. 188: the dramatic soprano Faustina:] her execution was articulate and brilliant. She had a fluent tongue for pronouncing words rapidly and distinctly, and a flexible throat for divisions, with so beautiful and quick a shake, that she could put it in motion upon short notice, just when she would. The passage might be smooth, or by leaps, or consist of iterations of the same tone, their execution was equally easy to her, as to any instrument whatever.'

(b) The following quotations have a more direct bearing on technique.

(670) Marin Mersenne, *Harmonie Universelle*, Paris, 1636–7, Livre Premier de la Voix, p. 40:

'It is a certainty that the windpipe of the larynx (l'anche du larynx), that is to say the little tongue (languette) or its opening, contributes more directly to the [performance of florid] passages and divisions than the other parts, in as much as it has to mark the degrees and the intervals which are made in sustaining the passage; which can only occur from the different openings of the little tongue (languette), as I have shown in speaking of low and high sound. Thence it follows that those whose little tongue (languette) aforesaid is the most mobile, are the most suited to make passages and divisions, and that those in whom it is too hard and dry cannot make them. Now passages and divisions can be made either in the gullet (gorge) by means of the windpipe (anche), as I have said, or with the lips; but this last manner is distorted, and condemned by those who teach good singing. But of all the nations who learn singing, and who make passages of the gullet (gorge), the Italians themselves who make a special profession of Music and of declamation (des recits), avow that the French make passages the best . . .

'It is necessary for the muscles and the cartilages to be very responsive . . . those who make passages easily have a softer windpipe (anche) . . . [p. 44:] As to the Hard and rigid voice, it acquires this vice from the hardness of the windpipe (anche).'

(671) B. de Bacilly, *L'Art de Bien Chanter*, Paris, 1668, p. 137:

'[The Port de Voix is] the transition which is made by a stroke of the throat (*coup de gosier*) from a lower note to a higher and consists of the lower note to be sustained; the doubling from the throat, which is made on the upper note; and the sustaining of the same note after it has been doubled [*i.e.* subjected to a mordent].'

(672) Joachim Quantz, *Essay*, Berlin, 1752, XII, 52:

'A singer who [uses his chest voice for runs] is hardly able to perform them as rapidly as one who [uses his head voice], although the first will always excell the second in clarity, particularly in a large place.'

(673) Jean-Philippe Rameau, *Code de Musique Pratique*, Paris, 1760, p. 16:

'Yes, all the perfections of singing, all its difficulties, depend solely on the breath which comes out of the lungs.

'The *larynx*, the *windpipe* and the *glottis* are not at our disposal, we cannot see their different positions, transformations, to each sound we wish to give; but we do at least know that they must not be constricted in these differences, that they must be left at liberty to follow their natural movement, that we are only masters of the breath, and that in consequence it is for us to govern it so well, that nothing can disturb the effect.

'Immediately the breath is given with more force than the sound demands, the glottis closes, as when the reed of an oboe is pressed too much; if this excess of force is further given too precipitately, it stiffens the walls of the glottis, and robs it of all its flexibility; on the other hand, a torturing (gène), a constraint caused by attention to good grace, to gesture, to the taste of the song, to the inflections of the voice themselves —efforts of which an acquired habit prevents one from being aware— these are the true obstacles to beauty of sound, as well as to the flexibility of the voice: the sound(?) tient pour lors du peigne, de la gorge, du canard; the voice trembles and produces nothing more pleasant than bleating (le chevrottant).

[p. 17:] 'We give our attention, then, solely to spinning the sounds (filer les sons) by semitones, both ascending and descending, and when the habit is a little familiar, the exercise is extended by a semitone on each side, then at the end of two, four or eight days, again a semitone, and even so up to the impossible: you will be greatly astonished, after two months of this exercise at the most,. several hours a day, to find the voice perhaps extended by two tones at either end . . .

'When one feels a slight mastery at this exercise, one notices the degree of breath during which the sound has its greatest beauty, whether for power, or whether for colouring (timbre); one returns to it frequently, one tries to give this sound at the first impact of the breath (coup de vent), without forcing and without constriction; at last time brings the happy day when one reaps the success of one's efforts . . .

'Arrived at this last point of perfection, the rest is mere child's play; one tries florid passages (roulades) . . . trills . . . appoggiaturas taken ascending; slides are born from there, and these are the sources of all the ornaments of singing.

'The principle of principles is to take pains to take no pains . . .

'The breath must be so managed during the florid passages as not to force them beyond what one feels one can do without forcing oneself, diminishing the breath, and consequently the power of the sound, in the measure in which one increases the speed; yet to give more breath a few days later, to test if one can do so without forcing; then finally to augment and diminish it alternately during the same florid passage, to accustom oneself to give, so to speak, the shades of the picture, when the expression or sometimes even the simple taste of the song, demands it. The same applies to trills and appoggiaturas.

'Roualdes, trills and appoggiaturas are made all in one breath, in the same way as the spun sound (son filé), so that one does not at once take them at one's ease; but in the degree to which the thing becomes familiar, the duration of a single breath grows substantially.

'While the breath flows, one feels the sounds following one another at the opening of the glottis; but however little one tortures oneself, the glottis suffers for it; closes instead of opening; and what one should feel at its opening is felt for the moment at the bottom of the throat, whence are born the sounds of the throat (sons de gorge), *etc.*, of which I have spoken.'

(674–5) Charles Burney, *Present State of Music in Germany*, London, 1773, II, p. 174:

'[Francesco Bernardi, called Senesino] sung rapid *allegros* with great fire, and marked rapid divisions, from the chest, in an articulate and pleasing manner.

'[p. 179: Gaetano Orfini's] shake was perfect and his portamento, excellent. In allegros, he articulated divisions, particularly in triplets, most admirably, and always from the breast [chest]. In *adagios* he was so perfect a master of every thing which pleases and affects, that he took entire possession of the hearts of all that heard him; he was many years in the imperial service, and though he lived to an advanced age, he pre-served his fine voice to the last [a sure sign of good voice-production. A footnote adds:] He died at Vienna, about the year, 1750.

'[p. 241: of "one of the Baglioni", her compass] B on the fifth space in the base, to D in alt, fully, steady and equal; her shake is good, and her *Portamento* admirably free from the nose, mouth, or throat [*i.e.* ? not produced from those organs]. There was such a roundness and dignity in all the tones, that every thing she did became interesting; a few plain notes from her, were more acceptable to the audience than a whole elaborate air from any one else.'

3. THE TRILL

(676) M. Mersenne, *Harmonie Universelle*, Paris, 1636–7, II, vi, 355:

'Now when voice-production has been taught (après que l'on a enseigné à former le ton), and the adjustment of the voice to all sorts of sounds, familiarity with the making of cadences is imparted, which corre-spond to the trills and mordents (aux tremblemens et aux martelemens) made on the keyboard of the organ and the spinet, and on the finger-board of the lute and other stringed instruments. These [trilled] cadences are the most difficult part of all that has to be done in singing, because it is necessary simply to beat the air in the throat (battre l'air de la gorge), which must make a series of repercussions (tremblemens) without the help of the tongue. But they are as much more pleasing as they are more difficult, for if the other progressions are the colours and the shadings, the cadences can be called the rays and the light. Those who have not the constitution of the throat for the said cadences and florid passages, make use of movements of the tongue, which are not so pleasing, especially when they are made with the tip; for as to those which are made with the middle, they are necessary for certain passages which cannot be performed accurately enough without the help and repercussion (tremblement) of the middle of the tongue, because of the occurrence of the vowels, which must be pronounced, and rendered intelligible to the hearers.

'As for ornaments from the lips, they are not agreeable, nor permitted, any more than those which seem to be drawn from the stomach.'

We may compare with the above early baroque passage the two modern ones next following.

(677) Franklyn Kelsey, *Grove's Dictionary*, 5th ed., London, 1954, Vol. IX, *s.v.* 'Voice-training', p. 65:

'It is a fact known to all competent teachers that the trill cannot be produced by orthodox vocalization, for the tensioning muscles of the glottis simply will not oscillate rapidly enough to cause it. An attempt to trill by orthodox vocalization always results in what the Germans call a *Bockstriller* [and the French *chevrotter*]—a sound like a goat-beat. The trill is in fact caused by a controlled oscillation of air-pressure in the windpipe, the trachea acting like an accordion, stretching and shortening itself with extreme rapidity and so causing an oscillation of the entire larynx.'

(678) An 'old Italian singing-teacher in New York', quoted in a letter to *Musical Opinion*, July, 1946, and cited by Kelsey (*loc. cit.*, p. 48):

'You modern singers always seem to want to make your notes in your mouths. We old singers always made our notes in our throats, long before they came into our mouths!'

The rapidity of the trill is, of course, only relative. A very rapid vocal trill is necessarily tight and narrow, and is always to be avoided.

(679) Charles Burney, *Present State of Music in Germany*, London, 1773, II, p. 137:

'[Anfani's] shake is a little too close, otherwise I should venture to pronounce him a *perfect* tenor singer.'

The following suggests another view of the trill: namely that it is not produced by an 'unorthodox' technique, but by an intensive cultivation of normal agility. The authority cited is the great teacher Mancini; but Mancini may not have realised that agility carried to this point does change its technical basis in the way described by Kelsey at (677) above. That would, indeed, account for the difficulty found with the trill by 'many who can execute passages'.

(680) Charles Burney, *Present State of Music in Germany*, London, 1773, I, p. 334:

'For the shake he [Signor Mancini] thinks it ruined ninetynine times out of hundred by too much impatience and precipitation, both in the master and scholar; and many who can execute passages, which require the same motion of the larynx as the shake, have notwithstanding never acquired one. There is no accounting for this, but from the neglect of the master to study nature, and avail himself of those passages which, by continuity, would become real shakes.'

4. THE VIBRATO

A confusion of terms exists among singers: vibrato is used by some for a desirable oscillation of *intensity* (strictly a tremolo) which corresponds, in singing, to the instrumental vibrato; by others for an undesirable oscillation of *pitch* (strictly a vibrato).

An uncontrolled pitch-wobble is a distressing disturbance of technique which can arise from faulty voice-production, and which once it has arisen is appallingly hard to cure. It is condemned by all teachers. Not all teachers, however, realise that the true vocal 'vibrato' is not only an intensity fluctuation but also (though less conspicuously) a pitch fluctuation. The 'wobble' sounds weak, vacillating and out of control. The true vocal 'vibrato' sounds wonderfully alive, decisive and under control. It is an essential element of voice-production, as much so in early music as elsewhere. See also Ch. XIX above.

5. THE PORTAMENTO

The traditional Italian portamento is always *practised* as if on definite notes: chromatic if the interval bridged is less than about a fifth; diatonic if it is more. It is (except as a special coloratura effect) *sung* by almost running the notes together, but is still distinctly heard as notes, and not as a mere *glissando* scoop. The vocal apparatus is aimed towards the higher pitch in ascending, and held well up even in descending. The portamento itself ordinarily comes rather quickly, and should always sound (like the true vocal 'vibrato') as steady as a rock.

Caccini at (660) in Ch. LI, 5, above, refers to a slide from the third below, which in singing might mean the more or less *sotto voce* portamento from below with which so many notes are habitually attacked.

6. THE NECESSARY ELEMENT OF CHEST VOICE

The references to the chest voice at (672) and (674) above are exceedingly important. There can be no *bel canto* without an excellent chest voice to colour the bottom register and to blend upwards into the medium and head registers above.

(680a) Claudio Monteverdi, letter to the Duke of Mantua, 9 June 1610:

'A fine voice, strong and long [sustained]; and singing in the chest, he reached all places [in the voice] very well.'

(681) Joachim Quantz, Autobiography (1754) in Marpurg's *Historisch-kritische Beyträge*, I, Berlin, 1755, pp. 231–232:

'[Paita's tenor voice] would not have been by nature so fine and even, if he himself, through art, had not known how to join the chest voice with the head voice.

[p. 235: 'Carestini] had a great dexterity in [ornamental] passages, which he, according to the good school of Bernacchi, like Farinello, produced with the chest.'

It is skilled chesting which gives easy power, brightness and clarity to sopranos and mezzo-sopranos high up, transparent strength, sureness and colour low down. The colour is strong and went out of fashion, but is being admired again as we bring it back (Stignani retained a good deal of it, and indeed it is particularly needed for the mezzo voice). Men have usually enough chest voice, but have a problem in blending it into their high notes (it is this which gives the *Heldentenor* his true ring, and which distinguishes a genuine bass-baritone).

Voice teachers have a valuable part to play in developing this difficult but necessary reform. Strong chesting has its dangers, if the voice is forced; but not if it is placed and focused accurately, well supported and brought sufficiently forward. It will then sound almost quiet close by, but very open, and will carry through an orchestra to the back of the theatre at sixty years of age.

7. THE CASTRATO VOICE

The last castrato, Alessandro Moreschi, who died in 1922, can and should be heard on his recordings (available in collections of historical recordings). The power and beauty of this man's voice in woman's tessitura is unbelievably impressive: above all, it sounds unexpectedly but entirely masculine. Thus our substitution of a female soprano, mezzo-soprano or contralto, though it is what Handel himself did when short of a castrato, is inevitably a misrepresentation. A good counter-tenor (i.e. a male alto) makes a plausible substitute, if he has power and agility enough. A boy soprano is no use here, since while he may sound masculine, he cannot sound adult.

One alternative is transposition to the lower octave. In Handel operas, this has the unfortunate consequence of dropping the voice deep as a tenor (or still worse as a baritone) into an orchestration composed by Handel to support a soprano or an alto part. A female voice may well be the best compromise here, and can be musically although not quite dramatically satisfactory. In Monteverdi's *Poppea*, a tenor Nero at the lower octave goes mainly very well, because his orchestration has to be realised by us anyhow, and can therefore be suitably disposed (Monteverdi's *Orfeo* has a tenor and not a castrato hero, as Orfeo's tenor clef reveals). In Handel or Scarlatti, re-composing is a practicable though radical (certainly not an unbaroque) alternative. Gluck made his castrato Orfeo at Vienna into a tenor for Paris partly by transposing the voice down a fourth and the orchestra up a fifth; partly (at the original pitch) by considerable recomposing. Given the skill and courage, that might really be the proper treatment today.

(682) Charles Burney, *Music in Germany*, London, 1773, II, p. 179:

'*Domenico* had one of the finest soprano voices . . . it was so clear and penetrating, as to make its way through all obstructions, and with all this great force, was sweet, and well toned.'

8. THE MALE ALTO AND THE HIGH AND LOW COUNTER-TENOR

(a) A male alto is a bass or baritone singing high parts in a falsetto voice, apparently produced by using only the edges of the vocal cords.

(b) The counter-tenor is a natural voice often of extremely high tessitura, light and more or less unchested yet masculine in quality. The range is from g to d'' or even e''.

(c) A normal tenor may sometimes go extremely high, as in the magnificent voice and musicianship of Hugues Cuenod.

9. UNDERLAY OF THE WORDS

Most early texts are casual, incomplete and inaccurate in their under-laying of the words; it is for the performer to decide which syllable should go to which note or notes.

One curious but pleasing difference from modern methods was first thoroughly established by E. H. Fellowes (*English Madrigal Composers*,

Oxford, 1921, p. 112) for the Elizabethan and early Jacobean school; it was generally characteristic of the late renaissance and early baroque periods, and may be seen as follows.

Ex. 225. Elizabethan underlaying, cited E. H. Fellowes, *loc. cit.*, (a) Gibbons, Christ Church, Oxford, MS. 21; (b) Weelkes *Ayres*, London, 1608, No. 2; (c) Tomkins *Songs*, London, 1622:

10. A DECLAMATORY EDGE TO THE ARTICULATION

(683) Thomas Morley, *Plaine and Easie Introduction*, London, 1597, p. 179:

'Our church men . . . ought to studie howe to vowell and sing clean, expressing their words with devotion and passion.'

(684) Charles Butler, *Principles of Musik*, London, 1636, p. 91:

'[Singers should] sing as plainly as they would speak: pronouncing every Syllable and letter (specially the Vowels) distinctly and treatably.'

(685) Le Cerf de La Viéville, in *Histoire de la Musique*, Amsterdam, 1725, II, p. 25:

'The Italian singers pronounce badly . . . because . . . they close all their teeth and do not open the mouth enough: except in the florid passages, where they hold it open for quarter of an hour at a time, without moving the tongue, or the lips . . . it is only in France that they take the trouble to open the mouth as they should in singing.'

The above view was biased against the Italians, being expressed in furtherance of the national controversy opened up by Raguenet's *Comparison of the French and Italian Music* in 1702; but that French singing was particularly declamatory is confirmed from other sources, as also that it became in some respects less so at the end of the baroque period (Quantz would be less up to date than Rousseau here):

(686) Joachim Quantz, *Essay*, Berlin, 1752, XVIII, 76:

'The *Italian manner of singing* is refined and full of art, it moves us and at the same time excites our admiration, it has the spirit of music, it is pleasant, charming, expressive, rich in taste and feeling, and it carries the hearer agreeably from one passion to another. The *French manner of singing* is more plain than full of art, more speaking than singing; the expression of the passions and the voice is more strange than natural.'

(687) Jean-Jacques Rousseau, *Lettre sur la Musique Françoise* [Paris], 1753, p. 53:

'The old recitative was performed by the actors of that time quite otherwise than we do it today; it was more lively and less dragging; they sang it less, and they declaimed it excellently.'

These variations of period and nationality do not diminish our impression that a large proportion of baroque delivery was more highly dramatised than we tend to make it. The florid passages were slipped in lightly and easily; the cantabile never wavered; but the enunciation was incisive, especially on the consonants, and full of both musical and verbal point. This declamatory edge to the articulation is an important aspect of the interpretation.

11. POLYPHONIC MUSIC ALSO DECLAMATORY

Late renaissance and baroque church singers, especially of such famous bodies as the Vatican Sistine choir, were trained in *bel canto*, and used the same technique, often the same embellishments, as their secular colleagues.

The modern Sistine choir is still far more colourful and far more declamatory than our English choirs. It sings Palestrina or Vittoria with 'devotion and passion' as Morley desired at (683) in 10 above. The best English choirs are famous for their purity, balance and intonation, but the tone is white and the attack is mild. They convey the devotion, but not always the passion. If they could add the more dramatic qualities, they would be still more excellent.

12. THE WHITE VOICE

There is no evidence that the 'white voice'—the notorious *voce bianca* of traditional Italian teaching—was ever desired (except as a special effect) by any late renaissance or baroque musician. On the contrary, it is very much to be avoided.

CHAPTER LVI

The Viols

1. THE FAMILY OF VIOLS

The viols are a family of bowed instruments collateral with the violin.

The viol family is the older, with medieval origins; the violins evolved, as a cross between the rebec and the lyra da braccio, only in the sixteenth century. But the viols became obsolete in course of the baroque period, except for the bass viol or gamba, which was not discarded until the nineteenth century.

The name *viole da gamba* (It.: viols of the leg) applies to the whole family, of which even the smallest is played resting on the legs, with underhand bowing. *Viole da braccio* (It.: viols of the arm) applies to the whole violin family, of which all but the cello and double-bass are played held up by the arm, and all, now, with overhand bowing (during the eighteenth century the originally underhand bowing of the cello was changed in imitation of violin bowing; the double-bass followed, but still with the exception of certain orchestras). Colloquially, however, it is the bass viol which became known as the viola da gamba, often shortened, as it also is nowadays, to gamba.

The viols are more lightly constructed and strung than the violins. They have, therefore, a more freely resonant but less powerful tone. If this tone is well produced (an important consideration), it has a most attractive quality: glittering in the treble viol; glowing in the tenor viol; clean and golden in the bass viol (gamba).

The technique, like that of the violin family, is flexible and expressive. (688) M. Mersenne, *Harmonie Universelle*, Paris, 1636–7, II, iii, 106:

'Now the chest of viols is the most excellent of all those [instruments of] which [the sound] can be swelled.

[p. 195:] 'Certainly if instruments are prized in proportion as they imitate the voice, and if of all things artificial that is best esteemed which most imitates what is natural, then it seems impossible to refuse the prize to the Viol, which resembles the voice in all its inflexions, and even in its accents most expressive of joy, sadness, gaiety, sweetness and strength, by its vitality, its tenderness, its consolation, its support: just as the ornaments and the vibrato of the left hand, which is called the finger-board hand, represent naturally both dignity and charm . . .

'Those who have heard excellent players and good consorts of voices, know that there is nothing more ravishing after good voices than these dying strokes of the bow, which accompany the ornaments made on the finger-board; but because it is no less difficult to describe their gracefulness than that of a perfect orator, it is necessary to hear them in order to appreciate them.'

2. THE VIOLS IN CONSORT

When heard in consort, the viols sound more distinct from one another than do the instruments of a string quartet of violins. This distinctness, which derives from a certain almost nasal edge to their tone, fits them for their most important music in the late renaissance and early baroque periods: ricercari, fantasies, pavans and galliards in contrapuntal style, of which the interest may depend more on the play of parts than on the harmony; and the accompanying of vocal polyphony.

In the late renaissance, contrapuntal parts for instruments were usually not much different from vocal parts. The fantasy, in particular, resembled a motet or a madrigal. But in the early baroque period, when the continental countries were turning from the polyphonic structure, the English school retained it for most of the first half of the seventeenth century, during which time they produced the most valuable chamber music in the literature of the viols. The poorer specimens tend to monotony, but the masterpieces are of true chamber-music intimacy and intensity of feeling. Their harmony is unusually rich and noble; their counterpoint often most intricate. It is this intricacy, and a certain fullness of scoring in the lower registers, which depend for their effectiveness on the distinctness and light colouring of viol tone.

The less complex works are between the two idioms, and suit both families: viols and violins.

(689) John Dowland, title, London [1604]:

'Lachrimae, or Seaven Teares figured in seaven passionate Pavans, with divers other Pavans, Galiards, and Almands, set forth for the Lute, Viols, or Violons . . .'

It will, however, be found that these wonderful pavans, and indeed most border-line works between the viols and the violins, are better with a gamba on the bass-line even when violins and violas are used above. The sonority is kept lighter in this way; and the sound of violins and gambas combined has a brilliance all its own.

Purcell's magnificent contrapuntal fantasies, dated 1680, are genuinely transitional music. But his first published trio-sonatas of 1683 are true violin music.

Many modern consorts of viols have been trained—the first by Arnold Dolmetsch several decades ago. Their technical standards naturally vary, and so does their sense of the style; but there is no other medium in which the more complex fantasies and pavans can be satisfactorily performed, and a really good consort of viols is a delight to the ear as well as to the mind.

3. THE GAMBA, ETC., AS SOLOIST

The treble viol, when its tone is roundly produced, is an agreeable soloist, for which good music of the late baroque French school exists. But the gamba has always been the main soloist of the viol family.

The tone of the gamba, with its lighter construction and stringing, is more relaxed than that of the cello, and in its high registers, nearer to that of the violin. The following was written of the treble viol, but is partly relevant to the gamba also, though the latter is more versatile.

(690) Jean Rousseau, *Traité de la Viole*, Paris, 1687, p. 73:

'And you must be careful, in gay movements, not to stress the beat too much, so as not to depart from the spirit of the instrument, which is not to be handled after the fashion of the violin, whose role is to enliven, whereas the role of the treble viol is to caress.'

The technique of the gamba was highly developed by the sixteenth century, and further extended in the seventeenth and early eighteenth by Christopher Simpson (who takes it up to a'', a compass of four octaves on a 7-stringed gamba), Marais, Forqueray and others most of whose music calls imperatively for this instrument. J. S. Bach wrote three great sonatas for gamba and obbligato harpsichord; several obbligato gamba parts in his Passions and cantatas; two gamba parts in his Sixth Brandenburg Concerto, where they are very necessary to the unusually low sonority there used (violas in place of them sound too dark; cellos too intense). There are many good modern players, and the instrument is re-establishing itself, like the harpsichord, as a necessity for baroque music.

4. THE GAMBA AS A CONTINUO BASS

The cello replaced the gamba as the usual string bass by very gradual stages: first in Italy, later in England and Germany, last of all in France. For any ordinary baroque music, the choice remains with the performer: see Ch. LII, 2, above; also 7, below. Both the characteristic tone and the characteristic articulation of the gamba blend beautifully with the harpsichord, above all in trio sonatas.

5. THE CELLAMBA

The gamba can be turned into a hybrid irreverently known as the cellamba by depriving it of its frets, giving it strings of cello thickness and tension, and bowing it with a cello bow and technique. The tone, however pleasant, is not quite gamba tone and not quite cello tone; the articulation is entirely cello articulation. But this is to sacrifice the whole value of having different instruments. It is particularly unfortunate to be deprived of the distinct articulation of the gamba; but the adulteration of the tone is also a deprivation. This was a transitional aberration of the pioneering revival, now virtually discarded.

6. THE PURPOSE OF THE FRETS

The purpose of the gut frets tied round the necks of viols is to provide a hard edge against which the finger presses the string in taking stopped notes.

Except for teaching purposes, the violin family has at no time in its history used frets.

The difference between the two families in this respect reinforces the difference already existing between their qualities of tone. The fret defines the tone a little more sharply than the finger alone. The difference is not great, and diminishes as the string length is decreased (so that the high notes on each string are not in fact fretted, and do not seem to need to be); but it exists, and is missed if it is eliminated.

Frets correctly fitted are no impediment to rapid technique, and they are of considerable assistance for chords. They guide the fingers approximately into place, but fine intonation depends on the exact positioning of the fingers, as it does on the violins.

7. THE GAMBA IN THE POST-BAROQUE PERIOD

(691) Johann Friedrich Reichardt, *Geist des musikalischen Kunstmagazins*, Berlin, 1791, p. 89:

'A word to composers. Why do many of the most powerful instruments remain unused nowadays? [while] the most agreeable of the soft instruments also become lost. The Gamba, so lovely and sweetly touching in Abel's hand!'

Karl Friedrich Abel, the last international virtuoso of the gamba prior to modern times, died in 1787.

(692) J. J. Klein, *Lehrbuch der theoretischen Musik*, Leipzig and Gera, 1801, 'Die Violdegamba oder Kniegeige':

'[The gamba] has an attractive and penetrating tone. . . . You can play solo and in chamber music, also you can use it for accompaniment, when you can play several strings at once for the sake of the beautiful harmony resulting. This very refined instrument has however gone somewhat out of fashion and is becoming quite obsolete.'

(693) [J. S. Sainsbury] *Dictionary*, 2nd ed., London, 1827, *s.v.* 'Abel':

'The *viol da Gamba*, now hardly ever used.'

CHAPTER LVII

The Violins

1. A STYLE OF VIOLIN-PLAYING FOR BAROQUE MUSIC

Arnold Dolmetsch, who received fundamental training on the violin under Vieuxtemps, was the first violinist of modern times successful in developing a technique and style fitted to the needs of baroque music. He played on a violin of which the fittings (bridge, finger-board, bass bar, *etc.*) were of eighteenth-century pattern, and with a bow of pre-Tourte design.

Dolmetsch's basic tone on the violin was of a more fiery colouring and a less refined texture than we generally associate with this most versatile of instruments (almost as if 0.01 per cent of bagpipe chanter had got blended in). He played more into the string, and with a more slowly moving bow, than is general nowadays. His accentuation was almost entirely of the crisp variety (sharp attack, often preceded by silence of articulation) rather than of the massive variety (by arm-weight and pressure). His cantabile was exquisitely sustained; but the rest of his playing was highly articulated. Not only were the expressive silences numerous; notes not separated by silences were kept articulated by an incisive little bite of the bow-hair on (not off) the string. The result was piquant and cleanly-etched; it combined intoxicating lightness with solid strength and virility. It was at once vital and relaxed.

The most recent researches into the baroque treatises on violin-playing bear out this general style. The most thorough study of the evidence is that made by David Boyden, whose book, *The History of Violin Playing* (London, 1965), has put our entire knowledge of the evidence on a new level of reliability. On a practical basis, too, excellent work has been done by a variety of fiddlers and performing groups, with results to which I have referred in my Introduction, II, 3, above. We are reaping great benefit from this.

2. THE FITTINGS OF THE BAROQUE VIOLIN

(a) The neck of baroque violins was often (not always) shorter than is fitted to them now. It was normally set at an angle nearer to the straight.

This tends to give less string pressure for a given pitch; hence a

531

slightly freer, less massive tone. The tendency is increased where the bridge is low and the strings not very taut.

The difference, however, though appreciable, can only be had in practice by keeping a separate violin for baroque music, with a different neck-length and stop: this is desirable, but not essential.

(b) The bridge now fitted is higher and steeper than the baroque average.

This makes forceful passages easier to play without fouling a neighbouring string; chords harder to play without excessive pressure, resulting in harshness.

For unaccompanied violin music such as J. S. Bach's famous suites, a bridge somewhat less steeply arched than the modern average is really essential; for other baroque violin music, it is, perhaps, more suitable, but not essential.

(694) Marin Mersenne, *Harmonie Universelle*, Paris, 1636–7, II, iv, 240:

'[For full chords on the violin] the bridge would have to be lower than it [usually] is, and to imitate that of the Lyra [where chords are normal]. [p. 184: ordinarily] one can sometimes play two [but not more] strings on the violin to make a chord.'

(c) Mutes or objects employed as mutes were described by Mersenne (*Harmonie Universelle*, Paris, 1636–7, II, iv, 189). J. J. Rousseau (*Dictionnaire*, Paris, 1768, *s.v.* 'Sourdine'), says that the Italians made a great effect of them, but that the French could not be bothered to do so. Quantz (*Essay*, Berlin, 1752, XVI, 28) speaks of 'an arioso which is played piano or with mutes'. There are good examples in Lully and Purcell. But the effect of mutes on string tone is very drastic, and although there is nothing contrary to baroque style in using them, it would be undesirable on musical grounds to use them frequently. An unmuted string played piano is fundamentally more beautiful than the muted variety.

3. THE BAROQUE VIOLIN BOW

(a) The modern violin bow follows the design perfected by Tourte during the last quarter of the eighteenth century. A very good description of its mechanical properties will be found in an article by Eric Halfpenny (*Grove's Dictionary*, 5th ed., London, 1954, *s.v.* 'Bow').

The stick of the modern bow is incurved, and pulled a little nearer to the straight as the hair is screwed tighter. Its taper is not uniform, but follows a logarithmic curve. As pressure is brought to bear, in playing, this is compensated by the curvature, and the desired balance of stiffness with resilience maintained. A good specimen of such a bow is an ideal implement for sustaining a rich and massive tone, while permitting a remarkable variety of articulation by smooth, staccato or spiccato bowings.

The curve on most pre-Tourte bows, when they are screwed tight for use, is outwards, ranging from virtually straight (very frequent) to markedly curved (less frequent, especially in the baroque period). The length varies from very short (mainly for dance music) to very long, a common length being an inch or two less than the Tourte pattern, though bows a little longer than the Tourte are known. A good out-curved bow favours a transparent rather than a massive tone, and an easy, crisp articulation, which can be varied by springing bowings to an adequate extent.

An outcurved bow is not absolutely necessary for baroque violin music. A player who conceives the baroque transparency of tone and crispness of articulation clearly enough in his mind can produce them with a Tourte-pattern bow. But he can produce them better with an outcurved bow; and the difference is appreciable. It is therefore very desirable indeed for string-players taking part in baroque music to possess an outcurved bow. Early specimens are rare, but excellent modern reproductions can be bought from a number of good makers. *In either case* it is of the first importance to make sure of a good stick: straight, stiff, but not so stiff as to be insufficiently resilient.

(b) The date at which screw-nuts were first fitted is in David Boyden's opinion the last years of the seventeenth century. Mersenne (1636) shows knobs which look like screws but may as easily be ornamental. Other devices for adjusting the hair tension were certainly in use through the baroque period. There are no direct musical implications; a player finding a good early stick and desiring to have it fitted with a screw need not hesitate on musical grounds, though he may on archaeo-logical.

(c) The 'Vega Bach Bow' and similar 'Bach Bows' are not repro-ductions of any baroque type, but modern inventions for making J. S. Bach's unaccompanied violin music sound artificially smooth: see 9 below.

4. THE USE OF GUT STRINGS

Gimping (covering gut cores with finely-wound wire) is known to have been in use by the later seventeenth century, for the low strings of lutes, violins, viols, *etc.*, which were previously of very thick un-covered gut (decidedly unresponsive, especially on the smaller instruments).

Covered lower strings, but gut upper strings, favour the ideal colour-ing for baroque violin music. Normal modern stringing is, however, a compromise which has frequently to be accepted in practice.

5. HOLDING THE VIOLIN, ETC.

(a) Late renaissance and baroque pictures show rebecs, lyras and violins held either against the breast, which tends to make shifting down difficult for lack of any grip by the chin; or on the collar-bone, to left or right of the chin, and without chin-rest, but with the cheek or the chin resting on the instrument: hence the marks seen on the varnish of so many old violins. This grip or support may have been intermittent, chiefly for downward shifting, but was certainly sufficient to permit the very high position-work required for much virtuoso baroque violin music, with no technical impediment.

There are, however, no obvious musical advantages in departing from the normal modern grip.

(b) Late nineteenth-century illustrations still show cellos held on the calves of the leg. There is no musical objection, however, to using the comfortable modern end-pin, either for cellists or gambists.

6. HOLDING THE BOW

(a) The baroque bow-grip, as shown by pictures (see G. A. Kinsky, *History of Music in Pictures*, London, 1930) and descriptions, frequently approximates to the modern kind, but some players held the bow an inch or more in from the nut. A true Carl Flesch grip is occasionally shown. Leopold Mozart (*Violinschule*, Augsburg, 1756) has engravings showing the hand in both positions: Sol Babitz considers the modern position to be an engraver's error; but it was drawn specially, appears in both editions, and is far from unique. There is no need for the player to change his normal grip; but it may be tried for fast notes.

Folk-violinists often hold their bows some inches in from the nut, thus shortening its effective length for crisp playing in dance music.

(b) The cello was bowed underhand, like the gamba, until the eighteenth century, when increasing solo demands began to be made on it, in addition to some florid bass parts (*e.g.* in Vivaldi) which exploit its characteristic idioms. But in the Bologna school solo demands were made on the cello in the second half of the seventeenth century.

(695) Charles Burney, *Present State of Music in Germany*, London, 1773, II, p. 218:

'M. Grauel, a violoncello performer in the King's band, played a concerto; it was but ordinary music; however, it was well enough executed, though in the old manner, with the hand under the bow.'

The change to the modern bow-hold was very desirable, because it gives an articulation matched to that of the violins, and therefore makes the violin family more uniform in effect. But underhand bowing is what the earlier baroque cellists used, and for a fully authentic performance would have to be adopted. That would not be generally feasible, and the difference though appreciable is not crucial, provided that the cellist has a sensitive perception of baroque articulation.

7. LEFT-HAND TECHNIQUE

(a) The late renaissance applied an advanced technique to the lute and the bass viol (gamba); but the violin was then newly emerging as a dance and tavern instrument, and not until the early baroque generation of Monteverdi did it attract much serious attention.

Early instructions for the violin occur in Mersenne; but they are less detailed than we could wish.

(696) M. Mersenne, *Harmonie Universelle*, Paris, 1636–7, II, iv, 183:

'It is necessary so to adjust the fingers on each position of the fingerboard, that the sounds induce a proportion as well governed as if it had frets like the viol [keeping the fingers close to the fingerboard and pressing hard, for greater resonance].'

An advanced violin technique spread from Italy to Germany, and from there to England.

(697) Anthony à Wood, *Diary*, 24 July, 1658:

'Did then and there to his very great astonishment, heare [Thomas Baltzar] play on the violin. He then saw him run up his Fingers to the end of the Fingerboard of the Violin, and run them back insensibly, and all with alacrity, and in very good tune, which he nor any in England saw the like before.'

From the middle of the seventeenth century onwards, although average orchestral standards were, at least in some localities, modest, the standards of the virtuosi were high and continued to rise. Vivaldi's concertos in the early eighteenth century, like Geminiani's exercises (*Art of Playing on the Violin*, London, 1751) and compositions, demand very high left-hand positions and require in other respects a developed technique.

(b) Left-hand technique as taught by the baroque violinists was the same as ours in all important respects. There was, however, a greater disposition to use the second position, particularly in sequences (both upwards and downwards). This is in line with the tendency of keyboard fingering to follow the phrase as closely as possible, and is well worth cultivating.

Fourth-finger extension was greatly used, in all positions.

Finger-changing on the same note was taught by Geminiani, *op. cit.*

Positions higher than the third, though commonly fingered by virtuosos such as Vivaldi (*cf.* Geminiani, *Art of Playing on the Violin*,

London, 1751), should be avoided in ordinary orchestral and chamber-music parts (including most trio-sonatas), where the clearer, sharper colouring of the lower positions is mostly preferable: *cf.* Leopold Mozart's 'honest and manly tone' (701) in 8 below.

(698) Leopold Mozart, *Violinschule*, Augsburg, 1756, VIII, i, 2:

'[High positions may be taken from necessity, convenience and elegance;] consistency of tone-colouring is achieved by this means as well as a more even and singing execution.

'[V, 13: A virtuoso] soloist will do well to allow his open strings to sound rarely or not at all. His fourth finger on the next lower string will always sound more unobtrusive and refined, since the open strings are too loud compared with stopped notes, and penetrate the ear too keenly. In the same way, a soloist should make a point of taking all feasible passages on one string, in order to keep them in one tone-colouring.'

(c) Harmonics were familiar to the baroque violinists, but not encouraged by the better teachers.

(699) Leopold Mozart, *Violinschule*, Augsburg, 1756, V, 13:

'When [to insubstantial softs and rasping louds] the so-called flageolet tones ["natural" or "artificial" harmonics] are added, the result is a quite ridiculous kind of music and one which fights nature herself with its incongruity of tone-colouring.'

(d) Cello fingering included thumb positions from the first half of the eighteenth century, as the instrument came into virtuoso use. But again the lower positions are best except in solos.

(e) For vibrato see Ch. XIX, 4 above. It should not be very wide and heavy, nor very tight and rapid. But a relaxed, moderate vibrato not only can but must be used to keep the tone alive.

8. RIGHT-HAND TECHNIQUE

(a) Every string-player has in the back of his mind a conception of tone which he would regard as standard. The normal modern standard is more intense and less transparent than baroque descriptions suggest and than baroque music requires.

In the same way, the modern average of articulation is smoother, when it is not rather forcefully staccato.

In both these matters, it is very important to adapt the ordinary string style to the baroque methods. There is no other aspect which is quite so crucial to the successful performance of baroque music. It is not a question of special effects, but of the most commonplace successions of plain notes. If the strings can produce the appropriate tone and articulation for the most straightforward passages, by far the

greatest difficulty confronting modern performers has been overcome.
of they cannot, using small baroque forces merely exposes the failure
If style to full view. See also Chapter XLVIII, 7 above.

(700) M. Mersenne, *Harmonie Universelle*, Paris, 1636–7, II, iii, 177:

'The sounds [of the violin] have more effect on the spirit of the hearers
than those of the Lute or the other string instruments, because they are
more vigorous and indeed penetrating, by reason of the great tension of
their strings and their sharp sounds. And those who have heard the 24
Violins of the King, maintain that they have never heard anything more
ravishing or more powerful: whence it comes about that this instrument
is the most suitable of all to dance to, as is our experience in ballets and all
such other. Now the beauties and the charming refinements (gentillesses)
performed thereon are so numerous, that it can be preferred to all the
other instruments, for its bow-strokes are sometimes so ravishing that
there is no greater miscontent than to hear the end of them, particularly
when mingled with ornaments and vibrato in the left hand; which compels the hearer to confess that the violin is the king of instruments [but
for a similar eulogy of the viol, see (688) in Ch. LVI, 1 above].
[p. 183:] 'The bow hand must be at least as agile as the left . . . [often
many notes can be included] while continuing from top to bottom [of the
bow].'

It is striking how many baroque descriptions of the ideal of string
tone include the adjective 'clear' (*e.g.*: Christopher Simpson, *Division-
Violist*, London, 1659, ed. of 1667, p. 3; John Playford, *Introduction*,
London, 1654, ed. of 1674, p. 102; Thomas Mace, *Musick's Monument*,
London, 1676, p. 248). 'Natural and singing' is the description of
Corelli's tone given by Martinelli in 1766 (cited Thurston Dart, *Inter-
pretation of Music*, London, 1954, p. 92).

(701) Leopold Mozart, *Violinschule*, Augsburg, 1756, II, 5:

'[Keep the little finger on the stick because this helps] to draw an honest
and manly tone from the violin.
[6:] 'You should not confine yourself to the point of the bow with a
certain kind of quick stroke which hardly presses on to the string, but
must always play solidly.
'[11: Beginners should always play strongly;] the roughness of a strong
bowing which has not yet been purified is harsh to the ear. But with time
and patience the roughness of the sound will decrease, while purity will
be combined with the strength of tone.
[V, 12:] 'We must manage the bow from loud to soft in such a way
that a good, steady, singing, and as it were round, fat tone can always be
heard, which is to be done by a certain control in the right hand, and
especially by a certain skilful tensing and relaxing of the wrist by turns.'

(b) The average attack of the bow is well described as follows.

(702) Giuseppe Tartini, *Letter to Signora Maddalena Lombardini*, Padua, 1760, transl. Burney, London, 1771, 2nd ed. 1779, reprint. London, 1913, p. 11:

'Your first study, therefore, should be the true manner of holding, balancing and pressing the bow lightly, but steadily, upon the strings; in such a manner as that it shall seem to breathe the first tone it gives, which must proceed from the friction of the string, and not from percussion, as by a blow given with a hammer upon it. This depends on laying the bow lightly upon the strings, at the first contact, and on gently pressing it afterwards, which if done gradually, can scarce have too much force given to it, because, if the tone is begun with delicacy, there is little danger of rendering it afterwards either coarse or harsh [but Burney's "gradually" is a mistranslation of the Italian *subito*, "immediately"].'

This is reminiscent of Geminiani's 'Swelling of the Sound' (*Art of Playing on the Violin*, London, 1751), which he applies not merely to long notes (where he had in mind his favourite *messa di voce*: crescendo followed by diminuendo on one note) but also to fairly rapid notes (where this cannot be the intention, since an audible swelling would sound like a perpetual sforzando, which would be musically intolerable). The description is more cumbersome than the effect intended, which is merely to get the string into vibration by taking up the slight yield of the hair. This is not *heard* as a swelling, but merely as a clean start.

(703) Leopold Mozart, *Violinschule*, Augsburg, 1756, V, 3:

'Every note, even the most powerfully attacked, has a small, even if barely audible, softness at the start of the stroke; for otherwise no note would result, but only a harsh and incomprehensible noise. This same softness must also be heard at the end of every stroke.

[10:] 'The stroke has necessarily to be started gently and with a certain moderation, and, with no lifting of the bow, taken with so smooth a join that even the most powerful stroke carries the already vibrating string over one motion into another and different motion imperceptibly.'

(c) When to this clean start, which holds up the momentum of the bow so little that the listener should not be aware of it, there is added the slightest pressure of the forefinger on the stick of the bow, the result is that crispness of articulation which adds sparkle to so many allegro passages.

'To be play'd plain and the Bow is not to be taken off the strings' is Geminiani's advice (*loc. cit.*) for successions of rapid semiquavers, as opposed to 'a Staccato, where the Bow is taken off the Strings at every Note', which he recommends only for special effect, at a moderate speed, and not for very rapid notes.

Where no special effect is intended, and the passage is rapid, but of average intensity, a very relaxed and easy style is required. The bow should be allowed to ease off its pressure on the string between each note by its own natural resilience, without actually being allowed to spring clear of the string. This is half-way between the violinist's détaché (which is in fact a legato, but with separate bows) and his spiccato (with the bow springing clear of the string and back again): a convenient term for this is sprung détaché; and it will be found quite invaluable in countless ordinary baroque allegros. It can be combined with crisp finger-pressure or not, according to the degree of incisiveness desired. Tapering down the note is often better than holding it with full tone too remorselessly. Short last notes of phrases can be given away almost for nothing.

At slower speeds, a slightly sprung détaché will still be found useful, but beyond a certain slowness it is not suitable. The crisp finger-pressure can still be used; but the slower the passage, the greater the probability that its general character will be cantabile and legato.

(d) The best part of the bow at which to take an average succession of moderate or rapid notes is about one-third from the point of the bow. Nearer the point, they are apt to sound a little insubstantial; nearer the heel (nut) they are apt to sound too ponderous.

Tartini (op. cit., p. 17) recommends practising such passages at the point, mid-way between the point and the middle, and at the middle. He does not even mention practising them in the lower half of the bow; and there is no doubt at all that the frequent modern usage of taking them at the heel, in the hammered style with the bow lifted off the string between each note and returned to it with percussive force, is completely anachronistic and out of style. It produces an agitated impression far less brilliant and powerful, in spite of the energy displayed, than the relaxed but vital flow of notes intended.

(e) The cantabile style is well described as follows:

(704) Leopold Mozart, *Violinschule*, Augsburg, 1756, V, 14:

'You must therefore be at pains, where the singingness of the piece requires no separation, not only to leave the bow on the violin at the change of stroke, in order to bind one stroke to another, but also to take many notes in one stroke, and in such a way that the notes which belong together shall run one into another, and be distinguished in some degree merely by loud and soft.'

(f) The spiccato is an excellent effect in baroque music provided it is not introduced into plain passages which merely need a relaxed sprung détaché. Where justified by the expression, it can be freely used. We find quite an early reference to it as follows, though in the form of a complaint from a celebrated teacher of the viol who disliked it even on the rival instrument, and still more on his own.

(705) Jean Rousseau, *Traité de la Viole*, Paris, 1687, p. 73:

'[Avoid on the viol] those runs up and down the instrument with rebounding bow which are called "Ricochets", and which are hardly bearable on the violin.'

Leopold Mozart (*op. cit.*, VI, 11) gives typical examples of up-bow spiccato (bounding staccato of several notes), but not down-bow. He gives up-bow and down-bow pairs of staccato notes in one bow.

The spiccato with separate bows to each note (instead of several notes to a bow) is equally satisfactory in baroque music as a special effect, but had not the regular position which it later acquired.

(706) Leopold Mozart, *Violinschule*, Augsburg, 1756, XII, 18:

'Gay and playful passages must be lifted up with light and short strokes, cheerfully and rapidly; while in slow and sad pieces, you perform them with long bow strokes, simply and expressively.'

(g) The light staccato is taken with a silence of articulation between the notes, but this silence is modified by the fact that no pressure is exerted by the bow on the string in course of it, so that the sound to some extent rings through. This is the variety intended by Tartini at (621) in Ch. XLVIII, 6 above. The result is more articulate than plain sprung détaché, and more ordinary (less of a special effect) than spiccato; it is of very frequent value in baroque music.

(h) The heavy staccato is taken with a firm pressure of the bow on the string during the silence of articulation. The sound therefore starts and ends abruptly; and though such an effect may occasionally be useful, it is somewhat too massive for most baroque contexts.

The true martelé, in David Boyden's opinion, may have come in by about 1750, but cannot be confirmed before the late eighteenth century.

(i) Leopold Mozart (*op. cit.*, Ch. VII) and other authorities show a sophisticated range of legato slurrings, both mixed and unmixed with staccato notes. Some violin parts include similar indications. On the whole, the more sophisticated slurrings are typical of virtuoso parts, and plainer parts imply plainer bowings; but the performer has a reasonable liberty. See also Ch. XLVIII, 3 and 5 above.

(j) Changes of bow followed the same principles as today, except for a greater tendency to take two down bows, or two up bows, in succession, with the deliberate intention of enforcing a silence of articulation. The subject is mentioned by Mersenne (*op. cit.*, p. 185) and clearly illustrated by Leopold Mozart (*op. cit.*, Ch. IV and Ch. VII). But the *quality* of the change was different, being decidedly more articulated except in cantabile passages.

(k) Pizzicato was a recourse inherited from many medieval and renaissance stringed instruments of which the technique was both bowed and plucked. It was also familiar to viol players. It is indicated in Carlo Farina's *Ander Theil* (Dresden, 1627), and has always been part of violin technique. Long pizzicato basses, however, were not characteristic.

(l) The above section does little justice to the many refinements and nuances of the different bow strokes taught by Geminiani and Leopold Mozart. Since both their treatises are available in modern English editions, the reader is urged to study them for himself (see my Bibl.).

9. CHORDS AND POLYPHONY ON THE VIOLIN, ETC.

(a) Music for an unaccompanied violin in which chords and some simple polyphony appear was published by Carlo Farina (*Ander Theil newer Paduanen*, Dresden, 1627); he spent some years at Dresden, and may have started a fashion for such music in Germany, the culmination of which was J. S. Bach's famous suites for unaccompanied violin. Music of the kind was written elsewhere, but there is little to compare with Bach's for difficulty and complexity. The chords are full and numerous, and the polyphony is almost continuous. Any adequate performance is an achievement in virtuosity.

(b) With a bridge as highly curved as the present standard, and with strings as tense, it is not possible for the bow to hold down more strings than two except by great pressure. This leaves two alternatives: either the chords are arpeggiated, and the polyphony touched on but not sustained, which permits an easy style while leaving something to the imagination; or the chords are made as nearly simultaneous as possible and as much of the polyphony is sustained as can be held down, which fills in some of the gaps in the sound, but imposes a very strenuous style. The first alternative is historically correct and gives by far the most musical results; but it can be given greater continuity of sound by a somewhat flatter bridge.

(c) At the beginning of the present century, Arnold Schering noticed a seventeenth-century passage which he believed, in some excitement, to hold the explanation of this notorious problem. It is as follows:

(707) Georg Muffat, *Florilegium II*, Passau, 1698, preface:

'In Germany as in France, the majority of violins which play upper and middle parts [*i.e.* as opposed to cellos] hold the bow by pressing the hair with the thumb and by leaving the other fingers on the back of the bow.'

This statement probably means the first of two alternatives. It may describe a bow grip, for which confirmation is found in pictures, with the thumb actually holding the *hair* of the bow from underneath; it is very probable that German and some French violinists used this grip, though most perhaps in music of the dance type rather than the sonata type. Less probably, the statement may merely describe the fact, also clear from pictures, that the thumb in its normal position under the *stick* was sometimes pressed against the hair for greater control, the point of contact being about at the root of the thumb-nail.

There is no reference in Georg Muffat's preface to chords or polyphony (*i.e.* to 'multiple stopping'), nor are there examples of such writing in the music of this volume itself.

Nevertheless, Schering believed that the words 'by pressing the hair with the thumb' implied (they certainly do not say) that the tension of the bow-hair itself could be varied by varying the thumb-pressure. When the thumb was relaxed, he believed that the hair could curl over three or four strings at once, and thus play full chords and polyphony with no strain at all. When the thumb was pressed, he believed that the bow would again be tight enough to play normally on one string at a time. Unfortunately he did not put this belief to the test of experiment before publishing it in an article ('Verschwundene Traditionen des Bachzeitalters', *Bach-Jahrbuch*, Leipzig, 1904) which attracted the attention, among others, of Albert Schweitzer. In his turn, Schweitzer gave an enthusiastic account of the matter (*J. S. Bach*, 1905, *etc.*, pp. 209, 309, 388), in terms suggesting that Schering's belief rested on impeccable contemporary authority. From there, the belief was not unnaturally passed into general acceptance, and became widely held.

In reality, the thumb, whether resting on the stick or the hair, can exert no such influence on the tension of the hair as Schering's belief required. If the experiment is tried on any surviving baroque bow, or a reproduction of one, the impossibility is at once clear. If the hair is slackened enough to curl round the strings, not only can the thumb exert insufficient pressure to tighten it again, but the stick merely scrapes on the strings; for it must be remembered that while the out-curve of a baroque bow varies in steepness, it is seldom very much steeper than a straight line. If the hair is screwed a little tighter, and the pressure of the thumb relaxed in the hope of loosening the hair, either nothing happens or the bow drops from the hand. Schering's belief turns out to be wishful thinking; and in fact the passage from Georg Muffat has no bearing on the problem of violin multiple-stopping at all.

Schering did not cling obstinately to his mistake; he made honourable recantation in a footnote to an article by Andreas Moser ('Zu Joh. Seb. Bachs Sonaten und Partiten für Violine allein', *Bach-Jahrbuch*, 1920, p. 57, *f.n.*). But the sequel was curious.

In the first place, Schering's repudiation of his earlier belief attracted far less attention than the belief itself; and it is doubtful if many of those who are interested in the problem are aware that the originator of all the speculation had himself retracted. C. S. Terry (*Bach's Orchestra*, London, 1932, p. 132) and N. Bessaraboff (*Ancient European Musical Instruments*, Boston, Mass., 1941, p. 347) were both deceived.

In the second place, no one could make a baroque bow work on the method suggested, and it accordingly became necessary to invent a bow on which it would work.

This was duly done. One example was made by John Bolander for Roman Totenberg (described in the *New York Times*, 17 July, 1949); another was introduced by Ralph Schroeder (see Schweitzer, 'A New Bow for Unaccompanied Violin Music', *Musical Times*, Sept. 1933); another was made by Knud Vestergaard for Emil Telmanyi (the 'Vega Bach Bow': see Emil Telmanyi, 'Some Problems in Bach's Unaccompanied Violin Music', *Musical Times*, Jan. 1955; 'The Purpose of the Vega Bach Bow', *Musical Times*, July 1955; 'The Vega Bach Bow', *Strad*, Nov. 1955; 'The Bach Bow', *Strad*, Sept. 1956). The latter, which alone I have seen in action, has a very steep curve, like a segment of a child's hoop; and an ingenious lever or trigger, by which an effective difference in the tension of the bow can be produced almost instantaneously (a slight break in the music cannot be avoided). Wielded with great skill by Telmanyi, this bow, for all its awkward balance, approaches normal precision, when tightened, and genuinely curls round the strings, when relaxed. The sound of all four violin strings at once, in organ-like smoothness, affords a unique and by no means uninteresting experience. It also denatures the violin completely; and it would have considerably astonished J. S. Bach.

At this point in the first and second editions of my original version, a list of articles dealing with this ridiculous 'musicological red herring' was given, and can be turned up by those sufficiently curious. But it is enough now (1974) to read pp. 431–435 in David Boyden's *History of Violin Playing* (London, 1965); and from there to go on through pp. 436–443 for a clear account of what actually was done and needs to be done in order to perform polyphony and chords in baroque violin music successfully. As with so many problems of baroque violin playing, we are indebted to David Boyden for a more thorough investigation than we had before; and on this problem, he leaves us in no doubt at all. Violin chords were broken at need: three parts could sometimes be held simultaneously; four parts never. And indeed, as I wrote in 1963:—

(d) The baroque solution of this problem is not obscure.

(708) Jean-Philippe Rameau, *Pièces de clavecin en concerts*, Paris, 1741, preface:

'At places where one cannot easily perform two or more notes together; either one arpeggiates them, stopping on that [note] from the side of

543

which the melody continues; or one gives the preference, sometimes to the notes at the top, sometimes those at the bottom, according to the following explanation [instructions for two ensuing pieces follow].'

(709) J.-J. Rousseau, *Dictionnaire*, Paris, 1768, *s.v.* 'Arpeggio':

'Manner of performing the different notes in rapid succession instead of striking them at once. There are instruments on which a chord cannot be produced except by arpeggiation; instruments such as the violin, the 'cello and the viol, and all those played with a bow, because the convexity of the bridge prevents the bow from pressing on all the strings at once.'

As a further confirmation of the fact that Bach's violin chords were not meant to sound literally as written, but to be intelligently interpreted, Sol Babitz in the *Musical Times* for May, 1955 has well pointed out that very numerous passages cannot in any case be taken literally, because the fingering needed to hold them down does not exist on the violin, irrespective of the bowing problem.

The solution is in two parts. A bridge of lower curvature than the rather unnecessarily high modern average is a help; chords which cannot be sustained with any curvature actually in use should be un-fussily arpeggiated, the arpeggio ending on whichever note (top, bottom, or middle) continues the melody.

(e) A similar solution applies to chordal passages in J. S. Bach's unaccompanied cello suites, *etc.*

10. THE DOUBLE-BASS

(a) The original double-bass violin was a large and powerful instrument, used only when volume rather than refinement was needed. The present double-bass has been to some extent influenced by the more lightly resonant instrument which is the double-bass of the viol family: the violone, used in baroque ensembles much more frequently than the true double-bass violin.

A violone doubling a cello or gamba at the octave below produces a sound of peculiar silkiness, depth and warmth. In any thorough reconstruction of a baroque orchestra, this will undoubtedly give a more characteristic sonority. In a chamber ensemble, a certain mellowness and delicacy is gained, though nothing which a good player of our normal double-bass cannot match in his own somewhat different sonority, especially on a rather small 'chamber' bass.

(b) The term violone did not always mean an instrument of double-bass (sixteen-foot) register. It also (at least as often) indicated a bass of regular (eight-foot) register: *i.e.* a cello or a gamba. The musical context will best show which is intended.

CHAPTER LVIII

Plucked Instruments

1. THE LUTE

(a) The lute is the principal late renaissance and baroque representative of a species of instrument made with bowl-shaped body attached directly to the table—a method of construction which is particularly favourable to plucked sounds.

The construction of the lute is even lighter than that of the viol, and the stringing is light to correspond. The resonance is remarkably free, though the volume is comparatively small. The tone has an unsurpassed colourfulness and character; it is warm, but has a slight sharpness or astringency that adds greatly to its attractiveness; and it is capable of a rich variety of nuance.

The lute is technically, however, among the hardest of instruments. The fingers of the left hand may have some very awkward positions to take; yet unless they are placed with reasonable accuracy up against their frets, the resonance may suffer. The fingers of the right hand, which do the actual 'striking' (plucking) of the strings, need very delicate timing, placing and moving if the tone is to ring out as it should. Any inadequacy of technique deadens the sound and leaves it harsh and woolly.

(b) An important part of lute technique is to hold down as many fingers of the left hand as possible, so that their notes go on ringing: the effect of this, like the effect of holding down notes on the harpsichord, is to increase the sonority.

(710) Thomas Mace, *Musick's Monument*, London, 1676, p. 85:

'You are *not to take up That Finger, which you last Stopt, until necessity require.*'

(c) The right hand is supported by resting the little finger lightly on the table. Some modern lutenists, following a lead from guitarists, leave the hand unsupported so that the fingers can be pulled further from the strings; but the resulting gain in volume is sometimes at the expense of quality. It is necessary to accept the fact that the lute, unless electrically amplified, is effective only in small halls.

The classical technique is to strike with the soft ends of the fingers and thumb. The alternative of using the nails was regarded as cittern technique, not as lute technique. It can be developed to a high degree of refinement, and is favourable to velocity; it makes an interesting change of tone colouring; but it does not quite compare with the classical technique for subtlety of tone.

The entire right hand can be moved nearer to the bridge, for a more pungent and penetrating tone, or farther from the bridge, for a softer and more sonorous tone.

(d) The first extensive instructions in lute technique occur in Mersenne's *Harmonie Universelle* (Paris, 1636–7, II, ii, des Instrumens); they were supplied by Jehan Bassett. Mace goes into much greater detail still in his *Musick's Monument* (London, 1676); but he was writing when the classical age of lute playing was already in decline, and his instructions, which were largely based on the new French tunings of the mid-seventeenth century, need to be taken with this fact in mind. Later still, a revival in lute-playing occurred in Germany during the first half of the eighteenth century, heralded by Baron's *Untersuchung* of 1727, and represented, among other composers, by some beautiful solos and obbligato parts of J. S. Bach. Tunings and technique were by then, however, very different from the classic period.

(e) Lute-playing never quite died out; but it came near to doing so in the nineteenth century.

(711) Johann Friedrich Reichardt, *Geist des musikalischen Kunstmagazins*, Berlin, 1791, p. 89:

'The lute, so strangely moving in the hands of Leopold Weis or Pelegraski [is in danger of becoming obsolete].'

(712) Thomas Busby, *Dictionary of Music*, London, [1786], ed. of [1801], *s.v.* 'Arch-Lute':

'A Theorbo, or large Lute. . . . It is still used in Italy.'

(f) Instruments of modern manufacture, mostly German, are frequently encountered which have the outward form of lutes; but a somewhat heavy construction, so that they are not in fact lutes but guitars with lute-shaped bodies. But many modern lutes are excellent.

(g) The guitar proper makes the best substitute for the lute, and is by no means unsatisfactory in this role, particularly if it is an old enough instrument to be double-strung in the lute manner (the modern guitar is single-strung). Nevertheless, the tone is decidedly different, and does not quite equal in beauty and characterfulness that of a good lute well played. There are numerous excellent lutenists now performing professionally, and it is very well worth procuring their services either for Bach obbligato parts or earlier music. Consult my Bibliography for an article by M. W. Prynne, and for the tablatures in which lute music is notated, see articles by Thurston Dart (*Grove's Dictionary*, 5th ed., London, 1954, *s.v.* 'Lute', 'Lute Music', 'Tablature').

2. THE VIHUELA

This name is the Spanish for viol. It denotes an instrument in the shape of a guitar, which was used in three aspects: plucked with a plectrum (like the medieval but unlike the renaissance lute) when it was called the *vihuela de peñola*; plucked with the fingers (with the technique and essentially the musical effect of the lute) when it was called the *vihuela de mano*; and bowed (with the technique and effect of a viol) when it was called the *vihuela de arco*. Vihuela music may be played with complete success on the lute: the two varieties of music are in no significant way distinct.

3. THE GUITAR

The vihuela was slowly displaced by the guitar itself, which in its most typical baroque form is double strung (with two strings to each course) like the lute, and which then acquired a popularity it has not since lost. The guitar was and remains a valuable continuo instrument, either alone with a singer or two (especially for lively music) or with others in a larger continuo group.

4. THE CITTERN

The cittern or cithren is a flat guitar-like instrument with an outline shaped like a fig. Descended from the medieval citole, it acquired great popularity in late renaissance and baroque Europe, hanging on the walls of barbers' shops to while away the time of waiting customers, and becoming known as the poor man's lute. With a simplified tuning, and under the name of English guitar, it remained in favour well into the nineteenth century; and specimens of the latter instrument, which are commonly found, serve very well as citterns, with the proper tuning. The strings of the cittern are of wire, and it is played with the nails or with a plectrum.

5. THE HARP

The modern pedal-action harp has a louder and more massive tone than any variety of late renaissance or baroque harp, though in baroque orchestral music it serves very well when necessary. Virtuoso harpists were given important shares in seventeenth-century opera performances, presumably improvising parts similar to the famous written-out example for the aria 'Possente spirto' in Monteverdi's *Orfeo* (Mantua, 1607). Like the guitar, the harp is also a valuable instrument in a larger continuo group, and should be much used.

CHAPTER LIX

The Wind Department

1. THE CHANGED CHARACTER OF MANY WIND INSTRUMENTS

Our problem over early wind parts lies less in either the technique or the style than in the instruments themselves.

Superficially the most conspicuous change has been the evolution of key-work. In detail, this has revolutionised their technique, but not basically; and it has no direct bearing on style. Its advantages are evident. It aids facility, and makes freely available remote tonalities which were prohibitively difficult with keyless cross-fingering. Approximate intonation and even tone on different notes are made more reliable, though fine control always rests with the player. The weight of so much keywork clamped to the tube has been thought to modify the sonority, but only slightly.

The real changes are the structural changes in length and bore, in the embouchure size on flutes, the size and flexibility of reeds on oboes, the breadth and depth of brass mouthpieces, *etc.* Since all these variables can be graded imperceptibly, there have generally been intermediate grades between early wind instruments and modern ones; but the final difference is in many cases too wide to be ignored for purposes of interpretation.

2. HOW EFFICIENT ARE EARLY WIND INSTRUMENTS?

(713) Alessandro Scarlatti, quoted by Dr. Charles Burney, *Present State of Music in Germany*, London, 1773, II, p. 184:

'My son, you know I hate wind instruments, they are never in tune.'

(714) Dr. Charles Burney, *op. cit.*, I, p. 94:

'I found, however, an imperfection in this band [at Schwetzingen under Stamitz], common to all others, that I have ever yet heard, but which I was in hopes would be removed by men so attentive and so able; the defect, I mean, is the want of truth in the wind instruments. I know it is natural to those instruments to be out of tune, but some of the art and diligence which these great performers have manifested in vanquishing difficulties of other kind, would surely be well employed in correcting this leaven, which so much sours and corrupts all harmony. This was too plainly the case tonight, with the bassoons and hautbois, which were rather too sharp, at the beginning, and continued growing sharper to the end of the opera.

'My ears were unable to discover any other imperfection in the orchestra.

[I, p. 26:] 'The horns [at Brussels] were bad and out of tune . . . the first clarinet, which served as a hautboy, was, though a very good one, too sharp the whole night.

[II, p. 201:] 'A difficult flute concerto, very neatly executed.

[p. 312:] 'In his performance upon the French horn, [Mr. Spandau] has contrived, by his delicacy, taste, and expression, to render an instrument, which, from its coarseness, could formerly be only supported in the open air, or in a spacious building, equally soft and pleasing with the sweetest human voice.'

Burney certainly heard many ordinary performances in which the wind, being in tune, did not attract his attention; but it is his violent denunciations of bad intonation which get remembered. We know now from ample modern experience that early wind instruments can and should be got well in tune.

(715) Charles Butler, *Principles of Musik*, London, 1636, p. 103:

'[Because string instruments are less reliable for intonation] in our Church-solemnities only the Winde-instruments [are used].'

(716) Marin Mersenne, *Harmonie Universelle*, Paris, 1636–7, II, v, pp. 255 *ff.*:

'[On the trumpet, serpent *etc.* fine intonation and tone-quality depend on breath control, since (p. 281) the exact sounds are determined more by] the way you push the breath, than on the length of the instruments or the opening of holes.'

On flutes, the embouchure is turned to correct the intonation: Michel Corrette (*Methode pour la Flûte Traversière*, Paris-Lyon [*c.* 1730], p. 50) has a method of producing a *C* sharp not otherwise on the instrument 'by turning the embouchure'. Quantz gives full instructions (*Essay*, Berlin, 1752, Fr. ed., pp. 170 *ff.*), and lays frequent stress both on the difficulty and on the importance of good intonation.

(717) Joachim Quantz, *Essay*, Berlin, 1752, XVII, 18:

'[The leader] ought to take particular care that the instruments are exactly tuned and at the same pitch.

'[XVII, 4: There is often] great unevenness of playing, among the musicians in the same Chapel or in the same orchestra.

'[Fr. ed., p. 42:] To tune each note exactly, when passing from one to the other, it is necessary to have the embouchure firm and sure, the ear concentrated on the music, and a knowledge of the proportions which the notes have with one another. He who joins to these qualities that of

549

playing the flute well, is in a position to render a flute good and well in tune.'

3. BREATHING

(718) Joachim Quantz, *Essay*, Berlin, 1752, VII, 1:

'To know how to take timely breath, is a thing very necessary for wind instruments, in the same way as for song. Nevertheless it is to be noticed in a great many people that they fail in it, and it is hence that we find the most connected melodies interrupted; and that in short we find the ear deprived of part of its pleasure.

[2:] 'But as it is not always possible, to play in one breath all that belongs together, whether because the composition is not always constructed with the care which ought to be observed in this regard, or because the player has not skill enough to manage his breath [rules are needed].

[3]: 'Very quick notes, though of the same value, must be played with a certain inequality. . . . Hence follows the rule, that breath should be taken between a long note and a short. That should never be done after a little note, and still less after the last note of the bar. For it will be well to sound it with all possible shortness, it will always become long in taking breath on it. However we should make an exception for triplets, when they rise or fall by degree, and it is necessary to play them very quickly. It is then often necessary to take breath after the last note of the bar. But provided that there is only found an interval of a third, *etc.*, we can do it between this interval.

[4]: 'When a piece begins at up-beat (au lever) of the bar, whether the first note is the only one in this bar, or whether it is found preceded by a rest on the down-beat (au frapper); when there has been a cadence made, or there is an altogether new thought: it is then necessary to take breath, at the repeat of the subject, or at the commencement of the new thought; for the end of what precedes, and the commencement of what follows, should be well separated and distinguished one from the other.

[5]: 'When a note has to be held for one or more bars, breath can be taken before this note, even when preceded by a short note. If it is found tied to a quaver, and two semiquavers follow, and thereafter a tied note [Ex. 226 (a)] two semiquavers can be made of the first quaver, be it under-stood however on the same note [Ex. 226 (b)], and breath taken between them. The same can be done in case of need, with regard to all tied notes, whether they are crotchets, quavers or semiquavers. But if after this tie with the half note, no other follows [Ex. 226 (c)], breath can be taken after the note which is tied to the long note, without need to divide it into two notes.

[6]: 'However if it is found necessary to take breath between quick notes, the note after which this need arises must be made very short . . . the two or three following notes must be hurried a little, so that the tempo (la mesure) does not suffer at all, and that no note is lost [and don't wait for an extremity—breathe quietly in good time].'

Ex. 226. Quantz, *loc. cit.*, breathing places:

4. TONGUING

T and *K* are the commonest consonants today for articulating the notes of wind instruments where it is not desired to slur them: *T* for single tonguing; *T–K, T–K* for double-tonguing when the speed is too fast for the comfortable reiteration of a single consonant. The softer variants *L*, and *R* may also be used. *R* can be trilled as in the Italian *R* for 'flutter-tonguing', or rolled in the uvula, as in the French *R*.

Renaissance and baroque tonguings were to a greater variety of articulation syllables and combinations of syllables. The factors, being somewhat complex and technical, can best be studied in the writings of modern woodwind specialists, and the reader is referred to my Bibliography under the names of Anthony Baines, Betty Bang, Imogene Horsley, George Houle, David Lasocky and Mary Rasmussen. The general disposition would seem to have been towards using softer consonants, perhaps (Anthony Baines, *Woodwind Instruments*, London, 1957, p. 44) because there was then less orchestral opaqueness to cover them. '*Territory*' was a fashionable 18th century articulation; *titi, tutu, tiri, turu* (with French vowels) had extensive vogues; other combinations were *T– –R–T* ('slur two, tongue two'); *T–T–R–T/ R–T–R–T; T–R–T* (for equal triplets and certain syncopations); *T–T–R* (for dotted triplets, or equal triplets with the first two notes the same). Anthony Baines states (p. 42) that before about 1820, *T–K–* was thought too crude and explosive; *T–R–* (or *diri*) was preferred. Martin Agricola (*Musica Instrumentalis Deutsch*, Wittenberg, 1529) gave *de* (single-tonguing), *diri–diri–de* (double-tonguing) and *tellellell* (flutter-tonguing).

5. EARLY WIND INSTRUMENTS IN PRACTICE

Only when the strings of an orchestra have been reduced to baroque numbers and a baroque transparency of technique and style can most early wind instruments be used effectively. Under these circumstances, however, if instruments in good condition can be provided and if the players can give sufficient time really to master them, they can sound quite extraordinarily appropriate and beautiful. Some of them have a characteristic colouring to contribute which is necessary to any really idiomatic rendering of the scores in which they appear; others are nearer to their modern representatives, so that the need to reintroduce them is rather less. In these cases, the greater ease with which the modern instruments can be controlled give them an advantage not to be despised under ordinary circumstances. But under propitious circumstances, it can now (1974) be taken as certain that wind sections using instruments of baroque design are practicable and worth every effort and difficulty in achieving them. August Wenzinger has pioneered them at Basle and Brussels; other more recent groups in Vienna and elsewhere (*e.g.* the Concentus Musicus of Nikolaus Harnoncourt) have made great subsequent progress. It has now been shown conclusively that baroque wind instruments can be played with satisfactory control and intonation, and that their sonorities when well produced are extraordinarily different and extraordinarily fine.

The baroque flute as played by Gustav Scheck, for example, the baroque oboe as played by Michel Piguet, and the baroque bassoon as played by Hansjurg Lange, have qualities so characteristic and so beautiful that their recovery is welcome indeed. Don Smithers and Edward Tarr have been equally successful with the baroque trumpet, though the situation here still appears to be somewhat transitional, because the technique of high clarino playing is so very exacting and the design of the instrument so susceptible to small but critical modifications.

Most of our baroque performances continue to rely upon modern wind instruments, and are likely to do so for some time to come. But an orchestra with baroque wind and baroque strings is now, under propitious circumstances, a practicable proposition, and under sufficiently resonant acoustic conditions, a most desirable and enjoyable experience.

CHAPTER LX

Flutes

1. EMBOUCHURE AND FIPPLE

All flutes are alike in having their air-columns set in vibration by the eddies in an air stream which is directed across a sharp edge cut in the tube, or formed by one end of it.

If the air-stream is directed by the lips, it can be flexibly controlled, and we speak of an embouchure. This is the method in our transverse flutes.

If the air-stream is directed by a built-in whistle mouthpiece (fipple), this forms a rigid channel, and control is less direct. This is the method in our recorders.

2. TRANSVERSE FLUTES

The transverse flute in the late renaissance and early baroque periods had a straightforward cylindrical bore and a clear, relatively uncoloured yet fascinating tone. There were six holes, no joints and no keys. There is ample pictorial and other evidence of the popularity of this instrument, particularly in the small chamber groupings or 'broken consorts' of these periods. The intonation can be very good.

In the second half of the seventeenth century, the flute was redesigned, probably by the famous French family Hotteterre. A cylindrical head-joint was used; but the remainder of the bore was made conical, tapering inwards towards the bottom. The resulting tone is more veiled and colourful. A single key (E flat) was added. This is the famous one-keyed flute on which all the later baroque virtuosi performed; which Quantz taught; and for which Bach and Handel composed their great sonatas and obbligati. Mozart still composed his concertos for it in 1778, but in the ensuing period key-work was developed leading to the six-keyed flute of Beethoven's generation. The flute of this entire period is known as the conical flute.

In the mid-nineteenth century the flute was given another radical redesigning of which by far the most important part was the work of Boehm, the result being fundamentally our present flute. This has a modified (parabolic) conical head-joint, but the remainder of the bore cylindrical; every hole desirable for the acoustics of the instrument is placed in its best position and made to the best size, with most ingenious and elaborate key-work to give the necessary control. The tone is very open, capable both of expressive softness and of great loudness, though the peculiarly gentle charm and woody colouring typical of the older conical flute has been unavoidably sacrificed.

The following descriptions all draw attention to this gentle beauty. It is, indeed, of great attractiveness; both solos and obbligati reveal themselves in a different mood when this (their original) sonority is restored to them.

(719) François Raguenet, *Comparison*, 1702, transl. ? Galliard, 1709, ed. O. Strunk, *Mus. Quart.*, XXXII, 3, p. 415:

'The flute, which so many of our great artists have taught to groan after so moving a manner in our mournful airs, and sigh so amorously in those that are tender.'

(720) Jean-Laurent de Béthizy, *Exposition . . . de la musique*, Paris, 1754, 2nd ed., 1764, p. 304:

'The sound of the German [*i.e.* transverse] flute is tender and sad. It suits grief and lament.'

(721) John Hoyle, *Dictionary of Music*, London, 1770, ed. of 1791, *s.v.* 'German Flute':

'It is an instrument now much in use; it is found sweet and agreeable when a good performer blows it.'

In the main baroque period, the transverse flute is normally distinguished as the German flute or transverse flute. The word flute, unqualified, normally means recorder.

3. THE RECORDERS

The late renaissance and early baroque recorders had a conical bore tapering inwards to the bottom; no joints nor keys except where necessary for the largest sizes. The tone of this instrument is comparatively full but uncoloured, well suited to the consort music for which it was chiefly used.

The recorder, like the transverse flute, was redesigned in the second half of the seventeenth century, also in all probability by the Hotteterre family. Here, too, a cylindrical head-joint is joined to a conical body tapering inwards to the bottom; here, too, the tone became less open and more reedy. It is this, the normal baroque recorder, on which modern instruments are most often based; but modern makers (notably Carl Dolmetsch and his workshop) have opened up the tone and given it great brilliance, with some change of quality. The volume is still less than adequate for a full modern orchestral setting, and it would seem most probable that this limitation is inherent in a fipple-blown instrument (where sharpness due to harder blowing cannot be directly controlled, so that crescendos need careful handling); or possibly the bore could be redesigned (as that of all then current woodwind instruments was in the nineteenth century) for greater loudness but doubtful gain.

The recorder never acquired additional keywork, its cross-fingerings being reasonably satisfactory. Its tone and its technique are sufficiently distinct from the transverse flute for it to be most desirable to use it in baroque music where it is definitely intended. As an amateur instrument, it is now fully re-established, and there are also a number of brilliant professional players available, using both the renaissance and the late baroque varieties of recorder to excellent effect.

The names English flute, common flute, beak flute, *flûte douce, etc.*, are among those attached at various times to the recorder. Its parts, when not specifically designated, can sometimes be distinguished from those of the transverse flute by being written in the 'French violin clef' (G clef on the bottom line) or by being in the flat keys such as *F, etc.*, rather than the sharp keys such as *G, etc.*

On paper, the parts of a recorder consort correspond in range and register with the ordinary S.A.T.B. vocal disposition; but the instruments speak an octave higher than this. Perhaps because of the relatively strong fundamental and weak upper harmonics of this kind of tone, however, the ear accepts their pitch almost as if it really were at the vocal register. In mixed consorts a recorder (and the same is to some extent true of the early flute) can be treated as if it spoke at the octave below its actual sounds; it was habitually so treated in the late renaissance and early baroque periods. But as a solo instrument, it does not so readily create this illusion; hence for the solo sonatas and obbligatos of later baroque music, the standard recorder was never the soprano member of the family in *C* (known in modern England as the 'descant'), but the alto member in *F* (in England the 'treble'). The 'descant' as a soloist really does sound both objectively and subjectively very high; the 'treble' gives the impression of a very pleasant normally soprano register. (Yet there is an effective little recorder a fourth higher than the 'descant': the tiny 'sopranino'.)

4. PIPE AND TABOR

A fipple flute (and a relative, therefore, of the recorder) which has been revived very effectively by folk-dance musicians is the three-holed pipe played with one hand while the other beats a small snare-drum (tabor). The scale starts on the second harmonic, and is fully diatonic, with a few chromatic notes available by cross-fingering. The bore is narrow, so that it shall easily overblow to the third and fourth and even fifth harmonics needed to complete the scale. The tone is remarkably clear, pure and pleasing, by no means strident for so high a pitch; the tabor drum adds its dry timbre and sharp accentuation; and the combination is as exhilarating to dance to as it is attractive to the ear.

CHAPTER LXI

Reeds

1. THE INFLUENCE OF REEDS AND BORE

The influence on tone of the reed itself is very great, but more from its stiffness, size, shaping, *etc.*, than from whether it is single (beating against a channelled mouthpiece) or double (unsupported except by the lips). An even greater influence, however, is exerted by the design and dimensions of the bore. It is, moreover, necessary to use a reed capable of setting the air-column within the given bore into satisfactory vibration. Control of the reed by the lips can be very fine and accurate, but within relatively narrow outer limits, so that the reed itself must first be suitable.

2. THE SHAWMS

The most prominent late renaissance and early baroque reed instrument was the family of shawms in all its sizes (schalmey, shalmuse, shalmele, *etc.*; also, but especially for the larger members, pommer, bombard, bombart, *etc.*; from its use in town bands, wait, wayte, waight, *etc.*; from its loud volume, hautbois, hautboy, hoboy, *etc.*: hautbois being French for 'loud wood').

The shawm has a double reed, wide and stiff, and a conical bore of wide taper ending in a flared bell. The reed may be controlled directly by the lips, as with the oboe, or taken into the mouth with the lips resting on a ring or pirouette when the tone can be fiery, penetrating and reedy almost beyond belief (even more so than a Highland bagpipe), and more suitable for bands than for chamber music or refined ensembles. Anthony Baines (*op. cit.*) recommends introducing it into modern military bands, where it would be splendidly virile and colourful. The New York Pro Musica and other groups have made the shawms very welcome again in their gentler aspect.

In the band music of the late renaissance and baroque periods, the shawms were less often heard alone than in company with cornetts and trombones. Their revival has made possible an authentic dance orchestra for the renaissance *basse danse*, *etc.*, and the varied court dances of this and the next period.

(722) M. Mersenne, *Harmonie Universelle*, Paris, 1636–7, II, v, 303:

'[The tone of the shawms] is proper for large assemblies, such as balls [though the violins are now common in place of them], for weddings, for

village festivities, and for such-like public rejoicings, on account of the
great noise which they produce, and the great resonance which they set
up, for they have the most powerful tone of all instruments, and the most
violent, except for the trumpet.'

3. THE OBOE

The oboes are related to the shawms, but so refined as to constitute
a separate family. The names, however, were at first partly the same
(hautbois, oboe, etc.).

The true oboe was evolved in the middle of the seventeenth century
by the same school of French makers, centred on the Hotteterre family,
as redesigned the transverse flute and the recorder. The conical bore of
the treble shawm was narrowed (only slightly so at first); the holes were
reduced in size; the reed was narrowed very substantially. Three keys
were fitted, giving the three-keyed oboe; but one was a mere duplicate
for left-handed playing, and after about 1760 was often absent (two-
keyed oboe). The tone became singularly docile and sweet, actually a
little quieter, in the main, than a modern oboe. But the not very
different classical oboe of the generation of Beethoven is described by
Baines (*op. cit.*) as closely resembling in tone the present Austrian
(Viennese) oboe.

The oboe of the later baroque period is such a telling and efficient
instrument that its use in performance of Purcell, Couperin, Handel,
Bach, *etc.*, is quite practicable. The most suitable modern oboe may
well be the Austrian, both sweet and powerful, and next to that, the
fast declining German, a little rounder and less glittering. But the
French is now the normal oboe of the West; and very beautiful it is,
with its silvery timbre and refined sonority. It can be played in a variety
of styles, some broader than others, some reedier, according to the
player's individuality and the way in which he prefers to prepare his
reeds. For baroque music, it is probably best to avoid the most plaintive
and tenuous qualities of the modern French school, as not quite in
line with the traditional robustness of the older schools.

(723) François Raguenet, *Comparison*, 1702, transl. ? Galliard, 1709,
ed. O. Strunk, *Mus. Quart.*, XXXII, 3, p. 45:

'The hautboys, which, by their sounds, equally mellow and piercing,
have infinitely the advantage of the violins in all brisk, lively airs.'

(724) Jean-Laurent de Béthizy, *Exposition . . . de la Musique*, Paris,
1754, 2nd ed., 1764, p. 304:

'The sound of the oboe is gay and is particularly suited to open-air
entertainment.'

4. THE BASSOON

The bassoon is not strictly the bass of the oboe family (which would be a descendant of the bass shawm or pommer), but it sounds so admirable in that capacity that it has been accepted as such since the modern wood-wind group evolved—*i.e.* since the later baroque period. Its invaluable use as a tenor melodist in the orchestra is a more recent development.

Like the oboe, the bassoon has a conical bore, but expanding far less in proportion to its length. It appeared somewhat after the middle of the seventeenth century, as another French (and very probably Hotteterre) remodelling—in this case of the late renaissance and early baroque curtal, from which it differs far less in timbre, however, than the oboe from the shawm. There were ordinarily four keys during most of the eighteenth century, increasing to six, and by about 1800, eight. The bore, except for a wider crook, tended to be narrower than ours, and the reed larger.

The tone of the eighteenth-century bassoon is described by Baines (*op. cit.*, p. 287) as 'irresistably sweet and beautiful; something like a well-played modern French bassoon, but a little softer, more firm and compact, and rather cello-like. Like the old oboe, it blends supremely well with every other instrument'. It follows from this statement, which is based on expert practical experience, that of the two distinct varieties of modern bassoon, the French is more suitable to baroque music than the German. The French bassoon has never been fundamentally remodelled since the seventeenth century; the German has, by the great firm of Heckel, following tendencies already present in the German tradition. As with other wind instruments, the Germans have achieved a remarkably full, even tone, though at a slight cost in colourfulness and interest. But whereas the German oboe is on the decline, the German bassoon is now very much in the ascendant.

(725) Jean-Laurent de Béthizy, *Exposition . . . de la Musique*, Paris, 1754, 2nd ed., 1764, p. 305:

'The bassoon is the natural bass of the oboe. The sounds of this instrument are strong and brusque. A clever man nevertheless knows how to draw from it very sweet, very gracious and very tender sounds. . . . There is no more beautiful accompaniment than those in which a composer knows how to mingle tastefully the sounds of one or more bassoons with those of violins and flutes.'

5. THE CRUMHORN (CROMORNE)

Unlike the reed instruments hitherto mentioned, the crumhorn has a cylindrical bore, which is of narrow scale, but lacks a speaker hole to help it in overblowing, so that its compass is limited to nine notes. There is a double reed, completely covered by a reed-cap with a hole in the top for the breath to enter. As with the wind-channel (fipple) of the recorder, this lessens direct control, since the reed cannot be humoured with the lips; but it makes basic sound-production easier. The consort of crumhorns had a very similar function to the consort of recorders in late renaissance and early baroque chamber music (playing vocal polyphony with or without embellishment, dance tunes set in parts, *etc.*); and its modern revival has been facilitated by its having the same fingering. The tone is smoothly buzzing, and it has become well established in early music groups.

6. THE CLARINET

The sole professional representative in the modern West of the cylindrical reed instruments is the clarinet, which evolved at or before the beginning of the eighteenth century probably with a strong hint (rather than a structural descent) from the little cane chalumeau, by Johann Christoph Denner: a famous maker (especially of recorders) who had already, apparently, somewhat improved the chalumeau itself. There is some confusion between the two, and some genuine early clarinet parts are thought to appear under the designation chalumeau (see G. R. Rendall, *Grove's Dictionary*, 5th ed., London, 1954, *s.v.* 'Clarinet').

The clarinet is played with a single reed. The bore has never been wholly cylindrical (more nearly so, and also narrower, in early than in modern examples). Yet the tube functions acoustically as a closed cylinder in overblowing to the twelfth, not the octave; and in speaking an octave lower than a cone of equal length. Moreover, odd-numbered harmonics are largely suppressed, and the tone (especially at the bottom) has that slightly and almost literally hollow quality which this tonal spectrum produces. There is no more flexible or expressive instrument.

It was at one time thought that baroque music did not include designated clarinet parts, but this is incorrect: Handel, Vivaldi and Telemann are among those to have made some use of it. There were two keys; later in the eighteenth century, five (the classical form). The reed required was small, narrow and hard, the lay long and open; the tone was somewhat uneven at the bottom, and a little quiet at the top, where, however, it was of unsurpassed beauty and singing quality (Baines, *op. cit.*, pp. 300–302). It now seems possible that baroque oboe players doubled on clarinet much more often than the scores indicate, and that there was considerable unrecorded early use of clarinets.

CHAPTER LXII

Brass

1. BRASS CYLINDRICAL AND CONICAL, NARROW AND BROAD

Brass instruments are the hardest of all to classify in distinct families.

The species itself is more accurately called lip instruments, since the material itself is much less important than the method of exciting the air-column into vibration. This method is to use the human lips as a pair of highly flexible and adaptable reeds.

Two primary distinctions are found among lip instruments: cylindrical or conical tubing; and tubing narrow or broad in proportion to its length. Narrow cylindrical tubing makes for strong upper harmonics, and therefore a highly coloured tone as well as an ability to produce these upper harmonics as actual high notes. Broad conical tubing makes for strong lower harmonics, and therefore a thicker, less coloured tone as well as an ability to produce the fundamental and other low harmonics as good low notes. Any intermediate design (including a tube partly cylindrical and partly conical) produces intermediate effects; narrowness in the mouthpiece, and a sharp angle where it joins the shank, favour the upper harmonics, while wideness in the mouthpiece, and a tapering join to the shank, favour the lower harmonics.

2. THE CORNETTO

The Italian form cornetto (*plur.* cornetti) is now used for distinguishing this instrument from the modern cornet, to which it is not allied. The name, of course, merely means 'little horn'.

The cornetto (cornett, Zink, *etc.*) is normally a wooden instrument covered in leather, with a conical bore moderately but not very wide in proportion to its length; more often slightly curved than straight; no bell; a cup-shaped mouthpiece, fairly small, or alternatively a very small mouthpiece carved out of the end of the tube itself, and giving a softer and more veiled tone (mute cornetto).

The family has no very successful low member, and lower parts in consort were usually taken by trombones (sackbuts). Cornetti, shawms and trombones are also found in association, a fact which points to the very considerable volume the cornetto can produce when played loudly. It is also capable, however, of the most delicate piano. Its technique is uncommonly flexible, though difficult; and it was the

561

supreme virtuoso wind instrument of the late renaissance period, carrying off ornamental divisions and other embellishments with a brilliance not exceeded even by the human voice.

The tone of the cornetto is best described as silvery. It has (with its not dissimilar mouthpiece) something of the ringing clarity of the trumpet, though not the extreme brilliance and volume; it has a quality of sweetness (being, in one respect, a wood-wind instrument); and this combination is so rare and delightful that its revival is desirable on these grounds alone, and is now going well. In addition, the cornetto is pressingly required for performances of Monteverdi and his school, with others down to the period of J. S. Bach, who scored for the cornetti in eleven of his cantatas (as late as 1840 a cornetto was still heard with three trombones playing daily chorales from the church tower at Stuttgart). The cornetto is also very valuable in mixed consort-playing of the late renaissance and early baroque varieties. The 'velvet, horn-like quality of indescribable beauty' which Baines (*op. cit.*, p. 262) ascribes to the mute cornetto is a further argument in favour of this once celebrated instrument, whose modern use has already been shown to be practicable where a competent player has given its technique sufficiently concentrated attention.

(726) M. Mersenne, *Harmonie Universelle*, Paris, 1636–7, II, v, 274:

'[The sound of the cornetti] is like the brilliance of a sunray which appears in cloud or darkness, when one hears it among the voices in Cathedral churches, or in chapels.'

3. THE SERPENT

The serpent is to the cornetto family what the bassoon is to the oboe family: not strictly its own bass, but near enough to sound very much as if it were. But the serpent never in fact displaced the trombone in this role. Its earliest use (from the late sixteenth century onwards) was ecclesiastical, in support of the voice; and as a church instrument, it remained in England down to Thomas Hardy's time (*Under the Greenwood Tree*) and in France to within living memory. In the seventeenth and eighteenth centuries it had a considerable vogue in military bands, and in divertimentos, and some general orchestral employment, in the role now allotted to the tuba, which it equals in flexibility and docility and almost equals in volume, though its tone is certainly more woody and less brassy; for like the cornett, it is made of wood covered with leather. The bore is a widely tapering cone though with no bell; and the mouthpiece is large and cup-shaped.

(727) M. Mersenne, *Harmonie Universelle*, Paris, 1636–7, II, v, 278:

'[The serpent] is capable of sustaining twenty of the most powerful voices, though it is so easy to play that a child of fifteen years can sound it as powerfully as a man of thirty years. And its sound can be so sweetened that it will be suitable to join with the voice in soft chamber music, of which it so imitates the refinements, and the divisions, that it can make thirty-two notes to the bar.'

4. THE BUGLES (TUBAS, ETC.)

The present family of bugles (flugel horns, tubas, *etc.*; also saxhorns after 1845) did not come into musical prominence until well after the baroque period. But a tuba can at need substitute for a serpent.

5. THE HORN

The horn has a conical bore narrow in proportion to its length, the mouthpiece being narrow but in greater or lesser degree tapering.

A narrow conical bore gives rich upper harmonics, a little (but only a little) softened in this case by the lack of a sharp angle between mouthpiece and shank. The longer it is, the less its fundamental can be relied on to sound properly as a note or to weight the tone; the shorter it is, the less the very high harmonics can be relied on to sound as notes, or to colour the tone; hence such an instrument can only exist, without loss of character, in baritone-to-tenor registers. This fact is partially disguised by its exceptionally extensive upper compass: at least to the sixteenth harmonic, sometimes to the twentieth and higher.

The characteristic tone of the horn is as highly coloured as tone can be, but with a certain mellowness not found with its only real rival in this respect, the trumpet.

The horn makes only an occasional appearance in seventeenth-century music (Cavalli, Lully), but becomes important in the late baroque music of Bach and Handel's generation. Its parts in the eighteenth century are high, brilliant and exceedingly difficult. They were possible only because a tradition of virtuoso trumpet-playing could be called on for players expert in the production of very high lipped harmonics. As with trumpeters, horn-players took to specialising on a part only of the total harmonic compass: a *cor-alto* took harmonics about from the fourth to the twenty-fourth; a *cor-basse* from the lowest notes (five semitones 'forced' below the second harmonic) about to the sixteenth; later, a *cor-mixte* concentrated on the best solo two octaves in the middle, which is much what happens at present. Even with the full advantages of specialisation, these parts can never have been other than exacting; and they are on the extreme limits of modern technique.

Crooks for varying the tonality came in during the same period. After Haydn (who still wrote high parts) the technique was greatly modified by the development of hand-stopping. The pitch of notes is modified by inserting the hand into the bell, making the instrument partially chromatic and entirely melodic at a lower range of the compass than the very high harmonics previously exploited. Horn parts tended to a standard range up to the sixteenth harmonic, though sometimes (especially in chamber music) still of great difficulty. The natural horn thus used is called the hand horn. Haydn used this as well.

Valves making the instrument fully chromatic and generally more manageable became established during the second half of the nineteenth century, though hand stopping remains as a method of modifying the tone, which it renders more poetical and haunting than the fully open timbre.

The instrument itself was not vitally affected by any of these changes (not even by the proportion of cylindrical tubing rendered necessary by the valves), but it is being vitally affected by others occurring at the present time. For ease and certainty of control, shorter horns are becoming usual (B flat alto in place of F, nowadays usually in the form of the double F–B flat horn in which either the long F tubing or the much shorter B flat tubing can be brought into action instantly). On the same grounds, the broader bore typical of the German horn is becoming generally preferred to the narrower bore traditional in the French horn proper. Both these changes make the horn somewhat less of a horn, and somewhat more of a bugle, than it was before, for the reasons already mentioned: the very high harmonics characteristic both of its compass and of its tone-colouring result only from a bore of a certain narrowness in proportion to its length, and can moreover occur in full only when this length is such as to put the instrument into the baritone or tenor register.

The horn is and always has been so treacherous an instrument even in the most reliable hands that these changes are entirely understandable, and to a considerable extent their adverse effect on the quality of tone can be counteracted by the very great skill of the best modern players. But they are robbing the horn not only of its worst terrors but of its fullest perfection. Though still the most glowing sonority in the orchestra, the short, broad horn cannot glow with quite the unique character of the long, narrow horn which has always been the French horn proper, as crooked in F or E flat.

For early music, the best practically available instrument may well be the ordinary modern French F horn, and it is worth making an effort to use this if possible, in spite of the difficulty of producing the very high harmonics needed. The same very high notes can, of course, be produced as lower harmonics on the shorter, higher, B flat alto horn, but the difference in tone-colouring can never be quite disguised, particularly if the bore is the wider German bore. (A narrow B flat horn is, likewise, more suitable than a wide one.)

The use of a *B* flat alto crook, though it has always been widespread, has itself a marked effect on the tonal quality of the French horn.

6. THE TROMBONE

The trombone (Posaune, sackbut, *etc.*) has a cylindrical bore (except for the bell) of fairly narrow scale in proportion to its length. But it has been, and still is made in a variety of bores ranging from decidedly narrow (with a keen, ringing tone of no great power) to decidedly wide (with a richer, fuller tone but less ring and cutting edge). The thickness of the walls has also varied; baroque mouthpieces appear to have been not conical but cup-shaped, more or less sharply angled at the join to the tube. Great variations in the timbre and attack result from these physical variables; and perhaps even greater variations are introduced by the player, according to whether he cultivates the quieter, the more sonorous, the nobler, the more violent and explosive characteristics, *etc.* Since the musical situations in which the late renaissance and baroque trombone is found vary from outdoor bands in company with the powerful shawms to chamber consorts with the much subtler cornetti, most of these characteristics were presumably already exploited in appropriate contexts. It is possible, however, that the average ideal was mellower than it became in the nineteenth century, when trombone parts were often more forceful than imaginative.

The very wide trombones are, perhaps, a departure from true trombone colourfulness in the direction of tuba massiveness; they are especially a German predilection. Either the medium bore now favoured in English orchestras or the narrow bore of previous English and present French taste should be thoroughly satisfactory in early music. Reproductions of renaissance or baroque sackbuts are available and valuable, but this is not an instrument which has undergone fundamental change.

7. THE TRUMPET

The trumpet is a very close relative of the trombone. It has a narrow cylindrical bore and a more or less shallow mouthpiece, the angle at which this joins the tube varying from sharp to slightly tapered.

The most favoured trumpet in late renaissance and early baroque music was a long, 8-foot *C* trumpet, and in late baroque music, prominent among a choice of tonalities further extended by the use of crooks, was the long *D* trumpet, about 7 feet in tube-length, and able to produce very high harmonics both as separate notes and as colourfulness of tone. In both these respects it resembled the French horn; and its immensely skilled technique for playing ornate melody in natural high harmonics was the source of the similar technique on the late baroque horn. Parts were distinguished as, *e.g. clarino* (very high) and *principale* (low), the names, however, varying widely; and trumpeters specialised in one or another of the requisite techniques. Not till the generation of Mozart did this immense skill begin to disappear, when orchestral trumpet parts were reduced to a simplicity from which they were rescued during the nineteenth century by the development of valves.

The new technique based on valves works best in the lower and middle registers, since in the high register the closeness of the harmonics is actually an impediment, making it harder to pick out the one required. The lower natural harmonics are more widely spaced: but the valves fill in the intermediate notes, and with chromatic completeness. An obvious sequel was a gradual shortening of the standard trumpet length: to an *F* trumpet, later superseded by our modern *B* flat (or *C*) trumpet, at not much more than half the length of the baroque *D* trumpet, and still further modified by a cornet-like increase of conical tubing at the mouthpiece end to give greater legato flexibility. Shorter trumpets than these are coming more into use, and the pitch of the standard orchestral trumpet may not yet have reached its highest point. The higher the trumpet, the lower the harmonics of it which are needed to play high parts, and the normal modern method of playing the very high and difficult baroque trumpet parts is to use a very short trumpet for them. This has its own logic, and certainly its own convenience, but it is a reversal of the baroque method.

The baroque method was to use the highest harmonics of a low trumpet: *i.e.* the harmonics which lie close enough together to produce a melodic line on a natural trumpet without valves or slide. On such a trumpet, there was no other method; but it has a more positive advantage which the modern trumpet loses. As has already been mentioned in connection with the horn, only a tube narrow in proportion to its length, and moreover long enough to put the instrument into the baritone or tenor range, can produce the highest harmonics either as notes or as tone-colouring. The *F* trumpet was still long enough to retain most of the consummate tone quality of the baroque *D* trumpet: the most colourful of all the sounds which the range of musical instruments has to offer. The modern *B* flat or *C* trumpet is not, though it is a fine instrument. The yet smaller trumpets are not so satisfactory since they lack true trumpet character.

Efforts have been made to reverse this tendency for the purposes of early music. It was an expert cornet player, Julius Kosleck, who in 1871 played Bach parts on a natural trumpet in (low) *D*, and later used a somewhat shorter trumpet in *A* with two valves, with great success; it was improved by Walter Morrow, who with John Solomon popularised the so-called 'Bach Trumpet' in England, though later discarded in favour of a valved (high) *D* trumpet.

In the 1930s long *D* and *F* trumpets were reintroduced (with two valves for correcting the intonation) by Werner Menke, but not taken up. (There was an un-baroque bell flare, affecting the tone.)

It is to be noticed that Mersenne leaves no doubt about the uncanny skill already available in the best court trumpet-corps: skill in modifying the pitch and volume by the lips and wind-pressure alone (so as hardly to need the mutes which some used); skill in picking out notes, even some not theoretically possible (*i.e.* by forcing); skill in every subtlety of refined musicianship.

(728) M. Mersenne, *Harmonie Universelle*, Paris, 1636–7, II, v. 260:

'[Trumpeters] imitate the softest echo. [p. 260:] One meets men so skilful that they can sound all the [diatonic] degrees of *ut, re, mi, fa, etc.,* from the first note of the trumpet.'

I am indebted to Edward Tarr (private communication) for information about a moderately baroque coiled long trumpet designed in 1960 for the Cappella Coloniensis by Otto Steinkopf, having an ingenious series of three small holes of which one corrects the intonation of the notorious eleventh and thirteenth harmonics, while the other two will eliminate, alternately, all odd or all even harmonics, thus separating more widely and making more securely obtainable the difficult high harmonics. But Edward Tarr himself has got much nearer in subsequent experiments with various coiled or double-coiled long trumpets constructed by various makers. The real problem remains always the difficulty of the high technique. The trumpeter himself has to be so very good.

CHAPTER LXIII

Percussion

1. MILITARY, DANCE AND ORCHESTRAL PERCUSSION

Percussion instruments have an ancient history in military music and in dance music; their importance in baroque orchestral music lay mainly in the time-honoured association of trumpets and drums, which was itself of military origin.

A range of characteristic military drum rhythms (infantry) will be found in Thoinot Arbeau (Jehan Tabourot), *Orchesographie*, Langres, 1589, transl. C. W. Beaumont, London, 1925, pp. 29 *ff.*

2. THE KETTLEDRUM FOR ORCHESTRAL MUSIC

Kettledrums (nakers, *etc.*), at first small, but larger by the time of the late renaissance, became traditionally allotted to the cavalry; a pair of captured cavalry drums kept at the Tower of London were borrowed by Handel for certain of his performances. Through the baroque period, kettledrums were virtually inseparable from trumpets, and it was normal, at least from the middle of the seventeenth century onwards, for the court or municipal corps of trumpeters and drummers to supply the requirements of the local musical directors.

Two drums were customary in baroque music, tuned to the tonic and dominant of the trumpets' tonality, ordinarily *C* or *D* major. Where no part was written, the player improvised suitable rhythms, usually quite simple. There are drum parts notated, *e.g.* by Lully and Handel.

Modern kettledrums average a larger size, and are of various shapes; but there seems no particular reason for thinking them unsuitable for baroque music. Their tone is of great clarity and beauty, and capable of being tuned with the finest precision.

Mersenne (*Harmonie Universelle*, Paris, 1636–7, II, vii, p. 54) gives the sizes needed for a consort of four drums tuned to c^1, e^1, g^1, c^{11} and of eight tuned to the diatonic scale of *C*.

3. THE TABOR, ETC., FOR DANCING

The word tabor covers a variety of early drums, but especially the small or moderate snare-drum played with one hand by a piper who uses the other for a three-holed pipe, to accompany dancers. This combination, which has been very successfully revived by the modern folk-dance movement, was no doubt mainly used for rustic and popular dancing, especially Morris and Sword Dances.

A drum, however, though not necessarily a small one, nor necessarily with snares, was also a normal part of the ordinary orchestras or mixed consorts accompanying the more sophisticated court and society dances of the late renaissance and baroque periods.

(729) Thoinot Arbeau (Jehan Tabourot), *Orchesographie*, Langres, 1589, transl. C. W. Beaumont, London, 1925, p. 49:

'*Capriol*. Truly hautboys [shawms] greatly resemble trumpets and make a sufficiently pleasing harmony when the large ones, sounding the lower octave, are combined with the little hautboys which sound the higher.
'*Arbeau*. These two are excellent for making a loud noise, such as is required for village *fêtes* and large assemblies, but, if it be combined with the flute, it drowns the sound of it. It may well be combined with the tabor, or with the large drum.
[p. 50:] 'The tabor, accompanied by its long flute among other instruments, was employed in our fathers' time because a single musician could play them together in complete accord, thus avoiding the great expense of having many other players, such as violists [viol-players] and violinists and the like. Nowadays, the meanest workman must have hautboys and sackbuts [trombones] at his wedding, when many kinds of recreative dances are performed.'

Ex. 227. Thoinot Arbeau (a) *op. cit.*, p. 58, drum-rhythm for the pavan; (b) *op. cit.*, p. 61, drum-rhythm for the basse-danse:

Tambourines and castanets are further percussion instruments much used, in certain localities, in dance music, and still unchanged (see also 4 below).

4. TURKISH MUSIC: THE TRIANGLE, CYMBALS, ETC.

A fashion spread rapidly across Europe early in the eighteenth century for 'Turkish Music': a band partly of shawms and fifes, but predominantly of percussion instruments such as the Turkish Crescent (Jingling Johnny, Chinese Pavilion—a collection of jangling plates and small bells mounted on a pole with a conical 'hat' on top), triangle, cymbals and various drums large and small. This fashion had a persistent influence on military music, and during the second half of the eighteenth century brought the triangle, the cymbals, the side-drums and the bass-drum into orchestral use.

But Mersenne (*Harmonie Universelle*, Paris, 1636–7, II, iii, 175, and vi, 47 *ff.*) describes the triangle, a sort of xylophone, and the 'Jew's Harp', along with castanets and clappers and a variety of bells in different sizes.

CHAPTER LXIV

Keyboards

1. THE HARPSICHORD

(a) The starting-point for the harpsichord is its touch. Piano touch is in many ways quite different, and can make even a good harpsichord sound unsonorous. A bad harpsichord may be unavoidably unsonorous.

(730) Joachim Quantz, *Essay*, Berlin, 1752, XVII, vi, 18:

'Experience confirms that if two players of unequal abilities play on the same harpsichord, the tone will be far better in the case of the better player. There can be no reason for this except the difference in their touch.'

(b) The ideal approach is to feel the keys before depressing them. This is not peculiar to the harpsichord: pianists, especially those whose tradition descends along the great Czerny and Leschetizky line, recognise the same ideal. In practice, it cannot be done above a certain speed, but there is a certain feline smoothness which comes very near to it. The opposite to this is throwing the hands at the keys from a height, which sends the jacks up too violently for the quills to take a proper hold on the strings before plucking them. The result is a quite remarkably hard, metallic and jangling tone.

(731) François Couperin, *L'Art de toucher le clavecin*, Paris, 1716, ed. of 1717, p. 7:

'The sweetness of the touch depends on holding the fingers as near to the keys as possible . . . a hand which falls from a height gives a drier stroke than if it touches from close; and the quill draws a harder sound from the string.'

(732) Jean-Philippe Rameau, *Pièces de clavecin*, Paris [1724], preface on finger-technique:

'The greater movement should never be made except where the lesser will not suffice . . . even when the hand has to be moved to a certain part of the keyboard, it is still necessary for the finger used to drop on to the key by its own movement alone.

'The fingers must drop on to the keys and not hit them . . . never weight the touch of your fingers by the effort of your hand.'

This technique is much facilitated by an easy position at the keyboard, the elbows hanging loose, and the fingers curved each to the extent required to compensate for its difference in length. From Girolamo Diruta (*Il Transilvano*, Venice, 1597) to Jean-Philippe Rameau (*loc. cit.* [1724]) we read descriptions of these points which vary only in detail. The following later accounts are particularly vivid.

(733) Dr. Charles Burney, *An account of the Musical Performances . . . in Commemoration of Handel*, London, 1785, p. 35:

'[Handel's] touch was so smooth, and the tone of the instrument so much cherished, that his fingers seemed to grow to the keys. They were so curved and compact, when he played, that no motion, and scarcely the fingers themselves, could be discovered.'

(734) Johann Nikolaus Forkel, *On Joh. Seb. Bach's Life, Art and Works*, Leipzig, 1802, transl. C. S. Terry, London, 1920, p. 49:

'[J. S.] Bach placed his hand on the finger-board so that his fingers were bent and their extremities poised perpendicularly over the keys in a plane parallel to them. Consequently none of his fingers was remote from the note it was intended to strike. [So placed] the fingers cannot *fall* or (as so often happens) be *thrown* upon the notes, but are *placed* upon them. . . . We gather that the action of Bach's fingers was so slight as to be barely perceptible. Only the top joint seemed to move. His hand preserved its rounded shape even in the most intricate passages.'

(c) Though the approach must be smooth, the depressing of the keys must be firm even for soft effects, and very strong for loud effects. The dynamic contrast made by strengthening the touch is not great on the harpsichord, but it is sufficient to mould a phrase or give an impression of loud and soft playing. A touch which is less than firm, however, merely fails to get the string into proper vibration, and sounds not soft but weak. The hand *should grasp the keys with the grip of an eagle.*

(735) Joachim Quantz, *Essay*, Berlin, 1752, XVII, vi, 18:

'It is necessary for all the fingers to play with an equal force and with the right weight; the strings have to be given time enough to come into vibration undisturbed, and yet the fingers have to be pressed down not too slowly, but on the contrary, in one motion with a certain force which puts the strings into sufficient vibration.'

(736) C. P. E. Bach, *Essay*, II, Berlin, 1762, XXIX, 26:

'In accompanying, just as much as in playing solos, a continual playing on the surface of the keys must be avoided: on the contrary, they must be pressed down with decided force. . . . So long as it is not done after the fashion of a woodchopper, the lifting of the hands is not merely not wrong, but needful and good, in so far as they provide an obvious method of showing the tempo to the remaining performers, and allow the keys to be struck with due weight so that the notes sound clearly, as the rules of good performance demand.'

(737) [J. Mainwaring], *Memoirs of Handel*, London, 1760, p. 61:

'Though no two persons ever arrived at such perfection on their respective instruments, yet it is remarkable that there was a total difference in their manner. The characteristic excellence of SCARLATTI seems to have consisted in a certain elegance and delicacy of expression. HANDEL had an uncommon brilliancy and command of finger: but what distinguished him from all other players who possessed these same qualities, was that amazing fulness, force, and energy, which he joined with them.'

(d) The 'follow-through' is as important to good harpsichord touch as it is in golf or tennis (it probably minimises the faint impurity caused by the quill falling back into position again past the string).

(738) Joachim Quantz, *Essay*, Berlin, 1752, XVII, vi, 18:

'[In runs] the fingers should not be lifted brusquely; you must draw the tips back to the near end of the key, and slide them off in this way, which will secure the clearest possible performance of the runs. My opinion in this matter is founded on the example of one of the most accomplished harpsichordists, who used and taught it.'

In his index, Quantz named this accomplished harpsichordist as J. S. Bach; and his description is confirmed by Forkel's below with a closeness which increases our confidence in Forkel's necessarily second-hand account (he was not born till 1749) here and at (734) above.

(739) Johann Nikolaus Forkel, *loc. cit.* contd.:

'Since the force communicated to the note needs to be maintained with uniform pressure, the finger should not be released perpendicularly from the key, but can be withdrawn gently and gradually, towards the palm of the hand. . . . When passing from one note to another, a sliding action instinctively instructs the next finger regarding the amount of force exerted by its predecessor, so that the tone is equally regulated and the notes are equally distinct. In other words, the touch is neither too long nor too short, as Carl Philipp Emamuel [Bach] complains, but is just what it ought to be. . . . Stroking the note with uniform pressure permits the string to vibrate freely, improves and prolongs the tone.'

(e) The instrument itself may have a light touch (as recommended by Diruta, *op. cit.*, for music other than dance music, and by Couperin, *op. cit.*, generally); it may have a strong touch (as preferred by Quantz and C. P. E. Bach); but neither the very feeble touch of some modern or misrestored old instruments, nor the very stiff and hard touch of certain other highly efficient modern instruments, is satisfactory. C. P. E. Bach's description accords well with the average needs of baroque solo work and accompaniment alike.

(740) C. P. E. Bach, *Essay*, I, Berlin, 1753, Introd., 13:

'A good harpsichord should be evenly quilled as well as having a fine tone and the appropriate keys. . . . The action of the harpsichord should not be too light and emasculated; the keys must not sink too low; they must resist the fingers and return by [the weight of] the jacks. On the other hand, they must not be too hard to press down.'

(f) A point of harpsichord technique closely related to touch is the almost imperceptible spreading of all chords containing more than two or three notes. A correctly adjusted harpsichord plucks the strings of its different registers, when these are coupled, not simultaneously but in rapid succession, as may be tested by lowering the key with extreme slowness. The player applies the same principle to his fingers, starting from the lowest note, which takes the beat; but the successive notes of the chord follow so closely that they are not heard as coming after the beat. They are *heard* as simultaneous—unless, of course, they are more perceptibly spread for a deliberate effect of arpeggiation.

If this point is neglected, either in adjusting the action or in performance, so that more than at most three strings are plucked quite simultaneously, interference occurs among the high harmonics and combination tones, which is heard as painful harshness. Under these conditions, the harpsichord sounds unnaturally ruthless. The degree of spreading varies with taste and circumstances, from the least possible onwards; but a certain minimum is absolutely indispensable.

(g) The harpsichord, except in certain highly untypical modern developments, has no damper-raising pedal to allow a surging build-up of sympathetic vibration. A fundamental point in its technique, however, is holding down as many notes within the same harmony as the fingers can manage, irrespective of their written lengths, and subject only to the ordinary considerations of phrasing and articulation. This builds up sonority without blurring the progressions, and though very seldom indicated in the way suggested below, is of very general application. It is, indeed, an essential ally of good touch in giving the harpsichord its full sonority and sustaining power.

(741) Jean-Philippe Rameau, *Pièces de clavecin*, Paris [1724]:

'A slur which covers several notes shows that they must all be held from one end of the slur to the other for as long as one touches them [*i.e.*, till they require reiteration—the example making it clear, however, that only notes within the same harmony are intended].'

Ex. 228. Jean-Philippe Rameau, *loc. cit.*, notes held down to build up sonority:

(h) Registration has to be worked out by the performer in relation, first, to the mood and structure of the music; second, to the resources of his instrument.

Modern pedal controls make an almost unlimited interchange of registration possible; and this has certain baroque precedents.

(742) Thomas Mace, *Musick's Monument*, London, 1676, p. 235:

'An *Instrument* of a *Late Invention* . . . far beyond all [other] *Harpsicons* [with pedals giving twenty-four combinations of registration] either *Soft* or *Loud, according as he shall chuse to Tread any of them down.*'

This 'pedal harpsichord' appears to be specified in music by Hingston (Oxford, Bodleian Lib., late 17th cent., MS. Mus. Sch. e 382, p. 74) but was apparently not much taken up (possibly it was unreliable mechanically). Nearly a century later we hear of its re-invention.

(743) C. P. E. Bach, *Essay*, II, Berlin, 1762, XXIX, 5:

'The splendid invention of our noted Holefeld [Hohlfeld] which makes it possible to increase or decrease the registration by means of pedals, in the act of playing, has made of the harpsichord, especially in its one-manual form, a greatly improved instrument . . . if only all were thus made as a tribute to good taste!'

Yet neither pedals nor the knee-levers sometimes encountered became common enough for us to regard the demand for them as at all typical of the baroque period. In general, even the presence of a 16-foot register was not in favour; it can best be dispensed with, since it adds greatly to the pressure on the instrument and lessens its resonance. There can be no doubt that a moderate and restrained registration suits a great proportion of harpsichord music very much better than a continual dancing on the pedals. It is true that some pieces cry out for showy registration—the showier the better; but far more need a broad scheme of contrasts, mostly at section endings, without much use of sensational colourings and great crescendos and diminuendos. Quite often the only changes really required are those gained by moving from one keyboard to the other, for a contrast of colour, of volume, or of both. That is a particularly characteristic recourse on the harpsichord; yet even that must be foregone on a single-manual instrument. See also Chapter XXXI, 6c above.

The truth is that valuable as imaginative and well-planned registration can be, it is a secondary art. The primary art of harpsichord playing lies in touch, phrasing and articulation.

2. THE CLAVICHORD

(a) The action of the clavichord is nothing but a pivoted lever which when pressed by the finger at the nearer end thrusts a wedge-shaped brass tangent against the string (or pair of strings in the best examples) at the farther end. This contact is maintained so long as the note continues; and it gives what keyboard instruments ordinarily lack, a direct and sensitive vibrato. In every way, the player's control is the least mechanised and most responsive possible to a keyboard instrument. The range of tone is from almost nothing at the least to not very much at the most; but this not very much can sound by contrast violently loud in a passage such as the sudden great chords in J. S. Bach's Chromatic Fantasia. Such an instrument is at its best in a room, and can only just hold the attention in a small hall. With electric amplification, its intimate character is impaired, and it is unsuitable for large-scale public performance.

(744) Johann Nikolaus Forkel, *op. cit.*, p. 58:

'[J. S.] Bach preferred the Clavichord to the Harpsichord, which, though susceptible of great variety of tone, seemed to him lacking in soul. . . . Both for practice and intimate use he regarded the Clavichord as the best instrument and preferred to express on it his finest thoughts. He held the Harpsichord, or Clavicembalo, incapable of the gradations of tone obtainable on the Clavichord, an instrument which, though slight in quality, is extremely flexible.'

(744a) J. F. Reichardt, *Briefe eines . . . Reisenden*, II, Frankfurt and Breslau, 1776, p. 17:

'[Of] the extraordinary strength which [C. P. E.] Bach sometimes gives to a passage [on the clavichord]: it is the greatest fortissimo. Another clavichord [than his very fine Silbermann] would go to pieces under it; and in the same way with his finest pianissimo, which would not speak at all on another clavichord. [C. P. E. Bach, *Essay*, 1753, Introd., 12, says that the touch of the clavichord requires the strings to be "attacked" as well as "caressed". "Fortissimo" is of course here a relative term.]'

It was fairly common practice in Germany to found the player' touch on the clavichord before putting him on to the harpsichord, and C. P. E. Bach (*Essay*, I, Berlin, 1753, Introd., 15) recommends the sensitiveness of touch which a good clavichordist can bring to the harpsichordist. Experience confirms this recommendation.

(b) The vibrato on the clavichord is capable of a development which turns it into a modified kind of tremolo. By a slight exaggeration of the rocking of the finger by which vibrato is produced, the note is given a new emphasis which almost but not quite amounts to reiteration. Both vibrato and near-reiteration are given the German name *Bebung* (trembling); the latter may be distinguished as *Tragen der Töne* (sustaining the tone), but these names occasionally seem to be confused or reversed. Indeed, the two techniques merge so closely that it is not easy to distinguish them either in theory or in practice. Moreover, the near-reiteration very readily passes over into definite reiteration, when the effect, if regular, is simply a portato.

(745) C. P. E. Bach, *Essay*, Berlin, 1753, Introd., 11:

'A good clavichord, except for its softer tone, shares in the advantage of the pianoforte, and has moreover the further features of the *Bebung* and the *Tragen der Tone* [*sic*], which I effect by added pressure after each stroke.

[III, 19:] 'The notes of [Ex. 229 (a)] are taken legato but with a marked pressure on each note. The term for notes on the keyboard which are at the same time slurred and dotted is the *Tragen der Töne*.

[20:] 'A long, expressive note is taken with the *Bebung*. The finger holds down the key and so to speak rocks it. The sign for the *Bebung* is shown at [Ex. 229 (b)]. [Ed. of 1787:] The best result is obtained when the finger delays its rocking until half the duration of the note is ove r.

Ex. 229. C. P. E. Bach, *Essay*, Berlin, 1753, III, 20, *Tragen der Töne* and *Bebung*:

(746) Franz Rigler, *Anleitung zum Klavier*, Vienna [1779]:

'[*Tragen der Töne* is] when the key is somewhat slowly rocked [but *Bebung*] when the tone is rocked quite clearly according to the number of dots, without actual repetition of the finger stroke.'

(747) D. G. Türk, *Klavierschule*, Leipzig and Halle, 1789, Sect. 88:

'The *Bebung* (Fr. *Balancement*; It. *Tremolo*) can only be used to good effect on long notes, and in pieces of a melancholy character. It is usually indicated [as at Ex 230 (a) or (b)] or by the word *tremolo* [as at Ex. 230 (c)]. The rendering would be somewhat as shown at [Ex. 230 (d) and (e)].

'One holds the finger on the key for the full duration of the note, and tries by gently reiterated pressures to reinforce the tone. I need hardly say that there has to be a relaxation after each pressure, yet the finger must not leave the key.

'This ornament can only be performed on a clavichord, and indeed on a very good one.

'One must not use the *Bebung* too often, and must avoid the distressing exaggeration caused by using too much pressure.'

Ex. 230. Türk, *loc. cit.*, *Bebung* on the clavichord:

Ex. 231. Georg Simon Löhlein, *Clavier-Schule*, Leipzig and Züllichau, 1765–81, fifth ed., Züllichau and Freystadt, 1791, p. 19:

'The performance of this work, which is called Tragen der Töne, can only be done well on the clavichord' (aus dem Claviere).

In addition to its expressive value, the normal vibrato of the clavichord is useful in picking out an entry or leading part in contrapuntal solo music, by giving that part an additional significance.

3. THE PIANO

(a) The piano of Mozart's generation, now distinguished by its early name of forte-piano, has in its full-size concert version (not a very large instrument) a light efficient Viennese action and a small but extremely colourful tone of remarkable charm and beauty.

To produce this tone successfully requires a touch nearer to that of the harpsichord than to that of a modern grand piano. It can easily be killed by insensitive handling, when it becomes flat and muffled. The player has to feel his way to the right combination of delicacy and firmness. The proper sonority of the instrument is remarkably warm and generous, though not very loud.

(b) The grand piano of Beethoven's maturity is a more robust instrument, particularly if it has an English action of the kind which gave Beethoven so little pleasure as is now thought, when he was presented with a Broadwood in the year 1817. The tone still remains smaller, but also more colourful, than the present grand; the player must still adapt his touch until he can bring out the full, glowing sonority.

(c) The grand piano of Chopin's generation is the last to retain any of the old lightness and colourfulness of tone, and in this kind is an almost perfect instrument, lacking only the extremest rapidity of repetition. Both this and the foregoing are well worth cultivating.

(d) The little 'square' (actually oblong) pianos still often encountered in the sale-room under the flattering title of Spinet are quite agreeable if well restored, but of limited tone and expressive scope.

4. THE ORGAN

(a) The very rare specimens of unspoilt renaissance organs suggest a preference for voicing so forward that every attack is a small explosion of sound; while the tone favoured is fiery beyond belief, with a glorious medley of mixtures capable of maximum contrast but minimum gradation.

The baroque organ, of which quite a number of fine specimens survive, is considerably softened down, but by comparison with an organ of the nineteenth century is still a virile and responsive musical instrument. Particularly towards the end of the period, when baroque was merging into rococo, the variety of qualities and colourings became extremely numerous. In this respect, there were some remarkable anticipations of the 'orchestral' organ of the Liszt period; but the wind pressure was still much lower and the attack much more positive. The eighteenth century civilised the organ, but the nineteenth debased it. The twentieth has made remarkable amends, with a large and growing number of excellent new organs built on baroque principles and well-informed organists to make good use of them.

Even with low wind pressure, tracker action can grow heavy, but it has the great advantage of feeling more alive to the player than either pneumatic or electric.

(b) What we know of baroque registration suggests that bold contrasts continued to be more in favour than gradations. A baroque organ is likely to be rich in mixtures (stops combining intervals not at the unison or octave—e.g. tenths or twelfths) and mutations (stops producing one such interval, and therefore having the effect of mixtures when added to foundation stops). These lend themselves to strong colourings rather than to subtle blends and grades. The transparent baroque reeds are also full of clean, strong colour. Such an organ need never sound muddy or opaque; and the sharpness of the voicing makes it far more interesting than the bland tones and smooth attack subsequently favoured.

The swell-box was an early eighteenth-century invention, not much exploited till the nineteenth. Crescendos and diminuendos are not in the fundamental character of the organ. A skilful gradation of registers can give all the impression of climax or relaxation needed—especially if there is an assistant in the organ loft to help work the stops.

(c) Because of its sustained tone and lack of dynamic accentuation, the organ needs even more generous silences of phrasing and articulation than other instruments.

(d) In accompanying, the organ has to avoid not only being too loud, but too opaque for the accompanied parts.

(748) Friedrich Erhard Niedt, *Musicalische Handleitung*, *II*, 1706, ed. of 1721, XI, xiv:

'When only one or two parts sing or play, he needs on the manual merely the 8-foot Gedackt and no pedal at all; if there are more parts to accompany, he can bring in the Untersatz or sub-bass 16-foot [except in a bassetto passage; but] for a choir of eight, twelve or more . . . the 8-foot principal in the manual and in the pedal as sub-bass, another 8-foot octave. If the work is with trumpets and kettledrums, then in the pedal, besides the 8-foot octave, a trombone bass of 16-foot is brought in; the notes, however, must not be held on the whole or half of a bar [if written so], but rather just allowed to speak.'

(749) Johann David Heinichen, *Anweisung*, Hamburg, 1711, p. 226:

'In church recitatives, where one is dealing with sustained and humming pipe-work [the chords are held unembellished] till another chord follows, which is again held on [unless] the hands are quickly taken up again after striking a fresh chord . . . the better to hear and observe the singers or the instruments sometimes accompanying the recitative [or because] the bass sometimes stays on the same note and harmony for three, four or more bars and thus the pipe-work humming constantly through on one note can become unpleasant to the ear. All of which rests with the judgement and pleasure of the accompanist.'

(750) G. J. J. Hahn, *General-Bass-Schüler*, Augsburg, 1751, p. 57

'On organs [the chords in recitative] are struck simultaneously [*i.e.* not arpeggiated], and after they are struck the right hand is lifted and rests till the fresh chord.'

(751) C. P. E. Bach, *Essay*, II, Berlin, 1762, XXXVIII, 5:

'In a recitative with accompanying [orchestral] instruments of sustained tone, one holds on the organ only the bass-note in the pedals, one lifts up one's hands from the chords soon after striking them [because the tempering of the organ is unlikely to agree with the intonation of the orchestra if the passage is chromatic. See rest of passage at (411) in Ch. XXXII, 2 above].'

(752) J. S. Petri, *Anleitung*, Lauban, 1767, 2nd ed., Leipzig, 1782, p. 17:

'The organist [when accompanying] takes the chords short; [avoids reeds, mixtures and mutations; with a small church and organ, draws only] one 8-foot Gedackt, or, if this is too softly voiced, two 8-foot stops in the manual, and in the pedal a 16-foot or two at most, and again an 8-foot principal for the *forte*, and for the loudest *forte* a 4-foot, which however is better absent. And yet, when the singer comes in and the *piano* arrives, the 8-foot stop must be taken out, so that the bass does not overwhelm the *piano* of the violins and flutes. Moreover the notes must be taken off short. . . .' [But beware of exaggerating this as a mannerism.]

5. FINGERING

There is a very interesting general distinction between early systems of keyboard fingering and modern systems. The former exploit the natural differences of length and strength in the human digits, and their changes of position, as aids to good phrasing and articulation. The latter minimise these differences and changes, as an aid to facility and versatility.

All early systems assumed that there are good (strong) and bad (weak) digits, though not always quite agreed as to which is which. As far as possible, accented notes were to be allotted to good digits; unaccented notes to bad digits.

Modern systems assume that all the digits can be trained to sufficient strength and accuracy. Exceptions are allowed, but as far as possible the digits are treated on an equality.

In the early systems, it was customary to pass one of the middle fingers over another. On instruments with a light touch (and the majority of early keyboards were lighter than a modern piano) this can be done with great facility, but it is not fundamentally so smooth as passing the thumb beneath one of the middle fingers, or one of the middle fingers over the thumb, as in modern systems.

Very frequently indeed, original fingerings shown in early music make it not merely hard but impossible to make a smooth join between one hand position and the next. This was done with the deliberate intention of enforcing a silence of phrasing or articulation.

In the most advanced Spanish and English fingerings of the sixteenth and seventeenth centuries, the thumb was freely used, though not in its present function as the pivot on which changes of hand position are made. The French school of Couperin inherited these advanced fingerings, passing this legacy on to J. S. Bach, himself a partial but not a major innovator in this respect; thence C. P. E. Bach handed it down with further reforms which contained the seeds of modern fingering. But German fingering *before* J. S. Bach, and also to some extent Italian fingering, remained more primitive than elsewhere.

Because of their often very clear implications for phrasing and articulation, the early fingerings are always worth studying when they have been preserved. Is it also desirable to apply them in practice? Perhaps it is; but a practical compromise might be: no, with regard to passing one middle finger over another; mainly no, with regard to allotting important notes to 'good' fingers, but some use may be made of this often helpful principle; yes, with regard to using fingerings which enforce desirable silences of phrasing of articulation, wherever such fingerings can be worked out conveniently and effectively. See also Ch. XLVIII, 4, above.

Ex. 232. François Couperin, *L'Art de toucher*, Paris, 1716, ed. of 1717, (a), (c) specimen fingerings; (b), (d) the phrasing they imply:

[Right hand]

(752a) François Couperin, *L'Art de toucher le clavecin*, Paris, 1716, ed. of 1717, p. 10:

'A certain passage, being fingered in a certain way, produces a definite effect.

'The manner of fingering is a great help to good playing.'

On the harpsichord and clavichord, the principle of holding down notes of the same harmony for as long as fingers can be spared—see 1 (g) above—means that arpeggio-like figures will often need to be fingered as if for the corresponding chord.

POSTSCRIPT TO SECOND EDITION

There are full and excellent discussions of early keyboard fingerings both in Arnold Dolmetsch (*Interpretation . . .*) and in Eta Harich-Schneider's *Kunst des Cembalo-Spiels* (see my Bibl.).

The following confirms Rameau at (741) above.

(752b) C. P. E. Bach, *Essay*, I, Berlin, 1753, III, 18:

'When slurs appear over broken chords, one can keep the whole chord [sounding] at the same time.'

As with all such refinements, the occasions on which the notation shows any indication are few; the occasions on which they should be used are numerous. From the musical effects, I am certain that this building up of the sonority by holding down all possible harmony notes (except where considerations of phrasing or articulation preclude it) is fundamental to good harpsichord technique.

The harpsichord piece 'Les Bergeries' by Couperin appears in his Livre II, Ordre 6; a facsimile is included at the end of the Bach *Neue Ausgabe*, Ser. V, Bd. 4, *Kritischer Bericht*. It was copied by Anna Magdalena Bach into her famous notebook (Bach *Neue Ausgabe*, V, 4, p. 85). Couperin's notation (characteristically precise) shows at the start overlapping notes in the left hand; Anna Magdalena's copy shows only single notes. But if these are held down as they obviously should be held down, they overlap just as they are written in Couperin's own notation.

(752c) Michel de Saint-Lambert, *Principes du clavecin*, Paris, 1702, p. 41:

'There are passages, which without being Chords, become such by the manner in which the notes are managed, and by the rule which obliges one to hold down certain ones, until others have been touched.'

CHAPTER LXV

Choirs and Orchestras

1. LATE RENAISSANCE AND EARLY BAROQUE ENSEMBLES

The tendency of the sixteenth century was to complete the existing families of instruments. Whole (*i.e.* unmixed) consorts of voices, viols, recorders, crumhorns, shawms, *etc.*, were used for part music of which only the vocal was composed idiomatically, but the instrumental, even when it was borrowed vocal music or was composed in a vocal style, was often rendered idiomatic by its more or less impromptu embellishments. English seventeenth-century viol consorts are instrumentally composed.

Broken (*i.e.* mixed) consorts of shawms with trombones, cornetti with trombones and perhaps other combinations became to some extent standardised; but in the main this was an age of experiment. There was not yet any such concept as a standard orchestra.

(753) Francis Bacon, *Sylva Sylvarum*, London, 1626, Cent. III, Sect. 278:

'In that *Musick*, which we call *Broken Musick*, or Consort Music; Some *Consorts* of *Instruments* are sweeter than others. . . . As the *Irish Harp*, and *Base Viall* agree well: The *Recorder* and *Stringed Musick* agree well: *Organs* and the *Voice* agree well, *etc.* But the *Virginalls* and the *Lute*; Or the *Welch-Harp*; and the *Irish-Harp*; Or the *Voice* and *Pipes* alone, agree not so well; But for the *Melioration* of *Musick* there is yet much left (in this Point of *Exquisite Consorts*) to try and enquire.'

A characteristic broken consort of late Elizabethan England is seen in a painting (*c.* 1596) of scenes from Sir Henry Unton's life: his wedding banquet was enlivened by a masque accompanied by violin, gamba, flute, lute, cittern and (?) pandora, with a drummer among the masquers. This is virtually the same as:

(754) Thomas Morley, London, 1599:

'The First Booke of Consort Lessons, made by divers exquisite Authors, [and set with elaborately ornamental divisions for] the Treble Lute, the Pandora, the Cittern, the Base-Violl, the Flute and Treble-Violl.'

Philip Rosseter's *Lessons for Consort* (London, 1609) are for the same instruments; and they all appear in Praetorius' list of instruments which might be assembled in an 'English Consort' (*Syntagma*, III,

Wolfenbüttel, 1619, p. 5). His own suggestions for instruments to be combined in the half-improvised orchestration discussed in Ch. IX, 3 above include the following.

(755) Michael Praetorius, *Syntagma*, III, Wolfenbüttel, 1619, p. 140:

'Foundation [continuo] instruments, such as: wind organ; positive [chamber organ]; regal [small reed organ of special type]; great harpsichord.

'Ornamenting [melodic] instruments, such as: viols; violins; cornetti; flutes; recorders; shawms; trombones; cornamusas [? soft variety of crumhorn]; crumhorns; curtals [bassoons]; *etc.*

'Instruments in common [sharing in either function], such as: spinet; lute; theorbo [lute with extended bass strings]; double cittern [bass cittern]; harp; lyra [da braccio]; chitarrone [bass lute].' [See (129), Ch. IX, 3, above.]

Praetorius' list has a considerable similarity with the (not complete) list of instruments at the beginning of Monteverdi's *Orfeo* of 1607.

(756) Claudio Monteverdi, *Orfeo*, perf. Mantua, 1607, instruments:

'Two harpsichords, two double-bass viols [violones], ten violins, a double harp, two little violins in the French style [tuned higher than treble violins], two arch-lutes, two [chamber] organs with wood pipes, three gambas, four trombones, a regal [diminutive reed organ], two cornetts, a little flute "alla Vigesima seconda", a clarino [trumpet for high playing] and three muted trumpets [a few other instruments appear in the score].'

At only a few places in the score are instruments specified individually. There are some tuttis for 'all instruments'; various smaller groupings are sometimes mentioned; but the main disposal of the forces is left to the performers. Some of the most interesting specified passages are for two violins; for two cornetti; for chamber organ and lute; for the double harp.

In arranging music of this transitional period, we have a very free hand in our choice of instruments; and provided we produce effective orchestrations which lie within the contemporary possibilities and suit the music, we can hardly be too enterprising.

2. THE STANDARD BAROQUE FOUNDATION OF STRINGS

In Monteverdi's orchestra, the strings already take their modern function of providing the foundation, but often in five parts, like early baroque ensemble writing in the main. The French retained this preference through the seventeenth century; elsewhere, three essential parts became customary, with or without a fourth part for violas which tended to be less independent. This was in keeping with the baroque tendency to strengthen the interest of the outside parts at the expense of the middle. Frequently the violas were set to double the bass an octave up, with decidedly inopportune results when they were not alert enough to avoid getting above the melody. Concerti grossi with three concertante solo parts but four ripieni orchestral parts were even published for optional performance as trio sonatas, in which form the omitted viola part is very little missed.

(757) Arcangelo Corelli, Op. VI, ed. J. Walsh, London, early 18th cent.:

'XII Great Concertos or Sonatas, for two Violins and a Violoncello or for two Violins more, a Tenor [Viola], and a Thorough-Bass: which may be doubled at Pleasure.'

3. THE UNSTANDARDISED WIND

Adam Carse (*The Orchestra in the Eighteenth Century*, Cambridge, 1940), has established by an extensive examination of scores, parts, and lists of players that wind instruments not necessarily specified either on the title-page or in the music or even provided with parts were normally required, in suitable works of the main baroque period, to double existing string or voice parts (notes not on the instrument concerned could be left out, transposed an octave, or changed to other notes in the same harmony). This applies especially to oboes and bassoons; but also to flutes, clarinets, horns, trumpets, and associated with the trumpets in traditional rhythms, drums.

The doubling was not continuous. It might proceed for a movement or only for a passage; and it was intended as a deliberate contrast of sonority comparable to registration on the organ or harpsichord. Often the only written indication is an instruction to cease doubling, without previous notice that doubling was intended: *e.g.* senza oboi (without the oboes) or senza fagotti (without the bassoons) in a score not otherwise mentioning these instruments (we also find senza violini, violoncelli soli, *etc.*). There may be no indication whatsoever.

That is a different principle of orchestration from ours. We touch in a shade, withdraw it; blend a momentary mixture, follow it with another; use our instruments largely for passing coloration. Baroque musicians coloured entire melodic lines and preferred their contrasts mainly by long sections. Such broad contrasts as these are less affected than our kaleidescopic patterns by the substitution, for example, of a flute for an oboe or an oboe for a clarinet (still a comparatively rare instrument in the mid-eighteenth century). But they are affected if we fail to double with wind at all.

Having, unlike the solo wind of the present orchestra, mainly this ripieno function of doubling, baroque wind went usually two or more to a part. A strong force of oboes and bassoons added to a relatively small string department gives a pungent, clean sonority immensely effective in much baroque music, and confirmed by evidence such as the Foundling Hospital Minute books, which reveal the following orchestra for the last performance there of Handel's *Messiah* under his own direction: 14 violins (first and second); 6 violas; 3 cellos; 2 double-basses; 4 oboes; 4 bassoons; 2 horns; 2 trumpets with kettledrums; continuo. The four bassoons on the bass-line make a particularly magnificent contribution. No authenticated horn parts are known; they may have doubled or more probably alternated with the trumpets, reinforced choruses, *etc*. See also 6 below.

Besides their ripieno functions, wind instruments had solo or obbligato parts, sometimes (especially on the trumpet and the horn) of phenomenal difficulty. Here every effort should be made to use the instrument named, since it will have been chosen for special effect.

In the main baroque period, trombones were band and church instruments; Handel occasionally used them in oratorio, and J. S. Bach gave them doubling parts in a number of his cantatas, but they entered the regular orchestra, by way of opera, only during the second half of the eighteenth century.

4. THE INDISPENSABLE CONTINUO

In church music, the main baroque continuo instrument was the organ. It has been argued by Arthur Mendel ('On the Keyboard Accompaniments to Bach's Leipzig Church Music', *Mus. Quart.*, July, 1950, XXXVI, 3, p. 339) that even for the accompaniment of recitative in church music, the organ, not the harpsichord, was J. S. Bach's normal instrument; but played in a very light and detached style. See Ch. XXXII, 2 above; *but also* Ch. XXXI, 6a, third paragraph of (404).

In secular music, the normal baroque continuo instrument is the harpsichord, played as a rule by the musician in charge; in large ensembles, a second harpsichord might carry the bulk of the continuo, leaving him freer to direct as well as play.

(758) Joachim Quantz, *Essay*, Berlin, 1752, XVII, i, 16:

'I assume that the harpsichord is present in all ensembles, whether small or large.'

It is not always necessary for the continuo harpsichord to be heard very distinctly in the orchestra; it still has a binding effect and puts a certain edge on the sonority. On the other hand, it can be unduly obliterated by a large orchestra playing somewhat opaquely, and it should then be duplicated or amplified or both.

A keyboard continuo is still historically correct for Haydn, but it is not really necessary, owing to the added richness of the composed inner parts.

5. THE CONDUCTOR

Both larger and smaller ensembles are shown in baroque and pre-baroque pictures and descriptions as being conducted with the hand, with a baton (late 15th-cent. on), with a roll of paper (common baroque usage: Roger North, *The Musicall Grammarian*, Hereford Cathedral MS R.11 xlii, *f.* 36v., has 'for consort nothing like a roll of paper in the hand of an artist; without noise and above board'), with a long staff (Lully's downfall), or with the leader's violin bow often in a delicate division of authority with the harpsichordist's head. Conducting *in the normal modern manner* is extremely desirable under most circumstances. But the conductor should show great consideration for the singer's wishes, especially with regard to tempo and dynamics. The limits within which fine virtuoso singing is possible are often very narrow.

6. SOME TYPICAL BAROQUE CHOIRS AND ORCHESTRAS

(Trumpeters and drummers were usually drawn from the military retinue: hence they are often not listed below. Sometimes, on the other hand, the entire corps is listed.)

(759) J. S. Bach, memorandum, Leipzig, 1730, quoted in full by Spitta, *Bach*, Engl. tr. London, 1884–85, II, p. 240:

'[To each church choir] there must belong, at least, three trebles, three alti, three tenors, and as many basses . . . [as a minimum] a motet may be sung with, at least, two voices to each part. (N.B.—How much better it would be if the *Coetus* were so arranged that four singers could be available for each part, each choir thus consisting of sixteen persons.)

'[The orchestra should be] two or even three . . . Violino Primo. Two or three Violino . . . Secundo. Two Viola . . . Primo. Two Viola . . . Secundo. Two . . . Violoncello. One . . . Double Bass. Two or three according to need . . . Oboes. One or two . . . Bassoons. Three . . . Trumpets. One . . . Drum.

'In all eighteen persons, at least, for the instruments. N.B.—Added to this since church music is also written for flutes (*i.e.*—they are either *à bec* or *Traversieri*, held sideways), at least two persons are needed for that; altogether, then, twenty instrumentalists.'

(760) Johann Adolf Scheibe, *Critische Musikus*, Hamburg, 1737, *etc.*, collected ed., Leipzig, 1745, I, 78th article:

'[4 to 5 first and second violins, 2 violas, 3 to 4 cellos and basses, and a few bassoons, at the least if the music includes trumpets and drums, violins should be doubled by oboes, and if oboes are present, bassoons must double the bass.]'

TABLE XV: proportions of wind to strings recommended by Joachim Quantz, *Essay*, Berlin, 1752, XVII, i, 16:

Vn. I	Vn. II	Violas	Cellos	Basses	Flutes	Oboes	Bassoons	Horns
2	2	1	1	1	–	–	–	–
3	3	1	1	1	–	–	1	–
4	4	2	2	2	2	2	2	(2)
5	5	2	3	2	2	2	2	(2)
6	6	3	4	2	4	4	3	(2)

Compare 2 above. The proportions are somewhat short on violas, and may be contrasted with the proportions shown in 3 above for the orchestra performing Handel's *Messiah:* better balanced, and perhaps a better model for Handel or Bach, where the orchestra should not be too big but not too small either. Notice the strong bass section very rightly advocated below:

(761) Charles Avison, *Essay*, London, 1752, p. 113:

'[For concerti grossi:] And *1st*, I would propose, exclusive of the four [solo] principal Parts which must always be complete, that the Chorus of other Instruments should not exceed the Number following, *viz.*, six *Primo* and four *secondo Repienos*; four *Repieno Basses*, and two *Double Basses*, and a *Harpsichord*. A lesser Number of Instruments, near the same Proportion, will also have a proper Effect, and may answer the Composer's Intention; but more would probably destroy the just Contrast, which should always be kept up between the *Chorus* and *Solo*: For in this Case the Effect of two or three single Instruments would be lost and over-powered by the succession of too grand a *Chorus*, and to double the *Primo*, and *Seconds Concertino*, or *Violoncello* in the *Solo*, would be an Impropriety in the Conduct of our Musical Oeconomy, too obvious to require any thing to be said on that Head. It may be objected, perhaps, that the Number of *Basses*, in the above Calculations, would be found too powerful for the *Violins*: But as the latter Instruments are in their Tone so clear, sprightly and piercing, and as they rather gain more Force by this Addition, they will always be heard; However, if it were possible, there should never be wanting a *Double Bass*; especially in a Performance of full Concertos, as they cannot be heard to any Advantage without that NOBLE FOUNDATION of their Harmony. . . .

[p. 126:] 'When Concertos are performed [as trio sonatas, or as quartets] with three or four Instruments only, it may not be amiss to play the Solo Parts *Mezzo Piano*.'

This last is not very good advice: the effect is not to make the solo passages sound like solos as opposed to ripienos, but merely to make them sound weak. It is a better recourse to take out the string bass for the solo passage, and bring it in again for the ripieno passage; but in any case, not all concertos are suitable for this treatment.

(762) Friedrich Wilhelm Marpurg, *Historisch-kritische Beyträge*, Berlin, 1754, *etc.*, passim:

'[1754: Berlin, King of Prussia: Capellmeister Graun, eight singers, sixteen members of ballet, two decorators, one opera librettist; twelve violins, three violas, four cellos, one gamba, two double basses, five flutes, three oboes, four bassoons, two horns, two harpsichords, one theorbo; the king is mentioned specially as solo flute.

'Prince Heinrich: director and harpsichord Kirnberger; four violins, one viola, one cello, one double bass, one flute, one oboe, one bass singer.

'Prince Carl: five violins (probably including the director since none other is mentioned), one viola, one cello, one double bass, one flute, three oboes, one bassoon, two horns, one harpsichord, one harp.

'Gotha, chamber and chapel: Capellmeister, Georg Benda; two female singers; one male soprano, one male alto, one tenor, two basses; six violins, one double-bass (violone), two oboes, one bassoon, two horns, two organists, one lute.

'Breslau, Bishop's chapel: five male singers (including two sopranos and one alto); seven violins (including Konzertmeister Alexander Alberti), one viola, one double bass, two flutes/oboes, two bassoons, two horns, one harpsichord.

'Grafen von Branicki in Pohlen, chapel: four first violins, four second violins, one viola, one cello, one double bass, two flutes, two oboes, two bassoons, two horns.

'Paris, opera: eight female solo singers, four male altos, one tenor, seven baritones; chorus of seventeen women and twenty-one men; orchestra of two leaders, sixteen violins, six violas, twelve cellos, gambas and double basses (two were gambas), six flutes and oboes, three bassoons, two horns, one harpsichord; seven female and two male solo dancers, seventeen female and fifteen male chorus dancers.

'1755: Paris, Concerts Spirituels; "many of whom also belong to the opera": Director Roger, accompanist on the organ M. Cheron, four female and four male solo singers, choir of six female and six male sopranos, six male altos, seven tenors, five high basses, eight low basses; orchestra of sixteen violins, two violas, six cellos, two double basses, one flute, four oboes, three bassoons.

'1756: Dresden, King's chapel and chamber-music: Director von Dieskau, one poet, ober-Capellmeister J. H. Hasse, vice-Capellmeister vacant, two church-composers, one ballet-composer; five female and six male sopranos, one female and three male altos, three tenors, four basses, one Concert-meister, one Pantaleon (variety of dulcimer—in total disrepair by 1772), sixteen violins (including the Concert-meister), four violas, four cellos, two double basses, three flutes, five oboes, four bassoons, two horns, two organists.

'Mannheim, court chapel and chamber-music: one Intendant, Capellmeister for the church Grua, for the theatre Holtzbauer, Concertmeister and director of instrumental chamber music Stamitz, of instrumental church-music Toeschi; three female and three male sopranos, two male altos, three tenors, two basses; ten first violins (including Stamitz and Cannabich), ten second violins, four violas, two solo and two ripieno cellos, two double basses, two flutes, two oboes, two bassoons, four horns, two organists; corps of twelve trumpets and two kettledrums.

'1757: Schwarzburg-Rudolstadt, chapel; Capellmeister C. G. Scheinpflug, who also takes the role of Concertmeister and "in chamber-music and other concerts conducts with the violin"; one female and one male soprano, one male alto, one tenor (the Capellmeister), one bass; seven other violins (of whom three play solos, two compose and two play the trumpet), three violas (of whom two play the oboe), three cellos (of whom one plays the gamba and two play the trumpet), two double basses, two oboes (of whom one plays solos, composes, plays first violin and flute), one bassoon (who plays solos, composes, plays first violin, and flute), three trumpets (of whom one composes and plays the cello), two horns (of whom one plays solos)—but such "two-handedness", though not always mentioned, was general.

'Anhalt-Zerbst, chapel: Capellmeister J. F. Fasch, one Concertmeister, one male soprano, one male alto, one tenor, seven other violins, one viola, one cello (also plays organ), one double-bass (vacant), two oboes, one bassoon, one harpsichord.

'Salzburg, archbishop's music: Capellmeister E. Eberlin, vice-Kapellmeister Lolli, three court composers—Cristelli (also cello), Leopold Mozart (also violin and leads the orchestra), Ferdinand Seidl (also violin); eight other violins (one also flute, one also horn, one also bassoon, oboe, flute, horn, one also horn, one also cello), two violas (one also oboe) two cellos (both also violin), two double bass, three oboes and flutes (two also violin), four bassoon (two also oboe), two horns (one also violin, one also cello), one trombone (also violin, cello, horn), three organists (also harpsichord, one also violin and tenor); solo singers, five male sopranos (three vacant), three tenors, two basses, with additions from the choir; fifteen boy singers, their prefect and their preceptor; three male altos, nine tenors, nine basses (Chorherren) and one male alto, three tenors, four basses (Choralisten—four of these can play double bass); and three trombones (alto, tenor and bass, for church music); ten trumpets (seven also violin, one also viola, two also cello—two vacancies); two kettledrums (also violin); one organ-builder, one lute and violin maker, three beadles.

'Mecklenburg-Schwerin Hof-Capelle: a titled person as Capell-director; court-composer Hertel; one soprano, one tenor, one bass; soloists—one violin, one cello, one flute (also bassoon), one oboe (also flute); accompanists—six violins, two violas, two cellos, one double bass, two flutes, two oboes, one bassoon, two horns, four trumpets and drums, one harpsichordist (also composes), one organist (vacant), one copyist, one beadle.]'

I feel a particular attachment to that beadle. He was the last piece of contemporary evidence I originally introduced.

CHAPTER LXVI

Acknowledgements and Conclusion

1. PREVIOUS ACKNOWLEDGEMENTS

It is a pleasure to renew here my original warm thanks to my friends and colleagues: first to my old and much revered master, Arnold Dolmetsch, whose pioneering genius first set my young spirit in pursuit of early music; next to Marco Pallis, who fostered and guided my fresh enthusiasm, and to Richard Nicholson, who shared it; to my boyhood friend, Carl Dolmetsch; then to my first team-mates in the Donington Consort, Carl Pini, Penelope Howard and Niso Ticciati; thereafter to those many subsequent helpers who included H. K. Andrews, Anthony Baines, Eric Blom, David Boyden, Ray Byham, James Coover, Thurston Dart, Walter Emery, Vincent Duckles, Miss M. Fagadini, Paul Hamburger, A. Hyatt King, Rupert Bruce Lockhart, Arthur Mendel, Terence Miller, my wife Gloria Rose, my admirable typist Dolores Ryan, Mrs. Elizabeth Tomalin, Walter Rubsamen, Nicholas Slonimsky, and the publishing firms of Bärenreiter and Macmillan, and later Stainer and Bell, for permission to reproduce matter at their disposition, as well as to the Fellowes Memorial Fund for their grant towards my working expenses.

2. PRESENT ACKNOWLEDGEMENTS

To the University of Iowa, to the Director of our School of Music, Himie Voxman, and to the Director of our Department of Musicology, Albert Luper, I am under an ever-present obligation, for their sustained support and encouragement. I have, moreover, been awarded an Old Gold Summer Faculty Research Fellowship in 1966, and a Research Assignment during the first semester of 1970, together with further leaves of absence. I wish to state here my warm appreciation of this support, which has allowed me to keep abreast with the rapid development of this field of study, and also in my other field of opera. My friendship with the Voxman and Luper families has been warm indeed.

Our unusually fine Music Library, under the chief librarianship of Rita Benton, has been of crucial value. And I wish to thank personally members of our library staff who have been kind and helpful to me far beyond the mere call of duty: Beverley Bailey, Sara Ebert, Elizabeth

McWilliams, Martha Sacchini, Melody Scherubel. Librarians and directors elsewhere who have most notably assisted me include: Frank C. Campbell, Isabel Clark, Vladimir Féderov, Diana Haskell, Bernard Huys, A. Hyatt King, Karl-Heinz Köhler, William Lichtenwanger, Stanley J. Osborne, Susan T. Sommer. I also thank my most helpful graduate assistant, Sharon Kay Hoke.

I must next express a cordial debt of gratitude to my friend and colleague, Frederick Neumann, whose unusual kindness in allowing me to see his forthcoming work on baroque ornamentation helped me to bring myself up-to-date, both where we have been able and where we have been unable to reach the same conclusions; for it is a complex field.

The help for which I wish to thank the following of my friends and colleagues ranges from brief words snatched in the corridors of busy AMS meetings all the way to long and painstaking assistance, often with documentary support: Putnam Aldrich, Sol Babitz, Eva Badura-Skoda, Betty Bang, Janet Beat, David Boyden, George Buelow, Albert Cohen, Michael Collins, Frederick Crane, Sister Victorine Fenton, Howard Ferguson, Edward Foreman, David Fuller, Edwin Hanley, William Hibbard, Wiley Hitchcock, Paul Hodges, Erwin Jacobi, Harry Johnstone, Donald Katz, Gordon Kinney, Gerhard Krapf, David Lasocki, Lewis Lockwood, J. Buchanan MacMillan, Philip Miller, Jerrold Moore, Anthony Newcomb, Marco Pallis, William Pepper, Dean L. Quigley, Edward Reilly, Richard Rephann, Sandra Rosenblum, Don Smithers, Bernard Bailly de Surcy, Edward Tarr, Geneviève Thibault Comtesse de Chambure, Robert Warner, Neal Zaslaw.

My typist in Iowa City, Jerry Nyall, does work which not only looks very nice but is almost uncannily free of error. Her patience under my innumerable revisions and redrafts has never failed, and I thank her warmly here.

My late wife Gloria Rose was a colleague in a thousand. She made our bibliography into an instrument of precision, and my book all through is the better for our many discussions, shop talk at its happiest. How much her companionship meant to me I need hardly add, and it seems almost impertinent to thank her here. But I do. I miss her very much.

3. CONCLUSION

The only conclusion I wish to draw at the moment is that I have no conclusion I wish to draw. The interpretation of early music is so obviously a continuing experiment.

APPENDICES

Ligatures

I am indebted to the late Gerald Hayes for the following information
on ligatures, culled from Thomas Morley's *Plaine and Easie Introduction
to Practicall Musicke*, London, 1597, but compared also with other late
renaissance authorities. For full information, see Willi Apel, *The
Notation of Polyphonic Music, 900–1600.*

The large or Maxima [nota] having become virtually obsolete, the
main note-values were:

Ex. 233:

First Notes

   (a) When the first note has no tail:

   (1) if the ligature falls

Ex. 234:

the first note is a Long.

   (2) If the ligature *rises* to the second note

Ex. 235:

the first note is a Breve.

(b) When the first note has an upward tail on the left-hand side:
   If the ligature either rises or falls to the second note

Ex. 236:

then the first note, *and also the second note*, is a Semibreve.

(c) When the first note has a downward tail on the left-hand side:

If the ligature either rises or falls to the second note

Ex. 237:

the first note is a Breve.

Middle Notes

(d) With the exception of the second note mentioned in (b) all the 'inside' notes are Breves.

Ex. 238:

Final Notes

(e) When the final note is a 'square note':

(1) If the preceding note is above it

Ex. 239:

then the final note is a Long.

(2) if the preceding note is below it, and it has no tail

Ex. 240:

then the final note is a Breve. With a tail, it is a Long.

(f) If the note is oblique, rising or falling

Ex. 241:

then the final note is a Breve, unless rule (b) makes it a Semibreve.

Dotted Notes

(g) Any note in a ligature may have its value increased by one half by the addition of a dot.

Ex. 242:

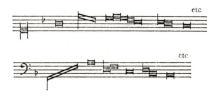

Ex. 243a from Morley would read as at Ex. 243b, or with the time values divided by four for modern convenience, as at Ex. 243c.

Ex. 243a:

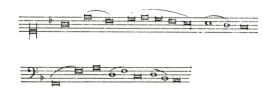

Ex. 243b:

Ex. 243c:

The above conventions are those which Gerald Hayes, on the basis of his wide knowledge of late renaissance treatises, considered to be as nearly standard at that period as can be established from the conflict of evidence. They may be considered in the setting of the findings summarized by Thurston Dart in his valuable article in *Grove's Dictionary of Music and Musicians*, 5th ed., London, 1954, Vol. VI, 'Notation', where the entire subject is covered in the most practical manner. He makes it as easy to understand as any one is ever likely to do; but no treatment of it can be very easy and at the same time true. Just interpreting the note values of pre-baroque music is a specialised and far from simple study.

Figured Bass: Three Realisations

Ex. 244: N. Pasquali, *Thorough-Bass Made Easy*, Edinburgh, 1757:

The above example illustrates exactly the following:

(763) Francesco Gasparini, *L'Armonico pratico al cimbalo*, Venice, 1708, ed. of 1754, p. 74:

'To introduce accompaniments in Recitatives with some sort of good taste, one must spread the Chords, almost [which to a modern performer means considerably] arpeggiating, but not continuously. For when the Harmony of the note has been heard, one must hold on to the keys, and allow the Singer to satisfy himself and sing as he pleases, and according to the expressiveness of the words; and not annoy him or disturb him with a continuous arpeggio or runs of passages up and down, as some do.'

Ex. 245: Right-hand imitation of subject, J. D. Heinichen, *General-Bass*, Dresden, 1728, I, vi, 40:

Ex. 245A. Aless. Scarlatti, cantata, 'Da sventura a sventura', as in Naples, Cons. MS 34.5.2. *ff.* 2–6v, Bologna, Cons. MS. BB/324, Cambridge, Fitz. Mus. MS. 24–F–17, *ff.* 57v. *ff.*, and other MSS; lightly imitative accompaniment by the composer or a contemporary:

Ornamentation

The following variants on Robert Johnson's 'Care-charming Sleep' were communicated to members of the International Musicological Society by Vincent Duckles and are reproduced here by kind permission.

Ex. 246:

Ex. 246A. M. de la Barre, *Airs a deux parties*, Paris, 1669, pp. 12 ff., slight additional ornamentation at 2nd couplet of vocal sarabande:

Ex. 247:

Ex. 248. J.-B. Cartier, *L'Art du Violon*, Paris, [1798] follows:

ADAGIO de Mʳ. TARTINI. Varié de plusieurs façons différentes, tres utiles aux personnes

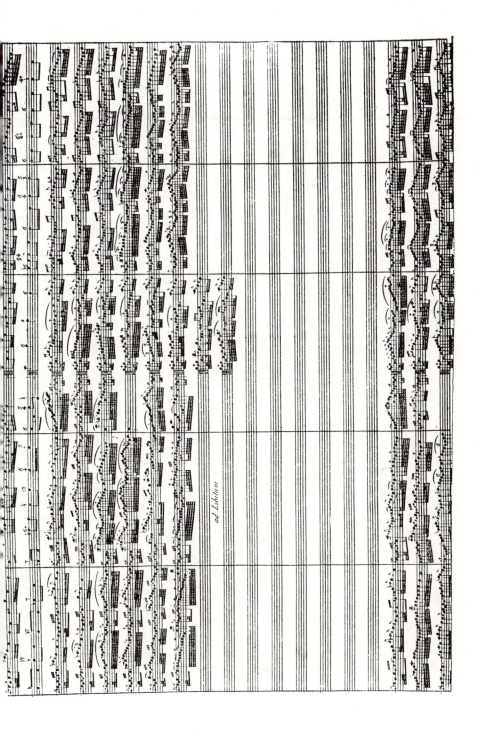

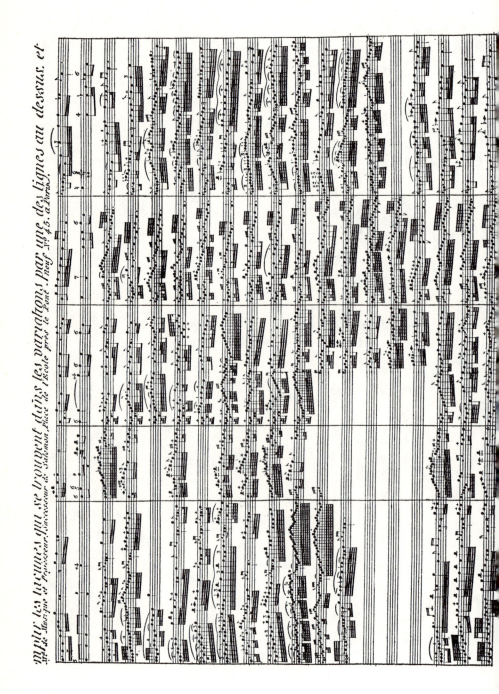

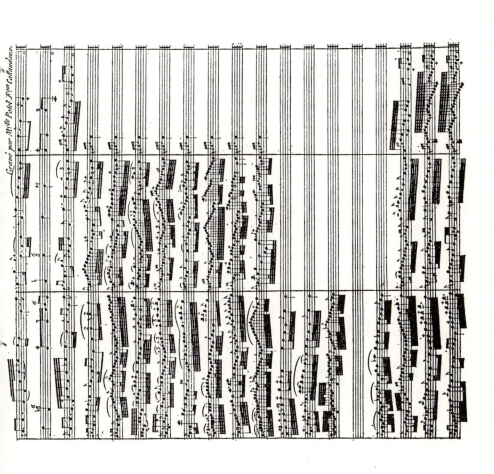

APPENDIX IV

Orchestral Improvisation

The following is a summary of an article by my wife, Dr. Gloria Rose, in the *Journal of the American Musicological Society* (JAMS), XVIII, Fall, 1965, pp. 382–393. The reader is referred to this article for the full evidence and argument.

Agazzari, at (129) on pages 171–172 above, like Praetorius a dozen years later in imitation of him, speaks of accompaniment in general. They certainly had opera in mind; but not only opera.

Agazzari's treatise of 1607 was reprinted entire in the continuo part of his *Sacrarum cantionum* (Venice, 1608): *sacred* motets 'cum basso ad organum'; yet the treatise must have been regarded as applicable. Agazzari's motets *Sacre laudes . . .* Lib. II (Rome, 1603) have 'Bassus ad Organum et Musica instrumenta'.

(764) Adriano Banchieri, *Ecclesiastiche sinfonie dette canzoni in aria francese, a quatro voci, per sonare, et cantare, et sopra un basso seguente concertare entro l'organo*, Venice, 1604, Preface:

'If you wish to perform them with voices and instruments . . . I should not neglect to say that within a few days [in fact three years!] Signor Agostino Agazzari, the very famous musician and organist, will publish a treatise which is a work useful for those who play concerted music, and necessary for those who wish to learn how to play freely over the basso seguente.'

Banchieri's *Conclusioni nel suono dell'organo* (Bologna, 1609) contains a letter from Agazzari, dated 25 April 1606 in Rome, 'from which one arrives at a knowledge of the style to be observed in concerting organ, voices and instruments'. It is substantially identical with the corresponding sections of Agazzari's treatise of a year later. He calls it 'a draft of the style which these Roman gentlemen musicians use in concerting voices, keyboard instruments, bowed and string instruments with organ'. (Peri, Caccini and Cavalieri, incidentally, were all born in Rome.)

Madrigals, too, were still performed in the seventeenth century, as they had been in the sixteenth, on voices, or on instruments, or on both voices and instruments. A typical title is Giovanni Valentini's *Fifth book of madrigals, divided into three parts: in the first, there are madrigals*

606

for three parts concerted with instrument; in the second, scherzi for six parts concerted with instrument; in the third, madrigals for six parts to be sung without instrument (Venice, 1625). Domenico Mazzocchi actually published his *Partitura de' madrigali* . . . (Rome, 1638) in score so that 'the madrigals can be sung more freely, and if it is anyone's taste (this being different in everyone) to give an instrumental accompaniment likewise to madrigals which do not require it, he will be able to do so without effort. And because of this distinction, I have placed a basso continuo under the concerted madrigals, but the others I have left bare and plain, since I wished them to be sung unaccompanied' (Preface). 'These last eight are variously concerted' (p. 134). Viols (among other instruments) are suitable in range, and one 5-part madrigal (pp. 166–172) with 'Basso continuo se piace' (if you wish) is entitled 'Ruggiero à 5. per le Viole'. The preface adds that performers should 'concert the madrigals with deliberation before presenting them in public'. This cannot refer to mere simple doubling; it must imply some complexity either in the parts or in the instrumentation.

Madrigals instrumentally accompanied were prominent in sixteenth-century *intermedi*, of which the orchestras were extremely similar to the famous one recorded in the score of Monteverdi's *Orfeo*. That orchestra was not exceptional: it was typical. Caccini, Peri and Cavalieri were all involved, for example, in the *intermedi* to the performance of *La Pellegrina* at Florence in 1589: the orchestra was almost that of Monteverdi's list; all these composers used such orchestras for their operas although the scores do not record them. Peri's *Euridice* lists only the noble-born players out of instrumentalists, and does not even mention some of the necessary singers; the score includes melodic parts although only instruments of harmony are mentioned. Caccini's *Nuove Musiche* (Florence, 1602) includes the 'Final Chorus of [his opera] the *Rapimento di Cefalo* [produced at Florence in 1600] concerted among voices and instruments by seventy-five persons'. Guidotti's instructions for Cavalieri's *Rappresentatione* (Rome, 1600) call for 'a very large number of instruments . . . and all the instruments, as many as possible, should play in the Ritornelli' (which are scored in melodic parts though the only instrument of melody mentioned is one violin).

The following is conspicuously reminiscent of Agazzari:

(765) Pietro della Valle, 'Della musica dell'età nostra', 1640, quoted in A. Solerti, *Le origini del melodramma*, Turin, 1903, pp. 159–160:

'Playing in the company of other instruments does not require the artifices of counterpoint so much as the graces of art; for if the player is good, he does not have to insist so much upon making a display of his own art as upon accommodating himself to all the others. . . . Those who sing and play well have to give time to one another [when performing] in company, and they have to sport with gracefulness of imitations rather than with too subtle artifices of counterpoints. They will show their art in knowing how to repeat well and promptly what another [player] has done before; and in then giving room to the others and fit opportunity for them to repeat what they have done; and in this way, with a varied and no less artful manner, though [a manner] neither so difficult nor [requiring] such deep knowledge, they will make known to the others their own worth. This is done nowadays not only by the most excellent, but also by the ordinary players, and they know how to do it so well that I do not know how it could have been done better by those of the past, whom I have not heard. When one plays in the company of voices, the same thing I said about [playing with] instruments must take place, and much more so: because instruments when serving voices, as it were the leaders in music, must have no other aim than to accompany them well. . . . Playing in order to support a chorus has to be the most simple of all, with no artifice of counterpoint, but only with good concordances and pretty accompaniments, which should follow the voices gracefully.'

The following are small clues, but they cover the entire seventeenth century, and not only its beginning. Instrumental parts for the Sinfonie and Ritornelli are written out, but no instruments are specified, in Peri's *Euridice* (1600), Cavalieri's *Rappresentatione* (1600), Domenico Mazzocchi's *Catene d'Adone* (1626), Marco da Gagliano's *Flora* (1628). In *Flora*, the note in Act IV, 'let them play', is without music at all. In Agazzari's own *Eumelio* (Venice, 1606), the solo voices have only an unfigured bass; the choruses no written accompaniment; the Ritornelli are written only as a few bars of continuo. (We can at least take it that Agazzari's instructions apply to Agazzari.) Two Ritornelli in the fourth Intermedio of G. Giacobbi's *Aurora ingannata* (1607) have only a basso continuo written. So has the opening Sinfonia of Luigi Rossi's *Palazzo incantato* (1642); it is followed by a prologue sung solo to a figured bass (according to MSS Lat. 4388 and Lat. 4389 in the Vatican Library, Fondo Barberini) or to seven written-out parts and figured bass, according to Vatican Lib., Fondo Chigiano, MS Q.V.51 (but there the seven parts drop out on folio 6, leaving the continuo and a tantalising remark: 'with the usual accompaniment'); Bologna, Civico Museo Bibliografico Musicale; and London, Royal Coll. of Music. The note 'all the instruments enter' in Cavalli's *Didone* (perf. 1641) is without any written instrumental parts, and an 'aria with all the instruments' is accompanied only by basso continuo in the written score. In Pagliardi's *Numa Pompilio* (perf. 1674) the note 'trumpets which sound' is without written music. The Sinfonia of Act III in

Legrenzi's *Totila* (perf. 1677) has only a bass part written. In Franceschini's *Oronte di Menfi* (perf. 1676), many instrumental sections such as Ritornelli have only a basso continuo written. It is common to find dances named, but no music written, or only a bass part. As late as 1679, the *Mercure Galant* for April wrote of the performance that year of Palavicini's *Nerone*: 'forty instruments, of the best that could be found, played the Simphonie . . . recorders, trumpets, drums, viols and violins'. The Contarini collection of operas produced in Venice from 1639 to 1692 specifically includes: harpsichord, organ, violins, viols, trumpets, flutes, bassoons, drums; from other MS. sources we can add for Venetian opera: horns, cornetts, trombones and theorbos.

Doni's *Trattato della musica scenica* (c. 1635) complains of composers who spare themselves 'the trouble of instrumental pieces written expressly', adding that there, 'the tablature of a simple Basso continuo suffices'—and was presumably the copy on which both foundation and ornamenting instrumentalists improvised whatever was necessary to complete the music.

I should add that I agree with Dr. Rose's conclusions in this important matter.

Responsibility for Accidentals

1. ACCIDENTALS STILL A BAROQUE PROBLEM

(a) Problems over accidentals leave us a legacy of uncertainty into and (though decreasingly) through the baroque period.

(b) Problems for which no certain solutions can be found are often, in early music, problems for which no one right solution exists. We should probably look for good and workable accidentals rather than for definitive accidentals, and one performance, though it should be consistent in itself, may not need to be the same as another performance.

Every accidental introduced carries implications for ensuing accidentals; and working these out satisfactorily may be our chief concern. If they will not work out, it may be necessary to change the earlier decision; but there is often a choice of solutions, each sufficiently consistent and satisfactory in itself.

On the other hand, when one decision is seen to be a virtual necessity, other decisions before and after may thereby become virtual necessities as well.

(c) In my *Performers' Guide to Baroque Music*, much more extensive examples are discussed of problematical baroque accidentals; and a series of rules of thumb is set up for working them out in practice. I believe we may not have been doing enough (i) in sharpening the seven as leading note, and the six in conjunction with the seven; (ii) in flattening the peak note of a phrase as *una nota super la*; (iii) in recognising the hexachordal persistence of accidentals; and (iv) in recognising retrospective accidentals.

2. HEXACHORDALLY PROSPECTIVE ACCIDENTALS

(a) Although the hexachord, with its six solmisation syllables, remained a standard teaching method through the seventeenth century, and was only overtaken gradually (as in Loulié's influential *Elements*, Paris, 1690) by our seven-syllable method repeating at the octave, it is hard to find direct references to the implied effect of the hexachordal method on accidentals. This effect certainly was implied, however, so long as hexachordal syllables were taught and practised; for it is the syllables which tell the learner where the semitone interval comes, and he could never correctly alter the semitone except by mutating into the appropriate different hexachord. And a musician who may have long since left behind him the learning of his part by singing it to the correct haxachordal syllables presumably could not altogether leave behind him the habit of thinking in a hexachordal way about accidentals.

In the complex tonality of baroque music, nobody can have rationalised hexachordally beyond a certain point, especially when embarking upon chromatic modifications of any considerable richness. Thus I have spoken only of a hexachordal *tendency* for accidentals to persist in a part so long as it does not exceed the compass of a given hexachord. But other things being equal, I believe this tendency may be quite strong in baroque music, at least through the seventeenth century and perhaps on occasion even subsequently to that.

(b) An explicit, late medieval statement of the rule is as follows:

(765a) Johannes Tinctoris, *Liber de natura et proprietate tonorum*, 1476, in Coussemaker, Scriptorum, IV, Paris, 1876, p. 22:

'If [the sign ♭] is placed at the beginning of the lines, the whole [piece] will be sung with *B* flat (*per ♭ molle*). But if it is placed in any other part [of the lines], for so long as the hexachord (*deductio*) to which it is attached shall endure, for so long will the piece be subject to the flat (*tamdiu cantus ♭ mollaris erit*).'

3. RETROSPECTIVE ACCIDENTALS

(a) Retrospective accidentals are a class which in the first and second editions of the original version I described, but with insufficient emphasis and conviction: see Ch. V, 5 above. Earlier than that, Jeppeson, as I pointed out, had noticed the phenomenon, but not followed it up; and earlier still, Rudolf von Ficker ('Beiträge zur Chromatik des 14. bis 16. Jahrhunderts', *Studien zur Musikwissenschaft* II, 1914, pp. 18–19) warned us against taking as chromatic two notes of the same written pitch with an accidental placed between them but affecting both (which is, of course, actually one type of retrospective accidental, and in fact the same type as that noticed by Jeppeson).

But I think I have now established that the class of retrospective accidentals is much larger than this particular type of it; and also that, like so many problems over accidentals, it continued much longer and more commonly into the baroque period than has previously been recognised.

(b) It is characteristic of our entire difficulty over early accidentals that retrospective accidentals may often be suspected, but seldom proved.

As much damage may be done by wrongly assuming an accidental to be retrospective as by wrongly overlooking that it is retrospective. The wrong assumption usually soon shows in the music, however, and should not be hard to detect. Where it is hard to detect, it is harmless anyhow; and here we can simply say that either decision probably lies within the performer's option.

This principle, whereby of two (or more) equally musical solutions, both lying within the boundaries of the style, either is taken to be legitimately within the performer's option, and neither is taken to be definitive, is of the utmost importance to early interpretation, and has often been invoked in this present book. It is the only principle which adequately meets the case of early accidentals; and it is now being applied to them by the best workers in the field, for example by Lewis Lockwood in his important recent studies, for which see my Bibliography. I am merely suggesting here that we should carry it over from the renaissance into the baroque period.

The same accidental may be taken either as having or as not having retrospective force in passages where the music will accept either solution with equal success. It would not be possible then to argue that one is right or the other is wrong, unless the further consequences of one solution proved unacceptable over the piece as a whole.

(c) Nevertheless, quite enough instances of the retrospective accidental can be proved in order to establish its importance in early music, and its continuance in baroque music. I have illustrated a number of them in my *Performer's Guide*; but here is one example, not there given, which has the advantage of proving both the presence and the absence of retrospective force in a single passage of the mid-seventeenth century. The passage is characteristic, though much later baroque examples also occur.

Ex. 248A shows two matching occurrences of the same passage, in different keys. At (a) the soprano is notated with sufficient accidentals to be unambiguous, but the bass is ambiguous; for the first F can either be influenced retrospectively, or not be influenced retrospectively, by the sharp notated before the second F. But at (b), the soprano is notated ambiguously, while the bass is notated unambiguously, because the change of key has made it necessary to notate a flat before the first B, in order to give the same progression as before. Thus (since matching passages can reasonably be taken as confirming one another) the soprano at (a) confirms the retrospective soprano accidental at (b); while the bass at (b) confirms the non-retrospective bass accidental at (a).

And indeed, this is just as well. We might have got the retrospective intention of the soprano accidental at (b) in any case, since this formula (an ornamental resolution with all its appearances of the leading note, and not only the main one, sharpened) is a very common one, and once known, is easily recognised. But the bass at (a) is genuinely misleading; for a retrospective force from the notated F would be plausible enough, and though it does not give quite so strong a progression, might very readily played, at least the first time round, by any accompanist familiar with the retrospective convention.

Ex. 248A. Giuseppe Giamberti, 'O belle lagrimette che da gli occhi', *Raccolta d'arie spirituali a una, due, e tre voci di diversi excellentissimi autori*, ed. Vincenzo Bianchi, Rome, 1640, pp. 4–5:

4. CHANGING CONVENTIONS FOR LATER
BAROQUE ACCIDENTALS

(a) We have to take into account a very gradual and inconsistent transition, during and after the baroque period, in the conventions loosely governing the use of accidentals.

(b) Praetorius (*Syntagma musicum*, III, Wolfenbüttel, 1619, Cap. VIII, p. 31, has a passage almost the same as that from Aaron in 1529, quoted at (82) in Ch. VI, 1 above. Praetorius advises composers to write in clearly (*klärlich darbey schreiben*) the required accidentals, to prevent singers from falling into confusion, and especially those un-sophisticated town musicians and organists 'who do not understand Music, still less are able to sing correctly'. The assumption that sophisti-cated musicians should know what accidentals to use, but nevertheless may get confused unless they are shown by the composer, is interesting at this date.

(c) It was the earlier baroque tendency to cancel previous accidentals by ♯ or ♭, and not (except sometimes, for historical but perfectly correct reasons, on the note *B*, which should strictly be either a round, flat ♭ or a square, natural ♮): see Ch. IV, 4 above.

One result was that accidentals did not define the pitch (as they do today), they inflected the pitch (by a semitone up or down from a prior position, so that the given position is merely relative to the prior posi-tion, and not absolute).

But gradually during the baroque period, the disposition grew (perhaps earliest in Italy) to cancel by ♮, thus leaving ♯ and ♭ free to indicate absolute positions of pitch, and not merely positions relative to what would otherwise have been the pitch. This disposition led to our modern convention, by which only one position is indicated by any one note with its accidental if any. But at no time during the baroque period can we count on that.

The following already (1696) modifies the (theoretically) simple rule quoted from Simpson (1665 onwards) at (79) in Ch. IV, 4 above.

(766) Étienne Loulié, *Elements*, Paris, 1696, transl. with additions and collations from the Amsterdam ed. of 1698, and from an unpublished *Supplément*, by Albert Cohen, New York, 1965.

[p. 11 of 1st ed.] 'The sharp is marked thus, ♯, and raises the note by a semitone.

'The flat is marked thus, ♭, and lowers the note by a semitone.

'The natural is marked thus, ♮, and removes a flat [or] a sharp.

'A Sharp or a Flat put before a Note, serves also for all those which follow immediately on the same Degree.'

[pp. 49–50 in Albert Cohen's ed., from the MS *Supplément*]:

'Some Italians and other [foreigners] use a ♮ after a ♯ to indicate that the note [thus marked] is natural again . . .

'Among the Italians:

'A sharp raises a note a semitone higher than a natural.

'A note is lowered a semitone beneath a natural by means of a flat.

A note is made natural by means of a ♮.'

The following Ex. 248B shows the complete arbitrariness of the notation of accidentals in this respect at the period of Loulié's book. We see here the same passage as notated in two manuscripts, not merely contemporary, but apparently from the hand of the same professional Roman copyist, around 1685; having (with two exceptions) the same number of bars on each page, similarly arranged; both describing their contents (anonymous *Lamentations* in a style of about that date) as having been 'sung in S. Apollinare in Rome'; both now in Oxford (Bodleian Lib., MS. Mus. d. 215; Christ Church Lib., Mus. MS. 995); actually the same in foliation, but *f.* 17 in the Christ Church copy was inadvertently left unnumbered, so that there is an apparent discrepancy of one folio thereafter. The bass of the Bodleian copy, however, is for the first few pieces more fully figured; and (what concerns us here), in the passage shown below, the Bodleian copy uses the correcting ♮ to cancel ♯ (though elsewhere it uses ♭ for that purpose), while the Christ Church copy uses ♭ to cancel ♯ (both copies have the same misplacement of the first 'P?', *i.e.* piano).

Ex. 248B. Anon. *Lamentations* (perf. Rome, *c.* 1685), (a) actual folio 38 in Oxford, Bodleian, MS. Mus. d. 215, (b) and in Oxford, Christ Church, Mus. MS. 995, different notation of same accidentals:

(b) The following quotation (766) shows Geminiani in 1751 reiterating the old rule as given by Christopher Simpson and others (for which see Ch. IV, 4 above) that ♯ and ♭ raise or lower a note by a semitone (*i.e.* inflect it but do not define it); he describes it, however, as an inexact rule, and also mentions ♮ as a cancelling accidental.

(766) Francesco Geminiani, *The Art of Playing on the Violin*, London, 1751, p. [3]:

'A Sharp (♯) raises the Note to which it is prefixed, a Semitone higher . . . A flat (♭) on the Contrary renders the Note to which it is prefixed, a Semitone lower . . . This Rule concerning the Flats and Sharps is not absolutely exact; but it is the easiest and best Rule that can be given to a Learner. This Mark (♮) takes away the Force of both the Sharp and the Flat and restores the Note before which it is placed to its natural quality.'

Moreover, Geminiani's music examples show him tending towards, though not entirely observing, the modern bar-line convention by which the force of an accidental persists during but not beyond the bar. We are thus still in the long period of transition with regard to the notation of accidentals.

(c) The following shows the transition in full progress, though not yet completed, from the early convention (many as its exceptions were) of one note, one accidental, to our modern convention (also now modified again by many exceptions) of one bar, one accidental.

Even in Beethoven sources, for example, the bar-line convention for accidentals is not quite consistent. In baroque music and earlier, it did not exist.

We also see below some indication of the more or less concurrent transition from interchangeably cancelling by ♯ or ♭ as well as by ♮ in the early manner, to regularly cancelling by ♮ in the modern manner.

(767) Daniel Gottlob Türk, *Klavierschule*, Leipzig and Halle, 1789, p. 46:

[Accidentals] 'are valid only through one bar; yet one must not wish to observe this rule too strictly, for such a modifying sign often remains valid through several bars, or indeed so long, until it is cancelled by a ♮ [especially if the same note is repeated after the bar line].'

[p. 47]: 'One still finds now and again, especially among the French and in older works, pieces in which a ♯ stands in place of our sharpening ♮ . . . In the same way one finds ♭ for a flattening ♮.'

5. ACCIDENTALS IN MODERN EDITIONS

(a) It is the proper wish of most modern editors nowadays to impart as much information about their original sources as can be imparted without making their editions too impracticable and difficult to use for ordinary performers.

A most usual compromise is to adapt the accidentals to our modern bar-line convention, and also to our convention of cancelling not by ♭ or ♯ but by ♮. A statement to this effect will generally be made, more or less explicitly, in the preface; any further accidentals added by the editor are set in small type, or within brackets, or distinguished through some other typographical device.

It is then assumed that information has been sufficiently imparted to enable the reader to reconstruct for himself, if he so wishes, the accidentals as given in the sources, and to make his own decisions in full possession of this information.

Such, however, is not the case.

(b) There is no possibility of knowing or reconstructing the original accidentals except (i) from seeing them in the original or in facsimile; (ii) from an exact transcription showing the accidental signs precisely as they were; or (iii) from a critical commentary so complete that it indicates every sign precisely as it was, in conjunction with a text which adds no sign whatsoever to the original signs without clear typographical distinction.

To modernise the signs for accidentals in any way involves an act, not of reproduction in another form, but of more or less precarious translation into another usage. A baroque accidental can carry so many meanings that any alteration constitutes an interpretation. It is not possible for the reader simply to subtract the bar-line convention, the cancelling ♮ convention, and the avowed editorial additions, with the expectation of arriving at the original accidentals. Even if we can arrive at an approximation, we cannot arrive at the signs; and until we arrive at the signs, we cannot know what were the original choices of interpretation, nor whether we should agree with the approximation or not.

Sometimes an editor will wish to add, for example, a precautionary accidental, because he anticipates that if he does not, the modern performers are likely to be misled; and he may well be right. It is not in the original, so he puts it in square brackets. So we assume he has introduced it as an editorial change. And we are right in that. But what then, in the substance of the music, has he editorially changed? Nothing: There is no change of substance, merely a precaution against misunderstanding. So he takes out the square brackets. So we assume that the accidental is not editorial, and that it was in the original. But it was not in the original. Wrong once more.

Or the editor may print a bar which includes repetitions of the same note, the first of them prefixed in the original by an accidental. He prints this, correctly, as it stands and without square brackets. Then within the same bar comes a rest, then the same note repeated, also prefixed with the same original accidental. But he has told us that he is adapting accidentals to the modern bar-line convention; so he takes out this reiterated accidental without saying any more about it. So we do not know that it was ever there, and cannot judge for ourselves whether there is the alternative of the rest having cancelled the force of the accidental according to one not unusual early convention; or whether this alternative is ruled out by the original having a reiterated accidental within the bar, but after the rest. Foiled again.

The differences between early and modern conventions for accidentals are so radical that we have no method of showing the one by means of the other. So soon as the accidentals are modernised, the originals are concealed. The only way of showing original accidentals is by printing original accidentals, either in the main text just as they come in the source selected, or in copious annotations. When more sources than one are being collated for the modern text, annotations for each source are the only means of conveying the complete information. In a complicated textual situation, the results of this may be not merely copious. They may be prohibitive for any but the most heavily subsidised and leisurely produced of scholar's editions.

(c) For straightforward performers' editions, these difficulties are immaterial. What is required is a simple and legible presentation, in completely modernised notation, of whatever text the editor, in the responsible exercise of his own skill, knowledge and judgement, wants the performer to play. Nothing of what has gone to the making of his final decisions needs to be or should be brought to the attention of his performers, most of whom are more likely to find it confusing than illuminating. That is the meaning of a performers' edition.

(d) For straightforward scholars' editions, all the facts about accidentals in the sources should be made available if possible; and if, for reasons of expense or time or other difficulty, this is not possible, then at least all the facts should be made available which could be envisaged as affecting any musical decision: as having, that is to say, any conceivable implication for performance.

(e) For combined-purpose editions, which raise inevitable problems but are nevertheless being increasingly found valuable in practice, we can only try for the best working compromise. It is not really sufficient to rely on a general statement that accidentals have been modernised to conform with present conventions; and it is as well to disillusion ourselves of the assumption that this statement allows the original accidentals to be reconstructed. Perhaps the most practical solution is to add full information, by annotation at the bottom of the page or elsewhere, about all original accidentals appearing in all the sources used, whenever a serious problem arises, but not for more or less unproblematical instances.

(f) A small but important question arises when the original key-signature (due to a notational legacy from transposed modes) lacks one flat or (by analogy) one sharp which the key actually requires.

The sources make up this deficiency by adding the missing flat or sharp as an accidental wherever required; but we have to watch out for omissions such as it was very easy to make inadvertently in this respect.

A modern performers' edition (and possibly but by no means certainly a combined-purpose edition also), but not a full scholars' edition, should have the last flat or sharp added to the signature, for modern convenience; but then, conversely, the modern editor has to be exceedingly careful not to leave out, inadvertently, any *correcting* accidentals thereby necessitated. For example, he may find G minor notated with a signature of one flat; and he may wish to modernise this by giving a signature of two flats. Then whenever he comes to an E in his source, he has to remember that this E, without having or needing to have an accidental ♮ affixed to it, nevertheless is E♮, and not E♭ as his signature (unlike the original signature) has now made it. He has to remember to affix the ♮ which the original did not have or require.

This is not in itself a problem of substance; but it is something of a trap for mere human inadvertence. It will be as well to double-check for accuracy here.

6. A RETROSPECTIVE LATE-COMER

The following typically retrospective accidental at Ex. 249 came to my attention just in time to slip in under the net at the end of this Appendix V: retrospective in more senses than one. I want to include it, however, for in the first place it is made quite certain by the imitation at the fifth, which gives the intervals correctly without the need for any accidentals; and in the second place, it is important to the music, which sounds very illogical indeed in its tonality unless the E♭ in the bass is taken back retrospectively to inflect the two *E*'s previously occurring within the theme, and also carried forward (by hexachordal persistence) through the remainder of the measures cited.

Ex. 249. Giralomo Frescobaldi, *Il primo libro delle fantasie a quattro*, Milan, 1608, 'Fantasia Seconda' (in *Works*, ed. P. Pidoux, Kassel and Basle, 1950–54, Vol. III), retrospective accidental confirmed by corresponding entry at the fifth:

New Thinking on Ornaments

1. FREDERICK NEUMANN'S CONTRIBUTION

(a) In course of re-working this book for its present, new version, I have had several occasions, in the chapters on ornaments, to avail myself of Frederick Neumann's kindness in allowing me to see the not quite finalised typescript of his forthcoming book (as I write early in 1973) on baroque ornaments. My own book is the better for it, and the reader could discover a number of passages in which, with due acknowledgement, my emphasis has become different, and several in which I have modified some conclusion, to meet a new discovery or valid argument of his.

With Frederick Neumann, the prevailing inclination is to anticipate the beat with almost everything, from trills to arpeggios, which the rest of us ever since Arnold Dolmetsch have found good baroque evidence for bringing on the beat. This evidence still remains, and a fair sampling of it has been presented earlier in this book. It is still preponderantly in support of that solid, clean style of baroque interpretation to which an on-the-beat performance of ornaments attached to the beat conduces. This preponderance in tables of ornaments approaches unanimity, with exceptions, carefully emphasised in this new version, which are significant for two ornaments. The first of these is that species of more or less unaccented passing note to which the misnomer of 'passing appoggiatura', as Frederick Neumann and I agree, should not have been but was given in the late baroque period. The second is the slide, which, when taken before the beat, has also the form of two more or less unaccented passing notes (as Arnold Dolmetsch already pointed out, *Interpretation*, London, [1915], pp. 243–44): yet it undoubtedly feels (unless quite slow) like the same ornament as when it is taken on the beat; and so also may the speedier kinds of 'passing appoggiatura'.

That is the feature which lends substance, as I now think, to Frederick Neumann's new insistence on the 'passing appoggiatura' and the anticipating slide as genuine before-the-beat ornaments in their own right.

(b) I was already aware of the 'passing appoggiatura' (Ch. XVIII, esp. Ex. 79, in the first and second editions, 1963 and 1965, of my original version), and was beginning to wonder if it was not more important than I thought, but it is Frederick Neumann who has now brought it into its proper prominence. He has done the same service for the anticipating slide (likewise already mentioned but underestimated in my original Ch. XVI, esp. Ex. 71).

(c) The slurring to the ensuing beat which lends their anticipatory character to these two ornaments is, of course, a fine distinction (which Quantz, for example, merely reverses to normal in his TAB. XVI, Fig. 27); and it may not altogether erase our impression that what we are actually hearing is not so much anticipatory notes *before* the beat as passing notes *between* beats, similar to springers and other unaccented changing notes, unaccented turns, unaccented tiratas and the like.

An ordinary note of anticipation, for example, such as terminates many trills (see Ch. XX, 6, and Ex. 198 in Ch. XLIII, 4 above), slips in at the last possible moment before the ensuing beat which it anticipates; but it is not slurred to nor felt as attached to that ensuing beat. It is felt as the last fragment of the previous beat, rather than as an anticipatory ornament.

All this is acceptable enough, and none of it is very crucially distinct.

(d) Among these somewhat fine distinctions, however, there is one distinction which is not fine at all, but of considerable musical importance. This is the distinction between a 'passing appoggiatura' of substantial length (as at my Ex. 79 in Ch. XVIII, 2 above) and an ordinary appoggiatura proper, which may be *identically notated* (as at my Ex. 47 in Ch. XIV, 6 above).

Sometimes either ornament will sound effective, but more often it is important to use the right one. Frederick Neumann has now demonstrated how very often, at least in French and French-influenced music, the right one is that wretchedly-named but practically significant 'passing appoggiatura'. It is no true appoggiatura, whether slurred backwards or forwards. It is truly passing, and has a function which is indeed the opposite of the appoggiatura proper. Hence the importance of distinguishing them apart, and the value of Frederick Neumann's new discussion in helping us to do so.

(e) The importance and gracefulness of between-beat ornaments has never been doubted. It is only before-the-beat ornaments which (unless they are of substantial length, as in the case just mentioned) can sound a little weak, and a little untidy, in music so powerfully harmonic as is much late baroque music.

So quickly may the moment pass, for example with a slide rapidly anticipating its beat, or with a trill anticipated (or begun on its main note), that one may not be quite sure which it is that one has heard. But there may be a fleeting impression of impreciseness, almost as if the ensemble were momentarily insecure. It is over in a flash; but what

Frederick Neumann enjoys here as an agreeable refinement, I disenjoy as a small blemish.

That was the view of C. P. E. Bach, quoted at (178) in Ch. XIII, 2 above, when he added in 1787 to his previous explanation of 1753: 'it might be thought unnecessary to repeat that the remaining parts including the bass must be sounded with the first note of the ornament. But as often as this rule is invoked, so often is it broken.' It happened, then; but he did not think it good style for it to happen, and I agree with that.

(f) I further think that Frederick Neumann has successfully indicated a larger range of fluctuating melodic ornamentation, chiefly vocal and chiefly French, than had so far been adequately appreciated. Unfortunately this is the very area where the extreme ambiguity of the evidence makes it hardest to be certain about anything, and impossible to be exact. We have therefore to make a virtue of necessity, and to regard this inexactitude as itself a part of the system. It has always been Putnam Aldrich's wise view, for example, that the ambiguous notation of so much French vocal ornamentation may have been a deliberate encouragement to flexibility (see his Harvard dissertation, 1942). In many directions, and always within the outer boundaries of the style, I have no doubt at all that this is true.

(g) In recognition of the new material and new thinking which Frederick Neumann has contributed, my working rule at Ch. XIII, 2, (k) above, which used to read 'baroque ornaments never anticipate the beat', has now been changed to read: 'obligatory ornaments never anticipate the beat'.

2. OBLIGATORY ORNAMENTS NEVER ANTICIPATE THE BEAT

(a) By an obligatory ornament I mean an ornament which, whether any sign for it appears or not, is so strongly implied by its context that to leave it out is in most circumstances equivalent to making a wrong note.

(b) Between-the-beat ornaments, not being attached to a beat, neither take the beat nor anticipate the beat, but float elegantly in between. None of them are obligatory.

(c) Ornaments attached to an ensuing beat by being slurred to it may reasonably be called before-the-beat ornaments. None of these are obligatory.

(d) Ornaments attached to a beat and taking that beat are on-the-beat ornaments. Of these, two in effect are obligatory: (i) the long appoggiatura in recitative; (ii) the cadential trill.

3. THE APPOGGIATURA BY DEFINITION AND
FUNCTION ACCENTED

(a) An appoggiatura properly so-called is by definition a 'leaning' ornament (*appoggiare*, 'to lean'), hence by function an accented ornament, *i.e.* on the beat.

(b) Frederick Neumann, who agrees with that, does not agree with the following, which I continue to believe: the appoggiatura proper, and above all the long appoggiatura, had by far the greatest share in late baroque music, with the partial exception of French music (especially vocal), where the 'passing appoggiatura' was more nearly on an equal footing.

Thus and only thus (*i.e.* long and on the beat) is the appoggiatura shown in J. S. Bach's own little table of ornaments (see Ex. 46 in Ch. XIV, 6 above), and in the tables of the French harpsichordists there approvingly reflected (compare Ex. 43 and Ex. 45).

It is therefore a mistake to deprive Bach or Handel or Telemann of their characteristic long appoggiaturas. And indeed, the best approach to a late baroque appoggiatura, where time and context allow, is still: try it long; try it longer; try it very long indeed. For other things being equal, it is so often a case of the longer the appoggiatura, the better the effect.

(c) The appoggiatura in recitative (Italian or Italianate) is always technically long, either occupying the half of one written note, or replacing the first of two written notes. Some expressive stretching of the tempo is usually desirable.

Singers are getting to recognise this obligation to introduce appoggiaturas in recitative, not as a special effect, but as a normal practice with very few if any exceptions. Some conductors are still sufficiently old-fashioned to insist on the notated though unintended text; but this situation is changing rapidly for the better. It cannot be too strongly reiterated that all late baroque and subsequent composers of Italian or Italianate recitative expected the customary appoggiaturas.

4. THE CADENTIAL TRILL LIKEWISE DEFINED AS ACCENTED

(a) When writing my article on 'Ornaments' for Grove V (London, 1954), I began by talking about trills 'on cadences', then about the trill 'as a cadential formula', and finally I settled for 'cadential trill' as a term for an ornament defined as enriching the penultimate harmony of standard baroque cadences, by turning a notated dominant 5–3 into a more interesting 5–4 or 6–3 or (with trills in two parts) 6–4, resolved to 5–3 as the main note is heard. This harmonic function required and requires an on-the-beat, accented and often prolonged upper note start (which produces the change of harmony). It was a familiar early baroque cadential formula, and it became the standard late baroque cadential formula, as evidence from different nationalities, sampled in my Ch. XX, 4 above, agrees in confirming.

The cadential trill is a bread-and-butter ornament of considerable utility in early baroque music, and of indispensable utility in late baroque music, my term for which has caught on as corresponding to a reality of some historical and artistic substance. We do not disagree about its interpretation, but solely about its pre-eminence.

(b) Frederick Neumann challenges the pre-eminence of the cadential trill, even at cadences, by proposing in addition: trills with a main-note start; trills starting before the beat on the upper or the main note; trills of which the actual repercussions start before the beat and 'straddle' (his vivid word for it) across the beat. These have it in common that none of them would produce a change of harmony on the beat, nor constitute a cadential trill defined as a trill which enters into a cadence to change its harmony.

(c) But any one of the regular preparations of the compound trill, as shown at Ch. XXV, 3 above, starting on the beat with some other note non-harmonic to the main note, will change the harmony of the beat as a cadential trill should.

(d) A standard cadential trill may occur as the resolution of a normal suspension, the consonant preparation of which on the previous un-accented beat is tied over to become the dissonant preparation of the trill on the accented beat.

The ensuing repercussions of the trill then resolve the dissonance on or across the next unaccented beat, in the usual way.

This structure is especially characteristic of late renaissance progressions, but it continued in use throughout the baroque period and subsequently. See Ch. XX, 3, esp. Ex. 91, above.

(e) A baroque cadenza may precede, and will then lead into, a standard cadential trill.

(f) Whatever precedes the standard cadential trill (whether the preparation of a suspension, or one or more anticipatory notes, or a longer elaboration, or a full cadenza) is no part of the cadential trill.

Whatever is part of the cadential trill (compound preparations included) accepts the standard behaviour of the cadential trill.

(g) For every cadence which can suitably be elaborated, there must be a hundred or a thousand which merely need to be trilled inconspicuously but firmly in the standard manner. You cannot improve on the bread-and-butter ornament for the bread-and-butter situation.

(h) There is no standard late baroque cadence which cannot at least be adequately approached by a standard cadential trill well proportioned to its speed and character.

Thus P. F. Tosi, quoted in Galliard's translation at (236) and (243) in Ch. XX, 3 and 4, wrote in 1723 (and I here give my own very literal translation of his Italian original, p. 25): 'Whoever has a very fine Trill, even though he were short on (*scarso di*) every other ornament, always enjoys the advantage of bringing himself without offence to the Cadences, where it is generally most essential'. (And p. 28): 'The Trill for its [full] beauty (*per sua bellezza*) wants to be prepared (*preparato*); nevertheless, its preparation (*preparazione*) is not always required (*non sempre esige*), since neither time (*Tempo*) nor taste (*gusto*) will always permit it; it is [however] called for in all final Cadences'.

5. THE PREPARATION OF THE BAROQUE TRILL

(a) We have now arrived at a critical point for all discussions of the baroque trill in general, and of the baroque cadential trill in particular.

For what Tosi meant by *preparazione*, and what such French contemporaries as Jean Rousseau, D'Anglebert, Loulié, Couperin and others meant by their corresponding term *appuy*, is crucial to our interpretation of the baroque trill, and our decision here affects all subsequent arguments. Here is indeed a parting of the ways.

(b) The explanation currently accepted is that given in my Ch. XX, 4 above; I believe it to be correct:

(i) The trill *sans appuy*, without preparation, means an upper-note start, on the beat, but not appreciably prolonged;

(ii) The trill *avec appuy*, with preparation, means an upper-note start, on the beat, and appreciably prolonged.

Thus at Ex. 95, for example, we saw the harpsichordist D'Anglebert illustrating his plain trill (*Tremblement simple*) by showing the upper-note start, on the beat, but not prolonged; and his prepared trill (*tremblement appuyé*) by showing the upper-note start, on the beat, and prolonged. At Ex. 94, we saw Purcell giving a similar illustration.

We saw Loulié, at (238a) telling singers to take the trill from an upper auxiliary to a lower main note; and 'when the Voice remains appreciably on the little sound of the first Appoggiatura (*Coulé*) [upper auxiliary] this is called preparing the trill (*appuyer le Tremblement*)', but 'when the Voice does not remain appreciably on the first Note [consisting] of the first Appoggiatura [upper auxiliary], the Trill is called unprepared Trill (*non appuyé*), or without Preparation (*sans Appuy*)'.

At Ex. 97 (a) and (d), we saw Couperin, a fine vocal as well as instrumental composer, illustrating for harpsichordists his 'Trill prepared and slurred (*Tremblement appuyé et lié*)' with a longer upper-note start, and his 'Trill slurred without being prepared (*Tremblement lié sans etre appuyé*)' with a shorter upper-note start.

At (240) we saw Quantz telling flautists that 'each trill starts with the appoggiatura [upper auxiliary] whether it is long or short'. At (243a) we saw Marpurg (over twenty years younger than Quantz, but likewise under considerable French influence), telling harpsichordists that 'the trill starts on the accessory [upper auxiliary]', and 'the trill *appuyé* or *préparé* [is] when one remains a little time on the accessory [upper auxiliary] before making the beating'. At (242) and Ex. 96, we saw Leopold Mozart, who was under the Italian influence of Tartini, instructing violinists to distinguish between trills with 'an appoggiatura [upper auxiliary]' so short that it is 'nothing but a strong attack on the trill', and trills of which 'the appoggiatura is held throughout half the duration of the note, while the trill [i.e. the beating] is not started until the remaining half'.

All these instructions, whether for voice or harpsichord or other instrument, refer, on our current explanation, respectively to unprepared and prepared upper-note trills.

(c) But the explanation now proposed by Frederick Neumann is:

(i) The Trill *sans appuy*, without preparation, is taken to mean without upper-note start, and therefore with main-note start;

(ii) The Trill *avec appuy*, with preparation, is taken to mean with upper-note start, whether uprolonged or prolonged.

Thus Frederick Neumann postulates (among other variants) main-note trills, which he sees as common late baroque practice, as well as upper-note trills, which he associates mostly with the French harpsichordists and 'the Berlin school'. His argument partly rests on his interpreting Tosi, with Jean Rousseau and certain other Frenchmen, as advocates of the main-note trill; and this may be a good point at which to pick up his thread. For here I think he goes wrong.

6. TOSI, GALLIARD AND AGRICOLA ON THE
BAROQUE TRILL

(a) Tosi, as cited at (243) in Ch. XX, 4 above (Galliard's translation), and again at the end of Sect. 4 just above (my translation), having said that the trill 'wants to be prepared (*preparato*)', added that 'neither Time nor taste will always permit it'.

Permit what? Frederick Neumann argues: permit an upper note start, which he thinks might indeed be against the singer's taste, should that singer prefer a main-note start. However, an upper-note start does not need any more time than a main-note start: but a prolonged upper-note start does need more time than an unprolonged upper-note start; and this is therefore the meaning which I think Tosi intended.

(b) My explanation of Tosi's meaning is supported by a curious but interesting circumstance, to which I attach importance because it concerns interpretations of Tosi by two of his own junior contemporaries.

The circumstance is that Tosi, in his influential singing-tutor of 1723, included no music examples. But both the English translation of 1742, and the German translation of 1757, have music examples added, independently, by their respective translators and editors: Galliard, for the English; Agricola, for the German.

J. E. Galliard (c. 1680–1749), a German-born composer and oboist, studied under Jean Baptiste Farinelli (director of the Hanover opera) and Steffani (the Italian opera-composer), at some time before migrating to England (probably around 1706) well acquainted with the tradition of Italian *bell canto* in which Tosi stood both as heir and as transmitter; and Galliard's comments in the footnotes to his translation, though not extensive, are comprehending.

J. F. Agricola, himself a singer, a teacher of singers, a composer of Italian opera and husband of the Italian singer and Porpora-pupil, Benedetta Emilia Molteni; having, moreover, the unusual distinction of having studied and played under J. S. Bach in Leipzig as well as worked (after 1741) with Quantz and C. P. E. Bach in Berlin; having there listened to the advice of Graun and Hasse; having, in short, much the same background of Italian *bel canto* as Tosi, Agricola not only translated him well but edited him with many extensively sympathetic and explanatory comments of his own.

Both Galliard and Agricola added a number of musical examples, though different ones, to illustrate Tosi's discussion of the trill. These examples without exception show an on-the-beat, upper-note start.

(c) Frederick Neumann, wishing to claim Tosi as an advocate of the main-note start for trills, is therefore pressed back into arguing (in the unfinalised typescript of his forthcoming book as he sent it to me) that Galliard and Agricola each independently misrepresented Tosi in this respect: whether because they misunderstood a tradition with regard to trills which had already changed; or because they were of a generation desirous of changing it.

The weakness in this argument is that it is circular. It rests on the same assumption which it is designed to prove: namely that the tradition with regard to trills did thus change between the generation of Tosi (born, according to Tagliavini's dating in MGG, c. 1653/4; died 1732) and the generation of Galliard (c. 1680–1749), or the considerably younger generation of Agricola (1720–1774).

With regard to Galliard, we have further to take it into account that

Tosi spent many years in London, during some of which Galliard was also there, and presumably forming that high and seemingly personal opinion of Tosi which is reflected throughout the preface to his (Galliard's) translation (p. viii): '[Tosi] had a great deal of Wit and Veracity, which he retained to his latter Days. His manner of Singing was full of Expression and Passion . . . The best Performers in his Time thought themselves happy when they could have an Opportunity to hear him . . . [it is desirable now] to make the Sentiments of our Author [Tosi] more universally known, when a false Taste in Musick is so prevailing . . .'

With regard to Agricola, the reader is recommended to Erwin Jacobi's comments in his magnificent facsimile edition (a model of how a facsimile can be introduced and set in context editorially) of Agricola's translation, with a facsimile of Tosi's original thrown in for good value (see my Bibl.). Jacobi believes (p. xxviii) that Agricola, in his own long and important extensions (more than doubling Tosi's text), incorporated much of what he had learned from J. S. Bach. There is certainly nothing to suggest that Agricola in 1757 any more turned against Tosi's teaching than Galliard in 1742. On the contrary, the Italianate *bel canto* technique and idioms, in the form perpetuated by Tosi's book, were conserved with remarkable tenacity, trills and all, for many more generations yet to come.

At no time or place during the second half of the baroque period, nor for as many decades afterwards, do we find any basic change with regard to trills. There was nothing to change: the upper-note start was already established as the basic habit. Even in the French authorities upon whom Frederick Neumann very much relies, this same basic consistency and continuity remained beneath the surface ambiguity, as may next be carefully considered.

7. JEAN ROUSSEAU AND THE FRENCH VOCAL SCHOOL ON THE BAROQUE TRILL

(a) Jean Rousseau (*Methode*, Paris, 1678, and *Traité*, Paris, 1687) altered his first term for the preparation of trills (*support*) to the more habitual term *appuy*, as used by D'Anglebert, Loulié, Couperin and others (see Ch. XX, 4 above), perhaps in order to show that he meant the same as they by this preparation of some but not of other trills.

'Preparation' is a convenient, but not a literal translation for either of these two terms. Brossard (*Dictionaire de Musique*, Paris, 1703), in his list of French terms, has unfortunately no such entries. But a more general seventeenth-century work, Randle Cotgrave, *A Dictionarie of the French and English Tongues* (London, 1611) has: 'Support: m. Support; a prop or stay; favour, maintainance; helpe, succour, assistance', and 'Appuy: m. A stay, buttresse, prop, rest, a thing to leane on./Appuyé: n. ée f. Stayed, propped, supported, sustained, held up; also, rested, or leaned on; built, or depended upon./Appuyer. To stay, prop, support, sustaine, underprop, hold, or beare up./s' Appuyer. To rest, or leane on; to build, or depend upon'.

From these shades of seventeenth-century meaning, I think the most significant in a musical context may be 'a thing to leane on' for *appuy*, and 'leaned on' for *appuyé*. Most educated French musicians would probably have known that the familiar Italian term *appoggiatura* also has this literal meaning of 'leaning'. At (238a) in Ch. XX, 4 above, we saw Loulié using one of the French words for appoggiatura (*coulé*) as a term for the upper auxiliary of the trill, evidently with its appoggiatura-like, 'leaning' potentialities in mind; for like some others, he explained the trill as a succession of such upper appoggiaturas.

Several authors used the term appoggiatura for the upper auxiliary when prolonged to form an *appuy*, or even when not so prolonged: see (240), (241), and (242) in Ch. XX, 4 above. When prolonged, the upper-note start has so much the 'leaning' effect of a long appoggiatura as to be musically indistinguishable from it, so that we may often today find ourselves talking of the appoggiatura of the trill. Occasionally, we find in baroque music a notated sign (a little note) for the appoggiatura, but serving to indicate just such an appoggiatura-prepared (i.e. *appuyé*) trill: see Ch. XX, 4 (f) above.

Thus a good literal translation for *appuy* might well be 'leaning'.

It is quite interesting that Quantz (*Essay*, XI, xii), when warning us not to prolong and stress (by inequality) the first of each pair of very fast notes, but only the first of each four, wrote of 'a very fast tempo, in which the time does not allow you to perform [pairs] unequally, and where you must only bring length (*Länge*) and strength (*Stärke*) to the first of four'; and that in the official (and simultaneous) French translation this appears (p. 108) as '*où l'on ne peut appuyer et employer de la force que sur la première note des quatre*'. From this it can be seen that the idea of prolonging was part of the eighteenth-century meaning of *appuyer*, as well as the more literal idea of leaning. For further confirmation of this meaning, see (586) in Ch. XLV, 7 above.

(b) Using this more literal translation, then, and noticing Jean Rousseau's explanation (*Traité*, Paris, 1687, p. 76) that 'by the word *Cadence* I mean the Trill (*Tremblement*) and by *Cadence finale* I mean the Cadence [in the sense of close]', so habitually associated with cadential trills, we read:

(769) Jean Rousseau, *Traité de la viole*, Paris, 1687, p. 76:

'There are two sorts of trill (*Cadence*); to wit, the Trill with leaning (*avec appuy*), and the Trill without leaning (*sans appuy*).

'The Trill with leaning is made when the finger which has to shake (*trembler*) the Trill, leans (*appuye*) for a little, before it shakes, on the Note which is immediately above the one which requires a Trill.

[p. 77]: 'With regard to Notes on the same degree, the leaning should be very slight (*leger*), at least if it does not fall on a final Cadence (*Cadence Finale*), and with regard to other Notes that should be leaned upon, it is always necessary to regulate (*regler*, time) the leaning according to the value of the Note, and according to the measure and the movement, which ought never to be altered, under any pretext of ornamentation.

[p. 78]: 'The Penultimate [note] of every final Cadence (*Cadence finale*), when descending by step, requires the Trill with leaning (*Cadence avec appuy*).

[p. 83]: 'The Trill without leaning is made like the foregoing, while curtailing the leaning (*en retrenchant l'appuy*).'

Cotgrave (*Dictionarie*, London, 1611) gives: 'Retrancher. To cut, strike, or chop off; to curtall [curtail], diminish, lessen, abridge'. But what is here being cut off, curtailed or diminished? The *appuy:* the 'thing to leane on'; the appoggiatura-like prolongation of the upper-note start. That leaves the on-the-beat, upper-note start unprolonged, but intact.

(c) Can we again confirm this explanation? Michael Collins attempted it, in a paper read to the American Musicological Society at Toronto in 1970. From a careful analysis of the solmisation syllables to Jean Rousseau's ambiguously notated music-examples in his singing-tutor (*Methode*), Michael Collins traced an upper-note start for each variety of trill, including one (apparently derived from the Italian *anticipazione della sillaba* through Caccini's visit to Paris or de Nyert's visit to Rome) 'by anticipation of the value and the sound (*par anticipation de valeur et du son*)'; for here, the little grace-note prior to the trill and constituting the 'anticipation' is shown by the syllables to be tied over the beat in such a way as still to supply there an upper-note start to the ensuing trill.

Only once, Michael Collins argued, does Jean Rousseau illustrate a trill in musical notation, of which the notes and their placing at least are unambiguous; and here Frederick Neumann does not allow the notation to be illustrating a trill at all, because its notes are not shown slurred, but are indeed described (*Traité*, p. 98) as being each bowed separately in 'Pieces of Harmony and of Melody', though slurred 'in playing accompaniments'. Now to bow the notes of a trill separately does, of course, denature it completely and is quite contrary to the baroque advice sampled at (238a), (239) and (240) in Ch. XX, 4 above. It does not increase our confidence in Jean Rousseau that he should recommend so finicky an aberration; yet I cannot help thinking that he did indeed intend this example to illustrate a trill, since he gives it the name of *Double Cadence*, and had himself, as we saw at (b) above, stated in this book (*Traité*, p. 76): 'by the word *Cadence* I mean the Trill (*Tremblement*)'.

Double Cadence in French tables of ornaments is ordinarily used for some form of compound trill, which may or may not itself be preceded by a four-note or five-note turn or (as in Jean Rousseau here, at Ex. 249A below, second measure) by a brief tirata; or which may include (as its 'compound' element) a turned ending (also as in Jean Rousseau here). See in Ch. XXV, 3 above: Ex. 161 from L'Affillard (*Principes . . . pour bien apprendre la musique*, 1694) and Ex. 162 from Georg Muffat (*Florilegium I*, 1695); also Ex. 158, where J. S. Bach (*Clavier-Büchlein*, 1720) translated (probably from D'Anglebert's *Pièces de Clavecin*, Paris, 1689, but condensed and with titles partly transposed) *Double Cadence* as *Doppelt Cadence*.

Similar instances of the *Double Cadence*, having it in common that the trill arrives with upper-note start, are to be seen in most French clavecin tables of ornament. The elaborations there and elsewhere are not always quite the same; but we are given no cause to doubt that *Double Cadence* does mean a trill with elaborations. Nor are we given cause to suppose that *Cadence* had a different meaning in a singing-tutor or a viol-tutor such as Jean Rousseau wrote, or in a general-purpose tutor like L'Affillard's or Loulié's; nor that the trills which Jean Rousseau did not illustrate by explicit notation differed in their upper-note start from the illustration spelt out in the second measure of (b) in Ex. 249A below.

My suggested interpretation at (c) for the trill not spelt out by Jean Rousseau in the first measure has of course no bearing on what he meant by the illustration which he did spell out in the second measure. I have, however, added for comparison, at Ex. 249B, three trills spelt out by Rameau.

Ex. 249A. Jean Rousseau, *Traité de la viole*, Paris, 1687, pp. 99–100, *double cadence*; (a) as notated by Rousseau; (b) as explained by Rousseau; (c) previous measure as explained by me, where Rousseau does not complete his explanation:

Ex. 249B. Jean-Philippe Rameau, *Pièces de clavecin*, Paris [1724], Table of Ornaments, unprepared trill, prepared trill and trill with turned ending (*double cadence*), all having upper-note starts:

Cadence   Cadence appuyée   Double Cadence

(d) In *L'Art de toucher le dessus et basse de viole*, by le Sieur Danoville, Paris, 1687, we read on p. 39: 'if there is a trill marked on the Mi, you anticipate (*anticiper*) on the Fa, putting the first finger on the Mi, and the second on the Fa, which is the substituted (*supposée*) note, and holding always the first [*i.e.* the Fa] leaned upon (*appuyé*), you let the bow slur (*couler*) for a moment, then you agitate the second finger with an equal agitation . . .'

This is not further clarified, since the accompanying music example does not translate the description into notation, but the sense is this: the upper-note start functions as an anticipation of the written note, since it comes first and substitutes for part of it. Nothing in the description or in the music example indicates an anticipation of the beat. We are not being told that the upper-note start anticipates the beat, which is not mentioned here; we are being told that the upper-note start anticipates the main note, which it does by taking the beat (with some prolongation, since it is to be leaned upon) and by therefore pushing the main note forward a little off the beat. This is the normal upper-note, on-the-beat trill, well prepared; and it is normally recommended (p. 40) for 'perfect, imperfect, middle and final cadences in all the modes'.

8. THE UPPER-NOTE HABIT IN LATE BAROQUE TRILLS

(a) It would be neither surprising nor disturbing to find in this French school of singing (on which Jean Rousseau evidently modelled his viol-tutor also) some continued use of main-note trills as ornaments of melody rather than of harmony. From the first edition (1963) of my original version onwards, I have always allowed for an occasional persistence of melodic, main-note trills after they had gone out of fashion in later baroque music (Ch. XX, 3 above), as well as for their quite regular and frequent appearance in earlier baroque music (Ch. XX, 2 above).

(b) The (melodic) main-note trill is not, like the (harmonic) cadential trill, an obligatory ornament. It is an optional ornament, and free to be used in any suitable context and with all appropriate flexibility. Can it therefore be used on an actual cadence of some weight and substance, to replace the standard cadential trill?

If this sometimes happened (and I should imagine that it did) it happened against the fashion of later baroque interpretation. For cadential situations there, we may regard the cadential trill as indeed the obligatory ornament: but we may perhaps do well to regard this obligation as having been less strictly honoured by singers than by others. That seems to be reasonable and is certainly practicable: singer's trills are apt to be less reliable; choral trills are always problematical, and on the whole best not attempted.

(c) The behaviour of the trill as an optional ornament is less critical than the behaviour of the trill as an obligatory ornament.

Hence it was also more variable, both by itself, and in free combinations with other ornaments and ornamental elements. These combinations, one might almost say (like dancers) these *enchaînements* of successive ornamentation have been explored for us by Frederick Neumann with great thoroughness and skill.

(d) It is all the more remarkable, then, that the variability of the trill itself in late baroque music still emerges as so insignificant in this particular matter of its on-the-beat, main note start.

From around the late seventeenth century onwards, treatise after treatise, and table after table, comes up with astonishing repetitiveness showing an on-the-beat, upper-note start for simple trills; a choice of ascending and descending preparations for compound trills; and no before-the-beat nor main-beat start for trills at all.

This prevailingly on-the-beat, upper-note start for melodic (as opposed to harmonic) trills was not a functional necessity of late baroque interpretation. But it certainly became a habit.

(e) Were there many exceptions to that prevailing habit? Frederick Neumann has found (besides the few earlier ones in Beyschlag) certain trills or trill-like groppi of just the melodic, on-the-beat but main-note pattern common in the early baroque period, notated sporadically into the eighteenth century by conservative (in particular Southern) German organists of the older tradition. These are a valuable though not an extensive nor altogether a novel discovery.

From there Frederick Neumann carries over such main-note trills to J. S. Bach, whose table does not show them, nor his style as I think invite them; and though as performer's options they would not be wrong, they would I think get out of style if often used, or if used where a standard cadential trill is in the context obligatory.

(f) As a method (among so many methods) of notating an upper-note start to a trill, the following, most kindly sent to me by Eva Badura-Skoda, requires further explanation.

Ex. 250. Vincenzo Manfredini, *Regole armoniche*, Venice, 1775, p. 27, upper-note start to a trill, notated separately:

An explanation of this notation may be supplied as follows:

(768) Jean-Philippe Rameau, *Pièces de clavecin*, Paris [1724], Table of Ornaments:

'The note slurred (*liée*) to that which carries a Trill or a Mordent, serves as a beginning to each of these ornaments.'

Ex. 250A. Jean-Philippe Rameau, *Pièces de clavecin*, Paris [1724], Table:

That is to say, the notated *E* natural (in both Exx. 250 and 250A) is one way of indicating 'the note', as Rameau puts it, which 'serves as a beginning' to the standard trill, when this beginning note is not merely present but prolonged. The slur is omitted from both Manfredini's and Rameau's notated interpretations, but Rameau's verbal explanation implies that we are intended to supply it, as we should anyhow mentally, at the keyboard, where it does not need notating; physically in singing, bowing or tonguing. See (238a), 239 and 240, in Ch. XX, 4 above.

The prolongation of the upper-note start thus shown in these examples, and others of their kind, extends to half the time available for the entire trill. This is quite a characteristic execution, as shown (more characteristically notated) below, with the written instruction to prepare (*en appuyant*) 'during half of the duration of the value of the note, and then beat (*fredonner*) during the other half'.

Ex. 251. Henri-Louis Choquel, *La musique rendue sensible par la méchanique*, Paris, 1759, 2nd ed. 1762, p. 166, prepared trill, (a) as notated by Choquel; (b) as illogically illustrated by Choquel; (c) as I would approximately interpret it on Choquel's written instruction:

An even more characteristic, refined and expressive execution may often be to carry the preparation just, but only just, across the second beat, for which see Ex. 97 (a) and Ex. 98 in Ch. XX, 4 above: the preparation is then just over half the trill.

(g) The following instructions were regarded as sufficient, at the beginning of the eighteenth century, by this unusually concise and lucid authority:

(770) Sébastien de Brossard, *Dictionaire de musique*, Paris, 1703, s.v. TRILLO:

'One should beat very quickly alternately, or one after the other the two Sounds on conjunct degrees [sample notes are named]; one starts with the higher, and one finishes with the lower, and this is properly the *Cadence* or *Tremblement* in the French manner [as opposed to the one–note Italian *trillo*, for which see Ch. XIX, 2 above].'

(h) Or in three pithy sentences from a brief set of 'Rules for Gracing' written, in a seventeenth-century hand, on the reverse of p. 67 in a copy of Christopher Simpson's *Division Violist* (London, 1659) now bearing the shelf-mark II.F.10 (1) at the Royal College of Music, London:

(771) Anon., English, 2nd half of the 17th-cent., on shakes (trills):

'Prepare all long shakes . . . The Note before a Close is to be Shaked . . . All shakes are taken from the note above . . .'

(i) Thus it does not seem to me that Frederick Neumann has been able to achieve for the trill the same reappraisal that he has achieved for the 'passing appoggiatura' and the anticipatory slide.

The early baroque trill begins on the beat: with its upper note, if cadential and harmonic; with its main note or its upper note indifferently, if non-cadential and melodic.

The later baroque trill begins on the beat: with its upper note, if cadential and harmonic (from functional necessity); likewise, and almost though not quite invariably, with its upper note, even if non-cadential and melodic (apparently from analogy and force of habit).

The cadential trill, being obligatory in contexts requiring it, is the most important; and no performer who has once got it into his own musicianship how firmly its upper-note start needs to be accented, and often prolonged to the utmost possible extent, will again be content to omit it or to weaken it. Wherever it is right, it is so very right.

The non-cadential trill, being optional, can be made the subject of more variability and experimentation, in which Frederick Neumann will be found an adventurous leader.

9. THE HARD CORE OF BAROQUE ORNAMENTS RELATIVELY SIMPLE

(a) It has long been my contention (see Ch. XIII, 1 above) that the enormous complexity of baroque ornaments, when studied in the detail necessary for specialists, need not weigh too heavily on the average student or performer, since the basic requirements sufficient for most though not all situations are relatively simple once they have been well taken into one's own musicianship. The hard core of baroque ornaments remains neither particularly uncertain nor particularly difficult.

(b) There are many further refinements of execution, many degrees of balance and proportion, many subtleties of context, to say nothing of rare situations or rare signs or rare ornaments, on which I can only do justice to Frederick Neumann's important new study by recommending the reader to acquaint himself with it at the earliest opportunity. And with that I take my leave of him for now. I have a high and affectionate regard for his scholarly persistence and integrity, and have no doubt that our fruitful discussions will continue.

10. HOW GRAMMATICAL HAVE BAROQUE ORNAMENTS TO BE?

(a) There is one other aspect of baroque ornaments which requires a measure of new thinking at the present time. This is the question: how grammatical, in practice, does our execution of any ornaments which we may find, or which we may bring in, have to be?

(b) It was the general understanding that ungrammatical progressions, i.e. progressions incorrect on the broadly accepted principles of harmony and counterpoint, should not be introduced by ornaments: see (183) in Ch. XIV, 2 above. But the following important reservations were made, with greater or lesser liberality by different authorities, but in some degree by all:

(i) the strictest standards of grammatical correctness are not applicable to ornamentation, just as they are not applicable to continuo realisation, and for the same good reason that progressions largely or wholly improvised cannot and do not need to move with the strictest correctness;

(ii) even the most blatant departures from correctness are not objectionable when they come and go, as in ornamentation they so often may, with a rapidity such that the listener either does not detect them, or if he does detect them, has not the time in which to object to them before the music has obliterated them in its forward movement.

11. WHEN CONSECUTIVE PARALLEL FIFTHS ARE CORRECT

(a) When, of two notes moving in parallel fifths, one is an accented passing note resolving by step before the other has changed, the progression is correct.

This rule, of which examples can be found notated in the music of the baroque and later masters, is of considerable importance for unnotated ornamentation. My formulation of it was supported by Klaus Hofmann in the pages of *Acta Musicologica* (XLIII, 1971, i–ii, pp. 106–108), where he cited Georg Philipp Telemann (*Musikalisches Lob Gottes*, Nürnberg, 1744) as including among acceptable 'eye-fifths' (and not among unacceptable 'ear-fifths') those produced 'by certain appoggiaturas and so-called ornaments'. By way of illustration, Telemann gives the following case as correct, notwithstanding the consecutive parallel fifths produced by its standard execution (but resolving in the acceptable manner just described); the explanations at (b) and (c) are mine:

Ex. 252. (a) Georg Philipp Telemann, *Musikalisches Lob Gottes*, Nürnberg, 1744, acceptable parallel fifths produced by standard appoggiatura; (b) no doubt because the progression resulting thus is heard (c) basically thus:

(b) Consecutive fifths of which one is diminished were quite commonly regarded as correct (especially if not between outside parts), for which see (339), (340) and (341) in Ch. XXIX, 5 above. They are always (and in any parts) acceptable in the execution of an ornament.

12. ORNAMENTS NOT TO BE FALSIFIED FOR THE SAKE OF GRAMMATICAL CORRECTNESS

(a) Certain other consecutive fifths, and any consecutive octaves, were regarded as always incorrect, but as often tolerable if well covered, either by the sounds of a big ensemble (336, 339); or by occurring between inside parts (337); or by occurring so quickly as to cause no real offence even to an ear sharp enough to hear them, for as Michel de Saint-Lambert put it (335), 'since Music is made only for the ear, a fault which does not offend it is not a fault'.

I must admit that my ear generally does hear such consecutive fifths or octaves, but that I find them offensive (either in ornamentation or in continuo realisation) only when they are somewhat blatant and without any very obvious musical justification or necessity. There is, however, a considerable musical justification for executing an ornament normally even at the cost of some grammatical incorrectness in the progression: it has a natural feel.

(b) If a grammatical incorrectness can be removed by adjusting, for example, the length of a long appoggiatura or of the preparation of a trill, or by substituting a short for a long appoggiatura, or a 'passing appoggiatura' for an appoggiatura proper, this should usually be done.

(c) But if that spoils a good sequence, it should not necessarily be done, since it has always been thought desirable to keep intact a good sequence once established, even at the cost of momentary incorrectness.

(d) If the grammatical incorrectness of the progression can only be removed by an incorrect execution of the ornament, that should probably not be done, since it will not have a natural feel, owing to the falsification of one's normal expectations of the ornament. It can never sound natural to falsify an ornament.

(e) But if the grammatical incorrectness or the harshness of the progression is more than the performer wishes to tolerate, rather than falsify the ornament he will probably do better to leave it out entirely, or to substitute another ornament.

Signs for ornaments were so casually, even carelessly, introduced by almost all baroque composers (including J. S. Bach, though not including François Couperin), that the performer is nearly always at liberty to follow his own taste and well-trained discretion in the matter.

When the composer has notated an ornament which produces a grammatical incorrectness unavoidable except by falsifying the ornament, either he did not notice that grammatical incorrectness, or he did not mind it. On neither view need his ornament be regarded as immovable. It is more in the baroque spirit to omit or replace an undesired ornament than to contrive an execution against its normal nature.

13. CLASHES OF ORNAMENTS TO BE TAKEN BOLDLY

(a) Ornaments normally and simultaneously executed in two separate parts may produce some surprises such as the consecutive seconds in a number of quite consistent passages from Kühnel kindly sent to me by Gordon Kinney, including the following:

Ex. 253. August Kühnel, *Sonate ô Partite ad una ô due Viole da gamba, con il basso continuo*, Cassel, 1698, No. 1, m. 14, simultaneous trills in consecutive seconds:

Academically, consecutive seconds may be unofficial, but they are not incorrect. They raise no problem here; but it is necessary to perform them with sufficient boldness and conviction, so as not to sound like a mistake. And since these pieces use them repeatedly in the same way, there can be no doubt that they are right. They cannot be dodged, so they may as well be enjoyed. They may, moreover, represent one possible solution for the so-called 'Corelli clash' shown in Ch. XX, 7 above; and if so, their practical importance may be considerable.

(b) When ornaments occur simultaneously in both hands on a keyboard, the practical difficulties can be much greater, but the principle is the same. Both the ornaments should be attacked in their normal execution, and any clashes resulting should be brought out and enjoyed rather than manipulated away by an abnormal execution.

If the difficulty or the harshness should seem to the performer excessive, it is probably better to omit or replace one or other of the ornaments. But it is amazing how convincing to the ear such clashings can sound, in a glittery kind of way, so long as they are taken with sufficient boldness and virtuosity. And that is generally true of baroque ornaments.

14. DOING THE OBVIOUS THING WITH ORNAMENTS

(a) Erwin Bodky, in his uneven but very interesting *Interpretation of Bach's Keyboard Works* (Cambridge, Mass., 1960), assembled small collections of problem trills and appoggiaturas. Most of his problems vanish on the considerations discussed above. Only one of the trills (his No. 16) might worry me for its unusually blatant consecutive octaves (perhaps the result of oversight); the others will all, I think, sound well enough in their standard execution if firmly played. Some of the appoggiaturas will need to be shorter than usual (his No. 11a, 11b): or longer (his No. 9 and 10); for which see my Ch. XIV, 6, b to d, above. In no case would it be helpful and in some cases there would not be time to anticipate the beat.

Out of Bach's vast production, this is not a very big or formidable list of problems: just enough, perhaps, to confirm how little pedantic he was in his use of ornaments; and how little pedantic we need to be in performing them.

(b) As with so many other aspects of baroque interpretation, the soundest approach to ornaments is first to know the boundaries of the style, and then without any particular cleverness, do the obvious thing. That is the most likely thing to have happened at the time; and the most likely to give a convincing and musicianly execution now. It may not always work; and then it may be necessary to think again. But time and again it does work.

A knowledge of the style may not come to us very easily at our distance of time. Once there, however, one of its chief advantages may be a certain gift for the obvious.

Tempo and Rhythm

1. FLEXIBILITY IN DECLAMATORY STYLES

(a) Recitative took several distinct though allied forms at different times and places within the baroque period. See Introduction, IV, 2, and Ch. XL, 4 above.

(b) The Italian recitative of the first great period of opera, during most of the seventeenth century, was only one aspect (the most declamatory) of a very fluid and expressive style of vocal solo music for which one modern (not contemporary) term is monody. Contemporary terms were *stile recitativo* and *stile rappresentativo*, of which the first can best be translated 'reciting style' (rather than 'recitative style') when it is being used for the style as a whole, which includes other idioms in addition to recitative. The second term can best be translated 'representative style' (rather than 'theatrical style') since it includes other music in addition to opera.

The reciting style as a whole is somewhat flexible in rhythm, though not by any means unmeasured; its declamatory aspect is especially flexible (but still not unmeasured in most instances), being nearer to arioso than to recitative of the later Italianate form. Its accompaniment must not be too melodious or symmetrical, but it does not have to be entirely free of all melodic quality. See Ch. XXX, 4 and Ch. XXXII, 2 above; and Introduction, V, 4–6.

(772) Severo Bonini, *Affetti spirituali a dua voci* . . ., Venice, 1615. Notice at end of both soprano parts:

'When the singer sometimes sings alone . . . he will be able to beat time by himself, so that he can, according to the needs of the words, sing quickly or slowly, now sustaining, now quickening the beat, for thus demands the Florentine style. And when the two sing together, the beat should be taken up by the first [of the two who again starts] to beat time; who, if he sometimes finds a run of quavers or semiquavers in the style of diminution, should quicken the beat much rather than slowing it down; for doing otherwise, the composition would give little pleasure to the listeners, and the singer would show that he has small skill.' [But contrast Frescobaldi's advice at (550) in Ch. XL, 6 above.]

(773) Claudio Monteverdi, *Madrigali guerrieri et amorosi*, Venice, 1638, 'Manner of performing the present song' ['Non havea Febo ancora']:

'The three parts which sing outside of the lament of the Nymph have been thus separately set out because they sing to the time of the hand. The other three parts, which proceed commiserating the Nymph in a weak voice, have been set out in score so that they follow her lament, which is sung to the time of the heart's feeling (*affetto del animo*), and not to that of the hand.' [Compare Monteverdi, *Settimo libro de madrigali*, Venice, 1619, 'Lettera amorosa', 'for solo voice, in representative kind (*genere rappresentativo*) and it is sung without beat (*senza battuta*)'.]

(774) Giovanni Bonachelli, *Corona di sacri gigli a una, due, tre, quattro, e cinque voci*, Venice, 1642, Preface:

'First they must be concerted together, and the feelings (*affetti*) of the words and the speed must be observed, and especially in the reciting styles, or representative, as others say, and in accordance with the feeling (*affetto*) [one must] guide the beat, sensing [it] now fast, now slow, according to the occasion, now liveliness, and now languor, as indeed anyone will easily know immediately who possesses the fine manner of singing.'

It will be noticed that the above quotations relate particularly to the reciting style. Other seventeenth-century styles require less flexibility, each according to its kind; and Anthony Newcomb has recently (paper to the National Conference of the American Musicological Society, Nov. 1971) drawn attention, with the support of late sixteenth-century and early seventeenth-century authorities, to the desirability of 'a constant pulse within autonomous sections of music, 1590–1625' in many contexts to which the above quotations might not apply. Nevertheless, the reciting style and its influence were of great importance in the modern music of the seventeenth century. In the following strong statement at (775), it is not quite clear whether 'the reciting style' or 'the recitative style' would best translate the meaning intended. At (776), the same ambiguity occurs, but clearly the description fits recitative or arioso more closely than aria.

(775) Giovanni Battista Doni, 'Trattato della Musica Scenica', [*c.* 1635], in *De' Trattati di Musica di Gio. Battista Doni*, II, ed. A. F. Gori, Florence, 1763, Appendix, *i.e.* first draft of the 'Trattato', p. 23:

'In the reciting style (*stile recitativo*) the Singer is not in the habit of confining himself to any beat'.

(776) Angelo Berardi, *Ragionamenti*, Bologna, 1681, p. 136:

'The representative style, that is, of the theatre, consists in this alone, that singing one speaks, and speaking one sings.'

The above two quotations are vividly suggestive, but rhythmic freedom is a relative matter, and recitative within the reciting or representative style of early Italian opera does not require so unmeasured a performance as the dry recitative in later Italianate opera. Berardi in 1681 was, however, writing at a moment when the transition between the earlier and the later forms of Italianate recitative was perhaps just perceptibly begun. Brossard in 1703 (or 1701—see Bibl.) at (777) below, was writing when it was just becoming conspicuous. (From the wording, he may even have read Berardi.)

(777) Sébastien de Brossard, *Dictionaire*, Paris, 1703, s.v. RECITA-TIVO:

'This is a manner of Singing which holds as much of *Declamation* as of *Song*, as if one *declaimed* in *singing*, or as if one *sang* in *declaiming*, hence where one has more attention to expressing the *Passion* than to following exactly a timed measure . . . one has the liberty to alter the beats of this measure, and make some longer or shorter than others . . .

[s.v. TEMPO]: 'One often finds after the Recitative of the Italians, these words, *à Tempo*, or *à Tempo giusto*, which indicate that it is necessary to beat the measure *exactly* (*juste*) and in making all the beats very *equal*, in place of which in the *Recitative* one has more regard to the *expression* than to the *exactness* or *equality* of *beats* of the measure.'

(c) The Italianate recitative of which Brossard was writing became still more declamatory and still less lyrical during the next fifty years, in the age of Bach and Handel. But during that same period, the French recitative in Rameau and others remained very much as Lully and others had established it during the second half of the seventeenth century. French recitative was always closer to early baroque Italian recitative than to late baroque Italian recitative. Its style of performance, as a natural consequence, was always of that more or less cantabile quality which matches this somewhat arioso variety of recitative. While the enunication has usually to be dramatic and indeed often declamatory, the melodic line should seldom, if ever, lose all lyrical smoothness; and while the rhythm has usually to be flexible, as the words require, the metre seldom, if ever, disappears altogether in unmeasured freedom.

2. TIME-SIGNATURES IN FRENCH RECITATIVE

(a) There is one very visible difference between Italian and French recitative of the baroque period.

Italian recitative never made a habit of changing the time-signature in order to follow small inflections of poetical rhythm or transient emphasis. French recitative always did. But since it was agreed in both cases that the singer takes his musical rhythm from the poetical rhythm and not from the notated rhythm, we may wonder how much practical difference in performance this visible difference in notation made.

Following the verbal pattern in their notated rhythms was certainly a matter over which French composers took much trouble, whereas Italian composers often notated their arias, at least, with time-signatures and barring which conceal rather than revealing the actual rhythm or even the actual metre: for a brief discussion of which, see Sect. 3 below. Italian recitative, on the other hand, goes to a perpetual C, but taken with 'more regard to the *expression* than to the *exactness* or *equality* of *beats* of the measure', as Brossard had it at (777) in Sect. 1 above. The singer's freedom was greatest in Italian recitative of the later, dry variety; but if we allow for the more arioso-like flow of French recitative, there was less difference in performance than the difference in notation appears to suggest.

(b) This leaves us, however, with one question to which a more definite answer is required. What is the effect of the continually changing time-signatures of French recitative on the tempo? What happens to the beat? What proportions are to be observed across the changes?

The only answer which seems to work out in practice is that there is no effect on the tempo; that nothing happens to the beat; that the proportion is therefore a one-to-one proportion. Though the number of beats in a notated measure changes, the value of the beats does not. Beat equals beat.

(778) Étienne Denis Delair, *Traité d'accompagnement*, Paris, 1690, p. (48:

'The measure of three simple beats corresponds to the measure of four beats, in that one crochet, or value, is made for each beat, in the one and the other measure, and the double triple measure, corresponds to the measure of two beats, in that one minim or value is made for each beat, they only differ in that triple measures have one beat more, or less than measures of two, or of four beats.'

(c) If this interpretation (beat equals beat) is correct, there was a very considerable element of affectation in the impressive array of different time-signatures which may occur even within a very short passage of French recitative. To a point, they may serve the convenience of the signer; but hardly to the extreme point to which composers carried them.

For modern performers, it may be desirable to transcribe in the simplest possible alternations of duple and triple metres: $\frac{3}{4}$ and $\frac{4}{4}$ with $\frac{2}{4}$ where needed to keep the barring straight, and $\frac{6}{8}$ should the recitative become sufficiently in aria style to require it in some passages.

For scholars, the original must be carefully retained or indicated in the critical commentary.

(d) More particularly, if this interpretation (beat equals beat) is correct, there was a tacit ignoring for French recitative of one of the most prominent if confused distinctions drawn in the baroque discussions of mensural proportions: the two-to-one proportion allotted in theory though not in practice to the distinction between C and ₵, for which see Ch. XXXVIII, 3 and 4 above.

We saw that no such numerical proportion was observed in ordinary practice: but that a more or less faster speed might be implied by ₵, especially when the change occurs in course of the music; and that a pulse of two in a bar rather than four in a bar might also be although it is not necessarily implied.

In French recitative, there may be a pulse difference; but if this interpretation (beat equals beat) is correct, there is not a tempo difference. Not only does ₵ move at the same tempo as 2 (a common though not invariable rule in French treatises); ₵ moves at the same tempo as C (against the common rule and to some extent against the common practice).

(e) Then is this interpretation (beat equals beat) correct? It is unexpected; but it is shown to be correct by passages where the music requires an identical figure to be maintained across such a change of time-signature.

The following brief passage in dialogue occurs as part of a scene all in recitative, with close and frequent alternations between 2, 3, C, ₵ and $\frac{3}{2}$, yet requiring a constant crochet to yield any kind of musical probability (*i.e.* crochet equals crochet, quarter note equals quarter note, beat equals beat).

But here what turns musical probability into certainty is the imitation between the two voices of the dialogue. At (a), Urgande sings 'Oriane' in 3-time; at (b), Amadis imitates her by singing the same name, 'Oriane', as an obvious echo, with the same rhythm intended and the same note-values written, but notated in ₵-time. If the ₵-time were interpreted, by the literal rule, as cut-time, then the tempo would be doubled, and Amadis would have to sing his imitation twice as fast as Oriane's original: *i.e.* a double-speed echo; which is absurd. Therefore the ₵-time cannot be taken as cut-time. Crochet does not equal quaver. Crochet equals crochet. The beat is the crochet, and beat equals beat. (For Ex. 253, see p. 646.)

Another case which affords not merely probability but certainty for the interpretation of beat equals beat (crochet equals crochet) across a change of time-signature is shown at Ex. 253A below. A section of arioso-like recitative has a first-time ending with repeat marks, and a second-time ending to lead on. In each ending, the same last two syllables of the same word occur, set to the same notes: *i.e.*, not merely

Ex. 253. Jean-Baptiste Lully, *Amadis*, Paris, 1684, ed. H. Prunières, Paris, 1939, p. 200: (a) phrase in 3-time, (b) imitation in ₵-time, same note-value retained and intended:

as a matching passage, but as the same passage notated twice. The note-values are written the same in both endings; but the first ending is in ₵-time, and the second ending is in 3-time. Therefore crochet equals crochet across the change of time-signature from 3-time to ₵-time. Beat equals beat.

Ex. 253A. Jean-Baptiste Lully, *Ballet des Nations*, Paris, 1670, ed. H. Prunières, coll. ed., 'Comédies-Ballets, III', Paris, 1938, p. 133, notation showing crochet equals crochet across change of time-signature to C-time.

In the same volume of Prunières' collected edition as the above, on p. 190, Lully's ballet *Les Amants Magnifiques* (1670) has a change from C-time to 3-time likewise necessitating the interpretation of crochet equals crochet. Similarly on p. 7, a passage in *Le Divertissement Royal de Chambord* (1669) changes from $\frac{3}{2}$ to ₵; on p. 192 of Prunières' collected edition, 'Les Motets, II' (Paris, 1935), a passage changes from 3-time to ₵-time to 3-time to 2-time; passages in Clerambault's *Cantates Françoises*, Livre X, Paris, 1710 have 2 on the last bar only of $\frac{3}{2}$-time, for no obvious reason at all, and changes from 3 to C to 2. These are merely sample references for the reader's convenience; they are all characteristic passages of French recitative, and they all suggest more or less clearly, from the continuity of their rhythm through multiple changes of time-signature, that whatever their subtle hints at various rhythmic nuances, nothing changes in the tempo intended by the written note-values.

(f) We may also notice from the examples given or cited above that, under whatever time-signature, the crochet (quarter-note) is the actual beat. Thus it is that the rule 'crochet equals crochet' and the rule 'beat equals beat' are in actual practice (though not in strict theory) synonymous for French recitative.

In strict theory, two beats of ₵ or 2 equal four beats of C, but at half the notated value and therefore twice the speed.

In practice, the two beats of ₵ or 2 may be slowed even to the extent of leaving the speed unchanged, so that a slow two-in-a-bar moves at the speed of a quick four-in-a-bar, only a difference of pulse perhaps remaining.

And again, in practice the difference of pulse may not remain, so that all distinction whatsoever may disappear.

This last represents the actual situation in French recitative.

(g) The following description, like so many, hovers uneasily between trying to give an account of the correct theory and of the actual practice. It is, however, especially valuable to us here because it does for once mention quite specifically the case of recitative; and if it still refrains from giving us precise information on the subject, at least it advances the very practical explanation that the words rather than the notation of recitative decides its actual movement.

(779) Henri-Louis Choquel, *La musique rendue sensible*, Paris, 1759, 2nd ed. Paris, 1762, pp. 109 *ff.*:

'[Crossed ₵ is] the ordinary sign of the measure with two common beats, that is to say with two slow beats (*temps graves*); it is only used in recitatives, and less often in sinfonias (*simphonies*); one semibreve is needed for this sort of measure, just as for the measure [*i.e.* his C] with 4 beats, and consequently we can use 2 minims or 4 crochets or 8 quavers, or 16 semiquavers.

'[2 is] the sign of the measure with 2 beats; when it is used in recitatives, the same notes are needed as for the [crossed ₵], but when it is used in airs or in quick sinfonias (*simphonies de legereté*), one semibreve is needed to the measure, or equally 2 minims or 4 crochets *etc.* [but] in that case we take them all very much more quickly than in the measure with 4 beats, [and] it is the taste of the Composer which decides this speed (*mouvement*); but when we use them in sinfonias such as Gavottes, Rigaudons or others, the speed of them is much quicker, the minims taking the place of crochets, the crochets of quavers, and the quavers of semiquavers.

[p. 118]: 'It will not be possible to fix the speed of the first Case of the measure with 2 beats, marked by a crossed C [*i.e.* ₵]. Since this sort of measure is only used for recitatives, [since] its movement is arbitrary and it is the words which decide it, I have consequently nothing precise to say on this point.'

As a matter of fact, Choquel has said much which, if not precise, is certainly useful, and becomes more so when compared with the following from half a century before:

(780) Étienne Loulié, *Elements*, Paris, 1696, p. 60:

'One uses the simple C for the sign of the Measure of four beats; again one uses it joined with figures or Signs of other Measures, to mark that the Strokes (*Battements*) or Beats (*Temps*) of them are as slow as in slow four Beats. Thus: C2, C3, C$_2^3$.

'One uses the stroked C (C *Barré*, *i.e.* ₵) for the Sign of the Measure of four quick Beats, or two slow Beats; again one uses it joined with figures or Signs of other Measures, to mark that the Strokes (*Battements*) of it are as quick as in quick four Beats (*Temps*). Thus: ₵2, ₵3, ₵$_8^4$.

[p. 61]: 'The [figure] at the top as Numerator, and the other at the bottom as Denominator.'

The last sentence shows the transition from the proportional signs and figures of mensural notation to the numerical signs and figures of modern notation well advanced, with the inevitable confusion resulting; and there is no mention of recitative. But we are told that ₵ can be four quick beats, as well as the slow two beats which Choquel mentioned at (779) above. And four beats it is in French recitative; only that they do not necessarily have to be quick, since Choquel also mentioned that 'for recitatives, its movement [*i.e.* the movement of ₵] is arbitrary and it is the words which decide it'. Indeed, Jean-Jacques Rousseau (*Lettre à M. Grimm*, [Paris], 1752, p. 2), brought up a biassed view of French recitative as both slow and monotonous; while [Rulhiere's] *Jugement* (see my Bibl.) said (p. 2) 'one could have nothing more ridiculous than French words with the speed of the Italian, and the Italian is not susceptible to the majesty of our song'.

Further confirmation of the practical interchangeability of four time and two time, given an adaptable tempo, can be found as follows, together with confirmation of this adaptability in recitative, where everyone is supposed to follow the singer, and the singer in turn to follow the words.

(780a) Charles Masson, *Nouveau Traité*, Paris, 1694, 2nd ed., Paris, 1697, p. 6:

'The Measure of four quick beats is the same thing as that of two slow beats . . .

'In the recitative of a Motet one beats the Measure, but in that of an opera one neglects it, because he who beats the Measure is obliged to follow the voice so as not to incommode the bass.'

That the composer should follow faithfully the prosody and accentuation and emotional content of the words in setting them to music, and that the singer should do likewise in singing them, interpreting the notated measure in the immediate service and over-riding interests of the poetry: this is the recurring theme of French treatises on singing. Bacilly, for example, began his *Art de bien chanter* (Paris, 1668) with detailed advice on word-setting as a musical embodiment of poetical prosody; continued it by discussing ornamentation in the light of true service to the words; and ended it with advice no less detailed on proper pronunciation as the very basis of the singer's art. A generation later, Jean-Léonor Le Gallois gave still more attention to the words and less to the music in his *Traité du récitatif dans la lecture, dans l'action publique, et dans le chant* (Paris, 1707) where he argued quite specifically (*e.g.* p. 228) that in recitative (and he had French recitative in mind) the singer's function is to follow the prosody and express the passions of the words with the finest of artistic license.

These facts do not reduce to meaninglessness the careful interchanges of different time-signatures used by French composers in their effort to match musical accentuation and duration with verbal accentuation and duration. It is merely that while pulse-values may subtly change, note-values do not.

Thus French recitative illustrates, but even more than other idioms, the general principle expressed by the following (which comes after a tabulation, pp. 26–29, of time-signatures, including instructions more systematic than realistic as to what note-values are equal and what unequal under each).

(780b) [Borin, ?], *La musique theorique, et Pratique*, Paris, 1722, p. 29:

'The different manners of beating the Measure do not in the least alter the tempo (*mouvement*); it is open to Musicians to choose that which seems to them suitable.'

(g) Thus beat equals beat (crochet equals crochet) under whatever change of time-signature in French recitative.

(h) The speed of this beat is variable, depending on the words; but experience shows that in practice the speed is likely to range from moderately slow to really quite quick. The reason for this is the declamatory character of all recitative, including French. It is legitimate and desirable to draw out the speed where an appropriately dramatic effect of lingering or of hesitation can be gained by this; and likewise to press on again where a dramatic effect of haste and agitation is appropriate. It is in the nature of recitative to be dramatically expressive, and in opera, theatrical.

Nevertheless, the sense of an underlying beat is not to be lost entirely. The basic continuity of the crochet value provides the constant foundation for the fluctuating expression; and the more arioso and tuneful the recitative, the greater the constancy of this underlying symmetry.

3. TACTUS AS DURATION AND METRE AS RHYTHM

(a) We have seen here, and in Ch. XXXVIII and Ch. XLII above, the confusion caused in time-relationships throughout the baroque period by remnants of mensural notation, including mensural time-signatures and mensural note-values. Certain other specific problems may be considered below.

(b) The tactus causes problems where its behaviour is otherwise than we might expect from our normal modern understanding of metre and rhythm.

The tactus or 'stroke' is that (double) stroke of the hand (down and up again) by which tempo could be conducted and time-keeping indicated. It is also that duration of time which is occupied by this double stroke of the hand. See Ch. XXXVIII, 1 (d) and (508), above.

The tactus is the only unit of time, in mensural notation, which remained constant within a moderately small range of variability. Its speed could vary from one piece to another, or from one passage to another, as the music requires; and it could fluctuate to accommodate any necessary rallentandos or other expressive departures from a steady tempo. But in order to keep the hand moving with a convenient motion, neither too fast nor too slow for comfort, the tactus could and did vary only to a moderate extent. The tactus is thus a moderately though not entirely stable unit of time, carrying some suggestion of an average normal tempo, but no mandatory or absolute control over tempo. Tactus adjusts to tempo, not tempo to tactus.

(c) Wider variations of tempo could be and were accommodated by changing (i) the number, (ii) the nominal value, (iii) the actual value of the note or notes going to the tactus.

(i) The number of notes may be, *e.g.* one breve or two breves or three breves, *etc.* to a tactus.

(ii) The nominal value of the notes may be, *e.g.* breve, semibreve, minim; and perfect (as we should notate it, dotted) or imperfect (as we should notate it, undotted).

(iii) The actual value of the notes may be standard (*integer valor*) or modified by augmentation (very rare) or by diminution (very common); *e.g.* (theoretically and sometimes practically) three times the speed (*tripla*) or one-and-a-half times the speed (*sesquialtera*).

In theory, all these variables were indicated by time-signatures, and also introduced by rules modifying the actual value of notes according to their immediate context (*i.e.* according to the nominal values of adjacent notes). These rules include perfection (making triple a note-value otherwise duple); imperfection (making duple a note-value otherwise triple); and alteration (doubling the duration otherwise applicable).

In practice, both signs and rules were used with extreme unreliability and inconsistency, so that the intention has often to be sought in the general context rather than in the detailed notation.

(d) Most commonly, an equal tactus (*tactus aequalis*), of which the down-stroke of the hand occupies the same duration of time as the up-stroke of the hand, yields duple rhythm; and an unequal tactus (*tactus inaequalis*) of which the down-stroke of the hand either occupies twice the duration of the up-stroke, or remains twice as long at the bottom, yields triple rhythm.

Less commonly, but still quite normally, an equal tactus yields triple rhythm in disguise, for the following reason.

(e) The tactus is a unit solely of duration. Tactus carries no implications for metre or rhythm, and thus no implications for accentuation.

It is therefore possible to conduct triple metre with equal tactus, as well as with unequal tactus; and under certain circumstances, the mensural structure causes this to occur.

When this does occur, the down-stroke of an equal tactus will come on the down-beat of one bar of triple metre. The up-stroke of an equal tactus will come on the down-beat of the next bar of triple metre. For each bar of triple metre will require one equal tactus and a half; and this brings the down-beat alternately on the down-stroke and the up-stroke of the hand, as it measures out the equal tactus.

That is no obstacle, since the down-stroke and the up-stroke of the tactus carry no metrical or accentual implications either way, and can therefore serve indifferently for down-beats or up-beats.

But what are the circumstances under which the mensural structure causes the equal tactus, rather than the unequal tactus, to be thus used for triple metre?

(f) No such circumstances arose with triple metre in quick or moderately quick tempo. Mensural notation as carried over into the early seventeenth century could and did show this as tripla proportion ($\frac{3}{1}$, often given incompletely as 3) or as sesquialtera proportion ($\frac{3}{2}$, sometimes given inconsistently or incompletely as $\frac{3}{1}$ or 3): *i.e.* by diminution of a prior (or supposed) duple metre whose speed they thus effectively increase.

Before these numerical signs on that level of the rhythmic hierarchy which is often known as prolation, there may be set, though commonly there is not, a time-signature on the next higher level, known as tempus. This should indicate what nominal note-value it is of which the numerical sign of proportion is supposed to be diminishing the actual value.

For example, O reckons one triple (perfect, or we should notate it, dotted) semibreve to a tactus, and C reckons one duple (imperfect, or as we should notate it, undotted) semibreve to a tactus; while ϕ reckons two triple and ¢ reckons two duple semibreves, faster though not in practice necessarily twice as fast, to a tactus.

Hence O_1^3 or ϕ_2^3 should go three semibreves to a tactus; so also should C_1^3 or $¢_2^3$. But O_2^3 or ϕ_1^3 should go three minims to a tactus; so also should C_2^3 or $¢_1^3$. Nevertheless, these relationships were not explained completely or consistently by the theorists, and they were used still less completely or consistently by composers, copyists and printers. It is commonly necessary to rely on the general context for an understanding of the situation.

But however confused they were both in theory and in practice, these simple numerical proportions were extremely familiar; and so long as it is realised that they do not always (though at times they may) imply a mathematical strictness of tempo relationship, they serve well enough as a means of notating quick or moderately quick triple metres.

(g) The circumstances were quite other in regard to slow triple metres.

These could have been, but in general practice were not, shown either by proportional signs of augmentation, or by signs of perfection (*i.e.* triple rhythm) on the tempus level, NOT followed by numerical signs of proportion on the prolation level. For in practice, signs of augmentation were not habitual by the seventeenth century; while signs of diminution (which were habitual) compel a faster tempo. They do this by grouping their rhythmic units within the tactus, which (for the convenience of the hand) cannot beyond a certain extent be slowed down. Signs of augmentation would likewise group their rhythmic units within the tactus, which cannot beyond a certain extent be quickened up. Thus proportions of augmentation would have imposed a slower speed, but were not used; while proportions of diminution were used, but imposed a faster speed.

But rhythm on the tempus level is not grouped within the tactus but within the measure. Slow triple metres grouped across the tactus could therefore be notated under tempus signs provided that these are not followed by numerical signs. Of these tempus signs, however, the per-

fect (triple-time) O and Ⓞ virtually always do occur followed by signs
of proportion which impose a grouping of threes within the tactus. That
leaves C and ₵, both of which freely occur not followed by signs of
proportion.

As a consequence, slow triple metres were quite normally and reasonably, from their point of view, notated under C or ₵. Since, moreover, the original barring, when present, will show the tactus rather
than the metre, we may find the bar-lines also showing an apparently
duple metre, thereby further disguising an actually triple metre.

(h) From our point of view, this disguise of an actual triple metre
under C or ₵ with an apparently duple barring can be, to say the least
of it, misleading.

For modern musicians, therefore, in any but a pure scholar's edition,
it is extremely desirable to change the notation visibly to triple-time
barring under a triple-time signature ($\frac{3}{2}$, or $\frac{3}{4}$). Examples may be seen in
Denis Stevens' edition (London, [1967]), as mentioned in his Preface,
of Monteverdi's *Orfeo*; and others, with a fuller explanation, in Putnam
Aldrich, *Rhythm in Seventeenth-Century Italian Monody* (New York,
1966), a rather difficult but important book on many aspects connected
with time-signatures and actual rhythms at this transitional period.

The practical conclusion here is: in Monteverdi, Schütz and others
of their generation or a little afterwards, be prepared to find an actual
three-time metre notated under the seeming appearance of a duple-
time signature (C or ₵) and barring; when it is found, do not hesitate to
change the time-signature to $\frac{3}{2}$ or (if transcribing with reduced note-
values) $\frac{3}{4}$, and to spread out the barring so that each one-and-a-half
bars of the apparent duple time gets redistributed as one bar of the
actual triple time.

(i) Because the first down-stroke of the first tactus merely represents
the start of the beating, and does not necessarily come on a down-
beat, it may easily happen in duple-time that the first and all subsequent
down-beats come with up-strokes of the tactus.

And because, as we have seen above, the original barring of this
period, when present, is likely to be distributed not by the metre, but
by the tactus (the bar-lines standing not necessarily before the down-
beat of the metre but before the down-stroke of the tactus), it may then
happen that every bar-line is half-a-bar out in relation to the actual
metre. Reasonable, again, from their point of view; unreasonable from
ours.

It is, for modern musicians, somewhat desirable to re-bar throughout
so that the barring and the actual metre coincide. And once again, the
practical point is simply that their barring followed the tactus, while our
barring follows the metre. Hence their barring has no implications

for the accentuation, while our barring has strong implications for the accentuation. But their barring, to us, is then misleading notation; hence the general desirability of altering it in modern performing editions.

It is possible to instruct a modern performer (*e.g.* in the preface): ignore the bar-line except merely for the purpose of counting and keeping the place; take the accentuation from the actual metre, and in vocal music take the actual metre from the words. But this is expecting a considerable skill from the average modern performer, who may not have had the special training or at least information required; and thus if such re-barring can be done regularly and consistently and without raising further problems, it is probably wise policy.

(j) On the other hand, it is very unwise policy to re-bar in irregular units continually changing, as for example Edmund Fellowes did in his generally valuable editions of Elizabethan polyphony. Since his modern changes of metre, being meant to show the actual rhythms, do not occur at the same time in the different parts, conducting is almost impossible, and even keeping one's place is quite difficult. In such music, four-in-a-bar for easy counting, and leave each singer to accent his part differently in accordance with what words he is singing at the time, is the only realistic method.

That is to say: the barring can well be modernised to coincide with the underlying metre, *provided that this is sufficiently uniform*; the subtle cross-rhythms between different parts at the same time should be left to the performers to bring out, in their superimposed accentuation as it is to be actually heard.

And the practical point here is: in equal-voiced polyphony, there may be cross-rhythms superimposed differently and simultaneously upon an underlying metre. It is important that the performers should make their cross-rhythms heard; the underlying metre, on the other hand, may be rather sensed than heard. Notation, however, is for the metre; not for the rhythms where these cross against the metre. Good training in the style, of course, is the real solution.

(k) In dances and forms derived from dances, assistance may also be had from the movements and particularly from the steps of the actual dances. The reader is directed to Putnam Aldrich's book just mentioned for a most careful and original investigation of both these sources of practical assistance.

4. BLACK AND WHITE NOTATIONS AS REMNANTS OF COLORATION

(a) Coloration was one resource of mensural notation which certainly became more trouble than it was worth in the seventeenth century.

(b) By the early seventeenth century, only one remnant of coloration retained any practical significance. This was the black semibreve (•) and the black minim ($\downarrow$) used as precautions against perfection, imperfection or alteration—see Sect. 3, (c, iii) above—in contexts where some lingering heritage of the once prominent rules of mensuration might otherwise cause hesitation in the mind at least of a traditionally trained musician.

The following example is undated, but of the first quarter of the seventeenth century (probably *c.* 1614). Triple-time sections in this volume introduce a blend of perfection with black notation (where perfection is not wanted), and do so under a variety of incomplete and rather uninformative time-signatures, or none. But the rules are at least comprehensibly applied, and the intention is in no way difficult to discern.

Ex. 254. Anon., [Welsh Dance], No. XVIII in *Parthenia In Violata*, London, [? *c.* 1614], perfection of the white minim and imperfection of the black semibreve:

[Harp'd, orig. on 6-line staves]

etc. [equals:]

[Gamba, on 5-line stave, unbarred]

In the above Ex. 254, under the rather vague encouragement of the time-signature 3 (which might be incomplete for C^3_2, *i.e.* sesquialtera, with a tactus of three black minims to each half-bar), we find the following note-values:

(i) In the right hand of the harpsichord, two measures, each comprising three black minims followed by a dotted black semibreve. This can be transcribed under $\frac{6}{4}$ as two measures each comprising three standard (black) crochets followed by a standard (white) dotted minim.

(ii) In the left hand of the harpsichord, top line, two measures, each comprising a black semibreve and a black minim, repeated. These can be transcribed as standard (white) minim and standard (black) crochet; but had they been thus notated, then by one of the lingering rules of mensuration, the minims would have been subject to perfection, which would have made them (in our notation) dotted. In order to prevent this, they had to be notated instead as black semibreves; for black notation was exempt from perfection, imperfection and alteration—see Sect. 3 (c, iii) above. But notice that the blackening has itself halved the nominal duration: the blackened nominal semi-breve has the actual value of a standard (white) minim, and the blackened nominal minim has the actual value of a standard (black) crochet.

(iii) In the left hand of the harpsichord, bottom line, the first measure has a black semibreve and a black minim, followed by a black-minim rest and a black semibreve. This can be transcribed as standard (white) minim, standard (black) crochet, standard (black) crochet rest, standard (white) minim; but had it been thus notated, then both the minims would have been perfected (to us, dotted) by the rules. The second measure has three black minims, a black-minim rest and a black semibreve. This can be transcribed as three standard (black) crochets, a standard (black) crochet rest and a standard (white) minim; but had it been notated thus, the minim would again have been perfected (to us, dotted) by the rules.

(iv) The gamba has, in the first measure, a black semibreve, a black minim, and a white minim. The white minim is perfected (which has to be given as dotted in our notation) by the rules; and this is exactly what is wanted here (and would have happened elsewhere without being wanted, had the notation been the same as here). The transcription is standard (white) minim, standard (black) crochet, and standard (white) dotted minim. In the second measure, there are three black minims, and a white minim which is again perfected by the rules; and the transcription is three standard (black) crochets and a standard (white) dotted minim.

Notice that in none of these transcriptions have I reduced the original note-values. On the contrary, I have merely set out in modern notation the actual values which the nominal values of the original represent. For the rules themselves, see Putnam Aldrich's book already mentioned, and Willi Appel's standard work, *The Notation of Polyphonic Music, 900–1600*, Cambridge, Mass., 1944, esp. pp. 108 *ff*. Neither account is altogether clear, since confusion and inconsistency are general in the sources; but the reader will be able to judge in what manner the rules, without being clearly understood or accurately applied even at the time, lie at least comprehensibly at the back of such a transitional piece of early seventeenth-century notation as Ex. 254 above.

(c) In other examples of blackened notation during the baroque period, and also in examples of whitened notation such as we sometimes find in Couperin and elsewhere, the rules, for what they were worth, seem more than ever to have receded into the dim and ill-recollected past, and mere musical common sense to be more than ever the necessary approach.

(d) The following may be noticed, but does not conform at all consistently with actual practice. There was no consistency in actual practice. We are dealing here with a much reduced remnant of mensural notation, though frequently enough encountered in baroque notation for us not to be able to ignore it. Fortunately, most situations yield to common-sense if not to rules.

(781) Étienne Loulié, *Elements*, Paris, 1696, p. 61:

'The Black Triple (*Triple Noir*) is a Measure in which they do not use White Notes (*Nottes Blanches*) at all, and that is the mark (*Signe*) of it.

'The White Triple (*Triple Blanc*) where they use Black Notes (*Nottes Noires*) not at all or very rarely.

'If one meets Black Notes in White Triple, they are worth as much as if they were White (*Blanches*) [for reasons] drawn from the Rules of the Ancients, which it would take too long to set out here [example under C_2^3, which should indicate *sesquialtera minore*].

'But one must admit that there is more caprice than reason in most of these Signs.'

(e) Whether in unmixed or (more usually) mixed passages of 'black' and 'white' triple notation, we are left essentially to decide from the context: do the blackened notes have the same value as if they were white; or do they have half that value?

In Ex. 254 above, we have seen that the blackened notes have half the value which they would have had if white. This is a common occurrence, and to us seems very logical; for just as blackening a white minim gives what looks to us like a standard (black) crochet, *i.e.* a note of half the duration, so blackening a white semibreve should give the equivalent of a white minim, *i.e.* again a note of half the duration. On this way of looking at it, blackening a normally white note would have the same effect on the value as adding a tail: *i.e.*, dividing the length by half. And so indeed it often does work out in practice.

On the same basis, whitening a normally black note should have the same effect on the value as removing a tail: *i.e.* multiplying the length by twice. And this, too, works out in practice, meeting many baroque instances successfully.

(f) We have seen that a reason for blackened notes was to insure against an undesired perfecting (in our notation, dotting), since white notes under mensural rules were liable to perfection, imperfection and alteration, but blackened notes were not.

Was there any reason, however, for whitening notes which are normally black? Choquel gives the interesting suggestion (*La musique rendue sensible*, Paris, 2nd ed., 1762, p. 107), that in the slow three-time signified by $\frac{3}{2}$, white quavers (*croches blanches*) may be used 'so as not to use crochets (*noires*) [literally 'blacks'] when it is a question of dividing the minims (*blanches*) [literally 'whites'] in relation to the song (*par rapport au chant*)'; by which I take him to mean that whereas crochets cannot be grouped by their beams, white quavers can, and that this may give an advantage to the whitened notation.

It is the assumption here that the note-value of the whitened quaver is the same as that of the standard (black) crochet; and experience shows that this is indeed the normal expectation. Choquel's reasoning may or may not be correct; but it is hard to see any other which might apply. Whitened quavers (with the value of crochets) and whitened semi-quavers (with the value of quavers) are by no means uncommon, and in most cases seemingly with no particular musical significance.

(g) Blackened semibreves and minims, however, cannot be dismissed so summarily, since they have each a choice of two possible values: half their white values, or the same as their white values.

A blackened minim is identical in appearance with a standard (black) crochet; and this raises no problem so long as their value is also identical. But there is a problem when a blackened minim has, on the contrary, the same value as if it were a standard (white) minim. And this alternative, unfortunately, is also quite likely to be the meaning.

The solution may have to be found mainly by musical intelligence; but this should not usually be difficult once the possibilities are known. The two cases at Ex. 255 take a little puzzling out, but their solution is in no respect uncertain, and is as I have shown it in square brackets above each part at the crucial places where mensural interpretation is involved. For modern performers, these interpretations should be written into the actual text; for a scholar's edition the notation should be left scrupu-lously as it appears in the original sources, which should also be collated for variant readings. (For Ex. 255, see p. 659.)

(i) Notice particularly the white notation (whitened crochets and quavers) in bars 3 and 7 of (a); the whitening doubles the value (standing for standard minims and crochets).

(ii) Also, in the voice part of (b), the standard (black) crochet at the end of bar 2, followed immediately by a black minim at the beginning of bar 3 (identical in appearance, but having twice the value); and the two standard (black) crochets at the end of the same bar.

(iii) Also, in the bass part of (b), the semibreve at the beginning of bar 5, perfected by mensural convention (in our notation, it would have to be dotted).

(iv) Also, in both parts of (b), the difference of notation between bar 3 and bar 6. Both these bars are of the same length, but they are of different metres: for bar 3 would in modern notation be $\frac{6}{2}$, but bar 6 would be $\frac{3}{1}$. That is to say, bar 6 is an example of hemiolia; for it goes not two perfect (in our notation dotted) semibreves to the tactus, but three imperfect (in our notation undotted) semibreves to the tactus. Black notation was therefore required to insure against unwanted

Ex. 255. (a) [Luigi Rossi], Cantata, 'Lascia speranza, ohimè', Harvard Univ., Houghton Lib., MS Mus. 106, *f.* 31 r; (b) anon., Cantata, 'Fugga amor chi teme affani', same MS, *f.* 61 v. to 62 r: examples of perfection and coloration (MS copied mid-17th cent.):

perfecting (dotting) of the semibreves by mensural convention; and this association between hemiolia rhythm and black notation was established practice.

But, of course, in baroque music there are incomparably more instances in which it is necessary to recognise, and to bring out clearly in performance, a hemiolia, without the slightly mixed blessing of black notation to draw attention to it.

(h) The following Ex. 256 illustrates both the indiscriminate confusion into which signs for mensuration had fallen by the middle of the seventeenth century, and the importance of understanding correctly what remnants of mensural notation are encountered (and they are by no means rare) in baroque music. (See p. 661 for Ex. 256.)

The principal manuscript here is accepted by my wife, Dr. Gloria Rose, as probably an autograph of Carissimi (she is exceedingly cautious in such a matter). The time-signature for the passage here is C_2^3. Of other mid-seventeenth century manuscripts collated by Dr. Rose for her *Giacomo Carissimi: Six Solo Cantatas* (London, 1969, p. 85), two have C 3, one has 3, and one rejoices in an impressive but perhaps a little redundant $\mathfrak{C}_2^3$. This last gives imperfect tempus, perfect prolation, sesquialtera proportion, and might therefore have been notated (though it is not) with undotted perfect semibreves of three minims each. The other collated time-signatures, C_2^3, C 3 and 3, however, were all at this period more or less debased but habitual manners of indicating sesquialtera. So low had the proud (but unfortunately never quite consistent) distinctions of the mensural time-signatures by then fallen.

In other respects, collation of six mid-seventeenth century manuscrips (out of a total of twelve known) shows no difference of notation at the place here illustrated; but it is worth mentioning that in bar 36 of the same cantata, four manuscripts (including the probable autograph) show the bass as a black minim followed by a black semibreve; one shows it has a white minim followed by a white semibreve (which is a valuable clue since it at least suggests that in this piece we do not have to regard blackening as diminishing the actual value); and one shows a white minim followed by a white minim, the second of which is correctly taken at double value as the result of alteration, *i.e.* at the actual value of a semibreve (which may put us on our guard once again for mensural influences).

In the passage here illustrated at Ex. 256 below, the only problem is the actual value of the three black semibreves. Dr. Rose in her transcription (p. 20, m. 28, and matching passage, p. 25, m. 116) took the value to be halved by the blackening, which as we have seen is very often the case in seventeenth-century notation; and there is nothing in the notation at this point to show that it is not the case here. But she was a little puzzled, afterwards, when she noticed that the word-accentuation was not up to Carissimi's usually impeccable standard; later still, she found the correct solution in a most unexpected source, a late 18th-century manuscript which includes this cantata in the hand of the celebrated organist William Crotch, of all people. The time-values are reduced by half throughout the composition; but the original black semibreves are transcribed in the same proportion as if they had been white semibreves: *i.e.* they are transcribed as three minims, the middle one bisected by a bar-line. It is a fine example of hemiolia; and Dr. Crotch knew it, and knew how to put it effectually into a modernised notation even though this bisecting of a note by a bar-line, too, has come to be a little unorthodox in our own modern notation. Unorthodox, but useful, and now again sometimes used.

Dr. Rose made no other such mistake; but that she could make this one several years ago, when neither of us knew enough about black notation, underlines the practical importance of this knowledge for modern editors and performers. I am happy to add that the word-setting, on this correct resolution of the hemiolia, is as good as ever.

Ex. 256. Giacomo Carissimi, Cantata, 'Bel tempo per me se n'andò', *c.* 1650, (a) in probable autograph, Rome, Vatican Lib., MS. Barb. lat. 4136, *f.* 44 v, virtually identical in Bologna, Conservatorio, MS. X234, *f.* 70 v., and other sources collated; (b) in William Crotch's hand, London, Brit. Mus. Add. MS. 31412, *f.* 76 r.; hemiolia shown (a) in black notation and (b) transcription:

5. TELESCOPED CADENCES IN RECITATIVE

(a) Just as the conventional appoggiatura was standard at cadences in late baroque Italianate recitative (for which see Ch. XIV, 10 above), so the conventional delay by the accompanist in bringing in his dominant $\frac{5}{3}$ resolution of the $\frac{6}{4}$ harmony (for which see Ch. XLII, 4 above) was standard.

A post-baroque confirmation of unusual clearness comes in Joseph Haydn's letter to a monastery about to perform his music, translated and ascribed to 1768 by H. C. Robbins Landon, *Correspondence . . . of Joseph Haydn* (London, 1959, pp. 9–11): 'in the accompanied recitatives, you must observe that the accompaniment should not enter until the singer has quite finished his text, even though the score often shows the contrary'. In 1873, Sir George Macfarren wrote (dated preface to Handel's *Belshazzar*, London [n.d.]) of his decision to discard 'the now obsolete plan, of writing the two final chords under the voice notes which are intended to precede them'. This is precisely the same misnotation which Scheibe categorically warned his readers against: see (565) in Ch. XLII, 4 above; and no one doubts that its standard interpretation for late baroque Italianate recitative was always the delayed accompaniment which Scheibe meant, which Haydn expected, and which Macfaren found passing into misunderstanding late in the nineteenth century.

(b) But J. A. Westrup has proved conclusively and with many striking examples ('The Cadence in Baroque Recitative', *Natalicia Musicologica Knud Jeppesen*, Copenhagen, 1962, pp. 243–52) the very important point that this standard interpretation was customarily modified in opera, where the entire cadence might be telescoped in order to gain speed and excitement. Sven Hostrup Hansell ('The Cadence in 18th-Century Recitative', *Musical Quarterly*, LIV, 2, April, 1968, pp. 228–48) seems to have confused some evidence concerning acciaccaturas, a quite different matter, and thus somewhat over-stated the circumstances admitting this cadential telescoping; but that it could be used at any (though not perhaps at all) suitably dramatic moments in opera is now certain, and continuo accompanists must cultivate this remarkable idiom among their other accomplishments.

(282) Johann David Heinichen, *General-Bass*, Dresden, 1728, II, i, 54, note dd (p. 674):

'By nature these recitative cadences ought always, I say always to resolve [after the singer has finished].

'Since however this kind of cadence, tedious, and yet occurring at every moment in theatrical music, would sound in the end annoying, yes and quite often the singer concerned seems to linger somewhat pointlessly; therefore it can happen that one takes occasion to shorten the matter, and [telescope the cadence].'

Ex. 257. J. D. Heinichen, illustrations of telescoped cadences discussed above at (282):

In his first two illustrations, Heinichen has shown his voice part (without words) as it is sung, and figured his harmonies as they would be played; and these cadences, although telescoped, are not actually ungrammatical, since the (written out) appoggiatura does fit with the figured 6–4 or 5–4, and the main note does fit with the figured 5–3 resolution.

But in his third illustration, Heinichen has shown his voice part not as it is sung, but as it would normally be notated; and has again figured his harmonies as they would be played. He has therefore (by a kind of visual though not aural deception common in such baroque circumstances) concealed to the eye though not to the ear the fact that the progression as actually heard is very ungrammatical indeed. For I have added at [*i.e.*] the appoggiatura which, though not notated, was certain to be sung, and of course should be sung: for which see Ch. XIV, 10 above. This appoggiatura in the melody is the 4 of an implied tonic 6–4 harmony; and it is heard simultaneously with the dominant 7–5–3, as figured and played. Tonic and dominant harmony thus clash in complete grammatical disarray. Yet that is just what is often going to happen to such telescoped cadences in recitative: experience shows that it sounds perfectly acceptable because of its dramatic suitability, and indeed that it is extremely desirable and effective in keeping the pace and the excitement going.

Heinichen only says of the telescoped cadence that in theatrical music 'it can happen'. The following is more strongly expressed.

Ex. 258. G. P. Telemann, *Singe-, Spiel- und Generalbass-Übungen*, Hamburg, 1733–34, No. 40, cadences (closes) in recitative, with the instruction: 'These closes would in opera be struck immediately, while the singer speaks the last syllables, in cantatas however one must strike them afterwards':

(783) Joachim Quantz, *Essay*, Berlin, 1752, XVII, vi, 59:

'[The bass] must generally, in all cadences of theatrical recitative, whether accompanied by violins, or merely ordinary [*i.e. secco*], begin its two [cadential] notes, which most often pass through a falling leap of a fifth, under (*unter*) the last syllable, and not strike them too slowly, but with liveliness.'

(784) C. P. E. Bach, *Essay*, Berlin, II, 1762, XXXVIII, 3:

'Fiery recitative in opera [where the orchestra is spread out and the singer distant from it, but under no other mentioned circumstances, may justify the first harpsichordist who] does not wait for the entire cadence of the singing part, but strikes already on (*bey*) the last syllable what should rightly be [struck] first on the following harmony, [with the intention] that the remaining basses or [other] instruments can enter correctly on time together'.

As sometimes happened, C. P. E. Bach seems to have had a passage of Quantz in mind, and to have contradicted it either from a personal difference of taste, or (if in his Part II, 1762) a subsequent change of taste.

There can have been no uniformity of practice in so eminently optional a matter, and we are certainly not obliged to take our operatic cadences this way all the time in late baroque Italianate recitative. But experience shows that the method works much better than one would suppose possible from the grotesque breaches of common musical grammar resulting, with dominant triads breaking in on six-four melody, and tonic triads breaking in on dominant triads, in an eager scramble to get the cadence over. But such eagerness may be just what the dramatic situation most aptly demands; and where this happens, which in baroque opera it habitually does, there is no good musician-ship in hanging around for the strict grammar of the case. The harpsi-chordist, with proper discretion as to when and where, can then best serve his duty by pressing theatrically ahead.

A Footnote to Inequality

(a) Evidence for the unequal performance of notes which are notated as equal has been uncovered for early music with remarkable impartiality of time and place; and it is this fact which precludes us from ascribing any monopoly of it to late baroque French circumstances, including those eighteenth-century German schools whose circumstances were largely modelled upon the French. At the most we might be inclined to suggest that the matter was more systematically pondered upon in such circles; but this was true of methods of performance generally, and not only of the rhythmic aspects of performance. It is always harder to find Italian authority than French or German, at any rate in the later portions of the baroque period.

(b) Since the first and second editions of the original version of this book, I have come across some further evidence, which, together with numerous findings by various of my colleagues, made the basis of my article 'A Problem of Inequality' (*Musical Quarterly*, LIII, 4, Oct. 1967). There, for example, I mentioned that Gio. Domenico Puliaschi ('L'autore a i lettori', last page of *Musiche varie a una voce*, Rome, 1618) spoke among other expressive resources of 'now pointing (*punteggiare*) the first note, now the second, as the passage requires'; and that Pier Francesco Tosi (*Opinioni*, Bologna, 1723, p. 114) likewise described, as part of a particular expressive effect, 'inequality of motion (*disuguaglianza di moto*)'. These are certainly Italian equivalents to the French *pointer* and *inegalité* respectively. See also Doni at (784), par. 5 of quotation, in App. IX below.

There is ample evidence for such customary though always optional inequality in Italian scores, large and small. A negative hint of it may be seen in the cautionary words 'here they play in equal time' under equally notated quavers (largo), which we infer might otherwise have been performed unequally, in Scarlatti's *Pirro e Demetrio* (perf. Naples, 1694), II, 15. A positive hint may be seen in the discrepancies of notation, but not of intention, between the Berlin score, the Madrid score and the London parts of Agostino Steffani's *Tassilone* (perf. Düsseldorf, 1709), III, 6, where in the aria *Tutta tremo* the dotting shown is variously inconsistent. Such inconsistencies are exceedingly common, and further examples are given during the longer discussion in my *Performer's*

Guide to Baroque Music (London, 1973), Ch. XIX, 5. The following samples may suffice here.

Ex. 259. Gio. Batt. Vulpio, cantata *Dolce zampogna mia*, Rome, Bibl. Naz. Cen. Vittorio Emanuele II, MS. Mus. 162, *ff*. 109r–110r, inequality notated inconsistently but intended consistently in matching phrase:

Ex. 260. Domenico Scarlatti, Sonata K.491 (L.164), consistent inequality implied though inconsistently notated (choice is optional but should be kept the same throughout; similar inconsistencies of notation are numerous):

The separate orchestral parts of operas, preserved in considerable numbers in the Bibliothèque Nationale and the Bibliothèque de l'Opèra in Paris (unlike Italy, where few survive) abound in similar discrepancies, though my extensive searches through this promising material led in other respects to more disappointing results, for clues on the actual performance of French opera, than I had hoped at first sight. There is, of course, no shortage of French evidence on inequality. The following makes an interesting story.

Lully's *Amadis* (perf. Paris, 1684) had a second edition with several impressions, taken from the same plates. There are impressions in the Bibliothèque Nationale in Paris, dated 1711, 1719 and 1721. The third of these has, on pages 54–5, *etc.*, equal notation changed in manuscript to dotted notation. On p. 74 the hand-written note appears: 'correct the middle parts of the orchestra and measure them according to the [dotted] Violins and Basses'. On pp. 75, 78, 96–7 we read 'very loud without dotting too much (*sans trop pointer*)'. On p. 108 we read: 'Equal quavers and very detached' (where they might otherwise be inequalised). On p. 118: 'Revise the Middle parts for the changes of the Measures and Value of the Notes'. On p. 139 *ff.*, under the top part: 'The sounds very firm and very detached', although here the equally notated notes are changed by hand to dotted. Conversely, at the Bibliothèque de l'Opèra, A.16.b., p. 8, bar 5 the dotted note of this print (and of the 1st ed.) has the dot scratched out by hand, and at bar 15 of the chorus 'Que le ciel annonce' has 'croches egales' written in ink; yet Lully's *Persée* (perf. Paris, 1682), Act III, prelude to Sc. iv, has in A.14.b., p. 143, the printed figure ♩ ♫ changed in ink to ♩. ♫ several times.

I take all this to hint at a very open situation, in which many passages notated equally were traditionally performed unequally (either 'not too dotted' or 'very detached' and therefore probably over-dotted); but that a conductor wishing partly otherwise in the 1721 revival of *Amadis* made his wishes known in rehearsal, from which this visible record of one particular performance (and there are others like it) comes down to us.

It is this openness in the rhythmic situation which we shall do well to bear in mind today.

(c) An unusual specimen of inequality is given below at Ex. 261; for here, equally notated triplets are shown alternating with triplets dotted in Siciliana rhythm, and that this should be among the options is remarkable indeed. It can hardly have been left to chance at rehearsal; presumably the director in charge expressed his wishes verbally as usual.

Ex. 261. Anon. opera (*c.* 1700), Rome, Bibl. Apost. Vat., (a) score in MS. Barb. lat. 4215, *f.* 11r, ritornello with equally notated triplets; (b) part for violins in MS. Barb. lat. 4217, *f.* 5r, same ritornello with Siciliana rhythm notated:

(d) A characteristic misnotation (for which see Ch. XLIV, 2 above) can be seen in Ex. 262 below, where the structure of the music makes it certainly necessary to adjust in performance the inconsistency in the notation (the over-dotting needed is exact double-dotting).

Ex. 262. G. F. Handel, autograph score of *Jephtha*, London, Brit. Mus., R.M. 20, *e.q.* 'Ouverture', inequality needed beyond that notated in order to synchronise with notated (*i.e.* as dotted) inequality:

Ouverture

(e) Inequality is mentioned in an anonymous English manuscript of the second half of the seventeenth century, 'Miss Mary Burwell's Instruction Book for the Lute' (ed. Thurston Dart, *Galpin Soc. Journ.*, XI, 1958, pp. 3–62) as (pp. 46 *ff.*) 'stealing half a note from one note and bestowing it upon the next note'; and again among the manuscript notes by Roger North (cited by John Wilson, in his *Roger North on Music*, London, 1959, p. 223) 'in short notes [the dot] gives a life and spirit to the stroke, and a good hand will often for that end use it, tho' not express't [in the notation]'.

Howard Ferguson in his excellent edition, *Eight Suites: Henry Purcell* (London, 1964), shows the following instructive comparisons, among others of the kind (by kind permission). (Ex. 263 on p. 669.)

With these variants (the crisper of which is in each case the better option and nearer to the probable intention) we may compare the following French example (where the same inference applies, as it also does to the two versions of J. S. Bach's French Overture, in *C* minor and *B* minor respectively, of which the latter more closely approximates in notation to the intention in performance). (Ex. 264 on p. 669.)

(f) It is as well to remember that while contemporary instructions for inequality, especially in French sources, are often quite explicit and even quite lucid, they are also quite inconsistent one with another. A particularly clear and simple explanation is found, for example, in

Ex. 263. Henry Purcell, Suite III, Almand, bars 5–7: (a) as in Oxford, Christ Church MS. 1117; (b) as in the ed. of London, 1696; and Suite IV, Corant, bars 1–3; (c) as in Paris, Bibl. Nat., MS Rés. 1186 bis, 1; (d) as in Oxford, Ch. Ch. MS. 1117; (e) as in ed. of 1696:

Ex. 264. Jean Henri D'Anglebert, *Sarabande grave*, ed. by M. Roesgen-Champion (Paris, 1934, pp. 141 and 145) from the *Pièces de Clavecin* (Paris, 1689) and Paris, Bibl. Nat., Bauyn MS., Res. Vm^7, 674), bar 2, (a) in equal notation; (b) in unequal notation, representing the preferred rhythm in performance:

Borin's *Musique theorique, et pratique* (Paris, 1722, pp. 26 *ff.*); but it is unfortunately too simple to be true. See also Ch. XLV above.

With our practical application of inequality, the difficulty lies not in knowing that it was done, nor even when and where it was done. It was done everywhere during the whole baroque period, not to mention before, and after until far into the nineteenth century. And it can be a most beautiful effect.

The difficulty lies in knowing just what are the musical contexts admitting or inviting inequality, and in just what form and degree. In the wrong contexts, inequality can do far more harm than it can do good in the right contexts. I have tried, both here and (still more) in my *Performer's Guide to Baroque Music* (London, 1972), to suggest where the crucial outer boundaries of style can approximately be traced. Within those boundaries, the great baroque principle of flexible interpretation (and no rigid rules) surely holds, as so often, the secret of success.

Ornamentation in the Reciting Style

The following passage has already been drawn upon in small part, in the Postscript to Ch. X above. It is given here at greater length for its value to editors and performers of early and middle seventeenth-century Italian opera, now so topical an issue in our pursuit of baroque music. The passages of ornamentation discussed are only those related to the reciting style (*style recitativo*): but in its various aspects, from little arias (*ariette*), on the one hand, all the way to big dramatic passages of recitative (in *stile rappresentativo*) on the other hand.

(784) G. B. Doni, 'Trattato della musica scenica' [about 1635] in his *Trattati di musica*, ed. A. F. Gori, Florence, 1763, II, 69:

'Passages (*passaggi*) [of ornamentation], then, under which name are included also short little passages (*passagetti brevi*), called Accents (*Accenti*) by some, [if] used as appropriate and in the proper places, bring a wonderful grace and sweetness to singing . . .

'[their most suitable place] really should be (against the usual belief) in Theatres [where] one tries, with costumes and with perfection of gesture and of speech and consequently also in the Music, to show how far human artifice can go, and to give that contentment which can be greatest to the eye and the ear; [whereas] in Churches, where above all one should use grave and moderate singing, and make well heard that which is said (although today this is little observed) long passages [of ornamentation] are extremely unsuitable.

'In chambers (*camere*), similarly, where one usually sings some sort of refined melody, and in the company of people who understand Music, it is necessary to use them there not so much as one says abundantly, but more sparingly. But in spite of the fact that Theatres are their proper places, Composers and Singers themselves should remember, nevertheless, that those [passages] so long that they interrupt the syllable too much and the understanding of the words, can never be pleasing to men of good sense and judgement.

'And what shall we say of those who, on account of their prolixity, cannot pronounce [their passages] with a single breath, but must interrupt them? . . . It seems to me that they are not much to be esteemed, and also because there is too much of the hop and the skip (*troppo del salterello*) about them: whence they can never adapt themselves well to grave subjects and continuous compositions [*modulazioni* in one of its seventeenth century senses] without such a kind of skipping notes; especially also because the movements and Rhythms of passages must not be different from or contrary to those of the whole song . . .

'Passages with beats and notes unequal and pointed (*passaggi di tempi, e note diseguale, e puntate*) can at the very most be allowed in certain little arias or songs for dancing (*ariette, o canzoni da ballo*), and not in other things, although some dotted and prolonged note (*puntata, e lunghetta*) at the beginning and at the end of them really turns out gracefully; especially in cheerful subjects, or indifferent. But in grave and sad [subjects] one should not in my judgement depart from quiet and equally performed (*quieti, ed egualmente tirati*) [passages], which present (*rappresentano*) better the unity of that syllable or note which they ornament (*diminuiscono*) . . .

'It is indeed true that those [passages] which unfold their passage-work (*spasseggiano*) little by little, and use quicker notes, are more graceful than uniform ones; but perhaps they are not so well suited to sad and languid matters as those which, on the contrary, start quickly, and very gently relax their pace; because they express better a certain languor, and lack of strength. But those which go like waves (*a onde*), that is, now they slacken and now they move on, yet not by jerks and at one blow, but gracefully, are the most beautiful and versatile; and this must be understood not less for soft and loud, than for slow and quick . . .

'Although Caccini says positively that reducing [the voice] little by little is more expressive than increasing it, nevertheless I should make distinctions there . . . One way and another, there is a place for what many call Exclamation (*Esclamazione*), because it adds power to the expressive effects (*affetti*) of both kinds: the which is a sudden increasing of the same sound (*voce*) after having pronounced the syllable more softly for a certain time, adding at the same time some small amount of that very short inflection of the voice (*piegamento di voce*) which is generally heard on the final conclusion (*ultime desinenze*) of the syllables of those who sing with grace and tenderness . . .

'As to the vocal tremolo (*Trillo*) which is a warbling (*increspamento*) [or] trembling (*vibratio*) of the voice, perhaps taken from Nightingales, which does not appreciably alter the Pitch (*Tuono*), since it increases liveliness, and certainly brilliance, it seems that it is more suited to cheerful subjects than to sad ones; but nevertheless one can use it almost for everything, especially at cadences, where prolonged or dotted notes (*note lunghette, o puntate*) are encountered; for it makes a fine effect (*fa bel sentire*). But that quavering (*tremolamento*) of the voice which some make, which is like an imperfect vocal tremolo (*Trillo*), is not to be used, unless in mild and womanly subjects; for it has too much of the effeminate, and is not in the least suitable for virile and heroic music.'

Select Bibliography

INTRODUCTORY NOTE

1. THE POLICY OF THIS BIBLIOGRAPHY

(a) I wish to set out here the working rules by which this Select Bibliography is constructed.

I include works mentioned (usually with abbreviated bibliographical information) in my text, even if there is little or nothing else in them which is likely to be useful, when a reader might well wish to look them up for himself.

I include wherever possible dates and places of the first edition of works used, even when I have myself used, and therefore mentioned in my text, a subsequent edition. I have done this even when the first edition appears to be no longer extant, but can be established with sufficient confidence on other grounds. I do this because it is often important to know just to what place and time the contents originally referred.

I include not only works of which I have myself made use or which I have usefully consulted, but also any other works, known to me and seen by me, which I would expect that some reader might find substantially useful.

I include English translations, but not translations into other languages, unless for some special reason: for example, the French translation of Quantz, authorised by himself, and issued concurrently with his German original, so that both his modern translator, Edward Reilly, and I have occasionally used it in preference to the German, and repeatedly consulted it where Quantz' German becomes a little difficult to understand. And for reasons somewhat similar, Marpurg's *Principes*.

But in my text, the English translations are my own, made with the most unremitting effort to get them just as literal as I possibly could. Any glosses and explanations which I felt to be helpful have been put within square brackets, by the usual convention. Where I have felt any doubts, I have put within round brackets the doubtful words in their original language. I wish to give the reader every opportunity to reach his own conclusions.

As an exception, however, I have used not my own translation, but an English translation made within the same period as the original, where I felt that the period flavour, and the nearness of the translator to the whole spirit and meaning of the original, might valuably outweigh any small departures from literal exactness: for example, J. E. Galliard's excellent English translation of Tosi. I have, of course, consulted such contemporary musical dictionaries as Brossard, Walther and Jean-Jacques Rousseau; and in addition, such general contemporary dictionaries as Randle Cotgrave's *Dictionarie of the French and English Tongues* (London, 1611, *etc.* to 1673), or the famous *Vocabolario degli Accademici della Crusca* (Venice, 1612, 3rd ed. Florence, 1691, *etc.*).

For primary sources, I include first editions, but not subsequent editions or impressions unless for special reasons, such as some confusion or uncertainty needing to be elucidated (*e.g.* Frescobaldi, Couperin, Masson, Hummel), or some substantial change of content (*e.g.* Brossard, Heinichen, Mattheson) or change of title (*e.g.* Aaron, Herbst, Simpson).

I include, however, modern editions, and in particular modern facsimile reproductions just so far as it has been possible to ascertain by seeing them (or occasionally from some exceptionally reliable source of information, such as the list of 'Books Recently Published' in *Notes*) that they have actually been published, as opposed merely to having been announced as having been published, since these two states of being are not invariably the same.

I exclude, on the other hand, many works, valuable in themselves, which are either somewhat marginal in their relevance to my present subject, or are concerned wholly or mainly with the useful but subsidiary function of the relaying of existing knowledge.

I have used bold-face type (Roman for articles, Italic for books) to pick out works which are of particular excellence and relevance in the context of my present subject, and not as a comparison of their intrinsic value, although this can then be assumed to be reasonably high. No work has been excluded because I do not agree with it in whole or part; but very many have been excluded because the standard of originality, accuracy, scholarship, musicianship, logic or just plain commonsense seemed to me too low for recommendation here. The field is already thick with a vast and rapidly expanding secondary literature; and for this reason alone I think that the more selective my list is made, the better it may serve my practical purpose of guiding the reader through the tangled undergrowth. I am, as always, extremely open to suggestions and corrections from interested readers.

2. TWO VALUABLE NEW TOOLS OF BIBLIOGRAPHY

(a) I should mention here two recent additions to our bibliographical armoury.

(b) The *Bibliography of Performance Practices* prepared by graduate students of the University of North Carolina at Chapel Hill under the supervision of William Newman (see my Bibl. under Vinquist, the name of its first editor-in-chief) is a most substantial and extensive achievement, forged for the manifold needs of those studying interpretation between the approximate dates 1100 and 1900. Its compilers made certain deliberate exclusions (*e.g.* notation, musica ficta) as explained in their preface, and certain others apparent by inference (*e.g.* dictionaries of music such as Brossard, Walther, Jean-Jacques Rousseau). Supplementary information includes an indication of the main relevant contents, where this is not evident from the title.

As an introduction to the literature, and a preliminary guide and check-list, the *Bibliography of Performance Practices* provides us with a very useful tool. It has to be understood that no such bibliography can be definitive to the extent of relieving the serious student of the need to investigate the bibliographical situation of his primary sources on his own responsibility; and this one is no more infallible than others of its kind. Its value lies not in any unrealisable ideal of finality, but in its sustained and largely successful attempt to be within its own terms inclusive.

The virtues of thus attempting to include everything on the subject, good, bad and indifferent, are just the opposite of those sought in my present Select Bibliography, which even within its narrower chronological limits tries so far as practicable to exclude the marginal and the inferior, and thus to edge the reader tactfully towards the regions of greatest profit. It is obvious that the services provided by both these approaches are complementary to one another.

(c) The two new volumes of RISM under the title *Écrits Imprimés Concernant La Musique* (*i.e.* 'Printed Writings Concerning Music') will be found listed in my bibliography under *Répertoire International des Sources Musicales* (RISM). Their editorial policy has not been explained clearly enough in the preface to prevent certain ambiguities as to what precise information is conveyed by the entries as printed. Thus, *e.g.*, Caccini's *Nuove Musiche* is dated 1601, the date on the title page; every reputable scholar knows that this date is incorrect (even on the assumption that it is Florentine Old Style, since the book was actually published in 1602 after 25 March, the Florentine New Year's Day at this period); but students may be much misled, since no explanation in the Preface or elsewhere warns them that dates are as on title pages and not necessarily correct. Nor, indeed, does such a policy, or any other, appear to have been consistently applied: the use of square, round or no brackets is particularly inconsistent; and there are further mysterious ambiguities, omissions and errors not by any means wholly explained by the inference (it is not stated) that reports from libraries holding copies were as a matter of policy accepted without investigation or comparison with existing works of reference.

Once again, then, we can feel the utmost gratitude for a powerful new tool of bibliography, without placing too unqualified a reliance on its dependability. RISM needs considerable caution in this respect.

3. OTHER ESSENTIAL TOOLS OF BIBLIOGRAPHY

The two bibliographical works just mentioned above are included in my Select Bibliography for pragmatic reasons: they are, at the present time of writing (1973), so recent that they may not be found in all of those invaluable books-about-books-about-books devised to introduce the reader to the literature of bibliography.

I do not, for example, include Eitner in my bibliography for almost the same reason that I do not include Grove or MGG: these are tools of a kind so basic, so necessary and so numerous that to do justice to them requires a bibliography on its own. Eitner, of course, remains indispensable for a vast quantity of bibliographical and supplementary information which it is not the policy of any of its successors to provide; and for this and other reasons, Eitner is not and will not be superseded. I certainly find myself consulting that monumental publication repeatedly, old and in many ways out-dated though it obviously is. But then, how many other great bibliographical authorities do we not require to consult: Emil Vogel; Claudio Sartori; Taddeo Wiel; Oscar Sonneck; Vincent Duckles; James Coover; Howard Brown; indeed they can be numbered by the score, and most of them have relevance to my present subject.

I have decided to deal with this crucial but formidable problem at a blow by recommending Vincent Duckles, *Music Reference and Research Materials: An Annotated Bibliography*, New York, 1964, 2nd ed. 1967. This is indeed a survey of surveys, and of all such the best: a perfect skeleton-key of a bibliographical tool, opening doors and windows in all sorts of what might otherwise remain unsuspected directions.

4. CORRECTIONS MADE, AND INVITED

Places (Anglicised) and dates (given in Arabic style) as shown in this Select Bibliography, and the form, spelling, accentuation and punctuation (but not necessarily the capitalisation) of titles, are (up to the limits practicable without disproportionate detail) as found on the title-pages of first editions, unless otherwise described; and they are as believed by us to be correct, unless information to the contrary is added. All such decisions have been taken jointly by my wife Dr. Gloria Rose, a very experienced bibliographer, and myself; but the solid four months of fresh enquiry and research which lie behind them have been entirely her doing, and she put aside her own book in preparation on the Chamber Cantata for this generous purpose.

Some portion of this labour has consisted of more or less routine but systematic checking against original sources, on the principle that seeing the book itself is always the best precaution. But it may not answer all questions. Not only were mere mistakes by author or printer as chronic a hazard then as now: more subtle complications not uncommonly arise. Bibliography is indeed a sophisticated skill, and full of difficulties.

There are problem-children in bibliography as elsewhere. Sometimes the problem is no more than the mere inexplicable failure of leading works of reference to incorporate corrections established many years ago (*e.g.* Geminiani's *Art of Playing on the Violin*, correctly dated at 1751, first edition, and severed from all supposed prior editions or imaginary links with Prelleur, by David Boyden twenty years ago; yet still, as I write in 1973, uncorrected in our major works of reference). Sometimes the problem has yielded to my wife's persistence and flair (*e.g.* Hummel, the date of whose first English edition she has found with certainty). And sometimes it has not yielded at all, nor seems very likely to (*e.g.* the true story of the Bérard, or Blanchet, *Art du Chant*).

But we have done our best, and now invite corrections in our turn.

SELECT BIBLIOGRAPHY

LIST OF ABBREVIATIONS

Act. Mus.	*Acta musicologica*
Ann. Mus.	*Annales musicologiques*
B-J	*Bach-Jahrbuch*
DDT	*Denkmäler deutscher Tonkunst*
DTO	*Denkmäler der Tonkunst in Österreich*
Erbe dM	*Das Erbe deutscher Musik*
Grove	*Grove's Dictionary of Music and Musicians*
GSJ	*The Galpin Society Journal*
HHA	*Hallische Händel-Ausgabe*
H-J	*Händel-Jahrbuch*
JAMS	*Journal of the American Musicological Society*
Jour. R&BM	*Journal of Renaissance and Baroque Music* (continued as *Musica disciplina*)
Jour. RME	*Journal of Research in Music Education*
MD	*Musica disciplina*
MfM	*Monatshefte für Musik-Geschichte*
MGG	*Die Musik in Geschichte und Gegenwart*
M&L	*Music and Letters*
MQ	*The Musical Quarterly*
MR	*The Music Review*
MT	*The Musical Times*
NBA	*Neue Bach-Ausgabe*
Proc. MTNA	*Proceedings of the Music Teachers National Association*
Proc. RMA	*Proceedings of the Royal Musical Association*
Pub. ält. Mus.	*Publikation älterer praktischer und theoretischer Musikwerke*
Rep. 8th IMS Cong.	*Report of the Eighth [I. M. S.] Congress, New York 1961*, ed. J. LaRue. Kassel, 1961.
Rev. de Mus.	*Revue de musicologie*
SIMG	*Sammelbände der Internationalen Musikgesellschaft*

Aaron, Pietro. *Thoscanello de la musica.* Venice, 1523.
[Name spelt Aron in later eds. Titled *Toscanello in musica* in 1529 and 1539 eds., *Toscanello* in 1562 ed.]
Facs. of Venice, 1523 ed. New York, 1969.
Facs. of Venice, 1539 ed., after-note G. Frey. Kassel, 1970.
Facs. of Venice, 1529 ed. Bologna, 1969.
Facs. of Venice, 1529 ed. announced Utrecht and Hilversum.
Tr. and ed. P. Bergquist. 3 vols. Colorado Springs, 1970.

Adam, Louis (Johann Ludwig). *Méthode de piano du Conservatoire.* Paris [1804].

—— *Méthode nouvelle pour le piano.* Paris, 1802.

—— and Ludwig Wenzel Lachnith. *Methode ou principle général du doigté pour le forté-piano.* Paris [? 1798].

Adlung, Jacob. *Anleitung zu der musikalischen Gelahrtheit.* Erfurt, 1758.
Facs., after-note H. J. Moser. Kassel, 1953.

—— *Musica mechanica organoedi,* ed. Johann Lorenz Albrecht. 2 vols. Berlin, 1768.
Facs., after-note C. Mahrenholz. 2 vols. in 1. Kassel, 1931; reissued 1961.
Facs. announced New York.

Agazzari, Agostino. ***Del sonare sopra 'l basso con tutti li stromenti e dell'uso loro nel conserto.*** Siena, 1607.
Facs. Milan, 1933.
Facs. Bologna, 1969.
In O. Kinkeldey, *Orgel und Klavier . . . ,* pp. 216–221.
Tr. in *Source Readings . . . ,* ed. O. Strunk, pp. 424–431.

Agricola, Johann Friedrich. *Anleitung zur Singkunst.* Berlin, 1757.
[Ger. tr., with extensive additions, of P. F. Tosi, *Opinioni de' cantori antichi, e moderni,* Bologna, 1723]
Facs. ed. E. R. Jacobi. Celle, 1966.
Facs. ed. K. Wichmann. Leipzig, 1966.

Agricola, Martin. *Musica instrumentalis deudsch.* Wittenberg, 1529.
Facs. Hildesheim and New York, 1969, as supplement to facs. of Agricola's *Musica figuralis deudsch.*
First and last (1545) eds., partly facs., ed. R. Eitner (Pub. ält. Mus. XX). Leipzig, 1896.

Alain, Marie-Claire. 'Appunti sulla "maniera francese" ', *L'Organo* V (1964–67) 6–19.

Albrechtsberger, Johann Georg. *Gründliche Anweisung zur Composition.* Leipzig, 1790.

Aldrich, Putnam C. 'The "Authentic" Performance of Baroque Music', *Essays on Music in Honor of Archibald Thompson Davison by his Associates* (Cambridge, Mass., 1957), pp. 161–71.

—— 'Bach's Technique of Transcription and Improvised Ornamentation', MQ XXXV (Jan. 1949) 28–35.
 (Illuminating)

—— 'On the Interpretation of Bach's Trills', MQ XLIX (July 1963) 289–310.
 (Extremely sound)

—— **Ornamentation in J. S. Bach's Organ Works.** New York, 1950.

—— **'The Principal *agréments* of the Seventeenth and Eighteenth Centures: A Study in Musical Ornamentation'.** Ph.D. diss., Harvard Univ., 1942.

—— **Rhythm in Seventeenth-Century Italian Monody.** New York, 1966.

Alembert, Jean le Rond d'. *Élémens de musique, théorique et pratique.* Paris, 1752.
 Facs. announced New York.

Allaire, Gaston G. *The Theory of Haxachords, Solmization and the Modal System* [n.p.] 1972.
 (Deals with accidentals)

Ammerbach, Elias Nicolaus. *Orgel oder Instrument Tabulatur.* Leipzig, 1571.
 Facs. announced New York.

Amon, Johann Andreas. *Recueil de vingt-six cadences ou points d'orgue pour la flûte* [?1820].

Amstad, Marietta. 'Das berühmte Notenblatt des Porpora', *Musica* XXIII (Sept.–Oct. 1969) 453–55.

Andrews, H. K. *An Introduction to the Technique of Palestrina.* London, 1958.
 (Particularly informative on proportional time-signatures)

—— 'Transposition of Byrd's Vocal Polyphony', M&L XLIII (Jan. 1962) 25–37.

Apel, Willi. *Accidentien und Tonalität in den Musikdenkmälern des 15. und 16. Jahrhunderts.* Berlin, 1936.

—— **The Notation of Polyphonic Music 900–1600.** Cambridge, Mass., 1942. 4th ed. 1949.

SELECT BIBLIOGRAPHY

Arbeau, Thoinot [i.e. Jehan Tabourot]. *Orchesographie*. Langres, 1589. [Privilege dated 22 Nov. 1588. Some copies, otherwise identical, undated on title-page.]
>Facs. announced Hildesheim.
>Ed. L. Fonta. Paris, 1888. Repr. Geneva, 1970. Repr. announced Bologna.
>Tr. C. W. Beaumont. London, 1925.
>Tr. M. S. Evans. New York, 1948. Repr., ed. J. Sutton. New York, 1967.

Arger, Jane. *Les agréments et le rythme*. Paris [1921].

Arnold, Denis. 'Brass Instruments in Italian Church Music of the Sixteenth and Early Seventeenth Centuries', *Brass Quarterly* I (Dec. 1957) 81–92.

—— ' "L'Incoronazione di Poppea" and Its Orchestral Requirements', MT CIV (Jan. 1963) 176–78.

—— 'Instruments and Instrumental Teaching in the Early Italian Conservatoires', GSJ, No. 18 (1965) 72–81.

—— 'Orchestras in Eighteenth-Century Venice', GSJ, No. 19 (1966) 3–19.

Arnold, Frank T. *The Art of Accompaniment from a Thorough-Bass as Practised in the XVIIth and XVIIIth Centuries*. London, 1931.
>Repr., introd. D. Stevens. 2 vols. New York, 1965.

Aron, Pietro. See Aaron.

Auda, Antoine. *Theorie et pratique du tactus: Transcription et exécution de la musique antérieure aux environs de* 1650. Brussels, 1965.

Avison, Charles. *An Essay on Musical Expression*. London, 1752.
>Facs. of 2nd ed. (London, 1753) announced Hildesheim.
>Facs. of 2nd ed. announced New York.

Babell, William. *Chamber Music. XII. Solos, for a Violin or Hautboy, with a Bass, Figur'd for the Harpsicord. With Proper Graces Adapted to Each Adagio, by the Author*. London [*c*. 1725].

Babitz, Sol. ' "Concerning the Length of Time that Every Note Must be Held" ', MR XXVIII (Feb. 1967) 21–37.

—— 'Differences Between 18th Century and Modern Violin Bowing', *The Score*, No. 19 (Mar. 1957) 34–55.

—— *The Great Baroque Hoax: A Guide to Baroque Musicians and Performance for Connoisseurs*. Los Angeles, 1970.
>(Erratic but sincere)

Babitz, Sol. 'On Using J. S. Bach's Keyboard Fingerings', M&L XLIII (Apr. 1962) 123–28.

—— 'A Problem of Rhythm in Baroque Music', MQ XXXVIII (Oct. 1952) 533–565.

Bach, Carl Philipp Emanuel. *Versuch über die wahre Art das Clavier zu spielen.* Berlin, 1753. Pt. II, Berlin, 1762.
>Facs. of Pts. I and II, ed. L. Hoffmann-Erbrecht. 2 vols. in 1. Leipzig, 1957. 2nd ed. 1969.
>Abr. ed. of Pt. I, 2nd ed. (Berlin, 1759) and Pt. II, 1st ed., ed. W. Niemann. Leipzig, 1906.
>Tr. and ed. W. J. Mitchell. New York, 1949.

Bach, Johann Sebastian. 'Clavier-Büchlein vor Wilhelm Friedemann Bach' [begun Cöthen, 1720].
>Facs. ed. R. Kirkpatrick. New Haven, 1959.
>Ed. H. Keller. Kassel, 1927.

>Ed. W. Plath (NBA, Ser. V, Bd. 5). Kassel, 1962. Krit. Bericht 1963.
>(Includes the table of ornaments)

Bacilly, Bénigne de. *Remarques curieuses sur l'art de bien chanter.* Paris, 1668.
>Facs. ed. N. Bridgman. Kassel, in preparation.
>Facs. announced New York.
>Facs. of Paris, 1679 ed. Geneva, 1971.
>Tr. and ed. A. B. Caswell, as *A Commentary upon The Art of Proper Singing.* Brooklyn, N.Y., 1968.
>(Long and detailed on early singing technique and style)

Bacon, Richard Mackenzie. *Elements of Vocal Science: Being a Philosophical Enquiry into Some of the Principles of Singing.* London [1824].
>Ed. E. Foreman. Champaign, Illinois, 1966.
>(Unusually lucid on *bel canto*)

Badura-Skoda, Eva. 'Textual Problems in Masterpieces of the 18th and 19th Centuries', MQ LI (Apr. 1965) 301–17.

Badura-Skoda, Eva and Paul. *Mozart-Interpretation.* Vienna, 1957.
>Tr. L. Black, as *Interpreting Mozart on the Keyboard.* London, 1962.
>(Excellent on ornamental embellishment, and full of other imaginative suggestions)

Baillot, Pierre Marie François de Sales. *L'art du violon.* Paris [1834].

——, Rodolphe Kreutzer and Pierre Rode. *Méthode de violon.* Paris [1802 or 1803]

Baines, Anthony. 'James Talbot's Manuscript . . . I. Wind Instruments', GSJ, No. 1 (Mar. 1948) 9–26.

—— 'A Barrel Organ Transcription', GSJ, No. 5 (Mar. 1952) 54–55.
(Transcription of 'God Save the King', highly ornamented, on a barrel organ built by Fentum, London, *c.* 1817)

—— 'Two Barrel Organ Transcriptions', GSJ, No. 12 (May, 1959) 94–98.
(Also highly ornamented melodies, on barrel organs of *c.* 1790 and of the early 19th century)

—— *Woodwind Instruments and their History.* London and New York, 1957. 3rd ed. 1967.
(The best general survey, special knowledge of early varieties)

——, ed. *Musical Instruments Through the Ages.* Harmondsworth, 1961.

Banchieri, Adriano. *L'organo suonarino.* Venice, 1605.
Facs. of 1605 ed., with excerpts from 1611 ed. and 1638 [reprint of 1622] ed., introd. G. Cattin. Amsterdam [1969].
Tr. of 1605 and 1622 eds., and partial tr. of 1611 ed.: Donald E. Marcase, 'Adriano Banchieri, *L'organo suonarino:* Translation, Transcription and Commentary', Ph.D. diss., Indiana Univ., 1970.

Bang, Betty. *Interpretation of French Music from 1675 to 1775, with Additional Comments on German and Italian Music: For Performers on Woodwind and Other Instruments.* New York, in the press.
(Especially for articulation syllables)

—— and David Lasocki. *Free Ornamentation in Woodwind Music 1700–1775.* London, in preparation.

Barbour, J. Murray. **'Bach and *The Art of Temperament'*,** MQ XXXIII (Jan. 1947) 64–89.

—— *Tuning and Temperament: A Historical Survey.* East Lansing, Michigan, 1951.

Baron, Ernst Gottlieb. *Historisch-theoretisch und practische Untersuchung des Instruments der Lauten.* Nuremberg, 1727.
Facs. Amsterdam, 1965.
Facs. announced New York.

Barre, M. de la [Joseph Chabanceau de La Barre]. *Airs a deux parties avec les seconds couplets en diminution.* Paris, 1669.

Barthe, Engelhard. *Takt und Tempo.* Hamburg, 1960.

Bassano, Giovanni. *Motetti, madrigali et canzoni francese . . . diminuiti per sonar con ogni sorte di stromenti.* Venice, 1591.
Facs. ed. C. Sartori. Kassel, in preparation.

Bassano, Giovanni. *Ricercate passaggi et cadentie, per potersi essercitar nel diminuir.* Venice, 1585.

Bate, Philip. *The Flute: A Study of Its History, Development and Construction.* London and New York, 1969.

—— *The Oboe: An Outline of Its History, Development and Construction.* London and New York, 1956.

—— *The Trumpet and Trombone: An Outline of Their History, Development and Construction.* London and New York, 1966.

Bathe, William. *A Briefe Introduction to the Skill of Song.* London [?1590].

Bauer, Robert. *Historical Records.* Milan, 1937. 2nd ed. as *The New Catalogue of Historical Records, 1898–1908/09.* London, 1947.

Beat, Janet E. 'Monteverdi and the Opera Orchestra of His Time', *The Monteverdi Companion*, ed. D. Arnold and N. Fortune (London, 1968), pp. 277–301.

Beck, Sydney and Elizabeth E. Roth. *Music in Prints.* New York, 1965.

Bedos de Celles, (Dom) François. *L'art du facteur d'orgues.* 4 pts. in 3 vols. [Paris] 1766–78.
    Facs., after-note C. Mahrenholz. 3 vols. Kassel, 1934–36 and 1963–66.

Bemetzrieder, Anton. *Leçons de clavecin, et principes d'harmonie.* Paris, 1771.
    Facs. New York, 1966. Facs. announced Bologna.
    Tr. G. Bernard. London, 1778–79.

—— *Traité de musique.* 2 pts. Paris, 1776.

Benary, Peter. *Die deutsche Kompositionslehre des 18. Jahrhunderts.* Leipzig, 1961.

Bent, Margaret. 'Musica recta and musica ficta', *Musica Disciplina,* XXVI (1972) 73–100.

Bérard, Jean-Baptiste (or Jean-Antoine). *L'art du chant.* Paris, 1755.
    Facs. New York, 1967. Facs. Geneva, 1972.
    Tr. and ed. S. Murray. Milwaukee, 1969.
    (Bérard's authorship was disputed by the Abbé Joseph Blanchet, who published a 2nd ed. of this book, with the title *L'art, ou les principes philosophiques du chant,* under his own name of Blanchet, in Paris, 1756. The question has not been settled, but it is well discussed by Murray, and the weight of evidence points to Bérard)

Berardi, Angelo. *Documenti armonici.* Bologna, 1687.
    Facs. Bologna, 1971.

Berardi, Angelo. *Miscellanea musicale*. Bologna, 1689.
Facs. ed. S. Clercx-Lejeune. Kassel, in preparation.
Facs. announced Bologna.

—— *Ragionamenti musicali*. Bologna, 1681.
Facs. ed. S. Clercx-Lejeune. Kassel, in preparation.

Bergmann, Walter. 'Some Old and New Problems of Playing the Basso Continuo', Proc. RMA, 87th Session (1960–61) 31–43.

Bernhard, Christoph. 'Tractatus compositionis augmentatus'; 'Von der Singe-Kunst oder Manier'. Printed in J. M. Müller-Blattau, *Die Kompositionslehre Heinrich Schützens in der Fassung seines Schülers Christoph Bernhard*. Leipzig, 1926. 2nd ed. Kassel, 1963.
(For 'doctrine of figures')

Bessaraboff, Nicholas. *Ancient European Musical Instruments*. Boston, Mass., 1941.

Béthizy, Jean-Laurent de. *Exposition de la théorie et de la pratique de la musique*. Paris, 1754.
Facs. announced New York.
Facs. of 2nd ed. (Paris, 1764). Geneva, 1972.

Beyschlag, Adolf. *Die Ornamentik der Musik*. Leipzig, 1908. Reprinted Leipzig, 1953.

Bianciardi, Francesco. *Breve regola per imparar' a sonare sopra il basso*. Siena, 1607.

Blades, James. *Percussion Instruments and Their History*. London, 1970.

Blainville, Charles Henri. *L'esprit de l'art musical, ou réflexions sur la musique*. Geneva, 1754.

Blanchet, (Abbé) Joseph (or Jean). See Bérard.

Boalch, Donald H. *Makers of the Harpsichord and Clavichord, 1440 to 1840*. London [1956].

Bodky, Erwin. *The Interpretation of Bach's Keyboard Works*. Cambridge, Mass., 1960.
(Idiosyncratic, but includes much valuable matter, especially on the detailed application of ornaments)

Bollioud de Mermet, Louis. *De la corruption du goust dans la musique françoise*. Lyon, 1746.

Bonnet, Jacques. *Histoire de la musique, et de ses effets*. 4 vols. Amsterdam [? 1721].

[Begun by Abbé Bourdelot, continued by Pierre Bonnet, completed and pub. by Jacques Bonnet. First pub. Paris, 1715. Vols. 2–4 of the Amsterdam, [? 1721], 1725 and 1726 eds. are a reprint of the *Comparaison* of J.-L. Le Cerf de la Viéville]

 Facs. of Paris, 1715 ed. Geneva, 1969.

 Facs. of Amsterdam, 1725 ed., ed. O. Wessely. 4 vols. in 2. Graz, 1966.

 (Poor as history but valuable as a contemporary picture)

Bononcini, Giovanni Maria. *Musico prattico*. Bologna, 1673.

 Facs. Hildesheim, 1969.

 Facs. New York, 1969.

 Facs. announced Farnborough.

[Borin, ?] *Le musique theorique, et pratique, dans son ordre naturel.* Paris, 1722.

Borrel, Eugène. *Contribution à l'interprétation de la musique française au XVIIIe siècle*. Paris, 1914.

—— *L'interprétation de la musique française (de Lully a la Révolution)*. Paris, 1934.

 [Partly drawn from his *Contribution* (1914) and *La réalisation* (1920)]

—— 'L'interprétation de l'ancien récitatif français', *Rev. de Mus.* XII (Feb. 1931) 13–21.

—— 'Les notes inégales dans l'ancienne musique française', *Rev. de Mus.* XII (Nov. 1931) 278–89.

—— *La réalisation de la basse chiffrée dans les œuvres de l'école française au XVIIIe siècle*. Paris, 1920.

 (Brief, good, has excellent 'Table of Figures')

Boston, Canon Noel and Lyndesay G. Langwill. *Church and Chamber Barrel-Organs: Their Origin, Makers, Music and Location; A Chapter in English Church Music*. Edinburgh, 1967. 2nd ed. 1970.

[Bottrigari, Ercole] *Il Desiderio overo, De' concerti di varij strumenti musicali*. Venice, 1594.

 Facs. Bologna, 1969.

 Facs. of 1599 ed., introd. K. Meyer. Berlin, 1924.

 Tr. of 1599 ed. by C. MacClintock. [Rome] 1962.

Bovicelli, Giovanni Battista. *Regole, passaggi di musica, madrigali, e motetti passeggiati*. Venice, 1594.

 Facs., after-note N. Bridgman. Kassel and Basel, 1957.

Boyden, David D. 'Corelli's Solo Violin Sonatas "Grac'd" by Dubourg', *Festkrift Jens Peter Larsen*, ed. N. Schiørring *et al.* (Copenhagen, 1972), pp. 113–25.

—— 'Dynamics in Seventeenth- and Eighteenth-Century Music', *Essays on Music in Honor of Archibald Thompson Davison by his Associates* (Cambridge, Mass., 1957), pp. 185–93.

—— 'Geminiani and the first Violin Tutor', Act. Mus. XXXI (1959) 161–70. 'A Postscript . . .', Act. Mus. XXXII (1960) 40–47.

—— *The History of Violin Playing from Its Origins to 1761 and Its Relationship to the Violin and Violin Music.* London, 1965.

—— 'The Missing Italian Manuscript of Tartini's *Traité des Agrémens*', MQ XLVI (July 1960) 315–28.

—— 'Monteverdi's *Violini piccoli alla francese* and *Viole da brazzo*', Ann. Mus. VI (1958–1963) 387–401.

—— 'The Tenor Violin: Myth, Mystery, or Misnomer?', *Festschrift Otto Erich Deutsch zum 80. Geburtstag am 5. September 1963*, ed. W. Gerstenberg, J. LaRue and W. Rehm (Kassel, 1963), pp. 273–79.

Bray, Roger. 'The Interpretation of Musica Ficta in English Music *c.* 1490–*c.* 1580', Proc. RMA XCVII (1970–71) 29–45.

Bridgman, Nanie. 'Giovanni Camillo Maffei et sa lettre sur le chant', Rev. de Mus. XXXVIII (July 1956) 3–34.

Broder, Nathan. 'The Beginnings of the Orchestra', JAMS XIII (1960) 174–80.

Brossard, Sébastien de. *Dictionnaire des termes.* Paris, 1701. [Enl. ed. as] *Dictionaire de musique.* Paris, 1703.
Facs. of 2nd ed. (Paris, 1705), introd. H. Heckmann. Hilversum, *c.*1965 (but introd. dated Feb. 1966).

Brunold, Paul. *Traité des signes et agréments employés par les clavecinistes français des XVIIe et XVIIIe siècles.* Lyon, 1925.

Buelow, George J. 'The Full-Voiced Style of Thorough-Bass Realization', Act. Mus. XXXV (1963) 159–171.

—— *Thorough-Bass Accompaniment According to Johann David Heinichen.* Berkeley and Los Angeles, 1966.

Bukofzer, Manfred F. *Music in the Baroque Era.* New York, 1947.

—— 'On the Performance of Renaissance Music', Proc. MTNA, Series 36 (1941) 225–35.

Burney, Charles. *An Account of the Musical Performances in Westminster-Abbey, and the Pantheon . . . 1784. In Commemoration of Handel.* London, 1785.
Facs. Amsterdam, 1964.

Burney, Charles. *A General History of Music, from the Earliest Ages to the Present Period.* 4 vols. London, 1776–89.
> Ed. F. Mercer. 2 vols. London, 1935. Reprinted New York, 1957.
> Ed. Othmar Wessely, in preparation.

—— Music articles in *The Cyclopaedia; or Universal Dictionary of Arts, Sciences and Literature,* ed. Abraham Rees. 45 vols. London, 1819–20. [Issued serially from 1802]

—— *The Present State of Music in France and Italy.* London, 1771.
> Facs. announced New York.

—— *The Present State of Music in Germany, the Netherlands, and the United Provinces.* 2 vols. London, 1773.
> Facs. announced New York.
> The two above books ed. Percy A. Scholes as *Dr. Burney's Musical Tours in Europe.* 2 vols. London, 1959.

Busby, Thomas. *A Complete Dictionary of Music.* London [1786].

Butler, Charles. *The Principles of Musik, in Singing and Setting.* London, 1636.
> Facs., introd. G. Reaney. New York, 1970.

Caccini, Giulio. *Le nuove musiche.* Florence, 1602.
> [Title-page 1601 (probably Florentine old-style for pre-March 25, 1602; but still erroneous, since publication was post-March 25; error is due to printing delay mentioned in printer's note). Caccini's dedication dated 1 February 1601, Florentine old style, *i.e.* 1602. Ecclesiastical 'licenzia de Superiori' last of June 1602. Imprimatur 1 July 1602 (*i.e.* earliest possible month of publication). License to print 1 June 1602 (probably in error for July). Last page has 1602, visibly changed from 1601.]
> Facs. ed. F. Mantica. Rome, 1930.
> Facs., introd. F. Vatielli. Rome, 1934.
> Facs. announced New York.
> Ed. H. Wiley Hitchcock. Madison, 1970.
> Dedication and **Preface** in *Le origini del melodramma,* ed. A. Solerti, pp. 53–71.
> **Preface** tr. in *Source Readings . . .,* ed. O. Strunk, pp. 377–392; and in the Hitchcock ed., pp. 43–56.

Cannon, Beekman C. *Johann Mattheson: Spectator in Music.* New Haven and London, 1947. Repr. 1968.

Carapetyan, Armen. 'The Concept of *Imitazione della natura* in the Sixteenth Century', Jour. R&BM I (Mar. 1946) 47–67.

Carse, Adam. *The Orchestra in the XVIIIth Century.* Cambridge, Eng., 1940.

Cartier, Jean-Baptiste. *L'art du violon.* Paris [1798].
Facs. announced New York.

Casa, Girolamo dalla. *Il vero modo di diminuir.* 2 bks. Venice, 1584.
Facs. 2 vols. in 1. Bologna, 1970.

Cavalieri, Emilio de'. *La rappresentatione di anima, et di corpo.* Rome, 1600.
Facs. ed. F. Mantica. Rome, 1912.
Facs., after-note M. Baroni. Bologna, 1967.
Facs. announced Farnborough.
Preface (probably by Alessandro Guidotti) in *Le origini del melodramma*, ed. A. Solerti, pp. 5–12.

[Cazotte, Jacques] *Observations sur la lettre de J. J. Rousseau, au sujet de la musique françoise.* [?Paris] 1753.

Cerone, Pedro [Domenico Pietro]. *El melopeo y maestro.* Naples, 1613.
Facs., introd. F. A. Gallo. 2 vols. Bologna, 1969.
Facs., introd. R. Stevenson, announced New York.

Cerreto, Scipione. *Della prattica musica vocale, et strumentale.* Naples, 1601.
Facs. announced Bologna.

—— *Dell' arbore musicale.* Naples, 1608.

[Choquel, Henri Louis] *La musique rendue sensible par la méchanique, ou Nouveau systeme pour apprendre facilement la musique soi-même.* Paris, 1759.
Facs. of [2nd] ed. (Paris, 1762). Geneva, 1972.

Chorley, Henry F. *Thirty Years' Musical Recollections.* London, 1862.
Ed. E. Newman. New York and London, 1926.

Clementi, Muzio. *Introduction to the Art of Playing on the Piano Forte.* London [1801].

Clutton, Cecil. 'The Virginalists' Ornaments', letter to GSJ, No. 9 (June 1956) 99–100.

—— and George Dixon. *The Organ: Its Tonal Structure and Registration.* London, 1950.

Cocks, William A. 'James Talbot's Manuscript . . . III. Bagpipes', GSJ, No. 5 (Mar. 1952) 44–47.

Coclico, Adrianus Petit. *Compendium musices.* Nuremberg, 1552.
Facs., after-note M. F. Bukofzer. Kassel, 1954.

—— *Musica reservata; consolationes piae.* Nuremberg, 1552.
Ed. M. Ruhnke (Erbe dM XLII). Lippstadt, 1958.

Cohen, Albert. '*L'art de bien chanter* (1666) of Jean Millet', MQ LV (Apr. 1969) 170–79.

Cohen, Albert. 'A Study of Instrumental Ensemble Practice in Seventeenth-Century France', GSJ, No. 15 (Mar. 1962) 3–17.

Collins, Michael B. 'The Performance of Coloration, Sesquialtera, and Hemiolia (1450–1750)'. Ph.D. diss., Stanford Univ., 1963.

—— 'The Performance of Sesquialtera and Hemiolia in the 16th Century', JAMS XVII (Spring 1964) 5–28.

—— 'The Performance of Triplets in the 17th and 18th Centuries', JAMS XIX (Fall 1966) 281–328.

—— **'A Reconsideration of French Over-Dotting',** M&L L (Jan. 1969) 111–23.

—— 'In Defense of the French Trill', JAMS XXVI (Fall 1973) 405–439.

The Compleat Musick-Master. Preface by T[homas] B[rown]. London, 1704.

> [Only known copy 3rd ed., London, 1722. A collateral descendant of *Nolens Volens*, London, T. Cross, late 1694 or early 1695. See David D. Boyden, 'A Postscript to "Geminiani and the first Violin Tutor" ', Act. Mus. XXXII (1960) 40–47]

The Compleat Violist. [Music by] Benjamin Hely. London, [c. 1700].

Conforti, Giovanni Luca. *Breve et facile maniera d'essercitarsi . . . a far passaggi.* Rome, 1593 [? possibly 1603: date blurred in printing].
> Facs. and Ger. tr., ed. J. Wolf. Berlin, 1922.

—— *Passaggi sopra tutti li salmi.* Venice, 1607.

Corelli, Arcangelo. *Sonate a violino e violone o cimbalo. Opera quinta, parte prima. Troisieme edition ou l'on a joint les agréemens . . . composez par M^r. A. Corelli comme il les joue.* Amsterdam [?1715].

> [The Joachim-Chrysander ed. of the Violin Sonatas, Op. V (*Les Œuvres de Arcangelo Corelli*, III [1890]) includes the ornamented version of the slow movements]

> [Geminiani's ornamentation of the *entire* sonata, Op. V, no. 9, is printed in Hawkins' *History*, ed. of London, 1875, II, 904–07]

> [Prof. David Boyden drew my attention to a MS. in the collection of the late Alfred Cortot entitled 'Correllis Solos Grac'd by Doburg' and including six sonatas from Op. V with ornamentation to the slow and to some of the fast movements: see under Boyden]

Corrette, Michel. *L'ecole d'Orphée: Méthode pour apprendre facilement à jouer du violon.* Paris, 1738.

—— *Le maitre de clavecin pour l'accompagnement.* Paris, 1753.

> Facs. Bologna, 1970.
> Facs. announced Hildesheim.
> Facs. announced New York.

[Corrette, Michel] *Methode pour apprendre aisément à joüer de la flute traversiere*. Paris and Lyon [*c.* 1740].

    Tr. and ed. Carol R. Farrar, in her *Michel Corrette and Flute-Playing in the Eighteenth Century*. Brooklyn, N.Y., 1970.

    Facs. announced New York.

    Facs. of 1780 [*sic*] ed. announced Hildesheim.

—— *Methode, théorique et pratique pour apprendre en peu de tems le violoncelle*. Paris, 1741.

    Facs. Geneva., 1972

    Facs. announced New York.

—— *Le parfait maitre à chanter*. Paris [1758].

Couperin, François. **L'art de toucher le clavecin**. Paris, 1716. [Enl. ed.] Paris, 1717.

    Facs. of 1717 ed. New York, 1969.

    Ed. P. Brunold in Couperin's *Oeuvres complètes*, I (Paris, 1933), pp. 19–68.

    Ed. and Ger. tr. A. Linde, with Eng. tr. M. Roberts. Leipzig, 1933.

—— *Le Parnasse ou l'Apothéose de Corelli*. Paris, 1724.

—— *Pièces de clavecin. Premier livre*, Paris, 1713; *Second livre*, Paris [1717]; *Troisième livre*, Paris, 1722; *Quatrième livre*, Paris, 1730.

    Ed. K. Gilbert. 4 vols. Paris, 1969–72.

    Facs. announced New York.

Courcy, Florence de. *The Art of Singing*. London [*c.* 1868].

Coverdale, Myles. *Goostly Psalms*. London [?1539].

    (For its interesting preface)

[Coxe, William] *Anecdotes of George Frederick Handel, and John Christopher Smith*. London, 1799.

Coxon, Carolyn. 'Some Notes on English Graces for the Viol', *Chelys: The Journal of the Viola da Gamba Society* II (1970) 18–22.

Cramer, Carl Friedrich, ed. *Magazin der Musik*. 2 Jahrg. Hamburg, 1783–86. [Continued as] *Musik*. Copenhagen, 1789.

    Facs. of the 1783–86 issues. 4 vols. Hildesheim and New York, 1971.

Cudworth, Charles. ' "Baptist's Vein"—French Orchestral Music and Its Influence, from 1650 to 1750', Proc. RMA, 83rd Session (1956–57) 29–47.

—— 'Handel and the French Style', M&L XL (Apr. 1959) 122–31.

Curtis, Alan. *Sweelinck's Keyboard Music: A Study of English Elements in Seventeenth-Century Dutch Composition*. Leiden and London, 1969. 2nd ed. 1972.

    (Appendix III, pp. 205–12: 'English and Dutch ornament symbols')

Cyr, Mary. 'A Seventeenth-Century Source of Ornamentation for Voice and Viol: British Museum MS. Egerton 2971', *R.M.A Research Chronicle*, No. 9 (1971) 53–72.

Czerny, Carl. *Complete Theoretical and Practical Piano Forte School* [*Vollständige theoretisch-praktische Pianoforte-Schule*, Op. 500]. London [1839].

    Facs. of Vol. IV, Ch. 2 and 3 (Vienna, 1842) as *Über den richtigen Vortrag der sämtlichen Beethoven'schen Klavierwerke*. Ed. P. Badura-Skoda, Vienna, 1963.

Dadelsen, Georg von. **'Verzierungen'**, MGG XIII (1966) cols. 1526–56.
——, ed. *Editionsrichtlinien musikalischer Denkmäler und Gesamtausgaben*. Kassel, 1967.

Dahlaus, Carl. **'Zur Entstehung des modernen Taktsystems im 17. Jahrhundert'**, *Archiv für Musikwissenschaft* XVIII (1961) 223–240.

Dannreuther, Edward. *Musical Ornamentation*. 2 vols. London [1893–95].

Dart, R. Thurston. 'Francesco Geminiani and the Rule of Taste', *The Consort*, No. 19 (July 1962) 122–27.

—— *The Interpretation of Music*. London, 1954. 4th ed. 1967.

—— 'Miss Mary Burwell's Instruction Book for the Lute', GSJ, No. 11 (May 1958) 3–62.
    (Explanation of rhythmic inequality pp. 46–47)

—— 'Ornament Signs in Jacobean Music for Lute and Viol', GSJ, No. 14 (Mar. 1961) 30–33.

—— 'Performance Practice in the 17th and 18th Centuries: Six Problems in Instrumental Music', Rep. 8th IMS Cong., I, 231–35.

——, Walter Emery and Christopher Morris. *Editing Early Music: Notes on the Preparation of Printer's Copy*. London, 1963.

Daube, Johann Friedrich. *General-Bass in drey Accorden*. Leipzig, 1756.

David, Hans T. *J. S. Bach's Musical Offering: History, Interpretation, and Analysis*. New York, 1945.

—— and Arthur Mendel. **The Bach Reader: A Life of Johann Sebastian Bach in Letters and Documents.** New York, 1945. Rev. ed. 1966.

Dean, Winton. *Handel and the Opera Seria*. Berkeley and Los Angeles, 1969.

—— **Handel's Dramatic Oratorios and Masques.** London, 1959.

Dean, Winton. 'Vocal Embellishment in a Handel Aria', *Studies in Eighteenth-Century Music: A Tribute to Karl Geiringer on His Seventieth Birthday*, ed. H. C. Robbins Landon and R. E. Chapman (London, 1970), pp. 151–59.

Degrada, Francesco. 'Giuseppe Riva e il suo "Avviso ai compositor ed ai cantanti" ', *Analecta musicologica* IV (1967) 112–23.

Descartes, René. *Musicae compendium* [1618]. Utrecht, 1650.
    Facs. Strasbourg, 1965.
    Facs. New York, 1968.
    Another facs. announced New York.
    Tr. [William Viscount Brouncker] as *Renatus Des-Cartes Excellent Compendium of Musick: With Necessary and Judicious Animadversions Thereupon. By a Person of Honour*. London, 1653.
    Tr. W. Robert; introd. and notes by C. Kent. [Rome] 1961.

Diruta, Girolamo. *Il Transilvano. Dialogo sopra il vero modo di sonar organi, & istromenti da penna*. Venice, 1593. Pt. II, Venice, 1610.
    [Pt. II title-page is dated 1609, *i.e.* presumably Venetian Old Style dating for 1610 prior to 1 March as New Year's Day there; but publication evidently delayed until after 25 March 1610, since the dedication is thus dated.]
    Facs. announced Bologna.
    Facs. announced New York.

Döbereiner, Christian. *Zur Renaissance alter Musik*. Berlin-Halensee, 1950. 2nd ed., Tutzing, 1960.

Dolmetsch, Arnold. **The Interpretation of the Music of the XVIIth and XVIIIth Centuries Revealed by Contemporary Evidence.** London [1915]. New ed. London [1944].
    Repr. of the 1946 [*sic*] ed., introd. R. Alec Harman. Seattle and London, 1969.

Dolmetsch, Mabel. *Dances of England and France from 1450 to 1600*. London, 1949.

—— *Dances of Spain and Italy from 1400 to 1600*. London, 1954.

Doni, Giovanni Battista. *De praestantia musicae veteris*. Florence, 1647.
    Facs. announced Bologna.
    Facs. announced Hildesheim.

—— **'Trattato della musica scenica'** [ca. 1635], *Trattati di musica*, ed. A. F. Gori (Florence, 1763), II, 1–144 and App.

Donington, Robert. 'Geminiani and the Gremlins', M&L LI (Apr. 1970) 150–55.

Donington, Robert. *The Instruments of Music*. London, 1949. 4th ed. [incorrectly given as 3rd ed. by publisher's error; very greatly rev. and enl.] 1970.

—— 'James Talbot's Manuscript . . . II. Bowed Strings', GSJ, No. 3 (Mar. 1950) 27–45.

—— *A Performer's Guide to Baroque Music*. London, 1973.
   (For a description of this smaller book in its relationship to the present book, see pp. 34ff. above.)

—— **'A Problem of Inequality'**, MQ LIII (Oct. 1967) 503–17.

—— *Tempo and Rhythm in Bach's Organ Music*. London, 1960.

Dreetz, Albert. *Czerny and Beethoven*. Stolp [1932].

Duckles, Vincent. **'Florid Embellishment in English Song of the Late 16th and Early 17th Centuries'**, Ann. Mus. V (1957) 329–45.

—— 'The Gamble Manuscript as a Source of *Continuo* Song in England', JAMS I (Summer 1948) 23–40.
   (Gives ornamented and plain versions from Brit. Mus., Add. MS. 11608)

—— *Music Reference and Research Materials: An Annotated Bibliography*. New York, 1964. 2nd ed. 1967.
   (See Introductory Note to this Bibliography)

—— and Minnie Elmer. *Thematic Catalog of a Manuscript Collection of Eighteenth-Century Italian Instrumental Music in the University of California, Berkeley, Music Library*. Berkeley and Los Angeles, 1963.
   (Indicates sources for embellished versions of slow movements, and for cadenzas, pp. 380–84)

Duey, Philip A. *Bel Canto in Its Golden Age: A Study of Its Teaching Concepts*. New York, 1951. Repr. Ann Arbor, 1968.

[Edgcumbe, Richard] *Musical Reminiscences of an Old Amateur*. London, 1824. 2nd ed. 1827.

Eggebrecht, Hans H. 'Arten des Generalbasses im frühen und mittleren 17. Jahrhundert', *Archiv für Musikwissenschaft* XIV (1957) 61–82.

Einstein, Alfred. *The Italian Madrigal*. Tr. A. H. Krappe, R. H. Sessions and O. Strunk. 3 vols. Princeton, 1949.

Emery, Walter. **Bach's Ornaments.** London, 1953.

—— *Editions and Musicians* [cover subtitle]: *A Survey of the Duties of Practical Musicians & Editors Towards the Classics*. London, 1957.

—— 'The Interpretation of Bach', MT XCVI (Apr. 1955) 190–93.

—— *Notes on Bach's Organ Works: A Companion to the Revised Novello Edition*. 2 vols. London, 1952 and 1957.
   (Detailed and valuable)

Emery, Walter. Review of Fritz Rothschild's *The Lost Tradition in Music*, M&L XXXIV (July 1953) 251–64. Reply about the same, M&L XXXV (Jan. 1954) 80–88.

Engel, Hans. **'Diminution'**, MGG III (1954) cols. 489–504.

Engramelle, Marie-Dominique-Joseph. *La Tonotechnie, ou l'art de noter les cylindres*. Paris, 1775.
    Facs. Geneva, 1971.

Eppelsheim, Jürgen. **Das Orchester in den Werken Jean-Baptiste Lullys.** Tutzing, 1961.

Fabbri, Mario. 'Appunti didattici e riflessioni critiche di un musicista preromantico: Le inedite "Annotazioni sulla musica" di Francesco Maria Veracini', *Quaderni della Rassegna musicale* III (1965) 25–54.

—— 'Nuova luce sull'attività fiorentina di Giacomo Antonio Perti, Bartolomeo Cristofori e Giorgio F. Haendel', *Chigiana* XXI (1964) 143–90.

Fantini, Girolamo. *Modo per imparare a sonare di tromba*. Frankfurt, 1638.
    Facs. Milan, 1934.

Fasano, Renato. *Storia degli abbellimenti musicali dal canto gregoriano a Verdi e guida alla loro interpretazione*. Rome, 1947.

Fellowes, E. H. *The English Madrigal Composers*. Oxford, 1921. 2nd ed. London and New York, 1948.

Ferand, Ernest T. 'Didactic Embellishment Literature in the Late Renaissance: A Survey of Sources', *Aspects of Medieval and Renaissance Music: A Birthday Offering to Gustave Reese*, ed. J. LaRue (New York, 1966), pp. 154–72.

—— 'Embellished "Parody Cantatas" in the Early 18th Century', MQ XLIV (Jan. 1958) 40–64.

—— 'A History of Music Seen in the Light of Ornamentation', Rep. 8th IMS Cong., I, 463–69.

—— 'Improvisation', MGG VI (1957) cols. 1093–1135.

—— *Die Improvisation in Beispielen aus neun Jahrhunderten abendländischer Musik*. (*Das Musikwerk*) Cologne, 1956. Eng. ed. (*Anthology of Music*) Cologne, 1961.

—— *Die Improvisation in der Musik*. Zurich, 1938.
    (A thorough and exhaustive study)

—— **'Improvised Vocal Counterpoint in the Late Renaissance and Early Baroque',** Ann. Mus. IV (1956) 129–74.

Ferand, Ernest T. 'Die Motetti, Madrigali, et Canzoni Francese . . . Diminuiti . . . des Giovanni Bassano (1591)', *Festschrift Helmuth Osthoff zum 65. Geburtstage*, ed. L. Hoffmann-Erbrecht and H. Hucke (Tutzing, 1961), pp. 75–101.

Finck, Hermann. *Practica musica*. Wittenberg, 1556.
    Facs. Bologna, 1969.
    Facs. Hildesheim and New York, 1971.
    Bk. V in Ger. tr. by R. Schlecht, MfM XI (1879) 130–41; mus. exs. ed. R. Eitner, *ibid.*, 151–64.

Fitzpatrick, Horace. *The Horn and Horn-Playing and the Austro-Bohemian Tradition from 1680 to 1830*. London, 1970.

Flesch, Carl. *The Art of Violin Playing*. Tr. F. H. Martens. 2 vols. Boston, 1924–30.

Forkel, Johann N. *Musikalisch-kritische Bibliothek*. 3 vols. Gotha, 1778–79.
    Facs. 3 vols. in 1. Hildesheim, 1964.

—— *Über Johann Sebastian Bachs Leben, Kunst und Kunstwerke*. Leipzig, 1802.
    Facs. Frankfurt, 1950.
    Ed. J. M. Müller-Blattau. Augsburg, 1925. 4th ed. Kassel, 1950.
    Tr. Stephenson as *Life of J. S. Bach*; *With a Critical View of his Compositions*. London, 1820. [Printed in *The Bach Reader*, ed. H. T. David and A. Mendel (New York, 1945), pp. 293–356]
    Tr. C. S. Terry. London, 1920.

Fortune, Nigel. 'Continuo Instruments in Italian Monodies', GSJ, No. 6 (1953) 10–13.

—— 'Giustiniani on Instruments', GSJ, No. 5 (1952) 48–54.

—— 'Italian 17th-Century Singing', M&L XXXV (July 1954) 206–19.

[Fréron, Élie-Catherine] *Lettre sur la musique françoise*. [Paris, 1753]

Frescobaldi, Girolamo. *Toccate e partite d'intavolatura di cimbalo . . . Libro primo*. Rome, 1615. [2nd ed.] Rome, 1615–16 [title-page dated 1615, preface engraved 1616].
    Prefaces in Claudio Sartori, *Bibliografia della musica strumentale italiana stampata in Italia fino al 1700* (Florence, 1952), pp. 207 and 219.
    Preface of 2nd ed. tr. A. Dolmetsch, *The Interpretation . . .*, pp. 4–6.

Frotscher, Gotthold. *Aufführungspraxis alter Musik*. Locarno, 1963.
    Repr. 1971.
    (Mainly German sources; no Bibl.)

Gafori, Franchino. *De harmonia musicorum instrumentorum opus.* Milan, 1518.
    Facs. announced Bologna.
    Facs. announced New York.

Gai, Vinicio. *Gli strumenti musicali della corte medicea e il museo del Conservatorio 'Luigi Cherubini' di Firenze: Cenni storici e catalogo descrittivo.* Florence, 1969.

Galilei, Vincenzo. *Dialogo . . . della musica antica, et della moderna.* Florence, 1581.
    Facs., introd. F. Fano. Rome, 1934.
    Facs. announced New York.
    Excerpts ed. F. Fano. Milan, 1947.

Ganassi, Sylvestro di. **Opera intitulata Fontegara, la quale insegna a sonare di flauto.** Venice, 1535.
    Facs. Milan, 1934.
    Facs. announced Bologna.
    Ed. H. Peter, with Ger. tr. E. Dahnk-Baroffio and H. Peter. Berlin-Lichterfelde, 1956.
    Ed. H. Peter, with Eng. tr. from the Ger. ed. of 1956 by D. Swainson. Berlin-Lichterfelde, 1959.

—— *Regola Rubertina. Regola che insegna. Sonar de viola darcho tastada.* Venice, 1542. Pt. II as *Lettione seconda pur della prattica di sonare il violone d'arco da tasti.* Venice, 1543.
    Facs. of Pts. I and II, introd. M. Schneider. 2 vols. Leipzig, 1924.
    Facs. of Pts. I and II. Bologna, 1970.

Garcia, Manuel. **École de Garcia: Traité complet de l'art du chant.** Paris, 1840. Pt. I, 2nd ed. and Pt. II, 1st ed., Paris, 1847.
    (Several translations and subsequent eds.)

—— *Hints on Singing.* Tr. from Fr. by B. Garcia. London and New York, 1894. Repr., introd. B. Cantrell, Canoga Park, Calif., 1970.

Garnsey, Sylvia. 'The Use of Hand-Plucked Instruments in the Continuo Body: Nicola Matteis', M&L XLVII (Apr. 1966) 135–40.

Garros, Madeleine. 'L'art d'accompagner sur la basse-continue d'après Guillaume-Gabriel Nivers', *Mélanges d'histoire et d'esthétique musicales offerts à Paul-Marie Masson* (Paris, 1955), pp. 45–51.

Gasparini, Francesco. **L'armonico pratico al cimbalo.** Venice, 1708.
    Facs. New York, 1967.
    Tr. F. S. Stillings, ed. D. L. Burrows. New Haven, 1963.

Geminiani, Francesco. *The Art of Accompaniament.* 2 pts. London [1756–57].

Geminiani, Francesco. *The Art of Playing on the Violin.* London, 1751. Facs., introd. D. Boyden. London [1952].

[Bibliographical information diversely incorrect in all major dictionaries of music examined with publication dates between 1954 and March 1972. See Boyden's introd. to the facs. ed. [1952]; Boyden, 'Geminiani . . .' 1959 and 1960; and Donington, 'Geminiani . . .' (1970). Riemann Suppl. A–K (1972) is correct.]

—— *Rules for Playing in a True Taste on the Violin, German Flute, Violoncello and Harpsichord, Particularly the Thorough Bass.* [London, 1745?]

—— *A Treatise of Good Taste in the Art of Musick.* London, 1749. Facs., introd. R. Donington. New York, 1969.

Geoffroy-Dechaume, A. *Les 'Secrets' de la musique ancienne.* Paris, 1964.

Gerber, Ernst Ludwig. *Historisch-biographisches Lexicon der Ton-künstler.* 2 vols. Leipzig, 1790–92.
Facs. ed. O. Wessely. Graz, in preparation.

Gérold, Théodore. *L'art du chant en France au XVIIe siècle.* Strasbourg, 1921. Repr. Geneva, 1971.

Gerstenberg, Walter. *Die Zeitmasse und ihre Ordnungen in Bachs Musik.* Einbeck, 1951.

Gill, Donald. 'The Elizabethan Lute', GSJ, No. 12 (May 1959) 60–62.

[Giustiniani, Vincenzo] 'Discorso sopra la musica' [1628].
Ed. S. Bonghi-Lucca, 1878.
In *Le origini del melodramma,* ed. A. Solerti, pp. 103–128.
Tr. and ed. C. MacClintock in MD XV (1961) 209–25.
Tr. and ed. C. MacClintock. [Rome] 1962.

Goldschmidt, Hugo. *Die italienische Gesangsmethode des XVII. Jahrhunderts.* Breslau, 1890.

—— *Die Lehre von der vokalen Ornamentik.* Bd. 1. Charlottenburg, 1907.

Gough, Hugh. 'The Classical Grand Pianoforte, 1770–1830', Proc. RMA, 77th Session (1950–51) 41–50.

Grassineau, James. *A Musical Dictionary.* London, 1740.
[Mainly but not wholly borrowed from Brossard's *Dictionaire*]
Facs. New York, 1966.
Facs. announced Amsterdam.

Grétry, André Ernest Modeste. *Mémoires, ou essai sur la musique.* Paris, 1789.

Grout, Donald J. 'On Historical Authenticity in the Performance of Old Music', *Essays on Music in Honor of Archibald Thompson Davison by his Associates* (Cambridge, Mass., 1957), pp. 341–47.

Guthrie, John. *Historical Dances for the Theatre: The Pavan and the Minuet.* Worthing, 1950.
    (A skilled dancer's point of view, who was also a Dolmetsch pupil)

Haas, Robert M. *Aufführungspraxis der Musik.* Wildpark-Potsdam, 1931.

—— *Die Musik des Barocks.* Wildpark-Potsdam, 1928.

Haböck, Franz. *Die Gesangskunst der Kastraten.* Erster Notenband. Vienna, 1923.

—— *Die Kastraten und ihre Gesangskunst.* Stuttgart, Berlin and Leipzig, 1927.

Hahn, Georg Joachim Joseph. *Der wohl unterwiesene General-Bass-Schüler.* Augsburg, 1751.

Halfpenny, Eric. 'Bow (1)', Grove, 5th ed. (London, 1954) I, 853–54.

Hall, James S. and Martin V. Hall. 'Handel's Graces', H-J III (1957) 25–43. (Ger. tr. pp. 159–71.)

Hansell, Sven H. 'The Cadence in 18th-Century Recitative', MQ LIV (Apr. 1968) 228–48.

—— 'Orchestral Practice at the Court of Cardinal Pietro Ottoboni', JAMS XIX (Fall 1966) 398–403.

Harding, Rosamond E. M. *Origins of Musical Time and Expression.* London, 1938.

Harich-Schneider, Eta. *The Harpsichord: An Introduction to Technique, Style and the Historical Sources.* Kassel and St. Louis, 1954.

—— *Die Kunst des Cembalo-Spiels.* Kassel, 1939. 2nd ed. 1958.
    (Full of excellent and important matter, especially on registration, fingering and phrasing)

—— 'Über die Angleichung nachschlagender Sechzehntel an Triolen', *Die Musikforschung* XII (1959) 35–59.

Harley, John. 'Ornaments in English Keyboard Music of the Seventeenth and Early Eighteenth Centuries', MR XXXI (Aug. 1970) 177–200.

Hawkins, Sir John. *A General History of the Science and Practice of Music.* 5 vols. London, 1776.
    Repr. of London, 1853 ed., introd. C. Cudworth. 2 vols. New York, 1963.
    Repr. of London, 1875 ed., ed. O. Wessely. 2 vols. Graz, 1969.

[Hawkins, Sir John] *Memoirs of the Life of Sig. Agostino Staffani.* [?London ?1740]

Hayes, Gerald R. **Musical Instruments and their Music, 1500–1750.** 2 vols. London, 1928–30.

[Hayes, William] *Remarks on Mr. Avison's Essay on Musical Expression.* London, 1753.

Heaton, Wallace and C. W. Hargens, eds. *An Interdisciplinary Index of Studies in Physics, Medicine and Music Related to the Human Voice.* Bryn Mawr, Pa., 1968.

Heck, Johann Caspar. *The Art of Fingering.* London [177–].

—— *The Art of Playing the Harpsichord.* London [1770].

—— *The Art of Playing Thorough Bass.* London [177–].

Heinichen, Johann David. **Der General-Bass in der Composition.** Dresden, 1728.

[A greatly expanded and improved version of the same author's *Neu erfundene und gründliche Anweisung . . . Erlernung des General-Basses*, Hamburg, 1711]

Facs. Hildesheim and New York, 1969.

Tr. of excerpts in G. J. Buelow, *Thorough-Bass Accompaniment According to Johann David Heinichen*, Berkeley and Los Angeles, 1966.

Helm, E. Eugene. *Music at the Court of Frederick the Great.* Norman, Okla., 1960.

Hely, Benjamin. See: *The Compleat Violist.*

Henderson, William J. *Early History of Singing.* London and New York, 1921

Herbst, Johann Andreas. *Arte prattica et poëtica.* Frankfurt, 1653.

—— *Musica poëtica, sive compendium melopoëticum.* Nuremberg, 1643. Facs. announced New York.

—— *Musica practica sive instructio pro symphoniacis.* Nuremberg, 1642. [2nd ed.] as *Musica moderna prattica, overo maniera del buon canto.* Frankfurt, 1653.
Facs. announced New York.

Heriot, Angus. *The Castrati in Opera.* London, 1956.
(An unsystematic book, but full of interesting quotations)

Herrmann-Bengen, Irmgard. **Tempobezeichnungen: Ursprung, Wandel im 17. und 18. Jahrhundert.** Tutzing, 1959.

Hickmann, Hans, Wilhelm Niemeyer, Hans-Peter Schmitz and Wilhelm Stauder. 'Flöteninstrumente', MGG IV (1955) cols. 311–61.

Hiller, Johann Adam. *Anweisung zum Violinspielen*. Leipzig [1792].

Hirschfeld, Robert. 'Notizen zur mittelalterlichen Musikgeschichte (Instrumentalmusik und Musica ficta)', MfM XVII (1885) 61–67.

Hitchcock, H. Wiley. 'Vocal Ornamentation in Caccini's *Nuove Musiche*', MQ LVI (July 1970) 389–404.

——, ed. *Giulio Caccini: Le nuove musiche*. Madison, 1970.
(Valuable introduction and commentary)

Hofmann, Hans. **'Aufführungspraxis'**, MGG I (1949–51) cols. 783–810.

Holder, William. *A Treatise of the Natural Grounds, and Principles of Harmony*. London, 1694. Facs. New York, 1967.

Hollander, John. *The Untuning of the Sky: Ideas of Music in English Poetry 1500–1700*. Princeton, 1961.

Holst, Imogen. 'Purcell's Dances', *Henry Purcell, 1659–1695: Essays on his Music*, ed. I. Holst (London, 1959), pp. 98–102.

Horsley, Imogene. 'Improvised Embellishment in the Performance of Renaissance Polyphonic Music', JAMS IV (Spring 1951) 3–19.

—— **'The Solo Ricercar in Diminution Manuals: New Light on Early Wind and String Techniques'**, Act. Mus. XXXIII (1961) 29–40.

—— 'Wind Techniques in the Sixteenth and Early Seventeenth Centuries', *Brass Quarterly* IV (Winter 1960) 49–63.

Hotteterre le Romain [Jacques Martin]. *Principes de la flute traversiere, ou flute d'Allemagne; de la flute à bec, ou flute douce, et du haut-bois*. Paris, 1707.
Facs. and Ger. tr. of Amsterdam [1728] ed., after-note H. J. Hellwig. Kassel, 1941. 2nd ed. 1958.
Facs. of Paris, 1713 ed. announced Hildesheim.
Tr. P. M. Doublas. New York, 1968. Tr. D. Lasocki. London, 1968.

Houle, George L. **'The Musical Measure as Discussed by Theorists from 1650 to 1800'**. Ph.D. diss., Stanford Univ., 1960.

—— 'Tongueing and Rhythmic Patterns in Early Music', *The American Recorder* VI (Spring 1965) 4–13.

Hoyle, John. *Dictionarium musica, Being a Complete Dictionary: or, Treasury of Music*. London, 1770.

Hubbard, Frank. *Three Centuries of Harpsichord Making*. Cambridge, Mass., 1965.

Huber, Anna G. *Takt, Rhythmus, Tempo in den Werken von Johann Sebastian Bach*. Zurich, 1958.

Hughes, Andrew. *Manuscript Accidentals: Ficta in Focus, 1350–1450*. [n.p.], 1972.

Hummel, Johann Nepomuk. *Ausführliche theoretisch-practische Anweisung zum Piano-Forte-Spiel, vom ersten Elementar-Unterrichte an bis zur vollkommensten Ausbildung.* Original-Auflage. 3 pts. Vienna, 1828.

    Facs. announced New York.

    Tr. as *A Complete Theoretical and Practical Course of Instructions, on the Art of Playing the Piano Forte, Commencing with the Simplest Elementary Principles, and Including Every Information Requisite to the Most Finished Style of Performance.* London [1829].

    [Preface dated December, 1827 at Weimar, in Ger., Fr. and Eng. eds.; hence, perhaps, the mistaken entry in NYPL Catalogue of a presumed Eng. ed. London, 1827. No such ed., however, exists at NYPL or elsewhere. Title-page of 'Original-Auflage' (Vienna, 1828) already names the subsidiary publishers 'London, bei Boosey und C^{omp} .... Paris, bei A. Farrenc' beneath the main publisher 'Wien, bei Tobias Haslinger', the date 1828 coming immediately above. Frontispiece of Eng. ed. is a signed portrait of Hummel, with the caption: 'London. Published May 12.th 1829 by T. Boosey & C.° 28 Holles Street'. Lib. of Congress copy of Eng. ed. lacks this frontispiece, but retains an added slip, undated, informing 'The Subscribers to Hummel's Pianoforte School' that a portrait of Hummel 'will shortly be presented to them gratuitously by the Publishers'. Eng. ed. not entered at Stationers Hall (though claiming so on title-page); but advertised explicitly as 'This day is published', *The London Literary Gazette*, No. 643, Saturday, May 16, 1829, p. 326.

    First publ. ('Original-Auflage') of Hummel's treatise was therefore Vienna, 1828, in Ger. A 2nd ed. ('Zweite Auflage') was publ. in Ger., Vienna, undated, but first listed March 1838 in the *Musikalisch-literarischer Monatsbericht* (Leipzig) of 1838, p. 42.]

Hunt, Edgar. *The Recorder and Its Music.* London, 1962.

Jackson, William. *Observations on the Present State of Music, in London.* Dublin, 1791 and London, 1791.

Jacobi, Erwin R. 'G. F. Nicolai's Manuscript of Tartini's *Regole per ben suonar il violino*', MQ XLVII (Apr. 1961) 207–23.

—— 'Neues zur Frage "Punktierte Rhythmen gegen Triolen" und zur Transkriptionstechnik bei J. S. Bach', B–J XLIX (1926) 88–96.

—— ' "Über die Angleichung nachschlagender Sechzehntel an Triolen": Bemerkungen und Hinweise zum gleichnamigen Artikel von Eta Harich-Schneider', *Die Musikforschung* XIII (1960) 268–281.

——, ed. *Carl Philipp Emanuel Bach, Giuseppe Tartini: Kadenzen zu Instrumentalkompositionen.* Kassel, in the press.

Jacobs, Charles. *Tempo Notation in Renaissance Spain*. Brooklyn, N.Y., 1964.

Jander, Owen. 'Concerto Grosso Instrumentation in Rome in the 1660's and 1670's', JAMS XXI (Summer 1968) 168–80.

Jeans, Susi. 'English Ornamentation of the 16th to 18th Centuries (Keyboard Music)', *Musica Antiqua, Colloquium Brno 1967; On the Interpretation of Old Music*, ed. R. Pečman (Brno, 1968), pp. 128–36.

—— 'The Pedal Clavichord and Other Practice Instruments of Organists', Proc. RMA, 77th Session (1950–51) 1–15.

Jeppesen, Knud. *Palestrinastil med särligt henblick paa dissonans-behandlingen*. Copenhagen, 1923.
    Tr. M. W. Hamerik, as *The Style of Palestrina and the Dissonance*. Copenhagen and London, 1927. 2nd ed. 1946.

Johnson, Jane Troy. 'How to "Humour" John Jenkins' Three-Part Dances: Performance Directions in a Newberry Library MS', JAMS XX (Summer 1967) 197–208.

Johnstone, H. Diack. 'Tempi in Corelli's Christmas Concerto', MT CVII (Nov. 1966) 956–59.

Kahl, Willi. *Selbstbiographien deutscher Musiker des XVIII. Jahrhunderts*. Cologne and Krefeld, 1948. Repr. Amsterdam, 1972.

Kapsberger, Johannes Hieronymus (Giovanni Girolamo). *Libro primo di arie passeggiate*. Rome, 1612.

—— *Libro primo di motetti passeggiati*. Rome, 1612.

Keller, Hermann. *Die Klavierwerke Bachs: Ein Beitrag zu ihrer Geschichte, Form, Deutung und Wiedergabe*. Leipzig, 1950.

—— *Die musikalische Artikulation, insbesondere bei Joh. Seb. Bach*. Stuttgart, 1925.

—— *Die Orgelwerke Bachs: Ein Beitrag zu ihrer Geschichte, Form, Deutung und Wiedergabe*. Leipzig, 1948.
    Tr. H. Hewitt. New York, 1967.

—— *Phrasierung und Artikulation*. Kassel and Basel, 1955.
    Tr. L. Gerdine. New York, 1965.

—— *Schule des Generalbass-Spiels*. Kassel, 1931. 4th ed. 1956.
    Tr. and ed. C. Parrish, as *Thoroughbass Method*. New York, 1965.

Kellner, David. *Treulicher Unterricht im General-Bass*. Hamburg, 1732. Facs. of 4th ed. (Hamburg, 1767) announced Kassel.

Kelsey, Franklyn. 'Voice-Training', Grove, 5th ed. (London, 1954) IX, 43–66.

Kinkeldey, Otto. *Orgel und Klavier in der Musik des 16. Jahrhunderts.* Leipzig, 1910. Repr. Hildesheim and Wiesbaden, 1968.

Kinney, Gordon J. 'Problems of Melodic Ornamentation in French Viol Music', *Journal of the Viola da Gamba Society of America* V (1968) 34–50.

Kinsky, Georg, ed. *Geschichte der Musik in Bildern.* Leipzig, 1929.
    Tr., with introd. E. Blom. London, 1930. Repr. New York, 1951.

Kirby, Frank E. 'Hermann Finck on Methods of Performance', M&L XVII (July 1961) 212–20.

Kircher, Athanasius. *Musurgia universalis.* 2 vols. Rome, 1650.
    Facs. ed. U. Scharlau. 2 vols. in 1. Hildesheim and New York, 1970.
—— *Phonurgia nova.* Kempten, 1673.

Kirkendale, Ursula. **'The Ruspoli Documents on Handel'**, JAMS XX (Summer 1967) 222–73.

Kirkpatrick, Ralph. *Domenico Scarlatti.* Princeton, 1953.

—— 'Eighteenth-Century Metronomic Indications', *Papers of the AMS*, 1938, 30–50.

——, ed. *J. S. Bach: Goldberg Variations.* New York, 1938.
    (Valuable preface)

Kirnberger, Johann Philipp. *Grundsätze des Generalbasses als erste Linien zur Composition.* Berlin [1781].
    Facs. Hildesheim, 1972.
    Tr. and ed. R. M. Fling, 2 vols., as M.A. thesis, Univ. of Iowa, 1964.

—— *Die Kunst des reinen Satzes in der Musik.* 2 vols. Pt. I. Berlin, 1771. Pt. II. Berlin and Königsberg, 1776–79.
    Facs. of 1776–79 ed. 2 vols. in 1. Hildesheim, 1968.

Kittel, Johann Christian. *Der angehende praktische Organist.* 3 pts. Erfurt, 1801–08.

Klein, Herman. *The Bel Canto, with Particular Reference to the Singing of Mozart.* London, 1923.
    (By a pupil of Manuel Garcia)

Klein, Johann Joseph. *Lehrbuch der theoretischen Musik in systematischer Ordnung entworfen.* Leipzig and Gera, 1801.

Klenz, William. *Giovanni Maria Bononcini: A Chapter in Baroque Instrumental Music.* Durham, N.C., 1962.

Knecht, Justin Heinrich. *Bewährtes Methodenbuch beim ersten Klavierunterricht.* Freiburg [c. 1800].

—— *Kleine theoretische Klavierschule.* 2 vols. Munich [c. 1800].

Kolneder, Walter. *Aufführungspraxis bei Vivaldi.* Leipzig, 1955.

—— *Georg Muffat zur Aufführungspraxis.* Strasbourg and Baden-Baden, 1970.

Kreutz, Alfred. 'Ornamentation in J. S. Bach's Keyboard Works', *Hinrichsen's Musical Year Book*, VII (1952) 358–79.
[Tr. by R. Snell of Kreutz's Introd. to Bach's English Suites, Peters ed.]

Kuhn, Max. *Die Verzierungs-Kunst in der Gesangs-Musik des 16.–17. Jahrhunderts, 1535–1650.* Leipzig, 1902. Repr. Wiesbaden, 1969.
(Valuable on free ornamentation)

Kullak, Franz. *Beethoven's Piano Playing, with an Essay on the Execution of the Trill.* Tr. T. Baker. New York, 1901.

Kutsch, K. J. and Leo Riemens. *Unvergängliche Stimmen: Kleines Sängerlexikon.* Bern and Munich, 1962. 2nd ed. 1966.
Tr. H. E. Jones, as *A Concise Biographical Dictionary of Singers from the Beginning of Recorded Sound to the Present.* Philadelphia, 1969.

L'Abbé le fils [i.e. Joseph Barnabé Saint-Sevin]. *Principes du violon pour apprendre le doigté . . . et les différens agrémens.* Paris [1761].
Facs., introd. A. Wirsta. Paris, 1961 [has title-page of 2nd ed. on cover].

[La Borde, Jean-Benjamin de] *Essai sur la musique ancienne et moderne.* 4 vols. Paris, 1780.

Lach, Robert. *Studien zur Entwicklungsgeschichte der ornamentalen Melopöie.* Leipzig, 1913.
(Really a massive study of figuration, with valuable examples)

L'Affillard, Michel. *Principes tres-faciles pour bien apprendre la musique.* Paris, 1694.
Facs. of 5th ed. (Paris, 1705). Geneva, 1971.

La Fond, Jean François de. *A New System of Music.* 2 pts. London, 1725.

La Laurencie, Lionel de. *L'école française de violon de Lully a Viotti: Études d'histoire et d'esthétique.* 3 vols. Paris, 1922–24. Repr. Geneva, 1971.

Landon, H. C. Robbins. *The Symphonies of Haydn.* London, 1955. 'Addenda and Corrigenda', MR XIX (1958) 311–19; XX (1959) 56–70.
(Has some valuable matter on interpretation)

705

Landowska, Wanda. 'Bach und die französische Klaviermusik', B-J VII (1910) 33–44.

—— *Musique ancienne*. Paris, 1909. 4th ed. 1921.
    Tr. W. A. Bradley, as *Music of the Past*. New York, 1924.

Landshoff, Ludwig. 'Über das vielstimmige Accompagnement und andere Fragen des Generalbassspiels', *Festschrift zum 50. Geburtstag Adolf Sandberger* (Munich, 1918), pp. 189–208.

Lang, Paul H. Editorial in MQ XL (Jan. 1954) 50–55.
    (A devastating review of Rothschild's *Lost Tradition*)

—— Editorial in MQ LVIII (Jan. 1972) 117–27.
    (On certain dangers of a historical approach to early interpretation)

Langwill, Lyndesay G. *The Bassoon and Contrabassoon*. London and New York, 1965.

Lasocki, David. *The Cadenza for Woodwind Instruments in the Eighteenth Century*. London, in preparation.

[Laugier, Abbé Marc-Antoine] *Apologie de la musique françoise, contre M. Rousseau*. [Paris] 1754.

Le Blanc, Hubert. *Defense de la basse de viole*. Amsterdam, 1740.
    Ger. tr. and ed. A. Erhard. Kassel, 1951.

[Le Cerf de la Viéville, Jean-Laurent, Seigneur de Freneuse] *Comparaison de la musique italienne et de la musique françoise*. 3 pts. Brussels, 1704–06.
    Reprinted as vols. 2–4 of Bonnet's *Histoire de la musique*, Amsterdam, [? 1721], 1725 and 1726 eds.
    See under Bonnet for the facs. ed.
    (Written in answer to Raguenet's *Paralele*, Paris, 1702)

Lehmann, Lilli. *How to Sing*. Rev. ed. tr. C. Willenbücher. New York, 1924.

Le Huray, Peter. *Music and the Reformation in England, 1549–1660*. London, 1967.

Lesure, François. *Musik und Gesellschaft im Bild: Zeugnisse der Malerei aus sechs Jahrhunderten*. Tr. from Fr. by A. M. Gottschick. Kassel, 1966.
    Tr. D. and S. Stevens, as *Music and Art in Society*. University Park, Pa. and London, 1968.

Lloyd, Ll. S. Articles in Grove, 5th ed. (London, 1954) *s.v.* Acoustics; Intervals; Just Intonation; Pitch, Absolute; Pitch Notation; Pitch, Standard; Sound; Temperaments; Theory, Scientific and Pseudo-Scientific; Tuning-Fork.
    (Excellent combination of the scientific and the musical approaches)

Locke, Matthew. *Melothesia: Or Certain General Rules for Playing upon a Continued-Bass.* London, 1673.
Facs. announced New York.

—— *Observations upon a Late Book, Entituled, An Essay to the Advancement of Musick.* London, 1672.

Lockwood, Lewis. **'A Dispute on Accidentals in Sixteenth-Century Rome'**, *Analecta musicologica* II (1965) 24–40.

—— **'A Sample Problem of *Musica Ficta*: Willaert's *Pater Noster***', *Studies in Music History: Essays for Oliver Strunk*, ed. H. Powers (Princeton, 1968), pp. 161–82.

Löhlein, Georg Simon. *Anweisung zum Violinspielen.* Leipzig and Züllichau, 1774.
Facs. announced New York.

—— *Clavier-Schule, oder kurze und gründliche Anweisung zur Melodie und Harmonie.* Leipzig and Züllichau, 1765. *Clavier-Schule, 2. Bd. Worinnen eine vollständige Anweisung zur Begleitung.* Leipzig and Züllichau, 1781.
Facs. announced New York.

Loulié, Étienne. **Elements ou principes de musique.** Paris, 1696.
Facs. Geneva, 1971.
Facs. announced New York.
Facs. announced Utrecht and Hilversum.
Tr. and ed. A. Cohen. Brooklyn, N.Y., 1965.

Lowinsky, Edward E. **'Early Scores in Manuscript'**, JAMS XIII (1960) 126–73.

—— 'Matthaeus Greiter's *Fortuna:* An Experiment in Chromaticism and in Musical Iconography', MQ XLII (Oct. 1956) 500–19; XLIII (Jan. 1957) 68–85.

—— 'On the Use of Scores by Sixteenth-Century Musicians', JAMS I (Spring 1948) 17–23.

—— *Secret Chromatic Art in the Netherlands Motet* Tr. C. Buchman. New York, 1946.

—— *Tonality and Atonality in Sixteenth-Century Music.* Berkeley and Los Angeles, 1961.

—— **'A Treatise on Text Underlay by a German Disciple of Francesco de Salinas'**, *Festschrift Heinrich Besseler zum sechzigsten Geburtstag* (Leipzig, 1961), pp. 231–51.

McClure, A. R. 'Studies in Keyboard Temperaments', GSJ, No. 1 (Mar. 1948) 28–40.

Mace, Thomas. *Musick's Monument.* London, 1676.
  Facs. Paris, 1958. Transcriptions by A. Souris, Commentary by J. Jacquot, vol. 2, 1966.
  Facs. New York, 1966.

McIntyre, Ray. 'On the Interpretation of Bach's Gigues', MQ LI (July 1965) 478–92.

Mackerras, Charles. **'Editing Mozart's Operas',** interview with Stanley Sadie, MT CIX (Aug. 1968) 722–23.

—— 'Sense about the Appoggiatura', *Opera* XIV (Oct. 1963) 669–678.

Maffei, Giovanni Camillo. *Delle lettere . . . v'è un discorso della voce,* comp. Don Valerio de' Paoli (Naples, 1562), Bk. 1, pp. 5–81: Letter 1, to Count d'Altavilla.
  Ed. in N. Bridgman, 'Giovanni Camillo Maffei et sa lettre sur le chant', Rev. de Mus. XXXVIII (July 1956) 10–34.

Maillart, Pierre. *Les tons, ou discours, sur les modes de musique.* Tournai, 1610.

[Mainwaring, John] *Memoirs of the Life of the Late George Frederic Handel.* London, 1760.
  Facs. Amsterdam, 1964.

Majer, Joseph Friedrich Bernhard Caspar. *Museum musicum theoretico practicum.* Schwäbisch Hall, 1732.
  Facs., after-note H. Becker. Kassel, 1954.

Malcolm, Alexander. *A Treatise of Musick, Speculative, Practical, and Historical.* Edinburgh, 1721.
  Facs. New York, 1970.
  Facs. announced Hildesheim.

Mancini, Giambattista. *Pensieri, e riflessioni pratiche sopra il canto figurato.* Vienna, 1774.
  Ed. of Milan, 1777 in *Canto e bel canto,* ed. A. della Corte. Turin, 1933.
  Tr. P. Buzzi. Boston, 1912. Repr., introd. P. Miller, announced New York.
  Tr. and ed. E. Foreman. Champaign, Illinois, 1967.
  Facs. of Milan, 1777 ed. Bologna, 1970.

Manfredini, Vincenzo. *Regole armoniche o sieno precetti ragionati per apprendere i principj della musica, il portamento della mano, e l'accompagnamento del basso sopra gli strumenti da tasto.* Venice, 1775. 2nd ed. [enl., esp. on singing] Venice, 1797.
  Facs. of 1st ed. New York, 1966 [actually 1971].

Marais, Marin. *Pièces à une et à deux violes.* 5 bks. Paris, 1686–1725.
Facs. announced New York.

Marmontel, Jean François. *Essai sur les revolutions de la musique en France.* [Paris, 1777]

Marpurg, Friedrich Wilhelm. *Abhandlung von der Fuge.* 2 pts. Berlin, 1753–54.
Facs. 2 vols. Hildesheim and New York, 1970.

—— *Anleitung zum Clavierspielen.* Berlin, 1755. Fr. ed. as *Principes du clavecin.* Berlin, 1756.
Facs. of 2nd ed. (Berlin, 1765) New York, 1969.
Facs. of 2nd ed. Hildesheim and New York, 1970.
Facs. of Fr. ed. Bologna, 1971.

—— *Clavierstücke mit einem practischen Unterricht für Anfänger und Geübtere.* 3 vols. Berlin, 1762–63.

[——] *Des critischen Musicus an der Spree erster Band.* Berlin, 1750.
[Issued weekly from 4 March 1749 to 17 February 1750]
Facs. Hildesheim and New York, 1970.

—— *Handbuch bey dem Generalbasse und der Composition.* 3 pts. Berlin, 1755–58. Supplement, Berlin, 1760.
Facs. announced Hildesheim.

—— *Historisch-kritische Beyträge zur Aufnahme der Musik.* 5 vols. Berlin, 1754–62, 1778.
Facs. 5 vols. Hildesheim and New York, 1970.

[——] *Kritische Briefe über die Tonkunst.* 3 vols. Berlin, 1760–64.
[Issued weekly, 1759–63]
Facs. announced Hildesheim.

[——] *Die Kunst das Clavier zu spielen.* Berlin, 1750. *2. Theil, worinnen die Lehre vom Accompagnement abgehandelt wird.* Berlin, 1761.
Facs. of 4th ed. of Pt. I (Berlin, 1762) and Pt. II (Berlin, 1761). Hildesheim, 1969.

Marx, Hans Joachim. 'Die Musik am Hofe Pietro Kardinal Ottobonis unter Arcangelo Corelli', *Analecta musicologica* V (1968) 104–77.

Masson, Charles. *Nouveau traité des regles de la composition de la musique.* Paris, 1697.
[2nd ed. appeared in 3 impressions dated 1699, 1700 and 1701, with title . . . *regles pour la composition* . . .]
Facs. of 2nd ed. (Paris, 1699), introd. I. Horsley. New York, 1967.
Facs. of 3rd ed. (Paris, 1705). Geneva, 1971.

Mattheson, Johann. *Critica musica*. 2 vols. Hamburg, 1722–25.
Facs. 2 vols. in 1. Amsterdam, 1964.

—— *Exemplarische Organisten-Probe im Artikel vom General-Bass*. Hamburg, 1719. 2nd, enl. ed. as **Grosse General-Bass-Schule**. Hamburg, 1731.
Facs. of 2nd ed. Hildesheim, 1968.
2nd ed., ed. W. Fortner. 2 vols. Mainz, 1956.

—— *Das neu-eröffnete Orchestre*. Hamburg, 1713.
Facs. ed. M. Reimann. Kassel, in preparation.

—— *Der vollkommene Capellmeister*. Hamburg, 1739.
Facs., after-note M. Reimann. Kassel, 1954.
Tr. and ed. E. C. Harriss, as Ph.D. diss., George Peabody College for Teachers, 1969.

Maugars, André. *Response faite à un curieux sur le sentiment de la musique d'Italie. Escrite à Rome le premier octobre* 1639. [? Paris, 1639 or 1640.]
Repr., ed. E. Thoinan, in his *Maugars: Célèbre joueur de viole*. Paris, 1865. Thoinan's book repr. London, 1965.

Mellers, Wilfrid H. *François Couperin and the French Classical Tradition*. London, 1950.

Mendel, Arthur. 'A Brief Note on Triple Proportion in Schuetz', MQ XLVI (Jan. 1960) 67–70.

—— 'On the Keyboard Accompaniments to Bach's Leipzig Church Music', MQ XXXVI (July 1950) 339–62.

—— **'On the Pitches in Use in Bach's Time'**, MQ XLI (July 1955) 332–54; (Oct. 1955) 466–80.

—— **'Pitch in the 16th and Early 17th Centuries'**, MQ XXXIV (1948); (Jan.) 28–45; (Apr.) 199–221; (July) 336–57; (Oct.) 575–93.

[The two articles above reprinted in A. J. Ellis and A. Mendel, *Studies in the History of Musical Pitch*, Amsterdam, 1968]

—— Review of Fritz Rothschild's *The Lost Tradition in Music*, MQ XXXIX (Oct. 1953) 617–30.

—— 'Some Ambiguities of the Mensural System', *Studies in Music History: Essays for Oliver Strunk*, ed. H. Powers (Princeton, 1968), pp. 137–60.

——, ed. **J. S. Bach: The Passion According to St. John.** New York, 1951.
(Valuable preface)

Mersenne, Marin. *Harmonie universelle.* 2 pts. Paris, 1636–37.
Facs. of copy in Bibl. des Arts et Métiers, with Intro. by F. Lesure. 3 vols. Paris, 1963.
The books on instruments tr. R. E. Chapman. The Hague, 1957.

Mersmann, Hans. 'Beiträge zur Aufführungspraxis der vorklassichen Kammermusik in Deutschland', *Archiv für Musikwissenschaft* II (1920) 99–143.

Meude-Monpas, J. J. O. de. *Dictionnaire de musique.* Paris, 1787.

Meyer, Ramon E. 'John Playford's *An Introduction to the Skill of Musick:* A Study of All the Editions and Revisions from 1654 to 1730'. Diss., Ph.D. in Music Theory, Florida State Univ., 1961.

Millet, Jean. *La belle methode, ou l'art de bien chanter.* Lyon, 1666.
Facs., introd. A. Cohen. New York, 1973.

Milner, Anthony. *Music in Performance.* In preparation.

Mizler von Kolof, Lorenz Christoph. *Musikalischer Staarstecher.* Leipzig [1740].
[Issued monthly, 1739–40.]

—— *Neu eröffnete musikalische Bibliothek.* 4 vols. Leipzig, 1739–54.
[Vol. I was issued in 6 pts., 1736–38; vol. II in 4 pts., 1740–43; vol. III in 4 pts., 1746–52. Of vol. IV only pt. 1 was pub., 1754]
Facs. 2 vols. Hilversum, 1966. Facs. announced Hildesheim.

Montéclair, Michel Pignolet de. *Méthode facile pour aprendre à joüer du violon.* Paris [1711 or 1712].

—— *Nouvelle methode pour aprendre la musique.* Paris, 1709.

—— *Petite methode pour apprendre la musique aux enfans et même aux personnes plus avancées en âge.* Paris [c. 1730].

—— *Principes de musique.* Paris [1736]. Facs. Geneva, 1972.

Morley, Thomas. *A Plaine and Easie Introduction to Practicall Musicke.* London, 1597.
Facs., introd. E. H. Fellowes. London, 1937.
Ed. R. Alec Harman. London, 1952.
Facs. Westmead, 1971.
Facs. announced New York.

Morley-Pegge, Reginald. *The French Horn: Some Notes on the Evolution of the Instrument and of Its Technique.* London and New York, 1960. 2nd ed. Tonbridge, 1973.

Moser, Andreas. *Geschichte des Violinspiels.* Berlin, 1923. 2nd ed., rev. H.-J. Nösselt. 2 vols. Tutzing, 1966.

Mozart, J. C. Wolfgang Amadeus. *The Letters of Mozart and his Family*. Tr. and ed. E. Anderson. 3 vols. London, 1938. 2nd ed., ed. A. H. King and M. Carolan. 2 vols. London and New York, 1966.

—— *Neue Ausgabe sämtlicher Werke*. Kassel and Basel, 1955–.
(Excellent editorial policy on vocal appoggiaturas, etc.)

Mozart, J. G. Leopold. **Versuch einer gründlichen Violinschule**. Augsburg, 1756.
    Facs. of 1st ed., ed. B. Paumgartner. Vienna, 1922.
    Facs. of 1st ed. Frankfurt am Main, 1956.
    Facs. of 3rd ed. (1787), ed. H. J. Moser. Leipzig, 1956.
    Facs. of 3rd ed., ed. H. J. Jung. Leipzig, 1968.
    Tr. E. Knocker. London, 1948. 2nd ed., 1951.

Müller, August Eberhard. *Grosse Fortepiano-Schule*. 8th ed., ed. C. Czerny. Leipzig, 1825.

Muffat, Georg. *Auserlesener mit Ernst- und Lust-gemengter Instrumental-Music*. Passau, 1701.
    Ed. E. Luntz, DTO XI/2. Vienna, 1904.
    Preface tr. in *Source Readings* . . ., ed. O. Strunk, pp. 449–52.

—— *An Essay on Thoroughbass*. Ed. H. Federhofer. [Rome] 1961.
[Ed. of Muffat's 'Regulae concentuum partiturae', 1699]

—— **Suavioris harmoniae instrumentalis hyporchematicae Florilegium primum**. Augsburg, 1695. . . . **Florilegium secundum**. Passau, 1698.
    Ed. H. Rietsch, DTO I/2 and II/2. Vienna, 1894 and 1895.
    Preface of *Florilegium primum* tr. in *Source Readings* . . ., ed. O. Strunk, pp. 442–44.
    Preface of *Florilegium secundum:* beginning tr. in *Source Readings* . . ., ed. O. Strunk, pp. 445–47; remainder tr. Kenneth Cooper and Julius Zsako, in their 'Georg Muffat's Observations on the Lully Style of Performance', MQ LIII (Apr. 1967) 220–45.

—— Collected title-pages, prefaces, music examples, etc. in W. Kolneder, *Georg Muffat zur Aufführungspraxis*, Strasbourg and Baden-Baden, 1970.

Muffat, Gottlieb (Theophil). *Componimenti musicali per il cembalo*. Augsburg [?1735].
    Facs. New York, 1968.
    Ed. G. Adler, DTO III/3. Vienna, 1896.
    Ed. F. Chrysander, Supplement to Complete Works of Händel, V. Leipzig, 1896.

Murphy, Sylvia. 'Seventeenth-Century Guitar Music: Notes on *Rasgueado* Performance', GSJ, No. 21 (1968) 24–32.

Murschhauser, Franz Xaver Anton. *Fundamentalische kurz, und bequeme Handtleithung.* Munich, 1707.

M[ylius], W[olfgang] M[ichael]. *Rudimenta musices . . . Anweisung zur Singe-Kunst.* [Gotha] 1685. Most surviving copies Gotha, 1686.

Nathan, Hans. 'The Sense of History in Musical Interpretation', MR XIII (May 1952) 85–100.

Neumann, Frederick. **Baroque and Post-Baroque Ornamentation (France, Italy, and Germany 1600–1765).** In preparation.
(A major contribution)

—— 'Couperin and the Downbeat Doctrine for Appoggiaturas', Act. Mus. XLI (1969) 71–85.
(For answers, see Act. Mus. XLII (1970) 252–55 and Act. Mus. XLIII (1971) 106–8)

—— 'External Evidence and Uneven Notes', MQ LII (Oct. 1966) 448–64.

—— 'The French *Inégales*, Quantz, and Bach', JAMS XVIII (Fall 1965) 313–58.
(For answers, see JAMS XIX (Spring 1966) 112–14; JAMS XIX (Fall 1966) 435–39; and JAMS XX (Fall 1967) 473–85)

—— 'Misconceptions about the French Trill in the 17th and 18th Centuries', MQ L (Apr. 1964) 188–206.

—— 'A New Look at Bach's Ornamentation', M&L XL (Jan. and Apr. 1965) 4–15 and 126–36.

—— 'La note pointée et la soi-disant "manière française" ', Rev. de Mus. LI (1965) 66–92.
(For answer, see M. B. Collins, 'A Reconsideration of French Over-Dotting', M&L L (Jan. 1969) 111–23)

—— 'Notes on "Melodic" and "Harmonic" Ornaments', MR XXIX (Nov. 1968) 249–56.

—— 'The Use of Baroque Treatises on Musical Performance', M&L XLVIII (Oct. 1967) 315–24.

Newman, William S. 'Is There a Rationale for the Articulation of J. S. Bach's String and Wind Music?', *Studies in Musicology: Essays . . . in Memory of Glen Haydon*, ed. J. W. Pruett (Chapel Hill, N.C., 1969), pp. 229–44.

Newman, William S. *Performance Practices in Beethoven's Piano Sonatas: An Introduction.* New York, 1971.
   (Opens up an important field)

—— *The Sonata in the Baroque Era.* Chapel Hill, N.C., 1959. Rev. ed. 1966.

—— *The Sonata in the Classic Era.* Chapel Hill, N.C., 1963.

Niedt, Friedrich Erhard. *Musicalische Handleitung . . . Erster Theil.* Hamburg, 1700. 2nd pt. as *Handleitung zur Variation.* Hamburg, 1706. *Musicalischer Handleitung dritter und letzter Theil.* Hamburg, 1717.
   Facs. of the 3 pts., ed. A. Dürr. Kassel, in preparation.

Nohl, Ludwig. *Beethoven Depicted by His Contemporaries.* Tr. E. Hill. London, 1880.

[North, Francis] *A Philosophical Essay of Musick.* London, 1677.

North, Roger. *The Autobiography of Roger North* [*c.* 1695]. Ed. A. Jessopp. London, 1887.

—— Annotated transcriptions of Capt. Prencourt's 'Rules' for harpsichord, singing, and thorough-bass [*c.* 1710]. Brit. Mus., Add. MS. 32,531, foll. 1–41.

—— 'An Essay of Musicall Ayre' [*c.* 1715–20]. Brit. Mus., Add. MS. 32,536, foll. 1–90.

—— Essay on Sound, Harmony, and 'Aire' [*c.* 1710]. Brit. Mus., Add. MS. 32,537, foll. 66–109.

—— 'The Musicall Gramarian' [*c.* 1726]. Brit. Mus., Add. MS. 32,533, foll. 1–181.
   Extract ed. H. Andrews. London, 1925.

—— *Roger North on Music: Being a Selection from His Essays Written during the Years c. 1695–1728.* Transcribed from the MSS. and ed. John Wilson. London, 1959.

Oberdörffer, Fritz. 'Generalbass', MGG IV (1955) cols. 1708–37.

—— *Der Generalbass in der Instrumentalmusik des ausgehenden 18. Jahrhunderts.* Kassel, 1939.

—— 'Neuere Generalbassstudien', Act. Mus. XXXIX (1967) 182–201.

Oliver, Alfred R. *The Encyclopedists as Critics of Music.* New York, 1947.

Ortiz, Diego. *Trattado de glosas sobre clausulas y otros generos de puntos en la musica de violones.* Rome, 1553.
 Ed., with Ger. tr., M. Schneider. Berlin, 1913. 2nd ed. Kassel, 1936; repr. 1961.
 (Includes the best 16th century musical examples of free ornamentation)

Pasquali, Nicolo. *The Art of Fingering the Harpsichord.* Edinburgh [?1760].
 (Includes written-out ornaments)

—— *Thorough-Bass Made Easy.* Edinburgh, 1757.

Penna, Lorenzo. *Li primi albori musicali per li principianti della musica figurata.* 3 bks. Bologna, 1672.
 Facs. of Bologna, 1684 ed. Bologna, 1969.

Pepys, Samuel. *Diary.* Transcribed by Rev. M. Bright, with Lord Braybrooke's notes, ed. H. B. Wheatley. 10 vols. London, 1893–99.

—— *Diary.* New transcription ed. R. Latham and W. Matthews. In progress, 11 vols. planned. Berkeley and Los Angeles, 1970–.

Petri, Johann Samuel. *Anleitung zur practischen Musik, vor neuangehende Sänger und Instrumentspieler.* Lauban, 1767.
 Facs. of [2nd, enl.] ed. (Leipzig, 1782) Giebing, 1969.
 Facs. of [2nd, enl.] ed. announced New York.

Pilgrim, Jack. 'Tallis' "Lamentations" and the English Cadence', MR XX (Feb. 1959) 1–6.

Pincherle, Marc. 'Elementary Musical Instruction in the 18th Century: An Unknown Treatise by Montéclair', MQ XXXIV (Jan. 1948) 61–67.

—— 'L'exécution aux XVIIe et XVIIIe siècles: Instruments à archet', Rep. 8th IMS Cong., I, 220–31.

—— 'On the Rights of the Interpreter in the Performance of 17th- and 18th-Century Music', MQ XLIV (Apr. 1958) 145–166.

Pirro, André. *L'orgue de Jean-Sébastien Bach.* Paris, 1895.
 Tr. W. Goodrich, as *J. S. Bach: The Organist and His Works for the Organ.* New York, 1902.
 (Good on Bach's background, especially the French influence)

Platt, Peter. 'Perspectives of Richard Dering's Vocal Music', *Studies in Music*, I (1967) 56–66.
 (For written-out ornamentation)

715

Playford, John. *A Breefe Introduction to the Skill of Musick for Song and Violl.* London, 1654.

[19 and several unnumbered eds.; 1655 to 1730 as *A Brief Introduction . . .* or *An Introduction to the Skill of Musick*]

Facs. of 7th ed. (London, 1674). Ridgewood, N.J., 1966.

Facs. of 12th ed. (London, 1694), introd. F. B. Zimmerman. New York, 1972.

Pleyel, Ignaz. *Klavierschule.* Vienna and Leipzig [1801].

Pollini, Francesco. *Metodo pel clavicembalo.* 2nd ed. Milan, 1811.

Pook, Wilfrid. 'Bach's E Major Violin Concerto Reconsidered', M&L XXXVIII (Jan. 1957) 53–65.

(Changes of figuration made by J. S. Bach)

Poulton, Diana. *An Introduction to Lute Playing.* London, 1961.

Powell, Newman W. **'Early Keyboard Fingering and Its Effect on Articulation'.** M.A. thesis, Stanford Univ., 1956.

—— **'The Function of the Tactus in the Performance of Renaissance Music',** *The Musical Heritage of the Church* VI (1963) 64–84.

(Good on the variable speed of the tactus)

—— 'Kirnberger on Dance Rhythms, Fugues, and Characterization', *Festschrift Theodore Hoelty-Nickel*, ed. N. W. Powell (Valparaiso, Ind., 1967), pp. 66–76.

—— **'Rhythmic Freedom in the Performance of French Music from 1650 to 1735'.** Ph.D. diss., Stanford Univ., 1958.

Praetorius, Michael. *Syntagma musicum.* 3 vols. Wittenberg and Wolfenbüttel, 1614–20.

[Original pub.: I, 1, Wolfenbüttel, 1614; I, 2, Wittenberg, 1615; II, Wolfenbüttel, 1618; III, Wolfenbüttel, 1618. Most surviving copies: I, Wittenberg, 1615; II, Wolfenbüttel, 1619 (*Theatrum instrumentorum*, 1620); III, Wolfenbüttel, 1619. On the Tenbury copy, see Grove, 5th ed. (London, 1954), VI, 905–7.]

Facs., after-note W. Gurlitt. 3 vols. Kassel, 1958–59.

Facs. of vol. II, after-note W. Gurlitt. Kassel, 1929 and 1964.

Vol. II ed. R. Eitner (Pub. ält. Mus. XIII). Berlin, 1884.

Vol. III ed. E. Bernoulli. Leipzig, 1916.

Vol. II, pts. 1 and 2 tr. and ed. H. Blumenfeld. [New Haven] 1949.

Vol. III tr. and ed. Hans Lampl as D.M.A. diss., Univ. of Southern California, 1957.

[Prelleur, Peter] *The Modern Musick-Master.* London, 1730.

Facs. of 1731 ed., after-note A. H. King. Kassel, 1965.

Prynne, Michael. 'James Talbot's Manuscript . . . IV. Plucked Strings —The Lute Family', GSJ, No. 14 (Mar. 1961) 52–68.

Quantz, Johann Joachim. *Versuch einer Anweisung die Flöte traversiere zu spielen.* Berlin, 1752. Fr. ed.: *Essai d'une methode pour apprendre à jouer de la flute traversiere.* Berlin, 1752.

Facs. of 3rd ed. (Breslau, 1789), after-note H.-P. Schmitz. Kassel, 1953.

Abbr. reprint ed. A. Schering. Leipzig, 1906.

Tr. and ed. E. R. Reilly, as *On Playing the Flute.* London, 1966.

[Commentary by Reilly as *Quantz and His Versuch: Three Studies.* New York, 1971]

Extracts tr. as *Easy and Fundamental Instructions . . . How to Introduce Extempore Embellishments or Variations.* London [*c.* 1775].

The Quarterly Musical Magazine and Review [ed. R. Mackenzie Bacon]. 10 vols. London, 1818–28.

[Raguenet, l'abbé François] *Paralele des italiens et des françois, en ce qui regarde la musique et les opéra.* Paris, 1702 [misprinted as 1602].

Tr. as *A Comparison between the French and Italian Musick and Opera's.* London, 1709.

[Tr. attrib. to J. E. Galliard as 'conjecture' by Sir John Hawkins, contested by Dr. Burney, not since proved or disproved]

Facs. of [? Galliard's] tr. (London, 1709), introd. C. Cudworth. Farnborough, 1968.

[?Galliard's] tr. ed. O. Strunk, MQ XXXII (July 1946) 411–36.

Tr. in *Source Readings . . .* , ed. O. Strunk, pp. 473–488.

(Full of invaluable sidelights on interpretation)

—— *Défense du parallèle des italiens et des françois.* Paris, 1705.

Rameau, Jean-Philippe. *Code de musique pratique, ou méthodes pour apprendre la musique . . . pour former la voix & l'oreille, pour la position de la main . . . sur le clavecin & l'orgue, pour l'accompagnement.* Paris, 1760.

Facs. ed. E. R. Jacobi (Complete Theoretical Writings of Rameau, IV), n.p., 1969.

Facs. New York, 1965.

—— *Dissertation sur les différentes métodes d'accompagnement pour le clavecin, ou pour l'orgue.* Paris, 1732.

Facs. ed. E. R. Jacobi (Complete Theoretical Writings of Rameau, in V), n.p., 1969.

Facs. announced New York.

—— *Pièces de clavecin* [Paris, 1706, 1724, 1731, *c.* 1728, 1741, 1747]. Ed. Erwin R. Jacobi. Kassel, 1958. 3rd ed. 1966.

(Tables, prefaces, etc.: exceptionally well edited)

Facs. of 1724 ed. New York, 1967.

Facs. of *c.* 1728 ed. New York, 1967.

Rameau, Jean-Philippe. *Pièces de clavecin en concerts*. Paris, 1741. Ed. E. R. Jacobi. Kassel, 1961. 2nd ed. 1970.

Rasmussen, Mary. 'Some Notes on the Articulations in the Melodic Variation Tables of Johann Joachim Quantz's *Versuch einer Anweisung die Flöte traversiere zu spielen* (Berlin 1752, Breslau 1789)', *Brass and Woodwind Quarterly* I (1966–67) 3–26.

Reaney, Gilbert. 'The Performance of Medieval Music', *Aspects of Medieval and Renaissance Music: A Birthday Offering to Gustave Reese*, ed. J. LaRue (New York, 1966), pp. 704–22.

Reddick, Harvey P. 'Johann Mattheson's Forty-Eight Thorough-Bass Test Pieces: Translation and Commentary'. Ph.D. diss., Univ. of Michigan, 1956.

Reese, Gustave. *Music in the Renaissance*. New York, 1954. Rev. ed., 1959.

Reichardt, Johann Friedrich. *Briefe eines aufmerksamen Reisenden die Musik betreffend*. 2 pts. Frankfurt and Leipzig, 1774; Frankfurt and Breslau, 1776.
Facs. announced Hildesheim.

—— *Geist des musikalischen Kunstmagazins*, ed. I. A. [Alberti]. Berlin, 1791.

—— *Musikalischer Almanach*. Berlin, 1796.

—— *Ueber die Pflichten des Ripien-Violinisten*. Berlin and Leipzig, 1776.
Facs. announced Utrecht and Hilversum.

Reilly, Edward R. *Quantz and His Versuch: Three Studies*. New York, 1971.

Rellstab, Johann Carl Friedrich. *C. P. E. Bach's Anfangsstücke mit einer Anleitung den Gebrauch dieser Stücke*. 3rd ed. Berlin [?1790].

Remata, Daniel R. 'A Study of the Early Eighteenth Century Violin Bow'. M.A. thesis, Occidental College, Los Angeles, 1958.

Rendall, Francis G. *The Clarinet: Some Notes upon Its History and Construction*. London and New York, 1954. 3rd ed., rev. P. Bate, 1971.

Répertoire international des sources musicales (RISM), B VI: **Écrits imprimés concernant la musique,** ed. F. Lesure. 2 vols. Munich-Duisburg, 1971.

Rigler, Franz Xaver. *Anleitung zum Klavier für musikalische Lehrstunden*. Vienna [1779].

[Riva, Giuseppe] *Advice to the Composers and Performers of Vocal Musick. Translated from the Italian*. London, 1727.

[Publ. in It., also anon., as *Avviso ai compositori, ed ai cantanti*, London, 1728; and, attributed to Riva, in Ger. tr. by L. Mizler, in Mizler's *Musikalischer Staarstecher*, Anhang (Leipzig, 1740), pp. 111–17.]

It. text given by F. Degrada, 'Giuseppe Riva e il suo "Avviso ai compositori ed ai cantanti" ', *Analecta musicologica* IV (1967) 119–22.

[Rochement, de] *Réflexions d'un patriote sur l'opéra françois, et sur l'opéra italien*. Lausanne, 1754.

Rognoni Taegio, Francesco. *Selva de varii passaggi*. 2 pts. Milan, 1620.
Facs., introd. G. Barblan. Bologna, 1970.

Rognoni Taegio, Riccardo. *Passaggi per potersi essercitare nel diminuire*. Venice, 1592.

Rose, Gloria. **'Agazzari and the Improvising Orchestra'**, JAMS XVIII (Fall 1965) 382–93.

—— 'A Fresh Clue from Gasparini on Embellished Figured-Bass Accompaniment', MT CVII (Jan. 1966) 28–29.

—— 'A New Purcell Source', JAMS XXV (Summer 1972) 230–36.

Rothschild, Fritz. *The Lost Tradition in Music: Rhythm and Tempo in J. S. Bach's Time*. London, 1953. Pt. II. *Musical Performance in the Times of Mozart and Beethoven*. London and New York, 1961.
(Unsatisfactory. For reviews, see Emery, Lang and Mendel.)

—— *Stress and Movement in the Works of J. S. Bach*. London, 1966.

Rousseau, Jean. **Methode claire, certaine et facile, pour apprendre à chanter la musique.** Paris, 1678.

—— **Traité de la viole.** Paris, 1687.
Facs. Amsterdam, 1965.

Rousseau, Jean-Jacques. *Dictionnaire de musique*. Paris, 1768; also Amsterdam, 1768, 2 vols.
[In Paris, 1768 ed., Preface dated 20 Dec. 1764; Approbation dated 15 April 1765; Privilege dated 30 July 1765. Pre-publication copies have been reported, but supposed earlier eds. not confirmed.]
Facs. of Paris, 1768 ed. Hildesheim and New York, 1969.
Tr. W. Waring. London [*c*. 1775].
Facs. of Waring's tr., 2nd ed. (London, 1779), announced New York.

—— *Dissertation sur la musique moderne*. Paris, 1743.

[——] *Lettre à M. Grimm*. [Paris] 1752.

Rousseau, Jean-Jacques. *Lettre sur la musique françoise.* [Paris] 1753.

—— *Observations . . . sur la réponse qui a été faite à son discours.* [?Paris] 1751.

Rubsamen, Walter H. 'The Justiniane or Viniziane of the 15th Century', Act. Mus. XXIX (1957) 172–84.

[Rulhière, Claude Carloman de] *Jugement de l'orchestre de l'Opéra.* [?Paris, not before 1753].

Russell, Raymond. *The Harpsichord and Clavichord: An Introductory Study.* London, 1959. 2nd ed., rev. H. Schott, 1973.

Sabbatini, Galeazzo. *Regola facile, e breve per sonare sopra il basso continuo.* Venice, 1628.

Sachs, Curt. *Rhythm and Tempo: A Study in Music History.* New York, 1953.

[Sainsbury, John S.] *A Dictionary of Musicians.* 2 vols. London, 1824. Facs. of 1825 ed., introd. H. G. Farmer (taken from M&L XII, Oct. 1931). 2 vols. New York, 1966.

Saint-Lambert, Michel de. *Nouveau traité de l'accompagnement.* Paris, 1707.
Facs. Geneva, 1972.
Facs. announced New York.

—— *Les principes du clavecin.* Paris, 1702.
Facs. Geneva, 1972. Facs. announced New York.

Santa María, Fray Tomás de. *Libro llamado Arte de tañer fantasia, assi para tecla como para vihuela.* Valladolid, 1565.
Ger. tr. E. Harich-Schneider and R. Boadella. Leipzig, 1937.
Facs., introd. D. Stevens. [n.p.] 1972.
Facs. announced New York.

Scarlatti, Alessandro. 'Regole per cembalo' [*c.* 1715]. Brit. Mus., Add. MS. 14244, fols. 38v–46 and Add. MS. 31517, fols. 35v–38v.

Scheibe, Johann Adolf. 'Compendium musices' [ca. 1730]. Printed in Peter Benary, *Die deutsche Kompositionslehre des 18. Jahrhunderts,* Leipzig, 1961.

—— *Der critische Musicus.* 2 vols. Hamburg, 1738–40.
[Issued weekly, irregularly, 1737–40]
Facs. of [2nd] enl. ed. (Leipzig, 1745) announced Amsterdam.
Facs. of [2nd] enl. ed. Hildesheim, 1970.

Schering, Arnold. *Aufführungspraxis alter Musik.* Leipzig, 1931.
Repr. Wiesbaden, 1969.

—— 'Zur instrumentalen Verzierungskunst im 18. Jahrhundert'. SIMG VII (1905–6) 365–85.

Schlick, Arnolt. *Spiegel der Orgelmacher und Organisten*. [Speyer, 1511.]
Facs. ed. P. Smets. Mainz, 1937.
Facs. and tr. mod. Ger., ed. P. Smets. Mainz, 1959.
Ed. R. Eitner, MfM I (1869) 77–114.
Tr. mod. Ger. and ed. E. Flade. Mainz, 1932 and Kassel, 1951.

Schmid, Ernst F. 'Joseph Haydn und die vokale Zierpraxis seiner Zeit, dargestellt an einer Arie seines Tobias-Oratoriums', *Bericht über die internationale Konferenz zum Andenken Joseph Haydns*, ed. B. Szabolcsi and D. Bartha (Budapest, 1961), pp. 117–29.

Schmitz, Hans-Peter. **Die Kunst der Verzierung im 18. Jahrhundert.** Kassel, 1955. 2nd ed. 1965.
(Full-length examples, with an interesting preface)

—— *Prinzipien der Aufführungspraxis alter Musik: Kritischer Versuch über die spätbarocke Spielpraxis.* Berlin-Dahlem [1950].
(Brief but intelligent)

—— **Die Tontechnik des Père Engramelle: Ein Beitrag zur Lehre von der musikalischen Vortragskunst im 18. Jahrhundert.** Kassel and Basel, 1953.

Schneider, Max. *Die Anfänge des Basso continuo und seiner Bezifferung.* Leipzig, 1918. Repr. Farnborough, 1971.

Schnoebelen, Sister Mary Nicole [now Anne, O.P.]. 'The Concerted Mass at San Petronio in Bologna, ca. 1660–1730: A Documentary and Analytical Study'. Ph.D. diss., Univ. of Illinois, 1966.

Schnoeblen, Anne, O.P. [same as above]. **'Performance Practices at San Petronio in the Baroque',** Act. Mus. XLI (1969) 37–55.

Schott, Howard. *Playing the Harpsichord.* London, 1971.

Schünemann, Georg. *Geschichte des Dirigierens.* Leipzig, 1931. Repr. Hildesheim and Wiesbaden, 1965.

Schwandt, Erich P. 'The Ornamented Clausula Diminuta in the Fitzwilliam Virginal Book'. Ph.D. diss., Stanford Univ., 1967.

Schweitzer, Albert. *Jean Sébastian Bach, le musicien-poète.* Paris, 1905. Ger. enl. ed. Leipzig, 1908.
Tr. E. Newman. 2 vols. London, 1911.

Schwendowius, Barbara. *Die solistische Gambenmusik in Frankreich von 1650 bis 1740.* Regensburg, 1970.
(Good on French ornaments, including table of signs)

Scimone, Claudio, ed. *G. Tartini: Concerto, G major*, D. 78, Milan [1972] with partly autograph ornamentations.

Seagrave, Barbara A. G. 'The French Style of Violin Bowing and Phrasing from Lully to Jacques Aubert (1650–1730)'. Ph.D. diss., Stanford Univ., 1958.

Seiffert, Max. 'Die Verzierung der Sologesänge in Händel's "Messias" ', SIMG VIII (1906–7) 581–615.

Serauky, Walter. 'Affektenlehre', MGG I (1949–51) cols. 113–21.

—— Die musikalische Nachahmungsästhetik im Zeitraum von 1700 bis 1850. Münster, 1929.

Severi, Francesco. Salmi passaggiati per tutte le voci. Rome, 1615.

Shaw, [H.] Watkins. A Textual and Historical Companion to Handel's Messiah. London, 1965.
    (Confirms over-dotting)

Simpson, Christopher. The Division-Violist: or, an Introduction to the Playing upon a Ground. London, 1659. 2nd ed. as Chelys, minuritionum artificio exornata . . . The Division-Viol. London, 1665; also London, 1667.
    Facs. of 2nd ed., introd. N. Dolmetsch. London, 1955.
    (Includes the best examples of 17th century divisions)

—— The Principles of Practical Musick. London, 1665.
    [Later eds. under titles A Compendium of Practical Musick and A Compendium: or, Introduction to Practical Musick]
    [2nd, enl. ed.] A Compendium of Practical Musick (London, 1667), ed. P. J. Lord. Oxford, 1970.

Solerti, Angelo, comp. and ed. Le origini del melodramma: Testimonianze dei contemporanei. Turin, 1903. Repr. Hildesheim and New York, 1969. Repr. Bologna, 1969.

Spazier, [Johann Gottlieb] Carl, ed. Berlinische musikalische Zeitung. Berlin, 1794.
    [Issued weekly, 1793–94]

Spitta, J. A. Philipp. J. S. Bach. 2 vols. Leipzig, 1873–80.
    Tr. C. Bell and J. A. Fuller-Maitland. 3 vols. London, 1884–85. Reprinted in 2 vols. New York and London, 1951.

Spohr, Louis. Violinschule. Vienna, 1832.
    Facs. ed. F. Göthel. Kassel, 1960.
    Tr. F. A. Marshall, rev. and ed. H. Holmes. 2 vols. London [c. 1880].

Staden, Johann. 'Kurzer und einfältiger Bericht für diejenigen, so im Basso ad organum unerfahren', in Kirchen-Music, Ander Theil. Nuremberg, 1626.
    Repr. in Allgemeine musikalische Zeitung XII (1877) 99–103, 119–23.

Stadlen, Peter. **'Beethoven and the Metronome'**, M&L XLVIII (Oct. 1967) 330–49.

Stanley, Douglas. *The Science of Voice*. New York, 1929.

—— *Your Voice: Applied Science of Vocal Art, Singing and Speaking*. New York, 1945.

—— and J. P. Maxfield. *The Voice: Its Production and Reproduction*. New York, 1933.

Steglich, Rudolf, ed. *Georg Friedrich Händel: Klavierwerke I. Die acht grossen Suiten* (HHA, Ser. IV, Bd. 1). Kassel and Basel, 1955.
   (Notably helpful editing)

Stevens, Denis W., ed. **The Mulliner Book** (*Musica Britannica* I). London, 1951. 2nd ed. 1962.
   (Excellent editing and preface)

—— *The Mulliner Book: A Commentary*. London, 1952.

—— 'Problems of Editing and Publishing Old Music', Rep. 8th IMS Cong., I, 150–58.

Stratton, John. 'Operatic Singing Style and the Gramophone', *Recorded Sound: The Journal of the British Institute of Recorded Sound*, Nos. 22–23 (Apr.–July 1966) 37–68.

Strunk, Oliver. **Source Readings in Music History**. New York, 1950.

Sumner, William L. 'The Baroque Organ', Proc. RMA, 81st Session (1954–55) 1–12.

—— *The Organ: Its Evolution, Principles of Construction and Use*. London, 1952. 3rd ed. 1962.

T. B. See *The Compleat Musick-Master*.

Tabourot, Jehan. See Arbeau.

Tagliavini, Luigi Ferdinando. 'Prassi esecutiva e metodo musicologico', *Bericht über den neunten internationalen Kongress Salzburg 1964* [I.M.S.], ed. F. Giegling, I (Kassel, 1964), 19–24.

—— *et al.* 'Problemi di prassi esecutiva', *Studi Corelliani*, ed. A. Cavicchi, O. Mischiati and P. Petrobelli (Quaderni della Rivista italiana di musicologia, 3; Florence, 1972), pp. 111–25.

Talbot, James. MS notes [*c.* 1690] in Oxford, Christ Church Library, Music MS. 1187.
   (Valuable on instruments. See GSJ, Nos. 1, 3, 5, 14, 15, 16, 21)

Tans'ur, William. *A New Musical Grammar*. London, 1746.

Tartini, Giuseppe. *L'arte dell'arco o siano cinquanta variazioni.* Naples [?1750]. Fr. ed. Paris [?1780].
> Included in J.-B. Cartier's *L'art du violon* (Paris [1798]), pp. 194–201.
> (Valuable examples of free ornamentation on a Corelli Gavotte)

—— *A Letter from the Late Signor Tartini* [Padua, 5 March 1760] *to Signora Maddalena Lombardini* (*now Signora Sirmen*) *Published as an Important Lesson to Performers on the Violin. Translated by Dr. Burney.* London, 1771. 2nd ed. 1779. 3rd ed. as *An Important Lesson to Performers on the Violin.* London, 1879.
> Reprint of 2nd ed. London, 1913; New York and London, 1967.
> Contemp. Ital., Fr., Ger. and Eng. (Burney) texts printed in Jacobi's ed. of Tartini's *Traité des agrémens.*

—— **Traité des agrémens de la musique** [survives in two Ital. MSS, and dates from before 1756 at latest, when L. Mozart drew on it]. Fr. tr. P. Denis. Paris [1771].
> Ed. Erwin R. Jacobi, with Eng. tr. C. Girdlestone and facs. of orig. Ital. text. Celle and New York, 1961.
> Eng. tr. also S. Babitz, 'Treatise on Ornamentation', Jour. RME IV (Fall 1956) 75–102.

Telemann, Georg Michael. *Unterricht im Generalbass-Spielen.* Hamburg, 1773.

Telemann, Georg Philipp. *Harmonischer Gottes-Dienst, oder geistliche Cantaten.* 2 pts. [Hamburg, 1725–26]
> Ed. G. Fock in Complete Works of Telemann, vols. 2–5. Kassel, 1953–57.

—— *Singe-, Spiel- und Generalbass-Übungen.* [Hamburg, 1733–34]
> [Issued in installments, starting 20 November 1733. Appeared as complete 17 January 1735]
> Ed. M. Seiffert. Berlin, 1914; 4th ed., Kassel, 1935.

Terry, Charles S. *Bach's Orchestra.* London, 1932.

Tilmouth, Michael. 'The Appoggiatura in Beethoven's Vocal Music', MT CXI (Dec. 1970) 1209–11.

—— 'A Calendar of References to Music in Newspapers Published in London and the Provinces (1600–1719)', *R.M.A. Research Chronicle*, No. 1 (1961); No. 2 (1962) 1–15.

Tobin, John. *Handel at Work.* London, 1964.

—— *Handel's Messiah: A Critical Account of the Manuscript Sources and Printed Editions.* London, 1969.
> (A notable attempt at authentic performing suggestions)

Tomeoni, Florido. *Théorie de la musique vocale*. Paris [1799].

Torchi, Luigi. 'L'accompagnamento degl'istrumenti nei melodrammi italiani della prima metà del seicento', *Rivista musicale italiana* I (1894) 7–38.

Tosi, Pier Francesco. **Opinioni de' cantori antichi, e moderni.** Bologna, 1723.
> Facs. included in E. R. Jacobi's facs. ed. of J. F. Agricola, *Anleitung zur Singkunst* (Berlin, 1757). Celle, 1966.
> Facs. New York, 1968.
> Ed. L. Leonesi. Naples, 1904. Repr. Bologna, 1969.
> Ed. A. della Corte, in *Canto e bel canto*. Turin, 1933.
> Tr. and ed. J. E. Galliard as *Observations on the Florid Song*. London, 1742.
> Facs. of Galliard tr., 2nd ed. (London, 1743). London, 1926 and 1967.
> Facs. of Galliard tr., 2nd ed., introd. P. H. Lang. New York, 1968.
> For Ger. tr., see Agricola, Johann Friedrich.

[Treiber, Johann Philipp] *Der accurate Organist im General-Bass*. Jena, 1704.

Tromlitz, Johann Georg. *Ausführlicher und gründlicher Unterricht die Flöte zu spielen*. Leipzig, 1791.
> Facs. announced New York.

Trydell, John. *Two Essays on the Theory and Practice of Music*. Dublin, 1766.

Türk, Daniel Gottlob. **Klavierschule, oder Anweisung zum Klavierspielen für Lehrer und Lernende.** Leipzig and Halle, 1789.
> Facs. ed. E. R. Jacobi. Kassel, 1962. 2nd ed. 1967.
> Tr. and abr. C. G. Naumburger as *Treatise on the Art of Teaching and Practising the Piano Forte*. London [1804].

—— *Von den wichtigsten Pflichten eines Organisten*. Halle, 1787.
> Facs., after-note B. Billeter. Hilversum, 1966.

Turner, William. *Sound Anatomiz'd, in a Philosophical Essay on Musick*. London, 1724.

Ulrich, Ernst. **Studien zur deutschen Generalbass-Praxis in der ersten Hälfte des 18. Jahrhunderts.** Kassel, 1932.
> (Valuable and has good bibliography)

Vaccai, Nicola. *Metodo pratico per il canto italiano*. Florence [*c.* 1840].

Valle, Pietro della. 'Della musica dell'età nostra che non è punto inferiore, anzi è migliore di quella dell'età passata' (1640). In *Le origini del melodramma*, ed. A. Solerti, pp. 148-179.

Vanneo, Stephano. *Recanetum de musica aurea.* Tr. Vincentio Rosseto. Rome, 1533.
 Facs., after-note S. Clercx. Kassel, 1969.
 Facs. Bologna, 1969.

Viadana, Lodovico (Grossi da). *Cento concerti ecclesiastici.* Venice, 1602.
 Prima parte ed. C. Gallico. Mantua and Kassel, 1964.
 Preface tr. and ed. F. T. Arnold, *The Art of Accompaniment from a Thorough-Bass* (London, 1931), pp. 3-4, 10-19. This tr. in *Source Readings . . .*, ed. O. Strunk, pp. 419-23.

Vinquist, Mary, *et al.*, eds. **'Bibliography of Performance Practices'**, *Current Musicology*, No. 8 (1969). Supplements in *Current Musicology*, No. 10 (1970), No. 12 (1971) and No. 15 (1973). First listing and first suppl. publ. in book form as *Performance Practice: A Bibliography*, ed. M. Vinquist and N. Zaslaw, New York, 1971.

Wagner, Ernst D. *Musikalische Ornamentik.* Berlin, 1869.

Walker, D. P. 'Some Aspects and Problems of Musique Mesurée à l'Antique; the Rhythm and Notation of Musique Mesurée', MD IV (1950) 163-86.

Walther, Johann Gottfried. *Musicalisches Lexicon.* Leipzig, 1732.
 Facs., after-note R. Schaal. Kassel, 1953.

—— *Praecepta der musicalischen Composition.* Ed. P. Benary. Leipzig, 1955.
 [Ed. of MS. Q 341^c, dated 13 March 1708, in Landesbibliothek, Weimar]

Wangermée, Robert, *et al.* 'Principes d'interprétation', *Les colloques de Wégimont, IV–1957: Le "baroque" musical* (Paris, 1963) 223–40.
 (Bold but excellent on the editor's responsibilities in reconstructing early music, especially opera)

Warner, Thomas E. *An Annotated Bibliography of Woodwind Instruction Books, 1600–1830.* Detroit, 1967.

—— 'Indications of Performance Practice in Woodwind Instruction Books of the 17th and 18th Centuries'. Ph.D. diss., New York Univ., 1964.

Werckmeister, Andreas. *Harmonologia musica, oder Kurtze Anleitung zur musicalischen Composition.* Frankfurt and Leipzig, 1702.
 Facs. Hildesheim and New York, 1970.

SELECT BIBLIOGRAPHY

Werckmeister, Andreas. *Die nothwendigsten Anmerckungen, und Regeln wie der Bassus continuus, oder General-Bass wol könne tractiret werden.* Aschersleben [1698].

Westrup, Jack A. 'The Cadence in Baroque Recitative', *Natalicia musicologica Knud Jeppesen septuagenario collegis oblata*, ed. B. Hjelmborg and S. Sørensen (Hafniae, i.e. Copenhagen, 1962) 243–52.

—— 'Monteverdi and the Orchestra', M&L XXI (July 1940) 230–45.

—— *Musical Interpretation.* London, 1971.

Wichmann, Kurt. *Vom Vortrag des Recitativs und seiner Erscheinungsformen: Ein Beitrag zur Gesangspädagogik.* Leipzig, 1965.

—— *Der Ziergesang und die Ausführung der Appoggiatura: Ein Beitrag zur Gesangspädagogik.* Leipzig, 1966.

Williams, Peter. 'Basso Continuo on the Organ', M&L L (Jan. and Apr. 1969) 136–52, 230–45.

—— *The European Organ 1450–1850.* London, 1966.

—— *Figured Bass Accompaniment.* 2 vols. Edinburgh, 1970.

—— 'The Harpsichord Acciaccatura', MQ LIV (Oct. 1968) 503–23.

—— 'Some Developments in Early Keyboard Studies', M&L LII (July 1971) 272–86.

Winternitz, Emanuel. 'On Angel Concerts in the 15th Century: A Critical Approach to Realism and Symbolism in Sacred Painting', MQ XLIX (Oct. 1963) 450–63.

Wolf, Georg Friedrich. *Kurzer aber deutlicher Unterricht im Klavierspielen.* Göttingen, 1783.

Wolff, Helmuth C. 'Vom Wesen des alten Belcanto', *Händel-Konferenzbericht* (Leipzig, 1959), pp. 95–99.

Wulstan, David. 'The Problem of Pitch in Sixteenth-Century English Vocal Music', Proc. RMA, 93rd Session (1966–67) 97–112.

Zacconi, Lodovico. *Prattica di musica.* Venice, 1592. Pt. II. Venice, 1622.
    Facs. of Pt. I ed. A. Geering. Kassel, in preparation.
    Facs. of Pts. I and II announced Bologna.
    Facs. of Pt. I (1596 ed.) and Pt. II announced Hildesheim.

Zarlino, Gioseffo. *Le istitutioni harmoniche.* Venice, 1558. Vol. I of *De tutte l'opere* (Venice, 1589).
  Facs. of Venice, 1558 ed. New York, 1965.
  Facs. of Venice, 1573 ed. Ridgeway, N.J., 1966.
  Facs. of *De tutte l'opere* (Venice, 1588–89) announced Hildesheim.
  Pt. III of Venice, 1588 ed. tr. G. A. Marco and C. V. Palisca, as *The Art of Counterpoint.* New Haven and London, 1968.

Zaslaw, Neal A. 'Materials for the Life and Works of Jean-Marie Leclair l'aîné'. Ph.D. diss., Columbia Univ., 1970.
  (For late baroque French dance tempos)

Zuccari, Carlo. *The True Method of Playing an Adagio Made Easy by Twelve Examples. First in a Plain Manner with a Bass, Then with All Their Graces. Adapted for Those Who Study the Violin.* London [*c.* 1765].

Index of Ornaments (Signs)

No.	Sign	Ornament	Rough Guide to Use or Source
1	•	Vibrato, tremolo.	17th-cent. French & English
2	⫶	Curtailed note.	Mace.
3	∴	Single relish (virtually a brief trill with turned ending).	Mace (but also used in 17th-cent. England as a repeat sign).
4	⟋ ∴	Prepared long mordent.	17th-cent. English.
5	∴ (also:)	Double relish	17th-cent. English.
6	∴ \\ ∴		
7	✸	Ascending trill with or without turned termination.	17th-cent. English.
8	↑	(*a*) Curtailed note. (*b*) Staccato more generally	(*a*) Couperin, Rameau. (*b*) General 18th cent.
9	⅂	(Quaver rest sign over note): curtailed note.	D'Anglebert.
10	(also:) ↲	(Inverted quaver rest sign under note): the same.	
11	❘	(*a*) Upright stroke above note: mordent. (*b*) Upright stroke after note: *Nachschlag*.	(*a*) Mace. (*b*) Loulié.
12	✗	Rising stroke *through* stem if there is one: ·(*a*) Mordent. (*b*) Half-shake. (*c*) ? Trill. (*d*) Ascending slide.	English virginalists (late 16th to late 17th cents.). (Use not entirely certain.)

No.	Sign	Ornament	Rough Guide to Use or Source
13		Ascending slide.	Th. Muffat.
14		Through stem if there is one: ascending slide.	Edward Bevin (Engl. 17th cent.).
15		Through stem if there is one: ascending slide leading to trill.	Edward Bevin (Engl. 17th cent.).
16		(a) Accacciatura. (b) Short appoggiatura.	(a) Marpurg and subsequently. (b) 19th cent. (Spohr, Czerny, &c.).
17		Acciaccatura.	C. P. E. Bach, Marpurg, &c.
18		(a) *Through* stem; or (b) *Before* stem: both = arpeggio. (usually but not invariably ascending).	(a) Chiefly French, 17th cent. and subsequently. (b) Marais.
19		*Between and above* notes: springer.	17th-cent. English.
20		*Before* note: (a) Lower appoggiatura. (b) Ascending slide. (c) Rising note of anticipation or similar *Nachschlag*.	(a) Widely current 17th cent. to mid-18th cent. (England, Italy, Germany). (b) Chiefly French, same dates, also given by Türk. (c) Later 18th-cent. German (esp. Türk).
21		Variant of 20 (b) above.	Th. Muffat.
22		Between heads of notes: (a) Ascending slide. (b) Slide-like accacciatura in chord or arpeggio.	(a) English, French, German; 17th–18th cent. (b) 18th cent. German (including J. S. Bach).
23		Variant of 22 above, but ? confined to (slide-like) accacciatura in a chord or arpeggio.	Late 18th and early 19th cent. (Türk, Clementi, L. Adam, *père*).
24		Falling stroke *across* stem; descending arpeggio.	Th. Muffat, Marpurg, etc.
25		*Before* note: (a) Falling note of anticipation (cadent). (b) Upper appoggiatura. (c) Descending slide.	(a) 17th-cent. English including Purcell; also Türk. (b) J. G. Walther; Th. Muffat. (c) Türk.
26		*Between* heads of notes: Descending slide.	Couperin.
27		Double rising stroke *through* stem if there is one: (a) Trill. (b) Half-shake. (c) Mordent.	English virginalists (late 16th to early 17th cents.). (Use not entirely certain.)
28		The same *above or below* the stem; probably a variant of 27 above.	English, 2nd half of 17th cent.; Geminiani; Kuhnau.
29		Probably a variant of 27 above.	Some Italians (Pasquali, Pollini); James Hook.
30		(a) Probably a variant of 27 above. (b) *Nachschlag*.	Marpurg, &c.

(a)

(b)

No.	Sign	Ornament	Rough Guide to Use or Source
31	＼＼	Probably a variant of 27 above.	Pollini, Clementi, &c.
32	＼≡	Appoggiatura — prepared trill.	English, late 17th cent.
33	↶	Trill with turned ending.	Edward Bevin.
34	↷	? A variant of 33 above: trill with turned ending.	Purcell.
35	c	Letter c above note: ascending slide.	Murschhauser.
36	g	*Groppo*: often in form of trill.	Italian, early 17th cent.
37	⌒	Mordent.	Murschhauser.
38	t	(a) *Trillo*=tremolo. (b) Trill. (c) Tremolo=trill.	(a) Late 16th–17th-cent. Italian. (b) Widespread. (c) Late 16th to 17th-cent. Italian.
39	t̖	Appoggiatura — prepared trill.	Th. Muffat.
40	tm	Trill full length of note.	G. Muffat.
41	ꝥ or	Trill with turned ending.	G. Muffat. Th. Muffat.
42	tᴗ		
43	tr∿	Trill with turned ending.	Occasionally encountered.
44	ꝥ	Mordent.	G. Muffat.
45	tr (early form sometimes tri)	(a) *Trillo*=tremolo. (b) Trill (of any length or variety).	(a) Late 16th–17th-cent. Italian. (b) Exceedingly common and widespread.
46	tr∿∿∿	Continuous trill	Couperin; Tartini; and subsequently well-established.
47	＋ (*Cf.* 49 below; the two are largely interchangeable.)	(a) Ascending slide. (b) Lower appoggiatura. (c) Trill. (d) Unspecified hint to ornament	(a) English 17th cent.; also French and German 18th cent. (b) Chambonnières. (c) Very common, esp. among violinists and flautists: the main usage. (d) Unfortunately not uncommon.
48	⌓͏꜀	Appoggiatura — prepared trill.	L'Affilard.
49	✕ (*Cf.* 47 above; the two are largely interchangeable.)	(a) Ascending slide. (b) Upper appoggiatura. (c) Trill. (d) Mordent. (e) Unspecified hint to ornament.	(a) Heinichen. (b) Marpurg. (c) Lully, Mondonville: not uncommon. (d) French and German 18th cent.: the main usage. (e) Unfortunately not unknown.
50	⌃	Springer.	German 18th cent.
51	＞	Upper appoggiatura. (Very like accentuation sign.)	Murschhauser.

(d)

No.	Sign	Ornament	Rough Guide to Use or Source
52	∨	(a) Mordent (prepared or unprepared). (b) Inverted springer. (c) Lower appoggiatura.	(a) L'Affilard; Loulié. (b) J. G. Walther; Türk. (c) Murschhauser.
53	～	(a) Trill. (b) *Pralltriller* (half-shake). (c) *Schneller* (inverted, *i.e.* upper mordent).	(a) Ubiquitous French and German from 17th cent.: the correct usage. (b) Türk. (c) Türk, Spohr, Czerny, etc. (a misappropriation).
54	～～	(a) Trill (variant of 53 above, sometimes but by no means always implying more repercussions, giving a longer duration). (b) Double mordent. (c) Appoggiatura—prepared lower mordent. (d) Prepared trill. (e) Ascending trill. (f) Vibrato. (g) Tremolo.	(a) Ubiquitous French and German from 17th cent.: the correct usage. (b) Loulié. (c) ? Locke, Purcell. (d) L'Affilard. (e) Th. Muffat. (f) Mace. (g) L'Affilard.
55	～～～～	(a) Long trill. (b) Long mordent. (c) Vibrato in general. (d) A special form of vibrato.	(a) German, later 18th cent. Subsequently well established. (b) Couperin. (c) A few violinists down to Spohr, &c. (d) Marais.
56	～ – ～	Trills on one main note separated by recurrence of the main note plain.	Geminiani.
57	ໂ～	Appoggiatura — prepared trill.	French and German 17th and 18th cents.
58	ໂ～	Appoggiatura prepared trill with turned ending.	Marpurg.
59	ໂ～	Variant of 58 above.	Marpurg.
60	～ᵗ	Trill with turned ending.	German 18th cent. (including J. S. Bach).
61	～	Trill with turned ending.	D'Anglebert.
62	～	Variant of 61 above.	French 18th cent.
63	～	Variant of 61 above.	Rameau, Marpurg (Fr. Ed.), Türk.
64	∾	(a) Trill with turned ending. (b) A special telescoped form of (a): "trilled turn" (*Prallender* or *Getrillerter Doppelschlag*).	(a) Couperin, J. S. Bach, and common in 18th cent. to early 19th cent. (b) C. P. E. Bach, Türk.
65	～	Ascending trill with turned ending.	Marpurg.
66	～,	Trill with turned ending.	17th–early 18th-cent. French.
67	～)	Variant of 66 above.	D'Anglebert.
68	～	Ascending trill.	Th. Muffat.
69	～	Ascending trill with turned ending.	Th. Muffat.
70	～	(a) Ascending trill. (b) Appoggiatura — prepared trill.	(a) 17th–18th-cent. French and German (including J. S. Bach). (b) Marpurg.

(e)

No.	Sign	Ornament	Rough Guide to Use or Source
71		(a) Ascending trill with turned ending. (b) Appoggiatura — prepared lower mordent.	(a) 18th-cent. German (including J. S. Bach). (b) Dandrieu.
72		Ascending trill with turned ending.	Marpurg.
73		Variant of 71 above.	Marpurg.
74		Descending trill.	17th–18th-cent. French and German (including J. S. Bach).
75		Descending trill with turned ending.	18th-cent. German (including J. S. Bach).
76		Descending trill with turned ending.	Marpurg.
77		Variant of 76 above.	Marpurg.
78		Variant of 77 above.	Marpurg.
79		(a) Mordent. (b) Inverted (i.e. upper) mordent (Schneller).	(a) Ubiquitous French and German later 17th and 18th cents.: the correct usage. (b) Hummel.
80		(a) Mordent (variant of 79 above, sometimes but by no means always implying more repercussions, giving longer duration). (b) Inverted (i.e. upper mordent (Schneller; but under misnomer Pralltriller).	(a) Ubiquitous French (from 17th cent.) and German (from early 18th cent., including J. S. Bach): the correct usage. (b) Preface to Spohr's Violin School; but shown in music text as at 53 above (incorrect either way).
81		Mordent: variant of 80 (a) above.	Chambonnières.
82		Mordent: variant of 79 (a) above.	Couperin.
83		Continuous mordent.	Couperin.
84		" Triple mordent."	Loulié.
85		Slide (sometimes but not always implying ascending) [also the " direct " showing at end of line what note the next line starts with, &c.].[1]	18th-cent. German (including J. S. Bach).
86		Inverted variant of 85 above, occasionally used for descending slide.	J. G. Walther.
87		(a) Turn. (b) Inverted turn.	(a) English, French, German; the ubiquitous sign from 17th cent. to present day: the correct usage. (b) An aberration of Hummel and Spohr (the latter, following Leopold Mozart, calls it " mordent " !).

	No.	Sign	Ornament	Rough Guide to Use or Source
(f)	88		Inverted variant of 87 above: (a) Irregular turns. (b) Inverted turn. (c) Standard turn.	(a) One by Chambonnières, another by d'Anglebert. (b) Marpurg, C. P. E. Bach, Clementi, &c.: the correct usage. (c) An aberration of Hummel and Spont (the latter, as " mordent " !)
	89		(a) Turn. (b) Inverted turn.	(a) L'Affilard, Türk, Czerny. (b) Clementi, Hummel.
	90		Inverted turn.	Marpurg.
	91		Trill with turned ending.	Geminiani.
	92		Five-note turn.	C. P. E. Bach, Türk, Hummel.
	93		Ascending turn.	C. P. E. Bach.
(g)	94		Five-note turn.	German down to Beethoven.
	95		Comma over note, or above, but to the left: (a) Upper appoggiatura ("backfall"). (b) Trill (viewed as " backfall shaked ").	(a) English 17th cent. (b) English and French 17th cent. to early 18th.
	96		Comma after note: (a) Trill. (b) Lower appoggiatura. (c) Mordent.	(a) French 17th and 18th cents.: the main usage. (b) French 17th-cent. lutenists. (c) French 17th and 18th cents.
	97		Double comma: descending slide.	English 17th cent.
	98		Inverted comma between notes: springer.	L'Affilard.
	99		Inverted comma before note: appoggiatura.	French 17th to 18th cents. Also J. G. Walther.
	100		Inverted comma after note: mordent.	D'Anglebert.
	101		Comma-like curve before note: lower appoggiatura.	Early 18th-cent. German (including J. S. Bach).
	102		Comma-like curve before and above note: upper appoggiatura.	Early 18th-cent. German (including J. S. Bach).
	103		Double comma-like curve rising to note: lower appoggiatura.	Early 18th-cent. German (including J. S. Bach).
	104		Double comma-like curve falling to note: upper appoggiatura.	Early 18th-cent. German (including J. S. Bach).
	105		Small bracket-like curve to left of notes: (a) Ascending slide. (b) Appoggiatura. (c) Mordent. (d) Indicates the (slide-like) figuring of an arpeggio between the notes bracketed	(a) 17th–18th cents. French. (b) Dieupart. (c) Marpurg. (d) Fairly common: the most important usage.
	106		Small bracket-like curve to right of notes: descending slide.	D'Anglebert.

733

No.	Sign	Ornament	Rough Guide to Use or Source
107	or:	Small bracket-like curves or commas on *either* side of note: prepared mordent.	17th–early 18th-cents. French.
108		Double bracket-like curve before arpeggio: doubly figured (*see* 105 (*d*) above).	Marpurg.
109	or:	(*a*) Tremolo; (*b* Bebung (on clavichord).	18th-cent. German (including J. S. Bach).
110		Truncated note.	Couperin, Rameau.
111		Appoggiatura — prepared trill (a misuse of 110 above).	Mondonville.
112		The pause mark often implies a cadenza.	Explained by 18th-cent. authorities.
113	(	Large bracket-like curve before chord: arpeggio.	Purcell; Dieupart; Cramer.
·114	(*See also* 124 below).	(*a*) Before chord: arpeggio. (*b*) Before note: vibrato.	(*a*) Late 17th-cent. England (Purcell) and France (Le Bègue); becoming common generally in 18th cent. and the established sign during the 19th. (*b*) Marais.
115	or	Before chord: ascending arpeggio.	French 17th cent.; and common generally in 18th cent. and into 19th.
116		Hooked zigzag to left of chord; slur sign to right: variant of 115 above.	French 17th cent.
117		Before chord: descending arpeggio.	Couperin, Türk.
118		Placed as 116 above: variant of 117 above.	French 17th cent.
119		Before chord: arpeggio.	Türk.
120		Before chord: ascending arpeggio.	18th-cent. German.
121		Before chord: descending arpeggio.	18th-cent. German.
122		Between staves: notes so joined to be played simultaneously.	Used by Dandrieu in his unmeasured preludes.

No.	Sign	Ornament	Rough Guide to Use or Source
123		Between staves: notes so joined are *unisson*.	Couperin.
124	*(See also* 114 above).	*After* chord with rising or falling stroke across stem to indicate arpeggio: the arpeggio to be figured.	Rameau.
125	or: etc.	Between melodic notes: *tirata*.	Occasionally encountered 17th–18th cents. in various localities.

POSTSCRIPT

(a) No. 19: also 18th-cent. French as *accent*.

(b) No. 28: also 17th-cent. Dutch.

(c) No. 29: also Clementi.

(d) No. 50: also more vertically, as follows:

50ᴬ	∧	Upper appoggiatura (coulement)	Hotteterre

(e) No. 55: also (*e*), measured (or unmeasured) tremolo: mainly 17th-cent. to 18th-cent. Italian; also French, English (Purcell in *King Arthur*).

(f) No. 88: also in J. S. Bach (*Clavier-Büchlein*, 1720) as accented upper (standard) turn.

(g) No. 94: should read as follows:

94		Variant of 64	German down to Beethoven

Index

Index

compiled by Terence A. Miller

Page numbers in italics include verbal and musical quotations and examples, those in bold type denote more important references.

739

740

386–7; Mozart, L., on, 387, 388, *389–90;* Purcell, H., on, *388;* Quantz, J., on, *386–7,* 390–1; Rellstab, J. C. F., on, 388; Rousseau, J.-J., on, *391;* Saint-Lambert, M. de, on, *391;* table of, 391

Timpani, 71. *See also* Percussion *and under the names of drums*

Tinctoris, Johannes, *Liber de natura . . .,* accidentals, *611*

Tippett, Michael, 80

Tirade (tirata), 258

Tirata, **268–9,** 631

Tiret (mordent), 260

Toccata, arpeggiation in, 278

Toccatas (Muffat, G.): acciaccatura, 225; slide, 221

Toccate (Frescobaldi): broken chord, *278–9;* inequality of rhythm, 455, *456;* phrasing, *471;* omissions, *380–1;* tempo, *429, 432, 433;* trill, *237–8*

Tomás de Santa Maria, Fray, *Arte de tañer fantasia:* inequality of rhythm, *454–5;* mordent, *262;* trill, *237;* turn, *274*

Tomeoni, Florido, *Théorie de la Musique Vocale,* appoggiatura, *199*

Tomkins, Thomas: pitch, 507; underlaying, *525*

Tonotechnie, La (Engramelle), *see* Engramelle, M.-D.-J.

Tons, Les (Maillart), *408*

Tosi, Pier F., *Opinioni de'cantori, see* Galliard, J. E. (trans.), *Observations on the Florid Song*

Totenberg, Roman (*violinist*), 543

Totila (Legrenzi), 609

Tour de gosier (turn), 272

Tourte bow, 532–3

Tragen der Tone (tremolo), 231, **576–7**

Traité de la viole (Jean Rousseau), *see* Rousseau, Jean

Traité de l'accompagnement (Saint-Lambert), *see* Saint-Lambert, M. de

Traité d'accompagnement (Delair), *644*

Traité . . . du chant (Garcia): appoggiatura, *213;* ornamentation, *183*

Traité du recitatif (Gallois), 649

Transilvano, Il (Diruta), *see* Diruta, G.

Transposition, effect on pitch, 505–6, 511–12

Transverse flute, 553–4

Trattado de Glosas sobre Clausulas (Ortiz), *see* Ortiz, D.

Trattati di musica (Doni), *see* Doni, G.

Trauer-Ode (J. S. Bach), *219*

Treatise of Good Taste (Geminiani): acciaccatura, *222, 223;* expression, *376*

Treatise of Musick (Malcolm), *see* Malcolm A.

Treiber, Johann P., *Accurate Organist,* accidentals, 129

Tremblement (trill), 236

Tremblement coulé en descendant (descending trill), 284

Tremblement mineur (vibrato), 232

Tremolando, 231

Tremoletto (trill), 229, 236

Tremolo, 195, **229–32,** 235

Tremor Pressus (vibrato), 231

Tremulus (ornament), 260

Trepidatio (trill), 236

Triads: augmented and diminished, 299; perfect, 297–8

Triangle, 569–70

Trill, 195, **236–59, 623–35,** 639; Abbé le fils on, *258;* in accompaniment, 315–18; Adam, L., on, 256; Affillard, L', on, 631; Agricola, J. F., on, 627–8; Andersch, J. D., on, 259; Anglebert, D', on, *242, 625;* appoggiatura link with, 242–6, 251, 257; *appuy,* 197, 625, **628–30;** ascending and descending, 196; Bach, C. P. E., on, *243, 245, 247, 248, 251, 252(bis), 255, 258–9;* Bach, J. S., on, 631; Bach's (J. S.), *245–6;* Bacilly B. de, on, *241, 249;* Baillot, P., on, 256; baroque, main, **239–41;** baroque, post-, 255–9; baroque, pre- and early-, 236–9; baroque, speed of, 246–7; baroque, termination of, 247–50; Beethoven's, 257, 258; Brossard, S. de, on, 628, *635;* Busby, T., on, 258; Caccini, G., on, *238;* cadential, 189, 194(*bis*), 236, *243,* 245, 255–6, 622, 623 *et seq.,* 635; Cartier, J.-B., on, *256, 257–8;* Choquel, H.-L., on, *634;* Clementi, M., on, 256; Collins, M., on, *630–1;* comma sign, 316; compound, 196, 624, 631; Conforti, G. L., on, *238;* continuous, **253–5,** 259; 'Corelli clash', *250;* Cotgrave, R., on, *628–9,* 630; Couperin, F., on, *244,* 625–6; Courcy, F. de, on, 256, *257;* Cramer, J. B., on, 256; Czerny, C., on, 256; Danoville, le Sieur- on, *632;* Diruta, G., on, *238–9;* Doning, ton, R., on, 238; *Double Cadence,* 631–2; Frescobaldi, G., on, *237–8;* Galliard, J., on, 627–8; Ganassi, S. di, on, *237;* Garcia, M., on, 259; half-, 218, **250–3,** *258,* 259; Handel's, *250;* Haydn's, 257, 258; Herbst, J. A., on, *238;* Hiller, J. A., on, 256, 259; Hotteterre, J. M., on, 241, *243, 246;* Hummel, J. N., on, 256, 257, 258; Knecht, J. H., on, 259; Kreutzer, R., on, 256; Loulié, É., on, *242, 246,* 625; Manfredini, V., on, *643;* Marpurg, F. W., on, *244, 245, 246(bis), 250,* 626; Monteverdi's, *239;* Mozart, L., on, *243, 247, 248, 250, 253, 254,* 626; Mozart's (W.), 257, 258; Muffat, Georg, on, 631; Muffat, Gottlieb, on, 247; Neumann, F., on, 626–8, 633, 635(*bis*); obligatory, 241; Ortiz, D., on, *237;* Playford, J., on, *242,* 247; Pleyel, I., on, 257, 259; Pollini, F., on, 256; *Pralltriller, 251–2, 258–9;* preparation of baroque, **241–6,** 625–6, 628–9; 'prepared' and 'unprepared', 241–6; Purcell, H., on, *242, 247, 248,* 625;